new york
CITY

FODOR'S TRAVEL PUBLICATIONS

NEW YORK • TORONTO • LONDON • SYDNEY • AUCKLAND

WWW.FODORS.COM

Contents

KEY TO SYMBOLS

- ✚ Map reference
- ✉ Address
- ☎ Telephone number
- 🕐 Opening times
- 💷 Admission prices
- Ⓜ Subway station
- 🚌 Bus number
- 🚉 Train station
- ⛴ Ferry/boat
- 🚩 Tours
- 📖 Guidebook
- 🍴 Restaurant
- ☕ Café
- 🏬 Shop
- 🚻 Toilets
- ① Number of rooms
- 🅿 Parking
- 🚭 No smoking
- 🏊 Swimming pool
- 🏋 Gym

UNDERSTANDING NEW YORK

New York City is an international center for entertainment, fashion,
creative arts and finance. It has great shopping, dynamic theater,
superb concert halls and clubs, world-class museums, gorgeous parks
and gardens, and sports events all year long. The variety and quality
of restaurants is incomparable.
As a world financial center, it soars and plummets with the fluctua-
tions on Wall Street. New Yorkers move fast, talk fast and are pas-
sionate about politics and style. They come in all shapes, sizes, colors
and ethnicities; the city's
multiculturalism is part of its charm. Known for being brusque, New
Yorkers are often surprisingly warm. Sometimes infuriating, the city is
never dull. And chances are, with its vibrant whirl of activity,
it's nothing like home.

NEW
YORK

THE MANHATTAN LAYOUT
Manhattan is just one of five boroughs that
comprise New York City. The others, sometimes
known as the Outer Boroughs, include the Bronx,
Brooklyn, Queens and Staten Island.

Manhattan is the long, narrow island jutting
southwest off the mainland and is the smallest
borough at 13.5 miles (22km) long and 2.25
miles (3.5km) wide. On the east side of the
island is the East River. On the west is the
Hudson River. To the north is the Harlem River.
Upper New York Bay—the city's fine harbor—is to
the south.

In Manhattan, most streets are numbered and
laid out in a grid. The exception to this is Lower
Manhattan, south of 14th Street, which grew up
before the grid system was established. On the
grid, "avenues" run from north to south, and
"streets" run east and west. Broadway, a chief
exception to this rule, cuts across town diagonally
from northwest to southeast. First Avenue is on
the eastern side of town, while Twelfth Avenue is
on the western side. Fifth Avenue divides the city
into the East Side and the West Side (except
south of Washington Square, where Broadway
becomes the east–west divide).

No matter where you are in Manhattan, if you
are heading north you're going "uptown" and if
you're heading south you're going "downtown."

If you want to travel east to west or west to east,
you want to go "crosstown."

CLIMATE
From January to March, New York can be very
cold, and occasional blizzards can obliterate your
view of skyscrapers. But cheaper air fares and
hotel rooms can make it worth your while to visit
then—and sometimes the weather can be temperate. The best times to visit are in late April and
May, when temperatures are generally no lower
than 61°F (16°C), and attractions are crowded
only at peak times, and in September to early
November, when temperatures range from 77°F
(25°C) to 50°F (10°C). The city is hot and humid
in July and August, with extremes of 95°F (35°C)
or higher—but the pleasures of Central Park,
open-air concerts and ferry rides are compensa-
tions, and almost everything is air-conditioned.

STREET LIFE
Walking is the best way to fully appreciate the
city, with its architectural splendors, intriguing
sculptures, pretty fountains, beautiful parks and
iconic landmarks. The street life is entertaining
and colorful. New Yorkers speak Spanish, Chinese,
Russian, Yiddish, Korean, Greek and English, to
name just a few of the languages you will hear
on the streets.

Financial District Oldest part of the city and nexus of the securities industry anchored by the New York Stock Exchange and Wall Street.

TriBeCa It means *Tria*ngle *Be*low *Ca*nal and is defined by Canal and Barclay streets and Broadway and the Hudson River. A mixed-use neighborhood of gritty warehouse lofts, loft-style restaurants, and low-end retail.

Chinatown Stretching over about 30 blocks, from Kenmare and Delancey streets to East Broadway and Worth Street, and from Broadway to Allen Street. Throngs of people shop for fish, meat, vegetables and herbal remedies or dine in the many affordable restaurants.

Little Italy Consists largely of Mulberry Street, lined with tourist-oriented restaurants, plus one or two genuine delis and pastry stores.

SoHo An ultra-expensive, chic shopping mall that is crowded with non-residents on weekends.

Take the Staten Island Ferry for one of the best views of the Manhattan skyline

Lower East Side From 14th Street to Fulton and Franklin and from the East River to Broadway, the area takes in Chinatown, Little Italy and the East Village neighborhoods. Haunt of young professionals and artists.

Greenwich Village/West Village Stretches from 14th Street to Houston and from the Hudson River to Bowery and Fourth Avenue. Boutiques line the west end of Bleecker Street.

Noho Between SoHo and Greenwich Village (from Houston to Eighth streets and Mercer to Bowery/Third Avenue), this youth-oriented neighborhood has plenty of fashionable shopping, bars and restaurants.

East Village Filled with restaurants, bars and a youth-oriented street scene.

Union Square/Flatiron District Hot new neighborhood south of the Flatiron Building on 22nd Street and around Madison Square with plenty of bars, restaurants and clubs. From 14th to 23rd streets and Park Avenue to Sixth Avenue.

Chelsea Center of the gay community. Numerous warehouse/garage galleries along 24th Street, and a lively club and restaurant scene. Stretches from 14th to 30th streets and from Sixth Avenue to the Hudson River.

Midtown Commercial heart of the city between 34th and 59th streets on the West Side and from 40th to 59th streets on the East Side.

Times Square/Theater District The area around 42nd Street and Broadway is now occupied by major corporations and national chain stores, who share the area with new hotels, clubs and theaters.

Upper East Side From 59th to 96th streets and from Fifth Avenue to the East River. Madison Avenue is the ultra-chic shopping street.

East/Spanish Harlem From 96th to 142nd streets between Park Avenue and the East River. A mixed neighborhood of Italians, African-Americans and Hispanics.

Upper West Side Broadway cuts right through this section that extends from 59th to 125th streets between the Hudson River and Central Park West. Has become more fashionable as new upscale restaurants have opened. Sites include the American Museum of Natural History.

Harlem Stretching from 110th Street to the Harlem River and from Fifth to St. Nicholas avenues, Harlem is the city's most famous black community.

The Bronx North of and linked to Manhattan by bridges and subway. Home of the New York Botanical Garden, the Bronx Zoo and Yankee Stadium.

Brooklyn Southeast of Manhattan and connected by bridges, a tunnel and subway, it is New York's most populous borough. Take in great views of Manhattan from Brooklyn Heights.

Queens A 20-minute subway trip east from Manhattan takes you to the temporary home of the Museum of Modern Art and one of New York's most ethnically diverse areas.

Staten Island The most southerly and least populous borough with attractions such as Historic Richmond Town. Good views of Manhattan and the Statue of Liberty from the ferry.

Teaneck

Englewood

9W

Hudson

95

93

Palisades Park

5

Cliffside Park

63

Fairview

67

Fort Lee

WASHINGTON HEIGHTS

87

New York Botanical Garden

Bronx Zoo

BRONX

Yankee Stadium

895

87

278

HARLEM

Central Park

MANHATTAN

Weehawken

9A

West New York

East River

Rikers Island

ASTORIA

Westchester Creek

LaGuardia

SOUNDVIEW

Mount Vernon

New Rochelle

95

Pelham Park

Hart Island

City Island

BAYCHESTER

678

695

Eastchester Bay

Long Island Sound

678

395

Flushing

25A

Queens Museum of Art

New York Hall of Science

25A

Flushing Meadows

495

Long Island City

25

ELMHURST

LOWER MANHATTAN

278

QUEENS

GLENDALE

NEW YORK

JAMAICA

678

25

Brooklyn History Museum

New York Transit Museum

WILLIAMS-BURG

Brooklyn Museum of Art

Brooklyn Botanic Gardens

Prospect Park

478

27

Waterfront Museum

EAST NEW YORK

Spring Creek Park

Jamaica Bay

878

John F Kennedy International

FLATBUSH

BROOKLYN

SHEEPSHEAD BAY

Bergen Beach Park

Gateway National Recreation Area

Canarsie Beach Park

Far Rockaway

Coney Island

BRIGHTON BEACH

Featured place of interest

Toll motorway (Turnpike)

Motorway (Expressway)

Major road

Atlas section

BEST PLACES TO SHOP

B & H Photo (see page 184) The professional place for cameras, video equipment and film, all at great prices.

Barney's (see page 181) For cutting-edge fashion. Don't miss the handbag department.

Bloomingdale's (see page 181) A department store that's so very New York.

Century 21 (see page 183) For seriously discounted designer wear and a crowd scene worthy of the annals of shopping.

Dean & De Luca (see page 170) Everything in this fancy food emporium is absolutely the best of its kind. A sensuous browsing and tasting experience.

Tiffany's window displays on Fifth Avenue are worth a peek

FAO Schwarz (see page 184) The ultimate toy store, as seen in the film *Big* with Tom Hanks.

J & R (see page 170) Audiophiles and technophiles can satisfy every craving for audio components and CDs, computers and peripherals, cameras and other gadgets at good prices.

Jeffrey's (see page 172) The shoe department at this expensive clothing store is stellar, and the best place to see high-designer selections in a single location.

Sherry-Lehmann (see page 171) An education; the inventory of international wine selections is worth $10 million.

Tiffany (see page 180) Superb silver, crystal and other luxury gifts are the attraction at this famous American name, in business since 1837.

Big names on the bags: Barney's (top left) and FAO Schwarz (above)

BEST MUSEUMS AND GALLERIES

Metropolitan Museum of Art (see pages 114–119) 5,000 years' worth of art from around the world.

American Museum of Natural History (see pages 68–72) Not only for dinosaur fossils and moon rocks, but also a new planetarium complex that is out of this world.

Frick Collection (see page 100) A large collection of masterpieces by Rembrandt, Vermeer, El Greco and Goya housed in Henry Clay Frick's splendid mansion.

International Center of Photography (see page 101) More than 60,000 photographs by top names.

Gallery Tours New York One way to see ten modern art galleries in Chelsea, SoHo and other New York locations in two hours *(tel 212/946-1548 or visit www.nygallerytours.com)*.

BEST OUTDOOR SCULPTURES

Alice in Wonderland (see page 82) by José de Creeft (1959). In Central Park Alice perches on a giant mushroom while the March Hare holds out a watch and the Mad Hatter looks on.

The Immigrants by Luis Sanguino (1973). A heart-rending sculpture evoking the hardships of early immigrants. In Battery Park.

Prometheus by Paul Manship (1934). Rockefeller Center's (see pages 128–130) famous gold-leaf and bronze statue overlooks the ice-skating rink.

The Sphere Fritz Koenig's 22-ton symbol of global peace, rescued from the plaza between the twin towers after 9/11, is now a memorial to the victims. In Battery Park.

Statue of Liberty America's symbol of freedom. Take the ferry to Liberty Island for a close-up look at the colossal woman, sculpted by Frédéric-Auguste Bartholdi (1885).

Bronze Bull by Arturo de Modica (1989). Reminds many stock-market traders who pass by daily that better times are ahead. At Bowling Green.

Barosaurus at the American Museum of Natural History

The gilded figure of Prometheus at the Rockefeller Center

BEST PLACES TO EAT

Restrained elegance, in decor and cuisine, at Jean-Georges

Babbo (see page 271) Mario Batali's flagship is the place to sample his lusty cuisine.

DB Bistro Moderne (see page 274) Eating at one of Daniel Boulud's restaurants is a must for every food-loving visitor. This is the most relaxed and joyous of them all.

Four Seasons (see page 276) Even though it has been around since 1959, it remains supremely modern and the darling of the city's movers and shakers. Christian Albin's cuisine is another bonus.

Jean-Georges (see page 278) All of Jean-Georges Vongerichten's restaurants (Jo Jo, Vong, 66 and Mercer Kitchen) showcase his brilliance, but this is his flagship.

Le Bernardin (see page 279) Everything about this seafood specialist is perfect—the service, the flowers, and the exquisitely refined, thoughtful cuisine.

Nobu (see page 282) Nobu Matsuhisa's *sushi* is inspirational.

Patria (see page 283) You can't visit New York without tasting some Nuevo-Latino cuisine, and Patria is the hip place for it.

Tabla (see page 287) Seductive neo-Indian cuisine by master spice blender Floyd Cardoz.

BEST BARS

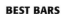

The bar scene lasts till dawn in the city that never sleeps

Flute (see page 214) A luxury subterranean retreat serving 20 champagnes by the glass. Perfect for pre- or post-theater.

King Cole Bar (see page 214) Where the Bloody Mary was invented. Maxfield Parrish's mural adds vibrant color. In the St. Regis.

P. J. Clarke's (see page 217) A beloved New York saloon, home to a rakish crowd.

Pen Top Bar (see page 215) Who can resist a rooftop bar in Midtown?

Pravda (see page 215) Sixty-five vodkas, plus caviar and Russian snacks at this trend setter.

Rainbow Grill Bar (see page 216) The bartenders mix a great cocktail at this romantic only-in-New York locale.

Top of the Tower (see page 216) A nostalgic 26th-floor piano-bar overlooking the East River.

XL (see page 220) Three terrific bars for a sophisticated gay crowd.

BEST PLACES TO STAY

The art deco Carlyle Hotel (above); welcome to the St. Regis (right)

Carlyle (see page 297) The city's most discreet retreat.

Four Seasons (see page 299) Legendary for its service and its immense bathtubs.

Le Parker Meridien (see page 301) Very French uptown hotel with hip downtown style. Pool with a view and a rooftop jogging track.

Library (see page 302) A book-lovers' haunt notable for its hip minimalist design and good service.

Metro (see page 303) and the **Marcel** (see page 302) Chic on the cheap (by New York standards).

Ritz Carlton (see page 305) The opulent Central Park star offers superb service, the latest techno amenities and the only La Prairie spa in the United States.

St. Regis (see page 306) A gilded Beaux-Arts beauty just off Fifth Avenue.

Soho Grand (see page 307) First of the hip downtown hostelries. Pets get the red-carpet welcome.

Wyndham (see page 309) Stay across from the Plaza Hotel for half the price.

BEST BUILDINGS AND SKYSCRAPERS

Ansonia Hotel (2101 Broadway) The Upper West Side's largest Beaux-Arts apartment-hotel. Soundproof partitions between floors attracted musicians and singers, many of them now famous.

Cathedral of St. John the Divine (see page 77) It dates from 1892 and still isn't finished, but the mix of architectural styles inside is amazing.

Chrysler Building (see page 85) An art-deco masterpiece, a shrine to the Chrysler automobile.

Flatiron Building (see page 99) New York's first skyscraper got its nickname from its triangular shape.

Guggenheim Museum (see pages 110–111) Frank Lloyd Wright's only New York building, a whirling wonder both inside and out.

42nd Street Studios Architecture as performing art with a luminous façade of pulsating color. Best at night.

New York Public Library (see page 127) Archetypal Beaux-Arts magnificence.

City icons: the Guggenheim (left) and the Chrysler Building

BEST FREE SIGHTS

Central Park (see pages 78–83) New York's green lung and Frederick Law Olmsted's masterpiece of landscape architecture.

Parades (see page 324) A festival of color and the city's best people-watching. There are many every year.

New York City Police Museum (see page 126) A small but interesting collection documenting the work of the NYPD. The Hall of Heroes is a touching reminder of the dangers faced daily by New York's finest, as the policemen are known.

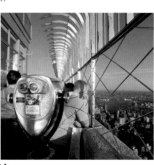

Staten Island Ferry (see page 54) A wonderful trip across the harbor. Just hop on.

Whitney Museum of American Art at Philip Morris A branch of the Whitney with wonderful exhibitions by living artists and a charming sculpture court. Worth a stop if you're in the Grand Central neighborhood.

New Museum of Contemporary Art (see page 124) Its Zenith Media Lounge is full of digital and media art technology with rotating installations.

Outdoor New York: Staten Island Ferry (left) and Central Park

BEST EXPERIENCES

Empire State Building (see pages 94–96) The Observation Deck offers a panoramic view of all Manhattan, very romantic at sunset.

A Broadway show Seeing one is quintessential New York and various discount pricing schemes make it more affordable for all.

M4 bus to the Cloisters (see page 252) A great trip past Columbia University (see page 77) and through colorful, ethnic neighborhoods.

Bronx Zoo (see page 157) Always entertaining—the people are sometimes as interesting as the animals.

Waldorf-Astoria Hotel (see page 308) A study in opulence. Ogle the amazing floral displays in the lobby.

A walk across the Brooklyn Bridge (see pages 74–75) A terrific view of the skyscrapers in Lower Manhattan and the East River.

Allow a day to visit the Bronx Zoo (left), and an hour or two for the Empire State Building

Living
New York

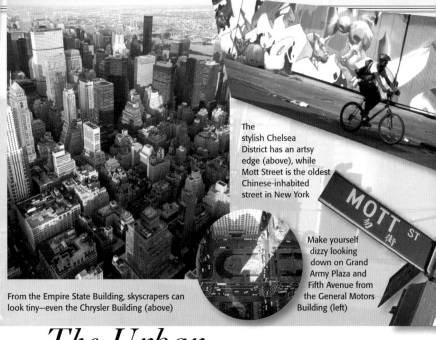

The stylish Chelsea District has an artsy edge (above), while Mott Street is the oldest Chinese-inhabited street in New York

Make yourself dizzy looking down on Grand Army Plaza and Fifth Avenue from the General Motors Building (left)

From the Empire State Building, skyscrapers can look tiny—even the Chrysler Building (above)

The Urban
Landscape

Commuting is part of daily life on the subway (above), as is taking a break in the park (below)

Manhattan is only 13.5 miles (22km) long and 2.25 miles (3.5km) wide. Geologically it consists of bedrock made of gneiss, marble or mica schist. These two factors, plus population density, have played major roles in shaping the city's land- and streetscape, making it more vertical than most. Tall buildings line the streets, and people think nothing of riding elevators to their 50th-floor offices. Daily the population swells as commuters pour into Manhattan from the suburbs creating a crowded environment that throbs with energy and excitement. Commuters access the city via ferry, tunnels and bridges, the most graceful of which are the Brooklyn (1883) and George Washington (1931) bridges. Above 14th Street the streets are laid out in a grid. There are few open spaces or green parks to provide relief— only one or two squares, such as Union, Washington and Madison, or small pockets of asphalt with benches, statues and fountains. Instead, there is one vast park, Central Park, separating East and West Sides uptown. It functions as the city's playground.

The Grid and the Warren

Most visitors to New York City quickly grasp the logic of the streetscape north of 14th Street. A series of broad north–south avenues is crossed by east–west streets, numbered logically. Below 14th Street things get more complicated. Here the narrow streets twist and turn, reminiscent of a medieval city, and have names rather than numbers. This came about because the city grew haphazardly and there were only a few long arteries connecting farms and villages. So in 1811 an orderly grid of 12 broad avenues and 155 streets was established, subdivided into lots measuring 25 by 100ft (7.5 by 30m). It was thought that traffic would be heaviest on the east–west routes, so more streets than avenues were planned. This pattern remains.

Central Park (right) is great for recreation: You can walk, jog, cycle, roller-blade, sail model boats, or just take a picnic and chill

With only one major park in the city, every space is turned into an outdoor haven (right); street vending (left); locally made produce (bottom)

Underground City

First-time visitors to Manhattan often notice the rooftop water towers, fire hydrants, potholes and, weirdest of all, steam-belching funnels. The last give an inkling of what lies below—a multilevel network of electric and telephone cables, plus steam, water, gas and sewage pipes, all laid above the subway. A large water tunnel under the subway supplies the city's drinking water. The subway alone has 700 miles (1,140km) of track and 469 stations. There's 100 million miles of telephone cable. City water comes from upstate New York reservoirs, and the 1,500 million gallons a day is delivered by more than 6,000 miles of tunnel and water mains. Installed before 1930 and made of cast-iron, they can rupture, which causes chaos. When the piped gases build up, they cause manhole explosions. The steam-belching funnels help to relieve the pressure and stop the 60,000 man-holes from erupting.

Robert Moses—New York's Baron Haussmann

Robert Moses (1888–1981), who served on the Parks and Planning commissions, had a huge impact on the city's overall design. Between 1924 and 1968, he transformed the city, building 17 parkways, 14 expressways (including the Brooklyn-Queens Expressway), the FDR and Harlem River drives, the Triborough and Verrazano bridges, Lincoln Center and Stuyvesant Town. In the process he destroyed whole neighborhoods, tearing down slums and relocating residents in dehumanizing public housing in Harlem, the Lower East Side, the Bronx and Brooklyn. The citizens got angry. And when he moved to route cars through Washington Square and put parking lots in Central Park they mobilized to preserve the small scale of their neighborhoods. Still, Moses left a gigantic imprint on the city.

Waking Up to the Waterfront

For years New York City's 580 miles (920km) of waterfront lay blighted, the site of rusting piers, crumbling warehouses and refuse-strewn lots. Suddenly it's as if the city has woken up to its potential pleasures, as citizens go kayaking, fishing and sailing. A 28-mile (45km) bike path now encircles Manhattan, and the waterfront has been converted into a park with promenade and gardens from the Battery to 58th Street. It's hard to pinpoint when it began. In the 1980s, South Street Seaport, Battery Park City and Chelsea piers were important beginnings, followed by Riverbank State Park (1993). The rest has followed, culminating in Stuyvesant Cove Park (2002) and Hudson River Park (2003).

Urban Gardens

New York City has one large park and only two important botanical gardens, so resident horticulturists create their own gardens in unlikely city corners. If you look up at the residential buildings you might see green fronds peeking out from the roofline. Some of these roof gardens are luxurious indeed, planted with trees and flowers and decorated with urns, benches and statues. In contrast are the hundreds of community gardens, usually created on vacant city-owned lots, which serve as neighborhood social centers. The impetus for such gardens can be traced to 1972 and a garden at Bowery and Houston tended by the Green Guerrillas. Mayor Giuliani sought to destroy such gardens and battled with neighborhood activists, but Mayor Michael Bloomberg has moved quickly to make peace.

You can join in with a game of softball on the Great Lawn in Central Park anytime

Shoe-shining outside Grand Central

Formal suit, fun transportation— New Yorkers like to be different

New York cops come from a wide range of backgrounds (left)

Peruvian celebrations in Bryant Park, Midtown (above)

The People

Playing chess in China-town (above); many immigrants take jobs as waiters, and earn most of their money from tips (below)

New York City is a city of immigrants. Between 1892 and 1924, 16 million immigrants poured through Ellis Island, many heading to the Lower East Side. Today, the gateways are Kennedy and Newark airports, and the immigrants' destination the ethnic mosaics of Brooklyn and Queens, where such high schools as New Town have students who speak 30 different languages, and where the Central Library caters to a population that speaks nearly 40 languages. The Dutch, of course, were the first immi-grants. They were not interested in build-ing a City of God. They cared about talent and enterprise and opened the city to immigrants of all sorts—Huguenots, Jewish, English, Germans, Scottish, French, Irish and Africans (slave and free). At the turn of the 20th century, large numbers of Jewish Italians and Russians arrived, and after 1965, people from the Caribbean, Central America and Asia. The percentage of foreign born has always fluctuated. At 40%, it is today at its highest. The lowest was in 1970 (18%). The population is 8 million, of which 35% are white, 27% Latino, 25% black and 10% Asian.

International Express—the Number 7 Train

In the census of 2000, Queens had the fastest-growing population, hav-ing risen by 11 percent in the preceding decade. Much of that rise can be attributed to the arrival of new immigrants from all over the globe— Indians, Colombians, Ecuadorians and Peruvians in Jackson Heights; Dominicans, Colombians and Mexicans in Corona; Chinese, Koreans and Vietnamese in Flushing. Queens is the city's new melting pot—the new gateway to America. A ride on the number 7 train will confirm this. The first few stations (40th to 61st streets and Queens Boulevard) are in Sunnyside and Woodside, where the most recent influx of Irish immigrants has set-tled. It then proceeds along Roosevelt Avenue, stopping in Jackson Heights (74th Street), Corona (111th Street) and finally, Flushing.

The Polish Day parade (left) takes place every October

A bright mural covers a wall in Chinatown (above); many early settlers were Jewish, and there is still a large Jewish community in New York, famous for their great sense of humor

Good clothing for a steamy New York summer's day (left)

Hispanics—Second in Strength

The 1961 movie *West Side Story* depicted the struggle of Puerto Ricans, the city's first Hispanic community. Today, joined by nationals from Cuba, Ecuador, Colombia, El Salvador, the Dominican Republic and Mexico, Hispanics are the city's largest minority, representing 27 percent of the population. The Hispanic influence can be seen and felt everywhere, from media and music to politics and cuisine. Turn on the TV and you'll find Telemundo and Univision offering Spanish talk shows and steamy soap operas. Scan a stand for newspapers *El Diario/La Prensa*, *Hoy*, *El Nacional* and *El Tiempo*. Baseball teams are peppered with Latin names; the Latino music craze continues, as more artists cross over in the footsteps of Ricky Martin; and chefs deliver the latest pan-Latino cuisine at such hot spots as Babalu and Noche.

Bollywood on the Hudson

Before 1965 only a few South Asian students lived in the city, but after 1965, the Indian, Pakistani, Bangladeshi, Sri Lankan and Nepalese presence increased noticeably. Asians ran the news-stands, and suddenly it seemed everyone who worked in a Duane Reade drug store was Asian. Gradually Asian cuisine, music and culture registered on the consciousness of New Yorkers. Now even fusion is occurring. Witness Panjaba MC and Jay-Z's hit *Beware of the Boys*, in which hip-hop meets British *bhangra*. In the 1970s more Asian professionals settled in Queens. Jackson Heights became the commercial center, with Sam and Raj opening in 1976 on 74th Street, a must-stop for all visiting Indians. Here are stores selling saris, South Asian videos, music and cooking staples. There are also several Hindu temples. And Madison Square Garden headlines Bollywood entertainers.

Tracing African-American Heritage

A scholar interested in the black experience would begin at the Schomburg Center on 125th Street. Documents here chart the growth of the community from 14,000 in 1830 to 1.96 million today, along with the lives of such famous black New Yorkers as abolitionists Henry Highland Garnet and Alexander Crummell, and civil rights leaders Adam Clayton Powell and Malcolm X. A casual visitor might start at the African Burial Ground at Broadway and Duane. Here, from 1712 to 1794, 10–20,000 blacks were buried as they were excluded from the Trinity Church graveyard. Few traces remain of Manhattan's 19th-century black communities, but much is found in Harlem: the Abyssinian Baptist Church where Adam Clayton Powell, Sr. and Jr. preached, at 138th Street; the mosque associated with Malcolm X; and many of the sites associated with the Harlem Renaissance.

Understanding Yiddish

Every New Yorker knows what *chutzpah, mensch* and *kvetch* mean, and what the difference is between *shlep, shlemiel* and *schmozzle*. New York has the largest Jewish community outside Israel, but it's not its size so much as its spirit that counts. The greatest number of Jews came in the late 19th century, fleeing pogroms in Russia and Eastern Europe and settling on the Lower East Side. Their story is told in Irving Howe's history, *World of Our Fathers*. A tale of struggle rewarded by success and assimilation, it's a journey seen in the contrast between Woody Allen's Jewish outsider and Jerry Seinfeld's totally assimilated incidental Jew. Successful Jews moved from the Lower East Side and Brooklyn to the Upper West Side and the suburbs. They became financiers, doctors, lawyers, stand-up comedians and school-teachers, and passed along Yiddish.

The 1959 Guggenheim Museum was designed as a flowing building to please the eye (right)

Brooklyn Bridge was the world's first steel suspension bridge (below)

The 1902 Flatiron Building is barely a skyscraper, measuring only 285ft (87m, above)

The New York skyline, now without the World Trade Center (above); Lee Lawrie's *Wisdom* at the G. E. Building (right)

New York Architecture

Beyond Signature Skyscrapers

Yes, the Empire State and the Chrysler buildings are two stunning skyscrapers, but they're not alone. The Bayard Condict building (1898) on Bleecker Street is the only example of Louis Sullivan's work in the city. Later skyscrapers often incorporated elements from earlier eras, as did Daniel Burnham's Renaissance Revival Flatiron Building (1902). Raymond Hood's Radiator Building is a beauty—black brick and blue-green tiles with gold ornamentation. The Seagram Building on Park Avenue, by Mies van der Rohe and Philip Johnson, is a good example of 50s modernism. Architects are still building the skyscrapers of tomorrow—Daniel Libeskind's design was chosen for the new complex to be built at the site of the former World Trade Center.

There are so many great buildings in New York that it can be overwhelming. Many great buildings have also been lost, and that too is overwhelming, but not surprising, given the city's commercial nature. Skyscrapers dominate the island of Manhattan, a building style made possible by the confluence of several factors—the geological bedrock, the availability of steel, and the techniques of engineering. City governments had always emphasized growth and innovation, which helped create such real-estate moguls as John Jacob Astor, William Zeckendorf, Harry Helmsley and Donald Trump. Zoning laws arrived only in 1916 and conservation came even later. Robert Moses razed whole neighborhoods, and between 1900 and 1965 many architectural gems were replaced with inferior substitutes. New Yorkers finally woke up in 1965, after Penn Station was demolished and replaced with the sorry station there today. A Landmarks Preservation Commission was founded, but it still had to be re-affirmed by the United States Supreme Court in 1978 when Grand Central Station was threatened.

The Chrysler Building, with its gleaming stainless-steel spire, is a 1930s art-deco masterpiece

Brownstones in TriBeCa (left); the Empire State Building (right)

Tenements with their fire escapes clearly visible (below left); vast columns decorate the former U.S. Custom House (right); a quirky statue in SoHo (below)

Brownstones and Tenements

Besides skyscrapers there are plenty of other building types to appreciate. Brownstones—named after the sandstone from the banks of the Connecticut and Hackensack rivers—line the streets of Greenwich Village, Chelsea and other districts. Today they make elegant residences. In the mid-19th century, cast-iron was used for the façades of factories, shops and warehouses, many in SoHo. They seemed to be carved in stone, but are in fact some of the first pre-fabs ever made. The most spectacular examples are at Nos. 260–561 Broadway and Mercer Street in SoHo.

Humble tenements with fire escapes are also city trademarks. Built to house the 19th-century immigrants, they were narrow, cramped and unsanitary, but cheap—$2–$3 per month. Examples still line the streets of the Lower East Side and East Village. Today the rent is 500 times more.

Mews, and Other Nooks and Crannies

Visitors soon discover Midtown's pocket parks and plazas, but if you wander farther you'll find more charming oddities. Pomander Walk (West 94th and 95th streets), for example, is 16 two-story Tudor-style cottages. Sniffen Court, 150–158 East 36th Street, is a beguiling collection of brick carriage houses now used as residences. The Village has several oddities. The enclaves of Patchin Place (1848), West 10th Street, and Milligan Place, on Sixth Avenue between West 10th and 11th streets (1852), were originally built to house Basque waiters, who worked at the Brevoort House on Fifth Avenue. Later residents were more famous —among them e e cummings. Along Bedford Street, between Morton and Commerce, stands the narrowest house in the city—it's only 9ft (3m) wide and was home to Edna St. Vincent Millay in 1924.

Sculptors and Painters Help to Gild the Lily

Visitors often focus on the number and size of Manhattan skyscrapers, failing to notice the many embellishments created by famous and not so famous stonemasons, sculptors and painters. Daniel Chester French adorned the U.S. Custom House with monumental portraits of Asia, America, Europe and Africa. Reginald Marsh painted the interiors, celebrating the maritime wealth of the city. The lower façades of the art-deco Rockefeller Center are encrusted with sculptures and bas-reliefs. Lee Lawrie's *Wisdom* hovers above the entrance to the G. E. Building, while inside José Maria Sert's mural, *Man's Conquests*, covers the walls. Portraits of Mary Pickford and Ethel Barrymore by Alexander Stirling Calder grace the Miller Building at West 46th Street and Seventh Avenue. French artist Marc Chagall adorned the Metropolitan Opera House.

Cass Gilbert

Cass Gilbert stands out as the designer of some of the city's most beautiful luxuriant buildings. Go into the Woolworth Building (1910–1913) at 233 Broadway, for example. Woolworth, who paid the $15.5 million price tag in cash, certainly got his money's worth. The exterior soars 792ft (240m) without a setback. The interior is stunning. The vaulted lobby is swathed in veined marble, gold leaf and mosaic, and decorated with humorous sculptures, including one of Cass Gilbert himself holding the building and another of Woolworth counting his dimes. Gilbert's other great building is the U.S. Custom House (1907), a suitably grand repository for the wealth of the early city. He also contributed the New York Life Insurance Building (1907) at 51 Madison Avenue, between 26th and 27th streets, and the Federal Courthouse on Foley Square (1936).

NEW YORK ARCHITECTURE   17

You can visit some famous graves in Trinity Church (above); a choir sings out loud and proud in Harlem (left)

Katz's Deli (above) serves Jewish deli food; hot dogs and bagels are part of the NYC experience

New York Way
of Life

Most New Yorkers are not born in the city. They come to it. They come for many reasons, most of which involve dreams of success and the money, power and fame that follow. So it is that the city is full of competitive people trying to make it on stage, in music, in real estate, on Wall Street, Madison Avenue or in any other arena. Even though many citizens are in "success overdrive," there are other factors that affect the rhythms of city life. New York is not monolithic. It's a cluster of neighborhoods, each with a different ambience and energy. The West Village wakes up late and operates at a slow pace; the East Village wakes up very late and parties very late; Washington Heights is loud and moves to a Dominican rhythm; Beekman Place is always subdued. The city may stay open 24 hours, but each neighborhood plays its own rhythmic variation.

Thousands of commuters pass through Grand Central Station every day

A hot dog with mustard and ketchup—lunch on the run

Worship at Your Choice of Altar

Many visitors are surprised to learn how religious Americans are and how many people attend religious services. New York City is no exception. From its founding it has offered an array of religious options, when Anglicans, Presbyterians, Quakers, Anabaptists, Jews, Catholics and Lutherans co-existed. Today, Christian denominations, plus Pentecostals, Greek and Russian Orthodox, Buddhists, Hindus, Sikhs, Jews and Muslims all have a place to worship in the city. If you want to understand a culture, attend a religious service. In New York, head to Harlem and hear the gospel choirs raising the roofs of the Baptist churches, or go to East 96th Street to the Islamic Cultural Center. Take the train to the Hindu temples or Sikh gurdawaras in Queens, or drop in to one of the Buddhist temples in Chinatown. Or visit St. John the Divine or St. Patrick's.

The first yellow cabs hit the streets in 1907 (above)

Sex and the City's four sirens of singledom: Kim Cattrall, Kristin Davis, Sarah Jessica Parker and Cynthia Nixon (below)

Doing weights at the gym is much more interesting with the Manhattan skyline to look at (above)

Roller-blading is a speedy and healthy option (right)

Convenience Greases the Daily Wheels

To the average New Yorker, speed and convenience take precedence over everything else. Time is, after all, money. So meals on the run are habitual. Workers en route to their offices, the women sporting Adidas, stop for an Egg McMuffin at McDonald's or coffee and a danish at Starbucks. At lunch, New Yorkers "order in" a sandwich or salad and soft drink, instead of going out for a leisurely meal. Or if they have a corporate cafeteria they go there. Some of these are extraordinary, the most famous being the Philippe Starck version at Condé Nast. If workers do go out, it will often be to "brown bag it," taking a sandwich to a pocket park.

At night, they may go home and order takeout from one of the many neighborhood menus that keep by their phone—Thai, Chinese, Mexican, Indian, Italian or Japanese.

Exercise, Exercise!

Although a recent study reported that 35% of New Yorkers are overweight or obese, you would not know it from the frequent sightings of earnest New Yorkers pumping iron or running on treadmills. Keeping fit is a serious business. Most executives receive a standard gym membership and many have personal trainers, who show them how to work the machines and set their fitness goals. Of course, the Old Guard have always had their clubs, where they go to swim, exercise or get a massage—The Knickerbocker, the Union, the Colony or the Harmonie are just some examples. After these come luxury gyms like the Sports Club/L. A. Average New Yorkers are more likely to join Bally Fitness or Crunch and take some aerobics classes. It's all part of the endless New York regimen of health and beauty.

Yellow Cabs— Love or Hate?

The average New Yorker rides the buses or the subways, but the highpowered prefer to hail a cab, one of the 12,184 licensed to cruise the city streets. You can't miss the yellow chariots. They have been in business since 1907. Early operators were so corrupt that in 1923 a Taxi and Limousine Commission began issuing licenses. LaGuardia sold the first medallion for $10 in 1937. Today they cost $227,000. Every immigrant group has driven cabs—initially Jewish settlers, Italians and Irish and more recently people from Russia, Africa, Haiti and South Asia. They receive only 24 hours of instruction and earn about $5 an hour. Some cabs perform some wild maneuvers to grab passengers. The bulletproof partitions separating passenger from driver were installed in 1967. A handful of televisions arrived in 2002 but were discontinued in 2003.

New York Solutions to the Single Problem

There are 100 million "singles" in the United States. Several million of them live in New York, and they are constantly looking for the perfect mate, supporting a veritable marriage market industry. Even in the 1860s, matrimonial broker's ads ran in the press. For example, John Johnson and Co. offered services to "ladies wishing agreeable and wealthy husbands," and to men desiring "beautiful, rich and accomplished wives." If you scan the ads in the local media, you'll find little has changed. Now, though, individuals advertise themselves, posting photographs in such publications as *New York Magazine*, revealing their most intimate data online at itsjustlunch.com, or signing up for TV shows such as "Perfect Partner" and "Boy Meets Boy." There are singles groups of all kinds, from speeddating specialists to one for tall people only.

The Metropolitan Opera House stages excellent performances (right); one of a series of Jackson Pollock's modern, some say agressive, pieces (below)

Everything from ancient Egypt to Van Gogh is in the Metropolitan Museum of Art (above); the all-singing, all-dancing 1980s musical *42nd Street* has been revived (right)

The Arts

New York City leads the nation in arts and entertainment. It's the world's center of contemporary art, and also has a phenomenal collection of performing arts companies in dance, music and theater. The city's cultural groups have also led the way in finding innovative ways to fund their endeavors. For years, although they have received some funding from government, city cultural institutions and groups have developed their own funding resources—private donors, memberships, book-stores and other ancillary profit centers. The arts scene is constantly chang-ing and evolving. There is an uptown mainstream scene and a downtown more experimental scene, and within each shifts are always occurring—SoHo galleries migrating to Chelsea, for example. Don't worry, whatever excites you in the arts can be found in New York.

Thoroughly Modern Millie is a big, bright, upbeat story of a young girl from Kansas arriving in New York in 1922 (above); modern art in SoHo (below)

Culture and Money

Wealthy dynasties have always served as patrons of the arts, and New York's are no different. Mayor Bloomberg donates a large part of his fortune to cultural institutions, as do many in the Social Register. Today, the money is likely to be dispensed by the 525 city-based foun-dations, which control $82 billion. These cultural donors are copying earlier magnates whose names still resonate throughout the city—Astor, Carnegie, Morgan, Rockefeller, Vanderbilt and Whitney. John D. Rockefeller gave away $1.5 million annu-ally and launched the Rockefeller Foundation in 1913 with $100 million. His son, John, Jr., founded Rockefeller University and donated the Cloisters, Fort Tryon Park and the site for the United Nations building. John Jacob Astor left $400,000 for a library, which Brooke Astor, the wife of his great-great grandson, supports.

New York and jazz are synonymous; this huge red cube by Noguchi is on Church Street (right); unmissable house number outside 9 West 57th Street (below)

Martin Scorsese's movie is about Irish immigrants in 1863 (above)

New York, New York, It's a Helluva Town

The film industry may have moved from New York to Hollywood after World War I, but it is still a film town, thanks to the renovation of old studios and the encouragement of the Mayor's Office of Film. Filmmakers have long conducted a love affair with the city, sometimes using fake studio backdrops, as they did in *King Kong*, and other times filming the reality on location. The directors most associated with New York are Martin Scorsese, Paul Mazursky, Sidney Lumet, John Cassavetes, Spike Lee and Wes Anderson (*The Royal Tenenbaums*). But the love affair goes back a long way to films such as *Miracle on 34th Street* (1947), *The Naked City* (1948), and *On the Waterfront* (1954).

If you want an architectural tour of New York plus an insight into its collective unconscious, treat yourself to any Woody Allen film.

They Still Make Steinways in New York

The name Steinway signifies the best pianos in the world, and it has done so since 1853, when Henry Steinweg started the company. The company was so successful that by 1873 the family was able to build a company town in Astoria, Queens, complete with factory, housing, a school and other amenities. At one time, the company made 6,000 grand pianos a year, but the industry collapsed in 1927 with the introduction of radio and the phonograph. The company survived, although the family sold it in 1972. Today it continues to operate with 450 workers, who handcraft about 2,000 grand pianos (and 500 uprights) a year, which cost from $25,000 to $147,000. Even though the eight-month process is the same, each one has a different musical personality, depending on the wood and other subjective factors.

Chelsea—New Center of Contemporary Art

In 1987 the Dia Center for the Arts opened on 22nd Street in Chelsea, making it the new vortex for contemporary art, surpassing SoHo and 57th Street. In 1991 it opened its innovative rooftop urban park. Since then, the area between 19th and 29th streets and 10th and 11th avenues has grown into a large gallery district with close to 200 spaces. All the former big names in SoHo and Uptown are now represented here—Matthew Marks, Larry Gagosian, Mary Boone, Pace Wildenstein, Paula Cooper, Robert Miller, Barbara Gladstone, Holly Solomon and Sonnabend. Some galleries have hangar-like spaces large enough to accommodate massive works by such artists as Richard Serra. In some cases entire buildings (529 West 20th and 526 West 26th Street, for example) now house multiple galleries.

The Challenge of Broadway

Every year Broadway is reported teetering on the edge of economic disaster and accused of abandoning serious theater for warmed-over revivals. It's tough to make money on Broadway. Back in 1866, *Black Crook*, a musical melodrama, ran for only 475 performances and took $1.1 million, easily recouping the $24,000 investment. Today a musical costs on average $8 million to put on, and the show has to run for at least 520 performances just to break even. When producers have to rely on tourists to fill the seats, it gets really tough. Success then depends on low costs, good press, a Tony Award and lots of luck. Few shows meet the test. In fact, about 80% of Broadway shows fail to recoup their investments. So producers of serious theater turn to Off- and Off-Off Broadway, where costs are lower and they can afford to nurture new playwrights.

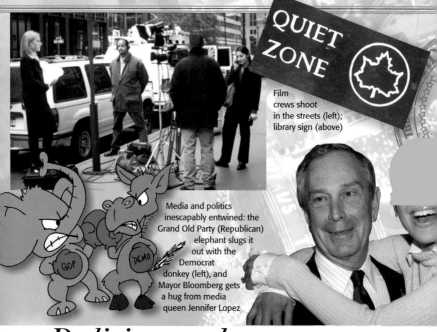

Film crews shoot in the streets (left); library sign (above)

QUIET ZONE

Media and politics inescapably entwined: the Grand Old Party (Republican) elephant slugs it out with the Democrat donkey (left), and Mayor Bloomberg gets a hug from media queen Jennifer Lopez

Politics and Media

Summarizing New York City politics is difficult. It's a complex city divided into five boroughs—Manhattan, Brooklyn, the Bronx, Queens and Staten Island—populated by eight million people of different races and religions and diverse socio-economic interests. As a consequence, city politics are often contentious, with ethnic rivalries playing such a large part in the political process that most mayors give up mediating between groups and instead favor some groups over others. The municipal employee unions—police, fire, teachers, sanitation and transit—also play a major role in city politics and can make the city a more, or less, pleasant place to live and work. As far as national politics goes, New York City is firmly Democratic, even though it has voted for two Republicans in the last three mayoral elections. Only Staten Island votes pretty solidly Republican. The print media cut across party lines. The *New York Times*, the *Daily News*, and *Newsday* lean toward the Democratic Party while the *Wall Street Journal*, the fledgling *New York Sun* and Rupert Murdoch's *New York Post* take a more Republican tack.

For some the alternating political processes are nothing but a failure

Will Work For Food May God Bless You People!

Who's in Charge?

It's hard for outsiders to determine who is in charge. Under the federal system, the responsibilities are divided among the federal, state and municipal governments. Although there have been many powerful mayors—LaGuardia, Koch, and Giuliani in particular, their power is limited by the state governor, the state assembly and senate, the borough presidents and the city council, to name the major challengers. Currently, for example, even though Mayor Bloomberg presides over a city containing 38% of the state's population, he is battling Governor Pataki over the redevelopment of Lower Manhattan and the building of a water filtration plant. The city lives under a tough set of fiscal rules imposed by the state 30 years ago, with four agencies monitoring city finances. If the city fails to balance the budget or pay its debt, the state will assume financial control.

The presidential seal (left); a New York cycling cop (right)

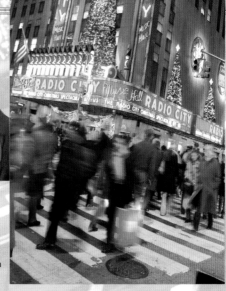

Mayor Michael Bloomberg's 2003 ban on smoking in all public places did not go down well with New Yorkers (below and left)

Radio City Hall, the world's largest theater in 1932, is lit up for Christmas (above)

Education is the Topic of the Day

From the 1960s to the early 1990s crime and race dominated the headlines, but under Mayor Guiliani crime dropped dramatically and although race continued to play a divisive role, it diminished as a headline issue. Today, education is such a compelling issue that among the wealthy even getting into the "right" nursery matters, as revealed when Citicorp analyst Jack Grubman did CEO Sanford Weill a favor in return for getting his two-year-old twins into the 92nd Street Y. Although there are top-notch schools (Stuyvesant, Bronx Science), the public school system is in crisis. It educates 1.1 million students in 1,200 schools, many of which are in disrepair, require students to pass through metal detectors, and have truancy problems. Bloomberg has staked his reputation on reforming it by streamlining the bureaucracy and imposing a standard curriculum.

The Smoking Edict

Mayor Giuliani told New Yorkers how to behave. He disciplined them for such "bad behavior" as jaywalking, panhandling, staging scatological art shows, squeegeeing and sleeping on, or occupying, two seats on the subway. New Yorkers grumbled, but came to appreciate the improvement in the quality of life that followed. Today, Bloomberg has not won over New Yorkers. One rule in particular has alienated them—the smoking edict, which has angered bar and nightclub owners, libertarians, smokers and the average New Yorker, who now has to elbow through crowds outside bars, and to tolerate their noise, which used to be confined to the interior. The Mayor insists that many lives will be saved.

Gossip

Gossip has a high profile in New York City because power, money, sex and celebrity drive society and gossip helps keep score on who's in and who's out. Gossip may have begun with Mrs. William Astor and her 400 and continued on the zebra-striped banquettes at El Morocco and at Walter Winchell's table at the Stork Club, but now it's everywhere. It's not confined to the tabloids, either. It may not be called a gossip column, but that's what it is. The New York Times has "boldface names;" New York Magazine has "The Intelligencer;" The New Yorker calls it the "Talk of the Town" and Town & Country insists that it's "Parties." Tina Brown leavened Vanity Fair with it. Everyone has to read the New York Post's Liz Smith, Cindy Adams and Page Six. And it's becoming even more center stage, as the Star moves into Manhattan and gossip drives the content of glossies U.S. and People.

Madison Avenue

Madison Avenue may be the Golden Mile of designer retailing, but it is also synonymous with one of the largest and most important city industries. In 2002, a massive $117 billion was spent on advertising, plus $6.8 billion on focus groups alone. With consumer spending accounting for 60% of the national economy and 22,000 new packaged products being launched annually, advertising plays a huge marketing role. New York City remains the advertising capital, because all the TV networks and publishing companies have their headquarters or offices here. Although the advertising companies are not necessarily on or near Madison Avenue anymore—Saatchi & Saatchi is at 375 Hudson in the West Village—they do need to be near the media buyers and sellers, so that they can easily participate in the seasonal media buying frenzy.

Alan Greenspan (above), Chairman of the Federal Reserve Board, is charged with balancing the U.S. economy between boom and bust

Nasdaq and Wall Street are familiar names in the world of money

The New York Stock Exchange (above) is the heart of financial America

Commerce and Finance

New York has always been a money-making city. The "robber barons" made their fortunes in commerce—John Astor in real estate, J. P. Morgan in banking and John D. Rockefeller in oil. Today new money is more in technology and communications. Manufacturing has shifted to Mexico and Asia, while the port business has moved to New Jersey. New York is still the global center of banking and insurance. The securities industry is vital to its economy. Since the collapse of the bubble in March 2000 and the tragedy of 9/11, the industry has suffered and is only now in recovery.

Financial Scandals Old and New

Wall Street has always attracted its fair share of scoundrels and con-artists since the Stock Exchange opened in 1792. After the crash on Black Tuesday in October 1929, when the Dow dropped 23%, the Securities and Exchange Commission (SEC) was established to regulate the markets. It had modest success until the recent scandals of the 1990s. Today Wall Street is still reeling from the financial meltdowns of Enron, Tyco and World-com and the prosecution of Martha Stewart for alleged insider trading.

In the 1980s, Michael Milken virtually invented junk bonds and benefited from the climate that generated so many hostile takeovers. He went to prison for fraud, one of only a few.

Seventh Avenue Hangs On

From the 1930s to the 1950s, the garment industry was the biggest in the city. Cutters, pattern-makers and sewing-machine operators, and button and zipper makers jammed the blocks between 36th and 38th streets between Madison and Eighth Avenues. (Seventh Avenue is also called Fashion Avenue between 23rd and 42nd streets.) Today the only evidences of the trade are the racks being pushed along the sidewalks and the "seconds" bins. Most manufacturing has gone to low-cost countries like China. What remains is on the Lower East Side, and in Chinatown and Queens, where Chinese, Thais and Dominicans staff sweatshops. The Garment Industry Development Corporation is working to reinvigorate the industry.

The NYSE, Amex and Nasdaq—the Three Pillars

The New York Stock Exchange, whose 1,366 seats are for sale by auction, is the most prestigious of the three. The first seats sold in 1868 for $4,000; in October 2002 a seat sold for $2.3 million. Only the most carefully scrutinized companies—2,783 of them—are listed on the NYSE, which has a global market capitalization of $13.9 trillion and trades on average 1.43 billion shares a day.

Those who could not afford to join the NYSE started the Amex, on Trinity Place. It lists only 696 companies. It was originally called the Curb Market because the brokers did their business at the curbside.

In 1971 the National Association of Securities Dealers Automated Quotation (Nasdaq) was launched as the world's first electronic stock market. It lists 3,663 mostly high-growth companies and is the world's largest market in trading volume.

The Story of New York

Early Colonial *Days*

In the 16th century the area now known as Manhattan was a land of natural beauty, populated by wild animals and Native American tribes. Early explorers' engravings and vellum maps depict the hilly terrain and early settlements, including the Indian longhouses near Coney Island. In the early 16th century, Giovanni da Verrazano, a Florentine navigator and merchant working for the French, attempted to find the supposed Northwest Passage, a more direct route between Europe and Asia. Instead, he found himself sailing into the wonderful natural harbor that is now New York Harbor on April 17, 1524, and was greeted by the astonished native Algonquians.

However, not much exploring went on until the arrival in 1609 of Henry Hudson, an English navigator working for the Dutch East India Company. He sailed up the river that now bears his name and reported back on the abundance of otter, beaver, mink and wildcat and on the possibilities of the fur trade. The Dutch, recognizing the potential, went into business and brought traders to settle the area. One farm belonged to Jonas Bronck, whose name has stuck firmly to the area known today as The Bronx.

Native Algonquians(left); Giovanni da Verrazano (right) has given his name to the Verrazano Narrow Bridge

Native Americans

During the early colonial days, the Algonquians were often at war with each other and with the Iroquois. To protect themselves, the tribes lived in tight-knit groups under strong chiefs.

In the beginning, the Algonquians were a friendly people and showed the Dutch colonists where to hunt, farm and fish. The Native Americans enjoyed trading just as much as the Dutch, but then, as the colonists tried to take land away, fighting broke out. The Dutch attacked two encampments, killing 80 Native Americans, and started a very bloody war. Reports of this fighting got back to Holland, discouraging emigration to the New World.

1500

Manhattan (right) was named New Amsterdam after the Dutch took control; the trial of John Peter Zenger (below) ended in victory for the press

Dutch Colony

Peter Minuit bought Manhattan Island in 1626 for a cool $24 worth of kettles, axes and cloth. However, the Native Americans he paid did not share his concept of land ownership and didn't understand the sale; furthermore, the transaction was made with the Canarsie tribe, who were merely passing by on that day. Dutch garrisons built a windmill, a fort, a barracks, a jail, a church, a tavern and a governor's house. There were about 120 houses by 1656, about 300 four years later. Merchants and traders ran the municipal government and everyone was happy until the Dutch governor tried civilizing the rowdy populace.

Peter Minuit purchased Manhattan illegally for next to nothing (below)

Peter Stuyvesant

The early colonists were a fairly lawless lot, and drunkeness and violence were common. Then, in 1647, the one-legged Peter Stuyvesant stepped in as governor. Under his strict control, law and order were established, along with a school, hospital, prison and post office. But Stuyvesant was not popular, and he eventually surrendered to English attackers, then returned to Holland in 1665 to defend himself against charges of misconduct. In 1667, he came back to his New York farm, the *bouwerij* that has given its name to New York's Bowery. Stuyvesant died in 1672 and was buried on his farm, now the site of St. Mark's in the Bowery Church (see page 131).

Peter Stuyvesant's lack of a limb never held him back (below)

The English

In 1664, with 8,000 unhappy Dutch colonists living on the island, now known as New Amsterdam, Colonel Richard Nicolls easily seized the territory from the Dutch on the orders of King Charles II of England. The king's brother, the Duke of York, took control and changed the colony's name to New York. The terms of the surrender were generous, and not a single Dutch resident took Nicolls up on his offer to repatriate them. Nicolls became governor and was both efficient and popular. In 1673, when a war between Holland and England broke out, New York returned to Dutch control, but it bounced back to the English in 1674 under the Treaty of Westminster.

King of New York: Charles II of England (below)

Freedom of the Press

German immigrant John Peter Zenger became the editor of the *New York Weekly Journal* in 1733 and quickly grew unpopular with Governor William Cosby. His opposition to the governor's arbitrary acts gained support from lawyers, merchants and others of independent spirit. In 1734 he was arrested for seditious libel. His lawyer, Andrew Hamilton, refuted the libel charge on the basis that the offensive article was not actually false. The court disagreed, stating that whether or not the publication was true was irrelevant and that merely publishing such wicked words about the government was enough to convict.

But Hamilton's eloquent appeal to the judge and jury resulted in Zenger's acquittal and a victory for freedom of the press, setting a precedent against judicial tyranny in libel suits and leading eventually to the First Amendment to the Constitution.

1750

A view of the early settlement of New York (above)

Revolutionary Period

King's College, now Columbia University (see page 77), was established in 1754 by royal charter of King George II with the twin aims of preventing the growth of republican principles and promoting the teachings of the Anglican Church. As the American colonies grew more independently minded, students such as Alexander Hamilton emerged to become America's patriot leaders.

In 1765 a Stamp Act passed by Parliament in London taxed marriage licenses, playing cards, newspapers and 40 other necessities of life, and infuriated the colonists. Leading opposition to the Stamp Act, New York sent a formal protest to the king; 28 delegates from nine colonies attended the Stamp Act Congress in New York. After protests that included the virtual suspension of all port activity for nearly two weeks, Parliament repealed the act in March 1766. New York joined the fight against taxation that eventually led to the American Revolution. Although New York did not see a great deal of action, it was Britain's military headquarters and was the only city occupied by the British throughout the conflict. When the war ended, many loyalists left America for the West Indies or Canada and the population dwindled to 12,000. But within six years of the British departure, New York had become America's most vibrant city.

You'll find Alexander Hamilton (left) on a $10 bill; the Stamp Act imposed by London (right)

1750

British Occupation

The city's Tories, who supported the British Crown, were jubilant when British troops entered New York in June 1776. Patriots surrounded the city, denying the British easy communications with other colonies. Under military occupation, the city suffered terrible fires and loss of life and property. A fire on September 21, 1776 destroyed a quarter of the city, including Trinity Church (see pages 142–143). On August 3, 1778, 100 houses burned. The guerrilla war between the two opposing sides involved cattle-rustling, abductions and deliberate burning of crops. American prisoners of war were either incarcerated in a crowded, appalling dungeon on Liberty Street or in ships anchored in the harbor. Almost 11,000 soldiers perished in the horrendous conditions.

The impressive entrance to the library at prestigious Columbia University (above)

Raging fires in New York in 1776 claimed many lives and destoyed parts of the city (right)

Defeat on Long Island

After forcing the British general William Howe to evacuate Boston in March 1776, General George Washington arrived in Manhattan on April 13. Knowing that he would meet General Howe's army again, forts were built in Brooklyn Heights and Lower Manhattan. On July 2, Howe's force landed on Staten Island. On July 9, the Declaration of Independence was read to Washington's soldiers on Bowling Green. The delighted soldiers and civilians tore down the statue of King George III and melted it down to make bullets—42,088 of them. Meanwhile, Howe's army moved to the south of Brooklyn, where his 20,000 British regulars surprised Washington's 7,000 militiamen. The Battle of Long Island, a terrible defeat for Washington, left 2,000 Americans dead.

Benedict Arnold

In today's United States, the name Benedict Arnold is synonymous with traitor. After Arnold had fought for General Washington against the British at Lake Champlain and in Connecticut, he was placed in command of Philadelphia in 1778. But he became disillusioned with Congress after he was overlooked for promotion. He knew British General Clinton was bribing Americans to desert and he began a treasonable correspondence with Clinton and was in the process of making plans to surrender West Point, the military academy then under his command, to the British when the plot was revealed. Arnold managed to escape and became a leader of British troops in New York. After the British surrendered, he and his wife moved to England, where they were deeply unpopular.

From General to President

On November 25, 1783, General Washington made his ceremonial entry into New York and gave a farewell address to his troops in front of Fraunces Tavern at 54 Pearl Street, then returned to his home at Mount Vernon in Virginia. On February 4, 1789, he was unanimously chosen as president of the new United States at a convention in Philadelphia.

On April 30, 1789, Washington took the oath of office on the balcony of L'Enfant's Federal Hall, on the site of today's Federal Hall National Memorial (see page 97). Thousands lined Murray's Wharf at the end of Wall Street as he arrived by ceremonial barge. The cheering crowds, waving their hats, then followed him on his route through the downtown streets.

The Tea Party

The British Parliament approved the Tea Act in 1773, giving the British East India Company a monopoly on all the tea sold in the colonies. The angry Manhattan Sons of Liberty encouraged the public to repel the tea ships; New Yorkers boycotted all establishments offering East India tea. On December 16, 1773, the Boston Tea Party, a protest in which a group of men masquerading as Mohawks dumped 342 cases of East India tea into Boston Harbor, further fueled radicalism in New York. Britain passed the Intolerable Acts which closed Boston's port, alarming New Yorkers. On April 22, 1774, New York had its own Tea Party and dumped 18 boxes of tea into the bay. This led to the establishment of the revolutionary government in New York State.

The hero and villain of the piece—George Washington (left)

Benedict Arnold (left) played a large part in the shaping of New York

1800

Troops were employed to escort the stamped paper for the 1765 Stamp Act to City Hall (below)

The inauguration of the United States' first president, George Washington, on the balcony of Federal Hall (above)

Commercial Growth

The first half of the 19th century brought New York conflict, epidemics and disaster, as well as an explosion of commerce and riches. During the War of 1812 between the United States and Britain, New York's port was blockaded. Ten years later, a yellow fever epidemic broke out in Front Street, and in 1832 a cholera epidemic killed 4,000. The Great Fire of 1835 gutted 700 buildings in a 17-block area below Wall Street; in 1845, another fire destroyed 300 buildings in Lower Manhattan.

The achievement that brought growth, prosperity and international commerce to the city was the building of the Erie Canal in 1825, a project of Governor DeWitt Clinton. In following years, powerful men went from rags to riches practically overnight. Cornelius Vanderbilt (1794–1877), an uneducated Staten Island farm boy, became one of the wealthiest men in America when he took control of much of the shipping business in the harbor and along the Hudson River to Albany.

The swelling city needed news. William Cullen Bryant, whose name is now associated with Bryant Park, became editor of the *New York Evening Post* in 1829. In 1834 Horace Greeley founded the *New Yorker*, a weekly literary and news journal unrelated to the modern magazine. In 1841, he became the founding editor of the *New York Tribune*, while other newspapers flourished.

Knickerbocker

The word knickerbocker was a literary invention of author Washington Irving (1783–1859) in his *Diedrich Knickerbocker's History of New York* (1809). A satire on pedantry, manners, politics and history told by an imaginary Dutch colonist, Knickerbocker, it won Irving much acclaim in the United States and Europe. New Yorkers of Dutch descent, and by extension the entire city, became known as Knickerbocker. The group of writers including Irving, novelist James Fenimore Cooper and poet William Cullen Bryant was known as the Knickerbocker Group.

1800

Writer Washington Irving (left) and editor William Cullen Bryant (above) left their mark

This was how New York appeared in 1849, looking south from Union Square (below)

Parts of the city were left in ruins after the Great Fire on December 16 and 17, 1835 (above)

John Jacob Astor

By 1808, John Jacob Astor—who emigrated to America from Germany in 1783—had amassed a fortune in the fur trade and was the sole owner of the American Fur Company. When he grew fat and his health deteriorated, he sold the company and took up real estate. After he invested in farmland north of New York City, in what is now the heart of Manhattan, the city's rapid expansion turned his farmland into a goldmine. Astor House, the biggest hotel in the world at the time, stood on what is now City Hall Park (see 77) and was the first building to bear the family's name. The Astor Library, which he bequeathed to the city, is now part of the New York Public Library (see page 127).

John Jacob Astor was the richest man in the world when he died

Grid System

New York City's grid system of streets was devised in 1811, at a time when the population was increasing rapidly. In need of new streets for the undeveloped land north of Washington Square, city officials accepted the plans put forward by engineer John Randel, Jr. The commissioners dismissed the idea of ovals, circles or stars and opted for the economy of straight lines and right angles. The Commissioner's Plan called for 2,000 long, narrow blocks, disregarded the contours of the land, and provided for neither parks nor open spaces.

Erie Canal

The Erie Canal, connecting the Hudson River and the Great Lakes, made New York the only eastern port with a waterway route to the farmlands of the mid-west, and instantly turned the city into America's center of commerce. It was New York governor DeWitt Clinton who oversaw the $7 million project, which skeptics at the time called "Clinton's Folly." The ten-day canal trip from New York to Buffalo meant that goods from around the world could be transported via New York to the interior of the New World. There was an explosion of new office space and warehouses along the harbor, and New York began its career as a major world trading center.

Artist and Inventor

By 1825, many of the most respected American painters were living in New York—that is the ones who stayed in the country and did not flee to Paris. A significant artist of the Romantic School and a successful portrait painter, Samuel F. B. Morse is best remembered as the inventor of Morse Code. He moved permanently to New York in 1824 and became a founder of the National Academy of Design in 1826. *The House of Representatives* (1822–23), one of Morse's most notable paintings, includes more than 80 portraits of politicians. By the early 1830s, he was more interested in electrical experiments than in painting, and in 1844 tapped out in code the famous message, "What hath God wrought."

City Hall (below), finished in 1812, gave the city a venue for meetings and events

DeWitt Clinton (above) was a governor with invaluable foresight

1850

The first barges arrived from Buffalo along the Erie Canal (above)

Social Unrest and Reform

By 1875 more than a million people lived in New York. The poor, many of them recent immigrants, lived in tenements that bred hatred, violence and disease, especially tuberculosis. Jacob Riis published a book of photographs, *How the Other Half Lives* (1890), which called the public's attention to the atrocious living conditions. As a result, reformers like Theodore Roosevelt and Frances Perkins joined a crusade to rid the city of these inhumane dwellings.

The enormous task of transportation in the growing city was a major problem. In 1858, about 35 million passengers used horse-drawn trams to move around. In the 1860s trains were a welcome improvement. Washington Bridge, opened in 1889, made it easier to go from Manhattan to the Bronx. Commissioner George Waring reorganized the sanitation system, and in 1893, New York began chlorinating its drinking water. Progressive reformers brought education to immigrant children and they were offered free medical examinations in 1895. The changes came too late for many immigrants, but at last something was being done to improve their lives

Immigrants poured into the city in the second half of the 19th century (right); Dr Elizabeth Blackwell was the first woman on the British Medical Register (far right)

Elizabeth Blackwell

Elizabeth Blackwell came from Bristol, England, to New York in 1832 to train as a doctor. She applied to eight medical schools before being accepted at Geneva Medical School, New York. Graduating in 1847, she was ostracized by the profession because she was a woman. With great determination, she opened a dispensary for the poor in the slums of the Lower East Side. In 1857 she founded the New York Infirmary for Indigent Women and Children (the New York Infirmary). In 1868, after creating a training school for nurses, she founded the Women's Medical College of the New York Infirmary. In 1910, she died in Hastings, England.

ELIZABETH BLACKWELL M D 1849

1850

A pictorial railway ticket (above); the elevated railway on Third Avenue (right)

Slavery

By the middle of the 18th century, New York had the highest concentration of slaves north of Virginia. They were sold at the slave market at the foot of Wall Street until slavery was abolished in New York State in 1827. But slavery was to continue, especially in the South, for another 38 years. New York provided a pivotal stage for its demise. On February 27, 1860, Abraham Lincoln arrived in New York City to give his celebrated antislavery address in the Great Hall of the Cooper Union Foundation Building on East 7th Street, now a designated historic landmark. His eloquent defense of the Constitution and the call for the freedom of slaves helped him secure the Republican presidential nomination.

The famous features of President Abraham Lincoln (below)

Tammany Hall

In 1850 William Marcy Tweed organized a volunteer fire department, a move which made him popular enough to get elected to city and state posts. In the 1860s and 1870s, under Tweed's direction, corrupt politicians at the Democratic Party headquarters, Tammany Hall, ran the party by bribery, coercion and vote rigging. Having swindled the city at every opportunity, Tweed was finally caught after the Tweed Ring reneged on a deal with the sheriff, who went to the press. *The New York Times* revealed the facts, and on November 19, 1873, Tweed was sentenced to 12 years in prison.

Draft Riots 1863

A dearth of volunteers for the Civil War led to conscription in 1862. In New York, as in other places, the draft met with great opposition and bounty hunters found substitutes for men who could pay. Others with $300 in their pocket could pay to be exempt. The cost of living in New York had doubled and the mostly Irish dock workers had gone on strike for higher wages; they were furious when black scabs were brought in to work. Under the circumstances the Irish could see no reason to fight for black freedom and bitterly resented conscription. Four days of rioting in scorching heat ended on July 17, 1863, but not before 120 men had died, mostly African-Americans killed by Irish immigrants.

Jewish Immigrants

The first Jewish people, 27 of them, arrived in New York in 1633. But the pogroms in Russia and eastern Europe resulted in the great influx of Jewish immigrants at the turn of the 19th century. In 1892, around 81,000 Jewish people arrived at Ellis Island (see pages 90–93) and 258,000 more between 1905 and 1906. They crowded into the tenements on the Lower East Side (see page 109), alongside the Irish, who had come earlier and who resented the newcomers. Given that many of the police officers of the day were Irish, it is not surprising that Mayor McClellan's police commissioner claimed that 50 percent of the city's crimes were committed by Jewish people. The outraged Jewish community forced him to make a public retraction.

A cartoon satirizing William Marcy "Boss" Tweed (1823–78), the corrupt politician who defrauded New York City of $30 million (left)

1900

The building on Ellis Island that was the first sight of New York for most immigrants (above)

Ulysses S. Grant, the Union and Republican President, tans the hides of Confederate generals and his electoral opponents (left)

World's Second-
Largest City

By 1900 Greater New York had a population of 3.5 million and was the world's second-largest city after London. In Manhattan, 42,700 tenements housed the 1.5 million poor in dire conditions. By the 1920s a campaign to restrict immigration resulted in legislation that brought a decline in the number of newcomers from Poland, Russia, and Italy.

The great metropolis experienced terrible disasters and celebrated remarkable triumphs. In 1901, a heat wave killed nearly 100 New Yorkers in just 24 hours. The first skyscrapers went up, starting with the Flatiron Building in 1902, symbolizing the city's wealth and hopes for the future. Meanwhile, Prohibition drove New Yorkers to illegal speakeasies. Many went uptown to Harlem for nights of pleasure. Then, on October 24, 1929, the New York stock market collapsed, bringing the Roaring Twenties to a sudden halt. A loudspeaker attached to a dirigible above the skyscrapers cried out to the employed, "Give until it hurts." Books like Theodore Dreiser's *Sister Carrie* (1900), and F. Scott Fitzgerald's *This Side of Paradise* (1920) and *The Great Gatsby* (1925) depicted a New York that had lost much of its sparkle.

The Empire State Building is a powerful symbol (left); At the Cotton Club (right) whites were entertained by blacks, who were banned from watching

Harlem
Jazz flourished in Harlem in the 1920s and 1930s as white New Yorkers discovered establishments such as the Cotton Club, famous for its "Colored Revues" and as the home of Duke Ellington, the Great Orchestrator of Jazz. Ellington's band, the Washingtonians, and his arrangements dominated big-band jazz for three decades. In 1932, he wrote a song whose title served as a slogan for the next ten years: *It Don't Mean a Thing If It Ain't Got That Swing*. Cotton Club owner Owney Madden, a gangster and bootlegger, strictly enforced segregation. The Depression took the swing out of these Harlem nightspots, and the Cotton Club moved downtown to West 48th Street, eventually closing in 1940.

1900

The subway in 1909 was only five years old (below)

Speakeasies flourished during Prohibition

IN THE NEW YORK SUBWAY. PICTURES BY G. W. PETERS.

THIS WAY TO SPEAKEASY

Triangle Shirtwaist Fire

Sweatshops in the Lower East Side at the beginning of the 20th century employed immigrant families in dreadful conditions at very low wages. These were increased after a series of strikes, but the tragedy of the Triangle Shirtwaist Fire in 1911 was to bring improvements in safety standards.

The factory, on the top three floors of a ten-story building at the corner of Washington Place and Greene Street, employed 600 workers, mainly young women. They were ready to go home when the fire broke out. Many doors to the fire escapes were locked, as was common during working hours, and 146 workers perished, some leaping to their deaths. Public outrage brought new legislation for safety in the workplace.

New Yorkers got their kicks on Coney Island's Boardwalk (below); Edwardian New York is apparent in the 20-story Flatiron Building (bottom)

Tin Pan Alley

By 1900 New York was the place to be for the young, ambitious songwriter. Theaters were flourishing and music publishers needed as many songs as they could get their hands on. Hundreds of composers and small publishing firms crowded into the abandoned brownstones on 28th Street, between Fifth Avenue and Broadway, and the area became known as Tin Pan Alley because of the cacophony coming from the open windows.

Two of the great songwriters of this era were George and Ira Gershwin, sons of Russian immigrants. At 15 years old, George was the youngest song demonstrator. The brothers' many hits included the classics *I Got Rhythm*, *Embraceable You* and *Somebody Loves Me*. George died of a brain tumor in 1937 at the age of 38.

The Subway

The elevated railways, financed by Jay Gould, Russell Sage and J. P. Morgan in the 1860s, improved public transportation, but were already inadequate by 1900. It was time to go underground. The Interborough Rapid Transit Company was born. The first line, 22 miles (35km) long, opened in 1904, carrying 600,000 passengers each day. It was a huge success and the profits enabled the city to expand the system. In 1921, New York and New Jersey joined forces to create the Port of New York Authority to develop and operate transportation. Delightful Coney Island, with its family entertainment, vaudeville and exhibitions, became accessible to everyone, thanks to New York's subways, which now total 722 miles (1,150km) in length, across 25 lines.

Organized Crime

Just before Mayor William O'Dwyer, first elected as New York's mayor in 1946, began a re-election campaign, the *Brooklyn Eagle* published some very damning news about the mayor's connection to organized crime in the city. The newspaper charged that policemen and judges were being paid off in return for protection for 4,000 bookies. The mayor fled to Florida "for health reasons." In the hope of avoiding prosecution, more than 110 policemen resigned. In August 1950, the mayor also resigned. Subpoenaed and left with little choice, O'Dwyer admitted he knew about the corruption and that he too had associations with mobsters. Yet for a lack of hard evidence of willful wrongdoing, he went unpunished.

George Gershwin (far left) wrote the classical *Rhapsody in Blue* (1924), while Irving Berlin (1888–1989) gave the world *White Christmas*, among other classics, before living as a recluse in Manhattan

Looking East from Steeplechase Pier, Coney Island, N. Y.

1950

Although America entered World War II in 1941 (below), New York City was physically unaffected

The Stock Exchange (above) is still a powerful financial institution

35

The Late 20th Century

The years between 1950 and 2000 swung back and forth between economic booms (1950s, 1980s, 1990s) and financial crises (1970s, 2002), and Wall Street struggled and soared with the times. New York's Abstract Expressionist painters inspired the art world in the late 1940s and 1950s; the Pop Artists shocked and thrilled the public from the late 1950s to the 1970s. Music and theater got a big boost when the Lincoln Center was built in the 1960s. The number of Asian and Hispanic immigrants swelled, with Hispanics overtaking the African-American population as the city's largest minority group. In 1989 the city elected its first black mayor, David Dinkins, who beat Rudolph Giuliani. Crime soared in the 1970s and 1980s, and vandals defaced city landmarks with graffiti. After Rudolph Giuliani was elected mayor in 1994, the number of recorded crimes dropped from 430,460 per year in 1993 to 161,956 in 2001, and the city had bright hopes for the future.

The Vietnam Veterans' Memorial (above) is a moving display of letters written home by the troops

Mayor David Dinkins (right)

Greenwich Village

By the 1950s, New York was America's cultural marketplace and Greenwich Village, with its cheap rents and bohemian flair, attracted America's finest artists and writers. Cedar Street Tavern at 24 University Place was the favorite Village hangout for Abstract Expressionist painters Jackson Pollock, Willem de Kooning and Franz Kline. Regulars at the San Remo bar on the corner of Bleeker and MacDougal streets included writers James Agee, James Baldwin, Allen Ginsberg, Jack Kerouac and William Burroughs. It was here that the word Beatnik entered the language. Writers Dylan Thomas and Norman Mailer preferred the White Horse at Hudson and West 11th Street. Mailer's disregard for the Beats produced the Hip Generation.

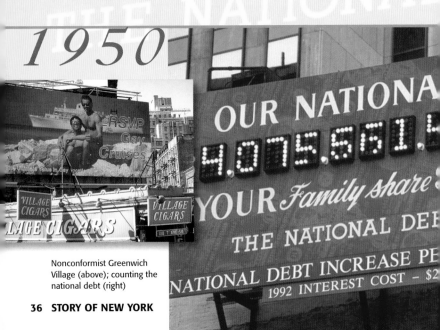

Nonconformist Greenwich Village (above); counting the national debt (right)

Sweet Success

In 1962, astronaut John Glenn arrived in New York and jubilant throngs lined Broadway for a tickertape parade, an honor bestowed only on visiting heads of state, generals, victorious baseball teams, athletes and great politicians. New Yorkers flung 3,474 tons of tickertape, more than anyone had ever seen before, from office buildings and skyscrapers along the route.

In 1969 the New York Mets rose from ninth place in the National League, defeating the Baltimore Orioles in the World Series and ending up with their first victory pennant. But they only received a tickertape flurry compared to the blizzard that welcomed John Glenn (below).

Andy Warhol

Pop Art changed the art scene when Andy Warhol (below) opened his Factory in 1963. His Coca-Cola bottle, Campbell's Soup cans and multicolor silk-screen images of icons Marilyn Monroe, Elvis and Jackie Kennedy were as astonishing at the time as the openly gay lifestyle he confidently espoused in an era when "homophobic" wasn't even a word. As a movie director he filmed *Kiss* and *Blow Job* in friends' apartments on the Lower East Side and in Greenwich Village. In June 1968, Warhol's Factory was visited by Valerie Solanos, the feminist author of the SCUM (Society for Cutting Up Men) manifesto; Warhol was shot, but survived. He lived as a recluse for the last 13 years of his life at 57 East 66th Street and died in 1987 rather bizarrely after routine gallbladder surgery.

Woody Allen

Allan Konigsberg changed his name when he started out as a comedian in Greenwich Village comedy clubs. He went on to make about a movie a year after 1965, most of them about New Yorkers. In 1977 *Annie Hall* took the brainy, scrawny actor and director to heights when he won Oscars for Best Director and Best Screenplay. But as luck goes, he did not attend the Academy Awards ceremony; he plays clarinet every Monday night at Michael's Pub (211 East 55th Street), no matter what. His 1992 affair with and later marriage to the adopted daughter of his partner Mia Farrow shook his fans and his career.

Ed Koch, Ronald Reagan and a large U.S. Treasury check

Ed Koch

The Big Apple was in such dire financial straits in the 1970s that it seemed only a miracle could prevent a collapse. In October 1975, for instance, the city was only 53 minutes from defaulting on its almost $477 million debt. After the Federal government proved unwilling to extend a hand, money from teacher pension funds inched the city back from the brink of disaster. When Ed Koch ran for mayor, he vowed to restore prosperity. He kept his promise after winning the 1977 election, and was re-elected by a landslide victory in 1981. His tax cuts, along with changes to investment banking , restored corporate America's confidence in New York.

2000

Public safety officers are on hand in Times Square, although its a lot tamer than it used to be (below)

The New Millennium

New York City's financial situation was not rosy at the start of the millennium. Mayor Rudolph Giuliani had cut taxes by $3 billion, and the city was heavily in debt. Then came the terrorist attack on September 11, 2001, that killed nearly 3,000 people, destroyed 25 million square feet (2.25 million square meters) of office space and closed the Stock Exchange for four days. Mayor Giuliani's courage and compassion immediately after the attack was admired by all. For plain-speaking Michael Bloomberg, elected mayor in 2002, Giuliani has proved a hard act to follow. The Republican billionaire businessman spent $70 million on his election campaign. With the Wall Street downturn cutting into tax revenues, spending cuts and belt-tightening have become routine—and predictions are rampant as to when, exactly, the recession will end.

strategy of implementing noise abatement laws and health statutes helped to close down brothels, gambling joints and massage parlors. A new zoning law banned "adult entertainment" from within 500ft of a residential district. In the 1990s Mayor Giuliani's tough policies made the area more desirable. Subsequent investment in the New Amsterdam Theater encouraged revitalization.

Crime

In 2003, New York happily boasted that it was America's safest large city, and given its history of disturbing crime statistics, this is good news. New York was ranked 160th in total crime among 205 American cities. The 15-year trend of crime reduction, with homicides at a 40-year low, is continuing. It was the controversial, aggressive policing during the Giuliani years that helped to cut crime by 62 percent. The mayor beefed up the police force with 4,000 new officers and sent them out to tackle jaywalking, sleeping on subways, defacing property, and other petty crime and quality of life issues. Mayor Bloomberg wants this trend to continue and is not letting up on criminals.

Cleaning Up

Between the 1960s and 1980s, the district from 40th Street to 53rd Street between 6th and 8th avenues was a sleazy area overrun by hookers, pimps and gamblers. In the 1970s and 1980s a

Grand Central Terminal (below); Mayor Giuliani (below left)

2000–today

Messages and prayers were everywhere after 9/11 (right); neon and color are de rigueur in Times Square (below)

On the Move

ARRIVING

BY AIR

You can fly direct to New York from most major European cities and from many other destinations around the world. International carriers fly into John F. Kennedy International Airport, 15 miles (24km) from Manhattan, on Jamaica Bay, and Newark Liberty International Airport, 16 miles (26km) west of town. LaGuardia Airport handles mainly domestic flights and is 8 miles (13km) from Manhattan in the borough of Queens.

John F. Kennedy International Airport (JFK)

There are nine passenger terminals at JFK. Terminals 2 and 3 are dedicated to Delta Airlines, Terminal 7 handles all British Airways flights, and jetBlue operates out of Terminal 6. All other terminals service major carriers for world destinations. There are information desks, restaurants and concession stands in all terminals. An AirTrain link between the airport

TRANSPORTATION FROM MAJOR AIRPORTS		
	JOHN F. KENNEDY INTERNATIONAL AIRPORT (JFK)	**LA GUARDIA AIRPORT**
Distance from Manhattan:	15 miles (24km).	8 miles (13km).
Journey time to Manhattan:	Taxi 45–60 minutes, Subway 60–100 minutes.	Taxi 20–35 minutes, Bus 40–50 minutes
Ground transportation information:	Baggage claim level of all terminals.	Baggage claim level of all terminals
Transport	**Shuttle/subway** • A free yellow, white and blue Long-Term Parking Lot shuttle bus runs to the Howard Beach Station, where you get the A subway train to Manhattan. • The free shuttle runs every 10 to 15 minutes during rush hour, every 20 minutes at all other times. • The subway costs $2 but you will need to buy a MetroCard (see page 43). **AirTrain** • Buy your ticket ($5 each way) at the station, or from a vending machine in the airport. • These connect to the LIRR at Jamaica station, subways at Howard Beach/JFK Airport station and Sutphin Blvd.-Archer Ave./Jamaica station, and local bus lines.	**Bus** • Follow the "Ground Transportation" signs out of the terminal. You will see the M60 bus stop sign at the curb. • The fare is $2, but you save on the transfer if you use a MetroCard (see page 43). • Take the M60 to 106th Street at Broadway. • Get off at Lexington Avenue to catch the 4, 5 and 6 subway trains; at Malcolm X Boulevard for the 2 and 3 trains; at St. Nicholas Avenue for the A, B, C and D trains; at 116th Street-Columbia University for the 1 train. • The bus runs daily between 4am and 1am, leaving every 30 minutes. • For more information, visit www.mta.nyc.ny.us/nyct.

and the New York subway, local bus lines, and the LIRR, opened in 2003.

LaGuardia Airport (LGA)
Most domestic flights go through LaGuardia airport, with TWA, United Airlines and Continental Airlines operating the lion's share. If you need assistance, look out for the Customer Service Agents in their red jackets or go to the information desk between concourse C and D on the departure level. Restaurants are in the USAir and Delta terminals, which are accessible via a free shuttle service.

TIP
Avoid airport hustlers offering taxi services. City cabs and car services are a better option and equally convenient—they wait outside terminals in designated areas.

Newark Liberty International Airport (EWR)
Major carriers that fly into Newark Liberty Airport include Virgin Atlantic, British Airways, Lufthansa and Continental Airlines. All passenger terminals, A, B, C and D, have restaurants on the concourse level, and the Information desk is in Terminal B, lower level. The AirTrain system, which opened in 2003, links the airport with the subway, NJ Transit, Amtrak and LIRR, and makes for a much quicker, and cheaper, journey into the city.

LEAVING THE AIRPORT
After collecting your bags and going through Customs, you can get into the city in several different ways.

TAXI
You will easily find taxi stands outside airport terminals. Dispatchers work during peak hours at JFK and La Guardia, 24 hours a day at Newark. For more

USEFUL TELEPHONE NUMBERS AND WEBSITES

John F. Kennedy International Airport (JFK)
718/244-4444
www.panynj.gov

La Guardia Airport
718/533-3400
www.panynj.gov

Newark Liberty International Airport
973/961-6000
www.panynj.gov

information about taxis, see page 51. Tip your drivers 15% to 20%.
● At JFK, you are charged a flat rate, plus tolls.
● At La Guardia, you pay by the meter, plus tolls.
● At Newark, dispatchers ask you where you are going. Give an exact address and you will be quoted the exact fare for the

ON THE MOVE

NEWARK LIBERTY INTERNATIONAL AIRPORT

16 miles (26km).

Taxi 35 to 50 minutes,
Airtrain 30 minutes.

On the baggage claim level.

AirTrain
• This modern speedy monorail/rail link operated by NJ Transit and Amtrak is comfortable and fast, and also easy, provided you do not have a lot of baggage.
• Follow signs to the AirTrain from any Newark arrivals terminal.
• Buy your ticket at the station (NJ Transit trains $11.55/children under 5 free; Amtrak trains $26) or from a vending machine in the airport or at the train station.
• These take you to Penn Station at Eighth Avenue and 31st Street in Manhattan.
• Do not get off at Newark's Penn Station if you want to go to Manhattan—stay on board until the next stop to reach New York's Penn Station. From there, you can easily catch a cab, the subway, or a bus to your hotel.
• NJ Transit trains run two to three times an hour during peak travel times, once an hour off-peak.
• It is easy to make connections to destinations beyond Manhattan from the Newark International Airport Station. For details, phone NJ Transit 800/626-RIDE or visit www.njtransit.com or phone Amtrak 800/USA-RAIL or visit www.amtrak.com.

ADDITIONAL INFORMATION

Telephone contact
The Air-Ride number, 800/247-7433, describing transportation to and from all three airports is answered by a live operator Monday to Friday between 8am and 6pm; at all other times you get recorded information.

NYC and Co.
810 Seventh Ave., New York, NY 10019
212/484-1200
www.nycvisit.com
Contact NYC and Co. to order the *Official NYC Guide* listing hotels, restaurants, theaters, attractions and events.
The visitor's kit also includes a map, brochures, a newsletter and information on services.

journey. They also give you a taxi information sheet with the rate, the amount for luggage, $1 per piece of luggage over 24 inches (60cm). Tolls are extra.

PRIVATE TRANSPORTATION FROM MAJOR AIRPORTS
New York Airport Service express bus
718/875-8200
www.nyairportservice.com
Follow the "Ground Transportation" signs to the pick-up point outside the terminal.
From JFK
This service runs between 6.15am and 11.10pm, and travel time is 45 to 65 minutes, longer during rush hour. The trip to the Port Authority Bus Terminal, at 42nd Street and Eighth Avenue, costs $13 ($23 round-trip): one way costs $10, but service is only three times daily, at 3.20pm, 5.20pm, and 6.50pm. The journey to Grand Central Terminal at Vanderbilt Avenue and 42nd Street, costs $13 ($23 round-trip), with a $2 additional charge to hotels between 31st and 60th streets. The journey to New York's Penn Station costs $13 ($23 round-trip).
From La Guardia
This service runs between 7.20am and 11pm, and travel time is 30 to 45 minutes, longer during rush hour. The journey costs $10 to $12 to Port Authority Bus Terminal at 42nd Street and 8th Avenue or Grand Central Terminal at Vanderbilt Avenue and 42nd Street, with a $2 additional charge to hotels

between 31st and 60th streets. The service to New York's Penn Station runs every 60 minutes from 8am to 8pm, takes 40 minutes, and costs $10.

SuperShuttle
800/451-0455 or 212/315-3006
www.supershuttle.com
Go to the Ground Transportation desk and dial SuperShuttle on the courtesy phone in the baggage claim area of JFK, La Guardia, or Newark airport. Vans runs 24 hours a day, throughout all five boroughs of New York City. Reservations are not required. The fares range from $13 to $22.

Coach USA
877/8-NEWARK
www.coachusa.com
Operating only out of Newark Airport, Coach USA takes passengers to Penn Station, at 34th Street and Eighth Avenue; to Grand Central Terminal, at Vanderbilt Avenue and 42nd Street; to the Port Authority Bus Terminal, at Eighth Avenue and 42nd Street; and to Chinatown and Lower Manhattan. The bus leaves every 15 to 20 minutes and costs $12 ($19 round-trip); children under 16 ride free.

SECURITY AT CUSTOMS
Since 9/11, security has been stepped up at airports, tunnels, bridges and train stations. To facilitate departure, do cooperate.

Do not carry sharp items on your person or in your carry-on bags. Empty your pockets before walking through the security detection scanner. Be prepared to open bags or remove your shoes for inspection or to allow a security officer to scan your body with a hand-held scanner.

BY ROAD
Driving into Manhattan is not for the feint hearted and once you've got into the city, you then have the problem of finding somewhere to park. Expect lengthy delays on the bridges and tunnels that cross to the island of Manhattan, especially on the bridges that cross the east river (repairs are ongoing). It is best to avoid the morning, lunchtime and evening rush hour traffic.

BY RAIL
Most commuter trains from Connecticut and the suburbs north of the city serve Grand Central Station (on 42nd Street at Park Avenue). Amtrak's long-distance trains from across the United States pull into Penn Station at 31st Street and Seventh Avenue and for journeys to and from Long Island and New Jersey, the Long Island Railroad and New Jersey Transit are the trains to catch, also operating out of Penn Station.

A New York Airport Service express bus

GETTING AROUND

The best way to see Manhattan is on foot. Streets in most Manhattan neighborhoods are safe both by day and after dark. However, walking takes time, and if you want to visit several museums or neighborhoods, or if the weather is inclement, the subways are a better option. They are easy to use, inexpensive, and relatively clean and safe. Buses are more pleasant than subways because you get a chance to see street life as you travel, although you need to pay with correct change, and during rush hour traffic slows your progress—sometimes it's faster to walk.

ON THE MOVE

OPTIONS

If you will be in New York for seven days or more, buy a MetroCard to save money on transit fares. You swipe the card at the subway turnstile or as you get on the bus, and you do not have to worry about having the correct change. Taxis are the quickest way for many to travel but the most expensive. When you take a cab, don't forget to tip the driver 15% or more.

Driving your own car in New York is not usually the best option. Besides the traffic, you count on parking on the street, and garages are expensive. If you do arrive in New York by car, the best course is to leave your car in a garage until you are ready to leave town (head for the eastern or western fringes of Manhattan if saving money matters more to you than convenience).

WALKING IN NEW YORK

Always use crosswalks; jaywalking is against the law. Stay to the right as you would when driving.
When the light changes and you are about to cross, check the intersection to make sure that no drivers or bicyclists have decided to make a dash through the light. This is not uncommon.

METROCARD

What is it?
A magnetically encoded card that debits the fare when you swipe it through the turnstile in the subway or the fare box on a bus.

What about transfers?
When you use a MetroCard for a trip, transfers between subways and buses within a 2-hour period are free.

Where can I buy one?
From staffed subway booths (cash only), special vending machines in most subway stations (cash, credit cards, debit cards), drugstores like Rite Aid, Hudson News at Penn Station and Grand Central Terminal, or at the Times Square Visitors Center at 1560 Broadway between 46th and 47th streets (cash, credit cards, debit cards). Many hotels sell them, too.

What's the cost?
Pay-Per-Ride MetroCard: $10 buys 6 rides, $20 buys 12 rides. These can be swiped four times

in succession, so are good for up to four people traveling together. Just swipe, walk through, and hand the card to the person behind you, who swipes, walks through, and hands it to the person behind. You can refill these cards—that is, put more rides on them—in the vending machines located in most subway stations. Just put the card in, indicate how much money you want to spend, and insert your credit card or cash.
Unlimited Ride MetroCard: $7 buys a 1-Day Fun Pass, $21 buys a 7-Day Card, $70 buys a 30-Day Card. These can't be used by

more than one person, an 18-minute interval must elapse between journeys. These cards go into effect the first time you use them, not the day you buy them.

Can I get a discount?
Seniors and people with disabilities can get reductions; phone 718/243-4999 or 718/596-8273.

How do you use a MetroCard?
When you swipe your card, the turnstile indicator shows how much money is left on the card. If you swipe the card too fast or too slowly, the indicator asks you to swipe it again. If this happens, swipe it again. Do not go to a different turnstile, as you may end up paying twice.

Where can I get more information?
Phone 800/METROCARD or 212/638-7622, from Monday through Friday between 9 and 5 or visit www.mta.nyc.us/metrocard.

Subways

The Metropolitan Transit Authority (MTA) runs the subway system. It runs 24 hours a day, seven days a week. Rush hour is between roughly 7.30 and 9.30am and again from 5 to 6.30pm Monday through Friday except holidays. The subway is quick, inexpensive, efficient, generally safe, and fairly easy to figure out.

> **TIP**
>
> New Yorkers refer to subway lines as trains. "Take the A train" means "Take subway line A."

Fares are $2 ($1 for seniors and people with disabilities); children under 44 inches (1.13m) ride free. The best way to pay is by MetroCard (see above).

A campaign promotes polite behavior, and posters ask passengers to give their seats to the elderly and infirm, to move to the center of the train so as not to block the doors, and to walk rather than run.

Stations are clearly marked

UNDERSTANDING THE SUBWAY MAP

MTA maps are free and easy to understand. You can get them in any subway station, at information centers and in hotel lobbies.

The map (see page 45) shows each line as a different color, but it is the number or letter that you need to know. No one refers to trains by color.

Black circles on the colored lines indicate stops for local trains, which make more stops than express trains.

Black and white lines connecting white and black circles indicate free subway transfers

White circles on the colored lines indicate express train stops. Express trains skip about three stops for every one they make.

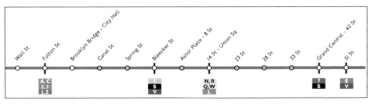

Below the name of every stop, the letters or numbers of the lines that stop there are indicated. Boldface type, for example **B**, indicates that the line offers a full-time service. Lightface type, for example B, indicates a part-time service. At 72nd Street, you see B, **C**, indicating part-time service on line B and full-time on line C.

ON THE MOVE

WARNING

The Lower East Side and the East Village are not well served by subways. If you are traveling to or from these areas at night, it is best to take a taxi.

SUBWAY HELP
- Station clerks are very helpful, and many subway stations are manned.
- For help in English, call 718/330-1234, 24 hours a day.
- For help in other languages, call 718/330-4847, between 7am and 7pm.

FINDING A SUBWAY
- Look for the signs in the station with colored circles showing the subway line letter (A, B, C, etc.) or the subway line numbers of the trains that stop there.
- If you need help finding a subway station, ask a policeman or step into a hotel lobby, museum or store to ask. Most people working in such places are used to helping tourists but even regular New Yorkers on the street do so quite happily.

FINDING THE RIGHT SUBWAY LINE
- After you have paid and walked through the turnstile, look for the colored circles. Find the line you want, and follow signs. Above the platform edge, signs indicate the trains that stop there, their destinations and hours of operation. Changes to the line's service are usually posted, but signs are not very large, so you need to look carefully.
- Uptown or downtown? If you want to go north of where you are, no matter where in the city you happen to be, you want an uptown train. If you want to go south of where you are, you want a downtown train. Some stations are Uptown Only or Downtown Only—clearly marked

A MetroCard ticket machine

HOW TO SURVIVE THE SUBWAY

- Although the New York subway once had a bad reputation for safety, trains are now safer and cleaner. However, pickpockets and beggars are perennial. Keep your money well hidden and do not wear expensive jewelry or even jewelry that looks expensive.

- Do not wait for trains near the edge of the platform; stand back a bit.
- If there are few people on the platform or if you are alone, stand under the yellow sign "During Off Hours Trains Stop Here." When the train stops, the conductor sticks his or her head out the window from a middle car, this is where he or she rides, and you should, too.

- Let passengers off first before getting on.
- Stay out of empty cars.
- After 11pm or midnight, take a taxi until you know your way around in the subway.
- If you find yourself on an express train speeding past your destination, get off at the next stop and either take the same line back to where you got on or ask the station clerk for directions. Be prepared to pay an extra fare to reenter the platform; at some stations, you may need to exit the station, cross the street, and reenter the station on the other side to catch the train that's going in the right direction for you.

at street level. If you find the color circle with the number or letter you want and know that you want to go north, for example, do not go into a subway entrance marked Downtown Only—any train you catch there will take you in the opposite direction. Trains headed your way are nearby—the entrance is usually across the street.

● On the front and side of every train, the route number or letter is displayed. Make sure you look for this before getting on the train to be sure it is the one you want.

● If you really want to be sure, stand in the middle of the platform, halfway between the two ends of the train, and when the train rolls into the station, look for the conductor leaning out a window in the center car—he can tell you definitively where the train is headed.

KNOWING WHEN TO GET OFF

● Conductors make announcements before each stop. On new trains, these are recorded.

● Every subway car has a map posted on the wall by a door, so you can check to make sure you are traveling in the right direction and can see how many stops you need to go.

● Look for signs on the station walls as you pull into the station.

LEAVING THE SUBWAY

After you get off the train, go upstairs (usually via stairway, but

sometimes via escalator). You have to go back through the turnstiles to exit, but you do not need to use your MetroCard again. Make sure you choose the right exit for your destination.

DISRUPTIONS

● The Cortland Street station, lines 1 and 9, damaged on 9/11, will remain closed while Ground Zero is under construction.

● Coney Island services on lines F, N, R, Q and W were being rerouted in 2003 owing to construction. Service may be restored by the time you use this guide, so check with the MTA for an update.

● Weekend service is sometimes altered on some lines to allow for maintenance work. Announcements are posted in the affected stations.

Passengers travel way above a Harlem street on an elevated section of the subway

IN CASE OF EMERGENCY

● Look for a police officer. The Transit Bureau Police patrol the subways.

● Look for a telephone and call 911. This is a free call.

● Go to the station clerk in the booth.

● On the subway train, go to the middle of the train to find the conductor or to the front of the first car to find the operator.

TRAVELERS WITH DISABILITIES

Not all subways are wheelchair accessible. To locate the 30 or more stations that are, visit www.mta.nyc.us.

TRAINS MOST USEFUL FOR VISITORS	
4, 5 and 6	The trains run up and down the east side of Manhattan, to the Bronx, and Brooklyn.
1, 2, 3, 9, A, B, C, D, E and F	The trains run up and down the west side of Manhattan, the Bronx and Brooklyn.
N, R, Q and W	The trains run diagonally east to west across Manhattan, then under Seventh Avenue to Queens.
S	The train runs between Times Square and Grand Central Terminal.
L	The train runs across 14th Street to Brooklyn.

Lexington Avenue subway

Buses

The Metropolitan Transit Authority (MTA) runs the city's buses, and fares are the same as for subways (see pages 44–48). You can use your MetroCard or exact change to pay for your ride. Bus drivers do not make change, so travel with plenty of quarters if you do not buy the more practical and economical MetroCard. Buses are slower than subways. Buses run 24 hours a day on most routes but less often at night, and on weekends. Drivers are helpful, so if you need advice, don't be afraid to ask.

FINDING A BUS

● Go to a designated bus stop, recognized by the yellow-painted curb and blue-and-white sign.
● Look at the posted Guide-A-Ride boxes, showing the route map and service schedule.
● Most major avenues have their own bus routes, running north or south.
● Crosstown buses, running east and west, are strategically located on major streets across Manhattan.

GETTING ON AND OFF

Board buses at the front. Swipe your MetroCard or pay in exact change. Leave seats in front for the elderly, the infirm, and adults with small children. You will notice a tape strip above and beside the windows. To indicate to the driver where you wish to get off, push on this about one block before your stop. Front doors open automatically; to exit by the back, wait for the green light to go on above the doors, then press the yellow tape on the doors to open them.

WHICH BUS TO TAKE

The routes given below are the ones most used by visitors who want to see the main attractions. If you need further guidance, use the map on pages 58–61 or pick up an MTA bus map from any visitor center (see page 324), subway station or hotel lobby.

ADDRESS LOCATOR

To locate the cross street of an address on an avenue
● Cancel the first digit.
● Divide by 2.
● Add or subtract the number given below.
● The answer is approximately the nearest number cross street (for example 54th Street).

AVENUES

A, B, C, D, First, Second		add 3
York		add 4
Third, Eighth		add 10
Fourth, Park Ave South		add 8
Sixth		subtract 12
Seventh	(above 1800)	add 20
Ninth		add 13
Tenth		add 14
Amsterdam		add 60
Eleventh		add 15
Broadway	754–858	subtract 29
	859–958	subtract 25
	1000+	subtract 30
Fifth	up to 200	add 13
	up to 400	add 16
	up to 600	add 18
	up to 775	add 20
	up to 1286	cancel last digit and subtract 18
	up to 1500	add 45
	above 2000	add 24
Central Park West		divide by 10 and add 60
Columbus		add 60
Lexington		add 22
Madison		add 26
Park		add 35

Bus routes criss-cross the city

North-South buses

● **M1**, **M2**, **M3** and **M4** basically run north up Madison and south down Fifth. These buses take you to the museums along Fifth Avenue, also called Museum Mile; M4 travels as far north as The Cloisters in Fort Tryon Park (see page 252).
● **M5** runs from Houston Street north along Sixth Avenue, then up Broadway to Washington Heights.
● **M6** runs from Central Park South down Broadway to South Ferry, through Times Square, Union Square, Greenwich Village, SoHo, and the Financial District, then back up.
● **M7** runs between Union Square and West 147th/Adam Clayton Powell Boulevard. It runs

The Coach USA sign

up Sixth Avenue, over Broadway, up Amsterdam Avenue, and across Central Park North, then up to 147th Street. On the return, it travels south on Columbus, Seventh Avenue, and Broadway back to Union Square.

M9 runs from Union Square to Battery Park along Manhattan's Lower East Side.

● **M10** runs from West 31st Street/Seventh Avenue (Penn Station) to West 159th Street/Frederick Douglass Boulevard. It travels up Central Park West, stopping at the American Museum of Natural History, and is a good bus for getting to Central Park.

● **M11** runs along the west side of Manhattan, north on Tenth Avenue/Amsterdam Avenue right up into Harlem.

● **M15** runs from South Ferry, north along the East Side to Second Avenue/East 126th Street.

● **M60** runs from West 106th Street/Broadway to La Guardia Airport.

● **M100** runs from West 220th Street/Broadway to East 125th Street/Second Avenue.

Crosstown buses

● **M8** runs from Avenue D to Christopher Street through the East Village and Greenwich Village.

● **M14A** and **M14D** run from the Chelsea Piers to the Lower East Side.

● **M27** runs between West 41st Street/Eighth Avenue (Port Authority Bus Terminal) and East 42nd Street/First Avenue.

● **M34** runs from Jacob Javits

ON THE MOVE

BUS BUSTER CHART

CHANGE AT OR WALK TO/FROM:

Union Square   Times Square   Broadway and E8/9 Sts.

Central Park South   South Street

w = walk   F = South Ferry from South Street

Use this chart to find out which buses will take you to your chosen destination. Follow the rows of squares horizontally and vertically from the name of the destinations until they meet. This square contains the number(s) of the bus(es) you'll need to catch. Bus numbers on white squares are direct. Numbers in shaded squares show that you have to change buses or take a bus some of the way and walk the rest. Start out on the first bus listed, then change to the second bus. Look at the key to find out where you must change buses or walk to/from. Note that the bus stop may be a few minutes' walk away from the destination.

Routes change regularly, and often differ on Sundays, so check an up-to-date timetable or bus map before setting out.

BUSES 49

MAIN TOURIST BUS ROUTES

Certain bus routes link key attractions. All routes shown are circular (north to south section of M15 shown only). Start and end point stops are given as well as stops near to main attractions.

M1

Jewish Museum, Cooper Hewitt, National Academy of Design, Guggenheim

Metropolitan Museum of Art

Rockefeller Center

Grand Central Terminal, Chrysler Building

Central Park

Frick Collection

Morgan Library

Whitney Museum

Harlem, Malcolm X Blvd./146 St. — Fifth Ave./(Central Park North — Fifth Ave./96–97 Sts. — Fifth Ave./84 St. — Fifth Ave./E79 St. — Fifth Ave./E72 St. — Fifth Ave./60 St. — Fifth Ave./49–50 Sts. — Fifth Ave./41 St. — Park Ave./E39 St. — Madison Ave./E43 St. — Madison Ave./E72St. — Harlem, Malcolm Blvd./W147

M7

Dakota Building

American Museum of Natural History

Madison Square Garden

Lincoln Center

Union Square

Central Park South

Schomburg Center

Times Square

Union Square, E13 St./University Place — Herald Square/W34 St. — Columbus Circle/W58 St. — Broadway/W65 St. — Amsterdam Ave./W96 St. — Harlem, Malcolm X Blvd./W135 St. — Harlem, Columbus Ave./W90 St. — Columbus Ave./W66 St. — Broadway/W42 St. — Union Square E13 St./University Place

M6

Empire State Building

Financial District

Carnegie Hall

Greenwich Village

Battery Park, Trinity Church; ferry to Ellis Island and Statue of Liberty

SOHO

Times Square

Flatiron Building

Ground Zero

6th Ave./(Central Park South — 7th Ave./W57 St. — 7th Ave./W42 St. — Herald Square/Broadway/W34 St. — Fifth Ave./23 St. — Broadway/E8–9 Sts. St. — Broadway/Fulton St. — South St./Whitehall St. — Church St./Vesey St. — 6th Ave./West Houston St. — 6th Ave./Central Park South

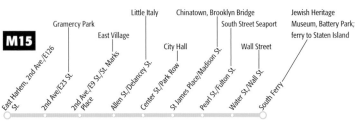

M15

Little Italy

Chinatown, Brooklyn Bridge

Jewish Heritage Museum, Battery Park; ferry to Staten Island

Gramercy Park

South Street Seaport

East Village

City Hall

Wall Street

East Harlem, 2nd Ave./E126 St. — 2nd Ave/E23 St. — 2nd Ave/E9 St./St. Marks Place — Allen St./Delancey St. — Center St./Park Row — St. James Place/Madison St. — Pearl St./Fulton St. — Water St./Wall St. — South Ferry

Convention Center at Eleventh Avenue/West 34th Street to East 34th Street/FDR Drive.
● **M42** runs along 42nd Street from Circle Line Pier to the United Nations Headquarters.
● **M72** runs from the Upper West Side to the Upper East Side from West 68th Street/Freedom Place to East 72nd Street/York Avenue.

● **M79** runs from West 79th Street/Riverside Drive to East 79th Street/East End Avenue.

SAFETY
Buses are safe throughout the day and the early hours of the night, but after 10pm it is best to take a taxi rather than wait for a bus on a deserted street. If a beggar asks you for money, just shake your head and do not get embroiled in conversation.

TRAVELERS WITH DISABILITIES
Buses are equipped with wheelchair lifts, and drivers can make the buses "kneel" by lowering the front step of the vehicle for people who have difficulty getting on.

Taxis and Car Services

New York's official taxicabs are licensed by the Taxi and Limousine Commission (TLC). They are easily recognizable; they are always yellow, always display the rates on the door, and always have a light on the roof and a flat bronze medallion on the hood. Do not get into any other taxi; only yellow cabs with the distinctive markings are legally licensed. Car services operated by private companies are available at an hourly rate and must be arranged in advance; they are not allowed to pick up passengers who hail them. Limousines are also available to rent.

A distinctive yellow New York taxi

HOW TO GET A TAXI

You can hail a taxi on any street by holding out your arm at the curb. When the light on the roof is turned on, the taxi is available. If the light is turned off, it is occupied. Usually you don't have to wait long before getting one, but it sometimes takes a while—after the theater, in the theater district and just about anywhere with the approach of rush hour time—4pm. Try to hail a taxi in the direction you would like to travel, which saves travel time and money. The best way to direct the driver is by giving the cross street and the avenue—for example, 42nd Street and Fifth Avenue. As you get closer to your destination, you can let the driver know the exact address. Most taxi drivers do not have a great command of the English language, so speak clearly and not too quickly when giving addresses or asking questions.

HOW MUCH IS THE FARE?

- As soon as you get into the cab, the meter is turned on; this flag-drop fare is $2.
- After that, it's 30 cents for every one-fifth mile (0.3km) or 20 cents per minute in stopped or very slow traffic.

- Tolls at tunnels and bridges cost extra. The driver may ask you for the toll money as you approach or may pay it from his pocket then add it to your fare at the end of the journey. Tolls range from $2 or $6, but there may be more than one. For more information on toll charges, visit **www.**panynj.gov.
- Between 8pm and 6am, you pay a night surcharge of 50 cents.
- Tip your driver between 15% and 20% on the fare excluding tolls.
- Note down the taxi driver's four-digit medallion identity number, which is posted on the divider behind the driver's head and ask for a receipt. These will be useful if you accidentally leave one of your possessions in the taxi or if you want to make a complaint.
- There is no extra charge per passenger, but taxis cannot take more than four people. There is also no extra charge for luggage.

KNOW YOUR RIGHTS

Drivers are required by law to:
- Be polite.
- Take passengers anywhere in the five boroughs, to Westchester and Nassau counties, and to Newark Airport.
- Provide air-conditioning.
- Turn off the radio if asked.
- Refrain from smoking while a passenger is in the taxi.

For full information on the Taxi Rider's Bill of Rights, call the 24-hour Consumer Hotline 212/NYC-TAXI or visit **www.**ci.nyc.ny.us/taxi.

Taxi drivers can be very helpful

Fasten your seatbelt. All taxis are required by law to provide them and passengers in the front seat are required to wear them.

TRAVELERS WITH DISABILITIES

Taxis are required to carry passengers with folding wheelchairs and with guide dogs and therapy dogs.

CAR SERVICES

Most car services have a two-hour minimum and rates start at $25 per hour. Allstate Car and Limousine Service 212/741-7440; 212/666-6666 for Carmel and 212/777-7777 for Tel Aviv are other options. The Yellow Pages has a complete listing. Alternatively, you can contract with a car service, through a concierge, perhaps for a specific trip at a pre-set rate.

TAXIS AND CAR SERVICES 51

Driving

Driving in New York City is not for everyone. Garage parking runs $25 a day or more, and finding on-street parking is nearly impossible; restrictions are designed to discourage drivers from using their cars. Plus tow trucks are out in force, and to get your car back if it's towed, you have to pay a hefty fine—in cash, often in a neighborhood you would rather not visit. Traffic is taxing during rush hours, between 7.30 and 9.30am and again from 4.30 to 6.30pm. Drivers are aggressive, unpredictable, or both.

DRIVING CUSTOMS AND LAWS

- Most streets in New York are

SPEED LIMITS	
Major streets	30mph (48kph)
Residential areas	25mph (40kph)
Major expressways	55mph (88kph)
Highways in rural areas out of town	65mph (104kph)

one-way. Newcomers from Britain and Australia need to remember that driving is on the right side of the road.
- No right turn is permitted on red lights in New York City.
- Drivers must wear seatbelts. By law, front-seat passengers and children ages 4–10 in the back seat must also wear them. Children under 4 ride in child safety-seats.
- Passing is permitted on the inside and outside lanes of Interstate Highways.

PARKING

- Check street parking signs carefully. For street cleaning parking is prohibited on alternate sides of the street on different days.
- For on-street parking you may need to feed the parking meter with change, sometimes on an hourly basis. In Midtown, look for Mini Meters, kiosks that dispense timed parking chits to leave locked inside your car, visible to parking inspectors.
- Do not park within 10 feet of a fire hydrant.
- Never leave anything inside a

Nose to tail on Madison Avenue

ROAD SIGNS

Regulatory information appears on signs with a white background
Warning information appears on signs with a yellow background

Left reverse turn ahead

Sharp curve to the right

Intersection within curve

Give way to other traffic

Intersection lane control

Y intersection ahead

T intersection ahead

Give way to other traffic ahead

High occupancy vehicle lane ahead

Divided highway

Divided highway ahead

Stop ahead

Advisory speed on deceleration lane for exit

Exits are clearly signed (above). Traffic policeman (below).

parked vehicle—even an empty shopping bag can provoke a thief's curiosity—and yield a broken window or locks.

● Parking garages are easy to find but expensive, in the range of $15 for the first hour to $40 a day, with special rates if you arrive before 10 or 11am. Midtown is the priciest area; to save, park closer to the rivers.

CAR RENTAL COMPANIES		
NAME	**TELEPHONE**	**WEBSITE**
Alamo	800/462-5266	www.alamo.com
Avis	800/331-1212	www.avis.com
Budget	800/527-0700	www.budget.com
Dollar	800/800-3665	www.dollar
Hertz	800/654-3131	www.hertz.com
National	212/875-8204	www.nationalcar.com

CAR RENTALS

Car rental companies are at all three major airports and at various locations around the city. Prices vary considerably, but as a general rule, a one-day weekday rental costs between $75 and $100, weekly rates run between $225 and $300, and weekend rates run around $65 for one day to $175 for two days.

If you require a specific type of car then make sure the rental company is aware of your needs because in a lot of cases you will be reserving the rental rate and not an actual car model when you make your booking. When working out costs, remember to consider the 13.25% tax in addition to the quoted price and remember that rates are calculated using the 24-hour clock. Most rental companies will offer various insurance packages which may include Collision Damage Waiver (CDW), Loss Damage Waiver (LDW), Physical Damage Waiver (PDW) or Additional Liability Insurance (ALI) in their cover. Another

charge to look out for is the "dropping off" charge levied when you want to leave the car in a different place to where you collected it. This charge is usually minimal but can be quite high if you decide to journey interstate. Most car rental companies have a stock of childrens' car safety seats but these need to be requested when you make your initial booking.

TIP

To rent a car you must
● Be 25 years old to rent a car from most companies (and be aware that some companies may have an upper age limit, too).
● Have a valid driver's license bearing your photo.
● Produce a major credit card and, if you're not an American citizen, your passport.
● Have your own insurance or purchase maximum insurance from the rental company.
● Return the car with a full tank of fuel or the company will fill it up and add the cost to your bill.

Alternatives

Depending on where you want to go, your journey can be a travel experience.

FERRIES

Ferries offer a comfortable journey with spectacular views. The free Staten Island Ferry has been running since 1905; it gives you a great view of the Statue of Liberty and New York Harbor. Boats depart from Whitehall Terminal 1 (Whitehall Street, tel 718/727-2508, www.ci.nyc.us/html/dot) and run 24/7 every 20–30 minutes on weekdays and less frequently on weekends and holidays. Taking your car costs $3. The journey, 5.2 miles (8.4km), takes 20 minutes. Listed below are only some of the ferry commuter services available. For sightseeing cruises, see page 260.

NY Waterway (tel 800/53-FERRY, www.nywaterway.com) operates commuter ferries to points in Manhattan, to Yankee Stadium and Shea Stadium, and to New Jersey from several piers: Pier 78 at West 38th Street, Pier 11 at Wall Street, and the World Financial Centre. Ferries run between 6am and 9.30pm, depending on location. Harbor sightseeing cruises also available.

New York Water Taxi (tel 212/742-1969, www.nywatertaxi. com) runs a shuttle between several locations throughout Manhattan, including Chelsea Piers on West 23rd Street and at the Circle Line at West 42nd Street. Packages are available.

Circle Line operates sightseeing cruises (see page 260)

NYC Department of Transportation (tel 311) can give you information on all New York City ferries.

PEDICABS

On weekends and evenings in Greenwich Village, SoHo, Times Square, Midtown, and the East Village, consider a pedicab for a unique view of town. Some drivers are licensed NYC tour guides. Most fares from Manhattan Rickshaw (tel 212/604-4729, www.manhattan-rickshaw.com) are approximately $8 to $15 within Greenwich Village, $20 minimum for reserved service, $150 for 4 hours or more during evenings. Consult a driver or contact the company by telephone. Pedicabs may be hailed, there are no stands.

CARRIAGES

A good old-fashioned carriage ride around Central Park can be idyllic. Carriages stand at Fifth Avenue and Central Park South. Most charge $40 for 20 minutes. For specific information call Central Park Carriages (547 West 37th Street, tel 212/736-0680, www.central parkcarriages.com).

Pedicab and driver

New York Water Taxi (below)

LEAVING NEW YORK

If you've had enough of the Manhattan hustle and bustle and want to sample life outside of the metropolis for a day then head out to the boroughs. If you have more time travel north into the beautiful Hudson Valley, with its pretty towns and historical buildings or go south to Philadelphia or the nation's political capital, Washington D.C. Trains and buses serve all major routes out of town if you decide not to take to the road yourself.

BY RAIL

New York has two train stations, Grand Central Terminal on the east side and Pennsylvania Station on the west.

● Local Metro-North commuter trains run in and out of Grand Central Terminal to New York and Connecticut suburbs. Information: 212/532-4900 or 800/METRO-INFO, www.mta.info/mnr.

● Long Island Railroad (LIRR) runs commuter trains to and from Long Island. Information: 718/217-5477; www.mta.nyc.ny.us/lirr.

● PATH connects Manhattan to many New Jersey cities. Information: 201/216-2677 or 800/234-7284; www.panynj.gov/path

● Amtrak's high-speed Acela trains serve Penn Station as well

as Boston, Philadelphia and Washington, D.C. Amtrak also has a daily service to cities throughout the US. Information: 800/872-7245 or 212/630-6400 or visit www..amtrak.com.

BY ROAD

Long-distance and commuter buses, as well as airport buses operate from the Port Authority

Travel by Greyhound bus is quick and comfortable

Bus Terminal (42nd Street and Eighth Avenue, tel 212/564-8484), which is New York's main bus station.

Greyhound buses travel to cities and towns across the US. Information: 800/231-2222, www.greyhound.com.

BUS VERSUS TRAIN

All prices are based on one-way tickets. To ensure availability, bookings should be made at least 24 hours in advance. Some train journeys involve transfers; contact Amtrak for further information.

ALBANY – HUDSON RIVER VALLEY
Train 2 hours 30 min. $43
Coach 2 hours 49 min. $32

HARTFORD
Train 2 hours 45 min. $41
Bus 2 hours 45 min. $24

BOSTON
Train Acela Express 3hr 30 min. $99
Bus 5hr. $30

PHILADELPHIA
Train Acela Express 1hour 15 min. $48
Bus 2 hours 50 min. $21

WASHINGTON, D.C
Train 3 hours 15 min. $72
Bus 4 hours 20 min. $35

CHICAGO
Train 19 hours, reservations only. $85
Bus 17 hours 15 min, reservations only. $85

ATLANTA
Train 18 hours, reservations only. $158
Bus 22 hours. $102

The mileages given on the chart below represent recommended driving routes and are not the shortest distances between cities.

ALBANY – HUDSON RIVER VALLEY
141 MILES (226KM)

BOSTON 194 MILES (310KM)

HARTFORD 120 MILES (192KM)

CHICAGO 807 MILES (1291KM)

NEW YORK

PHILADELPHIA 104 MILES (166KM)

WASHINGTON DC 235 MILES (376KM)

ATLANTA 888 MILES (1421KM)

TRAVEL WITH A DISABILITY

Thanks to the Americans with Disabilities Act, New York City is a fairly accessible place for wheelchair users. Most streets are level with curbs, cut at corners. Buses have lifts for wheelchairs, and taxis are required to pick up those with folding wheelchairs or service animals.

ON THE MOVE

GETTING ABOUT

All three airports serving New York are wheelchair accessible and have rest rooms for travelers with disabilities as well as TDD telephones in all terminals.

Most subway stations provide elevators and ramps, and there are tactile and audio features on ticket vending machines. If you use a wheelchair, alert the station clerk, who will collect your fare and buzz you through the entry gate near the turnstile; customers can enter the subway with a special Autogate MetroCard. (See page 43.)

The MTA buses are equipped with wheelchair lifts that are at the rear of most vehicles and are operated by the bus driver. Once on board, the driver makes sure that the wheelchair is secure. The buses are also fitted with a device that lowers the front of the vehicle so that people with impaired mobility are able to board and alight safely.

The car rental companies Avis and Hertz have some hand-operated cars for rent (see page 53). There are car rental desks at each airport.

Many theaters offer discounts to people with disabilities, and most cultural events are sign-language interpreted. Museums are accessible, but, some old buildings have not yet been converted.

USEFUL CONTACTS

If you have accessibility concerns and require information on visiting sights, contact individual venues or any of the following:

Mayor's Office for People with Disabilities
(tel 212/788-2830) will send the free book *Access New York* to people who phone in a request. This large-type book provides resources and reviews.

Metropolitan Transit Authority
(tel 718/596-8585, TTY 718/596-8273; 718/330-3322 for subway maps in Braille; 646/252-5252 for Access-a-Ride) provides information on New York's public transportation system.

Gray Line Air Shuttle
(tel 212/315-3006) provides transportation between the three major airports and area hotels with 24-hour notice.

Travel Information Center for Hearing Impaired Visitors
(tel TTY 718/596-8273) can help.

Society for Accessible Travel and Hospitality (SATH) (tel 212/447-7284; www.sath.org) gives information on travel worldwide.

Big Apple Greeter
(tel 212/669-8159, 212/669-3602, TTY 212/669-8273; www.bigapplegreeter.org) provides free tours of New York's neighborhoods with native New Yorkers. If you wish, you may ask for a volunteer guide with a disability. Reserve at least a week in advance.

Scoot Around (tel 888/441-7575; www.scootaround.com) provides wheelchairs and scooters for rental.

Hospital Audiences
(tel 212/575-7676, 888/424-4685, TTY 212/575-7673; www.hospitalaudiences.org) arranges seats at theaters, concert halls and other venues.

Hands On Sign Interpreted Performances (tel 212/740-3087; www.handson.org) can tell you where you will find sign language interpreters at exhibitions, performances and film screenings city-wide.

New York City Sports Commission (tel 877/NYC-SPORTS; www.ci.nyc.us/html/ sports) gives information on accessible sports leagues and venues.

AT&T Relay Operator
(voice 800/421-1220, TTY 800/662-1220; www.consumer.att.com/relay). operators act as interpreter between a TTY user and a voice telephone user. The operator reads the TTY user's typed message back to the other party.

This section is divided into three parts: Sightseeing Areas, consisting of five areas (shown on the map inside the front cover) highlighting what to see; A–Z of Sights, an alphabetical listing of places to visit in New York City, all located on the maps on pages 58–61; and Farther Afield, which describes attractions outside New York City (see map on pages 6–7).

The Sights

UPPER WEST SIDE

West 95th Street
West 94th Street
West 93rd Street
West 92nd Street
West 91st Street
West 90th Street
West 89th Street
West 88th Street
West 87th Street
West 86th Street
West 85th Street
West 84th Street
West 83rd Street
West 82nd Street
West 81st Street
West 80th Street
West 79th Street
West 78th Street
West 77th Street
West 76th Street
West 75th Street
West 74th Street
West 73rd Street
West 72nd Street
West 71st Street
West 70th Street
West 69th Street
West 68th Street
West 67th Street
West 66th Street
West 65th Street
West 64th Street
West 63rd Street
West 62nd Street
West 61st Street
West 60th Street
West 59th Street
West 58th Street
WEST 57TH STREET
West 56th Street
West 55th Street
West 54th Street
West 53rd Street
West 52nd Street
West 51st Street
West 50th Street
West 49th Street
West 48th Street
West 47th Street
West 46th Street
West 45th Street

Riverside Drive
Riverside Park
West End Avenue
BROADWAY
Amsterdam Avenue
Columbus Avenue
Central Park West

HIGHWAY 9A

Hudson River

86th Street
81st Street Museum of Nat Hist
American Museum of Natural History
New-York Historical Society
San Remo Apartments
Ansonia Building
The Dakota
79th Street
72nd Street

Freedom Place
West 69th Street
West 68th Street
Riverside Drive
West Side Boulevard

66th Street
Lincoln Center
Juilliard School
Lincoln Center

American Bible Society

De Witt Clinton Park

12th Av
12th Avenue
11th Avenue
10TH Avenue
9th Avenue
8th Avenue
BROADWAY
7th Avenue

Central Park
Sheep Meadow
Strawberry Fields
The Lake
Tavern on the Green
Central Park West
West Drive
65th

Columbus Circle
59th Street Columbus Circle
57th Street
50th Street
49th Street
Ca... Ha...

Intrepid Sea-Air-Space Museum
West 46th Street

BROADWAY

UNION SQUARE

Forbes Magazine Galleries

Ukrainian Museum

Grace Church

St Mark's-in-the-Bowery

EAST VILLAGE

Jefferson Market Library

Wanamaker Place

Astor Place 8th Street

NOHO

Washington Square Park

Merchant's House Museum

Tompkins Square Park

House of Oldies Rare Records

New Museum of Contemporary Art

Guggenheim Museum SoHo

St Patrick's Old Cathedral

Little Singer Building

SOHO

Haughwout Building

Lower East Side Tenement Museum

LOWER EAST SIDE

New York City Fire Department Museum

LITTLE ITALY

Tony Shafrazi Gallery

Seward Park

LOWER MANHATTAN

Museum of Chinese in the Americas

CHINATOWN

TRIBECA

Washington Market Park

US Courthouse

City Hall Park

City Hall and Civic Center

Woolworth Building

BROOKLYN BRIDGE

Avenue of the Finest

East River

Church of St Peter

St Paul's Chapel

Ground Zero

Fulton Street Market

BROOKLYN BRIDGE

BATTERY PARK CITY

Federal Reserve Bank

South Street Seaport

Trinity Church

Federal Hall National Monument

WALL STREET

Museum of American Financial History

Rectory of the Shrine of Elizabeth Ann Seton

New York City Police Museum

Battery Park

Fraunces Tavern Museum

Museum of h Heritage

Jeanette Park

61

Around Museum Mile

HOW TO GET THERE

🚌 M1, M2, M3, M4
🚇 4, 5, 6

Several of New York's finest museums are on the stretch of Fifth Avenue going north from 79th Street—an area known as Museum Mile.

This chic part of town, once known as Millionaires' Row, is also called the Carnegie Hill Historic District. Running from 86th to 98th streets between Fifth and Lexington avenues, Carnegie Hill is home to a concentration of imposing mansions by some of New York's most prestigious architects. Today's museums are housed in what were the great mansions of wealthy industrialists, who turned their attentions to this part of town in the 1890s. Central Park runs along the left-hand edge, and provided stunning views for the one-time residents.

The Guggenheim Museum is a masterpiece of architecture

MAIN SIGHTS

From 79th Street going north the main museums are the Metropolitan Museum of Art, the Guggenheim Museum and the Jewish Museum, but there are several others that are also worth a visit.

Metropolitan Museum of Art

The central hall of this enormous museum, the third-largest in the world, is one of the city's great public spaces. It costs nothing to walk in and spend a few minutes admiring it; the splendid collections could keep you awestruck for weeks. See pages 114–119.

Guggenheim Museum

To fully appreciate Frank Lloyd Wright's unsurpassable 1940s swirl, step inside, go to your right and look up. The fine collection and special exhibitions are ranged along a spiral staircase and are more than worthy of the setting. See pages 110–111.

Jewish Museum

This Loire Valley-style chateau, designed by Charles P. H. Gilbert, was completed in 1908 and was the home of financier Felix Warburg. Now it houses a museum of Jewish art and culture and offers an in-depth look into the lives of Jewish people through 19th- and 20th-century Europe and New York. See page 109.

OTHER PLACES OF INTEREST

Cooper-Hewitt National Design Museum

Built in 1902 to a design by the architectural firm of Babb, Cook and Willard, this 64-room Georgian mansion was originally the home of industrialist Andrew Carnegie and his wife Louise until his death in 1919. Now owned by the Washington, D.C.-based Smithsonian Institution, the industrialist's splendid home displays a superb design collection assembled by the Cooper and Hewitt families. See page 77.

National Academy of Design

This museum, also a school of fine art founded in 1825, owns the largest collection of 19th- and 20th-century American art in the country. See page 124.

Neue Galerie

Built in 1914 in the style of a place des Vosges mansion, and once the home of Mrs. Cornelius Vanderbilt III, the top society hostess of her time, the gallery

Go to the Great Hall of the Metropolitan Museum of Art to pick up information for your visit

was designed by Carrère & Hastings. Today it displays 20th-century German and Austrian works of art and design. See page 124.

WHERE TO EAT

Sarabeth's
Delicious breakfasts and filling lunches. See page 285.

TIP

● The Whitney Museum of American Art (see pages 148–151) and the Frick Collection (see page 100) are not far south along Fifth Avenue.

**Map labels:**
E13
Jewish Museum East 92nd Street
Cooper-Hewitt National Design Museum East 91st Street
East 90th Street
National Academy of Design
0 100 m
0 100 yds
Guggenheim Museum
Central Park Reservoir
East 88th Street F13
East 87th Street 86th Street
86th Street Transverse Road
Central Park
East 86th Street
Neue Galerie
East 85th Street
East 84th Street F14
East 83rd Street
The Metropolitan Museum of Art
East 82nd Street
East 81st Street
E14
5th Avenue
East Drive
PARK AVENUE
MADISON AVENUE
Lexington Avenue

THE SIGHTS

Around St. Patrick's Cathedral

HOW TO GET THERE
🚌 M1, M2, M3, M4, M5, M6, M7
🚇 B, D, F, S

When St. Patrick's Cathedral was built in 1878, architect James Renwick, Jr. must have had a premonition of the skyscrapers to come. Everything in this tightly packed area of Midtown Manhattan reaches to the heavens.

Unlike Lower Manhattan, where the streets tend to have names, Midtown is all numbered streets and avenues, which makes navigating easier for the visitor. Get caught up in the fast pace of life and you can easily spend an entire day here as there is so much to see and do. Aside from the sights, this is one of New York's main shopping districts, with the flagship store of the venerated national chain Saks Fifth Avenue.

The double-spired, Roman Catholic St. Patrick's Cathedral

MAIN SIGHTS

St. Patrick's Cathedral is right in the middle of this area, encircled by entertainments at the Rockefeller Center, the museums of Art and Design and Television and Radio, and the stunning, skyscraping Seagram Building.

St. Patrick's Cathedral

The twin towers and ornate white spires, reaching to 330ft (100m), remain impressive and are still often photographed, though dwarfed now by taller neighbors. The windows and stonework are beautiful and the space impressive. See page 131.

Municipal Art Society

New York's society for excellence in urban planning has been working to enrich the city's neighborhoods and physical design since 1893. Excellent walking and bus tours of the city are available. See page 120.

Seagram Building

The plaza of this bronze and glass giant, designed 1958, offers Midtown workers a place to soak up the sun over lunch. See page 141.

Trump Tower

The ultimate in shopping malls and decadence, with its many pricey shops, waterfalls and acres of marble and brass. See page 144.

Museum of Television and Radio

Access 75 years of programs and commercials through theaters, screening rooms and individual consoles. A good shop is the icing on the cake. See page 124.

Rockefeller Center

This city within a city is home to entertainment, shopping, dining, an ice-skating rink in winter and NBC's "Today" show. Some of New York's finest public sculptures, murals and friezes are here. See pages 128–130.

OTHER PLACES OF INTEREST
Dahesh Museum of Art

Dedicated to 19th- and 20th-century European academic art. See page 87.

Museum of Arts and Design

Huge exhibition of 20th-century crafts. See page 123.

Saks Fifth Avenue

Flagship store. See page 182.

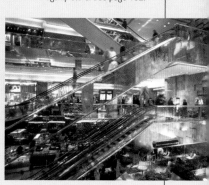

Trump Tower is about as ostentatious as it gets

WHERE TO EAT

Oceana
French-Asian cuisine and lots of wines by the glass. See page 282.

Le Cirque 2000
A legendary dining spot in the New York Palace Hotel, or there's Istana for olives, afternoon tea and tapas. See page 279.

TIPS

• Shopping at Saks Fifth Avenue, Thomas Pink or Cartier could liven up a visit.

• Try and catch a show at the Rockefeller Center.

THE SIGHTS

The Flatiron District, Union Square and Gramercy Park

HOW TO GET THERE

- M1, M2, M3, M5, M6, M7
- 4, 5, 6 or N, R Q, W

These three overlapping neighborhoods stretch east of Sixth Avenue (Avenue of the Americas) between 15th and 28th streets, south of Midtown Manhattan.

Each has managed to retain something of its historic charm. The Flatiron District has its early 20th-century classic skyscrapers around Madison Square Park, while Gramercy Park Historic District has leafy squares and fine old brownstones, and Union Square some of the first theaters. The area also provides some of New York's hottest restaurants (there's loads of choice) and hip, trendy shops like Emporio Armani and Diesel.

The Flatiron was built for the Fuller Construction Company

MAIN SIGHTS

The Flatiron Building, Gramercy Park, Theodore Roosevelt Birthplace and Union Square form a cluster of sights centered on the Flatiron Building.

Flatiron Building and District

When Daniel Burnham's triangular, steel-framed skyscraper went up in the city's most prominent site on Madison Square in 1902, it was dubbed "the Flatiron" because it was shaped like an iron (then called a flatiron). Painters and photographers have made it into one of the city's enduring symbols. See page 99.

Gramercy Park Historic District

Only residents around this lovely little park, or guests of the few hotels that front it, are allowed to enter the park; the gates are kept well locked. But you can see it well enough from the other side of the fence. Fine 1840s row houses line the west and south sides. See page 101.

Theodore Roosevelt Birthplace

The house is not the actual birthplace of Teddy Roosevelt, the 26th president, but a 1923 reconstruction. It was built for the Women's Roosevelt Memorial Association. Roosevelt is the only native New Yorker to have become president. See page 141.

Union Square

If you arrive at the Lincoln Statue in Union Square Park at 2pm on a Saturday, you can join a free walking tour of this neighborhood, a thriving theater, shopping, dining and entertainment area. If you go on Monday, Wednesday, Friday or Saturday and you will find one of the best of the city's green markets, farmers' markets that inspire New York's ambitious chefs and delight New York food lovers. See page 145.

OTHER PLACES OF INTEREST

Little Church Around the Corner

In 1870, when a minister of a nearby church refused to conduct an actor's funeral service, he suggested that mourners try "the little church around the corner." See page 109.

Metropolitan Life Insurance Tower

Designed in 1907 by Pierre Le Brun to be the world's tallest building, the Met Life skyscraper, at 700ft (214m), was soon over-

The National Arts Club in Gramercy Park Historic District

shadowed by the Woolworth Building. A four-faced clock is its most prominent feature. See page 120.

WHERE TO EAT

Eleven Madison Park
International menu and stylish decor. See page 275.

Veritas
Plenty of wines to choose from, and a tasty menu. See page 288.

TIP

• The Empire State Building is only a few blocks north, at East 33rd Street and Fifth Avenue.

THE SIGHTS

SoHo and Little Italy

HOW TO GET THERE

🚌 M1, M5, M6
🚇 4, 5, 6 or N, R, Q, W

In these adjacent neighborhoods, some of the best galleries display works by innovative contemporary artists from around the world, and there are also many historic landmarks.

SoHo, between Broadway and Sixth Avenue and West Houston and Canal streets, became of particular interest when mid-19th-century Italianate and French Second Empire cast-iron-fronted buildings were discovered. Its former manufacturing buildings are now apartments, and its artists' studios are still thriving, although today they're for wealthy artists only. Chic boutiques and restaurants ensure that the area is mobbed on weekends.

Little Italy, next door to SoHo to the east and bordered by East

of Contemporary Art where there's always something new happening that will be the talk of the town.

St. Patrick's Old Cathedral

This Gothic-style landmark has a grand interior with cast-iron columns supporting a timber roof. Construction began in 1809 on what is now the oldest Roman Catholic church in the city. In 1866, after suffering severe fire damage, it was restored. In 1879, after a new cathedral was built on Fifth Avenue, this building was renamed St. Patrick's Old Cathedral and it was demoted to parish church status. See page 131.

Haughwout Building

This building, on the corner of Broadway and Broome Street, is a classic example of the restored cast-iron buildings in SoHo, completed in 1857. See page 242.

Shopping for the unusual in SoHo's unique shops

Houston and Canal streets and Broadway to the Bowery, has at its heart Mulberry Street, once almost entirely inhabited by Italians, but now also home to a large Chinese community. Since the shrinking of Italian influence, trendy shops and restaurants have tended to moved just north of Little Italy, to an area known as NoLita (north of Little Italy).

MAIN SIGHTS

Aside from the many galleries that dot the streets in SoHo, St. Patrick's Old Cathedral is an early 19th-century landmark that contrasts well with the New Museum

New Museum of Contemporary Art

Contemporary art, including digital art and experimental video and sound, make this one of the city's most interesting museums. It offers international artists a venue for their experimental works of art. Programming is free in the Media Lounge, so step inside and see if you are tempted. See page 124.

OTHER PLACES OF INTEREST
Guggenheim Museum SoHo

On Broadway at Prince Street, this outpost of the Guggenheim occupies a warehouse and shows changing exhibitions drawn from the main museum's inspiring collection. See page 246.

Little Italy still exists but is also home to a Chinese community

WHERE TO EAT

Bread
Soups and salads. See page 273.

Honmura An
All kinds of noodles at this highly recommended establishment. See page 277.

Nyonya
A favorite for Malaysian cuisine. See page 282.

TIP

● Little Italy's Feast of San Gennaro in September is ten days of colorful festivities. Vendors offer tempting foods.

The Financial District

HOW TO GET THERE

🚌 M9, M15
🚇 4, 5, 6 or M, J, Z

The oldest part of Manhattan, the Financial District grew from the 1800s into a global focus for trade and commerce.

It is packed with historic landmarks, grand neo-classical buildings and contemporary high-rise steel and glass skyscrapers, and it's one area no visitor should miss. Come on a weekday to appreciate its vitality and robust flavor.

MAIN SIGHTS

Wall Street has become synonymous with high finance since the days of Dutch governor Peter Stuyvesant, and here too are the Federal Hall National Monument and Museum of American Financial History. In contrast, Trinity Church provides a peaceful interlude from all that money.

George Washington surveys the New York Stock Exchange

Wall Street

The skyscrapers lining this old, narrow street keep in shadowy gloom even on sunny days. But the passion for creating wealth that suffuses the offices overlooking this tunnel makes this little superhighway the city's most famous street. With many American flags waving overhead, it's a sight to see. The New York Stock Exchange is also on Wall Street. See pages 146–147.

Federal Hall National Monument

As you stroll along Wall Street, you can't miss the imposing bronze statue of the country's first president, George Washington, on the steps of the Federal Hall National Monument across the street from the New York Stock Exchange. On this site, Washington took the oath of office. Inside is an exquisite rotunda, among the finest Greek Revival rooms in the city. There are free exhibits, including the Bible on which Washington placed his right hand during the swearing-in. See page 97.

Trinity Church

At the west end of Wall Street is Trinity Church. Do pause for a look at this 1846 landmark's beautifully carved front door, white marble altar and wooden vault. At 284ft (86m), Trinity Church was Manhattan's tallest building from 1846 to 1890. See pages 142–143.

Museum of American Financial History

As you stroll down Broadway, you know you've reached the Museum of American Financial History when you see the bronze Charging Bull statue across from it. This Smithsonian affiliate displays some surprisingly interesting coins, documents and artifacts, and the interactive financial news terminals keep children amused. See page 123.

OTHER PLACES OF INTEREST

Fraunces Tavern Museum
On this site in 1783 General George Washington bade farewell to his officers at the end of the American Revolution. Fires in the 19th century all but destroyed the original building; what was left of it was bought by the Sons of the Revolution in 1904, who renovated it in Colonial Revival style. The tavern is now a museum and restaurant. See page 99.

Beautiful stained-glass windows adorn Trinity Church

New York City Police Museum

New York Police Department is proud of its achievements. This new museum offers a glimpse into the arrest records of famous criminals, a look at the weapons used, and an introduction to forensic science. See page 126.

WHERE TO EAT

Mark Joseph Steakhouse
The city's best steakhouse. See page 280.

TIP

● Century 21 is a designer discount heaven. See page 183.

The changing exhibitions at the American Bible Society explore Judeo-Christian art, both historical and contemporary

A 1795 $10 Eagle at the American Numismatic Society

AMERICAN ACADEMY AND INSTITUTE OF ARTS AND LETTERS

✚ Off map 58 C12 • Broadway at 155th Street 10032 ☎ 212/368-5900
🕒 Thu–Sun 1–4 🚇 M4, M5 🚊 C, D

One of America's first planned cultural centers, the Renaissance Revival complex now known as the Audubon Terrace Historic District was the brainchild of Archer M. Huntington, the son of Collis P. Huntington, builder of he Central Pacific Railroad, who founded the Hispanic Society of America in 1904 (see page 101). The American Numismatic Society (see below) was added in 1907, followed in 1921–23 by the American Academy of Arts and Letters.

The Academy gives grants and prizes to artistic causes and holds special exhibitions of works by member artists, composers or authors.

AMERICAN BIBLE SOCIETY

✚ 58 D16 • 1865 Broadway 10023
☎ 212/408-12 00 🕒 Mon–Wed & Fri 10–6, Thu 10–7, Sat 10–5 🚻 Free
🚇 M5, M7, M104 🚊 A, B, C, D 🏛
www.americanbible.org

Founded in 1816, the society has built up an extensive library of Bibles from all over the world. Its archives include an illustrated Armenian account of the Four Gospels dating back to the early 15th century. Displays upstairs are changed from time to time, but the reconstruction of a Gutenberg printing press is always on show, as is an exhibition on the Dead Sea Scrolls. Temporary exhibitions have included *From Gutenberg to the Internet: The Impact of the Word on the World* and *Symbols of Holy Russia*.

The postmodern cast-in-place concrete building dates from 1966 but the new steel-and-glass entrance, stairs and second-floor gallery were added in 1998.

AMERICAN MUSEUM OF NATURAL HISTORY
see pages 68–72

AMERICAN NUMISMATIC SOCIETY

✚ off map 58 C12 • Audubon Terrace at Broadway and 155th Street 10032
☎ 212/ 234-3130 🕒 Tue–Fri 9–4.30
🚻 Free 🚇 M4, M5, M100 🚊 1 🏛
www.amnusoc.org

The American Numismatic Society occupies one of the buildings in the four-building Audubon Terrace complex and was designed for serious collectors and researchers.

The society's superb ground-floor collection numbers an estimated 750,000 coins and related objects, and is comparable to the best in Europe. Displays document how the coins originated

A 14th-century Nepalese sculpture on display in the Asia Society and Museum

and were used around the world. Maps and photographs illustrate the history of money. Upstairs is a fine collection of medals.

ASIA SOCIETY AND MUSEUM

✚ 59 F15 • 725 Park Avenue at 70th Street 10021 ☎ 212/288-6400
🕒 Tue–Sun 11–6, Fri 11–9; closed major holidays 🚻 Adult $7, under 16s and members free, Fri 6pm–9pm free for all 🚇 M1, M2, M3, M4 🚊 6, F 🏛
🏛 🍽
www.asiasociety.org

Founded by John D. Rockefeller III in 1956 to promote relations between America and Asian countries, the society mounts exhibitions, lectures, conferences, concerts and workshops with specialists in Asian and world politics. A $30-million renovation of the 1981 building completed in 2001 doubled the exhibition space. The collection is based on Rockefeller's donation of acquisitions from all over Asia, and ranges from 11th-century BC Chinese ceramics to Japanese prints and Cambodian sculptures to 19th-century objects. The calendar of events includes films, lectures and discussions on Asian and global politics.

BATTERY PARK
see page 73

BATTERY PARK CITY

✚ 58 D25 • Southwest tip of Manhattan 🚇 M20, M22 🚊 N, R
www.batteryparkcity.org

From Pier A to Chambers Street, the $4-billion, 92-acre Battery Park City development was created using the earth excavated in the 1970s during construction of the World Trade Center. Admiral Dewey Promenade is a great place for a stroll along the waterfront, or sit on a bench to watch the boats on the Hudson. Cesar Pelli's World Financial Center (1987) sits amid residential towers, plazas and parks. The Gardens of Remembrance were planted here two months after the September 11 attack.

American Museum of Natural History

36 million specimens from dinosaur fossils to moon rock, and state-of-the-art exhibitions.

The main entrance to the museum on Central Park West

Biology and evolution of humans on Earth

Hanging around the Hall of Biodiversity

SEEING THE AMERICAN MUSEUM OF NATURAL HISTORY

There are three entrances to the museum: the main entrance on Central Park West, where you will see the impressive bronze statue of President Theodore Roosevelt on horseback; the Columbus Avenue entrance onto West 77th Street, temporarily closed at press time, and an entrance on West 81st Street into the Rose Center for Earth and Space, a planetarium with a narrated history of the universe. The museum has grown over the years and now has 40 grand exhibition halls, so you will have to decide what interests you most and save the rest for other visits. A good way to start a visit is to join one of the free Highlights Tours; you will hear about some of the museum's prized treasures and get orientation on the layout of the exhibits. Ask at the information desk inside the main entrance, where the tour begins. The tour guides are friendly, well-informed, usually very entertaining and easy to spot: They hold up a yellow flag as they proceed through the museum. You can join in along the way.

HIGHLIGHTS

ROTUNDA

Inside the main entrance is the Rotunda, a city landmark, where colorful murals depict great accomplishments of Theodore Roosevelt, the first New Yorker to become president of the United States. The *Barosaurus* in the middle of the Rotunda is the tallest mounted dinosaur in the world at 50ft (15m). The real bones are stored elsewhere; the ones you see here are casts.

RATINGS	
Good for kids	◗◗◗◗
Historic interest	◗◗◗◗
Specialist shopping	◗◗◗◗
Value for money	◗◗◗◗

TIPS

● Go on a free Highlights Tour

● On Friday evenings the museum is less crowded. On the first Friday of every month top jazz musicians entertain for free at 5.30 and 7.15. Tapas and drinks are available

● Purchase a CityPass (see page 317), good for nine days, to save money and avoid standing in line for tickets

● The gift shop has a wide range of jewelry, pottery, metalwork and glasswork from all over the world

The 563-carat Star of India sapphire in the Hall of Gems (left); the Barosaurus in the Rotunda (far left)

The gorilla diorama (top); the Hall of Northwest Coast Indians

Totem poles dominate the Native American exhibition

The Hall of the Universe, on the lower level of the Rose Center

ROSE CENTER FOR EARTH AND SPACE
Hayden Sphere
Part of the four-story, $210-million Rose Center for Earth and Space, opened in 2000, which occupies a glass cube designed by James Polshek, the great Sphere contains the planetarium. Take a 30-minute virtual ride through the Milky Way and find out about distant planets and superclusters elucidated through the fascinating commentary and stellar special effects. The spiral Cosmic Pathway winds down around the course of the Sphere.

FIRST FLOOR
Dzanga-Sangha Rainforest (Hall of Biodiversity)
The full-sized rain forest diorama, 90ft (27m) long, 26ft (8m) wide, and 18ft (6m) high, re-creates a forest in the Central African Republic. Visitors can go behind the glass into a world where high-resolution imagery, video, sound and smell take you into a rain forest experience. On the forest floor, insects, reptiles and small mammals scuttle through the saplings, shrubs, herbs, ferns and leaf litter; a stream runs past, and in the distance you may get glimpses of elephants moving about, while birds and primates hang around in the tangle of overhead vines, branches and trunks.

Blue Whale (Hall of Ocean Life)
One of the museum's favorite exhibits, the 94ft (31m) model of a blue whale dominates the state-of-the-art Hall of Ocean Life. Video projection screens and interactive computer stations help you to understand marine environments across the world.

Discovery Room
Designed to interest children between the ages of 5 and 12, the Discovery Room has puzzles and games, specimens to examine, and scientific challenges and investigations to explore.

SECOND FLOOR
Elephant Diorama (Akeley Hall of African Mammals)
This venerable diorama, constructed in the 1930s, set the standard for natural history museum displays. The group of elephants is

A decorative mask

KEY TO MAIN ROOMS

FOURTH FLOOR
1: Research library
2: Vertebrate origins
4, 5: Mammal fossils
7: Ornithischian dinosaurs (*Stegosaurus* and *Triceratops*)
9: Saurischian dinosaurs (*Tyrannosaurus* and *Apatosaurus*)

THIRD FLOOR
1: Pacific peoples
2, 3: Plains and Woodlands Indians
4: Primates
5: North American birds
6: New York state mammals
7: New York City birds
8: African mammals
9: Reptiles and amphibians (including the world's largest lizard the 10ft/3m Komodo dragon)
10: Hayden Planetarium Space Theater

SECOND FLOOR
1, 2: South and Central American peoples
3: Birds of the world
4: Asian peoples
5: Asian mammals
6: Main entrance and Rotunda
9: Cosmic pathway
10: Big Bang
11: African mammals
13: African peoples

FIRST FLOOR
1: Ross Hall of Meteorites
2: Human biology and evolution
3: Discovery Room
4: New York state environment
5: North American forests
6: Hall of biodiversity
7: Theodore Roosevelt Memorial Hall
8: Hall of Planet Earth
9: Cosmic pathway
10: Rose Gallery (space show boarding)
11: North American mammals
12: Hall of ocean life
14: Northwest coast Indians
15: IMAX theater
19, 20: Gems and minerals (Star of India sapphire)

Cafe on 4

Dinostore and More

10 (access only from 1st floor)

Dana Education Wing

Ross Terrace

The Museum Shop

COLUMBUS AVENUE

WEST 81st STREET

WEST 77th STREET

CENTRAL PARK WEST

THE SIGHTS

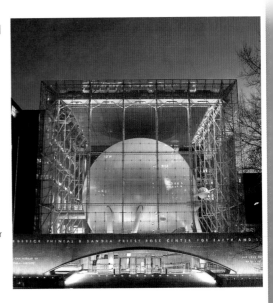

The Rose Center glass cube is made up of 736 panes of glass

set amid vegetation typical of their natural habitat. Other dioramas in the hall show more of Africa's stunning wildlife.

THIRD FLOOR

Passenger pigeon (Hall of New York City Birds)
Two centuries ago, the passenger pigeon was one of the most abundant birds in North America. Now extinct, the bird's life is traced through vivid displays.

FOURTH FLOOR

Stegosaurus and *Triceratops* (Hall of Ornithischian Dinosaurs)
These two huge dinosaurs were vegetarians, protected from rapacious attacks by massive bony jaw plates. Begin with a visit to the Wallach Orientation Center for an overview of the six fossil halls. Did you know that the word dinosaur means "terrible lizard?"

Tyrannosaurus and *Apatosaurus* (Hall of Saurischian Dinosaurs)
You may feel very small when you enter the Hall of Saurischian Dinosaurs and meet the giants displayed here. *Tyrannosaurus rex* is an awesome sight, with the horrendous teeth of a meat-eater.

BACKGROUND

Increasing interest in natural history and the discovery of fossils, particularly of dinosaurs, across the United States provided the inspiration for this great museum, founded in 1869 by Albert S. Bickmore. Originally the museum was in the Arsenal building in Central Park. Construction on this site began in 1874, to plans conceived by Calvert Vaux and J. Wrey Mould. President Ulysses S. Grant laid the cornerstone, and President Rutherford B. Hayes formally opened the museum in 1877. Additions in many architectural styles have expanded the museum since. The Theodore Roosevelt Memorial Hall, finished in 1936, was designed by John Russell Pope. Roosevelt, a keen hunter and collector, donated specimens from his many expeditions, including a bat and the skull of a red squirrel. The museum also includes a research center with numerous laboratories, teaching and other facilities, and a library that has the largest collection of natural history books in the western hemisphere. The collection of dinosaurs and other fossils is the largest in the world, and many of those on view are real, not cast reproductions.

THE SIGHTS

Heading for the relative peace and quiet of Battery Park

BATTERY PARK

Spectacular views take in New York Bay to the south and the Financial District skyscrapers rising to the north.

These 21 acres (8.5ha), at the southern tip of Manhattan are the site of Castle Clinton, a national monument, where you can buy tickets for the ferries to Liberty Island (see pages 136–137) and Ellis Island (see pages 90–93). The park's meandering paths are scattered with large, poignant memorials to more than 200 years of war dead and with its terrific view of the harbor, it is a pleasant place to get away from the busy, skyscraper-packed Financial District. Once a rocky ledge, Battery Park was created with landfill to protect the island from British attack in 1811, and it was named for the cannons that stood here.

The relocated Sphere *statue by Fritz Koenig*

RATINGS	
Good for kids	●●●●
Historic interest	●●●●
Photo stops	●●●●
Walkability	●●●●

BASICS
✚ 344 E26 • Southwest tip of Manhattan on the Hudson River
🚌 M15, M22
🚇 A, C, J, M

TIP

● If you enter the park from Bowling Green subway station, you will pass the damaged 22-ton bronze *Sphere,* which once stood between the twin towers of the World Trade Center. It was recovered and placed temporarily in the park as a memorial to the victims of the 9/11 attack.

CASTLE CLINTON

Castle Clinton was built in 1807–09 for defense. In 1823 the U.S. government ceded it to the city, and it became a center for theatrical and musical entertainment, hosting such events as the triumphal 1850 appearance of the Swedish soprano Jenny Lind. From 1855 to 1890 almost 8 million newly landed immigrants passed through Castle Clinton, when it was the immigration processing center, recalled by the statue in front of the castle, *The Immigrants* by Luis Sanguino. In 1889 immigration processing moved to Ellis Island. From 1896 to 1911, Castle Clinton was home to New York's first aquarium, now at Coney Island. Dioramas in the small museum depict Castle Clinton's history.

THE HARBOR

At the south end of Battery Park is the terminal for the Staten Island Ferry. From here, looking out across the city's harbor, you have a magnificent view of the Statue of Liberty, Ellis Island, Governors Island, and the Verrazano Narrows Bridge with the Atlantic Ocean beyond. Just past Slip 6 is a sculpture by Marisol, the *American Merchant Mariners Memorial,* dedicated to all merchant mariners who have served the United States since the Revolutionary War. Throughout the park vendors sell everything from T-shirts to ice cream.

Artruro Di Modica's bronze bull—Financial District landmark since the 1980s

Brooklyn Bridge

A walk across Brooklyn Bridge yields a memorable view of Lower Manhattan and New York Harbor. A symbol of true pioneering spirit.

The bridge has been described as the crowning glory of an age memorable for great industrial achievements

The walkway is a good place to enjoy the cityscape

RATINGS	
Good for kids	● ● ● ● ●
Historic interest	● ● ● ●
Photo stops	● ● ● ● ●

BASICS
✚ 61 G25 • From southern Manhattan over the East River to Brooklyn
🚇 Free
🚌 M9, M15
🚊 4, 5, 6

TIP

● Walk across the bridge at dusk on a summer evening as the sun slowly sets behind Liberty Island and the city lights begin to twinkle.

This remarkable feat of 19th-century engineering, designed by John Roebling and built between 1867 and 1883, was the world's first steel suspension bridge. It spans a mile (1.6km) across the East River, roughly between Cadman Plaza in Brooklyn and City Hall Park in Manhattan.

CONSTRUCTION CASUALTIES

The construction of the bridge cost several lives, including that of the chief engineer. While doing the final survey for the bridge, John Roebling suffered a severe injury to his foot. He survived the amputation of his toes, but died on July 22, 1869, of the resulting tetanus infection. His son, Washington Roebling, an engineer with the Union Army during the Civil War, took over as chief engineer. Working underwater on the caissons one day in 1872, Washington surfaced too quickly and was partially paralyzed by the resulting attack of the bends, also known as decompression sickness. He carried on, directing construction from his window in Brooklyn Heights with the aid of a telescope, while his wife Emily marched back and forth delivering his instructions to workers. Of the 600 laborers who worked on this project, 20 lost their lives in construction accidents.

When the bridge opened in May 1883, the public marveled at the Gothic-inspired span with its stone pylons and web of steel cables. Roebling's understanding of aerodynamic stability was very advanced for those days and he was the first to introduce radiating stays extending from the tops of the towers to the lower end of the suspender cables. It is estimated that 150,000 people walked across Brooklyn Bridge on opening day—but not Roebling, who refused to come after a bitter dispute with the company that financed the project. Disaster struck days later. A woman stumbled and fell while walking across. As people tried to see what was happening, there was much pushing and shoving. It was Memorial Day, a national holiday commemorating American servicemen killed in action, so there were great crowds on the bridge. A rumor began to spread that the bridge was about to collapse, and everyone panicked and rushed toward land. Twelve people were trampled to death and many were injured. On a cheerier note, in 1884 the great circus entertainer P. T. Barnum led 21 elephants across the bridge, which bore the weight without incident.

THE BRIDGE TODAY

As you walk along the wooden pedestrian walkway, you will come to a viewing spot where a bronze plaque gives information about the Roeblings. Take a look at the map etched in metal alloy, so that you know which skyscrapers loom ahead.

American poet Walt Whitman once described the bridge and the views as the best medicine his soul had ever experienced. He might balk at the number of skyscrapers, and probably at the number of bike-riders, roller-skaters and joggers racing across it today, but they have their own lane so pedestrians can stroll at their own pace and in safety.

The twin Gothic arches tower 277ft (84m) above the East River. The bridge was repainted in 1973, in its original beige and light brown. The walkway was reconstructed in 1983.

Jogging across the one mile span of the bridge is a popular way to keep in shape

Many famous conductors have appeared on this great stage, conducting music by names like Gershwin and Stravinsky

CARNEGIE HALL

The outstanding acoustics of this world-famous concert hall attract the world's most gifted musicians.

This superb Italian-Renaissance-inspired concert hall took seven years to build, opening in 1891. With 2,804 seats and excellent acoustics, it remains one of New York's most highly prized music centers. The Rose Museum next door *(Thu–Tue 11–4.30 and available to concert patrons in the evenings; free)* has archival treasures relating to the history of the building and famous figures who have performed here.

EARLY HISTORY

Late 19th-century New York was an important place but it did not have a concert hall. When the steel magnate Andrew Carnegie heard this, he put up the $2 million needed to construct the building, on the condition that the city provide the land on which to build it: At that time New York was a stretch of vacant lots, coal yards and row houses. Chief architect William B. Tuthill was a gifted amateur cellist, so was determined to get the acoustics right. Tchaikovsky opened the hall, making his American conducting debut in 1891. In the years since, the world's greatest musicians, including Rachmaninoff, Horowitz, Stravinsky, Ravel and George Gershwin have all performed here. The New York Philharmonic made this their home until moving to Lincoln Center (see pages 112–113) on the Upper West Side in 1962.

The second building, added in 1894, housed famous musicians, architects, dancing classes and agencies. In 1894 the green mansard roof of the main building was removed to build the studio floor. There is a small recital hall within the original building and an elegant auditorium, which was a movie theater until 1997.

THE HALL TODAY

In the 1960s, Carnegie Hall was saved from demolition when, in protest, violinist Isaac Stern joined fuming New Yorkers and put pressure on the city's state senator to convince the state legislature to authorize the city to issue bonds so that a non-profit organization could run the hall. The campaign worked. Between 1981 and 1990, Carnegie Hall underwent a $50-million renovation. The modern 60-story office tower next door, sensitively designed by Cesar Pelli, was built in 1990.

The distinctive redbrick exterior of Carnegie Hall

RATINGS

Good for kids	● ●
Historic interest	● ● ● ●
Value for money	● ● ● ● ●

BASICS

➕ 58 D17
• 156 West 57th Street at Seventh Avenue 10019
☎ 212/247-7800
For performance schedule, check website or phone 212/903-9765
Check website or phone 212/247-7800
One-hour tours Mon–Fri 11.30am, 2pm, 3pm when concert schedule permits
🚌 M7, M10, M20, M30
Ⓜ N, Q, R, W
🍽 🏛 🚻

www.carnegiehall.org

Detailed carvings front the Cathedral of St. John the Divine

The Civic Center dates from the 19th century

The Alma Mater statue, Columbia University

CATHEDRAL CHURCH OF ST. JOHN THE DIVINE

☩ Off map 58 C12 • 1047 Amsterdam Avenue at 112th Street 10025 ☎ 212/316-7540 ⏰ Services Mon–Sat 8, 8.30, 12.15, 5.30; Sun 8, 9, 11, 6 💲 Fee for tour, reservation required 🚇 M3, M4, M7, M11 🚇 B, C 🔲 🍽 Tue–Sat 11–noon, Sun 1–2 $3
www.stjohndivine.org

Seat of the Episcopal Diocese of New York, the cathedral covers 11 acres (5ha), and with a seating capacity of 5,000 is the largest Gothic church in the world. Building began in 1892 and has stopped and started many times, as funds for construction dried up; the end is still not in sight. Besides the dizzying scale and contrasting architectural styles, all in stone, admire the Mortlake Tapestries, woven from a design by Raphael in 1623, and the Barberini tapestries, woven on papal looms. Chapels around the cathedral are dedicated to other world faiths; memorials pay tribute to victims of genocide and racism, and most recently to those who died on September 11, 2001.

CENTRAL PARK
see pages 78–83

CHELSEA

☩ 60 D20 • Seventh to Tenth avenues between 14th and 28th streets 🚇 C, E 🚇 M20 🍽 🔲 🔲

Galleries, studios, and dance and media centers add the artsy edge to this now-stylish district. Before World War I the US movie industry developed in disused warehouses and theaters here before moving to California. The Kitchen, at 512 West 19th Street, has film, music and dance. Among the many galleries worth visiting are the Gagosian (555 West 24th Street, tel 212/741-1111) and Cheim & Read (547 West 25th Street, tel 212/242-7727). The Dia Center

for the Arts (548 West 22nd Street) hides wonderful exhibits behind an unappealing façade.

West of the West Side Highway, a series of piers on the Hudson, known as Chelsea Piers, forms a sports and entertainment complex with ice-skating, roller-skating, swimming and restaurants.

CHINATOWN
see page 84

CHRYSLER BUILDING
see page 85

CITY HALL AND CIVIC CENTER

☩ 61 E25 • Broadway and Murray Street 10007 ☎ 212/788-3000 🚇 M1, M6, M15 🚇 4, 6 🍽 Tours by appointment 212/788-6865

Built between 1802 and 1812 in the Federal style with French influence, City Hall is one of New York's most elegant buildings. The heart of the city's administration, it is where the City Council meets and where the Mayor has his office. It stands close to the foot of Brooklyn Bridge in City Hall Park. Since 9/11 it has been closed to the public and can be seen only from outside (though this may change). The surrounding Civic Center area includes City Hall Park and Foley Square, several city, state and federal government offices and police headquarters, including the New York State Supreme Court, the U.S. Courthouse and the New York City Criminal Courts Building (also known as the Tombs).

THE CLOISTERS
see page 86

COLUMBIA UNIVERSITY

☩ Off map 58 C12 • West 114th to 120th streets 10027 ☎ 212/854-4900 🚇 M4, M11, M60, M104 🍽 🔲 🔲 🚻 🍽 Free guided tours weekdays
www.columbia.edu

Founded as King's College in 1754 as a rival to the by then well-established Harvard and Yale, this was New York's first college and the fifth oldest in the nation, and is among the Ivy League's wealthiest universities. Originally located in the schoolhouse of Trinity Church (see page 142), the college has occupied several Manhattan locations, including the area that is now Rockefeller Center, sold for $400 million. It moved to the current 36-acre (15ha) campus, originally the site of Bloomingdale's Insane Asylum, in 1897. The heart of the campus is the magnificent Low Library, inspired by the Pantheon in Rome; academic buildings are arranged around it. In 1934 the Low became the university's administrative center, and the library was moved.

COOPER-HEWITT NATIONAL DESIGN MUSEUM

☩ 58 E13 • 2 East 91st Street 10128-9990 ☎ 212/849-8400 ⏰ Tue–Thu 10–5, Fri 10–9, Sat 10–6, Sun noon–6 💲 Adult $8, under 12s free 🚇 M1, M2, M3, M4 🚇 4, 5, 6 🍽 🔲 🚻
www.si.edu/ndm

This 64-room Georgian mansion, built in 1901, was the home of the industrialist and philanthropist Andrew Carnegie. Designed by the architectural firm Babb, Cook & Willard, it was the first private residence in New York to have an Otis elevator. Today it houses one of the largest design collections in the world, more than 250,000 items. The collection, originally from the Cooper Union School for the Advancement of Science, was donated in 1967 to the Smithsonian, which moved it here. It includes a drawing by Michelangelo, furniture designs by Frank Lloyd Wright and industrial design drawings by Donald Deskey and Henry Dreyfuss.

THE SIGHTS

Central Park

New York's "great green lung," designed by Frederick Law Olmsted and Calvert Vaux in 1851. Enjoy 843 acres (340ha) of green space with woods, gardens, playing fields and a zoo. Great for bird-watching, cycling, rowing, ice-skating, roller-blading, strolling or jogging along 58 miles (95km) of paths.

Softball games often take place on the Great Lawn

The city's 843 green acres are perfect for dog walking

Cyclists enjoy the park's car-free roads on the weekends

RATINGS

Good for kids	●●●●●
Historic interest	●●●
Photo stops	●●●●
Walkability	●●●●●

TIPS

● Don't stroll alone in deserted areas, and stay out of the park at night unless you are going to a play or concert. The park is now generally safe by day and after dark when there are crowds on hand. Police and park rangers patrol in vehicles, on skates and on horseback.

● Count on spending a half day or more, depending on what you want to see.

● On the roads, watch out for bicycle traffic, and always look carefully when crossing.

● The park has 21 children's playgrounds. Many are state of the art and no two are alike.

SEEING CENTRAL PARK

Several entrances lead into Central Park from Central Park South (59th Street) at the southern edge and 110th Street at the northern. The most popular entrance is at Grand Army Plaza, at 59th Street and Fifth Avenue. From Fifth Avenue on the east side, you can enter at 66th, 72nd, 79th, 85th, 97th and 102nd streets. On the west side, from Central Park West, you can enter at 66th, 72nd, 81st, 86th, 96th and 100th streets. North of 96th Street, the park is more rugged and less suitable for visitors with disabilities. Because there are so many different access points, study the map before entering, read about the highlights, then decide on a route through the park. Many roads that cut through the park are closed to vehicular traffic on weekends in summer, which makes it perfect for joggers, bikers, roller-bladers and baby-strollers. There are bronze statues throughout the park, including monuments to Beethoven, Christopher Columbus, William Shakespeare and Mother Goose in the south end. At the entrance to the Delacorte Theater are lovely statues of Romeo and Juliet, and from Shakespeare's *The Tempest,* Prospero with his daughter, Miranda. Bring binoculars; especially in the Ramble or on the lake.

HIGHLIGHTS

SOUTH QUADRANT

The Pond is a lovely first impression of Central Park for visitors who come in at Grand Army Plaza. The gilded bronze statue of Civil War Union General William Tecumseh Sherman by sculptor Augustus Saint-Gaudens is one of the most distinguished equestrian groupings in western art. Along Central Park South, drivers of horse-drawn carriages wait for passengers. Nearby, the wooded Hallett Nature Sanctuary juts into the Pond, which has an island inhabited by turtles and birds and a lovely waterfall.

The Wildlife Center fills 5.5 acres (2ha) just north of Grand Army Plaza, inside the park. This state-of-the-art zoo *(Mon–Fri 10–5, Sat–Sun 10–5.30, April–Oct; daily 10–4.30, rest of year; tel 212/439-6500; adults $6, 12s and under $1)* is home to more than 130 species as well as plants—from three climate zones—monkeys, crocodiles and snakes in the Rain Forest; Asian and North American animals in the Temperate Territory; polar bears, penguins and polar foxes in the Polar Circle. The sea lion pool in the central courtyard is very popular, especially at feeding times *(daily 11, 2 and 4)*. Young children can feed goats, sheep and a cow in the Children's Zoo. There are also daily shows about animals in the Acorn Theater here. North of the zoo, the George Delacorte Clock plays a nursery rhyme every hour on the hour as miniature animals glide around the base playing musical instruments. The café serves snacks.

Wollman Memorial Rink *(Mon–Tue 10–3, Wed 10–9.30, Thu 10–5, Fri–Sat 10am–11pm, Sun 10–9, tel 212/439-6900, www.wollman-skatingrink.com; adults $8.50, children $4.50, skate rental $4.75)* is filled with ice-skaters in winter. With its classic New York views of the Midtown skyline and its terrace overlooking the rink, this is one of the park's gems. Lessons are available; and there's a snack shop.

The Dairy *(daily 11–5, Apr–Oct, daily 11–4, rest of year)*, a 19th-century building overlooking the Wollman Rink, has an exhibit about the history and design of the park. There's a 12ft (4m) model of the park.

Friedsam Memorial Carousel *(daily 10–6, Apr–Nov, Sat–Sun 10–4.30, rest of year, weather permitting)*, in the middle of the park at 64th Street, is one of the largest carousels in the U.S., with 58 hand-carved, painted horses. Every year about 250,000 people mount a steed for a magical ride.

Mature trees surround the lake in the Ramble

Dine at the Tavern on the Green, perhaps before the theater

Horse-drawn carriage rides are popular with visitors year round

BASICS

⊞ 58 D14 • Central Manhattan from 59th Street to 110th Street between 5th and 8th avenues

☎ Administration 212/794-6564

🕐 30 min before sunrise to 1am

🚌 M1, M2, M3, M4 to 5th Avenue (East Side) and M10 (West Side)

🚇 A, B, C, D, 1, 9 to Columbus Circle (southwest corner)

ℹ Look for park lampposts to find out where you are in relation to city streets. The first two digits on the lamppost are those of the nearest street. There are direct-line emergency phones throughout the park and a 24-hour Park Line you can call from mobile phones 212/570-4820

🍴 The lavish Tavern on the Green at West 67th Street, tel 212/873-3200, Mon–Fri noon–3, Sat–Sun 11–3, Sun–Thu 5.30–10.30, Sat 5–11.45, pretheater dinner Mon–Fri 5–6.30, brunch Sat–Sun at 10, reservations advised

☕ The open-air Boathouse Café serves contemporary American cuisine from early spring to late October. Other cafés and food stalls throughout the park 🍴

🚶 Guided Central Park Conservancy Walking Tours 212/360-2726 and Central Park Bicycle Tours 212/541-8759; horse-drawn hansom cabs 212/246-0520

www.centralparknyc.org
Excellent online tours include particulars of the park's highlights, detailed maps and information on events and things to do

There are plenty of places to stop for a snack or a drink

The park is a favorite with joggers (top); Bow Bridge (above)

MID-PARK QUADRANT

The Sheep Meadow is 15 acres (6ha) of lush, green grass where you can have a picnic, fly kites and sunbathe. Some 300 sprinkler heads now keep the grass green and lush. A flock of sheep grazed here until 1934; their sheepfold is now a restaurant, the Tavern on the Green. On the east side of the meadow is a patch of pavement where you can watch talented roller-skaters practice their moves.

Bethesda Terrace, in Olmstead and Vaux's original design, was "the heart of the park." By the 1980s it had fallen into disrepair and was rebuilt. Stand on the Upper Terrace for a splendid view of the lake and the wooded area known as the Ramble. The fountain, *Angel of the Waters* (1870), was the work of sculptor Emma Stebbins.

Strawberry Fields was created in 1981 with funds provided by Yoko Ono, widow of musician John Lennon, after his 1980 murder, and named after his song *Strawberry Fields Forever*. Italian craftsmen made the black and white mosaic embedded in the path near the entrance at West 72nd Street, directly across the street from the Dakota apartment building where he was killed. It is centered around the word "imagine," recalling another of Lennon's most popular songs. Yoko Ono provides $1 million annually to the Central Park Conservancy for the upkeep of these 2.5 acres (1ha). Fans often stop to pay their respects and leave flowers or candles, and a huge crowd gathers every year on the singer's birthday (October 9) to sing, pray and celebrate his life and work.

Loeb Boathouse rents out rowboats and bicycles *(daily 10–5, Mar–Oct)*. Rowboats cost $10 for the first hour, $2.50 for each additional 15 minutes; each boat takes up to five people. A $30 cash deposit is required. Renting a bicycle costs between $9 and $15 per hour, and you must leave a credit card, driver's license or a passport as a deposit. In June and August (and weather permitting) another option is a gondola ride—not cheap at $30 per half hour, but memorable. A fast-food restaurant in the Boathouse offers cold drinks and snacks. The Park View Restaurant, open year-round, is a lovely spot, serving brunch, a buffet lunch and dinner *(reservations are a must,*

THE SIGHTS

Children love to climb on the bronze Alice in Wonderland *sculpture by Josef de Creefts, in Conservatory Water*

tel 212/517-2233). Bird-watchers record their observations in the Bird Register, inside the Boathouse, and other visitors' sightings also make for interesting reading.

Conservatory Water is the park's famous pond. On Saturdays at 10am from spring through fall, the Model Yacht Club races their radio-powered craft. A concessionaire rents miniature boats. North of the pond is the delightful *Alice in Wonderland* sculpture and to the west is the Hans Christian Andersen sculpture; children climb up on it to sit on his lap, and there are story hours on summer Saturdays at 11am.

Belvedere Castle (*Wed–Mon 11–4*) was Olmsted and Vaux's folly, an open-air flight of fancy that served as an elaborate scenic look-out across the lake. But during an extensive restoration in the early 1980s windows and doors were put in and it is now the Henry Luce Nature Observatory. Here you will find interesting displays—telescopes, microscopes, skeletons, feathers—intended to help children understand how naturalists observe the world. The U.S. Weather Bureau has been operating from here since 1919, and you can get up-to-the-minute weather reports on the second floor. Also on this floor is a tree loft with a wonderful collection of papier-mâché models of bird species found in the park.

The Delacorte Theater, built in 1962, is where Shakespeare in the Park performances delight large audiences in summer. Waiting in line for a free ticket is part of the theater. New Yorkers bring picnic baskets and books when they line up (starting around 10am) and make a day of it. The box office begins distributing tickets at 1pm. Tickets are also handed out at the Public Theater at 425 Lafayette Street on the day of the performance from 1 to 3pm.

RESERVOIR QUADRANT
The Jacqueline Kennedy Onassis Reservoir, named for the widow of President John F. Kennedy because of her fondness for the place and her contributions to the city, is noted for the 1.58-mile (2.55km) track around it. Joggers and walkers come here by the thousands every day. This 106-acre (43ha) body of water no longer supplies

Manhattanites with fresh water, but it still feeds the other ponds in the park. In spring glorious ornamental cherry trees blossom on the slopes.

NORTH QUADRANT

The Conservatory Garden is 6 acres (2.5ha) of formal gardens with lovely fountains in an area that has been landscaped in a more rustic, naturalistic style than the southern part of the park. If you enter from Fifth Avenue at East 104th Street, you will pass through giant Parisian wrought-iron gates from the mansion of Cornelius Vanderbilt II.

Harlem Meer, Dutch for "little sea," is a pretty pond, well stocked with about 50,000 fish. Catch-and-release fishing *(Tue–Sun 11–5, Apr–Oct)* is great entertainment for kids, big and small. Fishing rods can be rented at the Charles A. Dana Discovery Center.

Looking across at the city from Bow Bridge in the Ramble

The park's waterways provide different ways to relax

The Chess and Checkers House is a magnet for children

Lasker Memorial Rink and Pool *(daily 11–3, 4–7, tel 212/534-7639; adults $4, children under 12 $2)*, built in the 1960s, is a wonderful ice-skating rink from November through March and a great roller-skating rink for the rest of the year. Skate rental is available. Very popular in summer, the swimming pool opens on the July 1 and closes after Labor Day.

BACKGROUND

In the 1850s, many New Yorkers felt that their growing city needed a park. A large central site was chosen, and a competition in 1858 attracted 33 entries. A farmer and an architect, Frederick Law Olmsted and Calvert Vaux respectively, won the $2,000 commission. Olmsted was appointed superintendent of Central Park. Jacob Wrey Mould took on the ornamental side and designed the bridges, the Belvedere and the terrace. Construction took 16 years and cost more than $14 million. Three thousand workers, mostly unemployed Irish immigrants, and 400 horses moved stone and earth and planted 500,000 trees, shrubs and vines. The park got its own police force to discourage lawlessness. In 1925, the first of 19 playgrounds, the Heckscher Playground at 61st Street and 7th Avenue, was constructed. Between 1913 and 1919, decay took its toll on some of the fine designs. By 1934 Vaux's Marble Bridge was beyond repair and had to be demolished. In 1934, when parks commissioner Robert Moses moved the sheep from Sheep Meadow to Brooklyn's Prospect Park, the sheepfold, designed by Mould, was turned into the restaurant that's now the Tavern on the Green. The addition of the Wollman Skating Rink came in 1951 and the Delacorte Theater in 1963. Many statues were added along the way. The 1970s brought another period of neglect and lawlessness and the park was for a while not a safe place to visit. But that changed after the Central Park Conservancy, headed by Elizabeth Barlow Rogers, took the initiative in the 1970s and 80s to clean up the park and raise funds to establish a safer and cleaner space. The Sheep Meadow, the first area to be restored by the conservancy, was reopened in 1981 and remains one of the safest, most pleasant areas of the park.

PARK GUIDE

SOUTH QUADRANT

The Arsenal *(Mon–Fri 9–5)*, originally the New York State National Guard's munitions supply depot, was built between 1847 and 1851. Now a New York City Landmark, the Arsenal houses Olmsted and Vaux's original blueprint for Central Park, called the Greensward Plan. You can see it in a glass case on the third floor.

MID-PARK QUADRANT

The Dairy, a Gothic Revival cottage, was once a place where children could go for a glass of fresh milk. It now houses a visitors center with video information terminals and a permanent exhibit on the history of the park. To the west of the Dairy is the octagonal Chess and Checkers (draughts) House, where you can test your skills at one of the 24 chess tables.

RESERVOIR QUADRANT

As you walk, or run, around the reservoir, note the three pedestrian wrought-iron bridges, called 24, 27 and 28. New Yorkers call Bridge 28 the Gothic Arch because of its lace-like quality.

NORTH QUADRANT

The Charles A. Dana Discovery Center, opened in 1993 on the northern shore of the Harlem Meer, is a visitor and community center with free educational exhibits relating to Central Park.

Signs are in Cantonese and English along the busy shopping streets

CHINATOWN

The largest Chinatown in the United States—colorful, noisy and exotic, with 300 restaurants.

Chinatown, northeast of City Hall and below Canal Street, has been home to generations of immigrants from China, Hong Kong, Taiwan, Korea, Vietnam and other Asian countries for more than 150 years. Now covering 3 square miles (8sq km), it has all but crowded out its neighbors, Little Italy and the Lower East Side. For cheap restaurants, bargain clothing, souvenirs, and exotic herbs and spices, no other Manhattan neighborhood compares.

The district occupied by today's densely populated Chinatown was dominated by the hog and cattle industry in the 17th and early 18th centuries; many streets were named for prominent local butchers (including Joshua Pell and John Mott). During the 1800s, the area was populated by Irish and German immigrants; some of New York's dirtiest and most crowded tenements were around the intersection of today's Mosco, Worth and Baxter streets, then known as the Five Points—the setting for Martin Scorsese's 2002 movie *Gangs of New York*. Chinese immigrants arrived in the late 1870s.

PLACES TO VISIT

Visit the Church of the Transfiguration, a Georgian church with Gothic windows at 25 Mott Street, built in 1801 by the English Lutheran Church and later the Zion Protestant Episcopal Church, and a Roman Catholic church in 1853. Columbus Park, created in 1897 at Mulberry Street and Baxter Street below Bayard Street, is popular among Chinese women, who bring their swords to practice tai chi in the morning, and senior citizens, who meet for Chinese chess or mah jongg.

The Museum of Chinese in the Americas (see page 123) is dedicated to the history and culture of the Chinese and their descendants in the western world. The Kim Lau Chinese Memorial Arch, in Chatham Square, commemorates the Chinese-Americans who died in World War II. Facing the arch is a statue of imperial commissioner Lieutenant B.R. Kim Lau, who fought against the opium smuggling that led to the Opium Wars. The 15ft (4.5m) statue of Confucius at Confucius Plaza on the Bowery has been a landmark since 1976. It was sculpted by Liu Shih and a proverb inscribed on its base commends the virtues of a government that cares for the weak. The 1785 Edward Mooney House, at 18 Bowery, is the oldest townhouse in New York.

Street markets are an integral part of everyday life here

RATINGS

Historic interest	●●●
Specialist shopping	●●●●
Photo stops	●●●
Walkability	●●●●

BASICS

✚ 61 F24 • Between Little Italy and the Lower East Side, bounded by Canal and Worth streets between Broadway and Bowery

🚌 M1, M6, M101, M102

🚇 A, J, F, S

🍴 Hundreds of restaurants

☕ Saint's Alp Teahouse, 51 Mott Street 10013, tel 212/766-9889

ℹ️ Lower East Side Visitors' Center, 261 Broome Street between Orchard and Allen streets

🛍️ Dozens of souvenir shops; a few concentrate in the mini-mall at 15 Elizabeth Street

With its shining stainless-steel spire, the Chrysler Building is an icon

CHRYSLER BUILDING

New York's most stunning art deco skyscraper has a magnificent lobby with walls of African marble and steel.

The Chrysler Building's diamond-honed Enduro KA-2 steel is as incandescent today as it was in 1929. From the street, look up at the spire with its pattern of 30 radiating triangular windows. Note the 9ft (3m) pineapples on the spire and the mighty, gargoyle-like eagle heads in the corners of the building. Around the 30th floor, a brick frieze depicts hubcaps. Then go inside to view the lobby's sumptuous walls of African marble and steel and the Parisian-style elevators. The elaborate ceiling was painted by Edward Trumbull.

Walter Chrysler, the third biggest car manufacturer in America, spent $2 million of his own money to buy the skyscraper's site. Chrysler had been an automobile mechanic for most of his life and had very little formal education, but when it came to machines he was a genius. After saving General Motors a fortune with his new techniques, he moved to New York from Chicago at the age of 45. Already earning a million dollars a year, he produced his first line of Chryslers in January 1924. They appealed to the rich and were a symbol of wealth and luxury—they were the right product at the heart of the booming 1920s. For Chrysler, building a skyscraper more fantastic than anything anyone had ever seen was a challenge he could not resist.

THE TALLEST BUILDING IN THE WORLD

In late 1929, architect William Van Alen watched anxiously as the spire was raised above the 77-story structure to make it, at 1,048ft (320m), the world's tallest building, beating the Bank of the Manhattan Company Building at 40 Wall Street. It held the title for only a short time. Opened on May 1, 1931, the 1,250ft (381m) Empire State Building surpassed it. Securing an object at such a height had never been done before, and the job had been kept so secret that no reporters were around when it actually happened—probably on October 24, 1929, the day before the Wall Street Crash. The spire was as daring as it was ingenious and took the city by surprise. Many thought the building a crass bit of architectural advertising; today it is a symbol of an age when anything was possible.

In 1978, the Chrysler Building was designated a New York City landmark. In 1997, Tishman Speyer Properties took it over and restored the art-deco lobby. The lancet crown was first switched on in 1981.

The view from Lexington Avenue (above); the lobby (below)

RATINGS				
Good for kids	●	●		
Historic interest	●	●	●	
Photo stops	●	●	●	●

BASICS

✚ 60 F18 • 405 Lexington Avenue at 42nd Street
☎ 212/682-3070
🕐 Mon–Fri 8.30–5.30
🚌 M1
Ⓠ 4, 6, 7

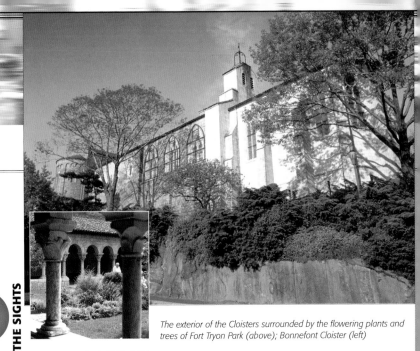

The exterior of the Cloisters surrounded by the flowering plants and trees of Fort Tryon Park (above); Bonnefont Cloister (left)

RATINGS

Historic interest	●●●●○
Specialist shopping	●●●○○
Photo stops	●●●●○
Walkability	●●●●○

BASICS

✚ Off map 58 C12 • Fort Tryon 10040
☎ 212/923-3700
🕐 Tue–Sun 9.30–5.15, Mar–Oct; Tue–Sun 9.30–4.45, rest of year; closed Jan 1, Thanksgiving, Dec 25
💵 Adult $12, under 12s free. Ticket includes same-day admission to the Metropolitan Museum of Art
🚇 M4
📷 A
🍴 New Leaf Café, tel 212/568-5323 on the grounds of Fort Tryon, Tue–Sat noon–3, 6–10, Sun 11–3, 5.30–9.30
📻 Free guided tours Tue–Fri 3pm, Sun noon; audioguide, adults $6, children under 12 $4
🏛

www.metmuseum.org

TIPS

● Take the subway ride if you are in a hurry. Get off at 190th Street and take the elevator to street level. Enter Fort Tryon Park and walk up the Promenade to the Cloisters.

● In summer there is a direct bus from the Metropolitan Museum of Art—more expensive than public transportation but quicker.

THE CLOISTERS

An outstanding collection of medieval art and architecture from Europe in idyllic Fort Tryon.

Perched high above the Hudson, the Cloisters is in delightful Fort Tryon Park in Washington Heights, at the northern tip of Manhattan, with spectacular views across the river to the steep rock-faced cliffs known as the Palisades. The Cloisters opened in 1938 as a branch of the Metropolitan Museum of Art (see pages 114–119) and is devoted to the art and architecture of medieval Europe. The building, in the style of a fortified monastery, includes large sections transported from five 12th- to 15th-century cloisters in southern France and Spain.

The collection is based on medieval sculptures and segments of architecture acquired by American sculptor George Grey Barnard during trips to Europe, and includes 5,000 sculptures, tapestries, illuminated manuscripts, paintings, stained glass and other priceless objects. He brought them to New York and exhibited them in a brick building on Fort Washington Avenue. In 1925, John D. Rockefeller donated a large sum of money to the Met to purchase the Barnard collection. Then in 1930, Rockefeller gave his beautiful Fort Tryon estate to the Met, stipulating that the Cloisters be built to fittingly house a medieval collection.

HIGHLIGHTS

On the main floor is the Fuentidueña Chapel, whose 1160 apse comes from the Church of San Martin in Castile, Spain. The capital on the right side depicts Daniel in the Lion's Den, while the one on the left shows the Adoration of the Magi. The Virgin and Child fresco in the semidome came from a small Catalan church in the Pyrenees. The Romanesque doorway in the nave of the chapel was carved in about 1175 in Tuscany. Also on this floor is the Saint-Guilhem Cloister, whose imposing covered walkway is from a Benedictine abbey near Montpellier, France. The columns have intricately carved capitals and date from the 12th to 13th centuries.

In the center of the main floor is the Cuxa Cloister, from a Benedictine monastery near Prades, France. The cloister was abandoned during the French Revolution and was later sold off in parts. Barnard managed to collect about half the original capitals, 25 bases and 12 columns. In the Nine Heroes Tapestries Room are some of the oldest surviving tapestries from a set dating from 1385.

Painting by Francois-Xavier Fabre, Dahesh Museum of Art

Detail above the entrance of the Daily News Building

The Dakota Building was the city's first luxury apartment block

DAHESH MUSEUM OF ART

➕ 58 E17 • 580 Madison Avenue 10017
☎ 212/759-0606 ⏰ Tue–Sat 11–6
🎫 Free 🚌 M1, M2, M3, M4 🚇 4, 5, 6
🍴 ♿ 📷 🚻
www.daheshmuseum.org

The museum occupies three floors of architect Edward Larrabee Barnes' black granite IBM Building. Established in 1995, the Dahesh is the only museum in America dedicated to 19th- and 20th-century European academic art.

Dr. Dahesh is in fact the Lebanese writer and philosopher Salim Achi; his collection of some 3,000 works of art was moved here from Beirut in 1975 to protect it from the civil war there. A subterranean concourse houses exhibitions, educational activities and public programs; visitor services and the museum store are at street level. The mezzanine, overlooking Madison Avenue and the IBM Building's bamboo-forest atrium, is the site of casual dining and public events.

DAILY NEWS BUILDING

➕ 338 F18 • 220 East 42nd Street 10036 ⏰ Daily 9–5 lobby only
🚌 M42, M104 🚇 4, 5, 6, 7

Founder of the *Daily News,* James Patterson commissioned this modernist steel-and-concrete song of praise to popular journalism in 1925. It was one of the first skyscrapers in New York not built in Gothic style. On the ground floor, outside and in, abstract art deco ornamentation contrasts with the modernist strips on the upper façade. Inside, the lobby is still mostly original. Note the revolving globe, 12ft (3.5m) in diameter; the frieze representing the early days of the paper; and the clock that gives the time in 17 different time zones; the floor is laid out like a giant compass.

In 1995, with *Daily News* circulation falling, the paper moved out and the building was renamed the News Building.

THE DAKOTA

➕ 58 D15 • 1 West 72nd Street 10023
🚌 M7, M10, M11 🚇 B, C

A vaguely Germanic Upper West Side landmark, commissioned in the 1880s by the president of the Singer Sewing Machine Manufacturing Company, Edward S. Clark, this marble-floored, mahogany-paneled structure was the first luxury apartment block on Central Park.

Far beyond the city's bright lights or even the power supply, it seemed as far away from the city as the Dakotas when it opened; the name was a joke on its remoteness. It wasn't long before the city moved uptown, however. Prices soared, and the rich and famous moved in—among them musician Leonard Bernstein and Lauren Bacall. John Lennon was tragically shot dead on the sidewalk outside the door as he returned home one night, and his widow, Yoko Ono, still lives here. In 2003, singer/songwriter Carly Simon found it difficult to be accepted as a resident when her plans to enlarge the bathroom in her apartment if her application was accepted got other residents in a lather. No one can move into this building without the agreement of all the other inhabitants.

EAST HARLEM

➕ Off map 59 E12 • Fifth to First avenues, East 97th to East 125th streets
🚌 M15, M101, M102, M103 🚇 4, 5, 6

Above the Upper East Side is East Harlem, once known as Spanish Harlem and now as El Barrio (the neighborhood). Unlike Central Harlem, this area developed in the 1870s and 1880s. Its poor-quality working-class dwellings were home to immigrants—first the Irish and then, from the 1890s, Italians. As the Puerto Ricans moved on up the social and employment ladder, they began to move in and soon made the area their own. The city's Puerto Rican population numbered 45,000 by the 1930s and 600,000 by the 1960s; today more than a million Puerto Ricans live in New York, and Spanish is an unofficial second language. El Barrio has a vibrant Hispanic flavor, with family-owned stores and restaurants lining the avenues and a busy street scene.

EAST VILLAGE AND NOHO
see pages 88–89

EL MUSEO DEL BARRIO

➕ Off map 59 E12 • 1230 Fifth Avenue 10029 ☎ 212/831-7272 ⏰ Wed–Sun 11–5; closed major holidays
🎫 Suggested donation: adults $5, under 12s free. Special exhibition rates apply 🚌 M1, M2, M3, M4 🚇 6 📷 🚻
www.elmuseo.org

Growing out of a classroom display and opened in 1969, this is the only museum in the United States dedicated to Puerto Rican, Latin American and Caribbean culture and art.

There is a permanent display of hand-carved religious statuettes known as *santos de palo*, and another of the Caribbean cultures that welcomed Christopher Columbus when he first arrived in the New World.

Changing exhibits of Latin American and Caribbean art and crafts regularly eclipse the permanent displays. With its lectures and workshops, the museum is a cultural focal point.

THE SIGHTS

East Village and NoHo

A funky area of vintage-clothing shops, ethnic diners, innovative restaurants and trendy clubs, with numerous historic sites.

The Joseph Papp Theater   *Hippy chic on St. Mark's Place*   *Music is a part of Village life*

RATINGS	
Historic interest	●●●●●
Specialist shopping	●●●●
Photo stops	●●●●
Walkability	●●●●●

The East Village and NoHo (North of Houston) extend between 14th Street and Houston Street, between Broadway and Avenue B. Once farmland owned by Dutch governor Peter Stuyvesant, this area was home to Irish, German, Jewish, Ukrainian and Italian immigrants in the 1800s and 1900s. Today you can visit the Ukrainian Museum (see page 144) to appreciate the culture of immigrants from Ukraine.

New York's second-oldest church, St. Mark's in the Bowery (see page 131), on Second Avenue at 10th Street, is on land that was once part of the Stuyvesant farm; the old governor is buried in the churchyard. Poet W. H. Auden, who lived at 77 St. Mark's Place from 1953 to 1972, was a parishioner at the church.

In the 1830s the richest of the rich lived at 428–434 Lafayette Street, south of Astor Place, known as Colonnade Row. Among them were John Jacob Astor, some of the Vanderbilts, and the Delano family. Today only four of the original nine houses remain. Cooper Union, at 51 Astor Place, was founded by one of America's great engineering geniuses, Peter Cooper. Now a designated New York landmark, it was completed in 1859 and was where Abraham Lincoln made the anti-slavery speech that helped earn him the Republican Party's presidential nomination. In the 1870s, wealthy New York women attended services at Grace Church (see page 99), by architect James Renwick, Jr., one of the finest examples of Gothic Revival architecture in the United States.

JEWS, RUSSIANS AND TURKS

At the beginning of the 20th century, Second Avenue between Houston Street and 14th Street became a center of Yiddish culture and came to be known as the Jewish Rialto. Edward G. Robinson and Walter Matthau got their start in the Yiddish theater here. At the Second Avenue Deli *(156 Second Avenue)*, known for its wonderful renditions of classic Jewish dishes, plaques in the sidewalk honor Yiddish theater stars. The Christadora House, on the corner of 9th Street and Avenue B, was where George Gershwin gave his first public recital. On 10th Street, between First Avenue and Avenue A, the Russian and Turkish Baths *(tel 212/674-9250)* opened in 1892; unlike many similar establishments, it has survived to become a New York institution. Inside, the baths are not glamorous but poignantly evoke 19th-century New York.

Artists sell their wares along the sidewalk in the East Village

A BOHEMIAN DISTRICT

In the 1960s and 1970s, the East Village was a focal point of the American hippie culture. Anarchist Abbie Hoffman lived on St. Mark's Place and poet Allen Ginsberg, drug guru Timothy Leary, Andy Warhol and a motley collection of Hell's Angels, Hare Krishnas and political rebels frequented the area, often meeting for protest rallies and rock concerts in Tompkins Square Park. For years, until a 1990s restoration, the area attracted the homeless and drug-users. Today it is lovely by day, but still best avoided after dark.

The Joseph Papp Public Theater on Lafayette Street is one of the city's most famous off-Broadway theaters. Impresario Joseph Papp rescued the old Astor Library from demolition, and his theater opened in 1967 with the original production of the musical *Hair*.

The mix of ethnic restaurants in the East Village gives visitors a choice of great food at budget prices. For more stylish dining at higher prices, head for NoHo, the area around Lafayette and Broadway betwen Bleecker and 4th streets.

The farthest area east, known unofficially as Alphabet City because the streets are designated by letters not numbers, is less accessible by subway, so it's best to arrive and leave by taxi. The area has some chic shops and fashionable bistros.

Book stalls on Avenue A are a reminder of the East Village's literary past

BASICS

⊞ 61 F22 • South of 14th Street, east of Bowery

🚌 M15, M8

Ⓜ 4, 5, 6

TIPS

● Skip the area east of Avenue B—it's not really worth visiting and can be intimidating.

● Check local listings to find out what's on at other theaters.

● Visit in late afternoon or early evening for a stroll and an inexpensive dinner.

Ellis Island Immigration Museum

A deeply moving memorial to the 12 million immigrants who arrived from distant lands between 1892 and 1924. Permanent exhibits include passports, clothing, baggage and family heirlooms donated by immigrants and their families.

THE SIGHTS

BASICS

✚ Page 6 • Ellis Island, New York 10004 ☎ Information 212/363-3200, ferry 212/269-5755; audiotours, café and gift shop 212/344-0996

◷ Daily 9.30–5, last outbound ferry departs 3.30; closed Dec 25

💵 Museum free, including film. Ferry ticket: adults $10, children 4–12 $4. Audiotours free

🎫 Buy tickets in Castle Clinton, Battery Park. Ferry runs approximately every 30 minutes daily 9–3.30, depending on season

🚌 M1, M6, M9, M15

Ⓜ 4, 5 to Bowling Green

🚶 Park Rangers periodically conduct tours; check schedules on arrival

🍴 Ellis Island Café serves burgers, pizza, sandwiches, soft drinks and beer and wine. Outdoor seating

🏛

www.ellisisland.com
The museum's website, complete with practical details, island map and a virtual tour. It's a little confusing to navigate but packed with useful information and links.

www.ellisisland.org
Website of the family history facility (in the museum on the first floor), which has passenger records for immigrants arriving between 1892 and 1924. You can search these online.

SEEING ELLIS ISLAND

To reach Ellis Island, buy a ferry ticket at Castle Clinton in Battery Park (see page 73). Boarding is on a first-come, first-served basis, so in spring and summer, catch the ferry early to avoid long lines. From Battery Park, take the Circle Line-Statue of Liberty ferry; en route you can stop at Liberty Island (see pages 136–137). Upon arrival at Ellis Island, walk under the glass-and-metal canopy from the ferry slip to the museum, an ornate Beaux-Arts building with fanciful copper-domed turrets. The magnificent arched portals must have been both imposing and intimidating to the arriving immigrants. There are three floors with permanent and changing exhibits about the immigration process, the living conditions of the detainees, memorabilia and displays on the building itself and its restoration. Upon entering, collect your free ticket for the 30-minute film *Island of Hope, Island of Tears*. The audiotour is well worth getting. Allow at least three hours for your visit.

HIGHLIGHTS

FIRST FLOOR

The Peopling of America Exhibit, located in the old railroad ticket office, provides statistical information on the history of immigration to the United States from as early as the 17th century. Trace migration patterns since the 18th century on the 6ft (180cm) globe.

The American Family Immigration History Center helps anyone to research their ancestors with high-tech facilities. Visit the website at www.ellisislandrecords.org

SECOND FLOOR

The Registry Room Climb up the stairs to the Great Hall, as every immigrant did, with doctors scrutinizing their walk for physical impairment. The voices of thousands of people speaking in many different languages filled this hall as inspectors and their interpreters questioned each adult and asked any child who looked old enough to give his or her name. The inspectors asked each immigrant up to 29 questions he or she had already answered on the ship's manifest. If the immigrants' answers did not match their previous answers, they were detained and questioned further. It was a harrowing experience for people who had traveled far, leaving family and possessions behind and enduring a long and difficult journey across the Atlantic. The railings that were here to keep the immigrants in orderly lines were removed in 1911 and replaced with benches. Today visitors pay tribute to the immigrants in this quiet space.

In 1916 the spectacular arched ceiling with Guastavino tiles and the red Ludowici tiled floor were added. During the 1980s restoration, only 17 of the 28,000 tiles needed replacing.

In the West Wing is an exhibit recreating the step-by-step immigration process. In the East Wing, photographs and memorabilia explore the

Study the moving portraits in Treasures from Home

immigrants' hopes and expectations, fears and hardships. You can also listen to first-hand accounts of the process.

THIRD FLOOR

Treasures from Home This exhibit displays more than 1,000 objects, including clothing, jewelry, family heirlooms and photographs donated by immigrants and their descendants. There are touching reminders of the life each person left behind and of the bright future they were hoping to find. A wedding dress, a grandmother's bracelet, a child's teddy bear—all testify to the heartbreaking sacrifices made by people desperate to find freedom and hoping for prosperity.

IN THE GROUNDS

The American Immigrant Wall of Honor displays the names of over 500,000 immigrants whose descendants made donations to the Ellis Island Restoration Project. It serves as a memorial to all those who passed through here as they fled persecution and disease, poverty and hopelessness.

BACKGROUND

Dutch settlers named this 3-acre (1.2ha) island Oyster Island because of the abundance of oyster beds in the area. In the 1760s, after the execution of pirates on the island, it was known as Gibbet Island. It then came under the ownership of Samuel Ellis, and when the city of New York bought it after his death in 1807, it was renamed again. Expanded by landfill to 272 acres (110ha), it became home to Fort Gibson and housed munitions. The original wooden fort burned down in 1897.

From 1892 onward Ellis Island replaced Castle Clinton as the inspection center for newly landed immigrants. The architectural firm Boring & Tilton designed its current Beaux-Arts buildings Until 1924, while the island was active, 70 percent of the immigrants to the United States passed through the receiving facility; it served as a hospital, detention facility and transportation station. First- and second-class passengers were processed on board ship in more comfortable quarters, but steerage passengers were herded onto the island. Because it was assumed that these huddled masses

TIP

● Allow at least three hours; the museum alone usually takes two to three hours. Add extra time to visit the gift shop if you are interested in immigration or genealogy.

The Registry Room is where arriving immigrants would have their first taste of America

Immigrants arriving with all their worldly belongings

The Baggage Room is the first room you will see

The copper-domed turrets stand out from the water

MAKE A DAY OF IT

Your ferry ticket is also good for a visit to Liberty Island to see the Statue of Liberty (see pages 136–137). Since 9/11 the Statue of Liberty has often been closed to the public, so call ahead. Even if you don't climb the 354 steps to the crown, you can walk around the island and see the statue up close.

The Circle Line-Statue of Liberty ferry passes Ellis Island

came from countries with substandard hygiene, no one was allowed to sleep on a bed provided by Uncle Sam without first having a bath. Public Health Service doctors examined every person and if they detected signs of heart problems, mental problems or moral degradation, they would return the individual to their homeland. Eyes were examined for signs of trachoma, a highly contagious eye disease that led to blindness and even death; doctors, who came to be called "buttonhook men," used their fingers or a button-hook to turn eyelids inside out in search of redness caused by inflammation. Via translators, immigrants had to answer questions about their finances, their intended residence, and any waiting relatives. They had to prove they were strong, intelligent and able to find work. Fearful, many immigrants gave contradictory answers and corrupt immigration officers took advantage of many by accepting bribes when they gave a "wrong" answer to one of the questions. Inspectors questioned 400 to 500 individuals each day, spending only a few minutes with each. The bureaucracy was daunting, and Ellis Island became known as the Island of Tears, although in the end, most new arrivals received the landing card that allowed them to enter the United States. Despite this, immigrants were often overcharged for their first train tickets in their new homeland so that many began their new lives in the poverty and squalor of New York City tenements.

During World War I, the island came under U.S. Army control and was used as a hospital. In 1924, after changes in legislation, prospective immigrants were checked in U.S. consulates abroad and Ellis Island became a deportation center for illegal aliens. A new immigration building, a ferry house and a recreation building were added between 1934 and 1936 under the Public Works Administration. During World War II, the U.S. Army used the island to detain enemy aliens. Between 1945 and 1954, the buildings were abandoned and deteriorated. In 1952, despite a proposal to convert the main building into a museum, it remained unused and was closed in 1954. In 1965, President Lyndon Baines Johnson designated the island part of the Statue of Liberty National Monument. In the 1980s architects Beyer Blinder Belle led a massive restoration project. The museum opened in 1990.

KEY TO MAIN ROOMS

THIRD FLOOR

17: Restoring a Landmark: photographs of the restoration
16: Silent Voices: large photographs of the abandoned building before restoration
15: Treasures from Home: immigrants' memorabilia
14: Ellis Island Chronicles: detailed models depicting the island's history 1897–1940
13: Dormitory Room: early 20th-century furnished room showing cramped conditions
12: Changing exhibits

SECOND FLOOR

11: Peak Immigration Years: photographs, memorabilia and recorded commentaries on immigration 1880–1924
10: Theater 2: shows *Island of Hope, Island of Tears* film, where immigrants tell their stories
9: Registry Room: the now empty great hall where immigrants were processed
8: Through America's Gate: 14 rooms with exhibits on the inspection process and the "Stairs of Separation"

FIRST FLOOR

7: Shop
6: Ellis Island Café
5: Theater 1: shows *Island of Hope, Island of Tears* film, where immigrants tell their stories
4: The Peopling of America: immigration patterns from 17th century to the present, and a Word Tree explaining the origins of words
3: Baggage Room: immigrants' suitcases and bags
2: Learning Center
1: American Family Immigration History Center

THE SIGHTS

Empire State Building

This New York City icon is the most famous skyscraper in the world.
Millions of visitors a year go up to the 86th-floor Observation Deck for spectacular
panoramas of the great metropolis.

THE SIGHTS

RATINGS					
Good for kids	●	●	●	●	●
Specialist shopping	●				
Photo stops	●	●	●	●	●
Value for money	●	●	●		

BASICS

⊞ 60 E19 • 350 Fifth Avenue 10118

☎ 212/736-3100

🕐 Daily 9.30am–midnight, last elevator ascends at 11.15pm

💵 Adult $11, child 12–17 $10, child aged 6–11 $6, military in uniform free, under 6s free

🚌 M1, M2, M3, M4, M6

🚇 6 to 33rd Street or B, D, F to 34th Street/Herald Square

📷 Observatory audiotour, $5, corresponds to signs on the Observation Deck so you know exactly what buildings you are seeing

🍴 ♿ 🚻

www.esbnyc.com
Listen to an audiotour sample, take an online tour, buy tickets and shop online, get the lighting schedule and a list of special events, and information about the ESB in the news and in the movies.

TIPS

● To avoid waiting in line for tickets, buy them online, or in advance at the NYC & Company Visitor Center at 810 Seventh Avenue between 52nd and 53rd streets, tel 212/484-1200.

● Come on a clear day and bring some quarters for the binoculars outside.

● The elevators carry only 16 people at a time, so be patient.

● Dusk is a popular time, so buy a ticket in advance if you can. Starry nights are magical and you can stay until closing time. There is no time limit on your visit.

SEEING THE EMPIRE STATE BUILDING

The main entrance is on Fifth Avenue. You pass through a security checkpoint similar to those at airports. There is no coat check, so you must carry your belongings. If you have not purchased a ticket in advance, take the escalator or elevator down to the Concourse level and the Observatory ticket office. Signs indicate the waiting time and visibility. After buying your tickets, go back up the escalator to the main floor and follow the signs to the Observatory elevators on the second floor. Elevators let you out on the 80th floor, where staff direct you to the Tower elevator to the 86th floor. Viewing areas are both indoors and outdoors.

HIGHLIGHTS

FIFTH AVENUE LOBBY
Interesting exhibits show off memorabilia from New York's museums, galleries and artists. The marble walls are stupendous and the metal relief sculpture of the building dazzling.

34TH STREET LOBBY
Eight huge color panels by artists Roy Sparkia and Renee Nemerov depict the Seven Wonders of the Ancient World and the eighth wonder from the modern world: the Great Pyramid of Cheops, the Hanging Gardens of Babylon, the Statue of Zeus, the Temple of Diana, the Lighthouse of Pharos, the Colossus of Rhodes, the Tomb of King Mausolus and the Empire State Building. The tallest Wonder of the Ancient World is the 600ft (183m) Lighthouse of Pharos.

CONCOURSE LEVEL
In addition to the Observatory ticket office, there is a collection of photographs of famous people who have visited the Empire State Building, including Queen Elizabeth II of Great Britain, Fidel Castro, and the great soccer player Pele.

SECOND FLOOR
Special exhibits about New York City and its museums, cultural institutions and tourist attractions are on this floor. NY SKYRIDE *(daily 10–10, tel 212/279-9777, www.skyride.com)* gives a thrilling simulated tour of the city via the same simulator hardware that is used to train 747 commercial pilots.

86TH-FLOOR OBSERVATION DECK
On the outside deck you can get close-up views of the surrounding buildings and area using the high-powered binoculars. There is also an indoor, enclosed deck, useful if it's raining.

FLOODLIGHTS
Powerful floodlights illuminate the upper 30 floors between 9pm and midnight every night. Significant colors are used for special occasions —red, white and blue for Independence Day on July 4; green on St. Patrick's Day (17 Mar); red, black and green on Martin Luther King Day (third Mon in Jun); yellow and white for Easter; lavender and

white on Gay Pride Day (Jun). The stainless-steel window frames glimmer by day and night. In spring and fall during the bird migration season, the lights are turned off on foggy nights because the light shining through the fog confuses them.

THE TOWER
Broadcast cameras and microwave antennae on the east and west sides of the building monitor city traffic conditions for major TV and radio stations. The National Broadcasting Company (NBC) sent out the United States' first experimental transmission from the TV station here on December 22, 1931. Since 1965, FM radio has been transmitting from the tower. The New York Telephone Company also has transmission facilities on the tower. It's not open to visitors.

The Empire State Building looks most dramatic at dusk (above); jostling for a good view on the 86th floor outside deck (inset left); the Fifth Avenue entrance lobby is dominated by the shining relief of the skyscraper (inset right)

The Empire State Building weighs 365,000 tons; took 7 million man-hours to build; and is made up of 60,000 tons of steel, 2.5 million feet (790,000m) of electrical wire, 10 million bricks, 62 miles (100km) of water pipes, 6,500 windows, 72 elevators, 7 miles (11km) of elevator shafts, 1,860 steps, and a foundation that extends 55 feet (17m) below street level.

The purchase price for the land, the site of the old Waldorf-Astoria Hotel, was $16 million; construction costs were $25 million. Construction time was an amazing 14 months. The building opened on May 1, 1931.

With 102 stories, the Empire State Building stands 1,454ft (436m) tall. Eighty-six stories are usable office space. The Observation Tower is 16 stories.

The TV antenna, installed in 1985, is 22 stories high.

Three million visitors ascend annually. The stupendous 360-degree view extends for around 80 miles (130km) on a clear day.

The Fleet Empire State Building Run-Up Race, a New York Road Runners Club event, was first run in 1978 and is now held annually in February. Competitors run up 1,567 steps, trying to break the record time. In 2003, the male winner completed it in 9 minutes 33 seconds; the female winner's time was 13 minutes 6 seconds.

BACKGROUND

In 1827, William B. Astor bought the farm where the Empire State Building now stands for $16,000 and erected the first Waldorf-Astoria hotel. In 1928 the hotel was sold for $20 million and demolished to make way for the present structure. Excavation began in 1930. The developer was General Motors' vice-president, John Jacob Raskob, who wanted to create the world's tallest structure as quickly as possible. As a result, designs to decorate the limestone façade and the chromium-steel windows were machine-stamped. Completed in 1931, and $5 million under budget, the Empire State Building replaced the Chrysler Building as the world's tallest building and held this title until surpassed by the World Trade Center in 1971. Since 9/11 it has again become the tallest building in New York City, but not the world.

In the 1930s and 1940s, the Depression and then World War II put an end to the city's prosperity and much of its office space stood vacant. The tallest building in the world was dubbed the Empty State Building. However, the Observation Deck was so popular that the income from admission charges paid the taxes on the building. In 1933 the thriller *King Kong* was released and the Empire State Building became a movie star for the first time. Concerns about the stability of the building were put to rest on July 28, 1945, when a U.S. Army B-25 bomber crashed into the 78th and 79th floors, killing 13 people and causing extensive damage.

Looking east towards the borough of the Bronx from the top of the Empire State Building

THE SIGHTS

The present Federal Hall building dates from 1842

FEDERAL HALL NATIONAL MONUMENT

The site of the nation's first capitol, where the first president of the newly created United States, George Washington, took the oath of office.

As you approach the Federal Hall National Monument there's no escaping the massive bronze John Quincy Adams Ward statue of George Washington on the front steps. This Doric-columned, Greek Revival building resembles a simplified Parthenon, and looks a bit out of place among Wall Street's massive structures. Inside, the rotunda has 16 marble Corinthian columns, a domed ceiling and ornate bronze railings. One exhibit explores the Constitution. Another showcases the Bible used to administer the solemn oath to Washington.

A HISTORIC SITE

New York's first City Hall was built on this site in 1699 and petty offenders were flogged in front of the building. In 1789 it was reconstructed by Pierre Enfant, who later designed Washington, D.C., and the First Continental Congress met here to draft the Bill of Rights, guaranteeing the rights to freedom of worship, speech, press, assembly, keeping and bearing arms, trial by jury, and the right against unreasonable searches and seizures. April 30, 1789, the day Washington took the oath of office, was an occasion for massive celebrations. The building remained the nation's first capitol until 1790, when the "famed deal" between Thomas Jefferson and Alexander Hamilton moved the seat of government along the Potomac River.

Many other important historic events took place on this site. Newspaper publisher John Peter Zenger was imprisoned here for seditious libel in 1734; a brilliant defense by lawyer Alexander Hamilton secured him victory in court and was an important step toward freedom of the press (see page 27). In 1765, the Stamp Act Congress assembled here to protest taxation without representation. In 1787, after the colonies won their independence, the First Continental Congress met here to establish procedures for the creation of new states. The state, war and treasury departments were established here, as was the Supreme Court. Customs stayed for 20 years before moving to Wall Street. The building became a National Historic Site on May 26, 1939, and a National Memorial to George Washington on August 11, 1955.

Doric temple on the outside and graceful rotunda on the inside

RATINGS	
Good for kids	● ● ●
Historic interest	● ● ● ● ●
Photo stops	● ● ● ●
Walkability	● ● ● ● ●

BASICS
✚ 61 F26 • 26 Wall Street, 10005
☎ 212/825-6870
🕐 Mon–Fri 9–5
💲 Free
🚇 M9
🚌 4, 5

Fifth Avenue—one of the most famous streets in the world

FIFTH AVENUE

One of New York's most fashionable avenues, with shopping, museums and a few landmark skyscrapers.

The Empire State Building was completed in 1931, on Fifth Avenue at 34th Street. From its 86th-floor Observation Deck all of Fifth Avenue stretches out below you. The avenue begins downtown in Washington Square Park, north of No. 47, the Salmagundi Club, the elegant Italianate brownstone where America's oldest club for artists met in the early 20th century. At No. 62 are the Forbes Magazine Galleries (see page 99). At 23rd Street is Manhattan's first skyscraper, the triangular Flatiron Building (see page 99).

St. Patrick's Cathedral (see page 131) is between 50th and 51st streets. At No. 645 is the Olympic Tower, the headquarters of Aristotle Onassis's empire, with shops, offices, apartments and restaurant. These two landmarks are at the heart of a section famous for its luxury shopping, between 49th and 59th streets. Tiffany & Co., founded in 1837, is now at 57th Street. Along with Saks Fifth Avenue, between 50th and 51st, and Bergdorf Goodman, also at 57th Street, are the Disney Store and many other retailers. Beyond the Trump Tower (see page 144), Central Park (see pages 78–83) spreads out on the west side.

MANSIONS AND MUSEUMS

In the 19th century, Fifth Avenue was the fashionable address for the very wealthy, such as coke-and-steel tycoon Henry Clay Frick, tobacco magnate James Duke and railroad baron Jay Gould, who built increasingly large mansions. Some of them were demolished in the 1920s to make way for luxury apartments, but many remain. The first one, at No. 998, built in 1912, was such a success that it became the model that hundreds copied in form and detail. The starched doormen are an indication of the wealth of the residents who enjoy spectacular views of Central Park. Henry Clay Frick's mansion at 70th Street is now open to the public, displaying his outstanding collection of European art in a residential setting. Andrew Carnegie's 64-room home at 91st Street is now the Cooper-Hewitt Museum (see page 77). The Jewish Museum, at 92nd Street, occupies another fine old home. The stretch between 79th and 104th streets is also punctuated by museums and has become known as Museum Mile. Here are the Metropolitan Museum of Art (see pages 114–119), the Guggenheim Museum (see pages 110–111) and the Museum of the City of New York (see page 123).

RATINGS

Historic interest	●●●●●
Specialist shopping	●●●●●
Photo stops	●●●●●
Walkability	●●●●●

BASICS

59 E16 • From Washington Square north to the Harlem River

M1, M2, M3, M4

4, 5, 6

TIP

● Be sure to catch a parade on Fifth. The St. Patrick's Day Parade on March 17 is the biggest, but there are others. Check the NYC & Company events calendar for details. Crowds are so thick on the sidewalks during parades that you will not be able to shop or sightsee.

The distinctive triangular Flatiron Building was built in 1902

The elegant façade of the Fraunces Tavern Museum

Ulysses S. Grant's tomb was completed in 1897

FLATIRON BUILDING AND DISTRICT

✚ 60 E20 • 175 Fifth Avenue at Broadway 10017 🚌 M2, M3, M5, M6 🚇 N,R

Squeezed into the angle where Broadway crosses Fifth Avenue, the Flatiron Building, at a mere 285ft (87m), never competed for New York's tallest-building status. The Park Row Building, erected in 1899, was already 391ft (119m) when the Flatiron, then known as the Fuller Building, went up to designs by architect Daniel Burnham, in 1902. The unusual proportions and elaborate architecture, however, have attracted the interest of photographers and the amazement of tourists for more than a century. Below 23rd Street, Fifth and Sixth avenues and Broadway were once the swankiest shopping district of New York, and this stretch of Sixth Avenue was called Ladies' Mile. Large department stores brought commercialism, a new style of architecture, and prestige to the area. Just northeast of the Flatiron Building is Madison Square Park.

FORBES MAGAZINE GALLERIES

✚ 60 E21 • 60–62 Fifth Avenue 10011 ☎ 212/206-5548 🕐 Tue–Wed and Fri–Sat 10–4 🎟 Free 🚌 M2, M3, M5, M7 🚇 F, L, N, V ♿
www.forbes.com/forbescollection

Publishing magnate and adventurer Malcolm Forbes (1919–1990) had a passion for collecting, and the former home of the Macmillan publishing house, now the offices of *Forbes* magazine, includes a gallery that displays the result: old Monopoly games, model boats, whole battlefields with model soldiers, about 3,000 historical documents (including Abraham Lincoln's *Emancipation Proclamation*) and, among a display of *objets d'art,* a dozen of the fabled, bejewelled Easter eggs crafted for Russian czars by the House of Fabergé.

Children enjoy the antique toy collection and the model boats and other watercraft.

FRAUNCES TAVERN MUSEUM

✚ 61 F26 • 54 Pearl Street 10004 ☎ 212/425-1778; restaurant 212/968-1776 🕐 Mon–Fri 10–4.45, Sat–Sun noon–4 🎟 Adult $3, child $2 🚌 M6, M15 🚇 4, 5 🍴 🚻 ♿
www.frauncestavernmuseum.org

The 18th-century Queen's Head Tavern on this site, run by one Samuel Fraunces, was visited in 1783 by George Washington himself. Here, in the Long Room, now reproduced in the style of a dining room of the period, he met with fellow officers and gave his famous farewell address at the end of the American Revolution. The current structure is a 1907 reconstruction sponsored by the Sons of the Revolution and now, together with adjacent 19th-century buildings, contains a museum of early American history and culture. Children can dress up in costume and try writing with quills. Separate from the museum is a restaurant busy at lunch serving all-American dishes to downtown workers.

FRICK COLLECTION
see page 100

GENERAL GRANT NATIONAL MEMORIAL

✚ Off map 58 C12 • Riverside Drive at West 122nd Street 10027 ☎ 212/666-1640 🕐 Daily 9–5; closed major holidays 🚌 M4, M5, M104 🚇 A

Generally called Grant's Tomb, this may be the nation's largest and most impressive sepulcher. Rising dramatically 150ft (46m) beside the Hudson River, the squat, dome-topped granite building fronted by six Doric columns proclaims the importance of wildly popular Civil War general, and later president, Ulysses S. Grant.

The design, chosen after a competition, was copied from the fourth-century BC tomb of Mausolus at Halicarnassus. Work began soon after Grant's death, with contributions from more than 90,000 people, many of them African-Americans, for whom Grant's achievements at the head of the Union army outweighed his less successful efforts as president.

Inside the massive bronze doors, below the domed rotunda and set off by the gleaming white marble, two 9-ton polished black sarcophagi hold the remains of Grant and his wife, Julia.

GRACE CHURCH

✚ 60 F21 • 800 Broadway 10004 ☎ 212/254-2000 🕐 Mon–Fri 10–4, Sun for services only 🚇 1, 2, 3 🚇 N, R, W, 6
www.gracenyc.org

By the time James Renwick, Jr. began building churches, the Gothic Revival was in full swing. Renwick, like Richard Upjohn, who designed Trinity Church (see pages 142–143) on Lower Broadway, took up the style with enthusiasm. Grace Church, completed in 1846, was one result, another was St. Patrick's Cathedral (see page 131), on Fifth Avenue at 50th Street.

The church's original wood steeple was replaced by marble in 1888. It stands on the first bend of Broadway, so that it anchors the view up Broadway from downtown. The complex that surrounds the church includes Renwick's Grace House (1881) and the Rectory, and, on Fourth Avenue South, Renwick's Grace Memorial House.

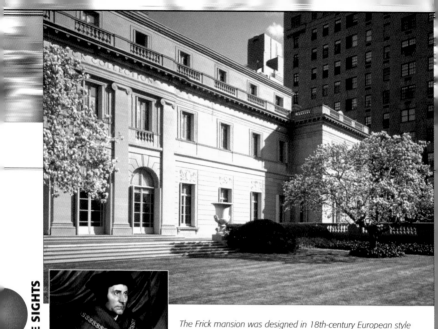

The Frick mansion was designed in 18th-century European style (above); Sir Thomas More *(1527) by Hans Holbein (left)*

FRICK COLLECTION

A striking collection of masterpieces tastefully displayed in Henry Clay Frick's luxurious mansion.

Henry Clay Frick (1849–1919), has gone down in history as a ruthless businessman, staunchly anti-union, obsessed with acquiring wealth—in other words, a master entrepreneur. Frick had his own successful business, the Frick Coke Company in Pittsburgh, when Andrew Carnegie made him his partner in the Carnegie Steel Company. Together they made the Carnegie steel empire one of the most important businesses in the country, and both men became multimillionaires. Frick's sole interest outside the world of steel and coke was art. He collected works painted by the world's masters from the 14th to the 19th centuries. At the age of 64 he had a palatial residence on Fifth Avenue built as his private home and gallery, to plans drawn up by Carrère & Hastings. Frick and his wife lived in the home until their deaths—his in 1919, hers in 1931. Frick, in an uncharacteristically generous move, bequeathed the house and paintings to the public.

After Frick's wife's death, the house was enlarged and became a museum in 1935. There is a reference library next door on East 71st Street, designed by John Russell Pope, the architect of the National Gallery in Washington, D.C. The house is set back from Fifth Avenue behind an elevated garden designed by Russell Page. As part of multi-million dollar improvements, the stone wall surrounding the site was replaced in 2002 and the wrought-iron fence was restored.

ARTISTIC HIGHLIGHTS
Through the 16 galleries, the paintings are not arranged by period or national origin, but in the way Frick would have had them displayed in his home. The Fragonard Room shows the large Fragonard paintings depicting *The Progress of Love* and contains 18th century French furniture and porcelain. In the Living Room are paintings by Holbein, El Greco, Titian and Bellini. Through the Library, past Italian bronzes and Chinese vases, is the West Gallery, where there are landscapes by John Constable and portraits by Rembrandt and Velázquez. Especially delightful is the East Gallery, with works by Degas, Goya, Turner, Van Dyke and Whistler. At the end of your visit, pause for a while in the peaceful Garden Court (the enclosed Palm Court is the perfect oasis on a cold New York day), which occasionally hosts special exhibitions.

RATINGS

Historic interest	●●●●●
Walkability	●●●●●
Value for money	●●●●●

BASICS

⊞ 58 E15 • 1 East 70th Street at Fifth Avenue 10021

☎ 212/288-0700

🕐 Tue–Thu, Sat 10–6, Fri 10–9, Sun 1–6; closed Mon, Jan 1, July 4, Thanksgiving, Dec 24–25; limited hours, 1–6, on Presidents' Day, Election Day and Veterans' Day. No children under 10

💵 Adult $12

🚌 M1, M2, M3, M4

🚇 4, 5, 6

🍷 Wine bar in the Garden Court Fri 6.30–9

📖 Books, cards, CDs, videos and museum-inspired gifts 🛍

www.frick.org

TIP

● Try to come for a chamber music concert (year round on occasional Sundays at 5pm). Check website for details.

Gracie Mansion has a prime location by the East River

The National Arts Club in Gramercy Park

Harlem's most famous club, now on 125th Street

GRACIE MANSION

⊞ 59 G13 • East End Avenue 10128
☎ 212/570-4751 Ⓖ Guided tour only Wed 10am, 11am, 1pm and 2pm, late-Mar to mid-Nov. Reservations required
🚋 $4 🚌 M15, M31, M86 Ⓜ 4, 5, 6

Nothing remains for long without modification in the city of permanent change, and Archibald Gracie's stately home is no exception. A fine example of Federal architecture, it has survived against the odds. A quiet country retreat overlooking the East River when it was built in 1799, it was enlarged in 1804. It was sold in 1823, when Gracie's shipping business went under, then bought by the city's Department of Parks in 1896 and converted into the Museum of the City of New York in 1924. In 1942, after renovation, it became the official residence of the mayor of New York. Major restoration renewed it in 1985.

GRAMERCY PARK HISTORIC DISTRICT

⊞ 60 F20 • Between Park Avenue South and Third Avenue from 18th to 21st streets 🚌 M2, M3, M6, M7 Ⓜ Q, N, R, 6

Copied from elegant London squares by the developer Samuel Ruggles in 1831, Gramercy Park is the only private park in New York City and is still surrounded by the original high iron railings. The elegant area, full of attractive buildings, has long been favored by well-to-do citizens. At No. 16 Gramercy Park South the actor Edwin Booth, brother of Lincoln's assassin, lived in a superb brownstone; here in 1888, he founded The Players, still a club for theatrical folk. Booth's statue is inside the park. At No. 15, now the National Arts Club, Samuel Tilden, opponent of the Tweed Ring, Governor of New York and failed presidential candidate, installed

steel doors and a tunnel to 19th Street in fear of the mob.

GRAND CENTRAL TERMINAL
see pages 102–104

GREENWICH VILLAGE
see pages 105–107

GROUND ZERO
see page 108

GUGGENHEIM MUSEUM
see pages 110–111

HARLEM

⊞ Page 7 • Fifth Avenue to Morningside Avenue north of 110th Street 🚌 M3, M10 Ⓜ B, 2, 5
🏛 Harlem Tourist Center and Gift Shop 2224 Frederick Douglass Boulevard
www.hatt.org

Harlem is forever linked with the speakeasies and jazz of the Prohibition era. Today the bleak landscape that saw the departure of middle-class families in the 1960s has given way to housing renovation and a growing, upbeat population. There is much of architectural interest, but many are attracted by the nightlife, jazz clubs and cultural attractions, including Manhattan's oldest residence, the Morris-Jumel Mansion Museum *(65 Jumel Terrace, tel 212/923-8008)*, and the Schomburg Center (see page 131). After completing his second term as president, Bill Clinton opened an office in Harlem.

HISPANIC SOCIETY OF AMERICA

⊞ Off map 58 C12 • 613 West 155th Street at Broadway 10032 ☎ 212/926-2234 Ⓖ Tue–Sat 10–4.30, Sun 1–4; closed major holidays 🚋 Free 🚌 M4, M5 Ⓜ 1 🏛
www.hispanicsociety.org

This museum, described as one of the best-kept secrets of New

York, is well worth the half-hour subway ride from Times Square. Audubon Terrace was the brainchild of philanthropist and Spanish scholar Archer Huntington, heir to the Central Pacific Railroad fortune. He founded the Hispanic Society in 1904 and commissioned his cousin to design the buildings, which also house the American Numismatic Society (see page 67). A little jewel devoted to the arts and culture of Iberia, the museum is a lavishly appointed showcase of all things Spanish, from Paleolithic tools to the masterpieces of Velàsquez and Goya. The first floor has a large exhibit of traditional and ritual artifacts, paintings and a research library.

INTERNATIONAL CENTER OF PHOTOGRAPHY

⊞ 60 E18 • 1133 Avenue of the Americas 10036 ☎ 212/857-0000
Ⓖ Tue–Thu 10–5, Fri 10–8, Sat–Sun 10–6 🚋 Adult $10 🚌 M5, M6, M7
Ⓜ B, D, F, V
www.icp.org

In the heart of midtown Manhattan, the ICP is both a school and a museum. Temporary exhibitions are always on view, and the permanent collection has 60,000 photographs ranging from old Daguerreotypes to iris prints, mainly from American and European reportage and documentation from the 1930s to the present. There are photographs by such well-known names as Henri Cartier-Bresson, Elliott Erwitt and Harold Edgerton, along with an impressive collection of 13,000 original prints by Weegee, who photographed crime scenes and New York nightlife in the 1930s and 1940s. Also on display are corresponding negatives, tear sheets from the newspapers where the photos first appeared, correspondence, and other personal memorabilia.

Grand Central Terminal

New York's most magnificent public space and one of the city's finest landmarks.
Full of sophisticated shops and interesting places for a quick bite.
Every day, trains running on 48 pairs of railroad tracks bring in half a million commuters
from the northern suburbs.

Thousands of commuters use the station every day

The brass four-faced clock tells the time from all angles

Passengers make a beeline for the central information booth

SEEING GRAND CENTRAL TERMINAL

Enter Grand Central on 42nd Street at Park Avenue in order to experience the full impact and grandeur of the main concourse. As you enter, the feeling of space, sophistication and city bustle creates an awesome introduction to Manhattan. The careful $200-million renovation project that has restored its grandeur fills even cynical New Yorkers with civic pride. Notice the 75ft (29m) windows, the Tennessee marble floor, the brass clock over the central kiosk, and the gold-and-nickel chandeliers. Stroll around the arcades leading to Lexington Avenue and the lower level where you'll find restaurants and shops, including The Children's General Store, The Discovery Channel Store, Banana Republic and Godiva Chocolatier. Off the main concourse is the Grand Central Market, packed with fresh produce. The New York Transit Museum Annex & Store is worth visiting if you've got time. A maze of underground tunnels and walkways links the terminal to surrounding streets; you can stay underground as far north as 48th and Park.

HIGHLIGHTS

THE MAIN CONCOURSE CEILING

With 59 electric stars replicating the zodiac constellations, in reverse, the design is based on an illustration from a medieval manuscript. It is not known whether the ceiling's French creator, Paul Helleu, was aware that depicting the heavens in reverse, or from God's point of view, was a common practice of medieval illustrators. The main concourse itself is 375ft long (114m) and 120ft wide (36m).

JULES ALEXIS COUTAN'S SCULPTURE

Mercury, the Roman god of travel and commerce, is the central figure of this 1935 sculpture over the south entrance. He is supported by Minerva and Hercules, representing mental and physical strength.

GRAND CENTRAL OYSTER BAR AND RESTAURANT

This restaurant, with its low-vaulted ceiling, is worth seeing. The tiles are by Guastavino. Order a bowl of clam chowder—either Manhattan (tomato-based) or New England (cream-based) style. See page 276.

RATINGS	
Historic interest	● ● ● ○
Specialist shopping	● ● ● ○
Photo stops	● ● ● ○
Good for food	● ● ● ● ●

TIPS

● Take one of the free area tours sponsored by Grand Central Partnership (GCP), one of the largest business improvement districts, every Friday at 12.30, rain or shine. Meet inside the Whitney Museum Annex at the Philip Morris Building at 42nd Street and Park Avenue.

● For lunch in New York, the food concourse on the lower level is fun with its many interesting options from Cajun pizza to Vietnamese sandwiches. But go early—after 12.30, it's next to impossible to find a seat.

● Don't rush, take your time to enjoy the shopping, restaurants and most of all the architecture. This is not just a train station, it's a New York experience.

● When you leave the building, walk a couple of blocks south to 40th Street, then turn around and look back at Coutan's neoclassical sculpture over the south entrance.

Make time for a shoeshine (above); the famous Oyster Bar and Restaurant (above right)

BASICS

⊞ 60 E18 • East 42nd Street at Park Avenue 10017

☎ 212/340-2210; for travel information 718/330-1234

🕐 Daily 5.30am–1.30am

💲 Free

🚌 M1, M2, M3, M4

🚇 4, 5, 6, 7

🍽 Grand Central Oyster Bar & Restaurant on the lower level; Mon–Sat, tel 212/490-6650, www.oysterbarny.com
Michael Jordan's The Steak House N.Y.C. serves just that, tel 212/655-2300, www.the glaziergroup.com
Métrazur serves Charlie Palmer's progressive American cuisine along with seafood and pasta, tel 212/687-4600, www.métrazur.com

🛍 50 specialist shops on the mezzanine and lower levels

🎫 Excellent free tour by the Municipal Arts Society on Wednesdays at 12.30. Meet at the information desk, under the clock, in the main concourse

www.grandcentralterminal.com
Phone numbers for stores and shops, menus and prices for all the restaurants, travel information, information on events.

THE CAMPBELL APARTMENT

This elegant (if pricey) cocktail bar was built by John Campbell as an office and pied-a-terre in the 1920s in the style of a 13th-century Florentine palazzo, with its stained-glass windows by Louis Comfort Tiffany and elegant dark paneling. Follow signs to the small staircase across from Jordan's restaurant off the west balcony.

NEW YORK TRANSIT MUSEUM GALLERY & STORE

Here you'll find changing exhibits on the history, impact and future of public transportation *(tel 212/878-0106, www.mta.nyc.us/museum)*.

SPECIAL EVENTS

Exhibitions, food tastings, treasure hunts and concerts take place regularly. The Christmas Market in Vanderbilt Halt showcases the work of dozens of innovative regional craftspeople and retailers.

BACKGROUND

New York Central Railroad magnate Cornelius Vanderbilt ordered the construction of Grand Central Terminal. Built between 1903 and 1913, it replaced the 42nd Street Terminal, an iron and glass train shed dating from 1871. At the turn of the 20th century, this area was the northern edge of the city, but as the new station flourished, stores, hotels, restaurants and offices grew up around it. By the 1920s it had become a fine boulevard graced with luxury apartment buildings.

Grand Central is an outstanding example of Beaux Arts design, with triumphal arches filled with glass and steel, a grand waiting room, sumptuous concourse, superb vaulted ceiling and imposing sculptures of Roman deities. The innovative design, by engineer William Wilgus and architects Reed & Stem, included extensive tunnels, a ramp system instead of stairs to facilitate pedestrian traffic, and upper and lower level concourses. Architect Whitney Warren, a Vanderbilt cousin, was responsible for the outstanding façades and interior. The public was delighted with this marvel, but by the 1970s, the station had acquired layers of grime and was not a place to linger. The steel was rusty, the asbestos was falling out and the stairways stank: It had become a symbol of decay.

In 1978, a New York City developer proposed building a 55-story office tower on top of the station, obliterating the façade. After a series of legal challenges, a U.S. Supreme Court decision sided with the New York City Landmarks law and saved it from this fate. Jacqueline Kennedy Onassis was a prime force in the battle against the tower and added her voice to thousands of New Yorkers who wanted to spare this magnificent building. Restoration was completed in 1998 under architects Beyer Blinder Belle, who examined 4,500 of Warren's original drawings and blueprints. Over a period of four years, 80-year-old wiring and plumbing were replaced, air-conditioning was installed and new entrances were built. All of this was done while the station continued to operate. MetroNorth, the commuter railroad operating out of the station, points out that not a single train was late or delayed owing to construction.

Greenwich Village

**A fascinating, once bohemian, now celebrity-studded area bursting with funky shops, unique bookstores, sidewalk cafés and cool clubs.
Where famous artists, writers and radical thinkers lived and hung out.**

George Segal's sculpture Gay Liberation *was installed in 1992*

Lively Bleecker Street has great shops and cafés

Chumleys' walls are lined with photos of its literary patrons

SEEING GREENWICH VILLAGE

Broadway divides Greenwich Village into the East Village (see pages 88–89) and the West Village. Bleecker Street is the main thoroughfare of the West Village and is full of cafés, restaurants and shops. Coffeehouses, music and poetry still thrive, and this definitely is a lively place for a late night out, whether you take in the bars and clubs, or just go for a stroll.

HIGHLIGHTS

CHRISTOPHER PARK

Bordered by Christopher Street, West 4th Street and Seventh Avenue, Christopher Park is home to George Segal's life-size sculpture *Gay Liberation,* which depicts a gay couple standing in front of a bench where two lesbians sit. Behind them is the Stonewall Bar & Grill, where riots in 1969 sparked the nation's Gay Liberation movement. Christopher Street is a focal point of gay life in New York City.

CHUMLEY'S

At 86 Bedford Street, near Grove Street, this former speakeasy is not easy to find—it has no sign outside and the number does not appear on the front of the building. Over time many New York writers, including John Steinbeck (1902–68) have found solace in a drop or two here. Photos of famous patrons decorate the interior walls. The bar has appeared in several movies, including Woody Allen's *Sweet and Lowdown.*

JEFFERSON MARKET LIBRARY

In 1885, a survey of architects found this Gothic building at 425 Sixth Avenue, designed by Calvert Vaux and Frederick Clarke Withers between 1874 and 1877) to be the fifth most beautiful building in the United States. The richly ornamented façades include a pediment depicting the trial scene from Shakespeare's *The Merchant of Venice.* The tower has been used as a fire watch, and originally, the building housed a police court and a district court. After years of neglect, it was about to be demolished when local activists saved it and it became a branch of the New York Public Library in 1967.

RATINGS				
Historic interest	●	●	●	●
Specialist shopping	●	●	●	●
Photo stops	●	●	●	
Walkability	●	●	●	●

BASICS

✚ 60 D22 • From Broadway west to the Hudson River, between Houston Street to the south and 14th Street to the north

🚌 M1, M5–8, M10–11

🚇 A, E, C, F

🍴 A huge number of restaurants on Bleecker Street, Greenwich Avenue and streets in between, provide a choice of cuisines including Italian, French, Middle Eastern, American, Indian and Japanese, and many others

🍽 Florent, 69 Gansevoort Street, tel 212/989-5779, open 24 hours Fri–Sun, until 5am Mon–Thu, French-American cuisine and a full bar

🏬 Shops on Bleecker Street and Greenwich Avenue and many others

ℹ Information centers at Sixth Avenue and Christopher Street and at Astor Place Triangle, both daily noon–6, Jul 1–Labor Day

ARTISTS

24 University Place: The site of the Cedar Street Tavern, where Jackson Pollock, Franz Kline and Willem de Kooning shared ideas, along with Beat writers Allen Ginsberg and Jack Kerouac.

8 West 8th Street: The first address of the Whitney Museum of American Art (see pages 148–151).

Garrick Theater, Bleecker Street: Crowds flocked here for seven months to see Andy Warhol's movie *Flesh*, which premiered in October 1968.

Skyscrapers north of Washington Square Park

WRITERS

145 Bleecker Street: Home to James Fenimore Cooper, author of *The Last of the Mohicans*, in 1833.

172 Bleecker Street: Where James Agee wrote the screenplay for *The African Queen*.

130–132 MacDougal Street: Louisa May Alcott stayed in this house, and it is believed, wrote *Little Women* here.

137 MacDougal Street: Home to the Liberal Club. Writers such as Upton Sinclair, Jack London, Theodore Dreiser and Sinclair Lewis regularly met in the house that once stood here.

85 West 3rd Street: Edgar Allen Poe lived on the third floor in 1845 (his was the last window on the right).

11 Commerce Street: Washington Irving wrote *The Legend of Sleepy Hollow* while living here.

14 West 10th Street: Home of Mark Twain when he moved to New York at the age of 65.

RADICALS

12 Charles Street: Home of suffragette Crystal Eastman and a gathering place for fellow suffragists.

91 Greenwich Avenue: Where *The Masses* was published. This left-wing publication backed the Communist Party and was a precursor to the counter-culture of the 1960s.

147 West 4th Street: John Reed rented a room in this house while he wrote *Ten Days That Shook the World*.

SHERIDAN SQUARE

Sheridan Square is at the point where Seventh Avenue, West 4th Street and Barrow Street intersect. Named after the Civil War general Philip Henry Sheridan, it is the site of the first protests that culminated in the Draft Riots of 1863 when 120 were killed, mostly African-Americans, by Irish immigrants (see page 33). You can see the statue of General Sheridan in Christopher Park.

WASHINGTON MEMORIAL ARCH IN WASHINGTON SQUARE

Built in 1889 as the entrance to the park at the base of Fifth Avenue, the original triumphal arch commemorated the centenary of George Washington's inauguration. Architect Stanford White designed the first arch, which was made of wood, plaster and papier maché. It was so successful that a fund to erect a permanent stone arch of the same design soon raised $134,000. The arch you see today, 30ft (9m) across and 77ft (23m) high, became the gateway to fashionable Fifth Avenue when cars passed directly underneath it in the 1950s when Fifth Avenue cut through the park, and remains a treasured city icon.

Many artists have painted or drawn the arch, including Childe Hassam in his 1894 *Washington Arch, Spring*. Many New Yorkers feel that New York University's 12-story Helen and Martin Kimmel Center on Fifth Avenue at Washington Square North detracts from the magnificence of the arch.

WASHINGTON MEWS

As you approach Memorial Arch from Fifth Avenue, on your left is a lovely little cobblestone street called Washington Mews. Originally the houses here were the stables and servants' quarters for the elite town houses on Washington Square North, known as "The Row," a street lined with fashionable homes built in 1833 by John Jacob Astor and Cornelius Vanderbilt.

The delightful old houses lining Washington Mews have long been sought as residences by artists and painters, including Gertrude Vanderbilt Whitney, founder of the Whitney Museum of American Art (see pages 148–151). Members of the faculty of New York University have more recently taken up residence here.

WASHINGTON SQUARE PARK

Washington Square is the heart of Greenwich Village. In warm weather the park is alive with street musicians, students, skateboarders, rollerbladers, the occasional film crew and chess players (bring your own set), so this lively little park is great for people-watching.

Originally the site was marshland and a hunting ground; until the 1820s, criminals were hanged from the large elm in the northwest corner, and from 1797 until 1926 it was a potters' field, where paupers were buried. The remains of about 10,000 people rest here in peace, if not quiet. Washington Square was eventually acquired by the city, cleared, and laid out as a military parade ground. The Common Council then purchased more land, and the 9 acres (3.5ha) became the city's largest park in the 1840s. In 1963 the city closed the park to traffic, making it even more attractive to the students in the area. By the 1970s, alcohol and drug abusers had taken over. A clean-up over the past decade has left it the mellow, genial place you see today.

BACKGROUND

By 1700 Greenwich Village, named after a town in England, had grown to become a small village of wood-framed houses and tree-lined, mud streets north of the city. A single grand estate, Richmond Hill, built by a British paymaster-general at what is today the intersection of Varick and Charleston streets, was George Washington's headquarters during the attempt to defend New York in 1776 and was later home to vice presidents John Adams (1767–1848) and Aaron Burr (1756–1836). Burr sold much of the land to John Jacob Astor, who divided it up into 456 lots, which he leased for a tidy little profit.

The streets grew up, sometimes along former cowpaths, before the grid street plan was introduced in 1811. When yellow fever struck in the 1820s, half the population fled the city, and prominent families looking for fresh air settled in Greenwich Village, tearing down most of the original frame houses and rebuilding in brick. The Village was a fashionable residential area by July 4, 1826, when Washington Military Parade Ground (Washington Square) was officially opened to celebrate the 50th anniversary of the signing of the Declaration of Independence. African-Americans moved in after the Draft Riots in 1863 and soon Italian immigrants from Little Italy were spilling over into the neighborhood. Tenements and factories were built, and wealthy New Yorkers moved north.

In the early 1900s, social changes and new zoning laws created cheap housing, attracting artists looking for studio space and low

TIPS

● If you're here on October 31, enjoy the outrageous costumes and festive partying up and down Sixth Avenue at the Village Halloween Parade.

● Stop at the Village Chess Shop at 230 Thompson Street, between Bleecker and West 3rd streets, for a friendly game of chess—or to buy anything to do with chess, Go or backgammon (www.chess-shop.com).

Regular jamming sessions still liven up the park

Pretty Brownstone townhouses characterize the streets

Bustling markets fill the streets on Sunday mornings

rents. Intellectuals, writers and rebels took up residence, creating a bohemian enclave. Social critics, including suffragists, anarchists and Communist sympathizers turned the Village into a hotbed of disaffection. Writers such as Henry James, O. Henry, Mark Twain, Edgar Allen Poe and Stephen Crane all lived here. The Village's artist-residents, including Edward Hopper, Jackson Pollock, Franz Kline and Willem de Kooning, created a new American style. Today, the Village is one of the liveliest parts of the city, and maintains its artsy overtones, despite being a very expensive place to live and therefore also popular with wealthy professionals.

Memorial Arch provides a sedate backdrop to performances in Washington Square Park

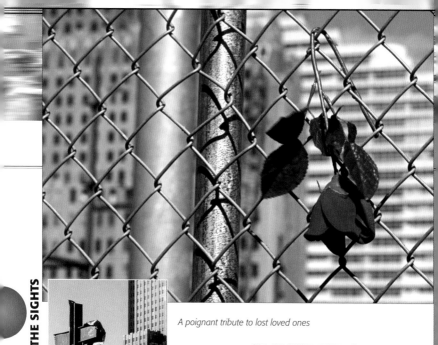

A poignant tribute to lost loved ones

GROUND ZERO

Ground Zero looks like nothing so much as a construction site. But seeing this corner of Lower Manhattan brings vividly home the horrors of 9/11.

The World Trade Center once filled seven buildings on the 16 acres (6.5ha) bordered by Church Street, Liberty Street, Park Place and West Street. The center's twin towers became the tallest buildings in the world in 1973, and for the next 28 years, more than a million visitors visited every year, thrilling to the views from the open-air rooftop observation level. Then, on the morning of September 11, 2001, New Yorkers and the rest of the world watched with horror on their televisions as two hijacked commercial jets slammed into the towers. A total of 2,752 people were killed, 343 of them firefighters. When the towers collapsed, six buildings were destroyed and about 100,000 jobs were lost. Mayor Rudolph Giuliani was on the scene within minutes. Streets like Church and Vesey were completely enshrouded in thick white dust, people were in shock, and emergency crews and firemen rushed to the scene, hoping to find survivors, but there were very few. When the fires were eventually extinguished, Ground Zero was all that was left.

A symbol of hope and strength, the iron cross at Ground Zero

RATINGS	
Historic interest	●●●●
Specialist shopping	●●
Photo stops	●●●
Walkability	●●●●●

BASICS
✚ 61 E25 • Church to West streets, Liberty to Vesey streets
🚌 M6, M9
Ⓜ E, N, R

LOOKING TO THE FUTURE

Within a year, clean-up crews had completed their gruesome task and workers had started rebuilding affected subway stations. The Lower Manhattan Development Corporation (LMDC) staged a design competition, inviting top architects around the world to create plans for the site. Six were unveiled in July 2002; all were rejected. Calling for more plans, the LMDC got responses from 406 teams of architects, and in March 2003 the governor and the mayor announced the winner: Daniel Libeskind, a Polish immigrant who arrived in the U.S. in 1960, aged 13.

An avant-garde architect, known for his commemorations of tragic events, Libeskind designed the Imperial War Museum in Manchester, England, and the Jewish Museum in Berlin. The heart of his underground memorial is the enormous slurry wall that kept the Hudson River from eroding the World Trade Center foundation. It surrounds the footprints of the two towers. Rising above is a symbolic 1,176ft (359m) tower with landscaped gardens. An elevated promenade allows visitors to view the memorial, and at ground level, a named marker will be put in the pavement for each rescue company that responded on 9/11. Commercial and cultural buildings are also planned.

One of the veteran aircraft in the Sea-Air-Space Museum

A Culture and Continuity gallery in the Jewish Museum

Go to Little Italy for the flavors and colors of the Mediterranean

INTREPID SEA-AIR-SPACE MUSEUM

⊞ 58 B18 • Hudson River Pier 86, west end of 46th Street 10036 ☎ 212/245-0072 🕐 Mon–Fri 10–5, Sat–Sun 10–7, Apr–Sep; Tue–Sun 10–5, rest of year; closed Thanksgiving, Dec 25 💷 Adult $13, child 6–11 $6, under 6s $2, under 2s/those on active duty with ID free 🚌 M42, M50 🚇 A, C, E 🎫 Free tours www.intrepidmuseum.org

The veteran aircraft carrier *Intrepid*, built in 1943 at a cost of $44 million, makes a fascinating museum. It is 898ft (275 m) long, weighs 42,000 tons, and had a crew of 3,500. The Hanger Deck is divided into four exhibits: Pearl Harbor and World War II, Life Aboard an Aircraft Carrier, the Story of *Intrepid*, and Space Exploration, Satellite Communication and Weaponry. On the Flight Deck you can inspect aircraft apparently ready for takeoff, including a Lockheed A-12 Blackbird, a Russian MIG and a Cobra helicopter. You can also tour the destroyer *Edson* and the submarine *Growler;* take a 7-minute SR-2 flight simulator ride; and rent a two-hour audiotour, during which veterans tell how they survived kamikaze attacks, and astronaut Scott Carpenter talks about the *Intrepid* scooping him up upon his return to Earth.

JEWISH MUSEUM

⊞ 59 E13 • 1109 Fifth Avenue 10128 ☎ 212/423-3200 🕐 Mon–Wed 11–5.45, Thu 11–8, Fri 11–3, Sun 10–5.45; closed Jewish and major holidays 💷 Adult $8, child free 🚌 M1, M2, M3, M4 🚇 6 🏧 💻 www.thejewishmuseum.org

A faux Loire Valley château, the former family home of banker Felix Warburg, this greystone mansion dating from 1908 contains the Jewish Museum's collection of Jewish ceremonial objects and works of art.

A generous philanthropist, Felix died in 1938 and his widow bequeathed the house to the museum in 1944. The permanent exhibit, entitled *Culture and Continuity: The Jewish Journey,* is based on Warburg's personal collection of artifacts, covering an impressive scale and time-span.

In a re-created 1900s café, oral histories reveal Jewish life in Europe at that time and explore the immigrant experience in the U.S. The Goodkind Resource Center shows classic TV and radio programs. Family workshops and other events celebrate Jewish culture, holidays and traditions.

LINCOLN CENTER
see pages 112–113

LITTLE CHURCH AROUND THE CORNER

⊞ 60 E19 • East 29th Street between Fifth and Madison avenues ☎ 212/684-6770 🕐 Daily 8–6 🚌 M2, M3, M4 🚇 6
www.littlechurch.org

The Episcopal Church of the Transfiguration is affectionately called the Little Church Around the Corner. Nothing could better demonstrate changed attitudes to all things theatrical than the way in which this charming little church acquired its nickname. In 1870, a nearby church declined to conduct funeral rites for actors, and directed one such request to "the little church around the corner." It has been favored by theater folk ever since.

An English-style lych-gate leads to the church, set back from the street in a quiet garden. The interior maintains the intimate, modest atmosphere with carved wooden pillars and beams.

LITTLE ITALY

⊞ 61 F23 • Between Canal, Lafayette, and Houston streets and the Bowery 🚇 6 🚌 M1, M103

Once the overcrowded destination of Italian immigrants coming from Ellis Island, Little Italy is shrinking under pressure from New York's burgeoning Chinatown (see page 84). A few blocks recall the friendly, festive area chockablock with Italian restaurants and grocery stores, where lavish displays of cheese, olives and salami entice visitors. Descendants of the initial immigrants still gather for family occasions, and tourists can wander the streets, savoring the atmosphere. In mid-September the Feast of San Gennaro, patron saint of Naples, fills Mulberry Street, the main artery, from Canal Street to Spring Street. With gaudy lights and carnival booths, it's definitely a scene to see if you don't mind crowds.

LOWER EAST SIDE

⊞ 61 G23 • East of the Bowery, south of East Houston to the East River 🚌 M14A 🚇 F, V

A slum tenement here was the next stop for most 19th-century immigrants after the ordeal of Ellis Island. The squalor, stench and disease in these overcrowded apartments during the area's heyday—from the mid-19th century until the 1920s—can barely be imagined today. Few of the original town houses survived the frenzied 19th-century building of tenement blocks, but most of these survived later rebuilding.

Today, although there is little to admire in the architecture, the area is thick with history. It is also one of New York shoppers' best bargain-hunting destinations, particularly on Sundays. Almost every day except Saturday (when stores are closed), the discount garment stores in the streets off Delancey Street and Orchard are crowded. Ethnic food shops in the area are wonderful; Essex Street Market *(Mon–Sat)* shows the changes in the ethnic mix of residents.

THE SIGHTS

Guggenheim Museum

A masterpiece of modern architecture designed by Frank Lloyd Wright. Exhibiting one of the world's finest collections of modern and contemporary art.

The dramatic sweeping curves of the Guggenheim's exterior

Permanent exhibit Still Life: Flask, Glass and Jug *by Paul Cézanne*

Under the rotunda (above) the ramp spirals downward (right)

RATINGS

Specialist shopping	● ● ● ●
Photo stops	● ● ●
Value for money	● ● ● ●

BASICS

✚ 58 E13 • 1071 Fifth Avenue 10028

☎ 212/423-3500

🕐 Sat–Wed 10–5.45, Fri 10–8; closed Thu

💰 Adult $15, under 12s free, Fri 6–8 pay-as-you-wish

🚌 M1, M2, M3, M4

🚇 4, 5, 6

📖 Free *Guggenheim Guide* containing listing of exhibits and programs available at admissions desk

🛍 Sat–Wed 9.30–5.45, Thu 9.30–3, Fri 9.30–8

🍴 Sat–Wed 9.30–6.15, Thu 11–6, Fri 9.30–8.30 👫

🎧 Free tours daily. Reservations are taken at the information desk from 1.30

www.guggenheim.org
Links to the Guggenheim's museums in Venice, Berlin, Bilbao and Las vegas; online listings of exhibitions with detailed information about each piece of art; museum store with innovative contemporary collectibles.

SEEING THE GUGGENHEIM

As you enter, to your right is the admission desk, where you can pick up a free exhibitions program with a floor plan. As you look up at the five levels above the low white walls bordering the ramp you see a tall empty atrium-like space so dramatic that it is easy to forget that you came here to see modern art. Frank Lloyd Wright designed this building with the belief that the eye should not be confronted with angles and sudden changes of form when viewing works of art. From a logistical point of view, the best way to see the works hung here is to take the elevator to the skylit top and meander down the spiral ramp. However, the exhibits are often hung with the opposite path in mind.

HIGHLIGHTS

PAUL CÉZANNE, *STILL LIFE: FLASK, GLASS AND JUG*
In this 1877 still life, Cézanne (1839–1906) perceives objects in space as being inter-related. He creates an illusion of objects resting and flowing simultaneously, calling attention to the two-dimensional canvas. This painting, and others, made Cézanne the foremost precursor of Cubism.

PABLO PICASSO, *WOMAN IRONING*
Painted in 1904 at the end of his Blue Period, *Woman Ironing* is Picasso's (1881–1973) quintessential work of labor and fatigue, reminiscent of the years he spent among the Paris working class. His expressionist style, with strong angular contours and attenuated proportions, expresses the woman's movement poetically, making her the metaphor for the pathos of the working poor.

MAX ERNST, *ATTIREMENT OF THE BRIDE*
This 1940s Surrealist painting by Max Ernst (1891–1976) evokes late 19th-century Symbolist painting, while the sleek, round-bellied figures recall motifs of 16th-century German art. The background architecture indicates the strong influence of the Italian painter Giorgio de Chirico. Ernst's invented alter-ego, the bird-man on the left, depicts the artist with a symbolic phallic spear. The picture-within-a-picture shows the same bride walking amid overgrown classical ruins, indicating the role

of the bride throughout history. Garish colors and beastly figures suggest something violent about to happen.

BACKGROUND

The Solomon R. Guggenheim Museum, designed by Frank Lloyd Wright, opened on October 21, 1959. The inverted-ziggurat design, with its ramp encircling the walls, is as surprising today as it was when it was created. Solomon R. Guggenheim, a wealthy New Yorker whose father was a prominent 19th-century mining and smelting capitalist, used some of his wealth to buy works of art. He was content with Old Masters until 1927, when at the age of 66 he met baroness Hilla Rebay von Ehrenwiesen. The baroness favored European abstract art and introduced Guggenheim to such artists as Wassily Kadinsky, Fernand Léger and Robert Delaunay. It was she who suggested that Wright design a museum to house the great collection Guggenheim was amassing. Guggenheim died in 1949 and never saw the wondrous building, but Wright took on the job with enthusiasm and later pronounced it his "Pantheon."

Jeanne in a Yellow Jumper by Amedeo Modigliani (1919)

Lincoln Center

The Upper West Side's performing arts center offers the best in opera, classical music, chamber music, jazz, ballet and theater.

Lincoln Center's fountains are dramatically lit at night

Take in a concert at Damrosch Park in summer

Colorful cafés line the Lincoln Center plaza

RATINGS	
Good for kids	● ● ●
Specialist shopping	● ● ● ● ●
Photo stops	● ●
Value for money	● ● ● ● ●

BASICS

✚ 58 C16 • 70 Lincoln Center Plaza 10023-6583 ☎ 212/546-2656 for main Lincoln Center

🚌 M5, M7, M11

🚇 1, 2

🍴 Avery Fisher Hall: Panevino Ristorante, tel 212/874-7000, Mon–Sat for dinner, lunch on matinée days

☕ Avery Fisher Hall: Café Vienna 5pm–intermission nightly, opens at noon for matinées

📷 The Performing Arts Shop, tel 212/441-1195, Metropolitan Opera Shop, tel 212/580-4090, Avery Fisher Hall Shop, tel 212/580-4356, New York Philharmonic Shop, tel 212/875-5437, Lincoln Center Theater Shop, tel 212/501-3178, The Gallery at Lincoln Center, tel 212/580-4673 ♿

🎫 One-hour tours daily from the concourse level of the Metropolitan Opera House 10.30–4.30, adult $10, child $5; backstage tours weekdays at 3.45, Sat 10am (reservations, tel 212/769-7020)

www.lincolncenter.org
Order tickets online, get visitor information about all events and performances.

With 14 venues offering everything from exceptional classical music to exhilarating performances for children, Lincoln Center is New York's premier center for performing arts. In the 1960s, a block of old tenements on the Upper West Side, where some of *West Side Story* was filmed, was demolished in a 12-block urban renewal project, and the Lincoln Center for the Performing Arts was built on the site. The initial investment for Lincoln Center was more than $165 million. The state contributed the site and the rest of the money came from private contributions.

In 1962 the New York Philharmonic moved here from Carnegie Hall (see page 76), which at the time was threatened with demolition. But the acoustics were never good, so in 1973 Avery Fisher donated $10 million to improve the hall's acoustics. The hall closed for a time to undergo this work, but musicians and music-lovers were still not satisfied, so in 1992 the hall underwent further renovation.

OPERA, BALLET, THEATER, JAZZ

The New York State Theater is home to the New York City Opera and the New York City Ballet. The theater seats 2,700.

The Metropolitan Opera House, affectionately known as the Met, is home to both the opera company and the American Ballet Theater and seats 3,800. General manager Joe Volpe started as an apprentice carpenter and has worked his way up; he knows what attracts crowds and what doesn't.

The Guggenheim Bandshell in Damrosch Park, on 62nd Street near Amsterdam Avenue, hosts open-air concerts in summer.

Lincoln Center Theater consists of the Vivian Beaumont Theater, with seating for 1,140, and the Mizi E. Newhouse Theater, an established Off Broadway venue.

Jazz, led by trumpeter and composer Wynton Marsalis, moves from Lincoln Center to the massive new Time Warner headquarters at nearby Columbus Circle in fall 2004, after receiving a $10 million gift from the Coca-Cola Company. The $128-million jazz venue is the focal point of the building, with three main performance spaces.

THE JUILLIARD MUSIC SCHOOL

The Juilliard School of Music is the top music school in the United

States. The campus includes Alice Tully Hall, a wonderful venue for chamber music and solo recitals, and the Walter Reade Film Theater, where the New York Film Festival sends up sparks every fall.

FUTURE PLANS

At the present time there is a plan to tear down Philharmonic Hall and start again; it is estimated that renovation of the existing building will cost half the amount of the projected $325 million reconstruction. When the New York Philharmonic is not in residence, leading orchestras stage shows in the house.

There are also plans to turn West 65th Street into a broad boulevard, much like a central artery of Lincoln Center. This will be the first step in the $150-million redesign of the public areas and the center's buildings and grounds. The avant-garde design team of Diller and Scofidio, who are described as "artist architects," and specialize in experimental installations, have been selected for the project. Other features of the plan include technologically sophisticated signs with information about events, a sweeping staircase into the plaza, and a new look to a number of the buildings.

Marc Chagall's murals are visible through the windows of the Metropolitan Opera House

TIPS

● There is a vast underground parking area, if you dare drive in New York.

● Special events take place all year, from summer's Mostly Mozart concert series and swing dancing to live jazz under the stars and the annual run of the Big Apple Circus, which pitches its tent in Damrosch Park at the beginning of November.

The Metropolitan Museum of Art

A spectacular collection spanning 5,000 years.

The entrance to the museum is imposing from any angle

Mary Cassatt's Lady at the Tea Table *(1885)*

The Petrie Sculpture Court is an idyllic spot for a rest

RATINGS	
Good for kids	◑ ◑ ◑
Cultural interest	◑ ◑ ◑ ◑ ◑
Specialist shopping	◑ ◑ ◑ ◑ ◑
Photo stops	◑ ◑ ◑ ◑

SEEING THE METROPOLITAN MUSEUM OF ART

The grand main entrance, with its impressive neoclassical façade, is on Fifth Avenue at 82nd Street. Take a moment to look at the three-story banners announcing exhibits. As you enter the Great Hall inside the main entrance, go to the information desk to pick up a museum plan, which lists special exhibitions and new installations, and ask about the day's activities, including gallery talks. Allow plenty of time—there is much to see. The collections number more than 3.3 million items, with around 100,000 on display at any given time. It can be confusing if you simply wander around, so begin by deciding which galleries you want to see and go straight to them. You may wish to rent an audioguide; some focus on special exhibitions, others on selections from the permanent collection. Or join a free guided tour; sign up at an information desk in the Great Hall.

HIGHLIGHTS

GREEK AND ROMAN ART
Statue of a *Kouros*
With more than 35,000 works ranging from the Neolithic period to AD312, in beautifully renovated galleries, the Greek and Roman Art collection is one of the most comprehensive in North America.

In the center of the Steinhardt Gallery is the marble statue of a *kouros* (youth), one of the earliest of such statues of boys to survive complete. Carved in Naxian marble in Attica, the boy's rigid stance reflects the influence of Egyptian art. It is believed to have marked the grave of a young Athenian aristocrat.

Other Highlights
In the Belfer Court is a collection of terra-cotta pots, gemstones, figures and sculptures from the Neolithic period to the fifth century BC. There are interesting pieces from the Minoan Palace of Knossos in Crete and Roman copies of Hellenistic sculptures from classical Greece.

Upstairs are bronze mirrors from the sixth century BC, painted amphoras from the fifth century BC, Corinthian and Hellenistic pottery, and bronze reliefs from the Etrusco-Roman period.

Enter via the Great Hall, with its large ornamental flower planters

Take in the view from the Roof Garden, where a modern sculpture overlooks the museum's environs

BASICS

✚ 58 E14 • 1000 Fifth Avenue at East 82nd Street 10028-0198

☎ 212/879-5500

🕐 Tue–Thu, Sun 9.30–5.15, Fri–Sat 9.30–8.45; closed Mon, Jan 1, Thanksgiving Day, Dec 25

💵 Suggested donation (includes main building and same-day visit to The Cloisters) adult $12, under 12s with adult free

🚌 M1, M2, M3, M4 to 79th Street

🚇 4, 5, 6 to 86th Street

🍽 Petrie Court Café, cafeteria on first floor behind Medieval Hall

🎁 The Met Store prides itself on being the largest museum bookstore in America and offers reproductions of the collection's jewelry, china and other objets d'art 🎨

🎧 Audioguide to special exhibitions and selections from the permanent collection in English, Chinese, French, German, Italian, Korean, Portuguese, Russian, Spanish or Japanese: adult $6, under 12s $4. The Key to the Met Audio Guide provides commentary on selected works of art

www.metmuseum.org
Informative introductions to collections. View highlights of 3,500 works of art online, get information on current exhibits, shop online from the Met Store.

EUROPEAN SCULPTURE AND DECORATIVE ARTS

Bacchanal: A Faun Teased by Children

With 60,000 exhibits ranging from the Renaissance to the early 20th century, European sculpture is one of the largest departments in the museum. In the Northern Renaissance and Florence galleries is a sculpture by Rome's Gian Lorenzo Bernini (1598–1680), which he created when he was only 18. Distinctive of his revolutionary style, it breathes life into the marble with profound emotional and spiritual intensity. The satin-like texture, strong accented lines and bacchic subject are typical Bernini.

Small Desk (bureau brisé)

In the Louis XIV Gallery, this little oak, pine and walnut veneered desk, engraved with tortoiseshell, brass, ebony and rosewood, is one of a pair made in France for Louis XIV. It was made to fit into the king's small study in the north wing of the Palace of Versailles by a little-known cabinetmaker by the name of Alexandre-Jean Oppenordt (1639–1715). On the closed top is a barely distinguishable engraved mask of Apollo above the crown, and inlaid Apollo lyres on the top's sides.

Other Highlights

In the English galleries are a rococo-style dining room from Kirtlington Park, Oxfordshire, and a lavish dining room from Lansdowne House, London. The French galleries include a Paris shopfront from 1775, a daybed made for Marie Antoinette in the boudoir of the Hotel de Crillon, and in the Louis XVI Gallery, the king's desk from his study at Versailles .

Petrie European Sculpture Court

Not to be missed is the beautiful Petrie European Sculpture Court. Fountains and greenery and a splendid view of Central Park and Cleopatra's Needle provide a peaceful setting for fine Italian and French sculptures. Cleopatra's Needle was a gift from the Pasha of Egypt.

THE AMERICAN WING

One of the Met's most popular areas, the American Wing has three floors and centers on the splendid Charles Englehard Court. Focusing on the development of art and design in America, the collection fills 25 rooms with period furniture and furnishings, more than 1,000 paintings by American artists, 600 sculptures, 2,500 drawings and numerous examples of the decorative arts.

Louis Comfort Tiffany Vase

This vase, one of the first pieces of American glass in the collection, came from Louisine and Henry Havemeyer in 1896. Tiffany (1848–1933) showed his talents as a colorist, designer and naturalist in this beautiful example of his Favrile glass peacock vases—the fan shaped like a peacock's outspread plumage, the eyes of sliced glass millefiori canes, and the graceful lines depicting each individual feather.

Emmanuel Gottlieb Leutze, Washington Crossing the Delaware

Painted in 1851 by the German-born painter E. G. Leutze (1816–68), this American icon depicts General Washington's surprise attack

KEY TO MAIN ROOMS

SECOND FLOOR
1: Modern art
2: 19th-century European paintings and sculpture
3: Islamic art
4: Cypriot art
5: Ancient Near Eastern art
6–7: Asian art
8: Musical instruments
9: American Wing: American paintings, sculpture, decorative arts and period rooms
10: European paintings
11: Special exhibitions

FIRST FLOOR
14: 20th-century paintings
15: Sculpture and artifacts from Africa, Oceania and the Americas
16: Greek and Roman art from prehistoric to classical
17: Egyptian art, Sackler Wing and Temple of Dendur
18: American Wing: American paintings, sculpture, decorative arts and period rooms
19: Arms and Armor: European, Islamic and Japanese armor, weaponry from Ottoman Turkish and Mughal Indian courts
20: European sculpture and decorative arts
21: Medieval art
22: Robert Lehman Collection: Old Masters, Impressionist, Post-Impressionist paintings
23: Library

GROUND FLOOR
25: Costume Institute: Late 16th-century to present clothing and costumes
26: Robert Lehman Collection

THE SIGHTS

THE METROPOLITAN MUSEUM OF ART   117

on the Hessians at Trenton, New Jersey on Christmas night 1776. Washington's physical stamina and indomitable spirit as he leads 2,400 men to victory is central. In attempting to mythologize, Leutze takes liberties with history and focuses attention on inaccuracies such as the flag, not adopted until six months after the crossing. Leutze painted three versions of this work: The original went to the Kunsthalle in Bremen, the second was made for engraving.

Hart Room
The earliest interior in the American Wing, the Hart Room is from the home of Thomas Hart of Ipswich, Massachusetts. Built sometime between 1639 and 1674, this is a typical example of homes of the early New England settlers. The post-and-beam construction, used much in England, was both simple and sturdy. The bed is a reproduction ash and pine frame. The handwoven and sewn wool hangings around the bed helped to keep drafts away from the sleeper.

Other Highlights
In the airy Charles Englehard Court, linger to study Tiffany's *Garden Landscape and Fountain* and the beautiful stained-glass *Autumn Landscape*. The former was inspired by the Byzantine churches Tiffany saw while traveling in Europe. Turn to the right to see Tiffany's extravagant loggia from Laurelton Hall. The dahlias at the top of the columns are in three stages of growth: bud, full bloom and seed pod.

The sculptures in this glass-enclosed garden are by American artists Augustus Saint-Gaudens, Frederick MacMonnies and Daniel Chester French. In Gallery 127 is the work of the world-famous architect Frank Lloyd Wright. Living Room from the Little House, a very modern design in 1912, was designed for Francis Little.

Paintings and sculptures by American artists on this floor include John Singleton Copely's *Midshipman August Brine*, *The Falls of Niagara* by S. F. B. Morse, James McNeill Whistler's *Arrangement in Flesh, Color and Black*, John Singer Sargent's *Madame X* (1884), Mary Cassatt's *Lady at the Tea Table* (1885), and from the Hudson River School Frederic Church's *Heart of the Andes*.

EUROPEAN PAINTINGS
Albrecht Dürer, *Virgin and Child with St. Anne*
Germany's greatest Renaissance artist portrays St. Anne with her daughter, the Virgin Mary, holding the infant Jesus. It is believed that Dürer (1471–1528) painted this in 1519, at the time he was becoming an ardent follower of Martin Luther. By including St. Anne, who was a much-venerated saint in Germany, the artist was perhaps questioning the veracity of a virgin birth.

Vincent Van Gogh, *Cypresses*
Painted in 1889 when Van Gogh (1853–90) began his year-long confinement in the asylum at St-Rémy, *Cypresses* was one of several paintings the artist produced of familiar landscapes during this time. The illuminating shades of the background contrast sharply with the tree's splash of black. The use of swirls evokes the unpredictability of weather and the possible threat of the unknown.

Claude Monet, *Terrace at Sainte-Adresse*
Painted in 1867 at a time when Monet (1840–1926) was exploring new ways of representing modern life, this painting shocked his contemporaries. The bold use of pure colors and strong contrasts combine to capture the blinding glare of the sun's reflection off the water, the paths and flowers. Giving balance and depth to the painting, the flags' movement give the impression that the painter has caught a moment in time, like photographers would later be able to do with the camera.

Other Highlights
Among the many Italian masters' works are Raphael's *Madonna Enthroned with Child and Saints* (1505), Titian's *Venus and the Lute Player* (c1560), Tintoretto's *Finding of Moses* (c1550), Botticelli's *Last Communion of St. Jerome* (c1450) and Caravaggio's *Musicians* (1504). Early Dutch painters include a Rembrandt *Self-Portrait* (1660),

The marble statue of a youth, kouros, in the Steinhardt Gallery

Stroll among the statues in the Petrie Sculpture Court

The Rocky Mountains, Lander's Peak, *by Albert Bierstadt (1863)*

Degas' The Dance Lesson *(c1879)*

Take an audiotour or a guided tour from the Great Hall

Vermeer's *Woman with a Water Jug* (1664) and works by de Hooch, van Goyen and others. French paintings include Poussin's *Rape of the Sabine Women* (c1635) and Jean Clouet's *Guillaume Budé*. Spanish works include El Greco's *View of Toledo* and *Grand Inquisitor Cardinal Don Fernando Niño de Guevara*. The English collection is represented by William Hogarth, Joshua Reynolds and Thomas Gainsborough.

European paintings of the 19th century include Millet's *Autumn Landscape with a Flock of Turkeys* (1872–73) and many Impressionist and Post-Impressionist paintings. Besides 100 works by Degas, there are paintings by Manet, Renoir, Seurat, Toulouse-Lautrec, Cézanne, Gauguin and Van Gogh. Worth seeing are one of Cézanne's best still lifes, *Still Life with Apples and a Pot of Primroses* (1895) and Monet's *Terrace at Sainte-Adresse* (c1867).

BACKGROUND

Members of New York's Union League Club—businessmen, artists and scholars—founded the Metropolitan Museum of Art in 1870. Originally at 681 Fifth Avenue, the museum moved to its present site in 1880. The original red-brick building, designed by Jacob Mould and Calvert Vaux, has been incorporated into the present museum and is visible in the Lehman Wing. The Richard Morris Hunt façade fronting Fifth Avenue was built in 1902. Beginning with a Roman sarcophagus, donations have continued over the years, but it was in 1904, when multimillionaire J. P. Morgan was elected president of the Board of Trustees, that world masterpieces became the main acquisitions. Morgan was not very interested in American art, nor in contemporary artists like Paul Gauguin and Henri Toulouse-Lautrec, but preferred the Old Masters. A former Cypriot consul sold his collection of 6,000 objects to the museum, and Catherine L. Wolfe handed over 143 paintings of the Dutch and Flemish schools. Louis Comfort Tiffany's work was first presented in 1896 with 56 Favrile glass vases and in 1951 the Tiffany Foundation donated spectacular pieces from a private collection. In 2003, more than 100 works of art by Henri Matisse were given to the museum. The Met has also been running excavations for more than 30 years, and the finds are added to the collection.

TIPS

● To avoid long lines at the main entrance, enter at 81st Street, where there is a ticket and information desk.

● If you plan to visit the Cloisters (see page 86) on the same day, it's best to visit the two sites on a Friday or Saturday, when the Met stays open later. Do the Cloisters in the morning and the Met in the afternoon.

● To avoid crowds, weekday mornings are optimal. Or plan a Friday or Saturday evening visit.

● Plan to take in the Roof Garden *(May–Oct)*. It's worth visiting not only for the splendid views of Central Park, the sandwiches and drinks, but also for the magnificent collection of sculptures.

An interior display from the Tenement Museum

The Metropolitan Life Insurance Tower stands proud

The elegant Ladies Parlour at the Mount Vernon Hotel

THE SIGHTS

LOWER EAST SIDE TENEMENT MUSEUM

✚ 61 G23 • 90 and 97 Orchard Street, between Broome and Delancey streets ☎ 212/431-0233 🕐 Guided tours only; available from the Visitor Center. Times vary but normally every half hour Tue–Fri 1–4, Thu 6 & 7pm, Sat–Sun 11–4.30, Apr–Nov. Interactive program Sat–Sun noon, 1pm, 2pm, 3pm 🎟 Adult $9, under 5s free. Interactive program: adult $8. Advance tickets (advisable), tel 800/965-4827 🚇 M9, M14A, M15 🚉 J, M, Z 🏛 👥 📷 Guided tours www.tenement.org

Four re-created apartments in a typical, five-story tenement dating from 1863 give a disturbing insight into how the other half lived, or at least managed to exist, in the overcrowded, unsanitary conditions common on the Lower East Side between the 1870s and 1920s.

Some 10,000 seekers of the American Dream and refugees from violent pogroms passed through this building through 70 years, as you learn on a guided tour. Fewer people go on each of these—never more than 15—than lived in a typical apartment. None of this is really for kids. For them, take in the interactive living history program, where they can try on period clothes and talk to "Victoria Confino," a Jewish teenager who lived here in 1916.

MERCHANT'S HOUSE MUSEUM

✚ 60 F22 • 29 East 4th Street 10003 ☎ 212/777-1089 🕐 Thu–Mon 1–5; closed Dec 25 🎟 Adult $5, child free 🚇 M1, M5, M6, M102 🚉 6, R, N 👥 📷 Tours every half hour Sat–Sun www.merchantshouse.com

This museum is an 1832 time capsule, one of six Federal-style row houses with a charmingly gracious Greek Revival doorway. Bought by wealthy merchant

Thomas Tredwell in 1835, the house was lived in by his daughter for 93 years. Renovated after her death in 1933, it was opened to the public as a museum in 1936 with the original furnishings intact, including personal family possessions. It is the only 19th-century house in Manhattan to be so completely preserved. Seven rooms on three floors and a secret garden are on view. Miss Tredwell is thought to have been the model for a character in Henry James' *Washington Square*.

METROPOLITAN LIFE INSURANCE TOWER

✚ 60 E20 • 1 Madison Avenue 🚇 M1, M3 🚉 4, 5, 6

Met Life's 1893 main building on 23rd Street stands on the site of the Madison Square Presbyterian Church, whose minister savagely attacked the corrupt politicians who ran the city in 1892. This 54-story tower, built in 1909, was their revenge. Planned as the tallest building in the world and a proud symbol of Met Life's prominence, it was soon overtaken by the Woolworth Building (see page 144). The Met's campanile was 700ft (214m); in 1913, the Woolworth surpassed it by 92ft (28m).

In 1962, the tower was stripped of its original ornamentation, leaving the gold dome and the huge clock faces.

METROPOLITAN MUSEUM OF ART
see pages 114–119

MORGAN LIBRARY
see page 122

MOUNT VERNON HOTEL MUSEUM AND GARDEN

✚ 59 G16 • 421 East 61st Street at York Avenue ☎ 212/838-6878 🕐 Tue–Sun 11–4, closed Aug 🎟 Adult $5, child free 🚇 M15, M31, M57 🚉 N, R, 4, 6 www.mountvernonhotelmuseum.org

In this splendid hotel, eight of the rooms were filled with Federal period furnishings by the Colonial Dames of America when they bought the structure in 1924. In the Gentlemen's Tavern Room, you're welcome to sit down and read a newspaper from 1828, and don't miss the museum's delightful 18th-century gardens. To get a feel for the place, visit the website and take a tour. The museum was a house that once belonged to Abigail Adams, the daughter of U.S. president John Adams and the wife of George Washington's aide, William Stephens Smith. The Smiths had to sell the property in 1798 before all the buildings were complete and so never lived here. In 1826 the building underwent substantial internal alterations to convert it into a hotel. There are regularly scheduled events such as talks on American furniture of the early 19th century.

MUNICIPAL ART SOCIETY

✚ 59 E17 • 457 Madison Avenue 10022 ☎ 212/935-3960 reservations; 212/439-1049 for tours and meeting places 🕐 Mon–Wed, Fri–Sat 11–5 🎟 Guided walking tour weekday $12; weekend walking and bus tour $15 www.mas.org

Founded in 1893, MAS is a non-profit, private, membership society aiming to promote a "more livable city." It advocates excellence in architecture, design and planning, public art and preservation of historic buildings, and organizes exhibitions and walking tours. The guides on these tours are highly qualified and give insights into the history and significance of the urban scene. Exhibitions are held at the headquarters, the Urban Center Galleries in one of the Villard Houses at the Helmsley Hotel, and are free and open to the public.

The view across town from the dizzying heights of the legendary Empire State Building

MIDTOWN MANHATTAN

Chic shopping, high-priced hotels, skyscrapers, landmarks and bright lights.

Midtown Manhattan stretches from 42nd Street to 59th Street, with Fifth Avenue splitting it into east and west, where shopping is a big attraction. Megastores have made it big in Times Square and the Theater District, while Fifth Avenue and 57th Street are lined with the most glamorous names like Gucci and Chanel. In the past few years, retailers Niketown, Banana Republic and Liz Claiborne have moved in, joining classic Saks Fifth Avenue, Tiffany & Co. and Bergdorf Goodman on the stretch of Fifth Avenue from 49th to 59th streets.

Midtown has New York's major train station, bus stations, the largest concentration of hotels, big stores and corporate headquarters. Midtown West includes the Garment District and the Theater District, with Times Square and Broadway (see pages 138–140) at the heart of it.

Bryant Park is where tents are set up in September for New York's Fashion Week, no matter what the weather. Here there are museums like the International Center of Photography (see page 101), Museum of Arts and Design (see page 123), the Museum of Television and Radio (see page 124) and, when it returns in 2005, the Museum of Modern Art (see page 125). Rockefeller Center (see pages 128–1300) and the home of the Rockettes, Radio City Music Hall (see page 129) are in Midtown. Along the Hudson River, there's the *Intrepid* Sea-Air-Space Museum (see page 109).

LANDMARK SIGHTS

Architectural landmarks in Midtown East include the Chrysler Building (see page 85), the Chanin Building and the Daily News Building (see page 87). Nearby is Grand Central Terminal (see pages 102–104). At 301 Park Avenue is the famous Waldorf-Astoria Hotel, where kings, queens and presidents have stayed. Along Madison Avenue are the stunning Villard Houses, notable for their turn-of-the-20th-century extravagance, now part of the Helmsley Palace Hotel. At the east end of 42nd Street is Tudor City, with 3,000 apartments and its own restaurants, parks, stores and post office. The U.N. Headquarters (see page 144) stands on the East River, not actually on U.S. land, but on international territory belonging to the member nations. It has a serenity that sets it apart here.

Broadway is synonymous with theater and entertainment

RATINGS				
Historic interest	●	●	●	●
Specialist shopping	●	●	●	●
Photo stops	●	●	●	●
Walkability	●	●	●	●

BASICS

➕ 59 E18 • 42nd Street to 59th Street

🚌 M1, M2, M3, M4, M6

🚇 4, 5, N, R

🍴 Oyster Bar Grand Central Terminal lower level, tel 212/490-6650

☕ Café Soleil, 135 East 56th Street, tel 212/832-0199; Bryant Park Café, 25 West 40th Street (behind New York Public Library), tel 212/840-6500, in summer eating outdoors

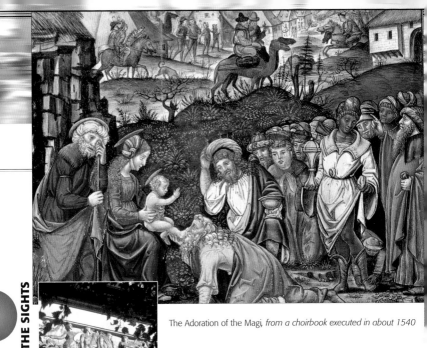

The Adoration of the Magi, *from a choirbook executed in about 1540*

The decorated façade of the Morgan Library

RATINGS	
Historic interest	●●●
Cultural interest	●●●●●
Specialist shopping	●●●●
Value for money	●●●●

BASICS

🔲 60 E19 • 29 East 36th Street 10016

☎ 212/685-0610

🕐 Tue–Thu 10.30–5, Fri 10.30–8, Sat 10.30–6, Sun noon–6

💷 Suggested admission: adult $7, under 16s with adult free

🚌 M1, M2, M3, M4

🚇 6

🍴 🔲 Morgan Court Café serves lunch and afternoon tea

📅 Bookshop closes 15 minutes before galleries

www.morganlibrary.org

MORGAN LIBRARY

An astonishing collection of rare books, manuscripts and drawings by the western world's most creative geniuses.

First, the bad news; the Morgan Library is closing to the public from spring 2003 until 2006, while it expands. The good news is that when it re-opens, it will have twice the gallery space, an enlarged auditorium, a café, a bigger shop and more open public spaces. The Reading Room will be better equipped and storage areas improved. At the time of writing the Morgan was planning to offer special programs and events during the closure and to lend objects to temporary exhibitions.

By the end of the 19th century, John Pierpont Morgan was one of New York's wealthiest financiers. To fulful his desire to match Europe's greatest libraries, he began his opulent private library of European cultural treasures: manuscripts, paintings, prints and furniture. His travels abroad resulted in this priceless collection of nearly 10,000 drawings and prints, including some by Leonardo da Vinci and Albrecht Dürer. In 1902, he commissioned Charles McKim to design the magnificent Renaissance-style building. Later additions include those by Benjamin Morris in 1928, the annex, which was Morgan's private residence, at 231 Madison Avenue, and the garden courtyard in the 1990s.

MORGAN'S STUDY

The West Room of the library remains as Morgan left it when he died in 1913. He used it as a study and his huge wooden desk is still here, along with the Italian Renaissance paintings lining the walls. From the study you pass green-veined marble columns as you proceed toward the rotunda and the East Room. The beautiful three-tiered, walnut and bronze bookcases are almost as amazing as the ceiling covered with frescoes and the signs of the zodiac. Notice the 16th-century Flemish tapestry above the fireplace. But it is the collection of letters and manuscripts that most intrigues.

Morgan acquired nearly 600 medieval and Renaissance manuscripts, including the 9th century *Lindau Gospels*, a rare vellum copy of the Gutenberg Bible, and the medieval Dutch masterpiece *The Hours of Catherine of Cleves*. He also purchased handwritten scores by Beethoven, Mozart and Puccini, which are under glass. The collection also includes manuscripts by Jane Austen, Charles Dickens, Henry David Thoreau and Mark Twain.

The Museum of Chinese in the Americas was founded in 1980

Modern and chic objects for daily use are on display in the Museum of Arts and Design

MUSEUM OF AMERICAN FINANCIAL HISTORY

61 E26 • 28 Broadway 10004
212/908-4110 Tue–Sat 10–4; closed Jan 1, Thanksgiving, Dec 25
4, 5 $2 contribution requested
www.financialhistory.org

On the site of Alexander Hamilton's law office, where John D. Rockefeller's Standard Oil Company was headquartered, this four-room, Smithsonian Museum affiliate celebrates America's spirit of entrepreneurship with exhibits of coins, tickertape from the Wall Street Crash of 1929, curiously interesting photographs and murals of Wall Street and other documents and artifacts. Interactive financial news terminals help children understand the stock market. Special exhibitions have included informative displays about high-value bills. The shop has interesting gifts for that person who has everything.

MUSEUM OF ARTS AND DESIGN

59 E17 • 40 West 53rd Street 10019
212/956-3535 Daily 10–6, Thu until 8 Adult $8, under 12s free, pay-as-you-wish Thu 6–8 M1, M2, M3, M4 E, V
www.americancraftmuseum.org

In this museum (formerly the American Craft Museum) the American Craft Council displays the nation's biggest exhibition of 20th-century American and international crafts. From jewelry to baskets, furniture to teapots, everything is carefully selected to represent the finest in form and function. Stimulating special exhibitions are chosen from the extensive, wide-ranging collections, augmented by loans from other collections, to illustrate contemporary trends in technique and design. It's all shown to great advantage in a spacious, three-story atrium. Past exhibitions have included a retrospective on U.S. design from 1975 to 2000 and another showcasing elaborate cake decorating.

MUSEUM OF CHINESE IN THE AMERICAS

61 F24 • 70 Mulberry Street, 2nd Floor 10013 212/619-4785
Tue–Sun noon–5 Adult $3
M15, M103 N, R, Q
www.moca-nyc.org

This museum exhibits photographs and other works of visual art, rare historical documents, musical instruments, clothing and artifacts that help to explain Chinese history and culture. MoCA's very moving core exhibit, *Where is Home?*, interprets themes such as migration, abandonment, customs, women and home. Temporary exhibits are equally interesting. Post 9/11, *Recovering Chinatown* displayed images, artwork and other materials documenting the experience of Chinatown residents during and after the attack on the World Trade Center. *Gotta Sing Gotta Dance!* offered insight into the world of Chinese-American performers from the 1930s and the 1940s.

MUSEUM OF THE CITY OF NEW YORK

Off map 59 E12 • 1220 Fifth Avenue 10029 212/534-1672 Wed–Sat 10–5, Sun noon–5. Preregistered groups only Tue 10.30–noon; closed major holidays Suggested admission: adult $7, child $4, family $12
M1, M2, M3, M4, M106 6
Highlights tour Sat noon
www.mcny.org

A neo-Georgian, colonial-style villa built in 1929 houses this museum devoted to New York's history and life. Six period rooms depict changing fashions and styles of furnishings from early days to the early 20th century, and exhibits explore New York's maritime history. The third floor has shows of a beloved collection of toys, dolls and dollhouses from the 18th to 19th centuries. John D. Rockefeller's master bedroom and dressing room were brought intact from his demolished mansion on West 54th Street and are displayed on the fourth floor. The basement houses a firefighting exhibit. Changing exhibits are on the main level, along with the information desk and museum shop.

MUSEUM OF JEWISH HERITAGE

61 E26 • 18 First Place 10280
212/509-6130 Sun–Wed 9–5, Thu 9–8, Fri and eve of Jewish holidays 9–3 (9–5 Apr–Sep); closed Jewish holidays and Thanksgiving Adult $7, under 6s free M1, M6, M9, M10 M15 4, 5
www.mjhnyc.org

This museum, opened in 1996 and designed by Kevin Roche and John Dinkeloo in a hexagonal shape to represent the Star of David, houses an exhibition of 20th-century Jewish history and culture. Presenting the story of Jewish tragedy and suffering, survival and renewal, the museum has three main sections: Jewish Life a Century Ago, The War Against the Jews, and Jewish Renewal.

Displays take you back to the now-vanished worlds of a century ago, through the horror of industrialized mass murder, to the resurgence of hope in a world not yet free of hatred and intolerance. Film clips, interspersed with displays of physical objects, include testimonies from Spielberg's *Survivors of the Shoah* project and footage from the museum's own archives.

THE SIGHTS

Statue of Diana the hunter in the National Academy of Design

Christian Schad's Maika *(1929) in the Neue Galerie*

Nineteenth-century fire carriages at the New York Fire Museum

MUSEUM OF TELEVISION AND RADIO

✚ 58 E17 • 25 West 52nd Street 10019
☎ 212/621-6800 🕐 Tue–Sun noon–6, Thu until 8, Fri theater programs until 9; closed major holidays 🎫 Adult $10, under 13s $5 🚇 M1, M2, M3, M4 🚊 E, V 🍴 ♿ 👥 📷
www.mtr.org

William S. Paley, former chairman of CBS and now chairman of the museum, donated the land for this 17-story building, erected in 1989 to a design by architects Philip Johnson and John Burgee. Theaters, screening rooms, three public galleries and individual viewing and listening consoles are your access to the museum's collection of tapes of 100,000 programs and commercials celebrating more than 75 years.

When you arrive, make a reservation to use the computer catalog on the fourth floor to locate what interests you, then reserve it and watch it in one of the museum's consoles. Or take in a show or two at one of the screening rooms or theaters. Seminars and classes, as well as exhibitions, are held throughout the year.

NATIONAL ACADEMY OF DESIGN

✚ 58 E13 • 1083 Fifth Avenue 10128
☎ 212/369-4880 🕐 Wed–Thu noon–5, Fri 10–6, Sat–Sun 11–6; closed public holidays 🎫 Adult $8 🚇 M1, M2, M3, M4 🚊 4, 5, 6 🚊 Wed–Thu 10–5, Fri 10–6, Sat–Sun 11–6 📷 Gallery talks Wed 12.30; docent tours Wed–Thu after 11am, Fri–Sun after 10am
www.nationalacademy.org

The National Academy of Design is both a museum and a school of fine art, and also owns the largest collection of 19th- and 20th-century American art in the country—an astonishing collection with more than 5,000 works ranging from portraiture of the

Federalist period, landscapes of the Hudson River School, gritty realism of the Ashcan Movement, and paintings representing movements from Fauvism to photorealism. The building was the home of Archer Milton Huntington and his wife, the sculptor Anna Hyatt Huntington. In 1913, they expanded and remodeled the house and lived here until 1939, when they gave it to the National Academy of Design, who moved in three years later. Tours covering the collection's highlights and Edith Wharton's New York are available.

NEUE GALERIE

✚ 58 E13 • 1048 Fifth Avenue 10028
☎ 212/628-6200 🕐 Fri–Mon 11–7
🎫 Adult $10, no children 🚇 M1, M2, M3, M4 🚊 4, 5, 6 🍴 ♿ 👥
www.neuegalerie.org

This museum, dedicated to early 20th-century German and Austrian art and design, has a marvelous collection of fine paintings, decorative arts and other media, including works by Gustav Klimt, Paul Klee, Egon Schiele, Josef Hoffmann and Adolf Loos.

On Friday nights there are cabarets in Café Sabarsky, which serves Austrian fare, including delicious pastries. Some of the furniture is by Adolf Loos, and lighting fixtures are by Josef Hoffmann. The 1914 Carrère & Hastings mansion housing the museum was built for Mrs. Cornelius Vanderbilt III, and is every bit as remarkable as the collection.

NEW MUSEUM OF CONTEMPORARY ART

✚ 61 E23 • 583 Broadway 10012
☎ 212/219-1222 🕐 Tue–Wed, Fri–Sun noon–6, Thu noon–8; closed major holidays 🎫 Adult $6 (Thu 6–8 $3), under 18s free 🚇 M1, M5, M6 🚊 N, C, F 🚊 👥
www.newmuseum.org

Installations in the museum's front window catch the eye, where international contemporary artists have been invited to mount shows of their innovative and experimental work since 1977. There are six major exhibitions each year and five Media Lounge shows.

The Zenith Media Lounge exhibits digital art and experimental video and sound works. There are five multimedia computer stations for online programming (free) and a lounge area where visitors can relax and view works presented on wall-mounted plasma screens. *Living Inside the Grid* was a popular 2003 exhibition that explored this significant 20th-century motif.

NEW YORK CITY FIRE DEPARTMENT MUSEUM

✚ 61 E23 • 278 Spring Street 10013
☎ 212/691-1303 🕐 Tue–Sun 10–4; closed major holidays 🎫 Contribution requested (adult $4, child $1) 🚇 M6, M20, M21 🚊 C, E 🚊 👥 📷 Tours by appointment
www.nycfiremuseum.org

A former firehouse of Rescue Company No.1, built in 1904, this museum packs three floors with firefighting paraphernalia, the most comprehensive collection in the United States. Equipment from the 1700s to the present includes buckets, pumps, horse-drawn fire engines, a fire hydrant, hose-pipes, axes, uniforms and helmets old and new, and there's an exhibit on fire safety and burn prevention. Firefighters are usually around to explain and share stories.

This is one of the best places in the city to pay tribute to the 343 firefighters who lost their lives on September 11, 2001 when the twin towers collapsed. You can also see exhibits relating to the disaster.

Among many fine works is Van Gogh's The Starry Night *(1889)*

MUSEUM OF MODERN ART

The world's greatest collection of painting and sculpture from the late 19th century to the present.

MoMA's West 53rd Street building, at the time of writing, has been undergoing a $650-million renovation to double the exhibit space. The completed building is expected to reopen in 2005. If you visit before then you will find the stunning permanent collections and temporary exhibitions in a redesigned former staple factory in Long Island City, Queens, a short subway or bus ride from Midtown. Look for the bright blue letters M-o-M-A. It looks more like a warehouse than a museum, with its concrete floors and raw open space, but it is welcoming and unpretentious, and the neighborhood is airy, bright, multi-ethnic, and full of good, inexpensive ethnic restaurants.

COLLECTIONS AND EXHIBITIONS

MoMA QNS certainly drew crowds in 2003, when the blockbuster Matisse Picasso exhibition, examining the development of the artists' close and complex relationship, came to town. Exhibitions on Max Beckman and Ansel Adams at 100 have also been popular; upcoming for 2004 are Tall Buildings and Lee Bontecou.

Works from the permanent collection are displayed in rotation, so it's difficult to say which works will be on view at any time: But the range is vast—approximately 100,000 pieces, including paintings, sculptures, photographs, architectural models and plans, prints and modern design.

Among the painting and sculpture collections, Van Gogh's mesmerizing *The Starry Night* and *The Bather* by Paul Cézanne stand out among many masterpieces; the Matisse paintings include *Dance*. Cubist paintings include Picasso's *Three Women* and Braque's *Man with a Guitar* and there are fine examples of Expressionism and Futurism, including Piet Mondrian's *Broadway Boogie-Woogie*. Joan Miró's works dominate the Surrealist collection. The photograph collection ranges from Henri Cartier-Bresson to Diane Arbus, highlighted by William Fox Talbot's *Lace* and Paul Strand's *Fifth Avenue, New York*. With 19,000 films and four million film stills, the Film and Media Department is impressive.

MoMA's first exhibition in 1929 was of post-Impressionist painters Cézanne, Seurat, Gauguin and Van Gogh. A modern art museum was a new adventure and skeptics scoffed. But MoMA was overwhelmingly popular and has continued to expand.

A model of the new Museum of Modern Art, designed by Yoshio Taniguchi

RATINGS	
Good for kids	●●●
Historic interest	●●●●
Specialist shopping	●●●
Value for money	●●●●

BASICS

341 J16 • 45 33rd Street, Long Island City, Queens
212/708-9400
Sat–Mon, Thu 10–5, Fri 10–7.45
Adult $12, under 16s with an adult free, Fri 4–7.45 pay-what-you-wish
Q32, Q60
7 local to 33rd Street
MoMA Store QNS, tel 212/708-9400, MoMA Design Store, 44 West 53rd Street, tel 212/767-1050, MoMA Design Store Soho, 81 Spring Street, tel 646/613-1367 Audioguide $5

www.moma.org

TIP

● Go around 10am, then grab a bite at one of the restaurants on Queens Boulevard, a block away. The museum distributes a list from the *New York Times*.

100 Old Slip in former days, now the New York City Police Museum

Indian, in the Henry Luce III Center, the NY Historical Society

The Gothic Revival interior of the Riverside Church

THE SIGHTS

NEW YORK CITY POLICE MUSEUM

61 F26 • 100 Old Slip 10005
212/477-9753 Tue–Sat 10–5
Suggested donation adult $5, child $2 M9, M15 N, R, 2, 3
www.nycpolicemuseum.org

This small museum exhibits a collection of uniforms, ceremonial batons, New York Police Department (NYPD) shields, handguns, and even the machine gun used by Al Capone's gang to assassinate Frankie Yale, the first homicide in New York by such a weapon.

Visit a prison cell and see the display on vintage weapons and notorious criminals, which includes arrest records. Learn about fingerprinting and forensics, then view the NYPD Hall of Heroes, which now has a memorial to the 23 policemen and women who lost their lives in the attack on the World Trade Center. Temporary exhibitions cover a range of subjects: one was *Women in Policing*. In 2003 the museum held its third annual Antique Police Car Show.

NEW-YORK HISTORICAL SOCIETY

58 D14 • 2 West 77th Street 10024
212/873-3400 Museum: Tue–Sun 10–6. Library: Tue–Sat 10–5 (summer Tue–Fri 10–5). Print Room by appointment only Adult $8, child $5 M10, M79 B, C
Audiotours, docent tours Tue–Sun at 1pm, 3pm
www.nyhistory.org

At Central Park West, this Upper West Side museum is a great place to spend a morning or afternoon. For nearly 200 years, the New-York Historical Society has been collecting, preserving and interpreting books, paintings, sculpture, photographs and newspapers. The fascinating Henry Luce III Center on the fourth floor displays lamps by Louis Comfort Tiffany, Hudson River School landscapes, a complete set of original watercolors by John James Audubon for *The Birds of America*, George Washington's inaugural chair, antique toys and much more. The library is the oldest research library in the country.

RECTORY OF THE SHRINE OF ELIZABETH ANN SETON

344 E26 • 7 State Street 212/269-6865 Mon–Fri, ring bell for admission

From 1801 to 1803, this redbrick town house was the home of the New York socialite and mother of five, Elizabeth Ann Seton, the first American-born woman to be canonized by the Roman Catholic Church.

Born in 1774, she converted to Catholicism as an adult and became a spiritual leader and educator. She founded the first order of nuns in the United States, the Sisters of Charity. Her legacy includes six religious communities with more than 5,000 members, hundreds of schools, and social service centers and hospitals in the United States and all over the world. Pope Paul VI declared her a saint in 1975.

RIVERSIDE CHURCH

Off map 58 C12 • 490 Riverside Drive 10027 212/870-6700 Gift shop hours Tue–Thu, Sat 10.30–5, Wed 10.30–7, Sun 9.45–10.45, noon–4 M4, M5, M60, M104 1, 9
www.riversidechurch.net

Philanthropist John D. Rockefeller, Jr., funded the construction of this 21-story, steel-frame Gothic Revival church. Designed to resemble Chartres Cathedral in France, and completed in 1930, it now serves as a venue for the large-scale weddings and funerals of the rich and famous. Nelson Mandela, Martin Luther King, Jr., and the Children's Defense funder Marion Wright-Edelman have all spoken from the pulpit. The bell tower houses the world's largest carillon, with 74 bells, as well as a 20-ton brass bell. A viewing platform on top of the tower gives a glorious view over the Hudson River (call ahead to check when it's going to be open). Inside are beautiful stained-glass windows and a cast of Jacob Epstein's *Christ in Majesty*. Another work by Epstein, *Madonna and Child*, is on the lawn.

ROCKEFELLER CENTER
see pages 128–130

ROOSEVELT ISLAND

59 G15 • In the East River between Manhattan and Queens Tram fare $2 Q102 F

You can take the subway to Roosevelt Island if you are afraid of heights, but the East 60th Street Heliport Aerial Tramway is a much more fun way to travel the 300 yards over the East River. Today there are 8,000 residents on the island, which is 2 miles (3.4km) long and only 800ft (250m) wide.

With its car-free streets, well-planned housing and great views of the Manhattan skyline, Roosevelt Island is a much sought-after area in which to live thanks to RIOC, which was created in 1984 to manage, develop and operate this "town-in-town." Up to the 19th century is was farmed by the Blackwell family, then it housed a prison, a mental health facility, the Octagon Building (1842), as well as the Smallpox Hospital (1854) and at the northern tip, a lighthouse (1872), both designed by James Renwick Jr.

Look down on the Main Reading Room, where the reading tables are often fully occupied

NEW YORK PUBLIC LIBRARY

Fascinating exhibits of New York culture inside a grand and beautifully restored Beaux-Arts building.

Some things in New York are surprises, and this amazing research library is one of them. The massive white marble building, one of the first major commissions of the firm Carrère & Hastings in 1911 is absolutely gorgeous. Half of its $9-million cost was donated by steel magnate and philanthropist Andrew Carnegie (1835–1918). The two lions at the foot of the staircase fronting the museum are New York icons affectionately named Patience and Fortitude by New York's 1930s mayor, Fiorello LaGuardia; in the giftshop they adorn tote bags, spoons, charm bracelets, bookends, paperweights and more.

Up the imposing staircase and through the triple-arched portico is beautiful Astor Hall, named after John Jacob Astor (1763–1848), whose private library, along with that of James Lenox, was the foundation of this great collection. (Former New York governor Samuel J. Tilden bequeathed the $2.4 million to combine the libraries and erect the building.)

WHAT TO SEE, AND WHERE

Upon entering, pick up a floor plan at the information desk and ask about free tours. Gottesman Hall, straight ahead, displays temporary exhibits. The DeWitt Wallace Periodical Room, to the left, is embellished with Richard Haas murals of New York magazine and newspaper offices. At the top of the marble stairs is the McGraw Rotunda. The stupendous Main Reading Room restored in 1998 so that the oak and brass gleam, is to your right. Across the hall is the Edna Barnes Salomon Room, where the very popular exhibit New York Eats Out attracted great attention in 2003. Other exhibitions have included Baseball at the Library, Prints of James McNeill Whistler (1834–1903) and The Charles Adams Mother Goose.

This is not a lending library, but there are more than 80 branches in Manhattan and the outer boroughs. Occasionally, you can see important items here from the vast collection, which include a Gutenberg Bible, a 1493 folio edition of a letter written by Christopher Columbus describing his discoveries in the New World, a first folio edition of William Shakespeare's from 1623, an early draft of Thomas Jefferson's Declaration of Independence, and much more.

One of two stone lions lounging on the front steps of the library

RATINGS	
Historic interest	● ● ●
Specialist shopping	● ● ● ● ●
Photo stops	● ● ●

BASICS

✚ 60 E18 • Fifth Avenue and 42nd Street 10018
☎ 212/221-7676
🕐 Mon, Thu–Sat 10–6, Tue–Wed 10–9
🎟 Free
🚌 M1, M2, M3, M4
Ⓑ B, D, F
🏛 🚻
🚩 Free tours Mon–Sat 11 and 2 from Astor Hall

www.nypl.org
The library catalog, Digital Library Collections, sections for teenagers, health information, an online exhibition archive and online shopping.

Rockefeller Center

●

**A vital urban enclave in the heart of Manhattan.
More than 100 art deco works by 30 artists, including Paul Manship's iconic gilded
bronze *Prometheus* and Lee Lawrie's *Atlas*.
Home of Radio City Music Hall, a spectacular art deco landmark and home of the Rockettes.**

Gilded sculpture on the front of the center

New Yorkers frequently take time out at Rockefeller Center

Radio City Music Hall is used for live concerts and film premieres

BASICS

✚ 58 E17 • West 48th to West 51st streets, between Fifth and Sixth avenues
☎ 212/664-3700
🎟 Free
🚌 M1, M2, M27, M50
🚇 B,D,F,Q
📖 Free walking-tour brochure from the main information desk in the lobby of the G. E. Building
🍴 Many eateries and restaurants including Cucina & Co., Mendy's Kosher Deli, Hale and Hearty, Ben & Jerry's. The Rainbow Room, 65th floor of the G.E. Building, tel 212/632-5000, is famous for its art deco designed revolving dance floor 🍴🍴
☕ Rockefeller Center Café, 20 West 50th Street, tel 212/332-7620

www.RockefellerCenter.com
View artwork from Rockefeller Plaza online; links to restaurants and cafés, Radio City Music Hall, NBC Store, ice-skating rink.

SEEING ROCKEFELLER CENTER

To get a good sense of the place begin at Channel Gardens, on Fifth Avenue between 49th and 50th streets, which are six pools surrounded by pretty flower boxes running between the Maison Francaise and the British Empire Building (hence the name). Straight ahead as you face the Channel Gardens, with your back to Fifth Avenue, is Rockefeller Plaza, with its sunken garden, which is turned into an ice-skating rink in winter and a restaurant in summer. The gilded *Prometheus,* stealing the sacred fire from the Greek gods to give to man, rises ahead, while flags flutter around the plaza's perimeter. At the top of the steps down to the Lower Plaza a bronze plaque from multimillionaire and philanthropist John D. Rockefeller, whose fortune built Rockefeller Center, praises the virtues of hard work. On the southeast corner of the Lower Plaza is a branch of the Metropolitan Museum of Art Store, full of elegant souvenirs and gifts. As the complex is large, it is best to pick up a walking-tour guide from the information desk in the lobby of the G. E. Building to help you decide what to see and do.

HIGHLIGHTS

THE G. E. BUILDING

Over the east entrance of this prominent tower, the former RCA Building, is Lee Lawrie's limestone-and-glass frieze, *Wisdom*, inspired by William Blake's painting of the same name. The beautiful granite and marble east lobby is worth visiting; it houses José Maria Sert's sepia mural *Man's Conquests*, commissioned to replace one by Diego Rivera, which was rejected because it included an image of Joseph Stalin. The anticommunist Rockefellers had insisted that Rivera remove the offending portrait, but Rivera refused and his mural was destroyed. The signature clock on the 51st Street corner has projecting arms grasping electric bolts (RCA was a subsidiary of General Electric). The stylized figures at the building's crown have halos of electric rays. The viewing platform is open to patrons of the elegant Rainbow Room restaurant on the 65th floor; for a drink and a view, stop in at the adjacent Rainbow Grill.

ICE-SKATING RINK

When this ice-rink in the Lower Plaza opened on Christmas Day 1933, it was a novelty made possible by new refrigeration technology. Today, a quarter of a million skaters test their blades here every year. The rink is small—only 122ft long (37m) and 59ft (18m) wide *(Mon–Fri 9am–10.30pm, Sat 8.30am–midnight, Sun 8.30am–10pm, mid-October to mid-March; adult $8.50/$11 weekends, child $7/$7.50, skate rental $6).*

RADIO CITY MUSIC HALL

With about 6,000 seats, Radio City was the world's largest theater when it opened in 1932. Impresario Samuel (Roxy) Rothafel's original plans were for live entertainment, but movies soon became the main fare, with the high-kicking Roxyettes, later called the Rockettes, performing before each feature film. Donald Deskey was the interior design co-ordinator. The great arched proscenium in the form of a setting sun is an art deco masterpiece. The Grand Foyer's 24-carat gold-leaf ceiling, sweeping staircase and elegant chandeliers are breathtaking. Radio City was designated a New York City Landmark in 1979 and a National Historic Landmark in 1987. Intensive renovation in the late 1990s then won it a National Preservation Award in 2000.

"LATE NIGHT WITH CONAN O'BRIEN"

To get standby tickets to join the studio audience of this popular late-night show, line up at 9am on the day of taping outside 30 Rockefeller Plaza on 49th Street under the NBC Studios awning. Or reserve tickets in advance by calling 212/664-3056. You must be 16 to attend.

"TODAY SHOW"

Every weekday between 7 and 9am, hundreds of people crowd the blue police barricades at the corner of West 49th Street and Rockefeller Plaza, just outside the ground-level NBC studio of the long-running morning "Today Show." The lure is a glimpse of anchors Katie Couric and Matt Lauer, a brief chat with weatherman Al Roker, or national exposure for a greeting for the folks back home scrawled on a piece of cardboard. Spirits are high and the mood almost giddy. In

In winter skaters show off their flashier moves at the Lower Plaza ice-skating rink

RATINGS				
Good for kids	●	●		
Specialist shopping	●	●	●	●	●
Photo stops	●	●	●	●
Walkability	●	●	●	●	●

TIPS

● If you're in town between early December and early January don't miss Rockefeller Center. An enormous Christmas tree is put up and decked with 20,000 tiny lights—a favorite New York tradition.

● Go early if you plan to ice-skate on the rink in the Lower Plaza. The rink can hold only 150 skaters at a time and it gets busy, especially at lunchtime. Skate rentals and rink fees are cash only—and not cheap.

● NBC Experience store, 49th Street and Rockefeller Plaza, offers one-hour tours of news and entertainment studios. See the "Saturday Night Live" set: arrive before noon in the busy holiday and summer period to get tickets, which are on a first-come, first-served basis.

The gilded Prometheus heralds the entrance to the center

WISDOM AND ✳ KNOWLEDGE
✳ ✳ ✳ SHALL BE THE ✳ ✳ ✳
STABILITY OF THY TIMES

Lee Lawrie's relief over the entrance to the G. E. Building (above right); one of Jose Maria Sert's sepia murals (above)

Six pools surrounded by flower boxes lead to the entrance

good weather, a segment or two may be presented outdoors on the street. In winter, you can get a good view of the action from the Dean & Deluca coffee shop across the street.

BACKGROUND

The land on which Rockefeller Center stands belonged to Columbia University at the beginning of the 20th century. The university rented the land to farmers, but eventually developers came along and put up brownstones. By the late 1920s, the area was noisy and unpleasant, with elevated trains rumbling down Sixth Avenue and many residents too poor to spend money on the upkeep of the buildings. During Prohibition, the area was known as the "speakeasy belt," and along 52nd Street police raids were common. When liquor regained its legal status, the area became a popular setting for jazz clubs, where great musicians like Count Basie and Harry James entertained.

In 1928, John D. Rockefeller leased 12 acres (5ha) from Columbia University in order to build a colossal new opera house for the Metropolitan Opera. Rockefeller had a 24-year lease, but the project was dropped when the stock market crashed in 1929. But the rent still had to be paid, so Rockefeller decided to build a commercial center. In all 228 buildings were demolished to make way for 12 new buildings to be designed by Associated Architects, a group directed by Raymond Hood. Between 1932 and 1940, this "city within a city," to use Rockefeller's words, was built. The central tower, the former RCA Building (now the G. E. Building) was planned with dense concentration of facilities for creation and broadcasting of sound, with a vision of television's bright future. Today NBC (National Broadcasting Corporation) occupies 11 floors.

Building Rockefeller Center was the largest privately sponsored real-estate venture in New York City's history. The complex was an instant success, and seven more buildings were added between 1947 and 1973. Today, 19 buildings cover 22 acres (9ha), about 65,000 people work in the offices here, and many more visit daily. In 1985 Columbia University sold the land underneath the buildings to Rockefeller Center, which had remained in the hands of the Rockefeller family; at the end of 1989, the family sold a half interest to Japan's Mitsubishi Estate Company.

The St. Patrick's Cathedral spires were completed in 1888

St. Paul's Chapel is the oldest church in Manhattan

St. Marks' in the Bowery's Greek revival steeple dates from 1828

ST. MARK'S IN THE BOWERY

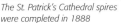 61 F21 • East 10th Street 10004
☎ 212/674-6377 ⏰ Events only
🚌 M8, M15 🚇 F, V

Peter Stuyvesant, New Amsterdam's last Dutch governor, had a *bouwerie* (farm) in the quiet countryside north of the bustling settlement. As the city expanded and land values soared, Stuyvesant's grandson sold off plots for development. In 1779, a year after the Stuyvesant mansion was destroyed by fire, his great-grandson sold the site of Stuyvesant's private chapel to the Episcopal Church for a nominal dollar. And so it was that St. Mark's in the Bowery was built and named. The original church was Federal-style; in keeping with the area's increasing affluence it later acquired a cast-iron portico. Stuyvesant and six generations of his descendants are buried in the graveyard.

ST. PATRICK'S CATHEDRAL

⊞ 58 E17 • Fifth Avenue (between 50th and 51st streets) 10022 ⏰ Daily
🚌 M1, M2, M3, M4 🚇 6, E, V
www.ny-archdiocese.org/pastoral/cathedral_about.html

Each year the largest Catholic cathedral in the United States, with seats for about 2,200, welcomes more than three million visitors. Designed by James Renwick, Jr., this Gothic Revival cathedral was inspired by European originals, most notably Cologne Cathedral in Germany. The spire is 330ft (100m) above street level. The *Pietà* inside is three times the size of the one in St. Peter's in Rome. Tiffany & Company designed the beautiful St. Michael and St. Louis altar. Work began on the church in 1853 and it was consecrated in 1879. The cathedral's arrival

encouraged the rich and powerful to move north and contributed to the development of Fifth Avenue's many sumptuous mansions.

ST. PATRICK'S OLD CATHEDRAL

⊞ 61 F23 • 260–64 Mulberry Street 10013 🚌 M15, M103 🚇 N, R, Q ⌨
www.oldsaintpatricks.com

French architect Joseph François Mangin had been busy with the building of City Hall until 1809, when he began work on this Gothic structure, the first Roman Catholic cathedral of New York. At 120ft long (36m) and 80ft (24m) wide, it opened in 1815, when the surrounding area was heavily populated by Irish immigrants. The work of enlarging the cathedral was well under way in 1866, when a disastrous fire destroyed it. Restored and completed by 1868, the cathedral remained the seat of the archdiocese until the dedication of the new St. Patrick's in 1879. At that time the old cathedral was demoted to the status of parish church. Now restored, the interior is grand and gloomy, the timber roof supported on iron columns, and the organ, built by Henry Erben in 1852, is one of only a handful of good instruments in New York City. The building was named a New York City Landmark in 1966, one of the first buildings to receive this designation.

ST. PAUL'S CHAPEL

⊞ 61 E25 • Broadway between Fulton and Vesey Streets 10007 ☎ 212/602-0800 ⏰ Mon–Fri 9–3, Sun 7–3; closed major holidays 🚌 M1, M22 🚇 4, 5
⌨ Classical music Mon noon–1pm $2

This church was one of the outbuildings of the wealthy Episcopalian parish of Trinity Church (see pages 142–143). Modeled on London's St. Martin-in-the-Fields, it was built of local stone

between 1764 and 1768, with the graceful spire added in 1796. In 1789 the inaugural prayer service for George Washington, the new nation's first president, was held here. Pierre l'Enfant, the soldier-architect who laid out the plan for Washington, D.C., as the new capital city and designed the Federal Hall, is credited with the altar. After his inauguration, Washington worshiped here regularly and his pew, together with Governor Dewitt Clinton's, is preserved. On Mondays at noon, you can come for a marvelous hour of classical music—it costs just $2.

SCHOMBURG CENTER FOR RESEARCH IN BLACK CULTURE

⊞ off map 59 E12 • 515 Malcolm X Boulevard 10037-11801 ☎ 212/491-2200 ⏰ Mon–Wed noon–7.45, Thu–Sat 10–5.45 💲 Free 🚌 M7, M102
🚇 2, 3 👥 ⌨
www.schomburgcenter.org

A research library that serves a national and international constituency, the Schomburg Center was founded in 1925 as a special collection in a branch of the New York Public Library (see page 127). Arthur A. Schomburg, a Puerto Rican black scholar and bibliophile, had collected 5,000 books, 2,000 etchings and 3,000 manuscripts, among other material on African-American culture, which was acquired by the library. The collection has now grown to more than five million items, including books, art, artifacts, photographs, prints, manuscripts, rare books, moving images and recorded sound.

The focus is on preserving and providing access to this important collection, documenting the lives of people of African descent throughout the world. Past exhibitions have included *The Art of African Women*.

SoHo

Stylish boutiques and stores, fashionable restaurants, fascinating architecture and plenty of art galleries.

Kors on Mercer Street keeps the designer fashions coming

The gilded Puck statue on the Puck Magazine Building

Shopping addicts should head for West Broadway

RATINGS	
Historic interest	● ● ● ● ○
Specialist shopping	● ● ● ● ●
Photo stops	● ● ● ● ○
Walkability	● ● ● ● ●

BASICS

⊞ 61 E23 • Canal Street to Houston Street, between Sixth Avenue and Lafayette Street

ℹ Lower East Side Visitor Center, 261 Broome Street, between Orchard and Allen streets

🚌 M6

Ⓜ C, E, N, R

🍴 Rocky's, 45 Spring Street, tel 212/274-9756 ☕ Le Pain Quotidien, 100 Grand Street, tel 212/625-9009 📷

www.lowereastsideny.com
Easy-to-navigate website with listings of local shops and restaurants.

There are still many art galleries

BACKGROUND

This area *South* of *Houston* (pronounced *how-sten*)—which actually extends as far south as Canal Street, and runs from Sixth Avenue on the west to Lafayette Street on the east—started out in the 19th century as an industrial zone. Architects kept catalogues of cast-iron window frames, balustrades and columns then pieced together what they liked; an Italian Renaissance motif was very popular. Fashion moved uptown in the early 20th century, taking industry and business out of the area. Development stalled; nothing went up—but nothing came down, either. Rents plummeted, opening up opportunities for artists and sculptors in need of cheap accommodation and studio space. Preservationists caught wind of the phenomenon and soon all New York was singing the praises of SoHo.

Today, there are 50 cast-iron structures on Greene Street alone. The most admired include the Haughwout Building at the corner of Broome Street and Broadway, the Little Singer Building at 561 Broadway, and the St. Nicholas Hotel, where Mark Twain met his future wife, at 521–523 Broadway. Across the street at 504 Broadway, Harry Houdini worked as a tie-cutter before his career as an escape artist took off. It was in the Haughwout Building that Elisha Graves Otis installed his first passenger elevator; unfortunately it is no longer in the building. (See pages 242–243 for a walk around this neighborhood.)

SOUGHT-AFTER NEIGHBORHOOD

By the 1970s, SoHo was one of the most desired addresses in town, rents shot up and struggling artists left. But many dealers and galleries remain, The Leo Castelli Gallery, which exhibited Andy Warhol, Frank Stella and Roy Lichtenstein in the 1960s, is at 420 Broadway.

By the end of the 20th century there were about 200 other art galleries, as well more photography galleries than anywhere else in New York. The New Museum of Contemporary Art (see page 124) is where you can see works by important new artists. The Alternative Museum *(Tue–Sat 11–6)*, on Broadway between Houston and Prince streets, exhibits works that are politically and socially inspired. Head for the SoHo Guggenheim *(Wed–Sun)* on Broadway at Prince Street to see displays from the main Guggenheim Museum, which are changed regularly. At 119 Wooster Street, the Tony Shafrazi

Gallery has exhibited artists such as Keith Haring and Julian Schnabel. Across the street at No. 120 is the well-established Howard Green-berg Gallery, devoted to 20th-century photography. The innovative New York Earth Room *(Wed–Sat),* at 141 Wooster Street, displays 14 tons of soil, rather intriguingly.

Stores followed the galleries and crowded many of the more original types out, often to TriBeCa (see page 141) or Chelsea (see page 77). But in the interim, many well-to-do New Yorkers moved into the loft spaces on the buildings' upper floors, attracting still other high-end retailers to SoHo, along with chic cafés and lots of bars and music venues. Rents for apartments here can rise to $15,000 per month.

No matter what the season, SoHo's streets offer the ultimate New York experience, for a couple of hours or the whole day.

Fashionable places to eat and be seen eating in are what SoHo is all about

South Street Seaport

A landmark district of historic buildings, a maritime museum, and more than 100 shops, cafés and restaurants on the waterfront.

Look out over the East River from South Street Seaport's Pier 17 sun decks

The inside areas at South Street have been attractively restored

RATINGS	
Good for kids	●●●○
Historic interest	●●●●●
Specialist shopping	●●●●○
Walkability	●●●●●

TIP

● If you plan to take a harbor cruise, reserve in advance to avoid disappointment.

Advertising the Titanic's *tragic maiden voyage to New York*

SEEING SOUTH STREET SEAPORT

This "museum without walls" is a 12-square-block landmark district at the tip of downtown Manhattan on the East River. Buildings include the Fulton Fish Market, Pier 17 Pavilion, the South Street Seaport Museum, and retail outlets on the surrounding blocks. Begin your visit at Pier 17, where the eateries and shops are concentrated. Pick up a visitors' leaflet from one of the many display racks at the entrance to the pier. The clear, well-labeled map and listing of the stores and restaurants will enable you to decide the route that appeals to you most.

HIGHLIGHTS

PIER 17
From this impressive three-story glass and steel pier, transformed into a shopping center with dozens of restaurants and eateries, you can enjoy the magnificent views of the East River from the outdoor terrace.

SOUTH STREET SEAPORT MUSEUM
Historic Ships
Berthed between piers 15 and 17 the collection of ships includes the 1911 *Peking*, a four-masted cargo vessel built by Blohm and Voss in Hamburg, Germany, which made several trips around Cape Horn. After numerous voyages between Europe and South America, then serving as a stationary school ship for the British, it came to New York in 1975. *The Pioneer*, an 1885 schooner, takes visitors on a 2.5-hour harbor cruise, including close-up looks at the Statue of Liberty and Governor's Island *(late May–late Sep, reservations tel 212/748-8786)*.

World Port New York
The museum's core exhibition, with 24 new galleries on the upper floors of the renovated Schermerhorn Row and the A.A. Low Building, explores the history of the port from colonial times to the present.

THE TITANIC MEMORIAL LIGHTHOUSE
At the Water Street entrance to the seaport, this monument to the victims of the *Titanic*, which sank on April 15, 1912 on its maiden

voyage from Southampton, England to New York, was put up in 1913 overlooking the East River. It was moved to its present site in 1968. John Jacob Astor, owner of the Astoria Hotel, which stood on the site of the Empire State Building, was one of the 1,513 people who died.

FULTON FISH MARKET

Restored in the 1980s, the Fulton Fish Market has been selling the local catch since the early 1800s. If you get there before 8am, you can witness the bustling activity and enjoy the briny aroma.

BACKGROUND

The South Street Seaport Museum, at 207 Front Street, opened in 1967 and was the original draw to this then-neglected area, leading to a complete restoration project. Schermerhorn Row is the most significant historical landmark in the South Street Seaport complex. Nos. 191 and 193 Front Street were built in the 1790s by Peter Schermerhorn, a leading merchant from a prominent New York family. He built further groups of four-story Georgian and Federalist warehouses and counting houses on Fulton Street in 1812. The stone warehouse at 167–71 John Street was built in 1849 for A.A. Low & Brothers. By the 1860s, the South Street area was no longer the hub of commercial port activity and only the Fulton Fish Market remained. In the 1980s the Rouse Company moved in to start restoring.

The collection of ships berthed between piers 15 and 17

BASICS

✚ 61 F25 • South of Brooklyn Bridge at Fulton Street

🛈 12 Fulton Street, daily 10–6, May–Sep; daily 10–5, rest of year, tel 212/669-9424

☎ Museum: 212/748-8600

🕐 Most shops Mon–Sat 10–9, Sun 11–8. Museum: daily 10–6, Apr–Sep; Wed–Mon 10–5, rest of year

💰 Museum: adult $6, child $3

🚌 M15

Ⓜ 2, 3, 4, 5

🍴 35 restaurants and food outlets

☕ Sago Tea Café, second floor of Pier 17 Pavilion, tel 212/267-8310

🎫 Guided walking tours: Ask at the ticket booth across from Pier 17

www.southstreetseaport.com
Events calendar, complete list of restaurants and shops.

www.southstseaport.org
Preview museum's permanent collection, information about exhibits and ships.

There is often some sort of street music or entertainment at South Street Seaport

Statue of Liberty

The city's most important landmark, in New York Harbor, recognized throughout the world as a symbol of freedom, a must-see for millions of visitors every year.

The statue is often affectionately referred to as Lady Liberty

Buy your very own statue headgear and wear it with pride

You can get up close on a ferry for a better look

RATINGS	
Good for kids	● ● ● ● ●
Historic interest	● ● ● ●
Photo stops	● ● ● ● ●

A symbol of freedom and democracy, the Statue of Liberty was the first sight for millions of immigrants as they approached their new homeland. As you sail toward her, it's easy to imagine how they felt.

A JOINT PROJECT

When the Statue of Liberty was unveiled on October 28, 1886, thousands of spectators were filled with awe. Nearly three times the height of the Colossus of Rhodes, one of the Seven Wonders of the World, this gift from the people of France was in recognition of the friendship established between the two countries during the American Revolution. The French statesman Edouard de Laboulay proposed that the statue be made in France, but that the pedestal be made by the Americans. Alexandre-Gustave Eiffel, who designed the Eiffel Tower in Paris, came up with the revolutionary support system of interlocking angle irons for the enormous statue, which was designed by Frédéric-Auguste Bartholdi.

Paying for the project was a problem for both nations and great effort was put into fundraising events, such as theatrical performances, art exhibitions, auctions and prize-fights. But the public showed little interest. Joseph Pulitzer, who established the Pulitzer Prize, criticized the rich in his newspaper *The World* for failing to help finance the pedestal construction. He also criticized the middle classes for expecting the rich to provide all the money. Donations came pouring in and the pedestal was completed in 1886. The French shipped the statue to New York in June 1885; it took four months to assemble.

VITAL STATISTICS

Lady Liberty, as she is often affectionately called, came to Bedloe's Island, renamed Liberty Island in 1956. By presidential proclamation the Statue of Liberty became a National Monument in 1924; the United Nations designated her a World Heritage Site in 1984. After almost 100 years, the statue needed some attention; an $87-million restoration project ended with fireworks to celebrate the statue's centennial, coinciding with Independence Day, on July 4, 1986.

Her measurements are impressive. She weighs 225 tons and measures 151ft 1in (46.05m) from the top of the base to the torch. Her hands measure a whopping 16ft 5in (5m) and even her nose is

The statue provides an inspiring welcome to the city

4ft 6in (1.37m). Richard Morris Hunt's magnificent pedestal measures 154ft (46.9m).

VISITING LADY LIBERTY

She can be fully appreciated only up close so it's unfortunate that the Statue of Liberty has been closed to the public for security reasons since September 11, 2001. Only the grounds are now open to visitors. Call ahead for the latest information or visit the website.

If the statue is open, you can take an elevator to either the pedestal level or to the crown, or go up the 192 steps to the top of the pedestal, or the 354 steps to the crown. At this level, 25 windows symbolize gemstones found on earth, and seven heavenly rays represent the seven seas, shining over the world. The museum, inside the pedestal, is also closed at present. Even if you can't visit the museum and go inside the statue, you can still see the tablet in her hand, with the date July 4, 1776, inscribed in Roman numerals, and get a sense of her size—and that alone makes the trip well worth your time.

To visit Liberty Island, take the Statue of Liberty & Ellis Island Ferry from Battery Park. In advance, buy tickets online, by telephone or at the ticket office. In person, use the CityPass (see page 317) or get your ticket from Castle Clinton ticket office (see page 73). Lines are long during peak season and as there are no reservations, arrive early.

The statue arrived in 350 pieces packed in 214 crates

BASICS

✚ Page 6 • Liberty Island in New York Harbor

☎ General information 212/363-3200; ferry tickets 212/269-5755

🕐 Daily 9.30–5, extended hours in peak season

🎟 Ferry tickets (good for a round-trip that includes a stop at Ellis Island) adult $10, 13+ $8, 3–12 $4, under 3s free. Free admission to Liberty Island and the Statue of Liberty

🚇 4, 5 🚌 M15

🍴 Refreshments on ferries; café on Liberty Island 🚻 🛗 On ferries

www.nps.gov/stli
History and statistics, museum exhibits and security updates.

Times Square and Broadway

New York at its flashiest.
Neon signs, gigantic billboards, live TV broadcasts, enormous stores and gigantic family-friendly theme restaurants, not to mention theaters.

THE SIGHTS

BASICS

➕ 60 D18
ℹ️ Times Square Visitors Center is the city's top information center at 1560 Broadway between 46th and 47th streets, daily 8–8
☎ Times Square Visitors Center 212/768-1560
🚌 M6–7, M27, M50
🚇 A, C, N, R
🍴 Broadway Joe's Steakhouse, 315 West 46th Street, tel 212/246-6513— steaks and seafood
🖥️ Planet Hollywood, 1540 Broadway at 45th Street, tel 212/333-7827, serves burgers and other American favorites, but movie memorabilia and giant projection screens are the real stars
👥 Times Square Visitors Center at 1560 Broadway between 46th and 47th streets, daily 8–8
🚶 Free walking tour every Friday at noon from the Times Square Visitors Center

www.TimesSquareBID.org
Get the latest news, events and tourist information, take a video tour, post a message.

SEEING TIMES SQUARE AND BROADWAY

Begin your visit at the Times Square Visitors Center, originally the attractive landmark Embassy Theater and now, unfortunately, dominated by a McDonalds. Even if you don't need information, take a look at the grand foyer. Over time, but especially during the last few years, many of the old theaters have been renovated and now have landmark status. A special security force patrols the streets, and the area is as safe as any crowded urban neighborhood can be. If your visit to New York happens to coincide with New Year's Eve and you don't mind dense crowds, join the throngs in Times Square to see the glass ball drop at midnight to ring in the New Year. It's a great New York tradition.

HIGHLIGHTS

ED SULLIVAN THEATER
697–699 Broadway between 53rd and 54th streets
Built by Arthur Hammerstein as a memorial to his father, Oscar Hammerstein I, this theater was formerly called the Hammerstein Theater. The neo-Gothic vestibules, lobbies and auditorium are unique on Broadway. Used as a dance hall for many years, it made history when it became a television studio. "The Ed Sullivan Show," the longest-running TV show in history, was broadcast from here during the 1950s and 1960s. Today it is perhaps even more famous as the home of "The Late Show with David Letterman."

LYCEUM THEATRE
149 West 45th Street ☎ 212/239-6280
The oldest New York theater, saved from demolition in 1939, it is Broadway's most imposing structure with its magnificent Beaux-Arts façade and powerful neo-Baroque columns. Inside are marble walls with murals by James Wall Finn. Many of Broadway's highly acclaimed comedies and dramas have been performed here, as well as classics by the National Actors Theatre. Such famous names as Ethel Barrymore, Bette Davis, Joseph Cotton, Melvyn Douglas, Alan Bates and Lauren Bacall have all performed at the Lyceum.

NEW VICTORY THEATER
209 West 42nd Street ☎ 212/382-4020
www.newvictory.org
Built by Oscar Hammerstein I in 1899 and once known as Minsky's, the New Victory was restored and remodeled in 1995 and is the city's first full-time family-oriented performing arts center.

PARAMOUNT THEATRE BUILDING
1501 Broadway ☎ 212/398-2563
The tallest building in Times Square when it was completed in 1927, the Paramount is crowned by a four-faced clock with a glass globe, a focal point of the area that is visible for miles when it's illuminated. The World Wrestling Entertainment's 2,000-seat theme restaurant, WWE New York, whose sign boasts the latest in fiber-optic technology, is in the old theater space; a 30ft (9m) video screen and 110 monitors

ensure that every diner can watch live broadcasts of shows like "Raw" and "Smackdown!", and appearances by WWE stars. Other entertainments vary from concerts to magic shows.

Transformed from a run-down, seedy area in the 1970s, Times Square is now respectable, safe and much cleaner

BACKGROUND

Called Heere Straat (Main Street) by Dutch settlers, Broadway is New York's longest and oldest street. As the city's population grew, seedy bars, brothels and gambling dens opened on both sides. Even in the early 1800s, it bustled with pedestrians and horse-drawn carriages; there were even traffic jams. In the 1860s, a row of minstrel halls opened along Broadway, and by 1900, the area on and off Broadway around Union Square had become the city's theater district. In 1880, the advent of electricity began to turn Broadway between 14th and 34th streets into the Great White Way. In the 1890s, when Oscar Hammerstein built the Olympia Theater on Broadway between 44th and 45th streets, the city's theatrical entertainment moved to the area that is now Times Square; it was then known as Longacre Square and was renamed only in 1904, when the *The New York Times* moved into Times Tower on 42nd Street. In 1928, 14,900 electrical lights were added to the four sides of the Times Tower, creating the first moving electrical sign.

After the subway came to the Theater District, beginning in 1900, the crowds poured in. By the 1920s, movies had taken over many theaters. After this, the theaters started showing pornography and the crowd turned seedy. Sex joints drove out reputable business, and by the 1970s the district was crawling with hookers, pimps, winos and tramps.

During the 1990s, an aggressive clean-up operation—which included legislation against noise, gambling and prostitution, as well as new zoning laws—transformed the area. There's no question that the current state of the square and surrounding area has been an amazing show of effective planning, and a great triumph for the city.

Broadway is by far New York's longest street

TV SHOW TICKETS GUIDE

Tickets for live tapings of TV shows are free but usually hard to obtain because of the high demand, especially the immensely popular "Late Show with David Letterman." If you are seriously addicted to a show and you know six months in advance that you'll be in New York, send a postcard with your name, address, telephone number, the number of tickets you want, and your preferred dates.

Many studios hand out stand-by tickets on the day of taping, but you have to get up early and stand in line. In the dead of winter, you stand a better chance as snow and cold winds put some people off. For more information call NYCVB at 212/484-1222. You can also phone or check show websites for information on ticket availability, waiting lists and stand-by tickets. When you attend a show, take ID, as it may be required.

"Late Show with David Letterman"
Send a postcard to Late Show Tickets, Ed Sullivan Theater, 1697 Broadway, New York, NY 10019, or register at www.cbs.com/latenight/lateshow or telephone 212/247-6497 for two standby tickets on the day of taping at 11am sharp. You must be 18 to attend.

"Total Request Live"
You can sometimes get tickets for the 3.30 taping by telephoning TRL Ticket Reservation Hotline on 212/398-8549. If that doesn't work, turn up by 2pm (earlier if the day's guest is a major celebrity) outside the 1515 Broadway studio. A producer often roams around asking trivia questions about musicians and hands out tickets to those who answer correctly. You have to be between 18 and 24 to attend.

"Good Morning America"
Fill out the online request at www.abcnews.go.com/sections/GMA or telephone 212/580-5176 and you may be lucky and get to join Diane Sawyer and Charlie Gibson in their street-facing studio on Broadway at 44th Street. The show runs Monday to Friday from 7am to 9am.

"Montel"
Tickets to join the audience to see the Emmy award-winning talk show host Montel Williams can be obtained by visiting www.montelshow.com or by emailing tickets@montelshow.com. Three shows a day are taped on Wednesdays and Thursdays.

TIPS

● Broadway extends from Lower Manhattan to beyond Manhattan's northern tip, but Broadway as most visitors understand it refers to the area north–south between West 53rd Street and West 40th Street and east–west from Sixth to Eighth avenues. Most theaters are not on Broadway but on side streets.

● The TKTS booth *(Broadway and Seventh Avenue, tel 212/768-1818, www.tdf.org, Mon–Sat 3–8, Sun 11–7 for 8pm performances; 10–2 for Wed and Sat matinées; only cash or travelers' checks)* sells day-of-show tickets for on and off-Broadway performances at 20–50 percent off face value. By 6pm the line is short.

● Times Square Visitors Center has a Metropolitan Transit Authority desk for transit maps and MetroCards; a Broadway Ticket Center sells full-price tickets; HSBC Bank Center with ATMs and currency-exchange machines; computers with free Internet access; free brochures and leaflets—some with discount vouchers.

The stratospheric Seagram Building, a fine skyscraper

Lucky commuters get to ride the Staten Island Ferry every day

An attractive promenade flanks the Hudson River Park in Tribeca

SEAGRAM BUILDING

59 F17 • 375 Park Avenue 10022
212/572-7000 Mon–Fri 9–5, closed major holidays

Erected in 1958 with interiors by Philip Johnson, this is New York City's only Mies van der Rohe building and one of the finest International-style skyscrapers in the world. The decision to set it toward the back of the granite-paved plaza was daring at the time, especially given real estate values, but it ignited a taste for pedestrian plazas that lingers in Manhattan to this day.

The building is also notable as the site of the esteemed Four Seasons Restaurant, famed venue for power lunches, and of the bustling Brasserie restaurant.

SOHO
see pages 132–133

SOUTH STREET SEAPORT
see pages 134–135

STATEN ISLAND FERRY

344 F27 • Whitehall Terminal, 1 Whitehall Street 10004 718/815-262 Daily 24 hours, every 20–30 minutes on weekdays, less frequently on weekends and off-peak Free, $3 for cars on certain ferries M1, M6, M9 N, R
www.ci.nyc.ny.us/html/dot

These commuter craft, which shuttle Staten Islanders to and from jobs in Manhattan, are—for tourists—a free, hour-long, round-trip excursion in the harbor—past the Statue of Liberty (see pages 136–137), Ellis Island (see pages 90–93) and Governors Island, with the Verrazano Narrows Bridge in the distance. In good weather, try for one of the old orange and green boats. The white boats are newer and have no outside deck. To get the best view, sit on the right side. Avoid rush hours, and disembark at Staten Island. On your right as you get off, look for the boat-loading sign, which directs you to the next loading dock.

STATUE OF LIBERTY
see pages 136–137

STUDIO MUSEUM IN HARLEM

Off map 59 E12 • 144 West 125th Street 10027 212/864-4500 Wed–Fri, Sun noon–6, Sat 10–6; closed holidays Adult $5, child $1 M2, M7, M60, M100 B, C, 2, 3
www.studiomuseuminharlem.org

Specializing in 19th- and 20th-century African-American art, and 20th-century African and Caribbean art and artifacts, this small but recently renovated museum has a lot to offer. Rotating exhibitions, a full calendar of events, and the annual exhibition from their Artists-in-Residence program, make this a museum well worth a visit. Exhibitions have included *Challenge of the Modern: African-American Artists 1925–1945*, which examined the modernist concepts adopted by black artists in the U.S. and the Carribean; *Veni Vidi Video*, the first in a 2003 series on video art; and *Harlem Postcards 2003*. The small sculpture garden is charming. The gift shop offers a good selection of books, postcards and other items.

THEODORE ROOSEVELT BIRTHPLACE

60 E20 • 28 East 20th Street 10003 212/260-1616 Visits only by guided tour (30 min) Mon–Fri 9–5; closed Federal holidays Adult $3, under 17s free M1, M6, M23 4, 5, N, R
www.nps.gov/thrb

Theodore (Teddy) Roosevelt, the great outdoorsman and 26th president of the United States, was born in New York in 1858 and spent his first 14 years in a fashionable brownstone just off Broadway. The house was demolished just before his death in 1919, but the lot where the house stood was acquired in 1923 by the Women's Roosevelt Memorial Association, which commissioned a female architect to reconstruct it as it had been in Roosevelt's youth. Rooms are furnished with objects preserved from the original house. The "lion's room" is filled with hunting and outdoor memorabilia. Roosevelt was sickly as a child, and a small gym that was intended to build up his health adjoins the nursery. There is also an exhibition about his eventful life.

TIMES SQUARE AND BROADWAY
see pages 138–140

TRIBECA

61 E24 • Between Hudson River and Broadway, Chambers and Canal streets M20 1, 2

TriBeCa (pronounced *try-beck-a*), the *Tri*angle *Be*low *Ca*nal Street, is where artists went after sky-rocketing prices made SoHo (see pages 132–133) unaffordable to all but the rich. They converted cast-iron warehouses into loft apartments, and now, predictably, a wealthy group has moved in along with antiques shops, design shops and some very fine restaurants. Actor Robert DeNiro brought the Tribeca Film Center to the area a few years ago. There are some notable buildings, especially 2 White Street, dating from 1809; the Fleming Smith warehouse at 451 Washington Street, home of long-established Capsouto Frères bistro; and the Corinthian-columned, cast-iron 47 Worth Street. The area was greatly damaged on 9/11, but got back into full swing remarkably quickly.

Trinity Church

A historic church tucked among Lower Manhattan's skyscrapers, and the final resting place of a handful of great Americans.

Many famous names are buried in the churchyard

Figures from the Bible mark the entrance to the church

Gothic romance authors have used the church as a setting

RATINGS	
Historic interest	● ● ● ○
Specialist shopping	● ● ● ●
Photo stops	● ● ● ○
Walkability	● ● ● ● ●

BASICS
✚ 61 E26 • Broadway at Wall Street 10006
☎ 212/602-0800
🕐 Mon–Fri 7–6, Sat and holidays 8–4, Sun 7–4
🚌 M6, M15
Ⓜ 4, 5, 6
☛ Free guided tours daily 2pm

www.trinitywallstreet.org

As you walk up Broadway, north of Bowling Green, you come to Trinity Church. Now dwarfed by the surrounding skyscrapers, Richard Upjohn's 1846 rose-pink sandstone masterpiece, with beautiful stained-glass windows and an eight-sided, 280ft (85m) spire, was once the tallest building in New York. The church bell was presented to the church in 1704 by the Bishop of London. As you enter, notice the biblical scenes on the bronze doors, designed by Richard Morris Hunt and donated in memory of John Jacob Astor III. Look for the white marble altar, the wooden vault and the screen of the Chapel of All Saints. To the left, at the back of the church, is a small museum (*Mon–Fri 9–11.45, 1–3.45, Sat 10–3.45, Sun 1–3.45*) selling postcards, pamphlets outlining the church's history, books and videos, and gifts. The 30-minute guided tours of the church start from this museum. Classical music concerts take place in the church every Thursday from 1 to 2pm. Men must remove their hats as a sign of respect, even in the dead of winter, or will be reminded to do so by one of the church's wardens.

THE FIRST CHURCH
In 1697, by Royal Charter, the Anglican parish of Trinity became one of the largest landholders in Manhattan, and the first church was put up the next year, only to burn in the great fire of 1776, when the British army occupied New York. You will find the original royal charter for the church on display in the museum. During the struggle for independence, Trinity Church was a Loyalist bastion, but when the revolution ended, so did the Loyalists' hold on the city. A second building on the same spot was structurally flawed and was torn down in 1839. British architect Richard Upjohn, together with James Renwick, Jr., were commissioned to build the third Trinity Church. In the process, Upjohn made his reputation and went on to design many more churches around the country.

Before you leave the church, stroll around the small churchyard, a green oasis that's now estimated to be worth several million dollars for its prime location. Here are the graves of steamboat inventor Robert Fulton, statesman Alexander Hamilton, killed in a duel with Aaron Burr and Francis Lewis, a signer of the Declaration of Independence. The large cross in the churchyard is dedicated to Caroline Webster Schermerhorn Astor, the queen of 1800s high society.

Looking down Wall Street toward the Gothic Revival Trinity Church, with its imposing spire (right)

The opulence of Trump Tower is now the stuff of legend

A symbol of peace and unity— the United Nations headquarters

Washington Heights is dedicated to an American Revolution battle

TRUMP TOWER

🏢 58 E17 • 725 Fifth Avenue 10022
☎ 212/832-2000 🚇 M1, M2, M3, M4
🚇 6, E, V ♿ 🚻

Not to be confused with the older Trump Building, originally the Manhattan Company Building, or with other Trump structures about town, this one rose in the 1980s as a glass monument to the affluent lifestyle. Upper floors contain 263 plush apartments. (Trump himself was one of the first to move in.) Below them, the interior is a six-story atrium with escalators, waterfalls and glittering boutiques surrounded by pink marble, mirrors and shrubbery. It's ridiculously ostentatious but still quite the sight.

UKRAINIAN MUSEUM

🏢 61 F21 • 203 Second Avenue 10003
☎ 212/228-0110 🕐 Wed–Sun 1–5
🚇 M
www.brama.com/ukrainian_museum

Ukrainian immigrants came to America in the 19th century and many stayed in New York and lived in the tenements on the Lower East Side, not far from this small but delightful museum. Committed to preserving the cultural heritage of Ukrainians, this well-documented museum displays an assortment of folk art items, including traditional costumes, decorative brass and silver jewelry, decorated Easter eggs, ceramics and woven and embroidered ritual cloths used as talismans at births, weddings, funerals and seasonal rituals. At the time of writing, the museum is moving to much grander premises on East 6th Street.

UNITED NATIONS HEADQUARTERS

🏢 59 G18 • United Nations Plaza 10017 ☎ 212/963-7713 🕐 Daily 9.30–4.45; closed Sat, Sun in Jan and Feb 🎫 Adult $10, child 5–14 $5.50, under 5s not admitted 🚇 M15, M27, M42 🚇 4, 5, 6, 7 🍴 🏛 🚻
📷 Tours every half hour Mon–Fri 9.30–4.45, Sat and Sun 10–4.30 www.un.org

At the end of World War II John D. Rockefeller, Jr. donated the $8.5 million to purchase this site, and six city blocks of slaughterhouses along the waterfront were cleared to provide space for the United Nations complex. The 544ft (166m) Secretariat building that dominates the site opened in 1950. Alongside are the General Assembly building, the Conference building (fronting the river), and the Dag Hammarskjold Library. Fittingly, architects from many countries contributed to the designs. A 45-minute guided tour covers the General Assembly Hall and Security Council Chamber. You can see donated exhibits such as stained glass by Marc Chagall, a replica Sputnik, and, in the park, sculptures by Barbara Hepworth and Henry Moore. Visit the landscaped grounds, with beautiful views. Arrive early at peak times.

UPPER WEST SIDE

🏢 58 C13 • Between 59th Street and 125th Street, west of Central Park
🚇 M7, M10, M11 🚇 B, C, 1, 2 🍴 🚻 🏛

The Upper West Side is a lively residential area with numerous historic districts, sumptuous landmark buildings, affordable hotels and excellent restaurants, and an affluent crowd that includes many actors, actresses, directors and musicians. The popular American Museum of Natural History (see pages 68–72) is here, as are the city's premier performing arts complex Lincoln Center (see pages 112–113) and the Cathedral of St. John the Divine (see page 77). While you stroll, note the San Remo Apartment Building at 145–146 Central Park West, and the Trump International Hotel/Tower on Columbus Circle.

WASHINGTON HEIGHTS

🏢 Page 7 • 155th Street to Dyckman Street 🚇 M4 🚇 A 🍴 🏛 🚻

At the northern tip of Manhattan, this neighborhood of Latinos, Dominicanos, Greeks and Armenians does not attract many visitors. Yet there are some excellent restaurants and interesting attractions, including the medieval collections at the Cloisters (see page 86) in Fort Tryon Park, which has spectacular views of the Hudson River. Washington Heights was the site of one of the earliest battles of the American Revolution, fought on November 16, 1776; Washington's troops lost to the British, who named the fort after the colonial governor, Sir William Tryon. John D. Rockefeller acquired the Cloisters property in 1917 and the museum opened in 1938.

WOOLWORTH BUILDING

🏢 61 E25 • 233 Broadway 10007
🚇 M1, M6, M15 🚇 4, 5, 6, A, C

Multimillionaire F. W. Woolworth, the department store mogul, hired fashionable architect Cass Gilbert to build the tallest building in the world in 1913. At 792ft (242m), this terra-cotta faced, neo-Gothic masterpiece held the record until 1929, with the completion of the Chrysler Building (see page 85). In the 1980s much of the terra-cotta cladding was replaced. Inside, the lobby is a marvel of Skyros marble, with murals of *Labor and Commerce* and plaster depictions of some of the builders, including Gilbert, with a model of the building and Woolworth himself counting his cash.

Relax in the shade under the trees in Union Square's gardens

UNION SQUARE

A focal point of the off-Broadway theater scene, with great restaurants, excellent art galleries and interesting museums.

On a sunny day, the park is a pleasant place to people-watch and relax. There are sculptures as well, Washington (1856) and Lincoln (1866), both by Henry Kirke Brown, and Lafayette by Statue of Liberty sculptor, Frédéric-Auguste Bartholdi. Nearby are the Center for Jewish History at 15 West 16th Street; the eclectic Forbes Magazine Galleries at 62 Fifth Avenue at 12th Street (see page 99; Theodore Roosevelt's reconstructed birthplace at 28 East 20th Street; and the Ukrainian Museum (see page 144).

At last count there were some 100 restaurants in the Union Square area, including some of the city's top tables. In September, at a Union Square Park fundraiser called Harvest, you can sample signature dishes of top neighborhood chefs. Also in September, the free outdoor Manhattan Short Film Festival screens 14 of the world's best short films and gives new filmmakers a chance to compete for prizes.

BACKGROUND

Run down and threatening in the 1970s, Union Square is thriving and proud today. Every Monday, Wednesday, Friday and Saturday, a green market—the best farmers' market in the United States—draws New Yorkers from all over the city and inspires local chefs. The bright idea of Barry Benepe (director of the green market)—who saw it as a way to simultaneously help Hudson Valley farmers and improve the neighborhood—it encouraged other communities to set up similar markets.

Union Square went residential in the 1840s, and America's greatest concentration of theaters, nightclubs, restaurants, hotels and luxury shopping followed. Union Square Park was laid out for the wealthy residents. In the 1800s, Ladies' Mile—Broadway and Sixth Avenue between 15th and 24th streets—was the height of fashionable shopping, until the turn of the 20th century when wealth moved uptown and the area deteriorated. In the late 1800s, Union Square was the center for demonstrations and political protests. In the early 1930s the editorial offices of The New Masses and the offices of the Communist Party's Yiddish-language paper moved here. A renovation of the square in 1936 discouraged further demonstrations.

The best chefs in town swear by the freshness and quality of produce at the farmers' market

RATINGS	
Historic interest	● ● ○
Specialist shopping	● ● ●
Photo stops	● ● ○
Value for money	● ● ●

BASICS

✚ 60 E21 • From East 12th Street to East 20th Street, between Third and Fifth avenues

🚌 M2, M3, M6, M7

Ⓜ Q, R, 4, 5

🍴 Old Town Bar & Restaurant, 45 East 18th Street between Broadway and Park Avenue, tel 212/529-6732

🚶 Free walking tour Sat 2pm, meet at the Lincoln statue near the Pavilion Building in Union Square Park

www.unionsquarenyc.org

Wall Street

●

**The heart of New York's financial center and the historic site of
first president George Washington's inauguration.**

*Shopping center underneath
Wall Street*

*Playing chess in the street is a
popular pastime today*

*The Stock Exchange, on the
corner of Wall and Broad streets*

This symbol of wealth is in fact a narrow 18th-century lane running from
Broadway to South Street. The New York Stock Exchange (closed to the
public since 9/11) stands on the corner of Broad Street and Wall Street.
At the west end of the street on Broadway, framed between towering
office buildings, is the Gothic Revival Trinity Church (see pages 142–
143)—an impressive sight, and a great photo opportunity, with the
many U.S. flags waving from their perches on the buildings along the
street. Stop in front of Federal Hall National Monument (see page 97);
a statue of George Washington marks the spot where the first president
took the oath of office. The two skyscrapers at Nos. 40 and 55 Wall
Street rise up 930ft (282.5m) and 951ft (290m) respectively. This is
an area steeped in history evidenced by the many historical plaques,
cornerstones, markers and notices. Take a look at the Morgan Bank
headquarters at No. 60. Its bold arcade vies for attention as one of the
tallest skyscrapers in the Financial District. Visit the white marble lobby.

Wall Street was named for the northern wall erected in 1653 to
defend New Amsterdam from Native Americans. North of this wall were
the *bouweries* (farms). After the English defeated the Dutch, and New
Amsterdam was renamed New York, the wall started to crumble and in
1699 it was torn down. The bastion stones from the Dutch wall were
carted off and used in the foundation of City Hall (see page 77).

THE FIRST TRANSACTION

In 1792, 22 brokers and merchants stood in front of a buttonwood
tree on Wall Street and made their first trading agreement. They were
actively trading government securities, seeking to establish fixed commissions on transactions and favoring brokers who were signatories.
This "Buttonwood Agreement," as it was called, eventually gave birth
to the New York Stock Exchange. Their open-air trading activities
moved indoors, probably to taverns, until premises on William Street
were acquired in the 1860s.

The telegraphic ticker, new in 1867, has been replaced by today's latest market information display technology. The adrenaline rushes as
hundreds of brokers on the trading floor, the size of a football field,
trade billions of shares in about 3,000 companies. This frenetic trading
viewed from the visitor's gallery will be worth a look when it reopens to
the public, but the long closure does not bode well, so phone ahead.

RATINGS	
Historic interest	●●●●○
Specialist shopping	●●○○○
Photo stops	●●●●○
Walkability	●●●●○

BASICS

✚ 61 F26 • Financial District

🚇 M1, M15, M22

🚇 4, 5

🍴 John Street Bar & Grill, 17 John
Street, tel 212/349-3278, daily 11.30–11

☕ Mangia, 40 Wall Street, tel 212/425-
4040, Mon–Fri 7–5

📷 Free 90-minute Wall Street walking
tour every Thu, Sat noon, meet on the
steps of the U.S. Customs House at 1
Bowling Green

www.downtownny.com
Up-to-date information on Lower
Manhattan's buses, subways, attractions,
shops, hotels and transportation

TIP

● As the Financial District is
deserted on weekends, visit on
a weekday when this little
street becomes a superhighway
for stockbrokers in dark suits.

*Wall Street is most famous
internationally for the
devastating Wall Street Crash
in 1929*

Whitney Museum of American Art

More than 11,000 works by 1,700 prominent 20th- and 21st-century American artists:
Georgia O'Keeffe, Jasper Johns, Edward Hopper, Mark Rothko and Jackson Pollock.
Provocative works by innovative and often controversial American independent filmmakers,
video artists, multimedia artists and photographers.

Taking a break at the museum

SEEING THE WHITNEY MUSEUM OF AMERICAN ART

Before entering the museum on Madison Avenue, take a few
minutes to look at the striking, granite, modernist building by
Marcel Breuer and Hamilton Smith. In a neighborhood of traditional brownstone, limestone and brick row houses, this Brutalist
architecture attracts attention, and when it was completed in
1966, many people thought it too heavy and dreary. Today, it is
generally esteemed as daring and innovative as it rises in a series
of inverted stairs above a sunken sculpture garden. As you enter,
the ticket desk is to your left. At the ticket desk and checkout
counter there are free Whitney calendars with the current exhibition schedule and leaflets about the current and upcoming
temporary exhibitions. The free audiotours can be picked up at
the end of the checkout counter.

Start your visit with the permanent collection either on the second floor, De Kooning to Today, or on the fifth floor, Hopper to Mid-Century. New exhibitions are also staged (in the past these have featured quilts made by African-American women and photographs by young artists).

Contemporary artists are displayed to good effect in the museum galleries

HIGHLIGHTS

FIFTH FLOOR: HOPPER TO MID-CENTURY

The Leonard and Evelyn Lauder Galleries, which make up part of this floor, contain more than 200 works from the first half of the 20th century. As you leave the elevator on this floor, you will see the Early 20th-Century Urban Realism Gallery, with several paintings by Robert Henri, including a lovely portrait dating from 1916 of the museum's founder, Gertrude Vanderbilt Whitney, donated by her granddaughter, Flora. If you have the free audioguide, listen to Mrs. Whitney's granddaughter's description of her. The portrait depicts a woman of leisure, which surprises the granddaughter who remembers her as an energetic woman always on the go. On the opposite wall is a fine painting by William J. Glackens, *Hammerstein's Roof Garden* (c1901), which depicts wealthy New Yorkers at the beginning of the 20th century enjoying watching tightrope walkers, acrobats and jugglers on hot summer evenings at Hammerstein's on the corner of Seventh Avenue and 42nd Street.

The Machine Age and Geometric Abstraction Gallery houses a collection of paintings of American factories and skyscrapers in a style called Precisionism. The artists' creations are a response to the explosion of industry in the early 20th century.

In the Early American Modernism Gallery are several paintings by Georgia O'Keeffe, including several of her dazzling flower paintings and *Summer Days* (1936), one of her many cow skull paintings. You will also find her gorgeous *Music Pink and Blue II* (1919) and *Black and White* (1930).

The superb collection in the Edward Hopper Gallery displays such favorites as *7am* (1948), and his earlier *Small Town Station* (1918–20) and *Italian Quarter From Gloucester* (1912), as well as his particularly haunting painting, *Early Sunday Morning* (1930).

RATINGS	
Good for kids	● ● ●
Historic interest	● ●
Specialist shopping	● ● ● ●
Value for money	● ● ● ● ●

TIPS

● Come Fridays from 6pm to 9pm. Admission is pay-what-you-wish and there are live musical performances.

● For a good cross section of the latest in American art and to see works by unknown but promising artists, visit when the Whitney Biennial is on (even-numbered years).

● There's a branch of the museum in the Philip Morris Building at 120 Park Avenue *(Mon–Wed and Fri 11–6, Thu 11–7.30, free).*

Notice the curtains and blinds in the windows above the storefronts in this picture. By making them different, some with yellow blinds and others with white curtains, he gives a sense that people live in each of these dwellings, and that something different is going on inside each one. Hold up your hands to block from your view the barber's pole and the fire hydrant, and notice how they give focus and balance to the painting.

The Realism in the 1930s Gallery has fine works by Thomas Hart Benton. *Poker Night* (1948) was a commissioned work based on the Broadway performance of "A Streetcar Named Desire."

In the Early Abstract Expressionism Gallery is a sculpture by Louise Bourgeoise called *Quarantania* (1953). The artist produced this work when she was feeling very homesick for her native France while she studied in the United States. Her longing for her loved ones comes

The entrance lobby is a riot of modern lighting

The fourth-floor gallery was used for temporary exhibitions during the 2000 Whitney Biennial

GALLERY GUIDE

Floors 1, 3, 4: Temporary exhibits
Floor 2: De Kooning To Today: Mildred and Herbert Lee Galleries include works by Jackson Pollock, Jasper Johns, Claes Oldenburg, Robert Rauschenberg, Roy Lichtenstein, Frank Stella, Robert Smithson, Alexander Calder and Paul Pfeiffer. Also temporary exhibits. Marisol's *Women and Dog* (1964) sculpture is four sculptures of the artist. The one with the green skirt and pink blouse has her photo stuck to the head.
Floor 5: Hopper to Mid-Century: Leonard and Evelyn Lauder Galleries include works by William Glackens and Robert Henri; Machine Age and Geometric Abstraction Gallery have works in the Precisionism style; Early American Modernism Gallery includes Georgia O'Keeffe; Edward Hopper Gallery; Realism in 1930s Gallery displays Thomas Hart Benton, John Stuart Curry and Joe Jones; Early Abstract Expressionism Gallery includes Louise Bourgeoise. Also temporary exhibits. *The Lord is My Shepherd* (1926), by Thomas Hart Benton, is a painting of a husband and wife who were the artist's deaf-mute neighbors on Martha's Vineyard.

out in this sculpture. The Surrealism in America Gallery contains Man Ray's *La Fortune* (1938), a statement about man's attempt to win at games.

SECOND FLOOR: DE KOONING TO TODAY

Roy Lichtenstein, *Little Big Painting*

In the Pop Gallery, *Little Big Painting* (1965) is a celebration of mass media and popular culture. The red, white and yellow with harsh black lines resembles an image of an abstract painting. With no trace of the artist's hand, no visible brushstroke, and the dot screen in the

Hail, Bright Aurora, *by an unknown artist*

background, Lichtenstein (1923–97) evokes mechanical printing, the culture of mass reproduction.

Alexander Calder, *Circus*
Calder's (1898–1976) fascination with the circus and his training as a mechanical engineer inspired him to create *Circus* (1926–31) and to breathe life into the tiny wire tightrope walkers, acrobats, weight-lifters and dancers in this mixed-media, miniature reproduction of an actual circus. The sculpture is accompanied by a continuous screening of a film of the affable ringmaster, Calder, in his studio with his wife, winding up the gramophone, as they performed for the Paris avant-garde in the 1920s.

Other Highlights
The Mildred and Herbert Lee Galleries, occupying almost all of this floor, displays works by American artists after 1945. In the Abstract Expressionism Gallery, Jackson Pollock's *Number 27* (1950) is one of the many pieces he created by placing the canvas on the floor and drizzling paint on it in a very controlled and deliberate manner. The Life Is Art Gallery contains Jasper Johns's *Three Flags* (1958), which he viewed as a deconstruction of this potent symbol of America.

BACKGROUND

Gertrude Vanderbilt Whitney (1877–1942), the daughter of Cornelius Vanderbilt (1843–1899), studied sculpture at the Art Students League in New York and went on to become one of the country's most generous patrons of the arts. In 1914, she launched the Whitney Studio Club, at 8 West 8th Street in the West Village, next to her MacDougal Alley studio, to exhibit works of young, avant-garde American artists. She was particularly fond of revolutionary artists such as John Sloan, Everett Shin and George Luks, realist painters Edward Hopper and Thomas Hart Benton, and early modernist painters such as Max Weber and Stuart Davis.

In 1929, after years of collecting, Whitney offered her personal collection to the Metropolitan Museum of Art. When the Met refused it, she established the Whitney Museum of American Art in 1931 with 700 objects, many from her personal collection. Thus the museum became one of the few museums anywhere in the world to be founded by an artist. The Whitney moved to its present building in 1966.

BASICS
✚ 59 E15 • 945 Madison Avenue at 75th Street 10021
☎ 1-800-WHITNEY
🕐 Tue–Thu 11–6, Fri 1–9, Sat–Sun 11–6; closed Jan 1, Thanksgiving, Dec 25
💷 Adult $12,under 12s free ($2.25 per ticket service charge online or by phone); pay-what-you-wish Fri 6pm–9pm
🚌 M1, M2, M3, M4
Ⓖ 6, B, D, F, N
🍴 🅳 Sarabeth's, a café, serves lunch Tue–Fri 11–4.30 and weekend brunch Sat–Sun 10–4.30 🏧
📷 Free exhibition tours start at the lobby information desk, tel 212/570-3676. Free self-guiding audiotours available in the lobby. Family audio guide; Saturday family programs (noon–1) free with museum admission for children aged 7–11 (reservations a must, 212/570-7745)

www.whitney.org
Highlights of the permanent collection, plus the latest on programs and events, shopping online, Whitney Biennial information.

Railroad Crossing, *by Edward Hopper*

Enjoying the last of the evening sunshine from the Brighton Beach Boardwalk in Brooklyn

The elegant Palm House in Brooklyn Botanic Gardens

Farther Afield

BROOKLYN

BRIGHTON BEACH

⊞ Page 7 • Southern tip of Brooklyn
🚇 B68, B1 🚊 Q 🍴 📷 ▦
www.brightonbeachbid.com

The influx of Russian immigrants to this area on Brooklyn's Atlantic-pounded shore has earned it the nickname Little Odessa by the Sea. You'll appreciate why as you stroll along the ocean's-edge boardwalk and Brighton Beach Avenue. The dozens of supermarkets and delicatessens are stocked with caviar, knishes, vodka, sausages and foods you just don't see back home unless home is Russia. The nightlife recalls Las Vegas, with its scantily-clad dancers crowned with elaborate plumage.

BROOKLYN BOTANIC GARDENS

⊞ Page 7 • 1000 Washington Avenue, Brooklyn 11225 ☎ 718/623-7200
🕐 Tue–Fri 8–6, Sat–Sun 10–6, Apr–Sep; Tue–Fri 8–4.30, Sat–Sun 10–4.30, rest of year 💲 Adult $5, 16s and under free. Free to all Tue 🚇 B41, B43, B48, B69, B71 🚊 Q to Prospect Park, 2, 3 to Eastern Parkway 📷 ▦ 🍴 📷 Guided tours weekends 1pm
www.bbg.org

These 52 acres (21ha), planted with more than 13,000 varieties from around the world, are a place for a quiet stroll when you've had enough of Manhattan. There are water-lily ponds, stately old trees and flowering shrubs, a local plantlife section and a conifer collection. The Cranford Rose Garden shelters more than 1,000 varieties of rose. The stunning Cherry

Esplanade draws large crowds in May for the blooming season and the Japanese hill-and-pond garden is one of the best of its type in the country. The Palm House, designed by McKim, Mead & White in 1914, and the contemporary greenhouses added in 1987, offer additional lovely spaces. You can see everything in two or three hours.

BROOKLYN HISTORICAL SOCIETY

⊞ 345 H26 • 128 Pierrepont Street, Brooklyn 11201 ☎ 718/222-4111
🕐 Wed and Thu 10–5, Fri 10–8, Sat 10–5, Sun noon–5 💲 Adult $6, members and under 12s free 🚊 M, N, 2, 3 🍴 📷 Guided tours available
www.brooklynhistory.org

The Brooklyn Historical Society, a National Historic Landmark, occupies a Queen Anne-style building designed by George B. Post and completed in 1881. It was the first New York building to use locally produced terra-cotta. Notice the busts of historic,

An early employee time recorder in Brooklyn's History Museum

heroic figures and representations of American plants on the façade. Inside, Post cleverly used a truss system to suspend the weight of the floors in order to create the open space you see in the galleried library.

BROOKLYN'S HISTORY MUSEUM

⊞ 345 H26 • 128 Pierrepont Street, Brooklyn 11201 ☎ 718/222-4111
🕐 Mon, Thu–Sat noon–5 💲 $2.50
🚊 M, N, 2, 3 🍴 📷
www.brooklynhistory.org

This museum, in the same building as the Brooklyn Historical Society, proudly displays 9,000 objects ranging from documents of Brooklyn's very early history to quirky personal belongings of local people. There are Native American tools, slave deeds, Dodgers and Coney Island memorabilia, and 3,000 prints that document the borough's history. Check out the Dodgers doll from 1948, which even has a leather mitt. There is a fine collection of paintings, including *Summer View of Brooklyn* (c1820) and *The Stage Sewanhackey* (1850). Guided tours should be reserved in advance (*adult $15, child $5, tel 718/222-4111*).

CONEY ISLAND

⊞ Page 7 • Southern tip of Brooklyn 11224 🚇 B36, B74 🚊 B, D, F, N 🍴 📷 ▦ 🍴

Known as Sodom by the Sea in the 1880s, this Atlantic-washed corner of Brooklyn was also called Playground of the World. Coney Island lost its historic Thunderbolt roller coaster and Kensington Hotel in 2000, and before that Steeplechase Park was closed in 1964. In spite of losing some of its famous

The Peaceable Kingdom *(1840–45), by Edward Hicks*

BROOKLYN MUSEUM OF ART

The second-largest art museum in New York City, and one of the largest in the country, attracts half a million visitors every year.

The Brooklyn Museum of Art is housed in a grand Beaux-Arts building designed by McKim, Mead & White in 1897, with an addition by Polshek Partners in spring 2004. The new plaza has two water features.

A sculpture in the grounds

THE COLLECTIONS

The museum prides itself on its fine collection of Egyptian, Classical, and Ancient Middle Eastern Art. It holds the third-largest collection of Ancient Egyptian artifacts dating from predynastic times to the Roman conquest. The renovated Morris A. and Meyer Schapiro Wing contains objects from 1350 BC, in the reign of Akhenaten and his wife Nefertiti, through to the time of Cleopatra. Jewelry, reliefs of major deities, decorated sarcophagi, coffins and a 2,600-year-old mummy are on display.

The Arts of Africa, the Pacific and the Americas galleries have astonishing collections. An ivory gong from the Edo people of Benin, works from Polynesia and Indonesia, and important textiles from the Andes are just some of the fascinating items. The Arts of Asia collection has objects from China, India, Iran, Korea, Japan, Tibet, Thailand and Turkey.

The collection of decorative arts, costumes and textiles features a 17th-century Dutch farmhouse and a 20th-century art deco library. The costumes of 19th-century America and Europe are a glimpse at finery we can hardly imagine today.

Paintings, sculptures, prints, drawings and photographs include works by Gilbert Stuart, Thomas Cole, George Caleb Bingham, Winslow Homer, Auguste Rodin, Edgar Degas, Camille Pissarro, Edward Steichen and Paul Strand, to name just a few.

EVENTS

First Saturdays of the month are enormously popular here. A free program of art and entertainment, with food and drinks supplied, attracts thousands. The entertainment starts with spoken-word artists and members of the Brooklyn Philharmonic in Shakespeare Live from 6.30 to 9. The program of Hands-on-Art from 6.30 to 8.30 allows you to create your own Egyptian-inspired necklaces.

RATINGS

Historic interest	● ● ●
Photo stops	● ● ●
Walkability	● ● ● ● ●
Value for money	● ● ● ●

BASICS

✚ Page 7• 200 Eastern Parkway, Brooklyn 11238-6052

☎ 718/638-5000

🕐 Wed–Fri 10–5, Sat–Sun 11–6, first Sat of the month (except Sep) 11–11; closed Jan 1, Thanksgiving, Dec 25

💵 Adult $6, under 12s free; 1st Sat each month free 5pm–11pm

🚌 B71, B41, B69

Ⓜ 2, 3

🍴 Museum Café Wed–Fri 10–4, Sat, Sun and holidays 10.30–4.30

🏛 BMA Shop 10.30–5.30, until 11pm on First Saturdays 🏛

📷 Free audiotour of permanent collection

www.brooklynmuseum.org
Floorplan, information on permanent and temporary collections, events, schedule for First Saturdays, online shopping.

Fun on the big wheel at Coney Island in Brooklyn

Henry Ward Beecher at the Plymouth Church of the Pilgrims

The Kennedy arch at the entrance to Prospect Park

THE SIGHTS

landmarks, Coney Island has a vibrant spirit of rebirth. The New York Aquarium, opened in 1957, is still going strong, Astroland Park still has its Cyclone roller coaster, and the Mermaid Parade is on the summer solstice.

Nathan Handwerker opened his hot-dog emporium here in 1916, and his famous hot dogs are now sold all over New York. Keyspan Park is the $39-million home of the Brooklyn Cyclones baseball team, behind Parachute Jump on the Boardwalk.

NEW YORK TRANSIT MUSEUM

✚ Page 7 • Boerum Place and Schermerhorn Street, Brooklyn 11201 ☎ 718/694-5100 ◷ Tue–Fri 10–4, Sat–Sun noon–5 💲 Adult $3, child $1.50 🚇 2, 3, 4, 5 🏛 Annex Gallery and Store at Grand Central, 212/878-0106 ♿ www.mta.info/museum

The New York Transit Museum occupies a decommissioned

Have a go at the exhibits at the New York Transit Museum

subway station in downtown Brooklyn. The permanent exhibition explores the history of buses and trolleys, using elements of a New York City intersection and a large display of more than 200 trolley models.

PLYMOUTH CHURCH OF THE PILGRIMS

✚ 345 H26 • 75 Hicks Street, Brooklyn 11201 ☎ 718/624-4743 ◷ Guided tour only (1hr 30 min) Sun 11–2, advance reservation required 💲 Phone for prices 🚇 A, N, M, 4 www.plymouthchurch.org

The Plymouth Church of the Pilgrims, built in 1849, was the first Congregational Church in Brooklyn and a focal point of the anti-slavery movement at the time. Abraham Lincoln worshiped here twice in 1860, and many eminent writers have spoken here. Elegant and beautiful stained-glass windows by Tiffany adorn this otherwise modest church, and in the courtyard next to it is a superb bronze statue of Henry Ward Beecher (1813–87) with slaves, sculpted by Gutzon Borglum (famous for his work on Mount Rushmore).

Beecher, the most famous preacher in America, preached from this pulpit for 40 years. He was not afraid to speak out on slavery and about Reconstruction issues after the Civil War.

PROSPECT PARK

✚ Page 7 • Flatbush Avenue at Grand Army Plaza. Information: Prospect Park Alliance, 95 Prospect Park West, Brooklyn 11215 ☎ Information: 718/965-8999; Lefferts Homestead Historic House Museum: 718/789-2822 ◷ Daily; closed 1am–5am 💲 Free 🚌 B41, B48, B69 🚇 Q, F 2, 3 🏛 ♿ 🚻 www.prospectpark.org

Designed by Frederick Law Olmsted and Calvert Vaux, the designers of Central Park (see

pages 78–83), this 526-acre (213ha) park is a pleasant place to spend a day. At the main entrance at Grand Army Plaza are a triumphal arch and a monument to President John Kennedy.

In Leffert's Homestead is a museum for children (tel 718/965-6505, Fri–Sun 1–4, Apr–Nov). A zoo, skating rink, boathouse and pond, playgrounds, and a lovely 1912 carousel (Apr–Oct, 50 cents) are very popular with visiting children, too.

The northeast corner has a rose garden, Japanese gardens, a sculpture garden and Brooklyn Museum of Art (see page 153). Entertainment events throughout the year draw large crowds.

The Audubon Center provides maps and guides for self-guiding tours, as well as free Discover Nature self-guiding tours (Sat–Mon, holidays at 3pm, Mar–Nov).

WATERFRONT MUSEUM

✚ Page 7 • 699 Columbia Street Marine Terminal, Brooklyn 11231 ☎ 718/624-4719 💲 Free 🚌 77 🚇 F, G www.waterfrontmuseum.org

An unusual museum in the last surviving railroad barge at Red Hook Garden Pier, the Waterfront stages a summer music series. The barge was designated by the U.N. in 1998 as the Regional Craft of the International Year of the Oceans. It's worth a visit to enjoy an unusual evening of live music, from blues to swing and country, in July and August.

To get here, take F or G train to Smith and 9th streets, then the 77 bus toward Red Hook. Exit at the Columbia Street stop, cross Lorraine Street, and walk south to Columbia Street. Bear left at the Todd Memorial Triangle and continue toward the Erie Basin Entrance along the esplanade.

Education through fun at the Hall of Science Playground

Staten Island's Conference House retraces American history

The Waterfront Museum is in the last old railroad barge

QUEENS

NEW YORK HALL OF SCIENCE

Page 7 • 111th Street, Flushing Meadows–Corona Park, Queens 11368 718/ 699-0005 Tue–Wed 9.30–2, Thu–Fri 9.30–5, Sat–Sun noon–5, Sep–Jun; Mon 9.30–2, Tue–Fri 9.30–5, Sat–Sun 10.30–6, Jul–Aug; closed major holidays Adult $7.50, preschool $2.50. Thu 2–5, Sep–Jun free. Science Playground (age 6 and up, with adult supervision, Mar–Dec, weather permitting) $3, $2 if in groups Q23, Q48 7 to 111th Street Queens Audio tours $2 www.nyscience.org

In this hands-on, interactive museum of science and technology, with more than 225 exhibits, trained Explainers answer questions about topics ranging from color or sound and light to microbiology and quantum physics. You can surf the net in the Technology Gallery, discover the wonders of science by conducting your own experiments in the Biochemistry Discovery Lab, or peer at the World of Microbes and the Realm of the Atom.

The Science Playground outside has more than 30,000sq ft (2,790sq m) of giant slides, windmills, waterplay features, kinetic sculptures and a 3-D spider web, where children can have fun.

QUEENS MUSEUM OF ART

Page 7 • New York City Building, Flushing Meadows–Corona Park, Queens 11368 718/592-9700 Tue–Fri 10–5, Sat–Sun noon–5 Suggested donation: adult $5, child free Q48, Q88 7 to Willets Point/Shea Stadium www.queensmuse.org

A $15-million renovation in 1994 by Rafael Viñoly expanded this museum for ambitious exhibitions of contemporary art.

The permanent collection includes beautiful glassware from the Tiffany Studio, which was in Queens from 1893 to 1938, and the Panorama of New York City, an 18,000sq ft (1,674sq m) minutely detailed scale model of New York City, with every building in place. The largest architectural scale model, it was created for the 1964–65 World's Fair, and it is regularly updated to reflect the changes in New York buildings.

The Unisphere outside the Queens Museum of Art

The museums's Art Moderne building was erected to house the 1939 World's Fair and was used again during the 1964–65 Fair, for which the adjacent Unisphere was created. It is the largest globe in the world, built by U.S. Steel. From 1946 to 1952 the museum building was home to the United Nations General Assembly.

STATEN ISLAND

ALICE AUSTEN HOUSE

Page 6 • 2 Hylan Boulevard, Staten Island 10305 718/816-4506 Thu–Sun noon–5, Mar–Dec; closed major holidays Adult $2, child free S51 to Hylan Boulevard www.aliceausten.8m.com

This unique museum is the restored Victorian house and garden of Alice Austen (1866–1952), one of America's early

female documentary photographers. A visit here is fascinating for the quality of Alice's photographs, but also to give an idea of what middle-class life was like at the turn of the 20th century. The house was declared a city landmark in 1971.

The photographs give you a glimpse into the world of a well-traveled young woman, who taught herself to operate the camera, develop heavy glass plates, and make prints. Alice took her equipment everywhere with her when she traveled, despite its weighing as much as 50 pounds (23kg), and photographed the world around her, including New York street scenes, using costuming and satire to create the desired effect.

Exhibitions and events take place throughout most of the year and often feature works by other local artists. Take the Staten Island Ferry from Manhattan, then catch the S51 bus to Hylan Boulevard.

CONFERENCE HOUSE

Page 6 • 7455 Hylan Boulevard 10305 718/984-2086 Wed–Sun 1–4, Mar–Dec $2 S78 to Craig Avenue www.nycparks.org

Originally called the Billop Manor House, Conference House was built around 1680. On September 11, 1776, Benjamin Franklin, John Adams and Edward Rutledge (a South Carolina governor and signer of the Declaration of Independence) came here for a meeting with Admiral Lord Howe, Commander of Her Majesty's Atlantic Squadron. Howe hoped to persuade the colonists to give up their fight for independence and to return to the Mother Country, but the meeting lasted no more than three hours. The three visitors made it clear that they were not interested in his

QUEENS: HALL OF SCIENCE–STATEN ISLAND: CONFERENCE HOUSE   155

The Garibaldi Meucci Museum is dedicated to two Italians

Restoration is widespread at Historic Richmond Town

There are plenty of beautiful buildings at Snug Harbor

offer to return to the fold. The two-and-a-half-story house has beautifully furnished period rooms and offers a look at life in Colonial America. Special events take place throughout the year.

GARIBALDI MEUCCI MUSEUM

Page 6 • 420 Tompkins Avenue 10305 ☎ 718/422-1608 ⏰ Telephone for opening times 💰 Telephone for prices 🚌 S52, S78
www.garibaldimeuccimuseum.org

The Italian national hero, and one of the founders of unified Italy, Giuseppi Garibaldi (1807–82) spent two years in this 1840s house after fleeing the conquering republicans in Italy. It was the home of one Antonio Meucci (1808–89), who in fact was the inventor of the telephone. He invented a prototype several years before Alexander Graham Bell got into the picture, but as he failed to patent his idea, he never got the credit.

After Garibaldi died in 1884, a committee decided to commemorate his stay in Staten Island and a plaque was placed on the house. After Meucci's death, the house was given to the Italian community to preserve as a memorial to Garibaldi.

Today the house is owned and operated by The Order of Sons of Italy in America and displays artifacts about the lives of these two men. From the Staten Island Ferry, take either bus S78 or S52.

HISTORIC RICHMOND TOWN

Page 6 • 441 Clarke Avenue, Staten Island 10306 ☎ 718/351-1611
⏰ Wed–Fri 1–5, Jan–Mar; Wed–Sun 1–5, Apr–Jun and Sep–Dec; Wed–Fri 10–5, Sat–Sun 1–5, Jul–Aug; closed Easter Sun, Thanksgiving, Dec 25
💰 Adult $4, child $2.50, under 6s free
🚌 S74 🍴 🍴 📷
www.fieldtrip.com/ny/83511611.htm

About 27 historic buildings spread out over 100 acres (40ha) at this museum complex that stretches across three centuries of daily life and culture on Staten Island, from its earliest days as a rural crossroad to its incorporation into Greater New York. The quaint atmosphere and helpful staff make the whole experience a very pleasurable day out. Special events take place throughout the year.

JACQUES MARCHAIS CENTER OF TIBETAN ART

Page 6 • 338 Lighthouse Avenue, Staten Island 10306 ☎ 718/987-3478

⏰ Wed–Sun 1–5, Apr–Nov; by appointment only, Dec–Mar 💰 Adult $3, child $1 🚌 S74 to Lighthouse Avenue 🏛 🍴
www.fieldtrip.com/ny/89873478.htm

This lovely museum is one of New York's best-kept secrets. The Dalai Lama, when he visited in 1991, attested to its likeness to a Tibetan temple, with its terraced sculpture gardens and an attractive fish pond. The museum exhibits Tibetan, Nepalese and Mongolian art from the 17th to the 19th centuries. The Nepalese metalwork, encrusted with jewels, and the metal figures of deities and lamas, are exquisite. Informative explanations help you understand the significance of the jewelry, dance masks, ritual objects, incense burners and paintings. Special exhibitions and activities enhance a visit.

SNUG HARBOR CULTURAL CENTER

Page 6 • 1000 Richmond Terrace. Staten Island 10301 ☎ 718/448-2500
⏰ Daily dawn-dusk; closed Jan 1, Thanksgiving, Dec 25 💰 Gallery $2, grounds free 🚌 S40 🍴 🏛 🍴 📷
www.snug-harbor.org

Snug Harbor, a National Historic Landmark District, spreads out over 83 acres (34ha). Its 26 buildings, a fine collection of Greek Revival, Beaux Arts, Italianate and Victorian architecture, housed homeless old sailors during the 1880s. By the 1960s, the buildings had fallen into disrepair. But demolishing was not in the cards. After a vast restoration project, it is now a focal point of Staten Island cultural life, with art exhibitions in the Newhouse Galleries (Wed– Sun) and other activities. Be sure to see the Main Hall (Tue–Sun), the oldest building, and its lavish ceiling mural, towering skylight dome and gilded weathervane.

Preparing flax at one of the Historic Richmond Town restoration projects

Seals bask in the sun in their landscaped habitat at the Bronx Zoo

BRONX ZOO

The largest metropolitan wildlife park in the country, with more than 4,500 animals representing 55 species housed on 265 acres (107ha).

Plan to spend a whole day at this wonderful and hugely popular zoo, which has no fewer than three names—Bronx Zoo (unofficial), New York Zoological Park and International Wildlife Conservation Park. The animals, including endangered and threatened species, are well cared for and their surroundings are as near as possible to their habitats.

HIGHLIGHTS
One of the most impressive areas is the Wild Asia Complex, where you can see Indonesian tigers and Asian elephants, but only from the Bengali Express monorail. Jungle World's indoor re-creation of an Asian forest will envelop you, and it's home to leopards, lizards, tree kangaroos and white-cheeked gibbons, among other exotic wildlife from jungles around the world. In the Himalayan Highlands there are extremely rare snow leopards as well as red pandas.

The Congo Gorilla Forest, a 6.5-acre (9ha) is re-creation of an African rain forest; among the treetop lookouts, wooded pathways and lush greenery are 400 animals, including western lowland gorillas, who can be entertaining. You'll also see okapi and red river hogs.

In the Butterfly Zone the size of some of the butterflies might surprise you, not to mention the enormous variety and beauty of these complicated insects.

The World of Darkness, as you might imagine, is devoted to the lives of noctural creatures, such as fruit-eating bats.

The Children's Zoo (Apr–Oct) has wonderful activities—kids learn to see like an owl and hear like a fox—and a petting-zoo.

The Bengali Express monorail (May–Oct) is a 25-minute narrated ride above the roaming Siberian tigers, Indian rhinoceroses, Asian elephants, and other animals of the Indian subcontinent. It's a good way to see a lot without wearing yourself out. Other rides include the Skyfari aerial tram, camel rides and the Zoo Shuttle (Apr–Oct).

In summer it can get very crowded, and if it is a very warm day the animals retreat from open sunny positions and it can be hard to see some of them.

RATINGS

Good for kids	●●●●●
Specialist shopping	●●●●●
Photo stops	●●●●●
Value for money	●●●●●

BASICS

⊞ Page 7 • Bronx River Parkway and Fordham Road, Bronx 10460

☎ 718/367-1010

🕐 Mon–Fri 10–5, Sat–Sun 10–5.30, Apr–Oct; daily 10–4.30, rest of year

💵 Tue–Thu adult $11, child 2–12 $6, under 2s free; Wed suggested donation. Congo Gorilla Forest and camel rides $3; Childrens Zoo, Skyfari, Zoo Shuttle, Butterfly Zone, Bengali Express $2 each. Pay-One-Price ticket that includes admission and all rides: adult $19, child $14

🚌 BxM11, tel 718/652-8400 for details

🚇 2 Express to Pelham Parkway

🍴 🛍 🏛 🚻

🎧 Tours by Friends of the Zoo, tel 718/220-5141

www.wcs.org/zoos

TIPS
● From Madison Avenue you can take the Liberty Lines BxM11 express bus directly to the zoo.

● Eat early or late or bring a picnic and drinks. Lines for the stands can be long and slow on a busy, hot afternoon.

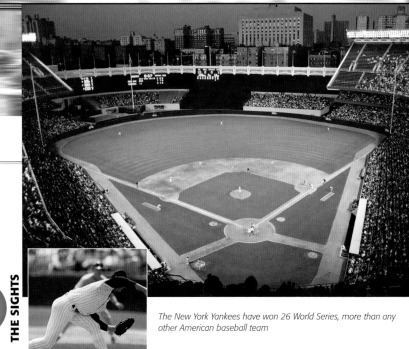

The New York Yankees have won 26 World Series, more than any other American baseball team

YANKEE STADIUM

Cheer the New York Yankees in their home stadium, the first to be labeled "stadium."

RATINGS

Good for kids	●●●●
Specialist shopping	●●●●
Photo stops	●●●
Value for money	●●●●●

BASICS

✚ Page 7 • 161st Street and River Avenue, Bronx 10451

☎ 718/293-6000

🕐 Baseball season Apr–Oct

🎟 Tickets for games $8–$65, tel Ticketmaster 212/307-1212 or Yankee Stadium

🚌 Bx6, Bx13

Ⓜ C, D, 4

🍴 Sidewalk Café on the Plaza next to Gates 4 and 6; snacks and drinks throughout the stadium

🎁 Gift shops are on the Field Level sections 24, 25. Yankee Clubhouse stores have five Manhattan locations. Get the location details and opening hours from the website 🔗

☞ One-hour behind-the-scenes tour, tel 718/579-4531, visit the website or buy tickets from one of the five Clubhouse Shops in Manhattan on the day of the tour

www.yankees.com

Yankee Stadium, America's first triple-decker stadium, has been home of the New York Yankees since April 18, 1923. The most famous player of them all, Babe Ruth, hit a three-run homer on that inaugural day in front of 74,200 fans and the Yankees were victorious 4–1. After that, the stadium quickly became known as The House That Ruth Built. The stadium got electric lighting in 1946 and the first electronic message board in 1959. After CBS became its new owner in 1967, the Yankees spent two seasons at Shea Stadium while their own stadium was renovated. Upon their return, the Yankees went on to host the World Series.

The stadium is used for other events, including football, soccer, religious conventions, political assemblies and concerts.

At Monument Park, on Field Level Section 36, you can see a special walk honoring players whose uniform numbers have been retired. Old Timers' Day, usually held in July, brings back the grand old players for a bow before their cheering fans.

SEEING A GAME

There are seven main entrances, so make a mental note of where you enter to avoid confusion when you leave. Make sure that you have no reason to leave once you are inside, because you cannot re-enter the stadium using the same ticket. Arrive an hour and a half before the game Mondays to Fridays, two hours ahead on weekends to watch the batting practice. It can take some time to get through the entrance, so allow plenty of time to see the beginning of the game.

To get a behind-the-scenes tour, which starts at the Press Gate, go to the Advance Ticket window or any of the Clubhouse stores on the day of the tour and you can find out more about Yankee history, get a good look at the field, the dugout area, the press box, the Clubhouse and Monument Park.

Alcohol is sold up until the seventh inning of each game, but drunkenness is not tolerated; you can ask to sit in an alcohol-free section when you buy your tickets. Other rules ban bottles, cans, coolers or containers, large bags and briefcases, noisemakers, laser pens, beachballs, firearms and knives; and there's no smoking.

This chapter gives information on things to do in New York other than sightseeing.

Shops and performance venues are located on the maps at the beginning of each section.

What to Do

East 95th Street
East 94th Street
Kitchen Arts and Letters
East 93rd Street
East 92nd Street
East 95th Street
East 94th Street

Jewish Museum

East 91st Street
Cooper-Hewitt National Design Museum
National Academy of Design
East 90th Street

Guggenheim Museum
East 89th Street
East 88th Street

East 91st Street
East 90th Street
East 89th Street
East 88th Street

13

Gracie Mansion

East 87th Street
86th Street
East 86th Street
Neue Galerie
East 85th Street
East 84th Street
East 83rd Street
East 82nd Street

The Metropolitan Museum of Art

East 81st Street
East 80th Street

East 87th Street
Carl Schurz Park
East 86th Street
East 85th Street
East 84th Street
East 83rd Street
East 82nd Street
East 81st Street
East 80th Street

14

East 79th Street
East 78th Street
East 77th Street
77th Street
East 76th Street

Whitney Museum of American Art

East 75th Street
East 74th Street
East 73rd Street
East 72nd Street

Conservatory Water

East 79th Street
East 78th Street
East 77th Street
John Jay Park
East 76th Street
East 75th Street
East 74th Street
East 73rd Street
East 72nd Street

15

ROOSEVELT ISLAND

Ralph Lauren
Frick Collection
Penhaligon's
Asia Society and Museum
East 71st Street
East 70th Street

Donna Karan
Dolce & Gabbana
68th Street Hunter College
East 69th Street
Moschino
East 68th Street
East 67th Street

Giorgio Armani
Jean-Paul Gaultier
East 66th Street
East 65th Street

Shanghai Tang
Jimmy Choo
East 64th Street

Floris
FIFTH AVENUE
East 63rd Street

Sherry-Lehmann
East 62nd Street

Calvin Klein
DKNY
East 61st St

Borrelli
Tod's
Barneys
Bloomingdale's
5th Street
59th Street

East 71st Street
East 70th Street
East 69th Street
East 68th Street
East 67th Street
East 66th Street
East 65th Street
East 64th Street
East 63rd Street
East 62nd Street
Mount Vernon Hotel Museum and Garden
East 60th Street

HIGHWAY 25
QUEENSBORO BRIDGE

FAO Schwarz
Crate & Barrel
Bergdorf Goodman
Chanel
East 58th Street
Border's Books, Music and Café
Hammacher Schlemer
East 57th Street

zoli
PK Fendi
WEST 57TH STREET
Tiffany
EAST 57TH STREET
Coach
Dahesh Museum of Art

Henri Bendel
Trump Tower
West 56th Street
Suarez Handbags
West 55th Street

Takashimaya
Gucci
Lacoste
West 54th Street

Manolo Blahnik
Thomas Pink
West 53rd Street

seum of Design
Museum of Television and Radio
Seagram Building
East 52nd Street

Jimmy Choo
West 51st Street

Cartier
St Patrick's Cathedral
Municipal Art Society
51st Street
East 51st Street

G E Building
Saks Fifth Avenue
West 50th Street

Cole Haan
Caswell-Massey
East 49th Street

Morrell & Company
West 48th Street

feller Center
West 47th Street

AMOND STRICT
MIDTOWN MANHATTAN
East 47th Street

16

Roosevelt Island Main Street

Main Street

EAST 57TH STREET

United Nations Headquarters

17

Paul Stuart
West 45th Street
East 45th Street

West 53rd Street
West 52nd Street
Museum of Arts and Design
Museum of Television and Radio
West 53rd Street
Seagram Building
West 51st Street
West 52nd Street
Cartier
Jimmy Choo
West 50th Street
Radio City Music Hall
St. Patrick's Cathedral
Municipal Art Society
West 51st Street
East 51st Street
Cole Haan
West 49th Street
50th Street
47th–50th Streets Rockefeller Center
G E Building
Saks Fifth Avenue
East 50th
West 48th Street
50th Street
Rockefeller Center
Morrell & Company
MIDTOWN MANHATTAN
East 48th Street
Caswell-Massey
West 47th Street
DIAMOND DISTRICT
East 47th Street
BROADWAY
West 46th Street
West 46th Street
Paul Stuart
West 45th Street
Int'l Center of Photography
West 44th Street
Grand Central Terminal
West 43rd Street
Times Square
Sephora
42nd Street
5th Avenue
Grand Central 42nd St
Chrysler Building

17
18
19
20
21
22

WEST 42ND STREET
Holy Cross Church
Reuters Building
42nd Street Port Authority Bus Terminal
New Amsterdam Theater
Times Square 42nd Street
Bryant Park
New York Public Library
Posman Booksellers
Chanin Building

West 41st Street
West 40th Street
FASHION AVENUE
AVENUE OF THE AMERICAS
East 41st Street
East 40th Street

West 39th Street
West 38th Street
Lord & Taylor
East 39th Street
East 38th Street

West 37th Street
West 36th Street
Morgan Library
East 37th Street
East 36th Street
PARK AVENUE

West 35th Street
Macy's
West 34TH STREET
EAST 34TH STREET
Empire State Building
34th Street Herald Square
23rd Street

B & H Photo
34th Street Penn Station
34th Street Penn Station

West 33rd Street
West 32nd Street
Madison Square Garden
Pennsylvania Station
East 33rd Street
East 32nd Street

West 31st Street
West 30th Street
Little Church Around the Corner
East 31st Street
East 30th Street

10TH AVENUE
9TH AVENUE
8TH AVENUE
7TH AVENUE
West 29th Street
28th Street
East 29th Street
28th Street

Chelsea Park
West 28th Street
West 26th Street
Jazz Record Center
East 28th Street
East 26th Street

Street
West 25th Street
West 24th Street
Madison Square Park
East 25th St
East 24th Street

23rd Street
23rd Street
Metropolitan Life Insurance Tower
23rd Street
Flatiron Building
23rd Street

West 22nd Street
West 21st Street
CHELSEA
Otto Tootsi Plohound
East 22nd Street
East 21st Street
Gramercy Park North
Gramercy Park
GRAMERCY PARK HISTORIC DIST

West 20th Street
West 19th Street
Theodore Roosevelt Birthplace
East 20th Street
East 19th Street
Gramercy Park South

West 18th Street
Bed, Bath and Beyond
ABC Carpet and Home
East 18th Street

West 17th Street
Loehmann's
Paragon Sporting Goods
Barnes & Noble
East 17th Street

Emporio Armani
West 16th Street
East 16th Street

Chelsea Market
West 15th Street
14th Street
14th Street Union Square
Union Square Park
UNION SQUARE
Union Square Green Market
3rd Avenue
Kiehl's

Jeffrey
Alexander McQueen
WEST 14TH STREET
8th Avenue
14th Avenue
EAST 14TH STREET
Diesel

Stella McCartney
Jussara Lee
West 13th Street
East 13th Street

Shelly Steffee
Decollage
6th Avenue
West 12th Street
Forbes Magazine Galleries
Strand Bookstore
Grace Church
Footlight Record

Jefferson Market Library
West 11th Street
East 11th Street

Constanca Basto
West 10th Street
East 10th Street
La Petite Coquette
99X

Three Lives
West 9th Street
East 9th Street
8th Street NYU
Wanamaker Place
Astor Place

Lucy Barnes
GREENWICH VILLAGE
Christopher Street – Sheridan Square
Christopher Park
WASHINGTON SQUARE NORTH
Macdougal Aly
Washington Mews
NOHO

McNulty's Rare Teas and Choice Coffee Shop
West 4th Street
Washington Square Park
Waverly Place
WASHINGTON SQUARE
Shakespeare & Co

Church St Luke-in-the-Fields
WEST 4th St – Washington Square
WASHINGTON SQUARE SOUTH
West 4th Street
Screaming Mimi's

L'Occitane
House of Oldies
Minetta Lane
Bleecker Street
Avirex
Bond
Jones Aly

C
D
E
F

Union Square Green Market
UNION SQUARE
Diesel
Strand Bookstore
Kiehl's
Filth Mart
Forbes Magazine Galleries
Ukrainian Museum
Footlight Records
Grace Church
St. Mark's-in-the-Bowery
99X
La Petite Coquette
8th Street NYU
Yona Lee
St. Mark's Bookshop
EAST VILLAGE
Macdougal Alley
Washington Mews
Tompkins Square Park
Jefferson Market Library
Washington Square Park
NORTH
Martin
NOHO
Shakespeare & Co
Merchant's House Museum
Eugenia Kim
L'Occitane
Screaming Mimi's
House of Oldies Rare Records
Avirex
Doyle and Doyle
Foley & Corinna
BCBG by Max Azria
Marc Jacobs
Eye Candy
Zara International
Me & Ro
Kelly Christy
Alife Rivington Club (shoes)
I, Claudia
Prada
Phat Farm
New Museum of Contemporary Art
Guggenheim Museum SoHo
Eddie Bauer
St. Patrick's Old Cathedral
Mary Adams the Dress
Nicole Miller
Dean & DeLuca
Zero
Sigerson Morrison
Cynthia Rowley
APC
Little Singer Building
Gas
INA
Le Sportsac
Eres
The Puma Store
Language
Resurrection Vintage
LOWER EAST SIDE
Hotel Venus
Kirna Zabete
Tracy Feith
Steven Alan
Helmut Lang
SOHO
Kate Spade
LITTLE ITALY
Forward
Broadway Panhandler
Alice Underground
Haughwout Building
Lower East Side Tenement Museum
Tony Shafrazi Gallery
Yohji Yamamoto
37=1
Pearl Paint
LOWER MANHATTAN
Kam Man Foods
Museum of Chinese in the Americas
Issey Miyake
CHINATOWN
Jacques Torres Chocolate
TRIBECA
Washington Market Park
Courthouse
US
City Hall Park
City Hall and Civic Center
Chambers Street
Brooklyn Bridge
BROOKLYN BRIDGE
Woolworth Building
J & R Music & Computer World
Church of St Peter
BROOKLYN BRIDGE
St Paul's Chapel
Fulton St
East River
GROUND ZERO
Fulton Street Market
Century 21
Federal Reserve Bank
South Street Seaport
Trinity Church
Federal Hall National Monument
WALL ST
Museum of American Financial History
Fraunces Tavern Museum
New York City Police Museum
Museum of Jewish Heritage

SHOPPING

They say that the national pastime of Americans is shopping. They also say that you can purchase anything you want in New York City. Both statements are true. New York's shopping ranges from large opulent department stores to tiny one-room boutiques and everything in between. Many visitors come to New York just to shop, especially pre-Christmas, uptown at the flagship designer stores that line Madison and Fifth Avenues, or downtown at the cutting-edge designers in SoHo and NoLita. More moderately priced merchandise can be found at stores around Herald Square and 34th Street, or in the branches of national chains scattered around Manhattan. Don't expect malls. There aren't any, of note. Stores accommodate shoppers by staying open seven days a week (with late night hours usually on Thursday). Note that American sizes differ from British and European sizes. Note too that the sales tax is 8.625%. Credit cards are accepted virtually everywhere.

Objets d'art and other decorative items from Greene Street, SoHo

116th and Lenox Avenue textiles, jewelry, bowls made from gourds, wooden stools and other artifacts from Africa are for sale. The Annex Antique Fair and Flea Market in the parking lots at Sixth Avenue and 26th Street is very popular. Get there early for the best pickings (it opens at 5am). The Sunday Columbus Avenue market (between 76th and 77th Streets is also fun (*tel 212-721-0900*). In summer, expect small neighborhood street fairs at which people sell all kinds of bric-a-brac, clothing, CDs, food, and books. Green

Vintage clothing for both sexes at Screaming Mimi's

Top-quality produce, packaged and fresh, from Dean & DeLuca

SALES

The largest sales take place in January and July, and also around legal holidays—Presidents' Day, Memorial Day and Labor Day, for example.

To keep abreast of current and forthcoming sales check the relevant sections of *New York* magazine and *Time Out* or go online to www.dailycandy.com or www.nysale.com. Some of the best deals are found at sample sales, usually held in the the spring and fall. Designers and manufacturers hold such sales to make space for their new design samples. Shopping fiends find

out about them by subscribing to S & B Report (*tel 877-579-0222*) or going online at www.lazarshopping.com. Online subscription is $75 a year. Www.nysale.com also lists them. For visitors the best way to locate these sales is to go to a favorite designer or store and ask if they hold them. Or try walking around the Garment District, where people often give out flyers announcing them. Bring cash and note you may not be able to try items on. No refunds either.

MARKETS

Unlike European cities, New York has few outstanding markets, although one or two are worth visiting. At the African Market at

markets have become very popular. The most storied is at Union Square (see listing), but there are smaller ones around town in Abingdon Square in the West Village or Tompkins Square in the East Village, for example.

Savvy New Yorkers also shop the thrift stores and consignment shops. Some of the best are: Housing Works, 143 West 17th Street (*tel 212-366-0820*) and at 306 Columbus Avenue (*tel 212-579-7566*), Encore, 1132 Madison Avenue (*tel 212-879-2850*) at 84th Street, and the Salvation Army, 112 4th Avenue (*tel 212-673-2741*).

SoHo

HOW TO GET THERE

🚇 4, 5, 6, or N, R, Q, W

🚌 M1, M5, M6

SoHo has some of the hippest loft-style stores in the city. Concentrate on Mercer, Greene, Wooster, Prince and Spring streets, between West Broadway and Broadway. Many stores are open seven days a week, and the area can be crowded with non-residents on weekends.

Emerge from the subway at Broadway and Prince and you'll find three destination stores. **Dean & DeLuca**, on the southeast corner, is a landmark of New York for food lovers. Displays are gorgeous, a café serves delicious pastries, and top-of-the-line cooking equipment is also for sale.

Across the street on the northwest corner, the **Prada** store was

Check out Eres for the ultimate in swimwear and lingerie

designed by Dutch architect Rem Koolhaas; rows of mannikins wear the latest must-haves of this fashion powerhouse.

On the southwest corner, **Victoria's Secret** sells romantic lingerie and swimwear. Farther down Broadway, **The Puma Store**, at No. 521 sells oodles of walking and running shoes, and at No. 481 the raucous **Alice Underground** is crowded with racks of fashions dating from the 1940s to the 1970s. Nearby, on Broadway, between Houston and Canal, branches of Seattle-based **Eddie Bauer** sell casual wear and the rapidly expanding Spanish chain **Zara**

International, among other brandname stores, sells fashion.

West along Prince Street look for more names. **Phat Farm** (No. 129) has hip-hop wear. Across the street at No. 134, **Nicole Miller** has a celebrity following for her feminine, lively clothing.

On Mercer, look for **Marc Jacobs** at No. 163, the hottest fashion name of the moment, and APC at No. 131, south of Prince, which sells welldesigned Parisian-style basics. **Kate Spade**, the famous bag designer, has a store at Mercer and Broome. At the corner of Mercer and Grand are the precise fashions of **Yohji Yamamoto**.

On Greene Street **Helmut Lang** sells his iconic jeans and other avant-garde fashions at No. 80 and **Kirna Zabete** at No. 96, shows fashions of the best of the current crop of international designers. If you appreciate kitchen and tableware, drop in at **Broadway Panhandler**, at 477 Broome Street between Greene and Wooster Streets, which sells top brands at discount prices, another landmark of a good cook's New York.

Turn off Prince Street and head south down Wooster, and you'll find BCBG by Max Azria at No. 120, **Cynthia Rowley** with witty cutting-edge fashion at No. 112, **Eres** selling beautiful swimwear and lingerie at No. 98, and **Steven Alan**, stocking the latest young designer names at No. 60.

WHERE TO EAT

Cupping Room Café, 359 West Broadway between Broome and Grand (tel 212/925-2898), a fixture of Soho, is casual and offers a menu of soups, burgers, salads and egg dishes.

Prada's store on Broadway is worth a visit just to see the design of the interior

At **Hampton Chutney**, 68 Prince Street between Crosby and Lafayette streets (tel 212/226-9996), tuck into Southern Indian specialties—dosas, pancakes made with lentil flour, filled with both Indian and western ingredients. You can get sandwiches on black, sourdough and other breads, too. (see page 277).

Fanelli's, 94 Prince Street at Mercer (tel 212/226-9412), is reminiscent of the days when SoHo was a hangout of artists. A good option for a burger or a plate of pasta, it also serves draft beer.

NoLita

HOW TO GET THERE

🚇 4, 5, 6

🚌 M1, M6, M21

NoLita stand for *North of Little Italy* and a warren of streets anchored by St. Patrick's Old Cathedral on Mulberry Street (between Prince and Houston), which was New York's original Roman Catholic cathedral. Dedicated in 1815, it was designed by Joseph Magnin, co-architect of City Hall. After a disastrous fire in 1868, the cathedral that stands on Fifth Avenue and 50th Street replaced it as the seat of the archdiocese.

The original congregation was largely Gaelic-speaking, poor Irish immigrants, in those days the St. Patrick's Day parade terminated at the Cathedral. At the turn of the 20th century Italians

Pick up some unique accessories in NoLita's boutiques

formed the majority; today most of the congregation is Spanish-speaking.

Several members of the famous restaurant family, the Swiss Delmonico's, are buried in the crypt.

Pierre Toussaint, a Haitian slave who came to America in 1787, was buried in the cemetery. He attained his freedom, subsequently worked as a hairdresser and donated most of his wealth to various charities— orphanages , seminaries and hospitals.

The area developed as a shopping district when SoHo rents became too expensive for new designers and artists. Here, along Mulberry, Mott and Elizabeth Streets between Kenmare and Houston streets are numerous small storefronts selling the latest fashions and accessories. From the Spring Street Station (6), walk east on Spring to Mulberry Street.

On Mulberry **Language** at No. 238 stocks an eclectic group of advanced designers assembled by owner Ana Abdul, while **Tracy Feith**, at No. 209, is famous for his ready-to-go party outfits. No. 257 used to be the Ravenite Social Club, a favorite John Gott hangout. today, of course, it's a boutique.

Mott Street, between Prince and Spring, shelters **Resurrection Vintage**, one of the city's finest vintage clothing stores, plus **Zero** at No. 225, where Maria Cornejo crafts her own avant-garde line, and **Gas** at No. 238, which displays this French designer's jewelry, made with brilliant colored semi-precious stones. **Sigerson Morrison**, around the corner on Prince Street, sells some ultra-fashionable shoes at No. 28—they're almost as good as Manolos at a fraction of the price. There are also more eye-catching boutiques on Mott between Prince and Houston streets.

Elizabeth Street has a couple of outstanding stores. **Kelly Christy** at No 235 is one of the city's new young milliners, while **Me & Ro** at No. 239 are a duo who make some fun, inspired jewelry, often with Eastern motifs.

Stores in NoLita tend to be one-of-a-kind rather than chains

WHERE TO EAT

Tiny Bread, at 20 Spring Street between Elizabeth and Mott (*tel 212/334-1015*), prepares soups, salads and Italian-inspired dishes. French-inspired **Café Gitane**, 242 Mott Street at Prince Street (*tel 212/334-9552*), serves good coffee plus salads, sandwiches and more substantial plates, such as couscous. Drop in to **Café Habana**, 17 Prince Street at Elizabeth (*tel 212/625-2001*), for some spicy tacos or a hefty Cuban sandwich.

You'll find designer jewelry aplenty in boutiques such as Me & Ro on Elizabeth Street

WHAT TO DO

Fifth Avenue

HOW TO GET THERE

🚇 A, C, E or N, R, Q, W
🚌 M1, M2, M3, M4, M5

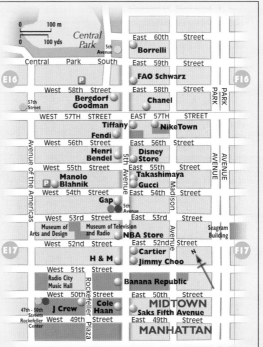

After Madison Avenue, Fifth Avenue is the city's other famous shopping street, at least from 48th to 59th streets. Leave the subway stop at Fifth Avenue and 59th Street around the corner from the Plaza Hotel and stroll down Fifth Avenue.

Across the street looms the old General Motors Building, At the northeast corner of 58th Street **FAO Schwarz** is the city's legendary toy store. Farther down the Avenue are several of the city's great stores—**Bergdorf Goodman** at No. 754, **Henri Bendel** at No. 714, between 55th and 56th streets and Japanese-owned **Takashimaya**, between 54th and 55th streets, with exquisite merchandise in

Go to Gap at No. 680 for practical, good quality casuals

Jimmy Choo shoe

ever yearned for. **Tiffany** and **Cartier** are the two heavy-weight jewelers on the Avenue, the first at No. 727, near 57th Street and the second at No. 653 at 52nd Street. There are others, too—Bulgari, Van Cleef & Arpels, Harry Winston, and Wempe. **Jimmy Choo** displays his fantastic footwear at No. 645, at 51st Street. (**Manolo Blahnik** is just a few blocks away on 54th Street between Fifth and Sixth avenues.) At No. 640 **H&M** rolls out the designer knock-offs for the young shoppers, while at No. 626 **Banana Republic** concentrates its efforts on a more mature, more conservative audience. **Cole Haan** sells soft leather shoes and accessories at No. 620. At No. 626 **Saks Fifth Avenue** culls the best of the world's designers, including many you know and the most promising newcomers.

exquisite settings. Duck off Fifth east along 57th to the French classic, **Chanel** and high-tech **NikeTown**, home of the swoosh. As you progress down the Avenue top-end designer showcases alternate with branches of national chains, making for sharp contrasts. At No. 720 **Fendi** sells its flamboyant, super-expensive accessories, while across the street a block farther south at No. 711, the **Disney Store** peddles character merchandise. **Gucci**, the premiere Italian designer at No. 685, stands across from the **Gap**, and a few blocks south at No. 666 is the **NBA Store**, which stocks everything a basketball fan

Well-cut, casual clothes for men and women at Banana Republic

In Rockefeller Plaza (between 49th and 50th streets), look for **J. Crew**, which caters to the college crowd, recent graduates and wannabes.

WHERE TO EAT

Xando Cosi, 320 Park Avenue at 51st (*tel 212/754-6144*), makes delicious flatbread, perfect for a quick morning pastry or sandwich. There's a branch at 60 East 56th Street between Park and Madison (*tel 212/588-0888*). **Emerald Planet**, on the concourse at 30 Rockefeller Plaza (*tel 212/218-1133*), fills its wraps with every conceivable ingredient.

Madison Avenue

HOW TO GET THERE

🚇 A, C, E
🚌 M1, M2, M3, M4, M5

Madison Avenue purveys to the crème de la crème of international fashion as well as to significant branches of national chains. From the 53rd Street and Fifth Avenue subway station, walk east to Madison Avenue and turn left (north) for a leisurely stroll.

At the northwest corner of 53rd, **Thomas Pink** sells beautifully cut shirts in rainbow hues. Across the street, **Talbots** at No. 525 sells comfortable, reasonably priced fashions to well-heeled women. Farther up the avenue at No. 543, **Lacoste** has complete wardrobes for cruising, golf and tennis. At No. 595 **Coach** sells attractive well-made bags and accessories. **Ann Taylor** caters

Bag from Coach

to the young professional woman at No. 645, while the huge **Crate and Barrel** at No. 650 sells smart tableware, furniture and other items for the home. Italian shoemaker **Tod's** at No. 650 sells some of the most comfortable walking shoes ever made. Quintessential American designer **Calvin Klein**, who has lent his name to every conceivable wardrobe and houseware item, displays his talent at No. 654 at 60th Street. Designer Donna Karan has her **DKNY** store across the street at No. 655. **Barneys** is famous for its windows and for its highly selective range of all that's cutting-edge in international design.

Between 62nd and 72nd Streets, famous names tumble one after the other—**Floris** at No. 703 with its alluring fragrances, **Shanghai Tang** displaying Asian-inspired fashions at No. 714, **Jean-Paul Gaultier** and **Giorgio Armani** (at 759 and 760 at 65th Street).

Farther up the avenue are **Moschino** at No. 803, **Donna Karan** at No. 819, **Dolce & Gabbana** at No. 816, **Penhaligon's** at No. 870 and **Ralph Lauren**, in a spectacularly renovated 19th-century town house at No. 867 at 71st Street—this store is worth seeing just for the architecture. Equally dramatic stores: Donna Karan, and Jean-Paul Gaultier.

WHERE TO EAT

Brasserie, 100 East 53rd Street between Park and Lexington avenues (*tel 212/751-4840*), is a frenzied, streamlined, ultramodern space, where you can linger over lunch or grab a bite at the bar. The broad menu offers crepes, burgers, salads and bistro classics, as well as baguettes for a lighter snack (see page 273). Food is served from early morning to late at night.

Pret à Manger, 400 Park Avenue at 54th Street (*tel 212/207-3725*) is one of the latest European chains to hit town. It delivers freshly made sandwiches and wraps filled with appealing ingredients.

### Map labels

East 72nd Street
Ralph Lauren
East 71st Street
Penhaligon
East 70th Street
Dolce & Gabbana
East 68th Street
Donna Karan
68th Street Hunter College
Moschino
East 67th Street
East 66th Street
Giorgio Armani
Jean-Paul Gaultier
East 65th Street
East 64th Street
Shanghai Tang
FIFTH
East 63rd Street
Floris
AVENUE
East 62nd Street
East 61st Street
Calvin Klein
DKNY
East 60th Street
Ann Taylor
Barneys
Tod's
Central Park South
East 59th Street
59th Street
Crate & Barrel
West 58th St
East 58th Street
Coach
WEST 57TH ST
EAST 57TH STREET
NikeTown
West 56th St
East 56th Street
West 55th St
East 55th Street
Lacoste
West 54th St
East 54th Street
Thomas Pink
Talbots
West 53rd St
East 53rd Street

Central Park
The Pond
East Drive
Park Drive North
Madison Avenue
Park Avenue
Lexington Avenue
5th Avenue

0 100 m
0 100 yds

E15 F15
E16 F16
E17 F17

SHOPPING

From large department stores and opulent designer stores to one-room boutiques, from diamonds to deck chairs and art supplies to zippers, you'll find it all in New York. Manhattan, though lacking the usual American city's bounty of malls, is itself like one huge open-air mall.

BOOKS

APPLAUSE THEATRE AND CINEMA BOOKS
Map 160 C15
211 West 71st Street between Broadway and West End Avenue
Tel 212/496-7511
www.applausebooks.com
Books about Broadway, plays and playwrights, dance and film fill the shelves.
Mon–Sat 10–9, Sun 12–6 72nd Street (1, 2, 3, 9) M5, M7, M104

BARNES & NOBLE
Map 162 E21
Union Square North at 17th Street between Broadway and Park Avenue South
Tel 212/253-0810
www.bn.com
Although not the original of this megachain with branches all over the country, it is large and comfortable enough to be considered the flagship store. The rise of this chain from a small store near New York University into this behemoth is certainly quite a story. Like most branches, this store has a café and comfortable chairs for reading, and sells music, software and magazines as well as books. The main college bookstore is at Fifth Avenue and 18th Street.
Daily 10–10 14th Street/Union Square (L, N, Q, R, W, 4, 5, 6) M1, M2, M3, M6, M7

BORDER'S BOOKS, MUSIC AND CAFÉ
Map 161 F16
461 Park Avenue at 57th Street (northeast corner)
Tel 212/980-6785
www.borders.com
The 'other' chain. It has a slightly more esoteric stock and more personal feel than its competitor Barnes & Noble.

Mon–Fri 9am–10pm, Sat 10–8, Sun 11–8 59th Street (4, 5, 6), 59th Street (N, R, W), M1, M2, M3, M4

HUE-MAN BOOKSTORE
Off map 160 D12
2319 Frederick Douglass Boulevard between 124th and 125th streets
Tel 212/665-7400
www.huemanbookstore.com
This bookstore stocks a large collection of classic and contemporary African-American fiction and nonfiction and holds author readings.
Mon–Sat 10–8, Sun 11–7 125th Street (A, C, B, D) M10

KITCHEN ARTS AND LETTERS
Map 161 F13
1435 Lexington Avenue between 93rd and 94th streets
Tel 212/876-5550
You can find all of the classic cookery writers here—Julia Child, James Beard and M. F. K Fisher—plus a host of others organized by category. Wonderful for rare and historic culinary volumes too.
Mon 1–6, Tue–Fri 10–6.30, Sat 11–6 96th Street (6) M98, M101, M102, M103

THE MYSTERIOUS BOOKSHOP
Map 160 D17
129 West 56th Street between Sixth and Seventh avenues
Tel 212/765-0900
www.mysteriousbookshop.com
An essential stop for the compulsive mystery reader as well as the collector of first editions and rare volumes. Sherlock Holmes, Raymond Chandler, P. D. James and Patricia Highsmith are all here. Recommendations from owner Otto Penzler and staff are surefire winners.
Mon–Sat 11–7 57th Street (N, R, Q, W), 57th Street (F) M5, M6, M7

POSMAN BOOKSELLERS
Map 162 E78
9 Grand Central Terminal (Vanderbilt and 42nd Street)
Tel 212/983-1111
www.posmanbooks.com
A general bookstore which offers a good selection of journals and sharp insightful staff recommendations.
Mon–Fri 8am–9pm, Sat 10–7, Sun 11–6 42nd Street (4, 5, 6) M1, M2, M3, M4, M42

RIZZOLI
Map 161 E16
31 West 57th Street between Fifth and Sixth Avenues (north side)
Tel 212/759-24241
www.rizzoliusa.com
This gorgeous store would make a worthy subject for any topnotch shelter magazine. Excellent stocks of art, design, and fashion books..
Mon–Fri 10–7.30, Sat 10.30–7, Sun 11–7 Fifth Avenue 59th Street (N, R, W), 57th Street (F) M1, M2, M3, M4, M5, M6, M7, M57

ST. MARK'S BOOKSHOP
Map 163 F22
31 Third Avenue between St Mark's Place and Ninth Street on east side
Tel 212/260-7853
www.stmarksbookshop.com
The original counterculture bookstore of the same name thrived on St. Mark's Place in the 1980s and '90s. It offers political and alternative titles plus a good general stock.
Mon–Sat 10am–noon, Sun 11am–noon Astor Place (4, 5, 6) M101, M102, M103

SHAKESPEARE & CO.
Map 163 E22
716 Broadway between West 4th Street and Astor Place
Tel 212/529-1330
www.shakeandco.com
One of the city's few surviving small (five stores) independent book chains. As the name suggests, it leans to literary and small press titles, plus other mid-list books.

Ⓒ Daily 10am–11pm ⓧ Astor Place (4, 5, 6), 8th Street (N, R, W), West 4th Street (A, C, E, F, V, S) 🚌 M1, M5, M6

STRAND BOOKSTORE
Map 162 F21
828 Broadway at 12th Street
Tel 212/473-1452
www.strandbooks.com
New Yorkers come to this extraordinary bookstore to pore over the stacks and tables of publisher's review copies, sold at half price. Although you can browse, it's best to come with a title in mind, and ask the staff where to find it. The management claims to shelve eight miles of books.
Ⓒ Mon–Sat 9.30am–10.30pm, Sun 11–10.30 ⓧ 14th Street/Union Square (L, N, Q, R, W, 4, 5, 6) 🚌 M1, M5, M6

THREE LIVES
Map 162 D22
154 West 10th Street at Waverly Place (southwest corner)
Tel 212/741-2069
www.threelives.com
The proprietor of this store provides super customer service and stocks an amazing variety of titles given the size of the place. A real neighborhood store, and one of the last personal bookstores in the city.
Ⓒ Mon–Tue 12–8, Wed–Sat 11–8.30, Sun 12–7 ⓧ Christopher Street (1, 9), West 4th Street (A, C, E, F, V, S) 🚌 M5, M6, M8, M20

FOOTLIGHT RECORDS
Map 162 F21
113 East 12th Street between Third and Fourth avenues
Tel 212/533-1572
www.footlight.com

You need hours to browse all of the categories at this music lover's store—from Big Band and Comedy to Rock and Spoken Word. There's even an Old and Cool section, which includes Dame Edna doing *Peter and the Wolf*.
Ⓒ Tue–Fri 11–7, Sat 10–6, Sun 12–5, closed Mon ⓧ 14th Street/Union Square (L, N, Q, R, W, 4, 5, 6) 🚌 M1, M2, M103

JAZZ RECORD CENTER
Map 162 D20
236 West 26th Street between Seventh and Eighth avenues (8th floor, room 804)
Tel 212/675-4480
www.jazzrecordcenter.com

This store stocks all the great jazz names and all the jazz labels, plus books, videos and ephemera. It specializes in rare and out-of-print recordings.
Ⓒ Mon–Sat 10–6, closed Sun ⓧ 28th Street (1, 9) 🚌 M20

J & R MUSIC AND COMPUTER WORLD
Map 163 E25
1-34 Park Row (one block south of City Hall).
Tel 212/238-9000
www.jandr.com
This store, opened in 1971, stocks every conceivable brand of audio, video, computer, camera and cell phone, plus software and household appliances. Prices are excellent, and the staff is knowledgeable and helpful. The Music Store has separate stores for jazz, classical and pop.
Ⓒ Mon–Sat 9–7.30, Sun 10.30–6.30 ⓧ Park Place (2, 3), City Hall (N, R, W), Brooklyn Bridge/City Hall (4, 5, 6) 🚌 M9, M15

CHELSEA MARKET
Map 162 D21
75 Ninth Avenue between 15th and 16th streets
Tel 212/243-6005
When you stroll through the first floor of this building, you can put together an entire meal including table decorations. You'll find bakers, fishmongers, florists, wine merchants, and such stores as Buon Italia, which sells superb cheeses, sausages, sauces, oils and other products from Italy. A good place to while away a rainy hour.
Ⓒ Hours vary from store to store ⓧ 14th Street (A, C, E) 🚌 M11, M14,

DEAN & DELUCA
Map 163 F23
560 Broadway at Prince Street
Tel 212/226-6800
www.deandeluca.com
A wonderful place to browse. Absolutely everything here is top quality—pastries, cheeses, meats, fishes, chocolates and packaged products, plus the baskets of handpicked fruits and vegetables. Coffee bar. There are five other branches in Manhattan.
Ⓒ Mon–Sat 9–8, Sun 9–7 ⓧ Prince Street (N, R, W) 🚌 M1, M5, M6

JACQUES TORRES CHOCOLATE
Off map 163 G24
66 Water Street
Brooklyn
Tel 718-875-9772
www.mrchocolate.com
Former Le Cirque dessert chef Jacques Torres is still the best chocolate maker in the city. The gems at his factory/shop and cocoa bar are sublime. The chocolates contain no preservatives, colorings, or additives, and he makes his own peanut butter, marzipan, walnut, praline and pistachio pastes. The pithiviers are heavenly, worth the 20-minute trip to Brooklyn from Midtown.
Ⓒ Mon–Sat 9–7, closed Sun 💰 $43 per pound ($95 per kilo) ⓧ High Street (A, C), York Street (F)

WHAT TO DO

KAM MAN FOODS

Map 163 F24
200 Canal Street at Mott Street
Tel 212/571-0330
This large Chinese food hall overflows with exotic products, from live fish and edible birds' nests to ginseng priced at hundreds of dollars. It also sells inexpensive Asian cookware.
🕐 Daily 9–9 🚇 Canal Street (J, M, Z) 🚌 M1, M103

MORRELL & COMPANY

Map 162 E17
1 Rockefeller Plaza
Tel 212/688-9370
www.morrellwine.com
Morrell, in business since 1947, is the other great wine shop in Manhattan after Sherry-Lehmann. It has its own wine bare and café next door.
🕐 Mon–Sat 10–7, closed Sun 🚇 47th – 50th streets/Rockefeller Center (B, D, F, V) 🚌 M1, M2, M3, M4, M50

SHERRY-LEHMANN

Map 161 E16
679 Madison Avenue at 61st Street
Tel 212/838-7500
www.sherry-lehmann.com

Even if you don't buy, this is a shop to browse. In business since 1934, it has a $10 million inventory of wines from every corner of the world, an attractive old-fashioned interior, and a friendly knowledgeable staff. Besides the premier cru Bordeaux and Burgundies, you'll find ice wines from Canada, Swiss and Lebanese varieties, and selections of sake, port and Madeira. Prices are good, too. Stop by for the Wednesday tasting from 3 to 6.

🕐 Mon–Sat 9–7, closed Sun 🚇 Fifth Avenue/59 Street (N, R, W), 59th Street/Lexington 4, 5, 6) 🚌 M1, M2, M3, M4, M30

UNION SQUARE GREEN MARKET

Map 162 E21
Union Square

Drop by this busy market to get a sense of the agricultural scene outside the city and to participate in a city happening.
🕐 Mon, Wed, Fri from 8am, Sat 🚇 14th Street/Union Square (L, N, Q, R, W, 4, 5, 6) 🚌 M2, M3, M5, M7

ZABAR'S

Map 160 C14
2245 Broadway between West 80th and 81st streets
Tel 212/787-2000
www.zabars.com
The countermen who wield the knives at this culinary landmark are legendary for their skills and their attitude. Look for exquisite smoked salmon and other smoked fish, terrific cheeses and, upstairs, cookware and tableware at great prices.
🕐 Mon–Fri 8–7.30, Sat 8–8, Sun 9–6 🚇 79th Street (1, 9) 🚌 M104

CLOTHING: BASICS AND SPORTSWEAR

APC

Map 163 E23
131 Mercer Street between Prince and Spring streets
Tel 212/966-9685
Atelier Production and Creation doesn't immediately suggest what you find here—good-looking, well-constructed Parisian-style basics. You can buy entire outfits, including

cotton T's, turtlenecks, sweat-shirts, dress shirts, leather jackets and very stylish jeans.
🕐 Mon–Sat 11–7, Sun 12–6 🚇 Prince Street (N, R, W) 🚌 M1, M6

BCBG BY MAX AZRIA

Map 163 E23
#1B, 120 Wooster Street between Prince and Spring streets
Tel 212/625-2723
www.bcbg.com
Bon Chic, Bon Genre brings you great style and fine quality from designer Max Azria. The women's fashions are stylish and sexy, suitable for day or night. Eye-catching accessories too, all at fair prices. Also at 770 Madison Avenue.
🕐 Mon–Sat 11–7, Sun 12–6 🚇 Prince Street (N, R, W) 🚌 M1, M6

BORRELLI

Map 161 E16
16 East 60th Street between Madison and Fifth avenues
Tel 212/644-9610
The ultimate Italian tailor favored by many a male film star offers exquisite shirts as well as a full line of beautiful suits, coats and sweaters, both custom-made and off the rack.
🕐 Mon–Sat 10–6, Sun 12–6 🚇 Fifth Avenue/59th Street (N, R, W) 🚌 M1, M2, M3, M4, M30

DKNY

Map 161 E16
655 Madison Avenue between East 60th and 61st streets
Tel 212/223-3569
www.dkny.com

Donna Karan delivers what New York women want—comfortable clothes that

coordinate easily. Black used to be her favorite color, but the current inventory offers plenty of colorful blouses, dresses, miniskirts, combat jackets and accessories. This striking glass-wrapped boutique opened in 1998. Also at 420 West Broadway and Spring Street.
🕐 Mon–Sat 10–8 (Thu until 9), Sun 10–7 🚇 Fifth Avenue/59th Street (N, R, W) 🚌 M1, M2, M3, M4, M30

EMPORIO ARMANI
Map 162 E21
110 Fifth Avenue at 16th Street
Tel 212/727-3240
www.emporioarmani.com
At this flagship of Giorgio Armani's less expensive line, you get the same great design at a fraction of the price. The store is in a lovely Stanford White building.
🕐 Mon–Sat 11–7 (Thu until 8), Sun 12–6 🚇 14th Street/Union Square (L, N, Q, R, W, 4, 5, 6) 🚌 M2, M3, M5, M7

HOTEL VENUS
Map 163 E23
382 West Broadway between Spring and Broome streets
Tel 212/966-4066
www.patriciafield.com
Patricia Field's latest and largest shop sells camp fashions made of rubber, PVC, leather, spandex, plastic and feathers. Styles range from bustiers and garter belts to micro minis. Not for the faint of heart, accessories, wigs and cosmetics are equally outrageous.
🕐 Daily 11–8 🚇 Spring Street (C, E), Prince Street (N, R, W) 🚌 M1, M6

JEFFREY
Map 162 C21
449 West 14th Street between Ninth and Tenth avenues
Tel 212/206-1272
It took courage for former Barneys shoe buyer Jeffrey Kalinsky to open this giant industrial-chic boutique in the blighted meatpacking district before it became so very hip. Naturally, the shoe department is stellar, chock full of Manolos

and other designer names. You will also find fashions by such leaders as Fendi, Jil Sander, Celine, Prada, Gucci and Dolce & Gabbana. Service is gracious.
🕐 Mon–Fri 10–8 (Thu until 9), Sat 10–7, Sun 12.30–6 🚇 14th Street (A, C, E) Eighth Avenue (L) 🚌 M11, M14

LACOSTE
Map 161 E17
543 Madison Avenue between East 54th and 55th streets
Tel 212/750-8115
www.lacoste.com
The alligator has been around since French tennis champion Rene Lacoste, nicknamed "alligator," sold his first polo shirt in 1933. Today, Christophe Lemaire is re-energizing the company, adding fragrance, home fabrics, eyewear, underwear and footwear to the selection of golf, tennis and yachting sportswear.
🕐 Mon–Sat 10–5 (Thu until 8), Sun 12–5 🚇 Fifth Avenue/53rd Street (E, V), 51st Street/Lexington (6) 🚌 M1, M2, M3, M4

PAUL STUART
Map 162 E18
Madison Avenue at East 45th Street
Tel 212/682-0320
www.paulstuart.com
This pricey haberdashery, which opened in 1938, feels like something from Savile Row. It sells fine-quality suits, Italian dress shirts, Irish argyles and other good-looking traditional fashions for men. Women will find similar—silk cashmere turtlenecks, pinstripe pantsuits and leather jackets.
🕐 Mon–Wed, Fri 8.30–6, Thu 8–7, Sat 9–6, Sun 12–5 🚇 42nd Street (B, D, F, V), 42nd Street/Grand Central (S, 4, 5, 6, 7) 🚌 M1, M2, M3, M4, M5

PHAT FARM
Map 163 E23
129 Prince Street between West Broadway and Wooster
Tel 212/533-7428
www.phatfarm.com
A newer name on the hip-hop fashion scene, this line includes urban safari shirts and

pants, scribble stitch jeans and jackets, plus hoodies, carpenter shorts and leather bomber jackets. Many bear the company logo.
🕐 Mon–Sat 11–7, Sun 12–8 🚇 Prince Street (N, R, W) 🚌 M1, M6

THE PUMA STORE
Map 163 E23
521 Broadway between Spring and Broome streets
Tel 212/334-7861
www.puma.com
The Puma has made a dramatic return to the fashion scene. with shoes in olive and beige, as well as hot colors like canary yellow and lime green.
🕐 Mon–Sat 10–8, Sun 11–7 🚇 Prince Street (N, R, W)

SHANGHAI TANG
Map 161 E16
714 Madison Avenue between East 63rd and 64th streets
Tel 212/888-0111
www.shanghaitang.com
Asian cut and styling inform the youthful fashions at this store. Piping, clasps, and Chinese frog closures detail the women's jackets and blouses fashioned from pagoda prints. Kung fu and Fuji jackets with mandarin collars and knot buttons are favorites for men. Great fabric bags and home accessories too.
🕐 Mon–Sat 10–6, Sun 12–6 🚇 59th Street (4, 5, 6), Lexington Avenue/53rd Street (F) 🚌 M1, M2, M3, M4

STEVEN ALAN
Map 163 E23
60 Wooster Street between Broome and Spring streets
Tel 212/334-6354
Radical fashions for daring fashionistas. The store stocks the very latest international designers—Vanessa Bruno, Alice Roi, Kateyone Adeli.
🕐 Daily 11–7 (Thu and Sun from 12) 🚇 Prince Street (N, R, W) 🚌 M1, M6

THOMAS PINK
Map 161 E17
520 Madison Avenue between East 53rd and 54th streets

WHAT TO DO

Tel 212/838-1928
www.thomaspink.co.uk

This British store sells formal, business casual and casual shirts for men and women in strikingly beautiful colors and patterns, as well as cufflinks—pretty ones for her and elegant ones for him.
🕐 Mon–Fri 10–7 (Thu until 8), Sat 10–6, Sun 12–6 🚇 Fifth Avenue/53rd Street (E, V), 51st Street (6) 🚌 M1, M2, M3, M4

CLOTHING: DESIGNER

ALEXANDER MCQUEEN
Map 162 C21
417 West 14th Street, between Ninth Avenue and Washington Street
Tel 212/645-1797
www.alexandermcqueen.com

The British fashion shock jock, who made his name at Givenchy and is now designing at Gucci, began his career on Savile Row and at theatrical costumer Angels and Bermans. So it's not surprising that he chose to open a boutique in this out-of-the-way neighborhood. His shows are famous for their theatricality and so are his fashions, which are fantastical but beautifully executed with whimsical details.

🕐 Mon–Wed, Fri 10–8 (Thu until 9, Sat until 7), Sun 12.30–6 🚇 14th Street (A, C, E), Eighth Avenue (L) 🚌 M11, M14

CALVIN KLEIN
Map 161 E16
654 Madison Avenue at East 60th Street
Tel 212/292-9000
The beloved Bronx-born American designer who remade the American fashion industry in the 70s has expanded beyond refined sportswear into shoes, accessories and home furnishings. He knows how to cut and he knows how to advertise. The boutique is a paragon of minimalism by British architect John Pawson, worth seeing in its own right.
🕐 Mon–Sat 10 – 6 (Thu until 8), Sun 12–6 🚇 Lexington Avenue/59th Street (N, R, W, 4, 5, 6) 🚌 M1, M2, M3, M4

CHANEL
Map 161 E16
15 East 57th Street between Madison and Fifth avenues
Tel 212/355-5050
www.chanel.com
Coco Chanel, the first woman to succeed in French couture, created the little black dress and added slacks to a woman's wardrobe. Now Karl Lagerfeld designs the styles that will last forever and the accessories (including the quilted purse), shoes and scents to go with them. Two other stores on Madison Avenue sell accessories and jewelry only.
🕐 Mon–Sat 10–6.30 (Thu until 7, Sat until 6), closed Sun 🚇 Lexington Avenue/59th Street (N, R, W, 4, 5, 6) 🚌 M1, M2, M3, M4, M57

CYNTHIA ROWLEY
Map 163 E23
112 Wooster Street between Prince and Spring streets
Tel 212/334-1144
Midwesterner though she may be, Cynthia Rowley has been wowing New Yorkers with her bold shows and her witty original fashions ever since she won the Council of

Fashion Designers New Fashion Talent award in 1995. Look for beaded or embroidered dresses and whimsical accessories.
🕐 Mon–Sat 11–7, Sun 12–6 🚇 Prince Street (N, R, W) 🚌 M1, M6

DOLCE & GABBANA
Map 161 E15
825 Madison Avenue between East 68th and 69th streets
Tel 212/249-4100
www.dolcegabbana.it

Domenico Dolce and Stefano Gabbana have dressed virtually every Hollywood and Broadway star in fashions that exude heat (distressed torn pants and shirts, lots of corset lacing). This spacious and beautiful store is their flagship.
🕐 Mon–Fri 10–7 (Sat until 6), Sun 12–5 🚇 68th Street (6) 🚌 M1, M2, M3, M4

DONNA KARAN
Map 161 E15
819 Madison Avenue between East 68th and 69th streets
Tel 866-244-4700
www.donnakaran.com
In the elegant and dramatic flagship of this very popular American designer, the floating staircase is worthy of Fred Astaire and Ginger Rogers.
🕐 Mon–Sat 10–6 (Thu until 7), closed Sun 🚇 68th Street (6) 🚌 M1, M2, M3, M4

GIORGIO ARMANI
Map 161 E16
760 Madison Avenue at 65th Street
Tel 212/988 9191
www.giorgioarmani.com
The ultimate designer for men and women makes suits in

understated fabrics with superb detailing.

🕐 Mon–Sat 10–6 (Thu until 7), closed Sun 🚇 68th Street (6) 🚌 M1, M2, M3, M4

GUCCI
Map 161 E17
685 Fifth Avenue at East 54th Street
Tel 212/826-2600
840 Madison Avenue between 69th and 70th streets
Tel 212/717-2619
www.gucci.com
Tom Ford has maintained the style and detailing implicit in the Gucci name as well as adding his own influence. Inspired by Calvin Klein and Ralph Lauren, he is expanding the brand.
🕐 Mon–Fri 10–6.30 (Sat until 7), Sun 12–6 🚇 Fifth Avenue/53rd Street (E, V), 68th Street (6) 🚌 M1, M2, M3, M4

HELMUT LANG
Map 163 E23
80 Greene Street between Spring and Broome streets
Tel 212/925-7214
www.helmutlang.com
Austrian Helmut Lang crafts clothes that are lean, spare and beautifully cut, whether it's a gorgeous cashmere coat with a sheepskin lining, biker- and surfer-style garments, or skintight leggings in an electric hue. His entire line is sold here, including the iconic jeans.
🕐 Mon–Sat 11–7, Sun 12–6 🚇 Prince Street (N, R, W) 🚌 M1, M6

ISSEY MIYAKE
Map 163 E24
119 Hudson Street at North Moore

Tel 212/226-0100
www.isseymiyake.com

This TriBeCa store, designed by Frank Gehry and his protégé Gordon Kipping, stocks all of Miyake's lines including the A-POC ("a piece of cloth"), each item created from a seamless cloth. A Gehry metallic sculpture defines the loft space.
🕐 Mon–Sat 11–7, Sun 12–6 🚇 Franklin Street (1, 9) 🚌 M20

JEAN-PAUL GAULTIER
Map 161 E16
759 Madison Avenue between East 65th and 66th streets
Tel 212 249-0235
www.jeanpaulgaultier.com

The first US store designed by Philippe Starck is luxurious indeed, with its taffeta-covered walls and clothing racks with crystal fixtures. The fashions are exciting, dramatic, beautifully draped and always au courant.
🕐 Mon–Sat 10–6 (Thu and Sat from 11), closed Sun 🚇 68th Street (6) 🚌 M1, M2, M3, M4

MARC JACOBS
Map 163 E23
163 Mercer Street between Houston and

Prince streets
Tel 212/343-1490
www.marcjacobs.com
Marc Jacobs is having his moment as the city's hottest designer, turning out luxurious, updated vintage designs in soft, feminine colors. He also has two stores on Bleecker Street, one selling strictly accessories (retro flats plus), the other his highly successful, less expensive Marc by Marc Jacobs line, which includes his must-have cargo pants.
🕐 Mon–Sat 11–7, Sun 12–6 🚇 Prince Street (N, R, W) 🚌 M1, M6

MOSCHINO
Map 161 E15
803 Madison Avenue between East 67th and 68th streets
Tel 212/639-9600
www.moschino.it

Style wizard Moschino creates flowing, Japanese-inspired silhouettes using rich and vivid prints, diaphanous materials, or ethnic fabrics. This store, which opened in 1996, also stocks his cheap and chic line.
🕐 Mon–Sat 10–6, closed Sun 🚇 68th Street (6) 🚌 M1, M2, M3, M4

NICOLE MILLER
Map 163 E23
134 Prince Street between Wooster Street and West Broadway
Tel 212/343-1362
www.nicolemiller.com
Nicole Miller's innovative, sexy and very wearable fashions attract a number of celebrity clients. She makes cowl-neck halter tops, distressed jersey tunics, bags and shoes, and simple evening gowns.

WHAT TO DO

Ⓖ Mon–Sat 11–7, Sun 12–6 🚇 Prince Street (N, R, W) 🚌 M1, M6

PRADA
Map 163 E23
575 Broadway at Prince Street
Tel 212/334-8888
www.prada.com

Dutch architect Rem Koolhaas designed this $40-million must-see store. The scooped-out ground floor functions as a stepped display area and performance space. Even the dressing rooms are very high-tech, and of the designer's five stores in Manhattan, this is the one to see.
Ⓖ Mon–Sat 11–7, Sun 12–6 🚇 Prince Street (N, R, W) 🚌 M1, M6

RALPH LAUREN
Map 161 E15
867 Madison Avenue between East 71st and 72nd streets
Tel 212/606-2100
www.polo.com

Bronx native Ralph Lauren sells his distinguished cowboy and English country heritage looks in the historic Rhinelander Mansion, one of a handful of turn-of-the-20th-century great houses in Manhattan,

luxuriously renovated to gleaming splendor from its amazing hand-carved staircase to its Baccarat chandeliers and 19th-century oil paintings.
Ⓖ Mon–Sat 10–6 (Thu until 8), closed Sun 🚇 68th Street (6) 🚌 M1, M2, M3, M4

STELLA MCCARTNEY
Map 162 C21
429 West 14th Street between Ninth Avenue and Washington Street
Tel 212/255-1556
www.stellamccartney.com
Since graduating from London's Central St. Martin's College of Art and Design in 1995, Stella McCartney began her rise to stardom at Chloe and continues in partnership with Gucci. In this store, which opened in 2002, fitting rooms are lined with marquetry or hand-printed fabric. Her full line of well-tailored but nicely draped fashions is for sale.
Ⓖ Mon–Sat 11–7, Sun 12–6 🚇 14th Street (A, C, E), Eighth Avenue (L) 🚌 M11, M14

YOHJI YAMAMOTO
Map 163 E23
103 Grand Street at Mercer Street
Tel 212/966-9066
www.YohjiYamamoto.co.jp
Impeccable design and draping informs the fashions, often black and white, of this serene designer. The store itself is an aesthetic gem.
Ⓖ Mon–Sat 11–7, Sun 12–6 🚇 Canal Street (A, C, E, J, M, N, Q, R, W, Z, 6) 🚌 M1, M6

CLOTHING: TRENDY BOUTIQUES

ALIFE RIVINGTON CLUB (SHOES)
Map 163 G23
158 Rivington Street between Clinton and Suffolk
Tel 212/375-8128
The unmarked steel door opens onto a space paneled in cherry wood, where sneakers are treated as high fashion, and you can find limited-edition American, European and Japanese lines in fantastic colors.

Ⓖ Tue–Sun 12–7, closed Mon
🚇 Delancey/Essex (F, J, M, Z) 🚌 M9

FORWARD
Map 163 G23
72 Orchard Street between Broome and Grand streets
Tel 646-264-3233
www.forwardnyc.com
This fashion incubator, supported by the neighborhood business association, regularly selects six emerging designers to create the merchandise and run the store. The stock changes constantly, so you might find dresses, jewelry, handbags, hats or lingerie.
Ⓖ Daily 12–7 🚇 Delancey/Essex (F, J, M, Z) 🚌 M9, M15

JUSSARA LEE
Map 162 C21
11 Little West 12th Street between Washington and Ninth Avenue
Tel 212/242-4128
www.caipirinha.com/jussara
This Korean-Brazilian designer's clothes have an edge but are eminently wearable. Coats, dresses, tops, pants, skirts, and bathing suits are elegantly displayed here and at her flagship store.
Ⓖ Mon–Sat 11–7, Sun 12–7 🚇 14th Street (A, C, E) 🚌 M11, M14

KIRNA ZABETE
Map 163 E23
96 Greene Street between Prince and Spring streets
Tel 212/941-9656
www.kirnazabete.com

Beth Buccini and Sarah Hailes assemble their choice of the avant-garde designers at this pretty store. You might find mohair and lace cardigans, sweatshirts by Matthew Williamson, Cacharel T's, frayed and patchwork pieces by Jessica Ogden, plus such other hard-to-find designers as Clements Riberro and Hussein Chalayan. Accessories, too.

🕐 Mon–Sat 11–7, Sun 12–6 🚇 Prince Street (N, R, W) 🚌 M1, M6

LANGUAGE

Map 163 F23

238 Mulberry Street between Prince and Spring streets

Tel 212/431 5566

www.language-nyc.com

Owner Ana Abdul stocks an eclectic group of clothes from advanced designers like Sophia Kokosalaki and Alice Lee, plus Share Spirit jeans, Koi cashmeres and accessories from D & G or Hermés. She also creates her own line.

🕐 Mon–Sat 11–7 (Thu until 8), Sun 12–6 🚇 Broadway-Lafayette (F, V, S) 🚌 M1

LUCY BARNES

Map 162 D22

117 Perry Street between Hudson and Greenwich streets

Tel 212/647-0149

Edinburgh-born Lucy Barnes has been collecting vintage materials for years and uses them beautifully either whole or in part to make her nostalgic, feminine clothes. The designs and colors are stunning and often feature gorgeous embroidery, beading, and patchwork. Prices are excellent considering the quality of the materials and the beauty of the designs.

🕐 Daily 11.30–7.30 🚇 Christopher Street (1/9), 14th Street (A, C, E) 🚌 M20

MARTIN

Map 163 F22

206 East 6th Street between Second and Third avenues

Tel 212/358-0011

Greek togas seem to have inspired designer Anne Johnston's clothes, whether soft Ts or hip street wear.

🕐 Tue–Sun 1–7, closed Mon 🚇 Astor Place (6) 🚌 M15, M103

MARY ADAMS THE DRESS

Map 163 G23

138 Ludlow Street between Rivington and Stanton streets

Tel 212/473-0237

www.maryadamsthedress.com

Neighborhood pioneer Mary Adams, who moved in during the early 1980s, sells beautifully light evening dresses in pastel hues.

🕐 Wed–Sat 1–6, Sun 1–5, closed Mon–Tue 🚇 Delancey/Essex (F, J, M, Z) 🚌 M9, M15

SHELLY STEFFEE

Map 162 D21

34 Gansevoort Street between Hudson and Ninth Avenue

Tel 917-408-0408

The sign outside reads Design Studio and that's how the clothes are displayed, in a museum-like fashion. The designs are sexy and fun. Capri pants have drawstrings at waist and calf; safari-style shirts are made from sheer material; and then there are more tailored separates.

🕐 Tue–Sat 12–10, Sun 12–6, closed Mon 🚇 14th Street (A, C, E) 🚌 M11, M14

37=1

Map 163 F23

37 Crosby Street between Grand and Broome streets

Tel 212/226-0067

Jean Yu makes dresses, lingerie and separates of the richest of silks. The garter belts are to die for. Prices are up there.

🕐 Tue–Sun 12–6, closed Mon 🚇 Canal Street (N, R) 🚌 M1, M6

TRACY FEITH

Map 163 F23

209 Mulberry Street between Spring and Kenmare streets

Tel 212 925-6544

Surf dude-turned-designer Tracy Feith dresses women in striking, playful, ready-to-party outfits. There's a gypsy glamour or ready-for-vacation air to all the clothes.

🕐 Daily 11–7 🚇 Spring Street (6), Broadway-Lafayette (F, V, S) 🚌 M1, M21

ZERO

Map 163 F23

225 Mott Street between Prince and Spring streets

Tel 212/925-3849

In this store you'll see capes, jackets and coats with an avant-garde look that Maria Cornejo sews in the back.

🕐 Mon–Fri 12.30–7.30, Sat–Sun 12.30–6.30 🚇 Prince Street (N, R) 🚌 M1, M6

ALICE UNDERGROUND

Map 163 E23

481 Broadway between Grand and Broome streets

Tel 212/431-9067

It takes patience to rake through the stuff displayed at this large vintage emporium. The fashions travel from the 40s to the 70s and include accessories as well as every kind of garment, plus shoes.

🕐 Daily 11–7.30 🚇 Prince Street (N, R), Canal Street (N, R) 🚌 M1, M6

DECOLLAGE

Map 162 D21

23 Eighth Avenue between 12th and Jane streets

Tel 212/352-3338

It's worth a visit just to look at the new and vintage clothing on display in this wonderful fashion-as-art venue in a town house.

🕐 Mon–Fri 10–5, Sat 12–6 (spring–fall only) 🚇 14th Street (A, C, E) 🚌 M20

FILTH MART

Map 163 G21

531 East 13th Street between Avenues A and B

Tel 212/387-0650

Clubbers come here to get their rhinestone glitter. There's plenty of 60s, 70s and 80s retro fashion to pick through, and prices are good.

🕐 Sun–Tue 1–7, Wed–Sat 1–8 🚇 14th Street/Union Square (L, N, Q, R, W, 4, 5, 6), First Avenue (L) 🚌 M9, M14, M15

WHAT TO DO

FOLEY & CORINNA
Map 163 G23
108 Stanton Street between Ludlow and Essex streets
Tel 212/529-2338
www.foleyandcorinna.com
Fashionistas and celebrities flock here to see the famous silk and vintage lace butterfly blouses, mohair and cashmere knit coats and other romantic hippie-chic fashions created by Dana Foley, who began her career at a city flea market. Partner Anna Corinna selects the vintage clothing and accessories.
🕐 Mon–Fri 1–8, Sat–Sun 12–8
🚇 Delancey/Essex (F, J, M, Z)
🚌 M15, M21

99X
Map 163 F21
84 East 10th Street between Third and Fourth avenues
Tel 212/460-8599
www.99xny.com
Most of the 60s to 80s fashions here come from the United Kingdom. Customers can pick up mod and rocker outfits, as well as punk stuff and even some slender Teddy Boy ties and pork-pie hats.
🕐 Mon–Sat 12–8, Sun 12–7 🚇 Astor Place (6) 🚌 M1, M103, M8

RESURRECTION VINTAGE
Map 163 F23
217 Mott Street between Spring and Prince streets
Tel 212/625-1374
www.resurrectionvintage.com

This store has great vintage designer clothes—Pucci slips, pieces by Miyake and Vivienne Westwood, and 80s

skateboard clothes from Alva, Thrasher and other brands. The owners also offer their own line of skirts and tops.
🕐 Mon–Sat 11–7, Sun 12–7
🚇 Broadway-Lafayette (F, V, S) 🚌 M1, M21, M103

SCREAMING MIMI'S
Map 163 F22
382 Lafayette Street between Great Jones and 4th streets
Tel 212/677-6464
www.screamingmimis.com

The stock at this old-timer ranges from 40s to 80s. It's well displayed and in good condition. Cool and hip still, even though "Sex and the City" made it famous beyond a select circle of cognoscenti.
🕐 Mon–Sat 12–8, Sun 1–7
🚇 Broadway-Lafayette (F, V, S)
🚌 M1, M103

YONA LEE
Map 163 G22
412 East 9th Street between First Avenue and Avenue A
Tel 212/253-2121
Good vintage fashions, mostly from the 60s and 70s, are carefully displayed here.
🕐 Daily 12–8 🚇 Astor Place (6)
🚌 M8, M9, M14, M15

SHOES AND ACCESSORIES
CARTIER
Map 161 E17
653 Fifth Avenue between 51st and 52nd streets
Tel 212/753-0111
www.cartier.com
Cartier opened in Paris in 1847 and has been famous for beautiful design ever since, creating such signature pieces

as the three-band ring and the Portico Mystery Clock. Richard Burton went to Cartier for the diamond for Elizabeth Taylor. Today, it sells beautiful jewelry and watches, plus leather goods and other luxuries.
🕐 Mon–Sat 10–5.30, closed Sun
🚇 Fifth Avenue/53rd Street (E, V)
🚌 M1, M2, M3, M4, M50

COACH
Map 161 E16
595 Madison Avenue between East 57th and 58th streets
Tel 212/754-0041
www.coach.com

This successful leather purveyor has a line of classics as well as seasonal collections. There are seven other branches in the city.
🕐 Mon–Sat 10–8, Sun 11–6 🚇 Fifth Avenue/59th Street (N, R, W), 59th Street (4, 5, 6) 🚌 M1, M2, M3, M4, M57

COLE HAAN
Map 161 E17
620 Fifth Avenue at 50th Street
Tel 212/765-9747
www.colehaan.com
Nike now owns this maker of traditional, good-quality shoes and is jazzing it up with new ideas, colors, and styles.
🕐 Mon–Sat 10–7 (Thu until 8), Sun 12–6 🚇 47th–50th streets/ Rockefeller Center (B, D, F, V) 🚌 M1, M2, M3, M4

CONSTANCA BASTO
Map 162 D22
573 Hudson Street between Bank and 11th streets
Tel 212/645-3233
www.constancabasto.com
This Brazilian shoe designer has a striking orange candy-

stripe boutique studded with gorgeous stilettos decorated with jewels, plus other beguiling footwear.
🕐 Tue–Sat 11–6, Sun 12–6 🚇 14th Street (A, C, E) 🚌 M20

DOYLE AND DOYLE
Map 163 G22
189 Orchard Street between Houston and Stanton
Tel 212/677 9991
Doyle and Doyle offers some very alluring, historic estate jewelry in prime condition.
🕐 Tue–Sun 1–7, closed Mon 🚇 Lower East Side/Second Avenue (F, V) 🚌 M9, M15

ERES
Map 163 E23
98 Wooster Street between Spring and Prince streets
Tel 212/431-7300
www.eresparis.com
In 1968 Eres opened in Paris on Place Madeleine selling the ultimate swimwear— bikinis, tanks and other one-pieces. Today it issues a cruise collection in November and a summer collection in January. Equally beautiful and flattering lingerie is offered as well now.
🕐 Mon–Sat 11–7, Sun 12–5 🚇 Prince Street N, R) 🚌 M1, M6

EUGENIA KIM
Map 163 G22
203 East 4th Street between Avenues A and B
Tel 212/673-9787
www.eugeniakim.com
Former *Allure* editor Kim fell into her career when she fashioned a hand-feathered cloche for herself, went shopping, and attracted attention from shop owners. Her hats— many with a retro look—are dashing, flamboyant, beautifully crafted, and expensive, made of straw and cotton in cowboy, fedora, caps and other shapes, and trimmed with feathers, leather and ribbons. On the wild side.
🕐 Mon–Sat 11–8, Sun 1–7 🚇 Astor Place (6) 🚌 M9, M14

EYE CANDY
Map 163 F22
329 Lafayette Street between Bleecker and Houston streets
Tel 212/343-4275
www.eyecandystore.com

The bags, costume jewelry, sunglasses here are the stuff of whimsical dreams.
🕐 Daily 12–8 🚇 Broadway-Lafayette (F, V, S) 🚌 M1, M5, M6, M21

PK FENDI
Map 161 E17
720 Fifth Avenue between 56th and 57th streets
Tel 212/767-0100
www.fendi.it.
The flashy Fendi label conveys the message of money and glitz, and women wear Fendi for that reason. This flagship store sells the full line: handbags, shoes, accessories and furs.
🕐 Mon–Sat 10–6 (Thu until 7), Sun 12–5 🚇 Fifth Avenue/53rd Street (E, V) 🚌 M1, M2, M3, M4, M57

GAS
Map 163 F23
238 Mott Street between Prince and Spring streets
Tel 212/334-7290
This outpost of the St. Tropez and Paris jeweler has lovely inspirational handmade jewelry made with semi-precious stones.
🕐 Daily 12–7 🚇 Broadway-Lafayette (F, V, S) 🚌 M1, M103

I, CLAUDIA
Map 163 G23
168 Ludlow Street between Houston and Stanton streets
Tel 212/533-4722

What Kelly Christy is to hats Claudia Porcelli is to shoes. She custom-makes them for the general shopper and for the stage. Prices start at $200.
🕐 Tue, Thu and Sat 2–7 🚇 Lower East Side/Second Avenue (F, V) 🚌 M9, M14, M15

JIMMY CHOO
Map 161 E16
716 Madison Avenue, between East 63rd and 64th Streets (west side)
Tel 212/759-7078
645 Fifth Avenue between 51st and 52nd streets
Tel 212/593-0800)
www.jimmychoo.com

Velvet-quilted sofas and satin-covered chairs set the tone at this flagship store selling the exquisite shoes and purses by this legendary Malaysian designer, who cobbled for Princess Diana. His line offers a variety of styles from pony boots and evening slides to kitten heels, stilettos and sandals made in all kinds of materials and fabrics, which are decorated with beads, crystals, embroidery, or just beautifully colored.
🕐 Mon–Sat 10–7 (Thu until 8), Sun 12–6 🚇 59th Street (4, 5, 6) or 68th Street (6) 🚌 M1, M2, M3, M4

KATE SPADE
Map 163 E23
454 Broome Street at Mercer Street
Tel 212/274-1991
www.katespade.com
The former *Mademoiselle* accessories editor, Kate started out in 1993, making handbags that emphasized utility, color and fabric. She opened her

first store in 1996, and now sells a full line of exquisite nylon, leather and fabric bags, plus wallets, luggage, stationery, eyeglasses, fragrance and beauty products.

⏰ Mon–Sat 11–7, Sun 12–6 🚇 Prince Street (N, R, W) 🚌 M1, M6

KELLY CHRISTY
Map 163 F23
235 Elizabeth Street between Houston and Prince streets
Tel 212/965-0686
www.kellychristyhats.com
Kelly Christy makes eye-catching hats in all kinds of fabrics and in every conceivable style, from fedora to beret. Prices vary according to style and fabric and start at about $200.

⏰ Tue–Sat 12–7, Sun 12–6, closed Mon 🚇 Broadway-Lafayette (F, V, S) 🚌 M21, M103

KENNETH COLE
Map 160 D14
353 Columbus Avenue between West 76th and 77th streets
Tel 212/873-2061
www.kennethcole.com
Good, clean styling and quality for the money have made Kenneth Cole a major fashion player. He started with urban shoes, but has expanded to include such fashionable footwear as satin pumps with ankle straps, plus sportswear, handbags, fragrance and other accessories.

⏰ Open Mon–Fri 10–8, Sat–Sun 11–7 🚇 79th Street (1, 9) 🚌 M7, M11

LA PETITE COQUETTE
Map 163 E22
51 University Place between 9th and 10th streets
Tel 212/473-2478
www.lapetitecoquette
This may well be the best lingerie store in the city. In a boudoir setting, it sells swimwear and sexy top-of-the-line, multi-hued lingerie (camisoles, corsets, garter belts and other scanties).

⏰ Mon–Fri 11–7 (Thu until 8), Sun 12–6 🚇 8th Street (N, R, W) 🚌 M1, M3, M6

LE SPORTSAC
Map 163 E23
176 Spring Street between West Broadway and Thompson Street
Tel 212/625-2626
www.lesportsac.com
Fold-in-a-pouch bags made of rip-stop parachute nylon made this name famous after they were introduced in 1974. Today the brand continues to deliver practical, affordable totes, messenger bags and backpacks, now in fun prints and patterns including batik. A couture line features such materials as sheared mink and fox.

⏰ Mon–Sat 11–7, Sun 12–6 🚇 Spring Street (C, E) 🚌 M6

MANOLO BLAHNIK
Map 161 E17
31 West 54th Street between Fifth and Sixth avenues
Tel 212/582-3007
The sexy, strappy sandals, plain stiletto pumps, sling backs and mules are beloved of the fashion and celebrity crowd, who pay $450 and up for these most glamorous accessories. They're fashioned from pony skin and other elegant materials in a brilliant palette.

⏰ Mon–Fri 10.30–6, Sat 10.30–5.30, closed Sun 🚇 Fifth Avenue/53rd Street (E, V) 🚌 M5, M6, M7

ME & RO
Map 163 F23
239 Elizabeth Street between Houston and Prince streets
Tel 917-237-9215
www.meandrojewelry.com

Michelle Quan and Robin Renzi are friends. Canadian Michelle trained at Parsons School of Design and worked as a fashion model, while Robin has been making jewelry since high school. Their collection uses precious and semi-precious stones in stackable rings, bangles, necklaces and other pieces with a lotus petal motif or Sanskrit and Tibetan calligraphy.

⏰ Mon–Sat 11–7, Sun 12–6 🚇 Broadway-Lafayette (F, V, S) 🚌 M21, M03

OTTO TOOTSI PLOHOUND
Map 162 E20
137 Fifth Avenue between 20th and 21st streets
Tel 212/460-8650
Who knows what the name refers to? But shoes are very cool and stylish. They're from European and American designers, plus the own-design Otto line.

⏰ Mon–Fri 11.30–7.30, Sat 11–8, Sun 12-7 🚇 23rd Street (N, R, W) 🚌 M2, M3, M5

SIGERSON MORRISON
Map 163 F23
28 Prince Street between Mott and Elizabeth streets
Tel 212/219-3893
www.sigersonmorrison.com
The shoes from this exciting designer are not as pricey as Manolos but are stunning nonetheless. Colors range across the spectrum, from red to lavender, and materials encompass everything conceivable—pony skin, suede, satin and metallic leather. Styles range from sling-back stilettos to flats and boots.

⏰ Mon–Sat 11–7, Sun 12–6 🚇 Broadway-Lafayette (F, V, S), Prince Street (N, R, W) 🚌 M21, M103

SUAREZ HANDBAGS
Map 161 E17
450 Park Avenue at East 56th Street
Tel 212/753-3758
Here, copies of designer handbags sell for a fraction of the price.

⏰ Mon–Sat 10–6, closed Sun 🚇 59th Street (4, 5, 6) 🚌 M1, M2, M3, M4

TIFFANY
Map 161 E17
Fifth Avenue at 57th Street
Tel 212/755-8000
www.tiffany.com

Tiffany is famous for its superb silver and crystal and its beautiful design (think Jean Schlumberger, Paloma Picasso and Elsa Peretti). Although some items are astronomically priced, it also displays more moderately priced luxury gifts—embossed note cards ($40 for 15) and singular silver pieces. All are packaged in the signature turquoise blue box tied with red or white ribbon, which was introduced when the store opened in 1837.
⏰ Mon–Fri 10–7, Sat 10–6, Sun 12–5
🚇 Fifth Avenue/59th Street (N, R, W), 57th Street (F) 🚌 M1, M2, M3, M4

TOD'S
Map 161 E16
650 Madison Avenue between East 59th and 60th streets
Tel 212/644-5945
www.tods.com
This Italian designer makes ultra-comfortable shoes for walking and driving, plus boots with equestrian styling. They are relatively expensive, but long lasting.
⏰ Mon–Sat 10–6 (Thu until 7), Sun 12–5 🚇 59th Street/Fifth Avenue (N, R, W) 🚌 M1, M2, M3, M4

HEALTH AND BEAUTY
CASWELL-MASSEY
Map 161 F17
518 Lexington Avenue at East 48th Street
Tel 212/755-2254
www.caswell-massey.com
This apothecary, founded in

1752, provided perfume to George Washington and Dolly Madison and continues to produce a range of delicious floral scents such as freesia, lilac, rose geranium and lily of the valley. You can find rose-water and glycerin soap, sandalwood massage oil and appealing gift sets.
⏰ Mon–Fri 8–7, Sat 10–6, Sun 12–5
🚇 51st Street (6) 🚌 M98, M101, M102, M103

FLORIS
Map 161 E16
703 Madison Avenue between East 62nd and 63rd streets
Tel 212/935-9100
www.florislondon.com
Floris has been refining the art of making fragrance since 1730, when it opened on London's Jermyn Street. It's said that Beau Brummell (and more recently James Bond) loved No. 89, named after the store's London address. Today's scents are for men, women and the home (grapefruit, rosemary and seasonal spice); men's shaving and grooming accessories are also available.
⏰ Mon–Sat 10–6 (Thu until 7), Sun 12–5 🚇 5th Avenue/59th Street (N, R, W), 59th Street (4, 5, 6) 🚌 M1, M2, M3, M4

KIEHL'S
Map 163 F21
109 Third Avenue between East 13th and 14th streets
Tel 212/677-3171
www.kiehls.com
Founded in 1851 and owned by L'Oréal since 2000, Kiehl's has been selling homeopathic remedies and natural cosmetics and treatment products since its inception. Natural herbal-based moisturizers, cleansers, shampoos, eye creams, masques, facial scrubs, talc, lipsticks and toners line the shelves.
⏰ Mon–Fri 10–6.30 (Thu until 7.30), Sat 10–6 🚇 14th Street/Union Square (L, N, Q, R, W, 4, 5, 6), Third Avenue (L) 🚌 M101, M102, M103

L'OCCITANE
Map 162 E22
247 Bleecker Street between Sixth and Seventh avenues
Tel 212/367-8428
www.loccitane.com
The great range of beauty and body products sold here incorporates almond, honey, apricot, bergamot and other natural ingredients. The most irresistible product has to be shea butter hand cream, made from the shea, fruit of a tree that grows in Burkina Faso.
⏰ Mon–Fri 11–8, Sat 10–8, Sun 11–7
🚇 West 4th Street (A, C, E, F, V, S), Christopher Street (1, 9) 🚌 M1, M5, M6

PENHALIGON'S
Map 161 E15
870 Madison Avenue between 70th and 71st streets
Tel 212/249-1771
www.penhaligons.com
Classic British style reigns at this wood-paneled emporium, the American outpost of the famous British perfumer, established in 1841. The seductive scents are handmade and have an almost cult following.
⏰ Mon–Sat 10–6, Sun 12–5 🚇 68th Street (6) 🚌 M1, M2, M3, M4

SEPHORA
Map 162 D18
1500 Broadway between 43rd and 44th streets
Tel 212/944-6789
www.sephora.com
If you have ever been intimidated, or overwhelmed by the typical make-up counter, then you'll appreciate Sephora. This European chain, which arrived in 1998, has an efficient self-service orientation and sells more than 200 brands of beauty products, from Adrienne Vittadini to Philosophy. There's a scent-testing bar, and treatments are arranged by skin type.
⏰ Daily 10am–midnight 🚇 Fifth Avenue/53rd Street (E, V) 🚌 M1, M2, M3, M4

WHAT TO DO

HOME FURNISHINGS

ABC CARPET AND HOME
Map 162 E21
888 Broadway between 18th and 20th streets
Tel 212/473-3000
www.abchome.com
Fabrics, furnishings and interior design artifacts from around the world are artfully displayed on 10 floors. Provençal armoires, Kashmiri silks, gorgeously dressed beds and Venetian chandeliers keep company with rugs from India, Nepal, Pakistan and China.
🚇 Mon–Fri 10–8, Sat 10–7, Sun 11–6.30
🚊 23rd Street (N, R, W) 🚌 M6, M7

BROADWAY PANHANDLER
Map 163 E23
477 Broome Street between Greene and Wooster streets
Tel 212/66 3434
www.broadwaypanhandler.com

Originally selling to professional kitchens, Broadway Panhandler now offers the very best cookware, tools, appliances and gadgets to domestic cooks at decent prices. There are hundreds of different types of pots, pans and skillets available—about 10,000 items in all. Special demonstrations bring in the likes of Jean-Georges Vongerichten, Eric Ripert and Jacques Pépin.
🚇 Mon–Fri 10.30–7, Sat 11–7, Sun 11–6
🚊 Prince Street (N, R, W) 🚌 M1, M6

DEPARTMENT AND SPECIALTY STORES

BARNEYS
Map 161 E16
660 Madison Avenue between East 60th and 61st streets

Tel 212/826-8900, warehouse 212/450-8400
www.barneys.com

Barneys stocks only what's newest and hippest, so you'll find designers whose names everyone knows, as well as those known only to cognoscenti of the fashion scene—say, Proenza Schouler, Behnaz Sarafpour and Tess Giberson. The windows always make a statement, and people flock to the sales at the warehouse on 17th Street, between Seventh and Eighth avenues, where prices are slashed.
🚇 Mon–Fri 10–8, Sat 10–7, Sun 11–6
🚊 Fifth Avenue/59th Street (N, R, W), 59th Street (4, 5, 6) 🚌 M30

BERGDORF GOODMAN
Map 161 E16
754 Fifth Avenue between 57th and 58th streets
Tel 212/753-7300

Some shoppers actually dress up to visit this luxurious store, which showcases classics and new talent. The store is beautifully laid out, the shoe department marvelous and the designer boutiques extraordinary. You'll find great

accessories throughout. The men's store is a just across the street.
🚇 Mon–Sat 10–7 (Thu until 8), Sun 12–6 🚊 Fifth Avenue/59th Street (N, R, W) 🚌 M5, M30, M57

BLOOMINGDALE'S
Map 161 F16
Lexington Avenue at East 59th Street
Tel 212/705-2000
www.bloomingdales.com

Bloomingdale's, opened in 1879, is one of the most venerable names in Manhattan yet keeps up with every trend. It's an icon among its fans, and tourists and locals alike buy logo items emblazoned with the store's name or sobriquet, "Bloomie's." On weekends locals come to schmooze.
🚇 Mon–Fri 10–8.30, Sat 10–7, Sun 11–7
🚊 59th Street/Lexington (4, 5, 6) 🚌 M98, M101, M102, M103

HENRI BENDEL
Map 161 E17
714 Fifth Avenue at 56th Street
Tel 212/247-1100
www.henribendel.com
Henri Bendel is synonymous with sophistication and elegance. The inventory and the clientele are similar to Bergdorf's, but the displays reveal the store's élan. If you want to see works by the hottest new designers, check out the New Creators boutique, which features such names as Michael Soheil, Peter Som, Alice Roi, Zac Posen and Behnaz Sarafpour.
🚇 Mon–Sat 10–7 🚊 Fifth Avenue/59th Street (N, R, W), Fifth Avenue/53rd Street (E, V) 🚌 M5, M30, M57

LORD & TAYLOR
Map 162 E18
424 Fifth Avenue between 38th and 39th streets
Tel 212/391-3344.
www.maycompany.com
This classic, established in 1826, targets traditional middle-aged shoppers from Greenwich matrons to young working women. The Christmas windows are a must-see.
◑ Mon–Tue 10–7, Wed–Fri 10–8.30, Sat 10–7, Sun 11–7 ▣ 42nd Street (B, D, F, V) ▣ M2, M3, M5

MACY'S
Map 162 D19
Herald Square at 34th Street and Broadway
Tel 212/695-4400
www.macys.com
Occupying an expansive block, Macy's calls itself the "world's largest department store." The Cellar stocks housewares and culinary delights, and clothing, generally mainstream, comes from a range of well-known names. The store has good seasonal sales, and is famous for sponsoring both the Thanksgiving Day parade and the July 4th fireworks.
◑ Mon–Sat 10–8.30, Sun 11–7 ▣ 34th Street/Herald Square (B, D, F, N, Q, R, V, W) ▣ M6, M7, M34

SAKS FIFTH AVENUE
Map 162 E17
611 Fifth Avenue between 49th and 50th streets
Tel 212/753-4000
www.saksfifthavenue.com
Comfortable Saks offers a very fine selection of clothing by an excellent range of established to up-and-coming designers for men and women.
◑ Mon–Fri 10–7 (Thu until 8), Sat 10–6.30, Sun 12–6 ▣ Fifth Avenue/53rd Street (E, V), 47th–50th streets/Rockefeller Center (B, D, F, V) ▣ M1, M2, M3, M4, M50

TAKASHIMAYA
Map 161 E17
693 Fifth Avenue between 54th and 55th streets
Tel 212/350-0100

CHAIN STORES

This chart tells you what to expect in many of the chain stores on New York's main shopping streets. Call the head office to find your nearest branch or check the website.

NAME	Clothing	Fashion accessories	Souvenirs	Books Music	Outdoor Sport	Shoes	Pharmacy Toiletries	Stationery	Food	Household and Electrical goods	HEAD OFFICE CONTACT NUMBER
Abercrombie & Fitch	✔	✔			✔	✔					614/283-6500 or 888 856 44
Anthropologie	✔	✔					✔			✔	212/627-5885 or 800-309-25
Ann Taylor	✔	✔				✔					212/541-3300 or 800-432-52
Banana Republic	✔	✔				✔					212/644-6678 or 888-277-89
Bed Bath and Beyond										✔	800-462-3966
Benetton	✔	✔				✔					800-535-4491
Bodyshop			✔				✔				800-263-9746
Brooks Brothers	✔	✔				✔		✔			800-274-1815
Club Monaco	✔	✔									888-580-5084
Crabtree & Evelyn			✔				✔		✔		860/928-2761 or 800-272-28
Crate & Barrel										✔	847-272-2888 or 800-967-66
Diesel	✔				✔						212/755-9200
Disney Store	✔		✔	✔							800-328-0368
Eddie Bauer	✔	✔			✔	✔					800-426-8020
Eileen Fisher	✔										800-345-3362
Gap	✔	✔				✔					800-333-7899
H & M	✔	✔									212/564-9922
J. Crew	✔	✔				✔					800-562-0258 or 800-932-0
NBA Store	✔	✔	✔								877-622-0206
Old Navy	✔	✔				✔					800-653-6289
Pier 1 Imports										✔	817/252-8000 or 800-245-45
Talbot's	✔	✔				✔					781/749-7600 or 800-992-9
Toys "R" Us				✔					✔		971-617-3500 or 800-869-77
Urban Outfitters	✔	✔				✔					215/564-2313 or 800-282-22
Victoria's Secret	✔	✔				✔	✔				800-411-5116
Virgin Megastore				✔							877-484-7446
Williams-Sonoma									✔	✔	877-812-6235 or 800-541-22

Step in to this beautiful branch of Japan's largest department store even if you're not a shopper. The flower shop on the first floor is a lovely retreat from Fifth Avenue. Look for gold-leaf cups, black lacquer saucers and silk pillows.
🕐 Mon–Sat 10–7, Sun 12–5 🚇 Fifth Avenue/53rd Street (E, V) 🚆 M1, M2, M3, M4, M5

DISCOUNT OUTLETS

New York magazine's "Sales and Bargains" feature highlights current sample and stock sales. On-line nysale.com and dailycandy.com keep up to date with what's on.

CENTURY 21
Map 163 E25
22 Cortlandt Street between Broadway and Church
Tel 212/227-9092
www.c21stores.com
Customers do their trying on in the aisles at this resource for discounted designer fashions. Look for Prada, Armani, Jil Sander and Moschino among other designers at 40 to 75 percent off or more.
🕐 Mon–Fri 7.45am–8pm (Thu until 8.30), Sat 10–7.30, Sun 11–6 Cortlandt Street (E) 🚆 M1, M6

INA
Map 163 E23
101 Thompson Street between Spring and Prince streets
Tel 212/941-4757
www.inanyc.com
The designer resale stock, discounted by 30 to 50 percent, changes daily, as models and the fashion set turn in their castoffs. Look for Diane Von Furstenberg and Anna Sui. There's usually a fantastic array of Manolos, Pradas and Sigerson Morrisons, too.
🕐 Daily 12–7 🚇 Spring Street (C, E), Prince Street (N, R, W) 🚆 M5, M6, M21

LOEHMANN'S
Map 162 D21
101 Seventh Avenue at 16th Street
Tel 212/352-0856
www.loehmanns.com
This place has been a name on the discount shopping scene ever since Frieda Mueller Loehmann began selling well-priced skirts and blouses out of her Brooklyn home in 1920. This flagship store has five floors of fashions to pick over. Discounts range from 30 to 65 percent.
🕐 Mon–Sat 9–9, Sun 11–7 🚇 14th Street (1, 2, 3, 9) 🚆 M14, M20

SUPERSTORES

AVIREX
Map 163 F22
652 Broadway between Bleecker and Bond streets
Tel 212/925-5456
www.avirex.com
Lusting for the bomber jacket worn by Tom Cruise in *Top Gun*? Head for Avirex, official

WHAT TO DO

LINE OF GOODS	WEB SITE
Stylish casual clothing for the American outdoors lifestyle	www.abercrombie.com
Ethnically inspired clothing and eclectic housewares	www.anthropologie.com
Elegant and casual women's fashion	www.anntaylor.com
Stylish fashion separates for men and women	www.bananarepublic.com
Everything and anything to go in the home	www.bedbathandbeyond.com
Contemporary fashions with Italian flair	www.benetton.com
Cosmetics and bath products made of natural ingredients	www.thebodyshop.com
Conservative and classic tailored fashions for men and women	www.brooksbrothers.com
Canadian chain selling chic basics and affordable high-fashion items	www.clubmonaco.com
Venerable British chain selling toiletries, and British-oriented products like teas and jams	www.crabtree-evelyn.com
High-quality products for the home with a distinct West Coast style	www.crateandbarrel.com
Latest trends for kids from hip-hop style to surfer	www.diesel.com
Disney paraphernalia including clothes and furniture	www.disneystore.com
Casual stylish fashions with an outdoor orientation	www.eddiebauer.com
Casual, comfortable clothes for women	www.eileenfisher.com
The ubiquitous reasonably priced, casual clothing store	www.Gap.com
ow-cost versions of trendy youth-oriented fashion	www.hm.com
Casual preppy and collegiate fashions and affordable accessories	www.jcrew.com
Souvenir jerseys, posters, mugs and more for basketball fans	
Moderately priced high-street fashions for adults and children	www.oldnavy.com
Affordable, stylish home décor–from tableware to bed linens	www.pier1.com
Fine-quality, practical and affordable ladies wear	www.talbots.com
Every toy imaginable plus a 60-foot (18m) Ferris wheel	www.toysrus.com
Practical casuals for the collegiate crowd	www.urbn.com
Sexy lingerie, sleepwear, and swimwear are the staples at this famous chain	www.victoriassecret.com
Classical, pop, and jazz CDs including plenty of imports	www.virginmega.com
Upscale kitchen equipment, condiments and specialty ingredients	www.williams-sonoma.com

supplier of the U.S. Air Force's A-2 leather flight jacket. It sells unisex military fashions, biker gear and varsity styles.
🕐 Mon–Sat 11–7, Sun 12–6
Ⓜ Broadway-Lafayette (F, V, S) 🚌 M1, M5, M6

B & H PHOTO
Map 162 D19
420 Ninth Avenue between West 33rd and 34th streets
Tel 212/444-5000
www.bhphotovideo.com
Even if you're not in the market for a new camera, you might want to make a detour to this vast store to pick up inexpensive film in bulk. You'll also find every conceivable brand and type of camera, plus darkroom equipment and other accessories. Don't expect service—come knowing what you want to buy.
🕐 Mon–Thu 9–7, Fri 9am–1pm, Sun 10–5 Ⓜ 34th Street/Penn Station (A, C, E) 🚌 M11

BED, BATH AND BEYOND
Map 162 E21
620 Sixth Avenue between West 18th and 19th streets
Tel 212/255-3550
www.bedbathandbeyond.com
It can be overwhelming to shop at this huge store, which sells absolutely everything for the bedroom, bathroom, kitchen and dining room, plus storage and cleaning accessories, lamps, and window treatments.
🕐 Daily 8am–9pm Ⓜ 18th Street (1, 9) 🚌 M5, M6, M7

CRATE AND BARREL
Map 161 E16
650 Madison Avenue at East 59th Street
Tel 212/308-0011
www.crateandbarrel.com
This chain sells affordable good-looking designs for your home. The focus is on tableware (from linens to glasses). It also sells attractive outdoor dining stuff.
🕐 Mon–Fri 10–8, Sat 10–7, Sun 12–6 Ⓜ 59th Street/Fifth Avenue (N, R, W) 🚌 M1, M2, M3, M4, M5

DIESEL
Map 162 E21
1 Union Square West
Tel 646-336.8552
www.diesel.com

This Italian clothes house always keeps one step ahead of the latest trends, whether it's hip-hop or surfer. Diesel jeans are de rigueur and so, too, are the shoes and bags. Also at 770 Lexington Avenue.
🕐 Mon–Fri 11–9, Sat 10–9, Sun 11–8 Ⓜ 14th Street/Union Square (L, N, Q, R, W, 4, 5, 6) 🚌 M2, M3, M5, M14

FAO SCHWARZ
Map 161 E16
767 Fifth Avenue between 58th and 59th streets
Tel 212/644-9400
www.fao.com

Tom Hanks helped make this store even more famous when it featured in the movie *Big*. Founded in 1862 in Baltimore, the store has been in Manhattan since 1876 and at this address since 1986. It stocks everything: action figures, stuffed toys, books, games, dolls, science and nature toys, and electronics, plus furniture and fashions.

🕐 Mon–Wed 10–6, Thu–Sat 10–7, Sun 11–6 Ⓜ 59th Street/Fifth Avenue (N, R, W) 🚌 M1, M2, M3, M4

HAMMACHER SCHLEMMER
Map 161 F16
147 East 57th Street between Lexington and Third avenues
Tel 212/421-9000
www.hammacher.com
Ingenuity meets the future. At this longtime innovator, which started as a hardware store on the Bowery in 1848, today you will find such items as the upside-down tomato garden and the Roomba, a robotic cleaning device that navigates whole rooms removing dust from carpet and floor.
🕐 Mon–Sat 10–6 Ⓜ 59th Street (4, 5, 6) 🚌 M57, M98, M101, M102, M103

PARAGON SPORTING GOODS
Map 162 E21
867 Broadway at 18th Street
Tel 212/255 8036
www.paragonsports.com
New Yorkers have been coming to this multilevel store for years to buy clothes and equipment for every conceivable type of sport or pastime. It stocks camping and hiking gear, binoculars for bird-watching, golfing gear, skis, snow and surfboards, tennis racquets and a terrific selection of name-brand clothing.
🕐 Mon–Sat 10–8, Sun 11–6.30 Ⓜ 14th Street/Union Square (L, N, Q, R, W, 4, 5, 6) 🚌 M6, M7

PEARL PAINT
Map 163 E24
308 Canal Street between Mercer and Broadway
Tel 212/431-7932
www.pearlpaint.com
You won't find a better place for fine arts supplies at discounted prices than this multilevel store. The selection of oils, acrylics and other mediums, brushes, easels, markers, pens, pastels, sketchbooks, photo frames, drafting and sculpturing tools is superb.
🕐 Mon–Fri 9–7, Sat 10–6.30, Sun 10–6 Ⓜ Canal Street (N, R) 🚌 M1, M6

WHAT TO DO

PERFORMANCE

The city's performance scene reflects the diversity of the metropolis. Theater patrons will find an array of options. There are 39 or so Broadway theaters, plus 450 nonprofit theaters operating in the city.

CINEMA

The city is a veritable cinema paradiso. Numerous art houses operate, frequently showcasing individual directors or focusing on particular themes or eras. First-run movies are shown all over town in grand movieplexes.

CLASSICAL MUSIC, DANCE AND OPERA

Musical riches abound, led by the Metropolitan and City Operas and Carnegie Hall and

the New York Philharmonic. All kinds of smaller groups and orchestras, plus independent opera companies, play at diverse venues—museums, music schools, and churches. The New York City Ballet and American Ballet Theatre lead the traditional dance scene, while Merce Cunningham, Mark Morris, Alvin Ailey, Paul Taylor, and Martha Graham are the leading modern dance companies.

COMEDY, POETRY, AND THE SPOKEN WORD

The spoken word can be heard throughout the city, as the intellectuals and literary lights meet, greet, and sign at bookstores, lecture at the 92nd Street Y, or deliver their poetry at poetry fests and St. Mark's in the Bowery. And don't forget stand-up comedy, a unique American cultural contribution, celebrated in New York City clubs, which gave birth to such brilliant comedians as Jerry Seinfeld, Jay Leno, Woody Allen, Rosie O'Donnell and Joan Rivers.

CONTEMPORARY LIVE MUSIC

Cabaret is flourishing in alluring rooms at the Carlyle and the Algonquin Hotels and producing such new voices as that of Peter Cincotti. Musically, uptown tends to be more traditional; downtown leans to the avant-garde. Indie rock clubs abound on the Lower East Side and in the East Village. Cool jazz and other exotica can be heard at the Knitting Factory and Tonic. Jazz continues to thrive as it has always in New York. The leading venue is still the Village Vanguard, now under the watchful eye of Lorraine Gordon, although jazz fans are eagerly awaiting the opening of the new $140 million Jazz at Lincoln Center in the AOL Time Warner building on Columbus Circle. World music programming is featured all over town at Town Hall, the new Zankel Hall at Carnegie, and Symphony Space.

THEATER

The Great White Way attracts the most visitors with its brightly lit marquees and gilded theaters named after such luminaries as Ethel Barrymore, David Belasco, and Eugene O'Neill. The Public Theater and BAM are the shining lights of Off-Broadway. The first, founded by Joe Papp, also delivers free summer Shakespeare in the Park, while BAM is famous for its New Wave Festival. Off-Broadway has nurtured many playwrights too, such as Wally Shawn, Lanford Wilson, and Tony Kushner, and several Broadway hits have emerged from here, notably *Rent*, *Avenue Q*, *A Chorus Line*, and the *Heidi Chronicles*. Off-Off-Broadway stages quirky experimental showcases in tiny theaters with less than 100 seats, but it has nurtured such players as Eric Bogosian, Karen Finley, Laurie Anderson, Paul Zaloom, and others.

PRACTICALITIES

Most box offices open from Monday to Saturday, 10am to 8pm, and Sun from 11am to 6.30pm. Tickets can be purchased here without paying a fee. Standing Room Only tickets, when available, go on sale on the day of the performance.

Tickets can also be purchased through Telecharge (*tel 212-239-6200*), Ticketmaster (*tel 212-307-7171*), and Smart Tix (*tel 212-206-1515*).

Best performance listings are found in *Time Out*, *New York* magazine, the *Village Voice*, and the Friday edition of *The New York Times*. A good online source is www.culture-finders.com.

Symphony Space
Leonard Nimoy Thalia

Cathedral Church of
St John the Divine
Sugar Hill Bistro

Manhattan School of Music
Miller Theatre
Cotton Club
Smoke

Showman's Jazz Club
Aaron Davis Hall
Apollo Theater
Classical Theater of Ha

UPPER WEST
SIDE

West 95th Street

West 94th Street

West 93rd Street

West 92nd Street

West 91st Street

West 90th Street

West 89th Street

West 88th Street

West 87th Street

West 86th Street

West 85th Street

West 84th Street

West 83rd Street

West 82nd Street

West 81st Street

West 80th Street

West 79th Street

West 78th Street

West 77th Street

West 76th Street

West 75th Street

West 74th Street

West 73rd Street

West 72nd Street

West 71st Street

West 70th Street

West 69th Street

West 68th Street

West 67th Street

West 66th Street

West 65th Street

West 64th Street

West 63rd Street

West 62nd Street

West 61st Street

West 60th Street

West 59th Street

West 58th Street

WEST 57th STREET

West 56th Street

West 55th Street

West 54th Street

West 53rd Street

West 52nd Street

West 51st Street

West 50th Street

West 49th Street

West 48th Street

West 47th Street

West 46th Street

West 45th Street

BROADWAY

Hudson River

Riverside
Park

HIGHWAY 9A

RIVERSIDE DRIVE

WEST END AVENUE

AMSTERDAM AVENUE

BROADWAY

COLUMBUS AVENUE

CENTRAL PARK WEST

CENTRAL PARK

CE
Re

CEN
PA

86th
Street

81st Street
Museum of
Nat Hist.

Shakespeare in the Park
(Delacorte Theater)

American Museum
of Natural History

New-York
Historical Society

San Remo
Apartments

The Dakota

Merkin
Concert Hall

Makor

Alice
Tully Hall

Juilliard School

Film Society of Lincoln Center
(Walter Reade Theater)

Bruno Walter
Auditorium

Lincoln Center for
the Performing Arts

Vivian Beaumont Theater

New York Society
for Ethical Culture

Mitzi Newhouse Theater

Lincoln
Center

Avery Fisher
Hall

Lincoln Plaza Cinemas

New York State Theater

Metropolitan
Opera House

American
Bible Society

Jazz at
Lincoln Center

COLUMBUS
CIRCLE

Beacon
Theatre

Ansonia
Building

Stand-Up
New York

Carnegie
Hall

WPP Theatre Four
(Women's Project Theatre)

De Witt
Clinton Park

Irish Arts
Center

Studio 54   Broadway

Virginia

Neil Simon   Roseland
Ballroom

Gershwin   Iridiun

Circle in the Square   Winte

Ambassador Theatre   Ca
Co
Cl

Eugene O'Neill   Walter Ke

Brooks Atkinson   Longacre

BROADWAY

Don't Tell Mama   The Supper
Club   Barrymo
Theatre

Firebird
Café

Danny's Skylight Room   Imperial   Richard Rog

Music Box   Marquis

Freedom
Place

Tavern on
the Green

Strawberry
Fields

The Lake

The She
Meadow

Central
Park

Riverside
Park

79th
Street

72nd
Street

86th
Street

Ind Sea-
Air-Space Museum

Intrepid Sea-
Air-Space Museum

Lenox Lounge
Schomburg Center for
Research in Black Culture

Jewish
Museum

Cooper-Hewitt
National Design Museum

National
Academy
of Design

Guggenheim
Museum

Neue
Galerie

Grace Rainey
rs Auditorium
Metropolitan
useum of Art)

Stanhope
Park Hyatt

Bemelmans Bar
& Café Carlyle

Whitney Museum
of American Art

Conservatory
Water

Frick
Collection

Asia Society
and Museum

Asia
Society

Kosciuszko Foundation

92nd Street Y
(Kauffman Concert Hall)

Gracie
Mansion

Carl
Schurz
Park

John Jay
Park

68th Street
Hunter College

Roosevelt
Island

ROOSEVELT
ISLAND

Café
Pierre

Feinstein's
at the Regency

Florence Gould Hall

Dangerfield's

Mount Vernon Hotel
Museum and Garden

Chicago City Limits

American Museum of
the Moving Image

QUEENSBORO
BRIDGE

Paris
Theatre

Trump
Tower

Dahesh Museum of Art

an Theatre Club

Central
Synagogue

York Theatre
St Peter's Church

Museum of
d Design

Museum of Television and Radio

Seagram
Building

YWCA Cine Club

o City
ic Hall

Donnell Media Center
New York Public Library

St Patrick's
Cathedral

Municipal
Art Society

G E
Building

Rockefeller
Center

DIAMOND
DISTRICT

MIDTOWN
MANHATTAN

Japan Society

United Nations
Headquarters

187

Daryl Roth Theater
Vineyard Theatre
Variety Arts Theatre
Detour
Quad Cinema
UNION SQUARE
Forbes Magazine Galleries
Ukrainian Museum
New School
Tishman Auditorium
Cinema Village
Grace Church
The Poetry Project (St Mark's Church in the Bowery)
Theater for the New City
The Ontological Hysteric Theater at St Marks
8th Street NYU
Cooper Union Great Hall
EAST VILLAGE
Jefferson Market Library
Cornelia Street Café
Waverly Place
Washington Square Park
NORTH
NOHO
Joe's Pub
Public Theater
New York Theatre Workshop
La Mama Experimental Theater Club
Two Boots
Pioneer Theater
Blue Note
Village Underground
Comedy Cellar
Lion's Den
Bitter End
The Judson Memorial Church
Terra Blues
Fez Under Time Café
Bowerie Lane
Bottom Line
Amato Opera Theatre
CBGB
Downstairs Lounge
Anthology Film Archives
Nuyorican Poets Café
Zinc Bar
Angelika Film Center
Bleecker Street Theatre
Bowery Poetry Club
Mercury Lounge
House of Oldies Rare Records
Minetta Lane
Film Forum
Joyce Soho
New Museum of Contemporary Art
Guggenheim Museum SoHo
Housing Works Used Book Café
St Patrick's Old Cathedral
Landmark Sunshine Cinema
Luna Lounge
Arlene Grocery
Little Singer Building
Kavehaz
Poets House
SOHO
Bowery Ballroom
LITTLE ITALY
Streb Action Invention Lab
LOWER EAST SIDE
Tonic
Gallery
Tony Shafrazi Gallery
Manhattan Ensemble Theatre
Performing Garage
Haughwout Building
Lower East Side Tenement Museum
Seward Park
LOWER MANHATTAN
CHINATOWN
Flea Theater
Museum of Chinese in the Americas
Knitting Factory
TRIBECA
Washington Market Park
US Courthouse
City Hall Park
City Hall and Civic Center
Blarney Star
Woolworth Building
Church of St Peter
Brooklyn Academy of Music (BAM)
BAM Rose Cinemas
Southpaw
GROUND ZERO
St Paul's Chapel
Cortlandt Street (under construction)
Fulton Street Market
Bargemusic
Federal Reserve Bank
Federal Hall National Monument
South Street Seaport
Trinity Church
WALL ST
Museum of American Financial History
New York City Police Museum
Fraunces Tavern Museum
Museum of Heritage

Cinema

Major cinema chains—AMC Empire, Cineplex Odeon, Loews and United Artists—have many theaters in the city showing first-run films. Those listed here screen art, foreign and independent films, documentaries, vintage films and series dedicated to a particular director or theme. Most open around noon and operate continuously until late night. You can get tickets in advance (for a surcharge) via websites such as fandango.com and movietickets.com. In fall, the New York Film Festival is held at Lincoln Center and other locations throughout the city. Spring is the time for the TriBeCa Film Festival.

AMERICAN MUSEUM OF THE MOVING IMAGE
Off map 187 G16
35th Avenue at 36th Street, Astoria, Queens
Tel 718/784-0077
www.ammi.org
This museum in Queens, built on the site of the Astoria Studio, a former Paramount movie production facility, hosts director festivals and retrospectives. Screenwriters answer questions at Wednesday night shows. Take a look at how films are made in the core exhibition "Behind the Screen."
🎟 $8.50 🚇 Steinway Street (34th Avenue) (R, V, G), Broadway (N, W)

ANGELIKA FILM CENTER
Map 189 E22
Mercer and Houston streets

Tel 212/995-2000
www.angelikafilmcenter.com
This multiplex shows foreign films with subtitles, plus films by such artists as Atom Egoyan and other independent movie makers. Pick up a latte at the café before or after the show.

🚇 Broadway-Lafayette (F, V, S), Bleecker Street (6) 🚌 M1, M5, M6, M21

ANTHOLOGY FILM ARCHIVES
Map 189 F22
32 Second Avenue at East 2nd Street
Tel 212/505-5181
www.anthologyfilmarchives.org
Shows new filmmakers along with old and rare vintage pieces and occasional tributes to particular directors.
🎟 Varies $7–8 🚇 Astor Place (6), Lower East Side/Second Avenue (F, V) 🚌 M15, M21

BAM ROSE CINEMAS
Off map 189 G25
30 Lafayette Street
Brooklyn
Tel 718/636-4100
www.bam.org
Screens at this house at the Brooklyn Academy of Music show contemporary first-run films, and tributes to American and foreign cinema, often with discussions with the directors.
🎟 $10 🚇 Nevins Street (2, 3), Dekalb Avenue (B, D, Q, N, R)

CINEMA VILLAGE
Map 189 E21
22 East 12th Street between University Place and Fifth Avenue
Tel 212/924-3363 or 4
www.cinemavillage.com
Renovated in 2000, this independent, housed in a former

fire station, now has three screens. Documentaries and old movies are the staples.

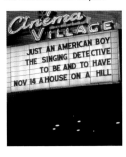

🎟 $9, students $7 🚇 14th Street/Union Square (L, N, Q, R, W, 4, 5, 6) 🚌 M1, M2, M101, M103, M103, M14

FILM FORUM
Map 189 E23
209 West Houston Street between Sixth and Seventh avenues
Tel 212/727-8110 or 212/727-8112
www.filmforum.com
The leading cinema for independent films, it also shows domestic and foreign documentaries, as well as revivals.
🎟 $9.75 🚇 Houston Street (1, 9) 🚌 M5, M6, M20, M21

FILM SOCIETY OF LINCOLN CENTER
Map 186 C16
Walter Reade Theater
165 West 65th Street
Tel 212/875-5600
www.filmline.com
This society hosts many different festivals—the New York Jewish Festival, Spanish Cinema Now, and Women in Film, for example.
🎟 $9 🚇 66th Street (1, 9) 🚌 M5, M7, M104, M66

LANDMARK SUNSHINE CINEMA
Map 189 F22/23
143 East Houston Street between First and Second avenues
Tel 212/358-7709 or 212/777-FILM (tickets)
www.landmarktheaters.com
This five-screener offers a medley of movies, from challenging documentaries such as *Bowling for*

WHAT TO DO

Columbine, foreign films, and oldies, to the better first-run movies. Seating is raked and more comfortable than at other movie houses with similar programming.
🎬 $10 🚇 Second Avenue (F, V) 🚌 M15, M21

LINCOLN PLAZA CINEMAS
Map 186 D16
1886 Broadway at 63rd Street
Tel 212/757-2280
www.lincolnplazacinema.com
A six-screener showing a select group of critically successful first-run movies and foreign films. For example, Gurinder Chadha's *Bend it Like Beckham* and Almodovar's *Talk to Her* both played here.
🎬 $10, seniors $6.50 🚇 66th Street (1, 9) 🚌 M5, M7, M104, M66

MAKOR
Map 186 D15
35 West 67th Street
Tel 212/601-1000
www.92Y.org
This club, part of a Jewish community center, hosts differ-ent programs, including mainly documentaries and oldies.
🎬 $9 🚇 66th Street (1, 9) 🚌 M 5, M7, M10, M104, M66

MOMA FILM AT THE GRAMERCY THEATRE
Map 188 F20
127 East 23rd Street between Lexington and Third avenues
Tel 212/777-4900
www.moma.org
MoMA's film program is show-ing its director tributes, oldies and documentaries here, while MoMA is being renovated.
🎬 $12 🚇 23rd Street (6) 🚌 M23, M1, M101, M102, M103

NEW YORK PUBLIC LIBRARY
Map 187 E17
Donnell Media Center
20 West 53rd Street between Fifth and Sixth avenues
Tel 212/621-0609
Foreign films, shorts and documentaries, plus tributes to directors.
🎬 Varies 🎬 Free 🚇 53rd Street/Fifth

Avenue (E, V) 🚌 M1, M2, M3, M4, M5, M6, M7

PARIS THEATRE
Map 187 E16
4 West 58th Street between Fifth and Sixth avenues
Tel 212/688-3800
The films that play here are mostly foreign.
🎬 $10, seniors $6 🚇 Fifth Avenue/59th Street (N, R, W) 🚌 M1, M2, M3, M4, M57

QUAD CINEMA
Map 188 E21
34 West 13th Street between Fifth and Sixth avenues
Tel 212/255-8800 or 255-2243
www.quadcinema.com

This four-screen art house shows foreign and independent films and works by new directors.
🎬 $9.50 🚇 14th Street (F, V), 14th Street/Union Square (L, N, Q, R, W, 4, 5, 6) 🚌 M2, M3, M5, M6

SCANDINAVIA HOUSE
Map 188 E19
Victor Borge Hall
58 Park Avenue between East 37th and 38th streets
Tel 212/779-3587
www.scandinaviahouse.org

Films by directors and actors from Denmark, Finland, Iceland, Norway and Sweden.
🎬 $8 🚇 42nd Street/Grand Central (4, 5, 6) 🚌 M1

SCREENING ROOM
Map 189 E23
54 Varick at Canal Street (northwest corner)
Tel 212/334-2100
www.thescreeningroom.com
Classics and independent movies.
🎬 $9.50 🚇 Canal Street (1, 9), Canal Street (A, C, E) 🚌 M20

SYMPHONY SPACE LEONARD NIMOY THALIA
Map 186 C12
Broadway at 95th Street
Tel 212/864-5400
www.symphonyspace.org
Brilliant gems, like Fritz Lang's *Metropolis* and David Lynch's *Blue Velvet,* plus more recent independent films are shown here. Director tributes, to Kurosawa for example, and frequent double features.
🎬 $9 🚇 96th Street (1, 2, 3, 9) 🚌 M96, M104

TWO BOOTS PIONEER THEATER
Map 189 G22
155 East 3rd Street at Avenue A
Tel 212/254-3300
www.twoboots.com
Opened in 2000 by the Two Boots pizza chain after they moved their East Village outlet to larger premises, this 100-seat house shows documentaries like *Bloody Sunday* and other foreign films, often followed by discussions with the director.
🎬 $9 🚇 Lower East Side/Second Avenue (F, V) 🚌 M14, M21

YWCA CINE CLUB
Map 187 F17
610 Lexington Avenue between East 52nd and 53rd streets
Tel 212/735-9717 or 735-9710
www.ywcanyc.org
Foreign films, director tributes and oldies.
🎬 $7 🚇 51st Street (6) 🚌 M98, M101, M102, M103

Classical music, dance and opera

CLASSICAL MUSIC

ALICE TULLY HALL
Map 186 C16
144 West 66th Street at Broadway
Tel 212/875-5050 or 212/721-6500
www.lincolncenter.org
This 1,096-seat hall is used for chamber music, vocal recitals, jazz and other musical events. The Chamber Music Society *(tel 212/875-5788)* resides here.
◉ Varies 🕐 $27.50–52 ($10 student rush) 🚇 66th Street (1, 9) 🚌 M5, M7, M104, M66

AVERY FISHER HALL
Map 186 C16
Lincoln Center
111 Amsterdam Avenue between West 64th and 65th streets
Tel 212/875-5030 or 721-6500
www.lincolncenter.org or
www.newyorkphilharmonic

Home to the New York Philharmonic *(tel 212/875-5656),* currently under the baton of Lorin Maazel, this hall seats 2,700. Many other groups perform here—the American Symphony Orchestra under Leon Botstein, the summer Mostly Mozart Festival and the JVC Jazz Fest. During its season, the Philharmonic opens its morning rehearsals to the public (usually on Thursdays at 9.45 for $12).
◉ Varies 🕐 Price varies $22–98 🚇 66th Street (1, 9) 🚌 M5, M7, M104, M66

BARGEMUSIC
Map 189 G25
Fulton Ferry Landing next to the Brooklyn Bridge
Tel 718-624-2083
www.bargemusic.org
Anchored under the Brooklyn Bridge, this old coffee barge-turned-125-seat concert hall is the brainchild of violinist Olga Bloom. A beguiling experience.
◉ Varies 🕐 Varies $20–35 🚇 High Street (A), Clark Street/Brooklyn Heights (2, 3)

BRUNO WALTER AUDITORIUM
Map 186 C16
The New York Public Library for the Performing Arts
111 Amsterdam Avenue between 64th and 65th streets
Tel 212/870-1630, 642-0142 (programs)
Lectures, seminars, concerts and films are the regular fare at this 212-seat hall. The library is a superb performing arts archive.
◉ Varies 🕐 Free 🚇 66th Street (1, 9) 🚌 M5, M7, M104, M66

CARNEGIE HALL
Map 186 D17
Seventh Avenue at West 57th Street
Tel 212/247-7800
www.carnegiehall.com
"Practice, practice, practice" is the answer to the old chestnut of a question, "How do you get to Carnegie Hall?" Many well-practiced conductors and artists have played in this famous hall, which was built with Carnegie money in 1891, from Tchaikovsky and Mahler to the Beatles and the Rolling Stones. Programming today includes all the great orchestras of the world, top-class

iinstrumentalists, the New York Pops under Skitch Henderson, and performers of jazz, folk, pop and comedy. A small museum on the second floor *(tel 212/903-9629)* displays associated memorabilia.
◉ Museum: daily 11–4.30; tours *(Tel 212/903-9765)* Mon–Fri 11.30, 2 and 3 🕐 Varies $10–102. Student and senior citizen tickets available two hours before the performance; museum $6 🚇 57th Street (N, R, Q, W) 🚌 M6, M7, M57

CATHEDRAL CHURCH OF ST. JOHN THE DIVINE
Off map 186 C12
1047 Amsterdam at 112th Street
Tel 212/316-7540
www.stjohndivine.org
Stop by to admire the still incomplete edifice, begun in 1892, and you may hear one of the sanctuary's five organs. The musical repertoire during arts events ranges from choirs singing Bach oratorios or chanting Tibetan monks to music made famous by Duke Ellington and Judy Collins.
◉ Varies 🕐 Varies 🚇 Cathedral Parkway/110th Street (1, 9) 🚌 M4, M11,

CENTRAL SYNAGOGUE
Map 187 F17
123 East 55th Street at Lexington Avenue
Tel 212/415-5500
www.92Y.org
Concerts at the synagogue often feature well-known or overlooked Jewish composers.
◉ Varies 🕐 Varies 🚇 51st Street (6) 🚌 M98, M1010, M102, M103

COOPER UNION
Map 189 F22
41 Cooper Square at 7th Street
Tel 212/353-4140
www.cooperunion.edu
Diverse array of musical performers and groups.
◉ Varies 🕐 Varies 🚇 8th Street (N, R, W), Astor Place (6) 🚌 M1

EOS ORCHESTRA
101 Fifth Avenue
Tel 212/691-6415
www.eosorchestra.com
The orchestra, named after the goddess of the new dawn,

takes a fresh approach to old and contemporary compositions, often combining music with film and other media. It performs at the New York Society for Ethical Culture (see below).

FLORENCE GOULD HALL
Map 187 E16
55 East 59th Street between Park and Madison avenues
Tel 212/355-6160
www.faif.org
Chamber groups, opera singers, pop and jazz artists, dance companies, and actors reading all entertain in this 400-seat auditorium associated with the Alliance Française.
🎫 Varies 💷 Price varies $20–25
Ⓜ Fifth Avenue/59th Street (N, R, W)
🚌 M1, M2, M3, M4, M5, M57

FRICK COLLECTION
Map 187 E15
1 East 70th Street
Tel 212/288-0700
www.frick.org

The recitals in this exquisite museum are a must .
🎫 Varies 💷 Varies Ⓜ 68th Street (6)
🚌 M1, M2, M3, M4, M72

GRACE RAINEY ROGERS AUDITORIUM
Map 187 E14
The Metropolitan Museum of Art
Fifth Avenue at 82nd Street
Tel 212/535-7710 or 570-3949
www.metmuseum.org
Small musical groups and individuals entertain in this mid-size 700-seat auditorium. And the Met always has chamber music in the Great

Hall Balcony on Friday and Saturday evenings.
🎫 Varies 💷 Varies $35–50 Ⓜ 77th Street (6) 🚌 M1, M2, M3, M4, M79

JUILLIARD SCHOOL
Map 186 C16
144 West 66th Street at Broadway
Tel 212/769-7406 or 212/721-6500
www.juilliard.edu
This world-famous performing arts school is especially well known for music. The young artists who train here can be seen in stimulating programs in two auditoriums. Juilliard also incorporates the School for American Ballet, which is the training ground for the New York City Ballet. Dance aficionados run to secure tickets for the school's annual workshop production in early summer *(tel 212/769-6600)*.
🎫 Varies 💷 Most are free except for opera programs and dance workshops
Ⓜ 66th Street (1, 9) 🚌 M5, M7, M104, M66

KOSCIUSZKO FOUNDATION
Map 187 E16
15 East 65th Street
Tel 212/734-2130
www.kosciuszko.org
Programs featuring Polish composers or artists.
🎫 Varies 💷 Varies Ⓜ 68th Street (6)
🚌 M1, M2, M3, M4

MANHATTAN SCHOOL OF MUSIC
Off map 186 C12
Broadway at 122nd Street
Tel 212/749-2802
www.msmnyc.edu
This institution with a world-class reputation has a large concert hall and several smaller venues. The programming is diverse—orchestras, chamber ensembles—and ticket prices reasonable.
🎫 Varies 💷 Varies $5–20 Ⓜ 125th Street (1,9) 🚌 M4, M104

MERKIN CONCERT HALL
Map 186 C15
129 West 67th Street
Tel 212/501-3330
www.ekcc.org
National and international

chamber groups perform here. You might find traditional classical, new music or even a group from Japan playing the 25-string koto.
🎫 Varies 💷 Varies $12–20 Ⓜ 66th Street (1, 9) 🚌 M5, M7, M104

MILLER THEATRE
off map 186 C12
Columbia University
Broadway at 116th Street
Tel 212/854-7799
www.millertheatre.com
Many cutting-edge classical groups and composers are presented here: John Zorn, Julia Wolfe and John King, for example.
🎫 Varies 💷 Varies Ⓜ 116th Street (1, 9) 🚌 M104

NEW YORK PHILHARMONIC
Avery Fisher Hall
Broadway at 65th Street
Tel 212/721-6500
www.newyorkphilharmonic.org
Established in 1842, this is the oldest orchestra in the United States. Currently under the baton of Lorin Maazel, the orchestra performs more than 200 concerts here annually. Dvorak's *New World Symphony* was premiered by the orchestra in 1893.
🎫 Varies 💷 Varies $24–108 Ⓜ 66th Street (1, 9) 🚌 M5, M7, M104, M66

NEW YORK SOCIETY FOR ETHICAL CULTURE
Map 186 D16
2 West 64th Street at Central Park West
Tel 212/874-5210 or 866/468-7619
www.nysec.org
All kinds of cultural events are held here, with lectures and discussions often preceding them. It's also home to the Eos Orchestra (see page 192).
🎫 Varies 💷 Varies Ⓜ 66th Street (1, 9) 🚌 M10

92ND STREET Y
Map 187 F13
Kauffman Concert Hall
1395 Lexington Avenue at 92nd Street
Tel 212/415-5500, 427-6000 or 996-1100
www.92Y.org
The 92nd Street Y offers some

of the city's most varied programming. It hosts music recitals (Guarneri and Tokyo string quartets, Janos Starker), jazz, pop and folk, poetry and literature readings (Thomas Keneally, V. S. Naipaul), and lectures on every conceivable subject by contemporary cultural leaders. A Jewish cultural organization, it celebrated its 125th anniversary in 1999.
🎬 Varies 💵 Varies 🚇 96th Street (6) 🚌 M98, M101, M102, M103, M96

WEILL RECITAL HALL
881 Seventh Avenue
Tel 212/247-7800
www.carnegiehall.org
Small groups perform in this 250-seat hall in the Carnegie Hall complex. Well known for its Distinctive Debuts Series.
🎬 Varies 💵 Varies $24–92 🚇 57th Street (N, Q, R, W) 🚌 M6, M7, M57

ZANKEL HALL
881 Seventh Avenue
Tel 212/247-7800
www.carnegiehall.org
This new 644-seat space in the Carnegie Hall complex, opened in 2003, offers programming, from early music and popular song to Afro-Cuban and other world music.
🎬 Varies 💵 Varies $25–65 🚇 57th Street (N, R, Q, W) 🚌 M6, M7, M57

DANCE AND OPERA

AMATO OPERA THEATRE
Map 189 F22
319 Bowery at 2nd Street
Tel 212/228-8200
www.amato.org
The company has been putting on tiny productions of five or six operas annually since 1948. Mignon Dunn and Jon Frederic West performed here early in their careers. Seats 107.
🎬 Varies 💵 $23–28 🚇 Bleecker Street (6), Lower East Side/Second Avenue (F, V) 🚌 M21, M103

AMERICAN BALLET THEATRE
890 Broadway at 19th Street
Tel 212/477-3030
www.abt.org

This company performs regularly at City Center (see below) and at the Metropolitan Opera House in the spring.

CITY CENTER
Map 186 D17
131 West 55th Street between Sixth and Seventh avenues
Tel 212/247-0430 or 212/581-1212
www.citycenter.org
The exotic Moorish-style building dating from 1922–24 is especially famous for dance productions. The Dance Theater of Harlem, Alvin Ailey American Dance Theater, Paul Taylor Dance Company, American Ballet Theatre, and the San Francisco Ballet have all performed here. The Gilbert and Sullivan Players are also residents. Originally a Shriner's temple, the building was converted by Mayor Fiorello LaGuardia into a "people's theater" in 1943.
🎬 Varies 💵 $35–65 🚇 57th Street (N, Q, R, W) 🚌 M5, M6, M7, M57

DANCE THEATER WORKSHOP
Map 188 D20
219 West 19th Street at Seventh Avenue
Tel 212/924-0077
www.dtw.org
In 1965 Jeff Duncan, Art Bauman and Jack Moore founded this choreographers' collective, and it still promises innovative performances here and at other city venues. Many famous dancers have begun careers here—Bill T. Jones, Mark Morris, Ann Carlson, Eiko and Koma—plus such theatrical talents as Bill Irwin, Whoopi Goldberg and Paul Zaloom.

🎬 Varies 💵 Varies 🚇 18th Street (1, 9) 🚌 M20, M14

DANCE THEATRE OF HARLEM
Everett Center for the Performing Arts
466 West 152nd Street between Amsterdam and St. Nicholas avenues
Tel 212/690-2800
www.dancetheatreofharlem.com
This exciting company presents a series at the New York State Theater and also has open house every second Sunday of each month. Their appearance at the August street festival is also fun. The repertory ranges from classical to contemporary.
🎬 Varies; July at New York State Theater 💵 Varies 🚇 155th Street (C) 🚌 M18, M100, M101

THE JOYCE THEATER
Map 188 D21
175 Eighth Avenue southwest corner of 19th Street
Tel 212/691-9740 or 212/242-0800
www.joyce.org
The city's premiere dance venue hosts important international and domestic dance companies and showcases such important dance series as Altogether Different. Expect to see the Eliot Feld Ballet, Pilobolus Dance Theater and many others.
🎬 Varies 💵 Varies 🚇 23rd Street (C, E) 🚌 M20, M23

JOYCE SOHO
Map 189 E23
155 Mercer Street between Houston and Prince streets
Tel 212/431-9233 or 212/334-7479
www.joyce.org
This theater offers cutting-edge dance, often with an alternative perspective. Rehearsals are open to the public.
🎬 Varies 💵 $15 🚇 Prince Street (N, R, W) 🚌 M1, M6, M21

THE JUDSON MEMORIAL CHURCH
Map 189 E22
55 Washington Square South,
Tel 212/777-0033
www.judson.org
For many decades this Baptist Church has nurtured avant-

garde artists. It's most famous for Judson Poets Theater but it still hosts experimental dance series. Movement Research performs a regular series here. Varies Varies West 4th Street (A, C, E, F, V, S) M5, M6, M8

LINCOLN CENTER FOR THE PERFORMING ARTS
Map 186 C16
Columbus Avenue between 62nd and 66th Streets
Tel 212/875-5000
www.lincolncenter.org
This 16-acre complex is home to the Metropolitan Opera House, the New York State Theater, Avery Fisher Hall, the Vivian Beaumont and Mitzi E. Newhouse theaters, the New York Public Library of the Performing Arts, the Walter Reade movie theater and the Juilliard School. In summer there is dancing under the stars on the plaza as well as the Lincoln Center Festival, a free event which presents hundreds of performing artists and companies of all kinds. For tours of the first three halls mentioned above call 212/875-5350 for reservations. Varies Varies 66th Street (1, 9) M7, M11, M104, M66

THE KITCHEN
Map 188 C21
512 West 19th Street between Tenth and Eleventh avenues
Tel 212/255-5793
www.thekitchen.org
At the fixture of the downtown scene established in 1971, the careers of such artists as Philip Glass, Laurie Anderson, Eric Bogosian, Robert Mapplethorpe and Cindy Sherman were nurtured. It's still going strong. Varies Varies 23rd Street (C, E) M11, M23

MERCE CUNNINGHAM STUDIO
Map 188 D22
55 Bethune Street at Washington Street (11th floor)
Tel 212/255-8240
www.merce.org

The Studio Performance Series for Emerging Choreographers uses this large studio space from September to July. It seats 99. Cunningham, now in his 80s, still teaches here. Varies $15 14th Street (A, C, E), 14th Street (1, 2, 3, 9) M11, M20, M8

METROPOLITAN OPERA HOUSE
Map 186 C16
30 Lincoln Center Plaza between 63rd and 64th streets
Tel 212/362-6000
www.metopera.org
The Metropolitan Opera, which had its first season in 1883–84, moved to this building on the western side of Lincoln Center Plaza in 1966. Although modern, it is glamorous with its Chagall paintings, plush crimson carpeting, chandeliers and gold leaf. The back of each of the theater's 3,800-seats has a screen that shows subtitles during performances. Most productions are spectacular, with the best international stars. Season ticket holders snap up most of the best seats (and the best-priced seats) but individual tickets are usually available. Beginning in May the American Ballet Theatre performs a traditional repertory plus more modern pieces by such choreographers as James Kudelka and Twyla Tharp. Varies Varies; $33–195, Student discount tickets $25–35 66th Street (1, 9) M5, M7, M11, M104, M66

NEW YORK GRAND OPERA
154 West 57th Street, suite 125
www.newyorkgrandopera.org
Founded in 1973, this company performs fully staged operas with full orchestra at Carnegie Hall and gives free performances at the annual SummerStage in Central Park. Varies $20–60 (Summer in Central Park free)

NEW YORK STATE THEATER
Map 186 C16
20 Lincoln Center Plaza at 63rd Street

Tel 212/870-5570
www.nycballet.com
www.nycopera.com
Home to the New York City Opera and the New York City Ballet, Philip Johnson's 2,792-seat auditorium stands on the south side of Lincoln Center Plaza. The New York City Opera is famous for its emphasis on the ensemble rather than soloists and for being the first major company in New York to display subtitles. Many opera mavens prefer the City Opera's exciting repertoire and stimulating productions over those of the Met.

The New York City Ballet got its start in 1933, when George Balanchine came to the United States and Lincoln Kirstein invited him to start a ballet school as an incubator for a company. Jerome Robbins joined the duo in 1948. Though Balanchine died in 1983, his company is still going strong under artistic director Peter Martins. Its 150-work repertory includes many works by both Balanchine and Robbins. The company performs for 23 weeks in the State Theater and then moves upstate to Saratoga. Varies City Opera $25–110, NY Ballet $30–78 66th Street (1, 9) M5, M7, M11, M104, M66

STREB ACTION INVENTION LAB
Off map 189 G23 (Brooklyn)
51 North First Street between Wythe and Kent
Williamsburg
Brooklyn
Tel 718-384-6491
www.billburg.com
Harry Houdini and Evel Knievel inspire Elizabeth Streb's daring energetic stunt-like "Popaction" dancing in which she crashes through glass and leaps from ledges. She performs at this 200-seat theater and supper club and also in Grand Central and at the Joyce Theater and the Kitchen. Varies Varies Bedford Avenue (L)

Comedy, Poetry & the Spoken Word

BARNES & NOBLE
Map 188 E21
33 East 17th Street at Union Square
Tel 212/253-0810 and other locations
www.bn.com
Barnes & Noble stores regularly sponsor readings, discussions and signings with numerous authors; the biggest names are most likely to appear at the Union Square branch.
🔘 Varies 🎫 Free 🚇 14th Street/Union Square (L, N, Q, R, W, 4, 5, 6) 🚌 M1, M2, M3, M6, M7, M14

BOWERY POETRY CLUB
Map 189 F22
308 Bowery between Bleecker and East 1st streets
Tel 212/614-0505 or 212/206-1515
www.bowerypoetry.com
All kinds of poets and performance artists play here. You might find *Communications from a Cockroach* and similar offbeat shows.
🔘 Varies 🎫 $5-15 🚇 Bleecker Street (6) Broadway/Lafayette (F, V, S) 🚌 M21, M103

CAROLINE'S COMEDY CLUB
Map 186 D17
1626 Broadway between 49th and 50th streets
Tel 212/757-4100
www.carolines.com
First opened by Caroline Hirsch as a cabaret in Chelsea in 1981, the club gained a name throughout the 1980s and 1990s for its comedy bookings. Now in its glitzy Times Square venue, it presents live entertainment 365 nights a year. Jerry Seinfeld and Rosie O'Donnell did their early stand-up here.
🔘 Mon–Wed 7.30, 9.30, Thu, Sun 8, 10, Fri–Sat 8, 10.30, 12.30am 🎫 Varies, plus 2-drink minimum 🚇 50th Street (1, 9) 🚌 M10, M20, M50

CHICAGO CITY LIMITS
Map 187 F16
1105 First Avenue between East 60th and 61st streets
Tel 212/888-5233
www.chicagocitylimits.com

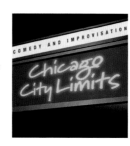

This comedy revue company relocated to New York from Chicago in 1979 The resident troupe puts on two-hour improv shows. Don't sit in the front row if you're worried about being heckled. Soft drinks served.
🔘 Wed–Sun 🎫 $20 🚇 59th Street (4, 5, 6) 🚌 M15

COMEDY CELLAR
Map 188 E22
117 MacDougal Street between West 3rd and Bleecker streets
Tel 212/254-3480
www.comedycellar.com
A down-home cave-like venue beneath the Olive Tree Café that features nationally known comedians from such shows as *Saturday Night Live*.
🔘 Sun–Thu 9, Fri 9 and 11, Sat 9, 10.45 and 12.30am 🎫 $10–15, plus 2-drink minimum 🚇 West 4th Street (A, C, E, F, V, S) 🚌 M5, M6

DANGERFIELD'S
Map 187 F16
1118 First Avenue between East 61st and 62nd streets
Tel 212/593-1650
www.dangerfields.com
Rodney Dangerfield is no longer a regular presence, but this classic seedy club, established in 1969, has hosted many a legend, from Jay Leno and Jim Carrey to Jackie Mason, Tim Allen and Andrew Dice Clay.
🔘 Sun–Thu 9, Fri 9, 11.15, Sat. 8, 10.30, and 12.30am 🎫 Cover varies, no minimum 🚇 59th Street (4, 5, 6) 🚌 M15, M57

DONNELL MEDIA CENTER
Map 187 E17
New York Public Library
20 West 53rd Street between Fifth and Sixth avenues
Tel 212/621-0609
www.nypl.org
Cultural events and readings.
🔘 Varies 🎫 Free 🚇 53rd Street/Fifth Avenue (E, V) 🚌 M1, M2, M3, M4, M5, M6, M7

THE DUPLEX
Map 188 D22
61 Christopher Street at Seventh Avenue South
Tel 212/255-5438
www.theduplex.com
A launching pad for Woody Allen, Joan Rivers and Rodney Dangerfield. The tradition continues in the upstairs cabaret room. Piano bar downstairs.
🔘 Varies 🎫 Cover varies, plus 2-drink minimum 🚇 Christopher Street/Sheridan Square (1, 9) 🚌 M20, M8

GOTHAM COMEDY CLUB
Map 188 E20
34 West 22nd Street between Fifth and Sixth avenues
Tel 212/367-9000
www.gothamcomedyclub.com

Old and new hands on the comedy scene play this upscale, elegant club in the Flatiron District, which opened in 1996.
🔘 Daily, showtimes vary 🎫 Varies 🚇 23rd Street (F, V) 🚌 M2, M3, M5, M6, M7, M23

HOUSING WORKS USED BOOK CAFÉ
Map 189 F23
126 Crosby Street at Jersey
Tel 212/334-3324

WHAT TO DO

This bookstore with a wrap-around gallery has become a major literary hub, attracting hipsters to readings, parties and events. Every third Friday of the month, there's an acoustic music concert. All monies support the homeless with HIV and AIDS.

Ⓞ Mon–Fri 10–9, Sat 12–9, Sun 12–7 (readings/events vary) Ⓥ Free–$20 Ⓢ Prince Street (N, R), Broadway-Lafayette (F, V, S), Bleecker Street (6) Ⓑ M1

NEW SCHOOL
Map 188 E21
Tishman Hall
66 West 12th Street between Fifth and Sixth avenues
Tel 212/229-5488
www.nsu.newschool.edu
This prestigious university stages concerts, lectures and other performances including a new poetry series. *Inside the Actor's Studio*, which airs on Bravo, is one of the school's most popular events, but no single tickets are available.

Ⓞ Varies Ⓥ Varies Ⓢ 14th Street (F, V) Ⓑ M5, M6, M7, M14

NEW YORK PUBLIC LIBRARY
Map 188 E18
Fifth Avenue between 41st and 42nd streets
Tel 212/930-0855
www.nypl.org

In addition to exhibitions, the Library also sponsors lectures by leading writers and critics. They are usually held in the Celeste Bartos Forum.

Ⓞ Varies Ⓥ Varies Ⓢ 42nd Street (B, D, F, V), Grand Central (4, 5, 6) Ⓑ M1, M2, M3, M4, M42

92ND STREET Y
Map 187 F13
1395 Lexington Avenue at 92nd Street
Tel 212/415-5500
www.92Y.org
This major cultural force in the city has four performance spaces, programming ranges everything from lectures given by heavy hitters like Bill Gates and Bill Clinton to readings sponsored in the Unterberg Poetry Center.

Ⓞ Varies Ⓥ Concerts $30–40; lectures $15–22 Ⓢ 96th Street (6) Ⓑ M98, M101, M102, M103, M96

NUYORICAN POETS CAFÉ
Map 189 G22
236 East 3rd Street between Avenues B and C
Tel 212/505-8183
www.nuyorican.org
Started as a living room salon and originally a platform for Puerto Rican poets and artists, the Café is still famous for its Wednesday and Friday night poetry slams. Expect to see theater, screenplay readings and even Latin jazz. Take a cab.

Ⓞ Tue–Sat 7–12, Sun 4–12 Ⓥ Varies Ⓢ Lower East Side/Second Avenue (F, V) Ⓑ M9, M21

PEOPLE'S IMPROV THEATER
Map 188 E19/20
154 West 29th Street between Sixth and Seventh avenues
Tel 212/563-7488
www.thepitnyc.com
Improvisation here comes with caustic social commentary and audience participation.

Ⓞ Varies Ⓥ Varies Ⓢ 28th Street (1, 9) Ⓑ M5, M6, M7, M20

THE POETRY PROJECT
Map 189 F21
St. Mark's Church in the Bowery
131 East 10th Street at Second Avenue
Tel 212/674-0910
www.poetryproject.com
This legendary outpost in the East Village, which hosted W. H. Auden, Allen Ginsberg and many others, has regular readings on Mondays and Wednesdays, among other events.

Ⓞ Varies Ⓥ Varies Ⓢ Astor Place (6) First Avenue (L) Ⓑ M15, M8

POETS HOUSE
Map 189 F23
72 Spring Street between Crosby and Lafayette
Tel 212/431-7920

This 40,000-volume poetry library sponsors a fall and spring lecture series.

Ⓞ Varies Ⓥ Free–$5 Ⓢ Spring Street (6), Spring Street (C, E) Ⓑ M1

QUEENS COLLEGE
Music Building
Tel 718-997-4646
www.qc.edu/readings
The college offers a fall and spring series of readings by international poets and writers. Past participants have included Paul Auster, Susan Sontag and E. L. Doctorow. No credit cards.

Ⓞ Tue at 7 Ⓥ $8–12 Ⓢ Main Street (7) and bus Q 25/34 (best to call for directions).

STAND-UP NEW YORK
Map 186 C14
236 West 78th Street at Broadway
Tel 212/595-0850
www.standupny.com
Stand-Up New York is a typical comedy club. Audiences can be hard on the comics, but comics that make it here today may well emerge tomorrow on late-night TV.

Ⓞ Varies Ⓥ Cover varies, 2-drink minimum Ⓢ 79th Street (1, 9) Ⓑ M104, M79

Contemporary Live Music

BLUES, COUNTRY, FOLK, REGGAE AND WORLD

ASIA SOCIETY
Map 187 F15
725 Park Avenue at East 70th Street
Tel 212/288-6400 or 288-4646
www.asiasociety.org
The downstairs auditorium showcases arts and culture—dance, film, lectures, and music—from Asia. Ravi Shankar made his American debut at the Asia Society.
Ⓘ Varies Ⓥ Varies Ⓢ 68th Street (6) 🚌 M1, M2, M3, M4, M72

B. B. KING BLUES CLUB AND GRILL
Map 188 D18
237 West 42nd Street
Tel 212/997-4144
www.bbkingblues.com
Little Richard and Roberta Flack, among others, have all entertained at this large bilevel club. On Sunday the Harlem Gospel Choir shakes up the Sunday brunch from 12.30 to 2.30. Dance floor.
Ⓘ Varies Ⓥ Cover $10–50 Ⓢ 42nd Street/Times Square (N, Q, R, S, W, 1, 2, 3, 7, 9) 🚌 M10, M20, M104, M42

BITTER END
Map 189 E22
147 Bleecker Street at Thompson Street
Tel 212/673-7030
www.bitterend.com
The cradle of the antiwar folk music scene in the 1960s, the Bitter End is much more rock-oriented today. Performances every night.

Ⓘ Varies Ⓥ Cover $5–15 Ⓢ West 4th Street (A, C, E, F, V, S) 🚌 M5, M6, M21

BLARNEY STAR
Map 189 E25
43 Murray Street
Tel 212/732-2873
Some big name traditional Irish musical entertainers perform here on Friday nights.
Ⓘ Daily 9am–4am (show time 9pm) Ⓥ Cover $12 Ⓢ City Hall (N, R, W), Park Place (2, 3) 🚌 M20

IRISH ARTS CENTER
Map 186 C17
553 West 51st Street between Tenth and Eleventh avenues
Tel 212/757-3318
www.irishartscenter.org

Comedy and music with a Celtic-Gaelic flavor are performed here the first Sunday of the month.
Ⓘ Varies Ⓥ Varies Ⓢ 50th Street (C, E) 🚌 M11, M50

JAPAN SOCIETY
Map 187 F18
333 East 47th Street between First and Second avenues
Tel 212/832-1155
www.japansociety.org
Traditional and contemporary Japanese music concerts and cultural events are held in the 278-seat Lila Acheson Wallace Auditorium.
Ⓘ Varies Ⓥ Varies Ⓢ 51st Street (6) 🚌 M15, M27, M50

LION'S DEN
Map 189 E22
214 Sullivan Street between Bleecker and

West 3rd streets
Tel 212/477-2782
www.cegmusic.com
Folk and rock artists are the staples.
Ⓘ Nightly (show times vary) Ⓥ Cover $8–30 Ⓢ West 4th Street (A, C, E, F, V, S), Bleecker Street (6) 🚌 M5, M6, M21

PADDY REILLY'S MUSIC BAR
Off map 188 F19
519 Second Avenue at 29th Street
Tel 212 686-1210
www.paddyreillys.com
The Celtic house band, the Prodigals, plays Friday nights. Thursday is open mike night, and visitors make an attempt to play the bodhran and the uillean pipes.
Ⓘ Daily 11am–4am Ⓥ Cover $5–10 Ⓢ 28th Street (6) 🚌 M15

RODEO BAR
Map 188 F20
375 Third Avenue at East 27th Street
Tel 212/683-6500
www.rodeobar.com
This Southern-style roadhouse serves up Tex-Mex food and margaritas, along with such musicians as singer-songwriter Cindy Bullens and Tex-Mex rockabilly artist Rosie Flores.
Ⓘ Daily 11.30am–2am (music Mon–Sat 10–4, Sun 10–2) Ⓥ No cover Ⓢ 28th Street (6) 🚌 M101, M102, M103

TERRA BLUES
Map 189 E22
149 Bleecker Street between LaGuardia Place and Thompson Street
Tel 212/777-7776
www.terrablues.com
At this second-floor club acoustic acts such as Honey Boy Edwards and Louisiana Red warm up the crowd. The bar has a good selection of bourbons.
Ⓘ Varies Ⓥ Cover $5–10, plus 2-drink minimum Ⓢ West 4th Street (A, C, E, F, V, S) 🚌 M5, M6

TOWN HALL
Map 188 E18
123 West 43rd Street between Sixth Avenue and Broadway
Tel 212/ 840-2824
www.the-townhall-nyc.org

This 1,500-seat theater, founded in 1921 by the suffragist League for Political Education, offers eclectic programming with Broadway songs, cabaret, opera, pop performances and world music as well as lectures and readings. McKim, Mead and White designed the Georgian-style building.

🕐 Varies 💷 $25–85 🚇 42nd Street/Times Square (N, Q, R, S, W, 1, 2, 3, 7, 9), 42nd Street (B, D, F, V) 🚌 M5, M6, M7, M42

VILLAGE UNDERGROUND
Map 189 E22
130 West 3rd Street between Sixth Avenue and MacDougal Street
Tel 212/777-7745
www.thevillageunderground.com
A subterranean club with a good lineup of artists ranging from salsa bands to blues artists. Sunday and Monday are open mike nights.
🕐 Varies 💷 Varies 🚇 West 4th Street (A, C, E, F, V, S) 🚌 M5, M6

WORLD MUSIC INSTITUTE
49 West 27th Street, Suite 930
Tel 212/545-7536
www.worldmusicinstitute.org
This organization sponsors world music concerts and series at venues around town (Symphony Space, Cooper Union, Town Hall).

JAZZ AND CABARET

ARTHUR'S TAVERN
Map 188 D22
57 Grove Street between Seventh Avenue South and Bleecker Street
Tel 212/675-6879

This funky down-home bar has jazz most nights—usually traditional Dixieland.
🕐 Showtimes vary 💷 Free 🚇 Christopher Street/Sheridan Square (1, 9) 🚌 M8, M20

BEMELMANS BAR
Map 187 E14
Carlyle Hotel
35 East 76th Street
Tel 212/744-1600
www.rosewoodhotels.com
The murals and the sophistication of the scene make this a classic New York experience.
🕐 Daily 11am–2am (entertainment from 5.30 usually) 💷 Cover $20 at table, $10 at bar; no minimum 🚇 77th Street (6) 🚌 M1, M2, M3, M4

BIRDLAND
Map 188 D18
315 West 44th Street between Eighth and Ninth avenues
Tel 212/581-3080
www.birdlandjazz.com
Perhaps the most elegant and comfortable jazz club in town. Charlie Parker inspired the original Birdland, which opened in 1949, and he was its first headliner. Expect to hear everyone from Roy Haynes and Lee Konitz to Diana Krall and Nicholas Payton.
🕐 Shows daily at 9pm and 11pm 💷 Cover varies $35–70, plus $20 minimum 🚇 42nd Street (A, C, E) 🚌 M10, M11, M20, M42

BLUE NOTE
Map 188 E22
131 West Third Street at Sixth Avenue
Tel 212/475-8592
www.bluenotejazz.com

Tiny and ultra expensive, the Blue Note is always jammed with fans grooving on the sounds of contemporary leaders in jazz, blues, Latin and R & B. It also sponsors a Latin Jazz Festival.
🕐 Daily at 9pm and 11.30pm 💷 Cover varies $20–65 at tables, $40–45 at bar, plus $5 minimum 🚇 West 4th Street (A, C, E, F, V, S) 🚌 M5, M6

CAFÉ CARLYLE
Map 187 E14
35 East 76th Street at Madison Avenue
Tel 212/744-1600
Bobby Short has been playing here since 1968, sashaying from Cole Porter to Bessie Smith with ease and entertaining Café Society in high style. On Monday night, Woody Allen occasionally shows up with his clarinet and the Eddy Davis New Orleans Jazz Band.
🕐 Sets: Mon 8.45pm, Tue–Sat 8.45pm and 10.45pm 💷 Cover $75, no minimum 🚇 77th Street (6) 🚌 M1, M2, M3, M4

CAFÉ PIERRE
Map 187 E16
Fifth Avenue at 61st Street
Tel 212/940-8185
www.fourseasons.com
Kathleen Landis and Nancy Winston play and sing jazz and cabaret standards, along with customer requests.
🕐 Tue–Sat 8.30–12.30, Sun–Mon 8.30–12 💷 No cover, $20 minimum 🚇 59th Street/Fifth Avenue (N, R, W) 🚌 M1, M2, M3, M4

CAJUN
Map 188 D21
129 Eighth Avenue between West 16th and 17th streets
Tel 212/691-6174
www.jazzatthecajun
One of the few places with traditional jazz bands every night.
🕐 Wed 12.30pm–2pm, Sun noon–4pm, Mon–Thu 8–11, Fri–Sat 8–12, Sun 7.30–10.30 💷 Free 🚇 14th Street (A, C, E) 🚌 M20

CORNELIA STREET CAFÉ
Map 188 D22
29 Cornelia Street between Bleecker and

West 3rd streets
Tel 212/989-9319
www.corneliastreetcafe.com

This subterranean space hosts
everything from structured free
jazz and cabaret to poetry and
performance art.
🕐 Varies 💵 Cover varies free–$10
🚇 West 4th Street (A, C, E, F, V, S)
🚌 M5, M6, M21

COTTON CLUB
Off map 186 C12
656 West 125th Street between
Broadway and Riverside Drive
Tel 212/663-7980
www.cottonclub-newyork.com

Although its heyday was from
1923 to 1935 (then on 142nd
Street), this famous Harlem
landmark still has blues, jazz
and gospel acts that seem
straight out of the 1920s.
Monday night is swing night.
🕐 Mon, Thu–Fri 8– 2, Sat–Sun
noon–2am 💵 Cover varies $15–32
🚇 125th Street (1, 9) 🚌 M104, Bx 15

DANNY'S SKYLIGHT ROOM
Map 186 D18
346 West 46th Street between Eighth and
Ninth avenues
Tel 212/265-8133
www.dannysgrandseapalace.com

Such cabaret artists as
singer-pianist Blossom Dearie
entertain in this elegant room.
🕐 Varies 💵 Cover varies none–$25,
plus $15 or 2-drink minimum; dinner-
show packages available 🚇 42nd Street
(A, C, E) 🚌 M11, M20

DETOUR
Map 189 F21
349 East 13th Street at First Avenue
Tel 212/533-6212
www.jazzatdetour.com
This tiny casual no-cover jazz
bar is the place to hear young
emerging musicians and
singers playing traditional
and experimental jazz.
🕐 Sun–Thu 4–2 (music 9–12.30),
Fri–Sat 4–4 (music 10–1.30) 💵 2-drink
minimum 🚇 14th Street/Union Square
(L, N, Q, R, W, 4, 5, 6), First Avenue (L)
🚌 M15, M14

DON'T TELL MAMA
Map 186 D18
343 West 46th Street between Eighth and
Ninth avenues
Tel 212/757-0788
Diverse singers and cabaret
artists perform at this
small venue.
🕐 Varies 💵 Cover varies none–$40,
plus 2-drink minimum 🚇 42nd Street
(A, C, E) 🚌 M11, M20

FEINSTEIN'S AT THE REGENCY
Map 187 E16
Regency Hotel
540 Park Avenue at East 61st Street
Tel 212/339-4095 or 307-4100
www.loewshotels.com
It's lush, elegant, and exclusive.
Michael Feinstein plays his
interpretations of Gershwin
classics. Dinner available.
🕐 Shows Tue–Sat, usually at 8
💵 Cover varies $45–75, plus $30 mini-
mum 🚇 Lexington/63rd Street (F), 59th
Street (4, 5, 6), 59th Street (N, R, W)
🚌 M1, M2, M3, M4, M57

FIREBIRD CAFÉ
Map 186 D18
365 West 46th Street between Eighth and
Ninth avenues
Tel 212/586-0244
www.firebirdrestaurant.com
Singer pianists entertain in the
downstairs café. Upstairs in the

opulent supper club the
entertainment ranges from
light musical fare to serious
operatic extravaganzas.
🕐 Tue–Thu 5–1, Fri–Sat 5–1.30 with
shows Wed–Thu at 9, Fri–Sat at 9 and 11
💵 Cover varies $20–30, plus $15 minimum 🚇 42nd Street (A, C, E) 🚌 M10,
M16, M20, M42

IRIDIUM
Map 186 D17
1650 Broadway at 51st Street
Tel 212/582-2121
www.iridiumjazzclub.com

Guitar legend Les Paul plays
every Monday night at this chic
good-looking club. Top rhythm
and blues and jazz names
appear, plus there are Cuban
jazz nights twice a month. On
Sunday there's a jazz brunch
buffet from 11.30 to 4, with
shows at 12.30 and 2.30.
🕐 Sun–Thu 5–12 (sets at 8 and 10),
Fri–Sat 7–2 (sets at 8, 10 and 11.30)
💵 Cover $25–95 ($5 minimum at bar,
$10 at table) 🚇 49th Street (N, R, W),
50th Street (1, 9) 🚌 M6, M7 M50

JAZZ AT LINCOLN CENTER
Map 186 D16
33 West 60th Street at Central Park West
Tel 212/258-9800
www.jazzatlincolncenter.org

In 2004. this Avery Fisher Hall concert series under the direction of Wynton Marsalis will move to a spectacular new facility in the AOL Time Warner complex on Columbus Circle, with performances in the 1230-seat Rose Theater, the 300- to 600-seat Allen Room (whose 50-foot-high (15m) glass wall overlooks Columbus Circle) and the more intimate Dizzy's Club Coca Cola, commemorating Dizzy Gillespie. Expect top-drawer jazz artists.
Varies Varies $45–100 66th Street (1, 9) M5, M104

JAZZ GALLERY
Map 189 D23
290 Hudson Street between Dominick and Spring streets
Tel 212/242-1063
www.jazzgallery.org
Opened in 1995, this exhibition and performance space, is used for jazz-oriented and jazz-influenced art, literature, drama and music.
Thu–Sat (sets at 9 and 10.30) Cover $12–65 Spring Street (C, E,) Houston Street (1, 9) M20, M21

JAZZ STANDARD
Map 188 F20
116 East 27th Street between Park Avenue South and Lexington Avenue
Tel 212/576-2232
www.jazzstandard.com
The Union Square Café's Danny Myers established this popular downstairs venue with food from his ground-floor restaurant Blue Smoke. It's a sleek, comfortable place for music and a meal.
Daily 6.30–3 (show times vary) Cover $20–25, plus minimum 28th Street (6) M1, M101, M102, M103

JOE'S PUB
Map 189 F22
Public Theater
425 Lafayette Street between Astor Place and East 4th Street
Tel 212/539-8770 539 8778
www.joespub.com
A favorite cabaret-club of many New Yorkers, named after

Public Theater founder Joe Papp. It's comfortable the way a club should be, with couches and tables. DJs spin during Late Night at Joe's.
Daily 6–4 (shows usually at 8.30) Cover $10–30, plus 2-drink minimum Astor Place (6) M1, M8

KAVEHAZ
Map 189 E23
123 Mercer Street between Prince and Spring streets
Tel 212/343-0612
www.kavehaz.com
The name means coffeehouse in Hungarian, and this long narrow gallery café has plenty of atmosphere. It serves light fare along with the cultural fare—usually two or three jazz bands per night and a monthly art exhibit.
Sun–Thu noon–11, Fri–Sat noon–2am (show times vary) Free Prince Street (N, R, W) M1, M6

LENOX LOUNGE
Off map 187 E12
288 Lenox Avenue between 124th and 125th streets
Tel 212/427-0253
www.lenoxlounge.com
This long time Harlem hangout for musicians has jazz every night except Tuesday.
Wed–Mon (8 and 10) Cover $20 125th Street (2, 3) M7, M102

OAK ROOM
Map 188 E18
Algonquin Hotel
59 West 44th Street between Fifth and Sixth avenues
Tel 212/840-6800
www.algonquinhotel.com
By nurturing such artists as Steve Ross, Michael Feinstein, Harry Connick, Jr., and Diana Krall, this room led a revival of cabaret. Dinner is available before the first show.
Tue–Thu 9, Fri–Sat 9 and 11.30 Cover $50, plus $15 munumum, late show $20 minimum, dinner packages 42nd Street (B, D, F, V) M1, M2, M3, M4, M5, M6, M7

ST. PETER'S CHURCH
Map 187 F17

Citicorp Center
619 Lexington Avenue at 54th Street
Tel 212/935-2200
www.saintpeters.org
The regularly held jazz vespers at this Lutheran church at Citicorp Center are well known among New Yorkers and musicians, along with the Wednesday jazz at noon.
Varies Varies 53rd Street/Lexington Avenue (E, V) M98, M101, M102, M103, M57

SCHOMBURG CENTER FOR RESEARCH IN BLACK CULTURE
Off map 187 E12
515 Malcolm X Boulevard at 135th Street
Tel 212/491-2200
www.nypl.org
This African-American cultural archive sponsors an annual Women's Jazz Festival and a performance of Langston Hughes' *Nativity* in December.
Varies Varies 135th Street (B, C) M7

SHOWMAN'S JAZZ CLUB
Off map 186 D12
375 West 125th Street between St. Nicholas and Morningside avenues
Tel 212/864-8941
In the 1940s and 50s, musicians often dropped in here after hours to jam or just hang out. Today musicians still frequent the place and you might find Grady Tate, George Benson, or Ed Bradley whiling away the hours.
Mon–Thu 8.30–12.30, Fri–Sat 10.30–3.30 No cover, 2-drink minimum 125th Street (A, B, C, D) M3

SMOKE
Off map 186 C12
2751 Broadway between 105th and 106th Streets
Tel 212/864-6662
www.smokejazz.com
Intimate and comfortable with its plush couches, red velvet barstools and heavy drapes, this club was opened in 1999. It has headlined many great jazz artists including organist Dr. Lonnie Smith and trombonist Slide Hampton.

⏺ Daily 9pm, 11pm, 12.30am 🅿 No cover, but $10 minimum Mon–Thu, cover varies $15–20 weekends ⓢ 103 Street (1, 9) 🚌 M104

STANHOPE PARK HYATT
Map 187 E14
995 Fifth Avenue at 81st Street
Tel 212/650-4737
www.parkhyatt.com

Dapper Steve Ross often entertains in the Melrose Room with his brilliant interpretations of Cole Porter, Noel Coward, Lorenz Hart and other classics.
⏺ Varies 🅿 Cover $35, plus required dinner, late shows $20 minimum
ⓢ 77th Street (6) 🚌 M1, M2, M3, M4, M79

SUGAR HILL BISTRO
Off map 186 C12
458 West 145th Street between Amsterdam and Convent avenues
Tel 212/491-5505
www.sugarhillbistro.com

At this Victorian town house, live jazz and R & B play in the first floor bar. Try the Sugar Hill ale from the Harlem Brewing Co. or one of the fancy cocktails, and keep an eye out for Bill Clinton, whose office is in Harlem.
⏺ Fri–Sat 9pm–1am 🅿 No cover
ⓢ 145th Street (A, B, C, D) 🚌 M18, M100, 101

THE SUPPER CLUB
Map 186 D18
240 West 47th Street between Broadway and Eighth Avenue
Tel 212/921-1940

On weekends DJs spin hip-hop, reggae and Latin at this swanky art-deco club with 50-foot high ceilings and a wraparound balcony. Plush couches, drapes and low lighting provide the ambience in the King Kong lounge, which is open daily.
⏺ Varies Fri–Sat 6–4 🅿 Cover $15–25
ⓢ 50th Street (1, 9), 50th Street (C, E) 🚌 M7, M10, M104 M50

SWEET RHYTHM
Map 188 D22
88 Seventh Avenue South between Grove and Bleecker streets
Tel 212/255-3626

The late Gil Evans played here when the place was called Sweet Basil. It's a casual spot where mainstream jazz artists play along with such singers as Carla Cook.
⏺ Varies 🅿 Cover $12–25, plus $10 minimum ⓢ Christopher Street/Sheridan Square (1, 9), West 4th Street (A, C, E, F, V, S) 🚌 M20, M8

TISHMAN AUDITORIUM
Map 188 E21
New School
66 West 12th Street between Fifth and Sixth avenues
Tel 212 229-5488
www.newschool.edu

The New School's Afro-Cuban Jazz Orchestra under Bobby Sanabria plays here.
⏺ Varies 🅿 Varies ⓢ 14th Street (F, V) 🚌 M2, M3, M5,M6

TONIC
Map 189 G23
107 Norfolk Street near Delancey
Tel 212/358-7051
www.tonicnyc.com

Very eclectic. This Lower East Side Club has fast become a landmark for avant-garde experimental music. Home for John Zorn's Masada, it has already completed many Live at Tonic recordings.
⏺ Varies 🅿 Cover $10–15 ⓢ Delancey Street (F, J, M, Z) 🚌 M9, M14

VILLAGE VANGUARD
Map 188 D21
178 Seventh Avenue at West 11th Street
Tel 212/255-4037
www.villagevanguard.com

Founded by Max Gordon in 1935, it's still the premier jazz club in the city, presided over by Lorraine Gordon since her husband died in 1989. The Vanguard is intimate, has terrific acoustics and features top-flight artists. All the great names have played here—Coleman Hawkins, Lester Young, and Thelonious Monk in the 40s, John Coltrane in the 60s, Keith Jarrett in the 70s, and Miles Davis and Bill Evans across the decades. Nowadays evenings often morph into a vibrant jam session. On Mondays, the Vanguard Jazz Orchestra, established by Thad Jones and Mel Lewis, plays.
⏺ Daily from 8 (sets Sun–Thu 9 and 11, Fri–Sat 9, 11 and 12.30) 🅿 Cover varies, plus $10 minimum ⓢ 14th Street (1, 2, 3, 9) 🚌 M14, M20

ZINC BAR
Map 189 E22
90 West Houston Street between LaGuardia Place and Thompson Street
Tel 212/477-8337

Music lovers and musicians come to this casual, tiny bar to hear newcomers as well as such famous names as George Benson and Max Roach. There's usually flamenco on Fridays and Brazilian music on Saturdays and Sundays.
⏺ Daily 6–3.30 (show times vary)
🅿 Cover varies ⓢ West 4th Street (A, C, E, F, V, S), Houston Street (1, 9) Bleecker Street (6) 🚌 M5, M6, M21

ROCK AND POP

AARON DAVIS HALL
Off map 186 D12
West 135th Street and Convent Avenue
City College of New York
Tel 212/650-7100
www.aarondavishall.org

Harlem's principal center for the performing arts presents established and emerging artists of color in music, dance, theater and multimedia performances. Ashford & Simpson, Craig Harris and Jose Mangual Junior Band are a few who have performed here.
⏺ Varies 🅿 Varies ⓢ 137th Street/Broadway (1, 9) 🚌 M4, M5

WHAT TO DO

APOLLO THEATER
Off map 186 D12
253 West 125th Street between Frederick
Douglass Boulevard and St. Nicholas
Avenue
Tel 212/531-5305 or 212/307-7171 (tickets)
www.apollotheater.com

Originally a vaudeville theater,
the Apollo has been a venue
for black entertainers since
1934. Everyone from Duke
Ellington and Billie Holiday to
Aretha Franklin and Stevie
Wonder have performed here.
The Wednesday Amateur Night
Competition is famous,
drawing crowds who register
their approval or disapproval
with gusto. Today the
entertainment ranges from
musicians and singers to
the Royal Shakespeare
Company's adaptation of
Salman Rushdie's novel
Midnight's Children.
🕐 Varies 💲 $25–35 🚇 125th Street
(A, B, C, D), Lenox (1, 2, 3) 🚌 M104

ARLENE GROCERY
Map 189 G23
95 Stanton St between Ludlow and
Orchard streets
Tel 212/358-1633
www.arlene-grocery.com
This former bodega is one of
the best rock clubs in the city.
The bar is pleasant, and the
back room casually comfort-
able. The place to hear
up-and-comers.
🕐 Daily 6–4 💲 Varies 🚇 Lower East
Side/Second Avenue (F, V) 🚌 M15, M21

BEACON THEATRE
Map 186 C15
2124 Broadway at 74th Street
Tel 212/496-7070 or 212/307-7171

Many different artists perform
here, from the Caribbean
calypso artist The Mighty
Sparrow to rock/pop groups.
🕐 Varies 💲 $33–75 🚇 72nd Street (1,
2, 3, 9) 🚌 M104, M72

BOWERY BALLROOM
Map 189 F23
6 Delancey Street at Bowery
Tel 212/533-2111
www.boweryballroom.com
When Patti Smith came out
of retirement, it was to this
rollicking tri-level venue in a
1929 Beaux-Arts building that
she returned. The club opened
in 1997 and has comfortable
lounges, good sound systems,
a large stage and excellent
sight lines. Beth Orton, Soul
Asylum, Chris Robinson, David
Byrne and Counting Crows are
just a few of the bands that
have played here.
🕐 Varies 💲 Cover varies $12–35
🚇 Delancey/Essex (F, J, M, Z) 🚌 M103

CBGB DOWNSTAIRS LOUNGE
Map 189 F22
315 Bowery at Bleecker Street
Tel 212/982-4052
www.cbgb.com
Ever since it opened in 1973,
this dark, funky place has
been the home of
underground rock (despite
the fact that the name stands
for "country bluegrass blues").
Here New Yorkers grooved to
the Ramones, Patti Smith,
and all of the most important
punk and post-punk bands
from Blondie to Television and
the Talking Heads. Sunday
night, there's jazz in the
downstairs lounge.
🕐 Varies 💲 Cover $7–10 🚇 Bleecker
Street (6) 🚌 M103, M21

COOPER UNION GREAT HALL
Map 189 F22
Seventh Street at Third Avenue
Tel 212/353-4195 or 212/279-4200
www.cooper.edu/ce
Everything from fado
(Portuguese folk music) and
contemporary classical music
to Afro-Brazilian drum groups
and samba bands can be

heard in this hall at a private
tuition-free college for the
Advancement of Science and
Art. Abraham Lincoln spoke
here in 1860.
🕐 Varies 💲 Varies $15–25 🚇 Astor
Place (6), 8th Street (N, R, W) 🚌 M101,
M102, M103, M8

FEZ UNDER TIME CAFE
Map 189 F22
380 Lafayette Street at Great Jones
Tel 212/533-2680
www.feznyc.com
This performance space
features theater, film, Celtic
singers, comedians and other
entertainers. Cocktail lounge.
🕐 Mon–Thu 6–2, Fri–Sun 6–4 (show
schedules vary) 💲 Varies $10–20
🚇 Broadway/Lafayette (F, V, S), Bleecker
Street (6) 🚌 M1, M8

KNITTING FACTORY
Map 189 E24
74 Leonard Street between Broadway
and Church Street
Tel 212/219-3006 or 219-3055
www.knittingfactory.com
Innovative owner Michael
Dorf opened this club in
TriBeCa in 1987 to headline
local and international bands
playing experimental music—
free jazz, rock and even
klezmer (a mix of eastern
European Jewish music with
other styles). Its dedicated
musical audience comes to
three performance spaces: the
Main Space, the smaller Old
Office and Alterknit Theater,
which hosts a weekly poetry
open mike, and the Tapas Bar.
The bar has plenty of beers on
tap and free shows at midnight. The club also sponsors
festivals and operates a record
label.
🕐 Show times vary 💲 Cover varies
$10–30; free live music in Tapas Bar
Sun–Tue 10pm–1am and Wed–Sat
11pm–2am 🚇 Franklin Street (1, 9)
🚌 M1, M6

LUNA LOUNGE
Map 189 G23
171 Ludlow between Houston and
Stanton streets
Tel 212/260-2323

Post punk and new wave bands perform here (usually three bands a night). Monday night is comedy.

🎧 Varies 🎫 $7 for comedy, free for music 🚇 Lower East Side/Second Avenue (F, V) 🚌 M9, M14, M15, M21

MADISON SQUARE GARDEN
Map 188 D19
4 Penn Plaza
Tel 212/465-6741
Located on top of Penn Station, this arena hosts sports events, concerts and other entertainment. Bob Dylan, Madonna, Michael Jackson, the Rolling Stones, Elton John and many other big star tours stop here.

🎧 Varies 🎫 Varies 🚇 34th Street/Penn Station (A, C, E, 1, 2, 3, 9) 🚌 M10, M16, M20, M34

MAKOR
Map 186 D15
35 West 67th Street at Columbus Avenue
Tel 212/601-1000
www.92Y.org
This venue associated with a Jewish community center offers an eclectic mix of musical entertainment ranging from rap to blues and gypsy to klezmer. It's strong on world music and brings in such performers as Nigerian Kofo the Wonderman and Maria del Mar Bonet from Mallorca.

🎧 Varies 🎫 Cover varies $15–30 🚇 66th Street (1, 9) 🚌 M5, M7, M104, M66

MERCURY LOUNGE
Map 189 G22
217 East Houston Street between First

Avenue and Avenue A
Tel 212/260-4700
www.mercuryloungenyc.com
A regular stop on the downtown music scene. Bands—both local or international—perform back to back in one raucous room. You might find Holly Go Lightly, who sang with punk Brit Billy Childish, doing garage rock, for example. The adjacent lounge is slightly more serene.

🎧 Daily 8–3 🎫 Cover varies $8–20 🚇 Lower East Side/Second Avenue (F, V) 🚌 M14, M21

ROSELAND BALLROOM
Map 186 D17
239 West 52nd Street between Broadway and Eighth Avenue
Tel 212/247-0200
www.roselandballroom.com
New Yorkers can wax nostalgic about this place. The original opened at 51st Street in 1919, during the big band era, but moved here in 1956. It was a legendary ballroom featuring the bands of Fletcher Henderson, Tommy Dorsey, Count Basie and Glenn Miller. Nowadays look for jambands, funk, hip-hop and jazz as well as the orchestras of Bob January and Don Glasser.

🎧 Varies 🎫 Cover varies $25–27.50 🚇 50th Street (1, 9), 50th Street (C, E) 🚌 M6, M7, M10, M20, M50

SOB'S
Map 189 D23
204 Varick Street at Houston Street
Tel 212/243-4940
www.sobs.com

Since 1982 this club (Sounds of Brazil) has been at the

forefront of Afro-Latino music. The featured band might play hip-hop and rap or driving Latin salsa. Monday nights include a free Latin dance class.

🎧 Varies 🎫 Cover $10–20, plus $20 minimum 🚇 Houston Street (1, 9) 🚌 M20, M21

SOUTHPAW
Off map 189 G25
125 Fifth Avenue between Sterling and St. John's Place
Park Slope, Brooklyn
Tel 718-230-0236
This club designed for rock shows has great acoustics, a good-size stage and a terrific sound system.

🎧 Daily 🎫 Varies 🚇 Fourth Avenue (F, M, R, W)

SYMPHONY SPACE
Map 186 C12
2537 Broadway at 95th Street
Tel 212/864-5400 or 864-1414
www.symphonyspace.org
Since 1978 this alternative space occupying a renovated movie theater has been offering eclectic programming in two theaters, the Peter Jay Sharp Theatre and the Leonard Nimoy Thalia. It's known for its free shows, Wall to Wall 12-hour marathons celebrating particular artists (Joni Mitchell, for example); for its Face the Music and Dance, which pairs musicians with choreographers; and for its Selected Shorts, an evening of major actors reading short stories. Companies that perform regularly include the New Amsterdam Symphony Orchestra, the Gilbert and Sullivan Players, and the Manhattan Chamber Orchestra. Many world music artists, including guitarist Djelimady Tounkara from Mali and Indian tabla player Zakir Hussain, also perform here under the auspices of the World Music Institute.

🎧 Varies 🎫 Varies $12–26 🚇 96th Street (1, 2, 3, 9) 🚌 M104, M96

Theater

No fee applies when you buy your tickets at the box office; most open from Monday to Saturday from 10am to 8pm and Sunday from 11am to 6.30pm. Standing Room Only tickets, which are sometimes available, go on sale when the box office opens on the day of the performance.

BROADWAY THEATERS

On Broadway, ticket prices range from $20 to $100 for major Broadway musicals and from $50 to $80 for dramas and comedies.

AL HIRSCHFELD
Map 188 D18
302 West 45th Street between Eighth and Ninth avenues
Tel 212/239-6200
Recently given the name of a theatrical caricaturist, this Moorish-style theater was built in 1924 and has lavish interiors. Avoid the side seats.
Tue–Sat 8, matinees Wed, Sat, and Sun 2 42nd Street/Eighth Avenue (A, C, E) M6, M7, M10, M11, M42, M104

AMBASSADOR THEATRE
Map 188 D17
219 West 49th Street between Broadway and Eighth Avenue
Tel 212/239-6200
Opened in 1921, this 1,125-seat auditorium is wider than it is deep, so viewing is good but with a mezzanine overhang.
Mon–Tue, Thu–Sat 8, Sun 7, matinees Sat–Sun 2 50th Street/Seventh Avenue (1, 9); 49th Street (N, R) M6, M7, M10, M27, M50, M104

AMERICAN AIRLINES
Map 188 D18
227 West 42nd Street between Seventh and Eighth avenues
Tel 212/719-1300
www.roundabouttheatre.org
This restored 1918 theater with 750 seats is now the home of the Roundabout Theatre Company, founded in 1965 to perform the classics and new plays at affordable prices.

Tue–Sat 8, matinees Wed, Sat, Sun 2 42nd Street/Times Square (N, Q, R, S, W, 1, 2, 3, 7, 9) M6, M7, M10, M42, M104

BARRYMORE THEATRE
Map 188 D18
243 West 47th Street between Seventh and Eighth avenues
Tel 212/239-6200
Ethel Barrymore starred in *The Kingdom of God* to open this theater in 1928. Fred Astaire gave his last stage performance here in *The Gay Divorcée* in the 1930s.
Tue–Sat 8, matinees Wed, Sat, Sun 2 50th Street (C, E), 50th Street (1, 9), 49th Street (N, R, W) M10, M20, M104

BELASCO
Map 188 E18
11 West 44th Street between Broadway and Sixth Avenue
Tel 212/239-6200
Named after the bishop of Broadway David Belasco, this gem of a theater with 1,018 seats has some gorgeous Tiffany lamps and lovely murals by Everett Shinn. Avoid the side orchestra if you can.
Tue–Sat 8, matinees Wed and Sat 2, Sun 3 42nd Street/Times Square (N, R, S, W, 1, 2, 3, 7, 9); 42nd Street/ Sixth Avenue (B, D, F) M5, M6, M7, M10, M42, M104

BOOTH
Map 188 D18
222 West 45th Street between Broadway and Eighth Avenue
Tel 212/239-6200
Numerous hits have played at this Italianate 781-seat theater dating to 1913 and named after actor Edwin Booth.
Tue 7, Mon, Wed, Fri–Sat 8, matinees Wed and Sat 2, Sun 3 42nd Street/Times Square (N, R, S, W, 1, 2, 3, 7, 9) M6, M7, M10, M42, M104

BROADHURST
Map 188 D18
235 West 44th Street between Broadway and Eighth Avenue
Tel 212/639-6200
Named after Anglo-American playwright George Broadhurst,

this theater was built by the Shuberts and has welcomed star-studded casts since opening in 1918. Seats 1,186.
Tue–Sat 8, matinees Wed and Sat 2, Sun 3 42nd Street/ Times Square (N, R, S, W, 1, 2, 3, 7, 9) M6, M7, M10, M42, M104

BROADWAY
Map 186 D17
1681 Broadway between 52nd and 53rd streets
Tel 212/239-6200
This 1,752-seat theater was built as a movie house in 1924. Avoid the back of the house if you can.
Tue–Sat 8, matinees Wed and Sat 2, Sun 3 50th Street/Eighth Avenue (C, E); 50th Street/Seventh Avenue (1, 9) M6, M7, M10, M27, M50, M104

BROOKS ATKINSON
Map 186 D18
256 West 47th Street between Broadway and Eighth Avenue
Tel 212/307-4100
www.nederlander.org
Built in 1926, this ornate theater is named after longtime *New York Times* theater critic Brooks Atkinson. With 1,086 seats, you may feel you're too far from the stage if you sit in the rear mezzanine .
Tue–Sat 8, matinees Wed and Sat 2, Sun 3 50th Street/Eighth Avenue (C, E); 50th Street/Seventh Avenue (1, 9) M10, M27, M50, M104

CIRCLE IN THE SQUARE (UPTOWN)
Map 188 D17
1633 Broadway at 50th Street
Tel 212/239-6200
Opened in 1972, this theater is in the same building as the Gershwin theater. All 681 seats have good sight lines.
Tue–Sat 8, matinees Wed and Sat 2, Sun 3 50th Street/ Eighth Avenue (C, E); 50th Street/Seventh Avenue (1, 9) M6, M7, M10, M27, M50, M104

CORT
Map 188 E17
138 West 48th Street between Sixth and Seventh avenues
Tel 212/239-6200

Named after producer John Cort, this 1,084-seat theater was modeled on the Petit Trianon and built in 1912. All seats have good sight lines. Tue–Sat 8, matinees Wed and Sat 2, Sun 3 47th–50th streets/ Rockefeller Center (B, D, F, V) M6, M7, M10, M27, M50, M104

EUGENE O'NEILL
Map 186 D17
230 West 49th Street between Broadway and Eighth Avenue
Tel 212/239-6200
Opened in 1926, the O'Neill was named after the great playwright in 1959. Tue–Sat 8, matinees Wed, Sat, Sun 2 50th Street/Eighth Avenue (C, E); 50th Street/Seventh Avenue (1, 9) M6, M7, M10, M27, M50, M104

FORD CENTER FOR THE PERFORMING ARTS
Map 188 D18
213 West 42nd Street between Seventh and Eighth avenues
Tel 212/556-4750 or 307-4100

The Lyric (1903) and the Apollo (1920) were renovated and combined to create this 1,839-seat house ideal for spectacular musicals. Most seats have good sight lines. Tue–Sat 8, matinees Wed and Sat 2, Sun 3 42nd Street/Times Square (N, Q, R, S, W, 1, 2, 3, 7, 9); 42nd Street/Eighth Avenue (A, C, E) M6, M7, M10, M42, M104

GERSHWIN
Map 186 D17
222 West 51st Street between Broadway and Eighth Avenue
Tel 212/307-4100
www.nederlander.org

Owned by the Broadway producers the Nederlanders, the Gershwin opened in 1972. The auditorium is on the second floor. It was renamed in 1983 after George and Ira. Tue–Sat 8, matinees Wed and Sat 2, Sun 3 50th Street/Eighth Avenue (C, E); 50th Street/Seventh Avenue (1, 9) M6, M7, M10, M27, M50, M104

GOLDEN THEATRE
Map 188 D18
252 West 45th Street between Broadway and Eighth Avenue
Tel 212/239-6200
A small theater, named for producer John Golden and opened in 1927. Tue–Sat 8, matinees Wed and Sat 2, Sun 3 42nd Street/Times Square (N, Q, R, S, W, 1, 2, 3, 7, 9); 42nd Street/Eighth Avenue (A, C, E) M6, M7, M10, M42, M104

HELEN HAYES
Map 188 D18
240 West 44th Street between Seventh and Eighth avenues
Tel 212/944-9450 or 239-6200
This small Colonial Revival-style theater was built in 1912 to house productions of new and experimental theater. Tue–Sat 8, matinees Wed and Sat 2, Sun 3 42nd Street/Times Square (N, Q, R, S, W, 1, 2, 3, 7, 9); 42nd Street/Eighth Avenue (A, C, E) M6, M7, M10, M42, M104

HENRY MILLER'S
Map 188 E18
124 West 43rd Street between Broadway and Sixth Avenue
Tel 212/239-6200
Playwriter Henry Miller helped design this space, and many of his plays premiered here. Tue–Sat 8, matinees Wed and Sat 2, Sun 3 42nd Street/Times Square (N, Q, R, S, W, 1, 2, 3, 7, 9); 42nd Street/Eighth Avenue (A, C, E) M6, M7, M10, M27, M50,

IMPERIAL
Map 188 D18
249 West 45th Street between Broadway and Eighth Avenue
Tel 212/239-6200
Gypsy, Fiddler on the Roof, and

Les Miserables played at this 1923 theater. Seats 1,421. Mon–Sat 8, matinees Wed and Sat 2 42nd Street/Times Square (N, Q, R, S, W, 1, 2, 3, 7, 9); 42nd Street/Eighth Avenue (A, C, E M6, M7, M10, M42, M104

LONGACRE
Map 188 D17
220 West 48th Street between Broadway and Eighth Avenue
Tel 212/239-6200
Named after Longacre Square, as today's Times Square was known before the *New York Times* moved into the area, this 1,095-seat theater opened in 1913. Orchestra seats have the best sight lines. Tue–Fri 8, Sat 5 and 9, Sun 3 and 7 50th Street/Seventh Avenue (1, 9); 49th Street (N, R); 47th–50th streets/Rockefeller Center (B, D, F, Q) M6, M10, M27, M50, M42, M104

LUNT-FONTANNE
Map 188 D18
205 West 46th Street between Broadway and Eighth Avenue
Tel 212/575-9200 or 307-4747
www.nederlander.org
Designed by Carrère and Hastings in 1910, the theater was gutted in 1958. It seats 1,475 and was the New York home of *The Sound of Music.* Tue–Sat at 8, Sun 6.30, matinees Sat 2, Sun 1 42nd Street/Times Square (N, Q, R, S, W, 1, 2, 3, 7, 9); 50th Street/Seventh Avenue (1, 9); 50th Street/Eighth Avenue (C, E) M6, M10, M27, M42, M50, M104

LYCEUM
Map 188 D18
149 West 45th Street between Broadway and Sixth Avenue
Tel 212/239-6200
Built in 1903 in Beaux-Arts style, it's the oldest theater still in use on Broadway. Tue–Sat 8, matinees Wed, Sat 2, Sun 3 49th Street (N, R); 47th–50th streets/Rockefeller Center (B, D, F) M5, M6, M7, M10, M42, M104

MAJESTIC
Map 188 D18
245 West 44th Street between Broadway

WHAT TO DO

and Eighth Avenue
Tel 212/239-6200
This theater seating 1,607, which opened in 1927, has hosted hits from *Carousel* to the *Phantom of the Opera*.
🕐 Mon–Sat 8, matinees Wed and Sat 2 🚇 42nd Street/Times Square (N, Q, R, S, W, 1, 2, 3, 7, 9); 42nd/Eighth Avenue (A, C, E) 🚌 M6, M7, M10, M42, M104

MARQUIS
Map 188 D18
1535 Broadway between 45th and 46th streets
Tel 212/382-0100 or 307-4100
www.nederlander.org
One of the newest large theaters on Broadway, with extra comforts, including well-raked seating. Seats 1,595.
🕐 Tue–Sat 8, matinees Wed and Sat 2, Sun 3 🚇 42nd Street/Times Square (N, Q, R, S, W, 1, 2, 3, 7, 9) 🚌 M6, M7, M10, M27, M42, M50, M104

MINSKOFF
Map 188 D18
200 West 45th Street between Seventh and Eighth avenues
Tel 212/ 307-4100
www.nederlander.org

This Nederlander theater, which was built in 1973, is rather impersonal. An escalator takes you to the fourth-floor Orchestra.
🕐 Mon–Sat 8, matinees Wed and Sat 2 🚇 42nd Street/Times Square (N, Q, R, S, W, 1, 2, 3, 7, 9) 🚌 M6, M7, M10, M42, M104

MUSIC BOX
Map 188 D18
239 West 45th Street between Broadway and Eighth Avenue
Tel 212/239-6200

Note the plaque, just inside the lobby, commemorating Irving Berlin, who built this theater in 1921 with producer Sam Harris to house his Music Box Revues.
🕐 Tue–Sat 8, matinees Wed and Sat 2, Sun 3 🚇 42nd Street/Times Square (N, Q, R, S, W, 1, 2, 3, 7, 9); 42nd Street/Eighth Avenue (A, C, E) 🚌 M6, M7, M10, M42, M104

NEDERLANDER
Map 188 D18
208 West 41st Street between Seventh and Eighth avenues
Tel 212/921-8000 or 307-4100
www.nederlander.org

When *Rent* moved from the East Village, it came here, and *Who's Afraid of Virginia Woolf* opened here. Seats 1,189. Avoid side seats.
🕐 Mon–Tue, Thu–Sat 8, matinees Sat–Sun 2 🚇 42nd Street/Times Square (N, Q, R, S, W, 1, 2, 3, 7, 9) 🚌 M6, M7, M10, M27, M42, M50, M104

NEIL SIMON
Map 186 D17
250 West 52nd Street between Broadway and Eighth Avenue
Tel 212/757-8646 or 307-4100
www.nederlander.org

This ornate theater, opened in 1927, has been home to many musicals, including *Porgy and Bess, Funny Face* and *Hairspray*. Named after the playwright. Seats 1,334.
🕐 Tue–Sat 8, matinees Wed and Sat 2, Sun 3 🚇 50th Street/Eighth Avenue (C, E); 50th Street/Seventh Avenue (1, 9) 🚌 M6, M7, M10, M27, M50, M104

NEW AMSTERDAM
Map 188 D18
214 West 42nd Street between Seventh and Eighth avenues
Tel 212/282-2900 or 307-4747; 282-2907 for tours
www.disneyonbroadway.com

Florence Ziegfeld commissioned this Art Nouveau beauty in 1903. In 1997 the Walt Disney Company restored the place with its murals, stucco, tiles and woodwork, and installed *The Lion King*. Avoid side seats.
🕐 Wed–Sat 8, Sun 6.30, matinees Wed and Sat 2, Sun 1. Tours Mon 9.30–5.30, Tue, Thu–Sat 9.30–11.30 💵 Tours: adult $10, children under 12 $5 🚇 42nd Street/Times Square (N, Q, R, S, W, 1, 2, 3, 7, 9); 42nd Street/Eighth Avenue (A, C, E) 🚌 M6, M7, M10, M42, M104

PALACE
Map 188 D18
1564 Broadway between 46th and 47th streets
Tel 212/730-8200 or 307-4747
www.nederlander.org
The Palace opened as a vaudeville house in 1913, and such legends as Bob Hope, Sophie Tucker, Jimmy Durante and the Marx Brothers all entertained here. The Nederlanders restored it in 1965.

Tue–Sat 8, matinees Wed and Sat 2, Sun at 3 🚇 50th Street (1, 9); 49th Street (N, R) 🚌 M7, M10, M27, M50, M104

PLYMOUTH
Map 188 D18
236 West 45th Street between Broadway and Eighth Avenue
Tel 212/239-6200
Drama amd comedy from Noel Coward's *Present Laughter* to the Royal Shakespeare Company's *Nicholas Nickleby* have played at this 1918 theater. Seats 1,078.
 Tue–Sat 8, matinees Wed and Sat 2, Sun 3 🚇 42nd Street/Times Square (N, Q, R, S, W, 1, 2, 3, 7, 9); 42nd Street/Eighth Avenue (A, C, E) 🚌 M6, **M7, M10, M42, M104**

RICHARD ROGERS
Map 188 D18
226 West 46th Street between Broadway and Eighth Avenue
Tel 212/221-1211
Guys and Dolls and other hits have entertained audiences at this Renaissance Revival theater, built in 1924. Named after the composer, it seats 1,400.
 Tue–Sat 8, matinees Wed and Sat 2, Sun 3 🚇 42nd Street/Times Square (N, Q, R, S, W, 1, 2, 3, 7, 9); 42nd Street/Eighth Avenue (A, C, E); 50th Street (1, 9) 🚌 M10, M27, M50, M104

ROYALE
Map 188 D18
242 West 45th Street between Broadway and Eighth Avenue
Tel 212/239-6200
Laurence Olivier starred in *The Entertainer* on this stage. Opened in 1927, the Royale is a perfect mid-sized theater. Seats 1,068.
 Tue–Sat 8, matinees Wed 2, Sun 3 🚇 42nd Street/Times Square (N, Q, R, S, W, 1, 2, 3, 7, 9); 42nd Street/Eighth Avenue (A, C, E) 🚌 M6, M7, M10, M42, M104

ST. JAMES
Map 188 D18
246 West 44th Street between Seventh and Eighth avenues
Tel 212/239-5800
Oklahoma, The King and I, Hello Dolly and *The Producers*

have all played in this Beaux-Arts theater, dating to 1927. Large but not deep, its mezzanine hangs over the orchestra.
 Tue–Sat 8, matinees Wed and Sat 2, Sun 3 🚇 42nd Street/Times Square (N, Q, R, S, W, 1, 2, 3, 7, 9); 42nd Street/Eighth Avenue (A, C, E) 🚌 M6, M7, M10, M42, M104

SHUBERT
Map 188 D18
225 West 44th Street between Seventh and Eighth avenues
Tel 212/944-3700 or 239-6200

This theater, opened in 1913, is the cornerstone of the Shubert family's empire.
 Mon–Tue, Thu–Sat 8, Sun 7, matinees Sat and Sun 2 🚇 42nd Street/Times Square (N, Q, R, S, W, 1, 2, 3, 7, 9); 42nd Street/Eighth Avenue (A, C, E) 🚌 M6, M7, M10, M42, M104

STUDIO 54
Map 186 D17
254 West 54th Street between Broadway and Eighth Avenue
Tel 212/239-6200
A discotheque from 1977 to 1988, today Studio 54 is a 920-seat theater. *Cabaret* has played here.
 Mon–Tue, Thu–Sat 8, Sun 7, matinees Sat and Sun 2 🚇 Seventh Avenue (B, D, E); 57th Street (N, R, Q) 🚌 M6, M7, M27, M50, M57

VIRGINIA
Map 186 D17
245 West 52nd Street between Broadway and Eighth Avenue
Tel 212/239-6200
The Theater Guild commissioned this striking theater with its Tuscan-style façade, and it opened in 1925.
 Tue–Sat 8, matinees Wed and Sat 2,

Sun 3 🚇 50th Street (1, 9); 50th Street (C, E) 🚌 M6, M7, M10, M27, M50, M104

VIVIAN BEAUMONT THEATER
Map 186 C16
150 West 65th Street
Tel 212/239-6200
Categorized as a Broadway theater despite its address. Its deep thrust stage allows for innovative directing.
 Tue–Sat 8, matinees Wed and Sat 2, Sun 3 🚇 66th Street (1, 9) 🚌 M5, M7, M104, M66

WALTER KERR
Map 186 D17
219 West 48th Street between Broadway and Eighth Avenue
Tel 212/239-6200
Named after the famous *New York Times* critic, this is an ideal house for serious drama and classic comedy. Seats 947.
 Tue–Sat 8, matinees Wed and Sat 2, Sun 3 🚇 50th Street/Eighth Avenue (C, E); 50th Street/Seventh Avenue (1, 9) 🚌 M7, M10, M27, M50, M104

WINTER GARDEN
Map 186 D17
1634 Broadway between 50th and 51st streets
Tel 212/563-5544
The building dates to 1885 when it served as an auction hall and stable. The Shuberts made it into a theater in 1910. Al Jolson first appeared here in blackface. Seats 1,482.
 Tue–Sat 8, matinees Wed and Sat 2, Sun 3 🚇 50th Street/Eighth Avenue (C, E); 50th Street/Seventh Avenue (1, 9); 49th Street (N, R, W) 🚌 M6, M7, M10, M27, M50, M104

Off-Broadway theaters have 500 seats or fewer, and are usually either in the East or West villages or along 42nd Street between Eighth and Eleventh avenues. Here you'll see showcases, experimental plays, musicals in development and innovative revivals. More than a few Broadway hits have emerged from these venues. Ticket prices typically range from $20 to $65.

WHAT TO DO

ACTOR'S PLAYHOUSE

Map 188 D22

100 Seventh Avenue South between Grove and Barrow streets

Tel 212/463-0060 or 239-6200

This small downstairs venue, which has been around for 40 years, presents musical revues, often with a gay theme.

🕐 Mon, Wed–Fri 8, Sat 7, 10, Sun 7, matinees Sun 3 🚇 Christopher Street/Sheridan Square (1, 9) 🚌 M20

BOWERIE LANE

Map 189 F22

330 Bowery at Bond Street

Tel 212/677-0060

www.jeancocteaurep.org

The Jean Cocteau Repertory Company (1971) presents five to seven masterworks from Euripides to Samuel Beckett between August and June at this beautiful old bank building. Seats 140.

🕐 Varies 🚇 Broadway-Lafayette (F, V, S) 🚌 M21, M103

BROOKLYN ACADEMY OF MUSIC (BAM)

Off map 189 G25

30 Lafayette Avenue

Tel 718/636-4100 or 212/307-4100

www.bam.org

New York's premier progressive cultural complex is in Brooklyn. It incorporates several performance spaces—the Howard Gilman Opera House, seating 2,100; the 1,000-seat Harvey Lichtenstein Theater; a café; and a four-screen film complex. Every fall, BAM stages the Next Wave Festival of experimental opera, music, theater, dance and film.

🕐 Varies 🚇 DeKalb Avenue (B, D, N, Q, R) 🚌 M51

CHERRY LANE

Map 188 D22

38 Commerce Street between Hudson and Bedford streets

Tel 212/989-2020

www.cherrylanetheater.com

In 1924 Edna St. Vincent Millay and others turned a warehouse into a theater. Today the Cherry Lane Alternative continues the theater's tradition of producing emerging playwrights. Seats 180.

🕐 Mon, Wed–Fri 8, Sat 5 and 9, Sun 3 🚇 Christopher Street/Sheridan Square (1, 9) 🚌 M20, M21

DARYL ROTH THEATER

Map 188 F21

101 East 15th Street at Union Square

Tel 212/375-1110 or 212/239-6200

Producer of many Pulitzer Prize winners, Daryl Roth owns this theater in an old bank building. The space is inherently dramatic, ideal for virtually anything.

🕐 Varies 🚇 14th Street/Union Square (L, N, Q, R, W, 4, 5, 6) 🚌 M14, M1, M2, M3, M6, M7

MANHATTAN ENSEMBLE THEATRE

Map 189 E23

55 Mercer Street between Broome and Grand streets

Tel 212/925-1900

www.met.com

Home to Manhattan Ensemble, founded by David Fishelson, this theater presents new plays that are often by well-known playwrights. Seats 140.

🕐 Varies 🚇 Canal Street (J, M, N, Q), Spring Street (E, C) 🚌 M1, M6

MANHATTAN THEATRE CLUB

261 West 47th Steet

Tel 212/581-1212 (tickets) or 212/399-3000 (info)

www.manhattantheatreclub.com

Founded in 1970 to perform new plays, this company performed in City Center since 1984 and moves to the Biltmore in 2004.

🕐 Varies 🚇 57th Street (N, Q, R, W), 57th Street (F) 🚌 M5, M6, M7

MINETTA LANE

Map 188 E22

18 Minetta Lane

Tel 212/420-8000

This charming theater with a mezzanine in Greenwich Village is a major off-Broadway player. Seats 407.

🕐 Varies 🚇 West 4th Street (A, C, E, F, V, S) 🚌 M5, M6, M8

MITZI NEWHOUSE THEATER

Map 186 C16

150 West 65th Street

Tel 212 239-6277 or 212/239-6200

www.lct.org

Spalding Gray performed his one-man *Swimming to Cambodia* (1996) at this Lincoln Center theater. It has a 3/4 thrust stage; the 299 seats are steeply raked.

🕐 Tue–Sat 8, matinees Wed and Sat 2, Sun 3 🚇 66th Street (1, 9) 🚌 M5, M7, M104, M66

THE NEGRO ENSEMBLE COMPANY

Map 188 D18

303 West 42nd Street at Eighth Avenue

Tel 212/582 58600

www.negroensemblecompany.org

Founded in 1967, this group holds workshops for actors and playwrights.

🕐 Varies 🚇 42nd Street (A, C, E) 🚌 M10, M20, M42

NEW YORK THEATRE WORKSHOP

Map 189 F22

79 East 4th Street between Second Avenue and Bowery

Tel 212/780-9037 or 212/239-6200

www.nytw.org

A significant player on the Manhattan theater scene. *Rent* began life here, and the workshop staged Caryl Churchill's *Far Away*. Seats 150.

⏱ Tue–Sat 8, matinees Sat and Sun 3 🚇 Broadway-Lafayette (F, V, S), Bleecker Street (6) 🚌 M1, M21

THE ONTOLOGICAL HYSTERIC THEATER AT ST. MARKS
Map 189 F21
131 East 10th Street between Second and Third avenues
Tel 212/420-1916 or 212/533-4650
www.ontological.com

An important home for the avant-garde. Richard Foreman presented his 35th anniversary production here in 2003.

⏱ Varies 🚇 Astor Place (6), Eighth Street (N, R, W) 🚌 M8, M15

PLAYWRIGHTS HORIZONS THEATER
Map 188 C18
416 West 42nd Street between Ninth and Tenth avenues
Tel 212/564 1235
www.playwrightshorizons.org

This company is dedicated to the production of new American plays and musicals. The main stage seats 198 and the studio 96.

⏱ Varies 🚇 42nd Street (A, C, E) 🚌 M11, M42

PUBLIC THEATER
Map 189 F22
425 Lafayette Street between Astor Place and East Fourth Street
Tel 212/539-8500 or 212/239-6200
www.publictheater.org

In 1967 producer Joe Papp got the city to lease him the old Astor Library and converted it into five theater spaces.

⏱ Tue–Sat 8, Sun 7, matinees Sat and Sun 2 🚇 8th Street (N, R, W), Astor Place (6) 🚌 M1, M8

RADIO CITY MUSIC HALL
Map 187 E17
1260 Sixth Avenue at 50th Street
Tel 212/247-4777
www.radiocity.com

This theater with plenty of art-deco paraphernalia opened in 1932, was saved from demolition in 1979, and was spectacularly refurbished in 1999 to the tune of $70 million. It has seats for 5,882 in the orchestra and on three mezzanines.

⏱ Varies. One-hour tours daily 11–3 🎟 Tours: adult $17, child (under 12) $10 🚇 47th-50th streets/Rockefeller Center (B, D, F, V) 🚌 M5, M6, M7

SECOND STAGE THEATER
Map 188 D18
307 West 43rd Street between Eighth and Ninth avenues
Tel 212/787-8302
www.secondstagetheater.com

Dutch architect Rem Koolhaas helped revamp the old bank building that is home to this company. Seats 299.

⏱ Tue, Thu, Sat 8, Wed, Sun 7, matinees

Wed and Sat 2, Sun 3 🚇 79th Street (1 9) 🚌 M104, M79

SHAKESPEARE IN THE PARK
Map 186 D14
Delacorte Theater
81st Street (West Side), 79th Street (East Side)
Tel 212/539-8500
www.publictheater.org

The Public Theater sponsors this summer festival in Central Park at the Delacorte Theater. Line up for free tickets from midday onward.

⏱ Summer only Tue–Sun 🚇 79th Street (1, 9) 🚌 M104, M79, M1, M2, M3, M4

THEATER FOR THE NEW CITY
Map 189 F21
155 First Avenue at East 10th Street
Tel 212/254-1109
www.theaterforthenewcity.org

Thought-provoking, often politically inspired dramas are the repertory of this community-oriented company, founded in 1970.

⏱ Thu–Sat 8, matinees Sun at 3 🚇 Astor Place (6) 🚌 M15, M8

VARIETY ARTS THEATRE
Map 188 F21
110 Third Avenue between East 13th and 14th streets
Tel 212/239-6200

Built in 1911, this theater stages eclectic theater, often featuring famous actors. Seats 498.

⏱ Varies 🚇 14th Street/Union Square (L, N, Q, R, W, 4, 5, 6) 🚌 M14, M101, M102, M103

VINEYARD THEATRE
Map 188 F21

108 East 15th Street at Union Square East
Tel 212/353-3366, 212/353-0303, or
212/239-6200
www.vineyardtheatre.org
Located in a residential tower,
this Off-Broadway theater has
staged Pulitzer Prize-winning
plays before they went to
Broadway. Seats 120.
🕐 Tue–Sun 8, matinees Sun 3 🚇 14th
Street/Union Square (L, N, Q, R, W, 4, 5,
6) 🚌 M101, M102, M103, M14

WPP THEATRE FOUR
Map 186 C17
424 West 55th Street
Tel 212/765-1706
www.womensproject.org
Founded in 1978 by Julia
Miles, the Women's Project
Theatre is the nation's pre-
eminent women's theater
company. Seats 199.
🕐 Tue–Sat 8, Sun 7.30, matinees Sat 2,
Sun 3 🚇 59th Street (A, B, C, D, 1, 9)
🚌 M11, M57

YORK (THEATRE AT ST. PETER'S)
Map 187 F17
619 Lexington Avenue at 54th Street
Tel 212/935-5824
The material presented at the
modern performing space in
this church at Citicorp Center
is often experimental and
challenging. Seats 147.
🕐 Fri–Sat 8, Sun 7.30, matinees Sat and
Sun 2.30 🚇 51st Street (6), Fifth
Avenue/53rd Street (E, V) 🚌 M98, M101,
M102, M103

OFF-OFF-BROADWAY
These small theaters seat 100
or under, offer contemporary
works or innovative
productions of traditional
works, and often feature
actors who don't belong to
Actors Equity, the professional
union. Performances range
from the mundane to the
inspiring, and ticket prices
from $10 to $55.

BLEECKER STREET THEATRE
Map 189 F22
45 Bleecker Street between Bowery and
Lafayette
Tel 212/253-9983 or 307-4100
www.45bleecker.com

Home of the Culture Project,
which produces eclectic works
by contemporary playwrights.
Stadium-style seating for 45.
🕐 Tue–Fri 8, Sat 5 and 9, Sun 3 and 7
🚇 🚇 Bleecker Street (6), Broadway/
Lafayette (F, V, S) 🚌 M1, M103, M21

CENTER STAGE/NY
Map 188 E20
48 West 21st Street between Fifth and
Sixth avenues, fourth floor
Tel 212/929-2228
www.labtheater.org
Thirteen actors founded the
Labyrinth Repertory Company
in 1992 to enable members
to write, direct and act. Now
it has 60 international
members, who produce
annual productions here.
🕐 Varies 🎭 Varies 🚇 🚇 23rd Street
(N, R, W), 23rd Street (F, V) 🚌 M2, M3,
M5, M6, M7

CLASSICAL THEATER OF HARLEM
Off map 189 D12
Harlem School of the Arts Theater
645 St. Nicholas Avenue near 141st Street
Tel 212/539-8828 or 212/206-1515
This company founded in 1988
has been recognized outside
Harlem only recently. Its reper-
tory ranges from *The Crazy
Locomotive* by Polish play-
wright Stanislaw Witkiewicz to
Jean Genet's *The Blacks*.
🕐 Varies 🚇 🚇 145th Street (A, B, C)

FLEA THEATER
Map 189 E24
41 White Street between Broadway and
Church Street
Tel 212/226-2407
www.theflea.org
Home to the Bat Theater
Company, which presents
works by playwrights who are
breaking new boundaries—
either society's or their own.
🕐 Varies 🚇 🚇 Canal Street (A, C, E)
🚌 M1, M6

LA MAMA EXPERIMENTAL
THEATER CLUB
Map 189 F22
74A East 4th Street between 2nd Avenue
and Bowery
Tel 212/475-7710
www.lamama.org

One of the most famous off-
off-Broadway theaters was
founded in 1961 by Ellen
Stewart to nurture new
playwrights. It has three
theaters: the Annex, the
First Floor and the Club,
a cabaret space.
🕐 Thu–Sun; show times vary. Matinees
Sun 🚇 🚇 Astor Place (6) 🚌 M8, M15

THE MINT SPACE
Map 188 D18
311 West 43rd St between Eighth and
Ninth avenues
Tel 212/315-9434 or 279-4200
www.minttheater.org
Home of the Mint Theater,
one of the most recognized
companies off-off-Broadway.
It performs stimulating plays,
which may drawn from foreign
traditions. Seats 74.
🕐 Varies 🚇 🚇 42nd Street (A, C, E)
🚌 M11, M20, M42

PERFORMING GARAGE
Map 189 E23
33 Wooster at Grand Street
Tel 212 966-9796 or 966-3651
www.thewoostergroup.org
Home to the Wooster Group,
an Obie-winning troupe
founded in 1975 by Jim
Clayburgh, Willem Dafoe,
Spalding Gray and others. The
group produces and develops
experimental entertainment
and theater.
🕐 Varies 🚇 🚇 Canal Street (A, C, E)
🚌 M6

THEATRE AT ST. CLEMENTS
Map 188 C18
423 West 46th Street between Ninth and
Tenth avenues
Tel 212/246-7277 or 212/279-4200
Playwrights such as David
Mamet and Terrance McNally
have premiered works here,
and many famous actors
appeared here early in their
careers. The plays often focus
on contemporary spiritual,
moral and ethical issues.
The space is in an Episcopalian
church and seats 151.
🕐 Wed–Fri 7.30, Sat 8, matinees Sat 2,
Sun 3 🚇 🚇 42nd Street (A, C, E)
🚌 M11, M42

NIGHTLIFE

WHAT TO DO

Many New Yorkers take their nightlife very seriously. You can always find a "scene" somewhere in the city that never sleeps. True, Giuliani clamped down on the big clubs, and Bloomberg's anti-smoking campaign has dampened some night clubbers' spirits, but the party goes on, shifting from bar to dance club and back, and then to the Meatpacking District at dawn. The night scene is constantly changing with clubs closing or undergoing makeovers, and name DJs flitting from one venue to another.

Some New York City clubs have a great deal of attitude. At the hottest dance clubs, there's a competition to get in, and people dress à la mode to ensure that they get past the velvet rope and the bouncer at the door. And there's always a VIP room and an A-list for guests (although you can often get on the list by calling in advance or going to www.newyorksheckys.com or www.promony.com). Still, there are plenty of more casual clubs available, especially the gay spots (see *Next*, *HX*, and *Metro Source* for listings), which are often a lot more fun.

There are bars to suit every taste. Great saloons with antique bars often have a lot of history attached. Cedar Tavern, for example, was associated with the abstract expressionists in the 1950s and P J Clarke's with many Damon Runyon types. In swank hotel bars such as the St Regis's King Cole or the Carlyle's Bemelman's you can lounge in luxury. Rooftop bars are spectacular trysting

places. Specialty bars serve up every liquor (beer, wine, champagne, vodka, and sake), and you'll find an extensive gay scene catering to different crowds and ages, the latter concentrated mainly in Chelsea and Greenwich Village. Many lounges now have DJs spinning music, but they don't allow dancing because they usually lack a cabaret license.

The city's nightlife hot spots are: Harlem, Chelsea, the East and West Villages, and the Lower East Side. There's also plenty of action across the East River in Williamsburg, which now draws its own bridge and tunnel crowd from Manhattan! Drinking age is 21 (always carry a picture ID). Note, too that whiskey is rye, not Scotch.

THE BAR AND LOUNGE SCENE

In addition to the outstanding hotel bars listed below, you might want to drop in at the following: The Villard at the New York Palace Hotel *(24 East 51st Street, tel 212/303-7757);* Thom's Bar at 60 Thompson Hotel *(60 Thompson Street, tel 212/219-2000);* The Whiskey, W Times Square *(1567 Broadway at 47th Street, tel 212/930-7444);* Underbar at W Hotel Union Square *(201 Park Avenue South, tel 212/358-1560);* the Monkey Bar at the Hotel Elysee, and the Rise Bar at the Ritz Carlton *(Battery Park, tel 917/790-2525).*

There is no cover for the bars listed here. Note too, that there is a strict no smoking law in the city, instituted March 30, 2003. Only bars that derive 10 percent of their revenue from cigars can opt out of the law and allow smoking.

ANGEL'S SHARE
8 Stuyvesant Street (2nd floor) between 9th Street and Third Avenue
Tel 212/777-5415
Tucked away upstairs in a Japanese restaurant, this tiny bar is named for the alcohol that evaporates while whiskey is aging. Try a lychee daiquiri.
Ⓖ Daily 6–2.30 Ⓜ Astor Place (6)

AUBETTE
119 East 27th Street between Park Avenue South and Lexington Avenue
Tel 212/686-5500
A fireplace makes this lounge a warm winter retreat. There are 28 wines by the glass, well-shaken cocktails and an appealing fellow crowd.
Ⓖ Mon–Fri 5–4, Sat–Sun 7–4 Ⓜ 28th Street (6)

THE AUCTION HOUSE
300 East 89th Street between First and Second avenues
Tel 212/427-4458
Sotheby's meets New Orleans bordello at this wood-paneled, split-level lounge. Patrons sip

cocktails on velvet sofas beneath gilt-framed portraits.
🕐 Daily 7.30–4 🚇 86th Street (4, 5, 6)

B BAR
40 East 4th Street at Bowery
Tel 212/475-2220
B Bar has cooled as a hot spot, but its Tuesday night extravaganza, Beige, still draws gay society and other beauties. Large outdoor summer patio.
🕐 Sun–Thu 11.30am–midnight, Fri–Sat 11.30am–3.30am 🚇 Broadway/Lafayette(F, V, S), Bleecker Street (6)

BARAZA
133 Avenue C between East 8th and 9th streets
Tel 212/539-0811
No wonder this place is crowded: Just look at the prices and taste the sunshine in the mojitos and caipirhinas, and listen to the merengue, salsa and Afro-Cuban rhythms.
🕐 Daily 7.30–4 🚇 Astor Place (6), First Avenue (L)

BARRAMUNDI
147 Ludlow Street between Rivington and Stanton streets
Tel 212/529-6900
For Manhattanites the fireplace and the garden are reason enough to stop by, despite its odd woodsy Adirondack accents. The martinis and caipirhinas taste fine, and the crowd is friendly.
🕐 Sun–Thu 7.30–4, Fri–Sat 6–4 🚇 Delancey/Essex (F, J, M, Z)

BEMELMAN'S BAR
Carlyle Hotel
35 East 76th Street between Park and Madison avenues
Tel 212/744-1600
Named for illustrator of the beloved Madeleine books Ludwig Bemelmans, this intimate bar attracts the city's most upscale tipplers with first-class cocktails and perfect piano music from Loston Harris or the Chris Gillespie Trio, on most evenings from 9.30 to 1.30.
🕐 Daily noon–2am 💲 Cover Fri–Sat $20 ($10 at bar) 🚇 77th Street (6)

THE BUBBLE LOUNGE
228 West Broadway between Franklin and White streets
Tel 212/431-3433
www.bubblelounge.com

This 1930s-style lounge celebrates champagne by serving more than 20 types by the glass and 350 by the bottle, amid luxurious red sofas, marble tables and chandeliers.
🕐 Mon–Thu 5–2, Fri–Sat 6–4 🚇 Franklin Street (1, 9)

D.B.A.
41 First Avenue between East 2nd and 3rd streets
Tel 212/475-5097
Serious drinkers appreciate the massive selection of single malts (130) and beers (20 on tap) at this old-fashioned friendly bar. The backyard garden is great in summer.
🕐 Daily 1pm–4am 🚇 Lower East Side/Second Avenue (F, V)

DECIBEL
240 East 9th Street between Second and Third avenues
Tel 212/979-2733
Subterranean, funky and cramped, this Japanese bar has a huge selection of sake. Take a booth and experiment.
🕐 Mon–Sat 8–3, Sun 8–1 🚇 Astor Place (6)

DIVINE BAR
244 East 51st Street between Second and Third avenues
Tel 212/319-9463
A young professional singles crowd turns this long tapas bar into late-night Madrid. Flights of the 60 wines are available along with 40 different beers.

🕐 Mon–Tue 5–12, Tue 5–12.30, Wed–Fri 5–1.30, Sat 7–2.30, Sun 7–12 🚇 51st Street (6), Lexington/53rd Street (E, V)

DOUBLE HAPPINESS
173 Mott Street between Broome and Grand streets
Tel 212/941-1282
This aptly named bar delivers on its promise, with well-made drinks, vibrant music and a beautiful young crowd.
🕐 Sun–Thu 6–2, Fri–Sat 6–4 🚇 Bowery (J, M, Z)

ELAINE'S
1703 Second Avenue between East 88th and 89th streets
Tel 212/534-8103
The writers, actors, politicians and socialites who gather here have their own tables, but everyone is welcome. Look for Liz Smith, Barbara Walters, Norman Mailer, Gay Talese, Woody Allen and many others.
🕐 Daily 6–2 🚇 86th Street (4, 5, 6)

ENOTECA I TRULLI
122 East 27th Street between Park Avenue South and Lexington Avenue
Tel 212/481-7372
This light and airy wine bar offers some 50 wines by the glass at the marble bar. Accompany them with some first-class cured meats, cheeses and olives from I Trulli next door.
🕐 Mon–Thu 12–10.30, Fri 12–11, Sat 5–11 🚇 28th Street (6)

EUGENE
27 West 24th Street between Fifth and Sixth avenues
Tel 212/462-0999
The razzle-dazzle of this restaurant, club, lounge—fluted columns, red-velvet club chairs, a glassed-in dining room—appeals to an international jet-set crowd.
🕐 Wed–Sat 6–4 🚇 23rd Street (F, V, N, R)

FEZ UNDER TIME CAFÉ
380 Lafayette Street between Great Jones and East 4th streets
Tel 212/533-7000; 212/533-2680 for events calendar

This casbah-style bar is plush and comfortable with pillow-studded sofas, under Moroccan-style hanging lamps, and whirling fans. The bar has a good selection of cognacs and single malts.

🕐 Sun–Thu 6–2, Fri–Sat 6–4
🚇 Broadway-Lafayette (F, V, S), Bleecker Street (6)

FIREBIRD
365 West 46th Street between Eighth and Ninth avenues
Tel 212/586-0244
Caviar and ice-cold vodka make perfect companions at this opulent Imperial Russian-style boite in two splendid gilded and flamboyant townhouses.

🕐 Sun–Thu 5–11, Fri–Sat 5–11.30
🚇 42nd Street (A, C, E)

FLUTE
205 West 54th Street between Seventh Avenue and Broadway
Tel 212/265-5169
Perfect, if pricey, for an after-theater celebration, this gilt-and-mirror subterranean bar serves 20 champagnes by the glass. Snag one of the private curtained alcoves.

🕐 Mon–Fri 5–4, Sat 7–4, Sun 7–2
🚇 Seventh Avenue (B, D, E)

GLASS
287 Tenth Avenue between West 26th and 27th streets
Tel 212/904-1580
This sleek modernist space is fun and futuristic—worthy of the arty neighborhood. Check out the two-way mirrors in the bathrooms, and other visual tricks.

🕐 Mon–Wed 5–2, Thu–Sat 5–4
🚇 28th Street (1, 9)

GRACE
114 Franklin Street at West Broadway
Tel 212/343-4200
Wall Streeters and politicos cozy up to the long mahogany bar for apple martinis and tangerine margaritas in this lofty elegant space.

🕐 Daily 11.30am–4am
🚇 Franklin Street (1, 9)

HAPPY ENDING
302 Broome Street between Eldridge and Forsythe streets
Tel 212/334-9676

This duplex lounge still reveals traces of its former life as a massage parlor, from the belly-button-level showerheads to the tiled sauna alcoves and the circular booths (which used to be tubs). Innovative drinks.

🕐 Sun–Wed 6–2, Thu 6–3, Fri–Sat 6–4
🚇 Delancey/Essex (F, J, M, Z)

HUDSON BARS
Hudson Hotel
356 West 58th Street between Eighth and Ninth avenues
Tel 212/554-6000
The two bars are central to this hipster hotel. In the Hudson, a long ornate table serves as the bar. Late night, the backlit floor becomes a dance floor. In the Library, there are leather chairs, ottomans and a fireplace.

🕐 Hudson Mon–Sat 4–2, Sun 4–1, Library noon–2am
🚇 59th Street/Columbus Circle (A, C, B, D, 1, 9)

IL POSTO ACCANTO
192 East 2nd Street between Avenues A and B
Tel 212/228-3562
A casual, friendly wine bar. Tile, wood and lace set the scene. Order appetizers to go with one of the 30 wines by the glass (all Italian).

🕐 Tue–Sun 4–2
🚇 Lower East Side/Second Avenue (F, V)

IZZY BAR
166 First Avenue between East 10th and 11th streets
Tel 212/228-0444
Distressed club chairs give the upstairs lounge here a grungy edge, but the crowd grooves on the music from acid-jazz, drum 'n bass and trip-hop and funk in the basement and to DJ-turns upstairs.

🕐 Mon–Sat 7–4, Sun 10.30–4
🚇 Astor Place (6), First Avenue (L)

KING COLE BAR
St. Regis Hotel
2 East 55th Street between Fifth and Madison avenues
Tel 212/753-4500
Named for the 1906 Maxfield Parrish mural *Old King Cole*, this bar claims to have invented the Bloody Mary (originally the Red Snapper). Excellent stock of cognacs, grappas and single malts.

🕐 Mon–Thu 11.30am–1am, Fri–Sat 11.30am–2am, Sun 12–12
🚇 Fifth Avenue/53rd Street (E, V)

KUSH
183 Orchard Street between Houston and Stanton streets
Tel 212/677-7328
In this dimly lit Moroccan-inspired lounge, Moroccan lamps make the tile and concrete walls glow. Monday nights patrons can smoke exotic-flavored hookahs. There's belly dancing on Tuesday, and on other nights DJs spin world music starting around 10. Sundays there's a reggae party.

🕐 Tue–Sat 6–4, Sun 8–4
🚇 Lower East Side/Second Avenue (F, V)

LIGHT
129 East 54th Street between Lexington and Park avenues
Tel 212/583-1333
Singles gather around the bar at this atmospheric red-velvet party spot. It is far from light.

🕐 Mon–Fri 5–4, Sat 8–4
🚇 Lexington Avenue/53rd Street (E, V), 51st Street (6)

LOT 61
550 West 21st Street between Tenth and Eleventh avenues
Tel 212/243-6555
This still-trendy lounge occupies a garage that once housed trucks. Sliding panels

divide the space into sitting areas, which are a pastiche of funky forties, fake zebra and posh Polynesian. Damien Hirst contributed some of the art.
🕐 Mon–Thu 6–3, Fri–Sat 6–4 🚇 23rd Street (C, E)

LUNA PARK
Union Square Park between Broadway and 17th Street
Tel 212/475-8464
The quintessential Manhattan summer scene, this open-air bar/restaurant occupies the northern end of Union Square Park. Decent Mediterranean fare, too.
🕐 Mon–Fri 12–12, Sat noon–1am, Sun 12–11, May–Sep 🚇 14th Street/Union Square (L, N, Q, R, W, 4, 5, 6)

MARION'S CONTINENTAL
354 Bowery between East 4th and Great Jones streets
Tel 212/475-7621
A steady clientele gathers for reasonably priced martinis and theme nights. On Monday, for example, the Pontani Sisters cavort around as if they were in the Ziegfeld Follies.
🕐 Daily 5.30–2 🚇 Broadway/ Lafayette (F, V, S), Bleecker Street (6)

MARKT
40 West 14th Street at Ninth Avenue
Tel 212/727-3314
In summer, the outdoor tables are always occupied at this Belgian-style bar. Belgian brews are on tap, to wash down mussels and shellfish.
🕐 Mon–Fri 11.30–4.30 and 5.30–1, Sat–Sun 9–4.30 and 5.30–1 🚇 14th Street (A, C, E)

MERC BAR
151 Mercer Street between Houston and Prince streets
Tel 212/966-2727
The ultra-hip have moved on, but this bar still has comfortable seating, seductive lighting and groovy music. The front banquettes are great for people-watching in summer.
🕐 Mon–Wed 5–1.15, Thu–Sat 5–3.30, Sun 6–1.15 🚇 Broadway/Lafayette (F,V,S), Bleecker Street (6)

METROPOLITAN MUSEUM ROOF GARDEN
Metropolitan Museum of Art
1000 Fifth Avenue at 82nd Street
Tel 212/879-5500
Classy all the way. What better accompaniment to a drink than a view of the sun setting over Central Park? The balcony bar is chic with its chamber music and jazz groups.
🕐 Roof Garden Tue–Thu and Sun 9.30–5.15, Fri–Sat 9.30–8; Balcony Bar Fri–Sat 5–8 🚇 86th Street (4, 5, 6), 77th Street (6)

MORGANS BAR
Morgans Hotel
237 Madison Avenue between East 37th and 38th streets
Tel 212/726-7600
This basement hideaway draws more than its fair share of celebrities. Sink into the leather chairs and enjoy the candlelight and well-made cocktails. Go after 10 to catch the place at its best.
🕐 Sun 6–12, Mon–Fri 5–2, Sat 6–3.15 🚇 33rd Street (6)

N
33 Crosby Street between Broome and Grand streets
Tel 212/219 8856
This narrow tiny bar serves sangria with tasty tapas. Good selection of sherry and Spanish wine.
🕐 Sun–Thu 5–2, Fri–Sat 5–4 🚇 Spring Street (6)

OPEN
559 West 22nd Street between Tenth and Eleventh avenues
Tel 212/243-1851
The minimalist setting shows art to good effect. Coffee and light fare as well as cocktails. In summer, the French doors are open to let in the river breezes.
🕐 Tue–Thu and Sun 11am–2am, Fri–Sat noon–4am 🚇 23rd Street (C, E)

THE PARK
118 Tenth Avenue between West 17th and 18th streets
Tel 212/352-3313
This gargantuan complex with an attractive outdoor courtyard

is famous for having hosted J Lo's birthday bash.
🕐 Daily 11.30am–1am 🚇 14th Street (A, C, E), Eighth Avenue (L)

PEN TOP BAR
Peninsula Hotel
700 Fifth Avenue at 55th Street
Tel 212/903-3097
Who can resist an invitation to a well-dressed outdoor rooftop bar in the middle of Manhattan? You'll pay dearly for the privilege, but that's what makes memories.
🕐 Mon–Thu 5–12, Fri–Sat 5–1 🚇 Fifth Avenue/53rd Street (E, V), 51st Street (6)

PLANT
217 East 3rd Street between Avenues B and C
Tel 212/375-9066
Spin meisters Marcus and Dominique draw crowds on Plant Saturdays. Most other times it's a place to enjoy a drink, groove on electronica and ponder the why of the long terrarium.
🕐 Daily 7–4 🚇 Lower East Side/ Second Avenue

PRAVDA
281 Lafayette Street between Houston and Prince streets
Tel 212/226-4944 4696
Caviar and other Russian snacks accompany the vodka at this classy lounge, which is more dacha than Imperial palace. Sixty-five vodkas are available, many infused with bizarre ingredients like ginger, mango and horseradish.
🕐 Mon–Thu 5–2, Fri–Sat 5–4, Sun 6–2 🚇 Broadway/Lafayette (F, V, S), Bleecker Street (6)

PUNCH AND JUDY
26 Clinton Street between Houston and Stanton streets
Tel 212/982-1116
Theater-style seating sets the scene up front at this sleek and comfortable wine bar, where you can sink back into red velvet couches and sample 32 wines by the glass.
🕐 Mon–Fri 6–2, Sat–Sun noon–2am 🚇 Delancey/Essex (F, J, M, Z)

RAINBOW GRILL BAR
30 Rockefeller Plaza at 49th Street
between Fifth and Sixth avenues
Tel 212/632-5000
www.rainbowroomny.com
You can spend a fortune dining
and dancing at the Rainbow
Room—or head to this bar and
dream among the starlit
towers of Midtown over some
of the most addictive cocktails
anywhere. Jackets required.
🕐 Sun–Thu 5–12, Fri–Sat 5–1, dining
and dancing selected Fri–Sat
🚇 47th–50th Streets (B, D, F, V)

ROYALTON VODKA BAR
Royalton Hotel,
44 West 44th Street between Fifth and
Sixth avenues
Tel 212/869-4400
Tucked away off the lobby of
the ultra-hip Royalton, this
cocoon-like bar is perfect for
pre- or post-theater drinks.
🕐 Mon–Thu 6–12.45, Fri–Sat 6–1.45
🚇 42nd Street (B, D, F, V)

RUSSIAN VODKA ROOM
265 West 52nd Street between
Broadway and Eighth Avenue
Tel 212/307-5835
A huge selection of flavored
vodkas, apple-cinnamon and
horseradish, for example, are
poured into martinis or drunk
straight, the preference of the
Russians who gather at this
old-fashioned basement bar.
Inexpensive menu.
🕐 Sun–Mon 4–1, Tue–Thu 4–2, Fri–Sat
4–3 🚇 50th Street (C, E)

SAKAGURA
211 East 43rd Street between Second and
Third avenues
Tel 212/953-7253
In the basement of a high-rise
building, this bar could have
been lifted from Japan. Shelves
are lined with 200 different
sakes, and you can order
flights of four selections.
🕐 Mon–Thu 12–2.30 and 6–1, Fri
12–2.30 and 6–2, Sat 6–2, Sun 6–12
🚇 42nd Street/Grand Central (4, 5, 6)

SERENA BAR AND LOUNGE
Hotel Chelsea
222 West 23rd Street between Seventh

and Eighth avenues
Tel 212/255-4646
Society and fashion doyenne
Serena Bass established this
cellar hot spot opulent with
lounges outfitted in velvet,
suede, marble and mirrors,
and a mover-and-shaker
crowd. On Wednesday nights
Seven Martini celebrates
downtown culture.
🕐 Mon–Fri 6–4, Sat 7–4 🚇 23rd Street
(1, 9)

SLIPPER ROOM
167 Orchard Street at Stanton
Tel 212/253-7246
The name captures the mood
of this lounge, where aspiring
cabaret artists entertain.
🕐 Sun–Wed 8–2, Thu 8–4 🚇 Lower
East Side/Second Avenue (F, V)

SPORTING CLUB
99 Hudson Street between Franklin and
Leonard streets
Tel 212/219-0900
The best sports bar in the city
shows sports around the clock
on large-screen TVs. If a local
team is in the playoffs, don't
even think of coming down—
it's hard to get even close to
the door.
🕐 Mon 5–2, Tue–Sun noon–2am
🚇 Franklin Street (1, 9)

SWIFT HIBERNIAN LOUNGE
34 East 4th Street between Bowery and
Lafayette
Tel 212/227-9438
Numerous brews are on tap
at this slice of Dublin in
Manhattan named after satirist
Jonathan Swift. Locals and Irish
expats are the main patrons.
🕐 Daily noon–4am 🚇 Broadway/
Lafayette (F, V, S), Bleecker Street (6)

TAO
42 East 58th Street between Madison and
Park avenues
Tel 212/888-2288
A large golden Buddha
presides over this loft space,
which is so crowded with
good-looking singles after
work that it made it into an
episode of "Sex and the City."
🕐 Mon–Tue 11.30am–midnight,

Wed–Fri 11.30am–1am, Sat 5–1, Sun
5–12 🚇 Fifth Avenue/59th Street (N, R,
W), 59th Street (4, 5, 6)

TEMPLE BAR
332 Lafayette Street between Houston
and Bleecker streets
Tel 212/925-4242
This ultra-expensive bar
attracts models and their mon-
eyed scene. A beautiful scene.
🕐 Mon–Thu 5–1, Fri–Sat 5–2, Sun 7–12
🚇 Broadway/Lafayette (F, V, S), Bleecker
Street (6)

THEO
325 Spring Street between Greenwich
and Washington streets
Tel 212/414-1344
A minimalist 50s second-floor
lounge with a very hip late-
night crowd.
🕐 Daily 6–2 🚇 Spring Street (C, E)

TOP OF THE TOWER
Beekman Tower
3 Mitchell Place on First Avenue at 49th
Street
Tel 212/980-4796
This 26th-floor aerie is neither
overhyped or overpriced—a
miracle considering how
romantic the place is and how
bewitching the views are.
🕐 Sun–Thu 4–1, Fri–Sat 4–2 🚇 51st
Street (6), 53rd Street/Lexington (E, V)

TORCH
137 Ludlow Street between Rivington and
Stanton streets
Tel 212/228-5151
Torch singers perform at this
club and French/Latin dining
room hidden behind metal
doors. Good selection of
martinis and cocktails.
🕐 Mon–Thu 6–1, Fri–Sat 6–3 🚇
🚇 Delancey/Essex (F, J, M, Z)

XUNTA
174 First Avenue between East 10th and
11th streets
Tel 212/614-0620
Flamenco and rippling guitar
music provide an atmospheric
setting for sangria and tapas
available at this lively bar.
Good selection of sherry, too.
🕐 Sun–Thu 4–12, Fri–Sat 4–2 🚇
🚇 Lower East Side/Second Avenue

WHAT TO DO

Traditional Old New York

CEDAR TAVERN

82 University Place between 11th and 12th streets

Tel 212/741-9754

In the 50s, the Cedar Tavern (then at No. 24) was the HQ of artists Jackson Pollock and Willem de Kooning. Today's crowd is likely to be NYU students. In summer, head to the glass-enclosed roof garden.

⏰ Daily 11.30am–3.30am, Sun 11.30am–3am 🚇 14th Street/Union Square (L, N, Q, R, W, 4, 5, 6)

CHUMLEY'S

86 Bedford Street between Barrow and Grove streets

Tel 212/675-4449

Originally opened in 1922 as a speakeasy, the bar attracted writers (note their book jackets), who have been replaced by locals and students.

⏰ Mon–Thu 5–12, Fri 5–1, Sat 12pm–1am, Sun 12–12 🚇 Christopher Street/Sheridan Square (1, 9)

EAR INN

326 Spring Street between Greenwich and Washington streets

Tel 212/226-9060

This 1817 bar near the Hudson River used to cater to sailors and stevedores and now attracts writers and artists.

⏰ Daily noon–4am 🚇 Spring Street (C, E,), Canal Street (1, 9)

FANELLI CAFE

94 Prince Street at Mercer Street

Tel 212/226-9412

Step through the etched-glass doors and you could be in London. A few artists still gather here, and you can get pub food in the back room.

⏰ Mon–Thu 10am–2am, Fri 10am–4am, Sat 10am–4am, Sun 11am–12.30am 🚇 Prince Street (N, R)

JOE ALLEN

326 West 46th Street between Eighth and Ninth avenues

Tel 212/581-6464

It's really a restaurant, but the bar is ideal for a pre- or post-theater drink. American menu.

⏰ Sun, Wed, Sat 11.30am–11.45pm, Mon–Tue and Thu–Fri 12–11.45 🚇 42nd Street (A, C, E)

LANDMARK TAVERN

626 Eleventh Avenue at West 46th Street

Tel 212/757-8595

At this 1868 bar you can cozy around the potbelly stove or perch at the mahogany bar and order Irish-American food.

⏰ Daily 12–12 🚇 42nd Street (A, C, E)

MCSORLEY'S OLD ALE HOUSE

15 East 7th Street between Second and Third avenues

Tel 212/473-9148

McSorley's, established in 1854, became infamous for refusing to admit women until 1970. The walls are plastered with old newspaper clippings. Students are the main patrons.

⏰ Mon–Sat 11am–1am, Sun 1–1 🚇 Astor Place (6), 8th Street (N, R)

OLD TOWN BAR

45 East 18th Street between Broadway and Park Avenue

Tel 212/529-6732

At this authentic hangout, dating from 1892, look for the private booths. Tiled floors, a long mirrored bar, pressed-tin ceiling and original gas lamps complete the look. No jukebox, conversation reigns.

⏰ Mon–Wed 11.30am–12.30am, Thu–Fri 11.30am–1am, Sat noon–1am, Sun 1–11.30 🚇 14th Street/Union Square (L, N, Q, R, W, 4, 5, 6)

P.J. CLARKE'S

915 Third Avenue at 55th Street

Tel 212/317-1616

A tiny building overshadowed by skyscrapers, the bar played a major role in Billy Wilder's 1945 film *The Lost Weekend*. A 2003 renovation preserved its old New York feel.

⏰ Daily 11.30am–3.30am 🚇 59th Street (4, 5, 6)

PETE'S TAVERN

129 East 18th Street at Irving Place

Tel 212/473-7676

The writer O'Henry supposedly wrote *The Gift of the Magi* in a beer-stained booth here. In summer, snag a sidewalk table if you can.

⏰ Mon–Sat 11am–2.30am, Sun noon–2.30am 🚇 14th Street/Union Square (L, N, Q, R, W, 4, 5, 6)

WHITE HORSE TAVERN

567 Hudson Street at 11th Street

Tel 212/989-3956

Dylan Thomas, Brendan Behan and Jack Kerouac all slaked their thirst here. In summer, the benches and picnic tables make perfect perches for Village people-watching.

⏰ Sun–Thu 11am–2am, Fri–Sat 11am–4am 🚇 Christopher Street/Sheridan Square (1/9), 14th Street (A, C, E)

Dance Clubs

New York has loads of attitude, and it is on display at its worst at the entrances to dance clubs. At a few places, the henchmen at the door are rude and obnoxious. At many places, as the week gets closer to the weekend the door policies get stricter. In some places, the action doesn't warm up until after midnight.

APT
419 West 13th Street between Ninth Avenue and Washington Street
Tel 212/414-4245
www.aptwebsite.com
You must be on the A-list to snag one of the sofas in the upstairs apartment-style lounge (with a big bed as well as coffee tables). The sleek basement lounge is more accessible, but you still need to look good at this designer nightlife spot.
🕐 Sun–Wed 6–2, Thu–Sat 6–4 (downstairs Sun–Wed 10–2, Thu–Sat 10–4)
💵 Cover varies $0–20 🚇 14th Street (A, C, E), Eighth Avenue (L)

BAKTUN
418 West 14th Street between Ninth Avenue and Washington Street
Tel 212/206-1590
www.baktun.com
A plain, but vibrant club, especially at the weekly Saturday drum 'n bass party, when club kids trance in to the double-sided video screens. Live instrumental and electronic music, plus special events (kodo drummers from Japan) are featured other nights.
🕐 Mon, Wed–Sun 9–4 💵 Varies
🚇 14th Street (A, C, E)

CENTRO FLY
45 West 21st Street between Fifth and Sixth avenues
Tel 212/627-7770
www.centro-fly.com
Named after the Milan store designed by Gae Aulenti in 1965, this club is called "shagadelic" by those who remember that kinetic era, because of the white sofas and black-and-white Op Art accents. The multi-level club offers top spin meisters, who mix house, techno and disco. Friday night's GBH (Great British House) is one of the best in the city. Tech from Plant takes over on Saturdays.
🕐 Thu–Sat 10–5.30 💵 Cover $20–25
🚇 23rd Street (F,V)

CHAOS
225 East Houston Street between Ludlow and Essex streets
Tel 212/475-3200
This club attracts a sexy chic crowd turned on by the latest techno.
🕐 Mon–Sat 10–4 💵 Cover $20
🚇 Lower East Side/Second Avenue (F, V), Delancey/Essex Street (F, J, M, Z)

CHINA CLUB
268 West 47th Street between Broadway and Eighth Avenue
Tel 212/398-3800
www.chinaclubnyc.com
This glitzy spot has been pulsating and attracting celebrities for 25 years. Today, sports figures and music heavies still head to its VIP lounge especially on Monday nights. Other nights are dedicated to house, salsa, merengue and R & B.
🕐 Mon–Sat 10–4 (doors open sometimes at 6 for after work events)
💵 Cover varies $15–35 🚇 49th Street (N, R, W), 50th Street (1/9)

COPACABANA
560 West 34th Street at Eleventh Avenue
Tel 212/239-2672
www.copacabanany.com
Serious dancers come to this flashy Latin club to dance to live bands playing salsa, merengue and other Latin rhythms. Tuesday includes free buffet from 6–8. No Ts for men, and no jeans or sneakers.
🕐 Tue 6–2.30, Fri–Sat 10–5 💵 Cover varies $10–25 🚇 34th Street (A,C,E)

DISCOTHEQUE
17 West 19th Street between Fifth and Sixth avenues
Tel 212/352-9999
www.discothequenyc.com
Soul, retro R & B and disco draw models and their banker escorts to this glitzy, hard-to-get-into club. The DJ lineup is always top drawer. Occasionally, there's a male revue for women and other entertainment.
🕐 Thu–Sun 10–4 💵 Cover varies $20–25 🚇 23rd Street (N, R, W), 18th Street (1, 9)

EL FLAMINGO
547 West 21st Street between Tenth and Eleventh avenues
Tel 212/243-2121
www.elflamingo.com or donkeyshow.com
This club/lounge is home to a hilarious musical revue called the *Donkey Show*. Afterward, the show patrons can join a disco diva party dancing with the scantily clad cast members.
🕐 Fri at 9, Sat 7.30, 10 💵 $39–45 including show and dancing 🚇 23rd Street (C, E)

EXIT 2
610 West 56th Street between Eleventh and Twelfth avenues
Tel 212/582-8282
www.exit2nightclub.com
Clubbers who mourned the closing of Twilo now repair to this huge dance warehouse to reconnect with DJ Junior Vasquez at his Sunday morning party Earth, starting at 6am. It can accommodate 5,000. Imagine!

⏰ Fri 11–4, Sat 9–4, Sun 6am–whenever 💲 Cover varies $15–30 🚇 59th Street/Columbus Circle (A, B, C, D, 1/9)

FLOAT

240 West 52nd Street between Broadway and Eighth Avenue
Tel 212/581-0055
www.floatnyc.com

This ultra-trendy club plays trance, reggae and R & B attracting a hip but well-heeled crowd of models and Euro-trash, who ogle the caged go-go dancers at this club that's loaded with attitude.
⏰ Thu 9–4, Fri–Sat 7.30–4, Sun 10–4 💲 Cover $25 🚇 50th Street (1, 9)

GO

73 Eighth Avenue between West 13th and 14th streets
Tel 212/463-0000

Dramatic lighting intensified by the all-white walls and an eye candy crowd makes this a current favorite. The sounds mix hip-hop, R & B and classic pop. Usual hassle to secure entry.
⏰ Fri–Sat 10–4 💲 Cover $10 🚇 14th Street (A, C, E)

LOTUS

409 West 14th Street between Ninth and Tenth avenues
Tel 212/243-4420
www.lotusnewyork.com

European jet setters flock to this chic supper club with attitude, attracted by the international DJs and the luxe balcony lounge and basement dance club. It's tough to get past the fu dogs at the door. Make a dinner reservation and bring the platinum.
⏰ Dinner Tue–Sat 6–11, Club Tue–Sat 11–4 💲 Cover $20 🚇 14th Street (A, C, E)

NELL'S

246 West 14th Street between Seventh and Eighth avenues
Tel 212/675-1567
www.nells.com

Nell's has been on the scene since the 80s, still offering eclectic music (soul to Latin). The lounge is laid-back—more convivial than other nightspots.

⏰ Mon 7–1, Tue 10–4, Wed 9–3, Thu–Fri 6–4, Sat–Sun 10–4 💲 Cover $10-15 🚇 14th Street (A, C, E), 14th Street (1, 2, 39), Eighth Avenue (L)

PANGAEA

417 Lafayette Street between Astor Place and East 4th Street
Tel 212/353-2992

This is an au courant club where an African safari theme attracts a Euro-trash and ex-dot.com crowd, who suavely negotiate the tough bouncers at the door to party to the house music.
⏰ Daily 10–4 💲 No cover 🚇 Astor Place (6)

PIANOS

158 Ludlow Street between Stanton and Rivington streets
Tel 212/505-3733
www.pianosnyc.com

Don't expect piano entertainment at this bi-level bar, because the name is a relic of a previous occupant. People show up for the alternative music on Friday and Monday. Sunday it's stand-up comedy.
⏰ Daily 5–4 💲 Cover varies $5 🚇 DeLancey/Essex Street (F, J, M, Z)

SHINE

285 West Broadway at Canal Street
Tel 212/941-0900
www.shinelive.com

At this shock-jock performance space of the TriBeCa night scene, you never know what you'll find. Entertainment ranges from acrobats and reggae bands to torch singers and belly dancers. Lounge and dance floor too.
⏰ Wed–Sat 10–4, Sun 6–4 💲 Cover $10–20 🚇 Canal Street (A, C, E)

SUPPER CLUB

240 West 47th Street between Broadway and Eighth Avenue
Tel 212/921-1940
www.thesupperclub.com

A good-looking, well-dressed crowd fills this 1940s lounge. The King Kong section opens most weeknights unless there's a private party. Once a month, Sunday is swing night.
⏰ Thu–Sat 10–2, Sun from 7 (King Kong room daily from 6) 💲 Cover $20 🚇 50th Street (C, E), 50th Street (1, 9)

SWING 46

349 West 46th Street between Eighth and Ninth avenues
Tel 212/262-9554
www.swing46.com

At this 40s-style jazz club, you can lindy and jitterbug to topnotch live bands. The management provides lessons to neophytes.
⏰ Daily 5–1 or 2 💲 Cover $5–12 🚇 42nd Street (A, C, E)

Gay and Lesbian Bars & Clubs

BAR D'O
29 Bedford Street at Downing Street
Tel 212/627-1580
Drag chanteuse Joey Arias channels Billie, while Raven-O, Sade Pendavis and Sherry Vine all croon to their own beat on Saturdays, Sundays and Tuesdays. Mondays is lesbian party night.
🕐 Sun–Thu 7–3, Fri–Sat 7–4 🍸 Cover varies $none–7 🚇 Houston Street (1,9)

CLUB SHELTER
20 West 39th Street between Fifth and Sixth avenues
Tel 212/719-4479
Upstairs the ultimate garage party has been playing for more than a decade. Downstairs is LoverGirlNYC, a major lesbian event.
🕐 Sat 11pm–noon 🍸 Cover varies $10–25 🚇 42nd Street (B, D, F, V), Fifth Avenue (7)

DON HILL'S
511 Greenwich Street between Spring and Greenwich streets
Tel 212/219-2850
Headquarters for gay rock. Live bands and regular parties mix against a backdrop of hardcore gay porn at this grunge club.
🕐 Tue–Sun (door times vary) 🍸 Cover $5–20 🚇 Canal Street (1, 9)

ESCUELITA
301 West 39th Street between Eighth and Ninth avenues
Tel 212/631-0588
www.enyclub.com

The big party is Sunday T-Dance, when Harmonica Sunbeam presides over stripper contests. Fever Friday is the hottest lesbian party in town, and Azucar Saturdays are mixed and throbbing.
🕐 Thu–Sat 10–5, Sun 7–5 🍸 Cover varies $10–15 🚇 42nd Street (A, C, E)

MARIE'S CRISIS
59 Grove St
Tel 212/243-9323
A mixed crowd of gays and straights gather around the upright piano and sing along to Broadway show tunes at this downstairs bar.
🕐 Daily 4–4 🍸 No cover 🚇 Christopher Street/Sheridan Square (1, 9)

MEOW MIX
269 East Houston Street at Suffolk Street
Tel 212/254-0688
The hub of the cutting-edge lesbian scene, this bar stages different nightly programs. It's aggressively women-oriented but not hostile to men.
🕐 Daily 5.30–4 🍸 Cover varies 🚇 Lower East Side/Second Avenue (F,V)

SBNY
50 West 17th Street between Fifth and Sixth avenues
Tel 212/691-0073
www.splashBar.com
A splash of beautiful muscular men undulates against a backdrop of video screens showing erotica and male go-go dancers.

🕐 Sun–Thu 4–4, Fri–Sat 4pm–5am 🍸 Cover varies $5–15 🚇 14th Street (F, V), 14th Street/Union Square (L, N, Q, R, W, 4, 5, 6)

STONEWALL
53 Christopher Street between Seventh Avenue South and Waverly Place
Tel 212/463-0950
www.stonewall-place.com
It's nondescript, but it's ground zero for the gay movement. Here in 1969 some transvestites, using their stilettos, took a stand against the police.
🕐 Daily 2.30pm–4am 🍸 No cover 🚇 Christopher Street/Sheridan Square (1, 9)

TOWNHOUSE
236 East 58th Street at Second Avenue
Tel 212/754-4649
www.townhouseny.com
Upscale professionals gather at three bars or around the piano in this club-dining room.
🕐 Sun–Wed 4–3, Thu–Sat 4–4 🍸 No cover 🚇 59th Street (4, 5, 6)

URGE
33 Second Avenue at East 2nd Street
Tel 212/533-5757
This large lounge is filled with gay males romping in front of large video screens, gathering around the central two-tier bar and ogling the go-go boys.
🕐 Daily 8–4 🍸 No cover 🚇 Lower East Side/Second Avenue (F,V)

WONDER BAR
505 East 6th Street between Avenues A and B
Tel 212/777-9105
www.wonderbarnyc.com
This grungy but no-sleaze spot gets so crowded on weekends that it's hard to elbow your way to the bar.
🕐 Daily 6–4 🍸 No cover 🚇 Astor Place (6)

XL
357 West 16th Street between Eighth and Ninth avenues
Tel 212/995-1400
www.xlnewyork.com
This upscale lounge has bars on three floors, but what bars they are! Sleek design, exciting cocktails, a flamboyant crowd and an ocean-inspired bathroom make this a must-stop.
🕐 Daily 6–4 🍸 No cover 🚇 Astor Place (6)

SPORTS AND ACTIVITIES

New York City is a major sports town. Local and regional rivalries drive the professional sports scene. In baseball it's the Yankees (Bronx) versus the Mets (Queens). In addition, whenever the Yankees play the Red Sox, it's a grudge game because Boston has never forgiven New York for stealing Babe Ruth. Baseball has not completely recovered from recent strikes. Attendance has been down at the stadiums, except in Coney Island where baseball purists are flocking to see the Brooklyn Cyclones and to enjoy the game as it used to be. The biggest sports are football (Giants and Jets) and basketball (Knicks and New Jersey Nets). Ice hockey has fanatical fans too, supporting the Rangers, Islanders, and New Jersey Devils, making for internecine rivalries between Manhattan, Long Island and New Jersey. Tickets to any of these sports are tough to get and/or expensive, but you can always take a seat in one of the many raucous sports bars around town and see the action there, or at the large ESPN Zone in Times Square. Despite the American women's global success in soccer, women's professional sports struggle for audience support, although such teams as basketball's Liberty have loyal fans.

Residents enjoy a variety of exercise and activities. They go to the gym, walk, run, bike, skate, rollerblade (even in the streets), and play tennis, softball, and street basketball. Equestrians can ride in Central Park. The citizenry has recently rediscovered the waterfront and now enjoys kayaking and sailing from several downtown piers. The more sedentary count bowling and pool as sports. Fitness goes hand in hand with beauty. The city has always had yoga studios and fancy hair salons, but it has seen an enormous growth of day spas and other pampering facilities. Some are world-class, like the new La Prairie in the Ritz; others cater to New Age constituencies, while still others hustle passers-by for a quick back massage. The Brazilian nail salons are considered extra-special.

Spectator Sports

Bear in mind that securing tickets for many of the following spectator sports can be difficult since most seats are sold in advance by subscription to corporations and individuals. Tickets are available without fee at the box office.

There's an additional fee for phone and online orders. Agencies like TicketMaster *(tel 212/307-7171 or www.ticket-master.com)* usually charge a fee of from $4 to $8 per ticket.

The major sports seasons are: baseball *April–October*; basketball *November–April*; soccer *March–October*; football and ice hockey *September–April*.

BASEBALL

BROOKLYN CYCLONES
Keyspan Park
1904 Surf Avenue, between 17th and 19th streets
Coney Island
Tel 718/449-8497 or 718/507-TIXX
www.brooklyncyclones.com
This minor-league club, which started in 2001, has the fans cheering, because going to the game here is the way baseball used to be. Sitting in the bleachers at this waterfront stadium is just the ticket, especially for old Dodgers fans.
🕐 Jun–Sep 💷 $5–11 (single tickets available mid–Apr) 🚇 Stillwell Avenue/Coney Island(W) 🚌 B36, B64, B74 (Stillwell/Surf Avenue)

NEW YORK METS
Shea Stadium
Roosevelt Avenue at 126th Street, Flushing, Queens
Tel 718/507-8499
www.mets.com
When the Brooklyn Dodgers left New York in 1957, the Mets in effect replaced them. Even though they haven't won a championship since 1986 and often finished at the bottom of their league, they continue to draw fans. You can usually get tickets unless they're playing the Yankees or the Boston Red Sox. Shea Stadium, right underneath the landing path to LaGuardia airport, is noisy.
🕐 Varies 💷 $8–53 🚇 Willets Pt/Shea Stadium(7) 🚢 On Sat–Sun only: New York Waterway *(Tel 800/533-3779)* operates from the South Street Seaport, East 34th Street, or East 90th Street for $16 round-trip. Reservations recommended.

NEW YORK YANKEES
Yankee Stadium,
East 161st Street and River Avenue, the Bronx
Tel 718/293-6000; 212/307-1212 for tickets; 718/579-4531 for tours
www.yankees.com
Since the Yankees began playing in 1903 as the New York Highlanders, they've racked up 26 World Championships, most recently in 1996, 1998, 1999 and 2000. Tickets are tough to get for certain games (opening day, games against the Mets, the playoffs, the series) but not for other games. Even if you don't go to a game, take the one-hour tour of the 1923 "House that Ruth built"—Ruth being, of course, Babe Ruth—to see the dugout, clubhouse, and scoreboard operations of a stadium associated with such legends as Joe DiMaggio, Lou Gehrig, Mickey Mantle, Roger Maris and Phil Rizzuto.
🕐 Varies 💷 $8–80 🚇 161st Street/Yankee Stadium (4, C, D) 🚢 New York Waterway *(Tel 800/533-3779)* operates from the South Street Seaport, East 34th Street, or East 90th Street for $16 round-trip. Reservations recommended.

STATEN ISLAND YANKEES

Richmond County Bank Ballpark at St.George
Tel 718/720-9265 or 718/720-9200
www.siyankees.com
This minor-league team plays in a brand-new stadium overlooking the harbor. It's fun to take the trip on the Staten Island Ferry.
🎫 Varies 💵 $8–10 🚇 South Ferry (1,9) to Staten Island Ferry 🚌 Staten Island Ferry

BASKETBALL

NEW JERSEY NETS

Continental Airlines Arena
East Rutherford, N.J.
Tel 201/935-3900 or 1800-7NJNETS
www.newjerseynets.com or www.meadowlands.com
This Atlantic Division basketball team has been on a winning streak thanks to All-star point guard Jason Kidd and Kenyon Martin and Richard Jefferson.
🎫 Varies 💵 $12–100 🚌 NJ Transit bus from 42nd Street/Port Authority Bus Terminal at Eighth Avenue

NEW YORK KNICKS

Madison Square Garden,
2 Pennsylvania Plaza,
Seventh Avenue between West 31st and 33rd streets
Tel 212/465-5867 or 212/465-6741(Madison Square Garden),
212/307-7171 for tickets
www.nyknicks.com or
www.thegarden.com
The Knicks are the city's hottest ticket. This team and the Boston Celtics are the only charter members of the NBA left. Walt Frazier, Bill Bradley and Willis Reed made them golden in the 1970s, and Patrick Ewing helped them to the playoffs in 1994 and 1999. Since Ewing left, they have struggled. Today Latrell Sprewell and Allan Houston are the guys to watch. The Knicks City Dancers are pure Americana. Spike Lee is just one of the celebrity fans in attendance. For tours, call 212/465-5802.

🎫 Varies 💵 $10–100 🚇 34th Street/Penn Station (A,C,E,1,2,3,9) 🚌 M20, M34

NEW YORK LIBERTY

Madison Square Garden,
2 Pennsylvania Plaza
Seventh Avenue between West 31st and 33rd streets
Tel 212/564-9622
www.nyliberty.com
This team, launched in the summer of 1997, has become a star in the Women's National Basketball Association (WNBA) and has played in four WNBA finals. Look for Tari Phillips, Tamika Whitmore and Teresa Weatherspoon to wow the crowds and get mascot Maddie waving and whooping.
🎫 Varies 💵 $10–229.50 🚇 34th Street/Penn Station (A,C,E,1,2,3,9) 🚌 M20, M34

CRICKET

VAN CORTLANDT PARK

Van Cortlandt Park, Park South and Bailey Avenue
The Caribbean communities brought cricket to the city and this is the best place to find a cricket game in progress.
🎫 Dawn–dusk in summer 💵 Free 🚇 242nd Street (1, 9)

FOOTBALL

NEW YORK GIANTS

Giants Stadium, The Meadowlands,
East Rutherford, N.J.
Tel 201/935-8111 or 935-8222 for tickets
www.giants.com or www.meadowlands.com
Also known as the Big Blue Wrecking Crew. Its fans are maniacally loyal and tickets are impossible to get. The team won their first NFL title in 1927; their golden years were in the late 50s and 60s when Frank Gifford, Roosevelt Brown and Sam Huff were in the lineup. The team made it to the Super Bowl in 2003 .
🎫 Varies 💵 Single tickets unavailable 🚌 NJ Transit bus from 42nd Street/Port Authority Bus Terminal at Eighth Avenue (30 minutes)

NEW YORK JETS

Giants Stadium, The Meadowlands,
East Rutherford, N.J.
Tel 516/560-8100 or 516/560-8200
www.newyorkjets.com or www.meadowlands.com
This American Football League team has been playing since 1960, but only gained credibility after they drafted Joe Namath in 1965 and won the Super Bowl in 1969. They moved to Giants Stadium in 1984. Tickets are hard to come by—you have to wait 15 years for season tickets.
🎫 Varies 💵 season ticket only 🚌 NJ Transit bus from 42nd Street/Port Authority Bus Terminal Eighth Avenue (30 minutes)

HORSE RACING

AQUEDUCT

108th Street and Rockaway Boulevard,
Ozone Park, Queens
Tel 718/641-4700
www.nyra.com
This racetrack, which opened in 1894, is only 30 minutes by train from Times Square.
🎫 Wed–Sun 1pm post time, mid-Oct to early May 💵 $1–4 🚇 Aqueduct Racetrack(A)

BELMONT PARK

2150 Hempstead Turnpike and Plainfield Avenue
Elmont, Queens
Tel 516/488-6000
www.nyra.com
This beautiful 430-acre racecourse is the largest in North America. In June, it hosts the Belmont Stakes, the third leg of the Triple Crown.
🎫 Wed–Sun, 1pm post time, May–Jul and Sep–Oct 💵 $2–5 🚇 Long Island Railroad's *Pony Express* from Penn Station

THE MEADOWLANDS

East Rutherford, New Jersey
Tel 201/935-8500
www.meadowlands.com
Trotters run from January through August and thoroughbreds from September through December at this track.

@ Wed–Sat 7.30 post time 🎫 Free–$2
🚌 Bus from 42nd Street/Port Authority bus terminal at Eighth Avenue

YONKERS RACEWAY

Yonkers, New York
Tel 914/968-4200
www.yonkersraceway.com

One of the premier harness racing tracks in the nation is in the city, just north of the Bronx. The track celebrated its centennial in 1999. The most illustrious race run here is the Night of Champions with a $1.2 million purse. Races are simulcast in the afternoons.

@ Wed–Sun, 7.40pm post time 🎫 $2
Ⓜ Woodlawn (4)and Beeline 20 bus

ICE HOCKEY

NEW JERSEY DEVILS

Continental Airlines Arena
East Rutherford, N.J.
Tel 201/935-3900, 201-507-8900 or 1-800-NJDEVILS
www.newjerseydevils.com or www.meadowlands.com

The Devils, who have won the Stanley Cup only twice, are currently the premier hockey team in the metro region, thanks largely to brilliant goalie Martin Brodeur and longtime players like Scott Niedermayer and Ken Daneyko. Tickets are easily available.

@ Varies 🎫 $20–90 🚌 NJ Transit bus from 42nd Street/Port Authority Bus Terminal at Eighth Avenue

NEW YORK ISLANDERS

Nassau Coliseum, Long Island
Tel 516/794-4100
www.newyorkislanders.com

Tickets to contests of this Long Island team are easier to come by than tickets to Rangers games, even though the Islanders won four straight Stanley Cups between 1980 and 1983. The two teams have an edgy rivalry even more cutting after the Islanders' place in the 2003 playoffs.

@ Varies 🎫 $19–120 (£40–265 during playoffs) 🚆 LIRR to Hempstead then bus or Westbury and cab

NEW YORK RANGERS

Madison Square Garden,
2 Pennsylvania Plaza,
Seventh Avenue between West 31st and 33rd Streets.
Tel 212/465 4459, 307-7171 for tickets, 212/465-6225 for guest relations, 212/465-5802 for tours and 212/465-6741 for the Garden
www.newyorkrangers.com or www.the-garden.com

The Rangers may have the highest payroll in the National Hockey League, but they still haven't made the playoffs in the last six seasons. They won their last Stanley Cup in 1993–94, and it was their first since 1940. Yet tickets are virtually impossible to get. Look to Bobby Holik to step up to the plate in the future. The institutionalized violence on the ice rarely extends into the stands, but it's wise not to cheer the other team.

@ Varies 🎫 $25–150 🚆 34th Street/Penn Station(A,C,E,1,2,3,9)
🚌 M20, M34

RUNNING

NEW YORK MARATHON

New York Road Runners Club
9 East 89th Street at Fifth Avenue
Tel 212/860-4455
www.nyrrc.org

Thirty thousand athletes compete in this Marathon, first run in 1970. Conducted by New York Road Runners Club, it's watched by 2.5 million spectators. Finish line is in Central Park.

@ First Sun in Nov

SOCCER

METROSTARS

Giants Stadium
Continental Airlines Arena
Tel 1-888-4METROTIX
www.metrostars.com

Despite the triumph of the women's soccer team in the World Cup, soccer has failed to capture the imagination of the American public. The MetroStars' dismal performance hasn't helped. New coach

Bob Bradley looks to a better future with newcomers Eddie Pope and Jaime Moreno.

@ Varies 🎫 $18–36 🚌 NJ Transit bus from 42nd Street/Port Authority bus terminal at Eighth Avenue (30 minutes)

NEW YORK POWER

Tel 646/282-0354
www.nypower.com

Tiffeny Milbrett and Christie Pearce both play on the national team, but that has not translated into financial success for this team, or the Women's US League launched after the US team won the World Cup in 1999. Still, with ESPN broadcasting some games, there is hope that women's soccer will eventually arrive. The team plays at the Mitchel Athletic Complex in Uniondale, Long Island.

@ Apr–Jul (starting time varies)
🎫 $12–25 🚆 LIRR to Mineola, then shuttle

TENNIS

U.S. OPEN TENNIS CHAMPIONSHIP

USTA National Tennis Center
Flushing Meadows–Corona Park, Queens
Tel 718/760-6200 or 516/354-2590
www.usopen.org or www.usta.com

This two-week tournament is one of four in tennis's Grand Slam. Tickets to any session admit you to major matches played in Arthur Ashe stadium, and to the many other men's and women's, and boys, girls and juniors singles and doubles matches played on other courts. You can see more tennis if you buy daytime tickets, since many of the outer courts are not used at night. Tickets go on sale at the end of April; most are sold via subscription and what remain are usually in the stratosphere—but that's less an issue for day sessions, when most of the action is on the outer courts.

@ Late Aug–Sep 🎫 $46–92 (day vs night are most expensive) 🚆 Willets Pt/Shea Stadium (7) 🚆 LIRR to Shea Stadium

Activities

BICYCLING

LARRY & JEFF'S
1690 Second Avenue between East 87th and 88th Streets
Tel 212-722-2201 This store rents road and mountain bikes and is conveniently close to Central Park.

⏰ Daily 10–7 (until 8 during daylight savings) 💲 $25 day (3 1/2hrs or more) 🚇 86th Street (4, 5, 6) 🚌 M15, M86

BIRDWATCHING

CHARLES A. DANA DISCOVERY CENTER
Central Park
110th Street between Fifth and Lenox Avenues
Tel 212/860-1370
www.centralparknyc.org or
www.nyc.gov/parks
Exhibits relate to the natural life in the park, and the center sponsors related activities in the park. For ranger-led activities call 1-866-NYCHAWK.
⏰ Tue–Sun 10–5 💲 Free 🚇 Central Park North (2, 3) 🚌 M4

NEW YORK CITY AUDUBON SOCIETY
Tel 212/691-7483
www.nycas.org
The New York Audubon Society allows visitors to join its bird-watching walks in Central Park for a fee of $5.

BOWLING

BOWLMOR LANES
110 University Place between 12th and 13th streets

Tel 212/255-8188
www.bowlmor.com
This funky bowling alley has 42 lanes with automatic scoring. At Monday's Night Strike (10pm–3am) DJs spin music as you bowl.

⏰ Mon and Fri 11am–4am, Tue–Wed 11am–1am, Thu 10am–2am, Sat 2pm–4am, Sun 2pm– 1am
💲 $5.95–7.95 a game ($5 for shoe rentals) 🚇 14th Street/Union Square (N, R, Q, W, L, 4, 5, 6) 🚌 M3

LEISURE TIME
625 Eighth Avenue at West 42nd Street (2nd floor)
Tel 212/268-6909
www.leisuretimebowl.com
Cocktails are prominently advertised at the entrance to this 30-lane alley in the Port Authority Bus Terminal. Sports bar and video arcade.
⏰ Sun–Thu 10am–1am, Fri–Sat 10am–4am 💲 $7 per game (shoe rental $4) 🚇 42nd Street (A, C, E) 🚌 M20, M42

GOLF

VAN CORTLANDT GOLF COURSE
Tel 718/543-4595
www.americangolf.com
The oldest public golf course in the US is not exactly grade A, but it will do at a pinch. Eighteen holes, 6,122 yards, with clubhouse and snack bar.
⏰ Dawn–dusk 💲 $34–42 for nonresidents 🚇 242nd Street (1, 9)

HORSEBACK RIDING

CLAREMONT RIDING ACADEMY
175 West 89th Street between Columbus and Amsterdam avenues

Tel 212/724-5100
Here, only experienced riders who can ride at all paces and post to the trot English-style can rent horses to ride in Central Park.
⏰ Mon–Fri 7am–10pm, Sat–Sun 7–5
💲 $50 per hr (lessons $60 for 30 min)
🚇 86th Street (B, C) 86th Street (1, 9)

JOGGING

CENTRAL PARK RESERVOIR
This 1.6-mile (2.6 km) gravel path is the favorite track for Upper West Siders and Upper East Siders.
💲 Free 🚇 86th Street (4, 5, 6), 86th Street (B, C) 🚌 M1, M2, M3, M4, M10, M86

KAYAKING

DOWNTOWN BOATHOUSE
Pier 26
241 West Broadway at North Moore Street
Tel 646/613-0375
www.downtownboathouse.org
This organization offers free kayaking trips and instruction on the Hudson River from Pier 26 and Pier 64.
⏰ Mid-May to mid-Oct 💲 Free
🚇 Franklin Street (1, 9) 🚌 M20

MANHATTAN KAYAK COMPANY
Pier 63 at West 23rd Street
Tel 212/924-1788
www.manhattankayak.com
This company offers instruction and over 30 local tours for beginners, intermediates and advanced paddlers. Longer tours go to the Verrazano Bridge and farther.
⏰ Mid-Apr to Oct 💲 Short tours $50–65, long tours $125–250 🚇 23rd Street (C, E) 🚌 M11, M23

NEW YORK KAYAK COMPANY
Pier 40 at Houston Street
Tel 212/924-1327
www.nykayak.com
This company offers classes and guided tours, which last two or three hours.
⏰ Tours early May to mid-Oct
💲 Classes: $40 per hr; tours: $80–120
🚇 Houston Street (1, 9) 🚌 M21

POOL

PRESSURE

110 University Place between 12th and 13th streets
Tel 212/255-8188
www.pressurenyc.com
This bubble on the roof of Bowlmor lanes is the ultimate pool hall/multimedia lounge. It has 21 tables, plus a huge bar/lounge with seven 42-inch plasma screens.
🕐 Thu 7pm–close, Fri–Sat 9pm–close
💲 Thu $21 per hr, Fri–Sat $24 per hr
🚇 14th Street/Union Square (N, R, Q, W, L, 4, 5, 6) 🚌 M2, M3, M14

SLATE

54 West 21st Street between Fifth and Sixth avenues
Tel 212/989-0096
www.slate-ny.com
This is one of the best billiard-pool halls in the city. It has 31 tables.
🕐 Mon–Sat 11am–4am, Sun 11am–2am
💲 $14–16 per hour 🚇 23rd Street (N, R,W), 23rd Street (F, V) 🚌 M2, M3, M5, M6, M7

ROWING

LOEB BOATHOUSE

Central Park near East 72nd Street
Tel 212-517-2233
www.thecentralparkboathouse.com
Weather permitting, you can rent bicycles and rowboats for use on the lake year-round.
🕐 Daily 10–dusk 💲 Bikes $6–21 per hour, rowboats $10 per hour 🚇 68th Street (6), 72nd Street (B, C) 🚌 M1, M2, M3, M4, M10

SKATING

BLADES BOARD & SKATE

120 West 72nd Street at Columbus
Tel 212/787-3911
www.blades.com
There are several of these stores in the city, but this is the most convenient to Central Park, where you can in-line skate. There's also a branch at Chelsea Piers.
🕐 Mon–Sat 11–8, Sun 11–7 💲 Rentals $21.65 for 24 hr 🚇 72nd Street (2, 3, 1, 9) 🚌 M7, M11, M72

EMPIRE SKATE CLUB

Tel 212/774-1774
www.empirestate.org
The club sponsors group skates, skating events and tours. Year-round skates include the Sunday morning roll from Columbus Circle at 11am and the Tuesday night skate from Blades at 120 West 72nd Street at 8pm.
💲 Club membership $25 (but you don't have to be a member to join group skates)

ROCKEFELLER CENTER ICE RINK

1 Rockefeller Center Plaza, Fifth Avenue between 49th and 50th streets
Tel 212/332-7654
www.restaurantassociates.com
This legendary rink is not expansive but it's dreamlike to glide under the golden statue of Prometheus in front of diners in the nearby restaurants. Live DJ Thursday 7–11pm.
🕐 Sun 8.30am–10pm, Mon–Wed 9am–10.30pm, Thu 9am–midnight, Fri–Sat 8.30am–midnight, Oct–late Apr
💲 Mon–Thu $8.50, Thu–Sun adult $11, child (under 12) $7/7.50, skate rental $6
🚇 47th–50th streets/Rockefeller Center (B, D, F, V) 🚌 M1, M2, M3, M4, M50

WOLLMAN RINK

Central Park at 62nd Street
Tel 212/439-6900
www.wollmanskatingrink.com
You can skate against the backdrop of the Manhattan skyline at this romantic outdoor rink—or, in summer, roller skate or blade.
🕐 Sun 10–9, Mon–Tue 10–2.30, Wed–Thu 10–10, Fri–Sat 10am–11pm
💲 Adult $8.50–11 (skate rental $4.75)
🚇 59th Street/Fifth Avenue (N, R, W)
🚌 M5

SPORTS CENTER

CHELSEA PIERS

Piers 59–62 between 17th and 23rd streets
Tel 212/336-6000 or 212/336-6400 for golf, 212/336-6500 for field house, 212/336-6100 for Skyrink
www.chelseapiers.com
This is the city's ultimate sports facility, where many sports are catered to. There's also a four-tiered golf driving range, basketball and sand volleyball courts, and a huge gym.
🕐 Daily 6am–midnight 💲 Day pass $60, golf $20 minimum for 80 balls after 5pm ($118 before 5pm), ice-skating adult $12.50 ♿ 🚇 23rd Street (C, E)
🚌 M23

TENNIS

DEPARTMENT OF PARKS AND RECREATION

830 Fifth Avenue at 64th Street
Tel 212/360-8111 or 212/408-0243 for pool information
www.centralparknyc.org
This office maintains and supervises the city's recreational facilities. The best tennis courts are: Central Park and 93rd Street (tel 212/280-0205), 30 hard courts; Riverside Drive and 96th Street (tel 212/496-2006), eight clay courts; Riverside Drive and 119th Street (tel 212/496-2006), eight hard courts.
🕐 Pools: Jul 1–Labor Day 11–7, tennis courts: early Apr–late Nov, office: Mon–Fri 9 - 4, Sat 9–12 💲 Tennis $5 pass for one-hour of play obtainable at office above or at Central Park courts ($100 adult a year). 🚇 Fifth Avenue/59th Street (N, R, W) 🚌 M1, M2, M3, M4

NEW YORK HEALTH & RACQUET CLUB

39 Whitehall Street at Broadway
Tel 212/269-9800
www.HRCBEST.com
There are ten indoor tennis courts at the Whitehall Street branch of this chain.
🕐 Mon–Fri 6am–10pm, Sat–Sun 9–6
💲 Day pass $50 plus $20 per hr
🚇 Whitehall Street (N, R ,W) 🚌 M1, M6

WHAT TO DO

Health and Beauty

Almost every neighborhood in New York has a selection of health clubs with fitness equipment, classes and assorted frills—sometimes a pool. Massages, nutrition consultations and personal trainers may be available by appointment. Most offer day passes for visitors for a price (anywhere from $22 to $50). It's best to go at off-peak hours. Between 12 and 2 and from 5 till 8, the clubs may be so crowded you have to sign up to use the machines.

HEALTH CLUBS

WHAT TO DO

ASPHALT GREEN
555 East 90th Street between York and East End avenues
Tel 212/369-8890
www.asphaltgreen.org

This 5.5-acre (2.25ha) sports complex has Manhattan's only Olympic-size pool. It also has indoor and outdoor running tracks, fields for team sports, a large rooftop terrace with views of the East River, and a multi-level fitness center with 50-plus exercise classes.
Mon–Fri 5.30am–10pm, Sat–Sun 8–8 Day pass $25 96th Street (6) M15, M31, M86

BALLY TOTAL FITNESS
335 Madison Avenue at 43rd Street
Tel 212/983-5320
www.ballyfitness.com
This national chain has eight facilities in Manhattan. The Madison Avenue club has an 80-foot swimming pool plus cardio equipment, weights, and aerobics classes (kick boxing, Pilates, step, yoga, spinning and kwando).
Mon–Fri 5.30am–9.30pm, Sat–Sun 9–6 Day pass $25 42nd Street (4, 5, 6) M1, M2, M3, M4, M42

CHELSEA PIERS
Piers 59–62 at 23rd Street and the Hudson River
Tel 212/336-6000
www.chelseapiers.com
The city's ultimate sports complex, built on four Hudson River piers, has facilities for 21 sports. In summer, the beach, sundecks, large pool and kayaking layout are inviting. There's a climbing wall as well as 200-meter and quarter-mile tracks, an ice rink, and rows of cardiovascular, circuit and strength-training equipment. There are courts for basketball, indoor sand volleyball, and touch football, plus a boxing ring, golf driving range and batting cages. Some 125 classes a week offer everything from aerobics to yoga. Sports medicine clinic, café and spa.
Mon–Fri 6am–11pm, Sat–Sun 8am–9pm Day pass $60 23rd Street (C, E) M23

CRUNCH FITNESS
54 East 13th Street between Broadway and University Place
Tel 212/475-2018
www.crunch.com
Crunch, which has ten locations in the city, is the very popular premier brand of Bally Fitness. Each has whimsy and pop style. The instructors are first-rate, and the studio is known for its innovative classes, from street stomp to cycle karaoke.
Mon–Fri 6am–10pm, Sat–Sun 8–8 Day pass $24 14th Street/Union Square (L, N, Q, R, W, 4, 5, 6) M1, M2, M3, M5

DAVID BARTON
552 Avenue of the Americas between West 15th and 16th streets
Tel 212/727-0004

This Chelsea gym attracts a substantial gay clientele and emphasizes toning and body building. The equipment includes weights and cardio machines, plus a sauna and steam room for men only.
Mon–Fri 6am–midnight, Sat 9–9, Sun 10am–11pm Day pass $20 14th Street (F, V), 18th Street (1, 9) M5, M6, M7

EQUINOX FITNESS CLUB
521 Fifth Avenue at 44th Street
Tel 212 972-8000
www.equinoxfitness.com
All 12 Equinox clubs in Manhattan are sleek and sophisticated and almost invariably offer spinning, Pilates, yoga, cardio-boxing and cardio machines.
Mon–Thu 5.30am–10pm, Fri 5.30am–9pm, closed Sat–Sun Day pass $35 42nd Street/Grand Central (4, 5, 6) M1, M2, M3, M4, M5

NEW YORK HEALTH AND RACQUET CLUB
24 East 13th Street between Fifth Avenue and University Place
Tel 212/924-4600
www.HRCBEST.com

The eight Manhattan branches of this chain offer sports, equipment, and classes from tai chi and karate to aqua-cise. Each branch has a pool, and the one at 57th and Lexington has a full spa. Members have access to a beach and tennis club in New Rochelle, plus a yacht docked at 23rd Street.
Mon–Fri 6am–11pm, Sat–Sun 8am–9pm Day pass $50 14th Street/Union Square (L, N, Q, R, W, 4, 5, 6) M1, M2, M3, M5

NEW YORK SPORT CLUBS

128 Eighth Avenue at 16th Street
Tel 212/627-0065
www.nysc.com

This chain has close to 30 locations around town, mostly aerobic studios with cardio-fitness machines and free weights, plus a full program of exercise classes—cardio-kick boxing, step, abs, Pilates and yoga. Massage treatments are usually available, too.

🕐 Mon–Thu 6am–11pm, Fri 6am–10pm, Sat–Sun 8am–9pm 💲 Day pass $25 🚇 18th Street (1, 9) 🚌 M20

SPORTS CLUB/LA

330 East 61st Street between First and Second avenues
Tel 212/355-5100
45 Rockefeller Plaza
Tel 212/218-8600
www.TheSportsClubLA.com

The spectacular 61st Street location of this urban country club occupies 150,000 square feet (13,500sq m) and offers 50 fitness classes, five squash courts, two basketball courts, a climbing wall, weights, and a cardio deck with more than 200 machines. There's even rooftop tennis and golf.

🕐 Mon–Fri 5am–11pm, Sat–Sun 7am–9pm 💲 Day pass $35 with member only 🚇 59th Street (4, 5, 6) 🚌 M15

WORLD GYM

232 Mercer Street between 3rd and Bleecker streets
Tel 212/780-7407
www.worldgymnyc.com
1926 Broadway between 64th & 65th streets
Tel 212/874-0942

World Gym's two large Manhattan locations have the latest exercise equipment and offer classes in spinning, yoga, Pilates, cardio-boxing, etc. The downtown club is large and not overcrowded.

🕐 Mon–Thu 5am–midnight, Fri 5am–1am, Sat 6am–10pm, Sun 7am–10pm 💲 Day pass $25 🚇 Bleecker Street (6), Broadway-Lafayette (F, V, S) 🚌 M1, M5, M6

ANUSHKA DAY SPA AND CELLULITE CLINIC

241 East 60th Street near Second Avenue
Tel 212/355-6404
www.anushkaonline.com

Anushka is the cellulite queen of the city. Clients come to her intimate brownstone for thermo-jet treatments and thigh contouring massage, as well as traditional massage, body treatments and facials.

🕐 Mon 9–6, Tue and Thu 10–8, Wed and Fri 10–7, Sat 9–6, closed Sun 💲 Presso-jet treatment $85, thigh contouring $35, massage $40–115, facial $70–95 🚇 59th Street (4, 5, 6) 🚌 M98, M101, M102, M103, M15

AVON SALON AND SPA

725 Fifth Avenue between 56th and 57th streets, sixth floor
Tel 212/755-2866
www.avonsalonandspa.com

Many clients come here for eyebrow shaping by the self-styled Queen of the Arch, Eliza Petrescu. There's also a hair salon. plus facials, massage, waxing and body treatments

🕐 Mon–Tue 9–6, Wed–Fri 9–8, Sat 8–6, closed Sun 💲 Facial $98–150, massage $98–130 🚇 59th Street/Fifth Avenue (N, R, W) 🚌 M1, M2, M3, M4, M57

CLAY

25 West 14th Street between Fifth and Sixth avenues
Tel 212/206-9200
www.insideclay.com

Sleek, serene and minimal, Clay combines bodywork therapies with exercise (weights,

cardio-boxing, yoga). The fireside lounge and rooftop deck are bonuses.

🕐 Mon–Fri 5.30am–11pm, Fri 5.30am–10pm, Sat–Sun 8am–9pm 💲 Massage $85 🚇 14th Street/Union Square (L, N, Q, R, W, 4, 5, 6) 🚌 M2, M3, M5, M14

THE GREENHOUSE SPA

127 East 57th Street between Park and Lexington avenues
Tel 212/644-4449
www.greenhousespa.com

This premier spa uses Elemis skin and body care products. Bask in relaxing treatments such as coconut rub and milk ritual wrap, and lime and ginger salt glow. Massage and hydro-massage are available.

🕐 Mon–Fri 10–7, Sat 12–6, closed Sun 💲 Facial $60–125, massage $60–135 🚇 59th Street/Lexington Avenue (N, R, W), 59th Street (4, 5, 6)

INSPARATIONS AT THE 92ND STREET Y

139 Lexington Avenue at 92nd Street
Tel 212/415-5795
www.insparations.com

People on the run appreciate the mini-facial, and hot-rock massages that are available.

🕐 Mon 11–7, Tue–Fri 9–9, Sat 12–8, Sun 10–7 💲 Facial $35–80, massage $45–95 🚇 86th Street (4, 5, 6) 🚌 M98, M101, M102, M103

J. SISTERS

35 West 57th Street between Fifth and Sixth avenues
Tel 212/750-2485
www.jsisters.com

In 1987, seven Brazilian sisters opened a nail salon to deliver "serious" Brazilian-style manicures and pedicures. They have now branched out to provide superb bikini waxing, facials and massage.

🕐 Tue, Fri–Sat 9–5.30, Wed–Thu 9–7.30, closed Sun–Mon 💆 Manicure $40, pedicure $60, facial $85, bikini wax $55 🚇 57th Street(F); 59th Street/Fifth Avenue (N, R, W) 🚌 M1, M2, M3, M4, M5, M6, M7, M57

JENIETTE
58 East 13th Street between University Place and Broadway
Tel 212/529-1616
www.jeniette.com
Since 1979 this East Village salon has been providing good manicures, pedicures, facials, and massage at much lower prices than uptown. It uses Dinur products.

🕐 Mon 11–7, Tue–Wed, Sat 10–7, Thu 10 – 8, closed Sun 💆 Manicure $10–15, facial $60, massage $40–90 🚇 14th Street/Union Square (L, N, Q, R, W, 4, 5, 6) 🚌 M1, M5, M6, M14

LE PETIT SPA
140 East 34th Street between Lexington and Third avenues
Tel 212/685-0773
www.lepetitspanyc.com
This small salon offers a full array of treatments. Fit in a mini facial or body polish when you're in a rush.

🕐 Daily 10–8 💆 Facial $100, massage $50–95 🚇 33rd Street (6) 🚌 M98, M101, M102, M103, M34

MILLEFLEURS
130 Franklin Street, between West Broadway and Varick Street
Tel 212/966-3656
www.spaaddicts.com
The best deal at this Egyptian-inspired spa in a handsome brownstone is the three-hour treatment, including a herbal mineral body wrap, mini aromatherapy facial and a one-hour massage for $225.

🕐 Daily 10–8 💆 Facial $100, massage $75–110 🚇 Franklin Street (1, 9) 🚌 M20

OASIS DAY SPA
108 East 16th Street near Union Square, 2nd floor

Tel 212/254-7722
www.nydayspa.com

Candlelight and soft music add to the charms of this popular spa, offering 15 massage treatments.

🕐 Mon–Fri 10am–10.15pm, Sat–Sun 9am–9.15pm 💆 Facial $60–120, massage $85–125 🚇 14th Street/Union Square (L, N, Q, R, W, 4, 5, 6) 🚌 M1, M2, M3

PAUL LABRECQUE SALON AND SPA
171 East 65th Street between Lexington and Third avenues
Tel 212/595-0099
www.paullabrecque.com
London-trained Labrecque has coiffed the rich and famous for decades. The ultimate facial at this attractive salon provides five levels of hydration. It also offers sensual body treatments and massage treatments (Thai, Reiki, rolfing, phyto-essence and acupuncture).

🕐 Mon–Fri 8am–9pm, Sat 9–8, Sun 10–8
💆 Facial $75–140, massage $65–120 🚇 68th Street (6) 🚌 M98, M101, M102, M103

RESCUE BEAUTY LOUNGE
34 Gansevoort Street between Hudson and Greenwich, second floor
Tel 212/206-6409
www.rescuebeauty.com
Rescue takes a medical approach to pampering, maintaining hospital standards of cleanliness. This is the place to get the ultimate manicure or pedicure.

🕐 Tue–Fri 11–8, Sat–Sun 10–6, closed Mon 💆 Manicure $23–50, pedicure $43–100, facial $85–160, massage $120

🚇 14th Street (A, C, E); Eighth Avenue (L) 🚌 M11, M20

SOHO SANCTUARY
119 Mercer Street near Prince Street
Tel 212/334-5550
www.sohosanctuary.com
This spa and yoga studio achieved a reputation when Julia Roberts made frequent visits. It offers facials, body wraps and massage.

🕐 Mon 3–9, Tue–Fri 10–9, Sat 10–6, Sun 12–6 💆 Facial $110, massage $110–115 🚇 Prince Street (N,R,W) 🚌 M1, M6

SPAS IN HOTELS
Many hotels in the city have spas and fitness centers. Below are some of the best.

AWAY SPA AND GYM AT THE W HOTEL
541 Lexington Avenue between East 49th and 50th Streets, fourth floor
Tel 212/407-2970
www.theawayspa.com

LA PRAIRIE SPA AT THE RITZ CARLTON

50 Central Park South at Sixth Avenue
Tel 212/521-6135
www.ritzcarlton.com/newyorkcentral-parksouth/spa

PLAZA SPA
Fifth Avenue at Central Park South
Tel 212/546-5444
www.fairmont.com

WOODSTOCK SPA AND WELLNESS CENTER
At the Benjamin Hotel
125 East 50th Street between Lexington and Third avenues, third floor
Tel 212/715-2517
www.woodstockspa.com

WHAT TO DO

CHILDREN'S NEW YORK

With its towering buildings, vibrant streets, sights and sounds, New York is wonderful for kids. Even a ride on the subway is exciting. A few of the family-friendly institutions are below. Also check the Sports and Activities chapter and the Shopping chapter (especially Niketown and the Disney Store). In addition, many seasonal events appeal to kids—performances of the Big Apple Circus and the *Nutcracker* at Christmas as well as the Radio City Christmas Spectacular; the Ringling Brothers' circus in spring; and the parades and fairs that take place throughout the year. As you research your visit, it's worth calling concert halls and museums in advance to find out what special events will be on while you're in town; reserve ahead for those that interest you.

Film, TV, Theater and Music

BACKSTAGE AT LINCOLN CENTER
Tel 212/769-7020
These one-hour tours, run by the Opera Guild, take you backstage to the shops where the sets and costumes are made and to rehearsal rooms and storage areas.
🕐 Oct–June (weekdays at 3.30, Sun at 10.30). Advance reservations needed 💵 Adult $10, student or child (6 and up) $5 (under 6 not admitted) 🚇 66th Street (1, 9) 🚌 M5, M7, M104

LITTLE ORCHESTRA SOCIETY
Avery Fisher Hall or Florence Gould Hall
Lincoln Center
Tel 212/971-9500
This company organizes two family concert series, Happy Concerts (children 6 to 12) and the Lollipops (tots 3 to 5).
🕐 Varies 💵 $15–35 🚇 66th Street (1, 9) 🚌 M5, M7, M104

LOEWS IMAX THEATER
1998 Broadway and 68th Street
Tel 212/336-336-5020
For some kids, the 3-D IMAX experience is too intense; those who tolerate it are usually enthralled. The screen is eight stories high. Programming changes roughly every two months.
🕐 Varies 💵 Adult $11, senior $10, child $9 🚇 66th Street (1, 9) 🚌 M5, M7, M104

NBC STUDIO TOUR
Rockefeller Plaza
Tel 212/664 3700
www.shopnbc.com
Hour-long tours of the NBC network's studios begin with a short video of Katie Couric and Matt Lauer tracing the story of NBC from its origins in radio days to the present. Visitors peek into studios and also see how shows are produced. The tour ends in a theater with a demonstration of HD TV.
🕐 Mon–Sat 8.30–5.30, Sun 9.30–4.30 💵 Adult $17.75, child (6–16) $15, (under 6 not admitted) 🚇 47th–50th streets/Rockefeller Center (B, D, F, V) 🚌 M1, M2, M3, M4, M5, M6, M7

NEW VICTORY THEATER
209 West 42nd Street between Broadway and Eighth Avenue
Tel 212/239-6200
www.newvictory.org

The city's first theater designed for family programming is an intimate space and a must. All types of theater take place here. Every show is age rated from 4 to 12-plus, but shows here suit all ages.
🕐 Varies 💵 $10–30 🚇 42nd Street/Times Square (N, Q, R, S, W, 1, 2, 3, 7, 9) 🚌 M6, M7

PAPER BAG PLAYERS
Sylvia and Danny Kaye Playhouse
Hunter College
East 68th Street between Park and Lexington avenues
Tel 212/772-4448
The members of this beloved troupe make their costumes and sets out of cardboard and paper bags and perform original offbeat plays and revues.
🕐 Sat 2, Sun 1 and 3, Nov–May 💵 $20–25 🚇 68th Street (6) 🚌 M1, M2, M3, M4, M98, M101, M102, M103,

TADA THEATER AND DANCE ALLIANCE
120 West 28th Street at Sixth Avenue
Tel 212/627-1732
www.tadatheater.com
Young professionals aged 8 to 17 put on entertaining shows and revues at this theater company-and-school.
🕐 Varies (weekends usually in summer, winter holiday time, and spring break) 💵 Adult $15, child $7 🚇 23rd Street (F, V) 🚌 M5, M6, M7

THEATREWORKS USA
Auditorium, Equitable Tower
787 Seventh Avenue between West 51st and 52nd streets
Tel 212/627-7373
www.theatreworksusa.org
This group puts on plays and musicals for children based on such favorites as *The Lion, the Witch and the Wardrobe* and *Charlotte's Web.*
🕐 Sat–Sun 12.30, Sep–Mar 💵 Adult and child $25 🚇 50th Street (1, 9), 49th Street (N, R, W) 🚌 M6, M7

THE "TODAY SHOW"
NBC Studios
Rockefeller Plaza
Kids may enjoy crowding against the barriers for a chance to be seen on nationwide TV. Just show up at dawn at the corner of 49th Street and Rockefeller Plaza.

⏰ Mon–Fri 7am–10am 🎫 Free
🚇 47th–50th streets/Rockefeller Center
(B, D, F, V) 🚌 M1, M2, M3, M4

YOUNG PEOPLE'S CONCERTS
Lincoln Center
Tel 212/875-5656 or 721-6500
www.newyorkphilharmonic.org or
www.lincolncenter.org
Sponsored by the New York
Philharmonic, these concerts
introduce kids to great artists
and great music. Children can
attend demonstrations and
workshops given by
members of the orchestra.
There's also a program
for teens.
⏰ Four Saturdays during the year
🎫 $5–25 🚇 66th Street(1, 9) 🚌 M5,
M7, M104

Game Center

BROADWAY CITY
241 West 42nd Street between Broadway
and Eighth Avenue
Tel 212/997-9797
www.broadwaycity.com
For teens, this tri-level game
center with a New York theme
is a hit.
⏰ Mon–Wed 10am–2am, Thu
10am–3am, Fri-Sat 10am–4.30am, Sun
10am–3am 🎫 25c–$1 per game (mag-
netically coded cards come in whatever
amount you choose) 🚇 42nd
Street/Times Square (N, Q, R, S, W, 1, 2,
3, 9) 🚌 M6, M7, M42

Museums and
Attractions

**AMERICAN MUSEUM OF THE
MOVING IMAGE**
35th Avenue at 36th Street, Astoria,
Queens
Tel 718/784-0077
www.movingimage.us
The permanent exhibit traces
the process of making,
producing and distributing
movies and TV programs.
Children enjoy the interactive
exhibits, and making their
own short animations.
⏰ Tue–Sun12–5 (Sat–Sun until 6),
closed Mon 🎫 Adult $10, students $7.50,
child (5–18) $5, under 5 free

🚇 Broadway (N), Steinway Street (R,G)
🚌 Q66, Q101, or Queens Artlink

**AMERICAN MUSEUM OF
NATURAL HISTORY**
See pages 68–72

BROOKLYN MUSEUM OF ART
See page 153

**CHILDREN'S MUSEUM OF
MANHATTAN**
212 West 83rd Street between Broadway
and Amsterdam Avenue
Tel 212/721-1223
www.cmom.org

The Children's Museum of
Manhattan was designed to
be a first museum experience
for kids from ten months to
ten years old. It has plenty
of sensory exhibits, plus a
regular schedule of sing-
alongs and other
wonderful programs.
⏰ Wed–Sun 10–5, Sep–late Jun;
Tue–Sun 10–5 late Jun–Aug 🎫 Adult $6,
senior $3, child (under 1) free 🚇 86th
Street (1,9), 81st Street (B, C) 🚌 M7,
M11, M104, M79

**CHILDREN'S MUSEUM OF THE
ARTS**
182 Lafayette Street between Broome
and Grand streets
Tel 212/274-0986
Children aged from 1 to 11
are welcome at this
playground-cum-museum,
which offers all kinds of
hands-on art projects.
⏰ Wed–Sun 12–5 (also Thu 5–6)
🎫 $6, child (under 1) free 🚇 Spring
Street (6), Prince Street (N, R) 🚌 M1

CONEY ISLAND
See page 152

ELLIS ISLAND
See pages 90–93

EMPIRE STATE BUILDING
See pages 94–96

FORBES MAGAZINE GALLERIES
See page 99

GUGGENHEIM MUSEUM
See pages 110–111

**INTREPID SEA-AIR SPACE
MUSEUM**
See page 109

MADAME TUSSAUD'S
234 West 42nd Street between Sixth and
Seventh avenues
Tel 800/246 8872
www.madame-tussauds.com
The New York version of this
famous London waxworks
museum opened in 2000. It
has the usual collection of life-
like figures (here, geared to a
New York audience—you'll see
Joan Rivers, Woody Allen and
Michael Jordan).
⏰ Daily 10–8 🎫 Adult $25, child (4–12)
$19, under 4 free 🚇 42nd Street (A, C,
E), 42nd Street/Times Square (N, R, Q,
W, S, 1, 2, 3, 7, 9) 🚌 M5, M6, M7, M42

**METROPOLITAN MUSEUM OF
ART**
See pages 114–119

**MUSEUM OF THE CITY OF NEW
YORK**
See page 123

MUSEUM OF MODERN ART
See page 125

**MUSEUM OF TELEVISION AND
RADIO**
See page 124

NEW YORK HALL OF SCIENCE
47-01 111th Street at 48th Avenue
Flushing Meadows–Corona Park, Queens
Tel 718/699-0005
www.nyscience.org
Built for the world's fair in
1968, this museum is one of
the first of the US's hands-on
science museums. The entire
basement is filled with interactive exhibits. Permanent

exhibits demonstrate biology, chemistry and physics, and special shows explore such topics as Optical Illusions. There's also a large outdoor science playground.

⏰ Tue–Wed 9.30–2, Thu–Fri 9.30–5, Sat–Sun 12–5, closed Mon 💷 Adult $7.50, child (5–17) $5, child (2–4) $2.50 🚇 111th Street (7) 🚌 Q23, Q48

NEW YORK TRANSIT MUSEUM

Boerum Place and Schermerhorn Street, Brooklyn
Tel 718/694-5100
www.transitmuseumstore.com

Vintage subway cars and other interactive exhibits are displayed in this old subway station.

⏰ Tue–Fri 10–4, Sat–Sun 12–5, closed Mon. Closed major holidays 💷 Adult $3, senior/child $1.50, under 3 free 🚇 Borough Hall (2, 3, 4, 5), Hoyt Street (A, C, G), Jay Street (F)

SONY WONDER TECHNOLOGY LAB

Sony Plaza
East 56th Street between Madison and Fifth avenues
Tel 212/833-8100
www.sonywondertechlab.com
Interactive exhibits on four floors here demonstrate the latest in communications, robotics, medical technology and entertainment. Not as much of a hard sell as you might expect. Reservations are needed and can be made two weeks in advance.

⏰ 10–6 (until 8 Thurs), Sun 12–6, closed Mon 💷 Free 🚇 Fifth Avenue/53rd Street (E, V), Fifth Avenue/59th Street (N, R, W) 🚌 M1, M2, M3, M4

SOUTH STREET SEAPORT MUSEUM AND MARKETPLACE

See pages 134–135

STATUE OF LIBERTY

See pages 136–137

TIMES SQUARE

See pages 138–140

Parks and Gardens

BROOKLYN BOTANIC GARDEN

See page 152

CENTRAL PARK

See pages 78–83

NEW YORK BOTANICAL GARDEN

Kazimiroff (Southern) Boulevard at 200th Street, Bronx
Tel 718/817-8700
www.nybg.org
This lovely retreat with 250 acres (101ha) has two special areas for kids—the 8-acre (3-ha) Adventure Garden, and the Family Garden. The conservatory is beautiful and so are the many specialty gardens.

⏰ Tue–Sun 10–6, Apr–Oct; 10–4 Nov–Mar 💷 Adult $10, students/senior $7.50, child (2–12) $4.50 (less for grounds only) 🚇 Bedford Park Boulevard (4, B, D) then walk, or take Bx 26 bus 🚌 Bx 19, Bx 26 🚊 Metro North to Botanical Garden Station

WAVE HILL

675 West 252nd Street at Independence Avenue, Bronx
Tel 718-549-3200
www.wavehill.org
The setting of this park in the toney Riverdale section of the Bronx is spectacular. So are the beautiful gardens and greenhouses. On weekends, there's often a Family Art Project scheduled.

⏰ Tue–Sun 9–5.30 (Wed until dusk in summer) 💷 Adult $4, senior and child $2, under 6 free (free Tue and mornings on Sat) 🚇 231st Street (1, 9), then Bx 7 or Bx 10 🚌 Bx 7, Bx 10
🚊 Riverdale (Metro North, tel 212/532-4900)

Toy Store

FAO SCHWARZ

767 Fifth Avenue between 58th and 59th streets
Tel 212/644-9400
www.fao.com
The toy store to end all toy stores. It's a fantasyland for kids and adults alike.

⏰ Mon–Wed 10–6, Thu–Sat 10–7, Sun 11–6 🚇 Fifth Avenue/59th Street (N, R, W) 🚌 M1, M2, M3, M4

Trips and Tours

CIRCLE LINE CRUISES

Pier 83
West 42nd Street and Hudson River
Tel 212/563-3200
www.circleline.com

Circling around Manhattan in a boat is the best way to grasp the contours of the island and the extraordinary city piled high upon it. Depending on the attention span of your kids, you can opt for the shorter two-hour afternoon trip or the longer three-hour version. The narration can be great or mediocre, but the fresh air, the passing river craft and the sights along the way make it fun. There are also day-long tours up the Hudson River.

⏰ Normally departs at 10, 12, 1.30 and 3.30 (2-hour trip), Fri–Sun also sunset cruises at 7 💷 Adult $25, child (under 12) $12.50 (20/10 for 2-hour cruise) 🚇 42nd Street (A, C, E) then M 42 🚌 M42, M50

LIBERTY HELICOPTERS

West 30th Street and Twelfth Avenue
Tel 212/967-6464
www.libertyhelicopters.com

Helicopters take off from the heliport on five, ten or fifteen minute tours hovering above the city and the Hudson River. If you can afford it, why not?
$56 (5 minutes), $101 (10 minutes), $162 (15 minutes) 34th Street (A, C, E) M11, M34

MADISON SQUARE GARDEN
4 Penn Plaza, Seventh Avenue between West 31st and 34th streets
Tel 212/465-5800
One-hour tours go to the locker rooms, the luxury boxes, and the sports bar and restaurant of this vast 20,000-seat arena, home to the Knicks and Liberty basketball teams and to the Rangers hockey team. Or just for for a game or special event. The Westminster Dog Show and the Westminster Cat Show are sure-fire hits.
Daily 10–3 Adult $16, child (2–12) $12, under 2 free 34th Street (A, C, E), 34th Street/Penn Station (1, 2, 3, 9) M10, M20, M34

ROOSEVELT ISLAND TRAM
Second Avenue at 60th Street
Tel 832-4540
www.rioc.com
Kids who have never ridden a tram at a ski resort will get a kick out of this cable-car trip across the East River and back.
Daily 6am–3am $2 59th Street (4, 5, 6) M15, M57

SMALL JOURNEYS
114 West 86th Street, between Columbus and Amsterdam avenues 10024
Tel 212/874-7300
Steven Kavee operates this top-of-the-line guide service

that manages to engage both children and adults on perfectly paced 4-hour tours. Tours can be typical or include puppet shows, backstage tours, DJ dances, and fun ethnic food stops, you name it. Transportation via mini coaches holding 10 or 21–24.
Year-round $500–550 for 4-hour tour 86th Street (1, 9) M7, M11, M104

STATEN ISLAND FERRY
Whitehall Terminal, 1 Whitehall Street
Tel 718/727-2508 or 718/815-2628

The view from the decks of the harbor, the Statue of Liberty and the Lower Manhattan skyline are stunning—and the trip is free.
Daily (24 hours) Free South Ferry (1, 9), Whitehall Street (N, R, W) M1, M6, M15

YANKEE STADIUM
See page 158

Wildlife Attractions

BRONX ZOO
See page 157

CENTRAL PARK WILDLIFE CENTER
Fifth Avenue and 64th Street
Tel 212/861-6030
www.wcs.org
A perfectly sized zoo for kids, this Manhattan classic is populated by youngsters' favorites—sea lions, polar bears, monkeys, pandas, penguins and tropical birds. The Tisch Children's Zoo is great for

little ones, offering fish, birds and llamas, and pigs and other domestic animals for petting.
Daily 10–5 (Sat, Sun and holidays until 5.30) Adult $6, senior $1.25, child (3–12) $1, under 3 free Fifth Avenue (N, R); 68th Street (6) M1, M2, M3, M4

NEW YORK AQUARIUM
Surf Avenue and West 8th Street, Coney Island, Brooklyn
Tel 718-265-3400
www.nyaquarium.com
Dolphin and sea lion shows are presented daily in summer at this small park, which also houses penguins, walruses, Beluga whales, sharks and seals – 300 species in all. Most exhibits are outside. There's a special Discovery Center where kids can pick up starfish, crabs and other small sea creatures.
Mon–Fri 10–5, Sat–Sun and holidays 10–7, summer; daily 10–5, spring/fall; 10–4.30 winter Adult $11, senior/child (2–12) $7, under 2 free Coney Is/Stillwell Avenue (W), Avenue X (F) B36, B64, B68, B74

CONCERTS FOR KIDS

The following venues offer musical and performing arts series or single performances for families at various times of year: Brooklyn Center for the Performing Arts at Brooklyn College *(tel 718-951-4500, www.brooklyncenter.com);* Carnegie Hall, Seventh Avenue and 57th Street *(tel 212/247-7800, www.carnegiehall.org);* Metropolitan Opera, Lincoln Center *(tel 212/769-7008, www.lincolncenter.org);* Jazz at Lincoln Center *(tel 212/258-9800, www.jazzatlincolncenter.org);* Chamber Music Society, Lincoln Center *(tel 212/875-5788, www.chambermusicsociety.org).*

FESTIVALS AND EVENTS

Note that the Convention & Visitors Bureau often has information about these events. Call 212 484-1222 or check www.nycvisit.com. Other useful websites are www.nyc.com and www.nyctourist.com.

FEBRUARY
Chinese New Year (depends on the lunar calendar) Firecrackers blast and dragon and lion dancers sashay through the streets of Chinatown, which are arrayed in red to welcome in the New Year. Tel 212/484-1222 or www.chinatown-online.com.

New York Armory Antiques Show (second weekend) The city's most prestigious antiques fair where 100 international - dealers display priceless furnishings and decorative objects in the Seventh Regiment Armory. Tel (during show only) 212/472-1180; otherwise 212/484-1222.

Westminster Kennel Dog Show (second weekend) More than 2,500 canines strut their stuff at Madison Square Garden competing for the Best in Show trophy. Tel 800/455-3647 or www .westminsterkennel-club.org.

MARCH
St Patrick's Day Parade (March 17) Bagpipers and bands, politicians and New York's finest march down Fifth Avenue from 86th to 44th streets celebrating the patron saint of Ireland. Tel 212/484-1222 or

www.saintpatricksdayparade .com.

APRIL
New York International Auto Show at Jacob Javits Convention Center (10 days including last two weekends in April). Futuristic concept cars, exotic classics and just plain good new cars, trucks, and SUVs are displayed for car enthusiasts' pleasure. Tel 800/282-3336, or www.autoshowny.com, or www.javitscenter.com.

Macy's Flower Show (last two weeks) More than 30,000 varieties of plants and flowers

are arrayed in the store in anticipation and celebration of spring. Tel 212/494-4495.

Easter Parade (March or April, depending on where Easter falls) People with a bent for fashion stroll down Fifth Avenue between 49th and 57th streets showing off their often wacky and wonderful hats.

Cherry Blossom Festival (late April, depending on when trees flower) Against a back-drop of gorgeous pink cherry blossoms in the Brooklyn Botanic Gardens, traditional Japanese dance, music and

drumming takes place along with haiku reading, tea ceremonies and craft demon-strations. Tel 718/623-7200, or www.bbg.org.

MAY
Ninth Avenue International Food Festival (second or third weekend) Between 37th and 57th Streets the Avenue is lined with booths and stands selling ethnic and street foods of all kinds. Musical entertainment, too. Tel 212/484-1222, or www. 9th-ave.com.

Fleet Week (third week) The tall ships and aircraft carriers sail in a majestic parade into New York Harbor and up the Hudson River. The festival includes military demonstrations, tugs of war, cooking fests, and culminates in a Memorial Day celebration. The best part are the posses of sailors roaming New York City streets in their crisp white uniforms. Tel 212/245-0072, or www.fleetweek.com.

Washington Square Outdoor Art Exhibit (Memorial Day weekend) The streets of the Village around Washington Square are lined with artists, photographers, and craftspeople showcasing and selling their work. Tel 212/982-6255, or www.nycgv.com.

JUNE
Belmont Stakes (first weekend in June) The last leg of the Triple Crown is run at Belmont on Long Island. It's rare that a horse wins the Triple Crown, but it's always an exciting chal-lenge. Tel 516/488-6000 or www.nyracing.com.

Puerto Rican Day Parade (sec-ond weekend) The city is awash in Puerto Rican flags, and cries of Boricua greet the revelers on Fifth Avenue. Tel. 212/484-1222.

Lesbian and Gay Pride Parade (last Sunday) The flamboyant parade from 52nd Street to Greenwich Village, via 5th Avenue, is the culmination of a week of gay-oriented celebrations memorializing The Stonewall riots. Tel 212/807-7433 or www.nycpride.org.

JULY

Independence Day Harbor Festival and Fireworks (July 4). New York City celebrates the nation's birth with a festival in Lower Manhattan and some spectacular fireworks launched from barges in the East River. Tel 212/484-1222.

AUGUST

Harlem Week (most of August) A host of Harlem events—film,

jazz, and food festivals among them—celebrate the culture and heritage of African-Americans and Hispanics. Tel 212/862-8477, or 212/484-1222 or www.harlemdiscover.com.

SEPTEMBER

West Indian Parade and Carnival (Labor Day) Thousands flock to Brooklyn to see the strutting flamboyant dancers and bands sashaying along to the beat of reggae, soca, and calypso. Caribbean food delights add to the festivities. Tel 212/484-1222.

Wigstock (Labor Day) An informal East Village gathering of vogueing transvestites has become a major drag queen event. Venues change, but the

biggest party is usually at the 13th Street pier on the west side of Manhattan. See www.wigstock.nu or ww.gaycenter.org.

Feast of San Gennaro (eleven days including the first and second weekend) The patron saint of Naples is paraded down Mulberry Street at this fiesta filled with all kinds of Italian food and popular street fair entertainment. Tel 212/484-1222, or www.san-gennaro.org.

New York Film Festival (17 days weeks in late Sept or early Oct) The Film Society of Lincoln Center organizes this major film festival, which shows new films by established and up-and-coming American and international directors. The hub is the Walter Reade Theatre and in past years the program has ranged from *About Schmidt* and *Talk to Her*, to *Bloody Sunday*. Tel. 212/875-5600, or www.filmlinc.com.

OCTOBER

Blessing of the Animals (First Sunday) At churches throughout the city, animals are blessesd on St. Francis day. The biggest event takes place at the Cathedral of St. John the Divine. People bring their pets (no matter how large or how weird). Tel 212/316-7540, or www.stjohndivine.org.

Halloween Parade What started as an impromptu procession of drag queens in Greenwich Village has become a huge event with big-name sponsors. The costumes are amazing, but you won't even get a glimpse if you don't line up really early. Tel 212/484-1222, or www.halloween-nyc.com.

NOVEMBER

New York City Marathon (first weekend) Thousands of runners thunder across the

Queensborough Bridge into Manhattan and race for the finish in Central Park as crowds roar their encouragement along the way. Tel 212/423-2249, or www.nyrrc.org.

Macy's Thanksgiving Day Parade (last Thursday) Families line the route from 77th Street and Central Park West to Herald Square to view the immense helium balloons representing many of the culture's favorite characters from Spider Man to Superman. Tel 212/484-1222.

DECEMBER

Lighting of the Christmas Tree at Rockefeller Center (date varies but is usually the first week in December). It's a media event, usually starring popular singers. Stake out your place early—or avoid the area altogether because crowds make it impossible to get through. Tel 212/332-6868 or www.rockefellercenter.com.

Radio City Spectacular (through December 30). Busloads of revelers come to the city to see the Rockettes kick up a storm in their stylish chorus line for this seasonal show, which always includes a Parade of the Wooden Soldiers. Tel. 212/247-4777. See www.radiocity.com

New Year's Eve Celebration (December 31) Times Square fills with thousands of partyers who show up to watch the ball drop announcing the official start of the next year.

New York is best explored on foot and this section describes ten walks that take in the most interesting parts of the city. The locations of the walks are marked on the map on the inside front cover of the book.

These pages also give suggestions for excursions outside the city center.

Out and About

42ND STREET TO THE UN HEADQUARTERS

This walk along 42nd Street is architecturally fascinating, taking you past some of the finest buildings in the city, including nine designated landmarks. It's a great stroll for families. Times Square is exciting, surprising and lots of fun, with its flashing billboards, electronic news and stock tickers, and theater marquees and posters. The walk ends at the United Nations complex in a quiet, peaceful spot alongside the East River.

THE WALK

Distance: 1.5 miles (2.4km)

Time: 2 hours

Start at: 42nd Street/Port Authority subway

End at: United Nations Building, 46th Street and First Avenue

HOW TO GET THERE

Subway: A

Bus: M15, M27, M42, M50

Leave the 42nd Street/Port Authority subway station and turn right, then proceed to the corner of West 42nd Street and Eighth Avenue.

❶ Times Square and 42nd Street are famous today for their theaters, giant neon advertisements and mega-stores. Look back toward Ninth Avenue and you will catch a glimpse of an older side of the area: Holy Cross Church, one of its oldest buildings, dates from 1887.

Face east toward Seventh Avenue and you'll see the gleaming spire of the Chrysler Building in the distance. Walk east towards it, passing the AMC 25-screen multiplex, formerly the Empire Theater, on your right. Next door is Madame Tussaud's and next to that the Candler Building.

❷ The Candler Building was named for a salesman for the Coca-Cola Company that built this white terra-cotta tower in 1914. Two doors farther east is the New Amsterdam Theater, lavishly restored by the Walt Disney Company with an outstanding Art-Nouveau foyer.

To see the building directly opposite, the New Victory Theater, you will need to cross this very busy street. So continue east to the traffic lights and use the crosswalk. The New Victory Theater, once known as Minsky's, was built in 1899 by Oscar Hammerstein I. Restoration in 1995 has retained the beautiful old-fashioned interior. Continue east along West 42nd Street on this side of the street. Two doors east of the New Victory is the Reuters Building, new in 2001, and just east of that, Times Square (see page 138), the triangle created by 42nd Street, Seventh Avenue and Broadway.

❸ The 25-story tower at No. 1 Times Square became the home of the *New York Times* on December 31, 1904; the inaugural fireworks display was almost outshone by the illuminated globe lowered from the roof to herald the New Year. Almost 100 years later, the globe is still lowered every New Year's Eve, and for many New Yorkers and visitors Times Square is still the place to celebrate the holiday. The tower now functions as an office block.

On the southeast corner of West 42nd Street and Broadway, on the right, is the former Knickerbocker Hotel, commissioned by Colonel John Jacob Astor. The songwriter George M. Cohan lived here for a time. It is now condominiums, but there is talk of returning it to its original use.

Continue east along 42nd Street, crossing Broadway and Sixth Avenue (now officially known as Avenue of the Americas).

❹ The flashy glass building leaning away from traffic on the north side of 42nd Street, 41 West 42nd Street, is the W. R. Grace Building, built in 1974 by architects Skidmore, Owings and Merrill.

Cross to the south side of the street and Bryant Park. Bryant Park sits on top of the subterranean stacks of the New York Public Library. During the World's Fair of 1853, the first to be held on United States soil, the park was the site of the Crystal Palace. To reach the library, continue east along 42nd Street to Fifth Avenue. Turn right. The library rises ahead of you on the south-west corner of 42nd Street and Fifth Avenue.

❺ The majestic Beaux-Arts New York Public Library (see page 127) is guarded by two stone lions, Patience and Fortitude, who sit at the base of an imposing front stairway. Inside the building, the marble entrance area on the ground floor and the usually packed second-floor Main Reading Room are well worth a look.

Return to 42nd Street and continue along east, crossing Madison Avenue. On your left at Park Avenue is Grand Central Terminal. Cross the street and plunge in.

❻ Inside Grand Central Terminal (see pages 102–104), the ceiling in the Main Concourse, decorated with the constellations of the zodiac, and the Dining Concourse downstairs, are a treat.

Back on 42nd Street, continue east to Lexington Avenue and the Chanin Building (on the southwest corner). Named for the brothers who developed the Times Square Theater District, the building has an art deco bas-relief on the façade, the work of Edward Trumbull. Continue to the northwest corner for the Chrysler Building.

❼ The Chrysler Building (see page 85) is one of the world's great 20th-century buildings—completed in 1929. Around the 30th floor a brick frieze depicts hubcaps and there are 9ft (3m)-high pineapples and giant stainless-steel radiator caps. The art-deco foyer is made of African marble and chrome.

OUT AND ABOUT

Neon signs in Times Square
(below and bottom right)

The magnificent Chrysler Building
(above); flags from all over the
world fly outside the United
Nations Building (above right)

Continue to 220 East 42nd Street and you'll come to the Daily News Building.

8 The Daily News Building (see page 87) was until 1995 the home of America's first tabloid newspaper.

Cross Second Avenue and continue on 42nd Street until you come to an area with steps on both sides of the street. These lead to the charming Tudor City apartments. From the top of the steps there's a splendid view of the United Nations Building, the East River and, beyond it, the borough of Queens. Turn left onto Tudor City Place, then right onto 43rd Street. Here, steps

lead down to Ralph Bunche Park. Cross United Nations Plaza (as First Avenue is called here) and turn left.

9 At the United Nations Headquarters (see page 144), view the General Assembly lobby (foyer) and stroll through the gardens. The entrance to the complex is on 46th Street. John D. Rockefeller, Jr. donated the $8.5 million needed for the site.

WHEN TO GO
Crowds will not be out in full force if you begin your walk on a weekday morning before 10. If you wish to visit the United Nations Building at the end of

the walk, arrive early—the last tour begins at 4.45pm.

WHERE TO EAT
The Dining Concourse at Grand Central Terminal, 42nd Street at Park Avenue *(tel 212/340-2210)*, is just the place to refuel; for variety at affordable prices, it can't be beaten. The Oyster Bar & Restaurant *(tel 212/490-6650)*, on the same level, offers excellent seafood, but at higher prices.

PLACES TO VISIT
Madame Tussaud's Wax Museum
✉ 234 West 42nd Street
☎ 212/512-9600
🕐 Daily 10–8
🎟 Adults $19.95, children 4–12 $15.95

NORTHEAST CORNER OF CENTRAL PARK TO GRANT'S TOMB

This northeast corner of Central Park boasts beautiful gardens, commissioned by parks commissioner Robert Moses in 1936. You will also find a pretty pond, meandering paths, woods and picturesque waterfalls. Just outside the park is the largest church in the United States, the Cathedral of St. John the Divine. Nearby is Grant's Tomb, where the great Civil War general, Ulysses S. Grant lies in rest.

THE WALK

Distance:	2 miles (3.2km)
Time:	2 hours
Start at:	Fifth Avenue and 105th Street
End at:	122nd Street and Riverside Drive

HOW TO GET THERE

Bus: M4 to Madison Avenue and 104th Street; walk one block west to Fifth Avenue

Leave Madison Avenue by turning left onto East 105th Street, and walk one block east to the entrance gate of the Conservatory Garden, across the street from El Museo del Barrio (see page 87) on Fifth Avenue.

❶ The Conservatory Garden—actually a complex of gardens — is at its best in July and August. As you enter, go straight toward the classical fountain in the area known as the Italian Garden. Walk to your left to tour the maze-like English Garden. To the right of the Italian Garden is the lovely French Garden, with the charming Untermeyer Fountain (also called "Three Dancing Maidens"). Go past this fountain and walk through the gate toward the pond on your right, whose Dutch name, Harlem Meer, means "little sea."

Skirt around the pond, keeping to the right, with the pond on your left.

❷ The Charles A. Dana Discovery Center, halfway around the pond, displays natural history exhibits in a Victorian-style building.

Continue around the pond and keep to the right of the Lasker Pool and ice-skating rink. Take the path up some steps, then down a few steps, then to the right and walk under the Huddlestone Arch. Still keeping right, with a pretty little waterfall on your left, walk about 300 yards (273m), and you'll come to a very small rustic wooden bridge on your left. Cross the bridge, keeping to the right and you'll come to the Glenspan Arch. There's a small waterfall beyond the arch and a small pool is just beyond that. Ahead of you, a couple of paths lead to Central Park West, which you can see. The path to the right takes you out to 103rd Street and Central Park West.
 On Central Park West, leave the park, turn right and follow the busy street, past Strangers Gate on the right, to Frederick Douglass Circle. Cross Central Park West at

110th Street and continue left around the circle until you come to the traffic lights. Cross 110th Street and immediately turn left. You are now in Harlem. Continue west on 110th Street for two blocks to Amsterdam Avenue, passing the entrance to Morningside Park. Turn right and walk north to 111th Street and the Cathedral of St. John the Divine.

❸ The enormous Cathedral Church of St. John the Divine (see page 77) is well worth exploring. The Peace Fountain in the Children's Sculpture Garden depicts a bronze Michael the Archangel slaying the devil.

Leaving the cathedral, cross to the west side of Amsterdam Avenue and follow 112th Street west one block to Broadway. Tom's Restaurant, familiar to fans of the TV show "Seinfeld," is on the right. If you are tired and do not want to continue, catch a bus on the west side of Broadway or take the M4 to Midtown East or the M104 to Midtown West. To continue the walk, go north up Broadway to 122nd Street, passing Columbia University (see page 77), New York City's oldest institution of higher learning, on your right. Turn left onto 122nd Street and walk two blocks west, passing the Manhattan School of Music on your left, to Riverside Drive. Riverside Church is on your left.

❹ From its 392ft (119m) tower, Riverside Church (see page 126) offers a magnificent view across the Hudson River.

❺ Nearby is General Grant National Memorial (see page 99), where Grant and his wife,

The "Three Dancing Maidens" Fountain in the French Garden, part of the Conservatory Garden

Cathedral of St. John the Divine (top); Columbia University is one of the most prestigious in the U.S.

Julia, rest side by side in two black sarcophagi. The Gaudi-style mosaic benches and tables surrounding the tombs are a good spot for a picnic.

From here you can walk back to Broadway and get the M4 or M104 bus downtown.

WHEN TO GO
Do this walk when the weather is pleasant and you want to have a quiet stroll away from crowds. Although the park is generally safe by day and is patroled, this is not a walk to do alone. Pack a picnic to enjoy along the way.

WHERE TO EAT
Tom's Restaurant, 2880 Broadway at 112th Street *(tel 212/864-6137).*

PLACES TO VISIT
General Grant National Memorial
✉ Riverside Drive at West 122nd Street
☎ 212/666-1640
🕐 Daily 9–5; closed major holidays.

Riverside Church
✉ 490 Riverside Drive
☎ 212/870-6700
🕐 Gift shop: Tue–Thu, Sat 10.30–5, Wed 10.30–7, Sun 9.45–10.45, noon–4

The tranquil waterfall at Glenspan Arch (above right); the façade of Ulysses S. Grant's majestic tomb

GREENWICH VILLAGE: WAVERLY CINEMA TO WASHINGTON SQUARE

Some of the country's finest literature and most radical ideas have developed in the area covered by this stroll. From the revolutionary Thomas Paine, who decried taxation without representation in Colonial times to the Stonewall rioters, whose protests sparked the gay liberation movement beginning in 1969, Village people have long been at the forefront of liberalism in America.

THE WALK

Distance: 1.9 miles (3km)

Time: 2 hours

Start/End at: West 4th Street/ Washington Square subway station

HOW TO GET THERE

Subway: A, C, E, F trains

Bus: M5, M6

Leave the subway on Avenue of the Americas (6th Avenue), cross the avenue at West 4th Street and position yourself in front of the Waverly Cinema. Turn to your left (as you face the theater) and head along the avenue to Carmine Street. Turn right.

❶ Along Carmine Street you pass first the Unoppressive, Non-Imperialist Bargain Books store on the left and then the House of Oldies Rare Records (on the right), both worth a browse.

Continue over to Seventh Avenue South, cross it, and turn right. At St. Luke's Place (also called Leroy Street), go left. On your left you will pass J. J. Walker Park, once a graveyard, which locals claim is the resting place of the lost son of Louis XVI and Marie Antoinette. The brick and brownstone houses along this street date from the 1850s. Theodore Dreiser wrote *An American Tragedy* while he was living at No. 16. At Hudson Street, turn right, and walk two blocks to Barrow Street where you turn left.

❷ On Barrow Street, take a look at the pretty garden behind the Church of St. Luke-in-the-Fields, built in 1822. The gate is on your right just before you reach Greenwich Street.

Backtrack along Barrow Street to Hudson, and stop for a snack or light lunch at the popular Belgian café, Petite Abeille. Go across

Hudson Street to 81 Barrow Street, where a plaque gives some architectural history of the area. Continue heading east on Barrow, then turn right onto Commerce Street. To the right at the bend in Commerce Street is the Cherry Lane Theater.

❸ Cherry Lane Theater, an Off-Broadway venue, was founded in 1924 by the Pulitzer Prize-winning poet Edna St. Vincent Millay. Samuel Beckett's *Waiting for Godot* and *End-game* both premiered here, as have plays by Edward Albee, David Mamet and many others.

Continue east on Commerce Street for one block and then turn right on Bedford Street. Notice the first two houses on your right.

❹ The Isaacs-Hendricks House, 77 Bedford Street, is the oldest in the West Village. The narrowest house in the city is at No. 75, which was home to Edna St. Vincent Millay in 1923–24. The actor Cary Grant also lived here when he was young.

Return along Bedford Street, past Chumley's, a famous speakeasy, which put in an appearance in Warren Beatty's *Reds* and Woody Allen's *Sweet and Lowdown*. John Steinbeck, Eugene O'Neill, e e cummings and F. Scott Fitzgerald are among past patrons whose book jackets hang on the walls. It's great for drinks or dinner. When you reach Grove Street, turn left.

❺ The pretty, leafy Grove Court, 10–12 Grove Street, was once dubbed "Ale Alley" because of the original Irish tenants' fondness for a brew.

Return to the corner of Grove and Bedford streets. The oldest

wooden house in the Village stands at 17 Grove Street. Continue one block roughly north on Bedford Street to Christopher Street, and turn right.

❻ The long-established McNulty's Rare Teas and Choice Coffee Shop is at 109 Christopher Street, and from its looks it hasn't changed much since it opened in 1895. Go in and enjoy the aroma.

Continue east on Christopher Street and cross Seventh Avenue South.

❼ Tiny Christopher Park, which was part of a tobacco farm from 1633–38 is to your right. Stop for a rest on the bench next to George Segal's sculpture *Gay Liberation*, then look behind you at the Stonewall Bar and Club, where gay resistance to police arrests provoked the Stonewall Riot in 1969, the start of the gay rights movement. There's a modest plaque on the building. Christopher Street is also called Stonewall Place from the park up to Greenwich Avenue.

Walk along the Stonewall's side of Christopher Street to Greenwich Avenue, and turn left. Go north one block, turn right onto West 10th Street and you'll come to Patchin Place; number four was famously the home of e e cummings. Continue on West 10th Street one block east.

❽ The ornate landmark Jefferson Market Library, at 425 Sixth Avenue, is a former courthouse built in 1877. The tower originally served as a fire-watching lookout.

Continue on West 10th Street, crossing Avenue of the Americas, until you come to Fifth Avenue.

OUT AND ABOUT

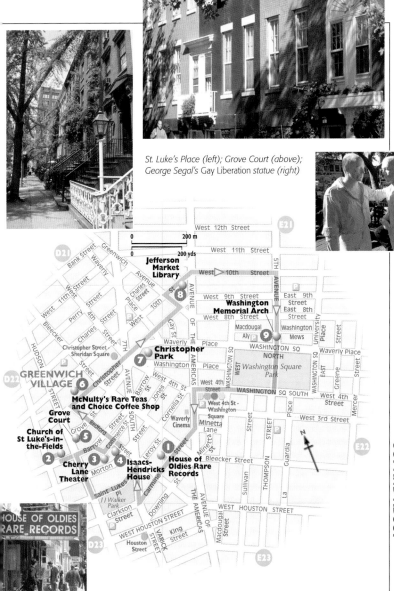

St. Luke's Place (left); Grove Court (above); George Segal's Gay Liberation statue (right)

Rare records to be explored on Carmine Street, Greenwich Village

Turn right and walk four blocks south on Fifth, through Washington Memorial Arch.

9 The original wooden arch was erected in 1889, in honor of George Washington 100 years after his inauguration. The marble Stanford White arch you see now was erected in 1895. The residential Washington Mews, on the east side of Fifth just north of the arch, were originally built as carriage houses for the wealthy residents of the fine town houses on Washington Square Park south of the arch. In the mews, John Dos Passos lived at No. 14A and Sherwood Anderson at No. 54. Washington Square Park, the focus of Greenwich Village, was once a potter's field and was the site of public executions until the 1800s.

Walk straight through the park to Washington Square South and turn right. This becomes West 4th Street, and ahead are the entrances to the subway on Avenue of the Americas.

WHEN TO GO

If you want to visit shops along the way, it is best to do this walk between 10 and 5 Monday to Saturday.

WHERE TO EAT

Petite Abeille, 466 Hudson Street *(tel 212/741-6479, open 24 hours)*.
Chumley's, 86 Bedford Street *(tel 212/675-4449)*.

OUT AND ABOUT

SOHO'S PUCK BUILDING TO THE SOHO GRAND HOTEL

If you enjoy gallery-hopping or architecture, put this walk at the top of your list. SoHo, *South of Ho*uston (pronounced *how-stun*), a landmark district famous for the prefabricated cast-iron façades of its buildings, is full of galleries where some of the city's most interesting contemporary artists show their work.

HE WALK

Distance: 2 miles (3.2km)
Time: 1.5 to 2 hours
Start at: Broadway/Lafayette subway station
End at: Canal Street subway station

HOW TO GET THERE

Subway: F and downtown 6
Bus: M6

Leave the Broadway/Lafayette Street subway and turn right (south) on Lafayette.

❶ The restored Puck Building is at 295 Lafayette Street. Don't miss the small statue of Puck, decorated with gold-leaf, above the door. Here the satirical magazine *Puck* was published, in German (1876–96) and in English (1877–1918). A much larger Puck can be seen at the entrance of the building on Mulberry and Houston. Inside is the office of Grace, the TV show character in "Will & Grace." A plaque on the West Houston Street side of the building relates its history.

Continue south along Lafayette, and turn right on Prince Street, then left on Broadway.

❷ The Little Singer Building at Broadway and Prince was designed by Ernest Flagg, who went on to design the Singer Tower, now demolished. An early skyscraper, the Little Singer was very avant-garde in 1904 with its curled steel, recessed glass and textured terra-cotta.

Walk to the end of the next block, to the corner of Broadway and Broome. Look on your left.

❸ The Haughwout Building, dating from 1857, is SoHo's oldest cast-iron beauty. Cast-iron façades were ornate, stylish, cheap, easy to assemble and recyclable. The Haughwout

Building architect based the façade on a window arch from a Venice library, repeating it 92 times. The first Otis elevator was installed here, inaugurating an era of ever-higher buildings.

Turn right onto Broome Street and right again onto Mercer Street. Go north on Mercer and don't miss Enchanted Forest at 85 Mercer Street *(tel 212/925-6677)*, a famously creative toy store.

❹ Stop for drinks at Bar 89, two doors down—and make sure you check out the now-you-see-through-them-now-you-don't doors on the toilet facilities on the mezzanine.

Continue to Prince Street and turn left (west), then go left again onto Greene Street, where there are more cast-iron buildings.

❺ Many of these structures started out as warehouses. By 1962, a lot of them had been abandoned, and there were plans to raze the neighborhood in order to accommodate a highway, but the area was saved from demolition when residents protested. Rents

were low here at the time so many artists, attracted to the huge, light-filled spaces, set up their homes and studios here; by the 1970s, artists had almost completely taken over. Landmark designation for the neighborhood came in 1973. As you walk south on Greene Street, watch for Nos. 72–76, known as the King of Greene Street, with cast-iron Corinthian columns, and Nos. 28–30, the Queen of Greene Street, with a Second Empire roof.

Return along Greene to Grand Street and turn right. Walk one block west to Wooster Street and turn right. On the corner of Broome and Wooster streets, a shop called Vintage New York has more than 200 wines for you to sample, many from New York State.

❻ On Wooster Street, the Tony Shafrazi Gallery is worth a visit at No. 119. Keith Haring and Julian Schnabel have exhibited here. At No. 120, the well-established Howard Greenberg Gallery is devoted to 20th-century photography. At No. 141, the innovative New York Earth Room exhibits great mounds of earth.

When you reach West Houston Street, turn left and walk one block west to West Broadway where you turn left again and walk south all the way down to Canal Street.

❼ Just north of Canal Street is The SoHo Grand Hotel. Have a look at the postmodern industrial interiors, then join the hip crowds at the bar.

Continue south on West Broadway, and turn right at Canal Street. You'll see the Canal Street

The gold Puck statue outside the building of the same name

OUT AND ABOUT

Cast-iron buildings on Greene Street (above); the Little Singer Building (right)

station for A, C and E subway lines two blocks along and, two blocks beyond that, the 1 or 2 train stations.

WHEN TO GO
To make the most of this walk, go when the art galleries are open, generally Tuesday to Sunday from 10 to 6.

WHERE TO EAT
Bar 89, 89 Mercer Street *(tel 212/274-0989).*

PLACES TO VISIT
New York Earth Room
✉ 141 Wooster Street
☎ 212/473-8072
⏱ Wed–Sat noon–3, 3.30–6, mid-Sep to mid-Jun
💰 Free

Take some time to watch the people at a café in SoHo (left); West Broadway is a typical SoHo thoroughfare

BOWLING GREEN TO SCHERMERHORN ROW

New York City began here in the 17th century, so if you are interested in the city's history, this is the walk for you. From Bowling Green to South Street Seaport, this area encompasses some of the city's greatest treasures.

THE WALK

Distance: 2.5 miles (4km)
Time: 2 to 2.5 hours
Start at: Bowling Green subway station
End at: Fulton Street subway station (A, 2, 3)

HOW TO GET THERE

Subway: 4, 5
Bus: M6

Leave Bowling Green station, and you'll see Battery Park ahead of you. Taking the path to the right, walk toward Castle Clinton.

❶ Castle Clinton *(tel 212/ 344-7220, Mon–Sun 8.30–5)* was the immigrant clearing center before Ellis Island. You'll pass a temporary memorial to the victims of the World Trade Center, *The Sphere*, a sculpture which stood between the towers as a symbol of world peace and is now a symbol of hope. In 1850, P. T. Barnum brought Europe's greatest soprano, Jenny Lind, to Castle Clinton, securing international stardom for both "the Swedish nightingale"—and for himself as her promoter. Inside the gate to your right, a small museum displays dioramas depicting the castle's various uses from fort and entertainment center to ticket office for boat trips to the Statue of Liberty (see pages 136–137) and Ellis Island Immigration Museum (see pages 90–93).

Leave through the gate straight ahead and walk to your right, keeping to the path as it veers left past Slip 6.

❷ In the water, just beyond slip 6, is the site of the *American Merchant Mariners Memorial,* a sculpture of a sinking ship by Marisol, dedicated to all merchant mariners

who have served the United States from the Revolutionary War to the present day.

Turn back and walk east past the ferries to Slip 3. Walk up the steps to your left.

❸ Albino Manca's sculpture of a bronze eagle with a funeral wreath, the *East Coast Memorial,* honors the memory of all people who died in American waters during World War II.

Take the path west back toward Castle Clinton and turn right at the east gate. Walk past the Hope Garden to the point where Battery Place, Broadway and State Street meet. This small park is Bowling Green, where a statue of King George III was torn down by fervent nationalists in 1776.

❹ The imposing neo-classical U. S. Custom House on the right houses the National Museum of the American Indian. The rotunda inside the Great Hall is well worth viewing.

Pass Bowling Green and walk north on Broadway, passing Arturo DiModica's bronze *Charging Bull* on your right outside the Museum of American Financial History. Continue past this symbol of stockmarket prosperity to Trinity Church, on your left.

❺ Trinity Church is historic (see pages 142–143). Many famous people are buried in the churchyard, including statesman Alexander Hamilton, steamboat inventor

Robert Fulton and Captain James Lawrence, whose last words ("Don't give up the ship") are now legendary.

As you leave the churchyard, cross to the east side of Broadway and continue east on famous Wall Street, straight ahead.

❻ Wall Street (see pages 146–147) is where you will find the New York Stock Exchange, now closed to the public, halfway down the street on your right. No. 40 is the Trump Building.

Walk east on Wall Street to William Street and go left, then left again onto Pine Street.

❼ On Pine Street, steps lead up to the Chase Manhattan Plaza, where sculptor Jean Dubuffet's *Group of Trees* takes center stage. Below the plaza is Isamu Noguchi's sunken sculpture garden.

Return to William Street by descending the steps to the right of the *Group of Trees*. Turn left to view the four abstract metal sculptures in Louise Nevelson Plaza. Across the street from the largest sculpture is the Federal Reserve Bank, designed to look like a Florentine palazzo. Just past the bank is Maiden Lane. Here turn left onto Maiden Lane, then right onto Nassau Street, and then right again onto John Street. At No. 44 is the United Methodist Church, with a fine Palladian front window. Continue east on John Street for five blocks, then left onto Water Street.

❽ The South Street Seaport Historic District (see pages 134–135) is full of boutiques and restaurants, more shopping mall than historic, but the atmosphere is festive and it's fun to be on the water; you have fine views of East River,

The Sphere, a memorial to the World Trade Center tragedy, temporarily in Battery Park

OUT AND ABOUT

Playing chess is one way to spend your lunch-hour on Wall Street; the American flag flies proudly outside many buildings on Wall Street

Fun is the watchword at South Street Seaport

the Brooklyn Bridge and the river craft. At the northern end of Water Street is Manhattan's oldest saloon, the Bridge Café, dating from 1847, where you can have a drink and a meal.

Turn right (east) onto Dover Street, then right again onto Front Street. When you get to Beekman Street, turn left to the city's fish market, Fulton Street Market. Go across South Street and walk to the end of Pier 17, and go up the steps for a spectacular view of Brooklyn Bridge (see pages 74–75). Then head toward South Street, cross over it and

continue straight ahead along Fulton Street.

❾ Schermerhorn Row, the Federal-style buildings along this street, were built as warehouses or counting houses in the early 1800s and named after the developer.

Continue west on Fulton Street to William Street and the subway station.

WHEN TO GO

To fully appreciate the bustle of Wall Street it is best to do this walk on weekdays.

WHERE TO EAT

Bridge Café, 279 Water Street *(tel 212/227-3344)*, or any of the eateries at South Street Seaport.

PLACES TO VISIT

National Museum of the American Indian
✉ 1 Bowling Green
☎ 212/668-6624
🕐 Mon–Wed and Fri–Sun 10–5, Thu until 8
💵 Free

OUT AND ABOUT

CITY HALL PARK TO WASHINGTON SQUARE PARK

Starting out from City Hall Park, you'll walk past the famous Woolworth Building, the world's tallest building until 1930 when the Chrysler Building spired even higher. Beyond lies Ground Zero, the site of the World Trade Center. You'll continue to SoHo and what remains of once-bustling Little Italy.

THE WALK

Distance: 3 miles (4.8km)
Time: 2 to 2.5 hours
Start at: Park Place subway station
End at: West 4th Street/Washington Square

HOW TO GET THERE

Subway: 2, 3
Bus: M6

When you leave Park Place subway station, City Hall and its park are on your right. Proceed south along Park Row, with the black iron fence on your right.

❶ The principal designer for City Hall (see page 77) was a Frenchman, Joseph Françoise Mangin, who also worked on the place de la Concorde in Paris. This mini-palace is where the mayor and city council have their offices. A wrought-iron fence keeps the rest of us out. In the park in front of City Hall is a statue of Nathan Hale, a spy for Washington's army, hanged by the English in 1776. Just before his execution he uttered his famous last words of regret that he had "but one life to lose for my country." The same area was the site of the 1863 Draft Riots (see page 33).

Across Broadway is Cass Gilbert's Woolworth Building (see page 144) between Park Place and Barclay Street, a skyscraper with lavish Gothic ornamentation and an amazingly rich lobby.

Turn left down Broadway and walk south.

❷ St. Paul's Chapel, on Broadway between Fulton and Vesey streets, is Manhattan's only remaining pre-Revolutionary building. George Washington worshiped here during the two years that New York was the nation's capital and inside you can see his pew.

Turn right on Fulton and continue west.

❸ Along the fence protecting the site of the World Trade Center (now known as Ground Zero, see page 108) at the end of Fulton Street, on Church Street, photos, flags, candles, flowers, teddy bears and other memorials to the victims of the tragedy can still be seen. Alongside the memorial, people sell T-shirts, photographs and hats to anyone willing to buy such reminders of the 9/11 disaster. Reconstruction on this site is already underway. If you wish to have a closer look, cross Church Street to the viewing wall.

Turn right on Church Street.

❹ At the corner of Church and Barclay streets is the Church of St. Peter, founded in 1785, and New York's oldest Catholic parish church.

Turn right on Park Place and you'll see City Hall Park ahead. Walk east through the park to get

The glistening Woolworth Building was built in 1913

a good view of Brooklyn Bridge. Back at Park Place subway station, take Park Row to Centre Street and walk north to the U.S. Courthouse.

❺ The U.S. Courthouse, designed by architect Cass Gilbert and also called Tweed Courthouse, is on the corner of Centre Street and Foley Square. In 1872, when Boss Tweed (see page 33) ran the city and milked taxpayers of millions of dollars, the estimated cost to construct the courthouse was $250,000. But by the time Tweed paid off friends and lined his own pockets to the tune of some $10 million, the tab was $14 million. Tweed died penniless in jail in 1878.

A little farther north are the criminal courts. As you approach Canal Street, the proximity to Chinatown becomes obvious: Open-fronted shops sell everything from Chinese lanterns to refrigerator magnets and made-in-China trinkets. When you reach the corner of Centre Street and Canal Street, turn right. Walk two blocks east, then turn left on Mulberry Street and walk north.

❻ You are now in the heart of Little Italy (see page 109), with a handful of Italian restaurants and cafés. Two blocks north, at 195 Grand Street, is Ferrara, founded in 1892, with strong coffee and sweet pastries.

Continue north on Mulberry to Prince Street, and turn left.

❼ On the corner of Prince Street and Broadway is the Guggenheim Museum SoHo, a branch of the famous art museum on Fifth Avenue, which offers many solo-artist shows by such famous names as Jeff Koons.

OUT AND ABOUT

City Hall was completed in 1802 in the Federal style

Chinatown canopies contrast with Ground Zero memories (above)

OUT AND ABOUT

Turn right on Broadway and walk half a block north.

❽ The New Museum of Contemporary Art (see page 124) displays paintings, sculpture and photography.

Go back to Prince Street and turn right along West Broadway. As you cross Houston Street, West Broadway becomes La Guardia Place.

❾ Three blocks north is Washington Square Park. Once a hanging ground and a burial site for more than 10,000 unidentified paupers, this space became a public park in 1828.

After a rest in the park, catch a downtown train from West 4th

Street/Washington Square back to Chambers Street near City Hall.

WHEN TO GO

The area around City Hall Park is at its liveliest on weekdays.

WHERE TO EAT

Ferrara, 195 Grand Street, between Mulberry and Mott streets *(tel 212/226-6150)*.

PLACES TO VISIT

Guggenheim Museum SoHo
✉ 575 Broadway
☎ 212/423-3500
🕐 Sun, Tue–Fri 11–6, Sat 11–8

Ferrara's, an Italian institution on Grand Street, where you can get great pastries and coffee (right)

MACY'S TO ROCKEFELLER CENTER

Some of New York's most striking sights are along this route—the Empire State Building, the Diamond District, and Rockefeller Plaza, where you may be tempted to stop in at the NBC Experience Store to pick up a "Will & Grace," "Friends" or "Law & Order" T-shirt.

THE WALK

Distance: 3 miles (4.8km)
Time: 2.5 hours
Start at: 34th Street/Penn Station subway station
End at: 34th Street/Herald Square

HOW TO GET THERE

Subway: 1, 2, 3, 9
Bus: M10

Leave the 34th Street/Penn Station subway station so you come out onto West 34th Street at Seventh Avenue (also known as Fashion Avenue).

1 You are standing in front of Macy's, arguably New York's most famous department store. Encompassing two entire city blocks, this store is so big you could spend days here.

The Empire State Building is east. Head east on West 34th Street. Continue to Broadway, cross it and turn left onto Sixth Avenue (Avenue of the Americas), keeping to the right as you go through the intersection. Six blocks north on Sixth, past lots of shops and banks, is Bryant Park on your right, where you can rest or get a coffee in the park. Continue north past the park. North of 43rd Street is the International Center of Photography (see page 101).

2 The Diamond District is concentrated on 47th Street between Fifth and Sixth avenues. Notice the diamond-motif street lights illuminating

the corners. Millions of dollars worth of gems are traded daily in the businesses here.

Continue north on Sixth Avenue.

3 At 49th Street you'll see the 70-story G. E. Building towers to the right at 30 Rockefeller Plaza. This building is the headquarters of General Electric and NBC (National Broadcasting Corporation) and is part of Rockefeller Center (see pages 128–130), a city landmark. The ground floor of the building is worth visiting; note José Maria Sert's sepia murals depicting the progress of man. At the Rainbow Room Restaurant on the 65th floor of the G. E. Building there are spectacular views of the city.

Continue on Avenue of the Americas to 50th Street.

4 Stop to admire the landmark art-deco Radio City Music Hall (see page 129), another city landmark and important element of the Rockefeller Center. Most famous for its Rockettes Christmas spectacular, it also hosts other music shows throughout the year. This was the world's largest indoor theater when it opened in 1932. Hour-long guided tours are worth the time and the money. The block-long entry, with its 24-carat-gold ceiling and two-ton glass chandeliers, is spectacular. Just past Radio City, at 1290 Avenue of

the Americas, is the AXA Financial Center. Stop in to view the foyer's magnificent multi-panel murals by Thomas Hart Benton depicting the nation's economic and social life on the eve of the Depression.

Back on Avenue of the Americas, go north a block to 52nd Street and turn right. The CBS Building, constructed in a dark granite in 1965, is on the corner of Avenue of the Americas and 52nd Street, a part of which is also known as Swing Street because of the many jazz clubs that flourished along here after the repeal of Prohibition.

5 At 25 West 52nd Street is the Museum of Television and Radio (see page 124). Next door at No. 21 is the 21 Club, a still-fashionable Prohibition-era hangout, now a fine restaurant. Note the jockeys above the door.

At the corner of 52nd Street and Fifth Avenue, turn right and walk south a block.

6 At St. Patrick's Cathedral, the largest Catholic cathedral in America (see page 131), the flying buttresses and 330ft (100m) twin towers vie for your attention.

Turn left on 51st Street, and walk east past the cathedral toward Madison Avenue. Cross Madison Avenue.

7 On the southeast corner of 51st and Madison is the New York Palace Hotel, which rises out of the Villard Houses, twin brownstone mansions built in 1884 by the Bavarian-born journalist, financier and railroad tycoon Henry Villard.

Continue walking east on 51st as far as Park Avenue. Turn left and walk one block north.

Macy's is the one everyone thinks of when they think stores

OUT AND ABOUT

8 The bronze-glass tower at 375 Park Avenue is the Seagram Building (see page 141), a lively place in summer and a delight at Christmas with a tree and lights. Diagonally across the avenue is Lever House, built in 1952 with an avant-garde metal- and glass-curtain wall that reflects everything around.

Go left on East 53rd Street, walk west to Sixth Avenue and turn left again. Walk four blocks south.

9 Rockefeller Center is a great place to shop, stop for a snack, or just wander around.

From here you can take the subway to Herald Square.

WHEN TO GO
Avoid this walk on Sunday if you want to shop and visit St. Patrick's Cathedral. Monday to Saturday from 10 to 6 is best.

WHERE TO EAT
Rainbow Room in the Rockefeller Center *(212/632-5000)* or Rockefeller Center Café, 20 West 50th Street *(212/332-7620)*

PLACES TO VISIT
Museum of Television and Radio
✉ 25 West 52nd Street
☎ 212/621-6800
🕐 Tue–Sun noon–6, Thu until 8

Radio City Music Hall
✉ 1260 Sixth Avenue
☎ 212/247-4777
🕐 Mon–Sat 10–5, Sun 11–5
▶ Hour-long behind-the-scenes tours every 30 minutes

Bryant Park is a pleasant green space to stop for a snack in summer (left)

Radio City Music Hall (top); St. Patrick's Cathedral (above)

Ice skating at the Rockefeller Center at Christmas

OUT AND ABOUT

CENTRAL PARK WEST HISTORIC DISTRICT

This walk begins with a quick look at the Dakota Building, where Beatle John Lennon was shot in 1980, then stops at his memorial across the street in Central Park. In the 1960s, with private contributions of about $165 million, Upper West Side tenements were razed and Lincoln Center was built in their stead, a very pleasant complex of pedestrian open spaces, theaters, concert halls, cinemas and museums. Many actors, actresses and movie directors work and live in the neighborhood—it's fun to see if you can spot any.

THE WALK

Distance: 1.5 miles (2.4km)
Time: 1.5 to 2 hours
Start/End at: 72nd Street subway station

HOW TO GET THERE

Subway: B, C
Bus: M10

Leave the 72nd Street subway at the corner of 72nd Street and Central Park West.

❶ The Dakota (see page 87) is on the northwest corner of Central Park West and 72nd Street. Look at the front of the building on 72nd Street, where John Lennon was shot. His wife, Yoko Ono, still lives in the building.

Walk east across Central Park West and follow the path straight ahead to Strawberry Fields.

❷ Here there is a memorial to Lennon, a black and white mosaic called *Imagine*.

Go back to Central Park West, turn left, and walk south. Note the residential streets lined with 19th-century brownstones to your right. Turn left into the park at West 67th Street.

❸ Here, at Tavern on the Green, celebrities show up for gala events and film premieres and tourists come (and pay the price) to enjoy the seating on the leafy patio in summer. The Sheep Meadow, straight ahead, is a 15-acre (6ha) expanse created as part of the Olmsted and Vaux design for Central Park; at the time it reminded many city-dwellers of the rural landscapes they had left behind when they emigrated to the United States.

Return to Central Park West and go south for two blocks. Turn right on 65th Street to Columbus Avenue. Cross Broadway and

Columbus Avenue. On the west of Broadway is Lincoln Center.

❹ Lincoln Center (see pages 112–113) includes Alice Tully Hall (on the northwest corner of 65th Street) and Avery Fisher Hall (on the southwest corner). Much of the movie *West Side Story* was shot in the tenements that once stood on this spot. Walk south from Avery Fisher about 300 yards (274m) to the Lincoln Center central plaza, with its fountain. On the south side of the plaza is the home of the New York City Ballet, the New York State Theater; rising over the plaza on the west is the Metropolitan Opera House with Austrian chandeliers and Marc Chagall murals visible through the glass façade. To the south of the Met is a pleasant open area where open-air concerts are held in summer and the Big Apple Circus holds forth over the year-end holidays. The pond sculpture is Henry Moore's *Reclining Figure*, and the Vivian Beaumont Theater lies to the west.

Go up the steps to the Juilliard School to the north, turn right then left down the steps to Broadway. Cross 66th Street, then cross Broadway to your right. Walk east on 66th to Columbus and turn left. On the right stands the contemporary ABC Building at No. 147 Columbus. Continue along Columbus to West 70th Street and turn left.

❺ At 135 West 70th, near the corner of 70th and Broadway is the Pythian Temple, now a condominium; designed by Thomas W. Lamb, and built in 1926, it was dedicated to Pythianism, the cult of the oracle at Delphi, and Assyrian sages still guard the entrance. Bill Haley and the Comets recorded "Rock Around the Clock" here in 1954. Across the

street, at 154 West 70th Street, is Café Mozart, with extravagant cakes and pastries.

Continue west to Amsterdam Avenue, turn right. As you approach West 72nd Street, you'll see one of the few remaining old subway buildings from the early 1900s on your left and a pleasingly harmonious new structure, an expansion of the venerable subway station, across 72nd on the north side of the street. Cross West 72nd Street.

❻ The magnificent Beaux-Arts Ansonia Building rises at 2109 Broadway between West 73rd and West 74th streets. Caruso, Stravinsky and Toscanini all lived at the Ansonia, and the soundproofing between apartments and floors continues to attract distinguished musicians, singers and conductors.

Turn right on West 73rd Street; 18 row houses, between Nos. 248 and 272, are the earliest houses in the neighborhood, dating from 1885. Turn left on Central Park West.

❼ Designed in 1930 by architect Emery Roth, the towers of the San Remo Apartments at 145–146 Central Park West grace the skyline. Residents have included Paul Simon and Dustin Hoffman.

Continue north on Central Park West to 77th Street.

❽ The New-York Historical Society (see page 126) is on the corner of 77th and Central Park West. The fascinating collections and unusual variety of gifts in the shop make this worth a stop.

Cross West 77th Street.

❾ The enormous American Museum of Natural History

OUT AND ABOUT

The fascinating American Museum of Natural History (above)

West 81st Street — West 81st Street

81st Street Museum of Natural History

West 80th Street

West 79th Street

American Museum of Natural History ⑨

West 78th Street

West 77th Street

New-York Historical Society ⑧

West 76th Street

The Dakota

0 — 200 m
0 — 200 yds

West 75th Street

San Remo Apartments ⑦

West 74th Street

The Lake

Ansonia Building ⑥

West 73rd Street

The Dakota ①

West 72nd Street

② **Strawberry Fields**

72nd Street

72nd Street

West 71st Street

Olmsted Drive

West 70th Street

Pythian Temple ⑤

West 69th Street

Central Park

West 68th Street

West 67th Street

The Sheep Meadow

66th Street Lincoln Center

West 66th Street

Juilliard School

③ **Tavern on the Green**

65th Street Transverse Rd

Lincoln Center ④

West 65th Street

BROADWAY

West 64th Street

Columbus Avenue · Amsterdam Avenue · BROADWAY · Central Park West

OUT AND ABOUT

(see pages 68–72) is on your left. Go to the main entrance to admire the bronze statue of President Theodore Roosevelt seated upon a horse, then step inside to look at William Mackay's beautiful murals depicting events from Roosevelt's life in the Roosevelt Memorial Hall.

After leaving the museum, walk up Central Park West, and at the 81st Street traffic lights take the entrance to the park straight ahead of you. As soon as you enter, take the path immediately to your right and walk south along this path to West 72nd Street and back to the 72nd Street subway station.

WHEN TO GO

This walk is very pleasant on Sunday afternoons. Most shops and restaurants are open then.

WHERE TO EAT

Café Mozart, 154 West 70th Street *(tel 212/595-9797)*.

PLACES TO VISIT

New-York Historical Society
✉ 2 West 77th Street
☎ 212/873-3400
🕐 Tue–Sun 10–5

American Museum of Natural History
✉ Central Park West at 81st Street
☎ 212/769-5100
🕐 Daily 10–5.45, Fri until 8.45

Sheep grazed in The Sheep Meadow until 1934

FORT TRYON PARK

Go to Fort Tryon Park for fresh air, a walk in the woods, spectacular views of the Hudson River from Manhattan's highest natural point, gardens and a medieval-style monastery.

THE WALK

Distance: 1.5 miles (2.4km)
Time: 1.5 to 2 hours
Start/End at: Margaret Corbin Circle at 190th Street subway station

HOW TO GET THERE

Subway: A
Bus: M4

Leave the M4 bus at 190th Street rather than taking it to the Cloisters, the last stop. If you arrive by the A train, get off at 190th Street and take the elevator to street level and turn to your right as you come out of the station.

1 One of the earliest battles of the American Revolutionary War was fought in Fort Tryon Park on November 16, 1776. General George Washington's troops were outnumbered 4,000 to 600 and lost to the British, who named the fort after the colonial governor, Sir William Tryon. Although the area around the park is known as Washington Heights, the British name for the fort was never changed.

John D. Rockefeller acquired the property in 1917 and in 1938 established the Cloisters, a branch of the Metropolitan Museum of Art, to house a large collection of medieval art. Frederick Law Olmsted, Jr. designed the gardens using more than 250 species of plants. Olmsted's stone walls, arches, terraces and stairs recall medieval Europe, making these 62 acres (25ha) a special spot.

Margaret Corbin Circle is named after a brave American woman who took over her husband's cannon after he was fatally wounded in the Fort Tryon battle, and the only woman buried at West Point. To your left, on the west side of the circle, stands a small stone building that was the gate-house for the Billings estate. Cornelius K. G. Billings was a weathy horseman from Chicago who spent more than $2 million building his Tryon Hill mansion between 1901 and 1905.

Make your way through the huge stone gateway ahead and onto the Promenade. Turn immediately to your left onto this walkway.

2 The 3-acre (1.2ha) Heather Garden here enjoys a breathtaking view across the Hudson River to New Jersey's Palisades and the George Washington Bridge. With its many heathers, brooms, perennials and shrubs, this garden is one of the largest heather gardens on the east coast. By May, 5,000 bulbs are in full bloom, with more than 30 varieties of daffodils and tulips, and 1,000 lilies are in flower from June to September.

From the Heather Garden, return to the Promenade and follow it for about 300 yards (273m) to Linden Terrace.

3 In 1909, Billings erected a stela in Linden Terrace as a memorial to the Continental Army's defense of the site. Linden trees shade the pretty spot, and there are benches, parapets and splendid river views. At the northeast corner of the terrace, steps lead up to a flagpole. Standing here, you are on the highest natural point in Manhattan.

Return down the steps you have just come up to the Promenade, which veers to the left and down some stone steps. At the bottom of the steps continue along the path to your right.

4 You can see the Cloisters (see page 86) straight ahead to the north. Stroll northward with the river on your left and, if you wish to have a quick look inside the museum, cross the road at the pedestrian crossing on your right and continue along the path straight ahead. The entrance on your left leads to the gift shop, which sells Tiffany-like glass, art books, educational children's toys, videos and CDs to a background soundtrack of medieval music.

Continue north on the path you left to visit the Cloisters and stroll through the very pleasant woods and lawns. If you stay on the path closest to the road (Margaret Corbin Drive) that runs through the park, you'll come to the New Leaf Café.

5 The stunning location, trendy food and affordable prices of the New Leaf Café, an enterprise of actress Bette Midler's New York Restoration Project, make it a very pleasant rest stop. Proceeds support ongoing work in the park.

The path leads back to the park's main entrance at Margaret Corbin Circle.

WHEN TO GO

It is best not to go on Mondays when the Cloisters and the restaurant are closed. Even if you do not spend time viewing the exhibits, a quick look at the Cloisers is well worthwhile

WHERE TO EAT

New Leaf Café, Fort Tryon Park (tel 212/568-5323; closed Mon).

PLACES TO VISIT

The Cloisters
✉ Fort Tryon Park
☎ 212/923-3700
🕐 Tue–Sun 9.30–5.15, Mar–Oct; Tue–Sun 9.30–4.45, rest of year

Margaret Corbin Circle, at the entrance to the park, is the start and finish of the walk (below); a blue jay in the park (below right)

OUT AND ABOUT

The impressive Cloisters; a walled walk around the park

One of the many beautiful walkways that make up the Cloisters, which houses medieval European art (below)

FORT TRYON PARK 253

BROOKLYN HEIGHTS TO MANHATTAN

If Brooklyn were not part of New York City, it would be America's sixth largest city. Historic Brooklyn Heights, with its many landmark churches, fine brownstones and leafy streets, remains one of the city's most distinguished residential areas. The walk across the Brooklyn Bridge provides stunning views of Lower Manhattan.

THE WALK

Distance: 2.5 miles (4km)

Time: 2 to 2.5 hours (allow time to enjoy the view of Manhattan from Brooklyn Bridge)

Start at: High Street/Brooklyn Bridge subway station

End at: Brooklyn Bridge/City Hall subway station

HOW TO GET THERE

Subway: A, C

Leave the High Street/Brooklyn Bridge subway station. As you come out of the station, you see Cadman Plaza Park, with its tall trees, paths and benches. On the right side of the park is Cadman Plaza West. Walk south on this street the length of the park.

❶ Stop for a moment at the large stone monument on your left, dedicated to the Brooklyn men and women who fought during World War II. With its trees and benches, this park is a pleasant place to sit.

Continue on Cadman Plaza West, crossing Tillary Street. Pass the Korean War Veterans Plaza on your left and continue to the Federal Building and the Romanesque Revival U. S. Post Office and Courthouse. Cross Johnson Street.

❷ The enormous building on the left is the Supreme Court of New York. Pause to admire the statue of Christopher Columbus in front of the building and the bronze bust of Senator Robert F. Kennedy, the assassinated brother of President John F. Kennedy.

❸ Straight ahead is an elaborate fountain and behind it is the Greek Revival Brooklyn Borough Hall, built in 1848.

Just past Borough Hall is Joralemon Street. Walk west on Joralemon a block and a half to Sidney Place, on your left. Look down this little street to the big red church, St. Charles Borromeo Roman Catholic Church, built in 1849. Three blocks farther west on Joralemon, turn right on Hicks Street. Walk one block north.

❹ Grace Church, at 254 Hicks Street, is one of many New York City churches designed by Richard Upjohn; it dates from 1849. Visit the charming entrance court off Hicks Street and cool off in the shade of the enormous elm tree.

Continue a block north on Hicks to Remsen Street, and turn right. Go one block east and cross Henry Street.

❺ On your left is Richard Upjohn's Cathedral of Our Lady of Lebanon, the first round-arched, Early Romanesque Revival ecclesiastical building in the United States. Notice the medallions on the entrance doors. Originally the dining room doors on the French luxury liner *Normandie*, they were bought at an auction in 1945.

Continue another block east on Remsen, and turn left on Clinton Street. Walking north, as you cross Montague Street, look at St. Ann and the Holy Trinity Episcopal Church, a major work of James Renwick, Jr., on your left; it is one of the most important Victorian Gothic churches in the

The statue of Bobby Kennedy outside the Supreme Court of New York

SENATOR ROBERT FRANCIS KENNEDY

NOVEMBER 20 1925
JUNE 6 1968

United States. At the end of Clinton Street, turn left on Cadman Plaza West, left again on Clark Street and then right on Henry Street. Walk two blocks to Orange Street and turn left.

❻ The Plymouth Church of the Pilgrims, built in 1849 on Orange Street between Henry and Hicks streets, was the center of anti-slavery sentiment during antebellum days. Abolitionist minister Henry Ward Beecher preached against slavery here. Abraham Lincoln worshiped here twice, and the building was a key part of the Underground Railroad, which helped get escaped slaves to freedom in the north. Beautiful stained-glass windows adorn this otherwise modest church, and in the courtyard next to it stands a bronze statue of Henry Ward Beecher by Gutzon Borglum, who sculpted the famous presidents' heads at Mount Rushmore.

Return to Henry Street and turn left. There are many cafés, restaurants and delis along here. At the traffic lights, turn right on Middagh Street and, at Cadman Plaza West, take the path ahead across the park. On your left is a plaque with information about the peregrine falcons that often roost here. At the fork in the path, keep left and you'll come to Washington Street. Turn left, and just before you come to the traffic lights at Prospect Street, go up the steps on your left.

❼ You now leave Brooklyn Heights across Brooklyn Bridge (see pages 74–75), on the wide wooden pedestrian walkway. In 1883 Brooklyn Bridge became the world's longest suspension bridge, spanning the East River and connecting Brooklyn to Manhattan. This spectacular bridge, with its web of steel cables, remains as much a marvel today as it did when it was first built.

OUT AND ABOUT

Brooklyn Borough Hall (above); Hicks Street brownstones (above right); the Plymouth Church of the Pilgrims (right)

Brooklyn Bridge 278

Vine Street
Middagh Street
Willow Street
Plymouth Church of the Pilgrims 6
Orange Street
BROOKLYN
Pineapple Street
HEIGHTS
Clark Street
Hicks Street
College Place
Love Lane
Pierrepont Street
St Ann and the Holy Trinity Episcopal Church
Montague Street
Cathedral of Our Lady of Lebanon 5
Remsen Street
Grace Court Aly
Grace Church 4
Willow Place

Adams Street
Pearl Street
Sands St
High St
Cadman Plaza East
High Street Brooklyn Bridge
Cadman Plaza Park
Federal Building
TILLARY ST
U S Post Office and Courthouse
Johnson Street
Supreme Court of New York 2
Court Street
Brooklyn Borough Hall 3
Joralemon Street
Livingston Street
Schermerhorn Street

McLaughlin Park
TILLARY STREET
Concord Street
Jay Street
Myrtle Av
Lawrence St
Borough Hall

FURMAN ST
Columbia Heights
BROOKLYN-QUEENS EXPRESSWAY
CADMAN PLAZA WEST
Clinton Street
Henry Street
Hunts Lane
Garden Place
Sidney Place

N

0   200 m
0   200 yds

Rows of tulips brighten up Columbus Park

OUT AND ABOUT

When you reach the other side of the bridge you'll see the Brooklyn Bridge City Hall subway, from where you can access lines 4, 5, 6 and J, M, Z.

WHEN TO GO

Any day of the week, morning or afternoon, but the walk across the bridge is especially romantic as the sun slowly sets behind Liberty Island and Lower Manhattan's city lights begin to twinkle.

WHERE TO EAT

Henry Street has a wide selection of cafés and restaurants.

BROOKLYN HEIGHTS TO MANHATTAN 255

HUDSON RIVER VALLEY

The Hudson River flows 315 miles (508km) from the Adirondack Mountains to New York and out into the Atlantic. The splendor of this valley can be seen in the paintings by the Hudson River School artists of the 19th century, and still today the area is lovely, especially in the fall, when the colorful foliage brightens the shoreline.

BASICS

Historic Hudson Valley
☎ 914/631-8200
www.hudsonvalley.org

National Trust for Historic Preservation
☎ 914/631-4481

National Park Service
☎ 845/229-9115

HOW TO GET THERE

By train: Most of the valley north of New York City is easily visited by train. From Grand Central Terminal, take the Metro-North Hudson Line to the closest station; local taxis meet trains at most stations, or you can book one for Yonkers North to Tarrytown through Rivertowns Taxi *(tel 914/478-2222)*.

By car: Follow the West Side Highway to the Henry Hudson Parkway and then the Saw Mill River Parkway (all one road, really, but with three different names). It's best to get specific directions from the Saw Mill by phoning each sight.

By river: The New York Waterway offers day-long excursions up the Hudson River, leaving from Pier 78 on Manhattan's west side *(www.newyorkwaterway.com)*.

HUDSON RIVER MUSEUM

The Hudson River Museum *(tel 914/963-4550, Wed–Sun noon–5, Fri noon–9, May–Sep)* is built around a historic house and a modern addition. Collections encompass art and history, and there's a planetarium. At the Museum Café, you can have a light lunch with splendid views of the Hudson River and the Palisades in New Jersey. Take Metro-North to Yonkers, then grab a cab (about $5).

SUNNYSIDE TO LYNDHURST

Sunnyside, a National Historic Landmark, was the home of Washington Irving, who wrote *The Legend of Sleepy Hollow* and was America's first internationally known author. The cottage *(tel 914/631-8200, Wed–Mon 10–5, Apr–Oct; Wed–Mon 10–4, Nov–Dec; Sat–Sun 10–4, Mar)*, was built in the 18th century and enlarged by Irving in 1835. Guided tours of the house and grounds are available up to one hour before closing time. There is a visitor center, museum shop and seasonal café. From Grand Central Terminal, catch a train to Tarrytown, where taxis are waiting.

Lyndhurst, a spectacular Gothic Revival-style mansion *(tel 914/631-4481, Tue–Sun 10–5, mid-Apr to Oct; Tue–Sun 10–4, rest of year)*, was the home of railroad tycoon Jay Gould. The surrounding lawns have amazing Hudson River views. You can call a local cab to take you to Sunnyside, or walk on the footpath.

PHILLIPSBURG MANOR AND KYKUIT

Phillipsburg Manor, on Route 9 in Sleepy Hollow, is a restored Colonial farm once owned by the powerful Phillips family *(Wed–Mon 10–5, Apr–Oct; Wed–Mon 10–4, Nov–Dec; Sat–Sun 10–4, Mar)*. Guided tours are available and houses and outbuildings like the barn and working grist mill are staffed by interpreters in period costume who explain early Hudson River Valley life.

Kykuit is a National Trust Historic Site that was home to four generations of the wealthy Rockefeller family. The sumptuous mansion is filled with priceless antiques and works of art, and sculptures fill the beautifully landscaped gardens. Guided tours *(Wed– Mon 10–3, mid-Apr to Oct)* begin at the Phillipsburg Manor; tickets go on sale at 9am and are issued on a first-come, first-served basis (children under 10 are not admitted).

VAN CORTLANDT MANOR

This 18th-century Hudson Valley mansion belonged to the Van Cortlandt family for more than 260 years. Pierre Van Cortlandt was the first lieutenant-governor of New York State. The house has many original furnishings, and the kitchen is a tour highlight with its original hearth and beehive oven *(Wed–Mon 10–5, Apr–Oct; Wed–Mon 10–4, Nov–Dec; Sat–Sun 10–4, Mar)*.

WEST POINT, FRANKLIN D. ROOSEVELT NATIONAL HISTORIC SITE TO VANDERBILT MANSION

Farther upstate, there are a handful of other landmarks on the east side of the Hudson. The

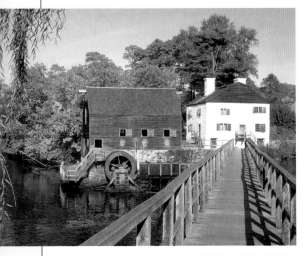

A long wooden footbridge leads to Phillipsburg Manor

United States Military Academy at West Point, is on the west side, two sites connected with President Franklin D. Roosevelt, a Beaux-Arts mansion, and a museum on the New York City art scene. Together they make for a full day's excursion; if you want to move at less than break-neck pace, however, allow two days. Either way, you should get your own wheels to visit.

Your first stop is the United States Military Academy at **West Point** *(tel 914/938-2368, daily 10.30–4.15)*. America's most respected academy has turned out some great generals, presidents and astronauts. The museum displays guns, uniforms, medals and flags from various conflicts, and the grounds are beautiful in their own right.

Franklin D. Roosevelt National Historic Site *(daily 9–5)* was the Depression-era president's birthplace. The house, library and museum have a large collection of family memorabilia. Franklin and his formidable wife, Eleanor, are buried in the rose garden; a white marble monument marks their graves.

From this point a shuttle bus will take you to the **Eleanor Roosevelt National Historic Site** *(daily 9–5, May–Oct, Thu–Mon 9–5, rest of year)* in the grounds of the Roosevelt estate.

Vanderbilt Mansion *(daily 9–5, May–Oct; Wed–Sun 9–5, rest of the year, visit by guided*

The Monument to the American Soldier in the U.S. Military Academy at West Point (above); Sunnyside, where Irving got his inspiration to write The Legend of Sleepy Hollow *(right)*

tour only), 2 miles (1km) north of the Roosevelt Historic Site, is a lavish Beaux-Arts mansion that was designed by architects McKim, Mead and White for the grandson of railroad magnate Cornelius Vanderbilt. Inside you will see all the splendors money can buy, from Renaissance to rococo furniture and works of art. The gardens are exquisite, and there are several walking trails that skirt the river.

WHERE TO EAT

In Tarrytown there are three good places to find something to eat: Equus Restaurant, The Castle *(tel 914/631-3646)*; Main Street Café, 24 Main Street, *(tel 914/524-9770)*; and Striped Bass, 236 Main Street *(tel 914/366-4455)*.

Fall foliage surrounds the Victory Monument in the U. S. Military Academy at West Point

OUT AND ABOUT

LONG ISLAND

Long Island measures 125 miles (202km) in length and between 12 and 23 miles (19 and 37km) in width. It lies east of New York City and is washed by the Atlantic Ocean on the south and Long Island Sound on the north. The rocky northern shoreline, scalloped with beaches, coves, bays, inlets and bluffs, and sometimes called the Gold Coast, has attracted the affluent since the late 19th century. The Hamptons, on the east end of the island, on the Atlantic shore, has become the playground of wealthy families, who have built fine summer houses and mansions. The delightful Atlantic-pounded beaches along the southern shore offer a refreshing escape from city heat in summer. The western part of the island is densely populated, and has a network of busy highways, but the farther east you go, the more rural it becomes. Here are historic homes, fishing ports, historic whaling towns, museums and state parks.

BASICS

🛈 NYC & Company
☎ 212/484-1222
🕐 Mon–Fri 8.30–6, Sat–Sun 9–5
www.nyc.visit.com

HOW TO GET THERE

By train: Go to Pennsylvania Station on 7th Avenue between 31st and 33rd streets. From here catch a Long Island Railroad train to the town nearest the place of interest.

By car: From New York, travel from Manhattan east through parts of Brooklyn and Queens. Buses and trains are often a better way to get to Long Island, but you usually need a car to get around the various sights, so it's best to take your own wheels.

OLD WESTBURY GARDENS AND SAGAMORE HILL HISTORIC SITE

Old Westbury Gardens *(tel 516/333-6807)* was the home of financier John S. Phipps (1874–1958), his wife Margarita and their four children. The Charles II-style manor house is furnished with English antiques and decorative arts. The surrounding 160 acres (64ha), with 88 breathtaking acres (36ha) of formal gardens, walkways, architectural follies and woodlands are dotted with ponds and lakes. The gardens are between the Long Island Expressway, also known as the L.I.E and I-495, and Jericho Turnpike (Route 25). By car, take Exit 39 (Glen Cove Road) off the I-495. Follow the service road east for 1 mile (1.5km), turn right on Old Westbury Road and continue for half a mile.

Sagamore Hill National Historic Site is northeast of Old Westbury, the home of President Theodore Roosevelt from 1885 until his death in 1919. The house is furnished as it was when he lived here *(tel 516/ 922-4788, Wed–Mon 10–5, May to mid-Dec).* Tours last half an hour and are offered on a first-come, first-served basis. They are limited in size, so arrive early if possible (by noon in summer they are often sold out). To get there by car, take Exit 41N (Oyster Bay) off I-495. Travel for 4 miles (6km) to Route 25A, where you will turn right and travel 2.5 miles (4km) to the third traffic light. At the bottom

Sagamore Hill House (left); the Atlantic Ocean washes onto Robert Moses State Park on Fire Island, south of Long Island

The Vanderbilt Museum was built in 1910 by William K. Vanderbilt

of a long hill, turn left onto Cove Road and continue for 1.5 miles (2.5km). Turn right onto Cove Neck Road for 1.5 miles (2.5km).

WALT WHITMAN BIRTHPLACE TO OLD BETHPAGE VILLAGE

Walt Whitman (1819–92) was one of America's finest poets and essayists. At his birthplace, south of Sagamore Hill, you will see Whitman memorabilia, including photographs and excerpts from his writings and letters *(tel 516/427-5240, Wed–Fri 1–4, Sat–Sun 10–4)*. To get there from I-495, take Exit 49N onto Route 110 North. Turn left onto Walt Whitman Road in Huntington Station. As the site is very popular with school groups, you may want to phone ahead.

Old Bethpage Village *(tel 516/572-8400, Wed–Sun 10–5, Mar–Oct, 10–4, rest of year)* is 100 acres (40ha) of vintage shops, farms, a one-room school-house, a church, gardens and homes filled with antiques, all staffed by costumed interpreters explaining what life was like on Long Island in the 19th century. Special events are lively and fun.

The Theodore Roosevelt Sanctuary at Sagamore Hill

OUT AND ABOUT

ORGANIZED TOURS

New York offers more tours than any city in the world. There are walking tours, bicycle tours, harbor tours, art and theater tours, behind-the-scenes tours, bus tours, limo tours, train tours, multilingual tours, and special-interest tours such as ethnic, food and shopping tours. Some major bookstores have shelves of books about New York, many of them with self-guiding tours themed around everything from nature to literary history. The list of tour operators below is a small sample of what's available.

Details: www.nycvisit.com (click on Visitors, Things To Do and Tours)

BICYCLE TOURS

CENTRAL PARK BICYCLE TOURS
2 Columbus Circle/Broadway at 59th Street
Tel 212/541-8759
www.centralparkbiketour.com
Rent a bicycle and ride around Central Park with a knowledgeable guide for two hours. Tours daily at 10am, 1pm and 4pm; adult $35, child $20. Rental only: $20 for 2 hours, $25 for 3 hours and $35 all day.

BUS TOURS

ON LOCATION TOURS
Tel 212/209-3370
www.sceneontr.com
Open-top buses depart from different locations. Reservations are recommended. Manhattan TV Tour (adult $20, child 6–9 $10, 5s and under free) departs from in front of McDonald's, 1560 Broadway between 46th and 47th streets, for a 2-hour tour to 20 locations; "Sex and the City" Tour (all tickets $25) departs from in front of the Pulitzer Fountain on Fifth Avenue by 58th Street; the "Sopranos" Tour (all tickets $30) departs from in front of Bryant Park Fountain on Sixth Avenue at 41st Street.

HELICOPTER TOURS
Helicopters leave from the Downtown Manhattan Heliport at Pier 6 and South Street and from the VIP Heliport at West 30th Street.

LIBERTY HELICOPTER TOURS
Tel 212/967-6464
www.libertyhelicopters.com
$56, 5–7 mins; $162, 15–17 mins
Fly over Manhattan's

skyscrapers, New York Harbor and the five boroughs.

RIVER TOURS

CIRCLE LINE
Tel 212/563-3200
www.circleline.com
Cruises from the Circle Line (Pier 83 at West 42nd Street/ 12th Avenue or Pier 16, South Street Seaport at Fulton Street and East River) are worth every penny. Take the 3-hour Full Island cruise, the 1-hour Semi-Circle cruise, 1-hour Seaport Liberty cruise, or a combination of packages. Prices are $13–$26 for adults, $7–$13 for children under 12, with combos more expensive. Cruises with live music (adults only) operate from May to September and cost $20–$40. In spring and fall remember that it's at least 10 degrees colder on the water—and more when you consider wind chill in a moving boat.

WALKING TOURS
Here are a few that are highly recommended. Call ahead for up-to-date schedules.

BIG APPLE GREETER
Tel 212/669-8159
www.bigapplegreeter.org
A free public service. The guides—volunteer New Yorkers—are matched with visitors according to language and interests. Give at least a week advance notice (longer during peak season).

BIG ONION WALKING TOURS
Tel 212/439-1090
Adult $12–$18, child $10–$16
www.bigonion.com
Two-hour tours. Guides have

degrees in American history. No reservations necessary.

EAST SIDE, WEST SIDE TOURS
Tel 718/549-7812
Adult $12, under 12s $10
www.eastsidewestsidewalkingtours.com
A variety of tours lasting two to two-and-a-half hours with licenced guides.

GRAND CENTRAL PARTNERSHIP
Tel 212/883-2420
www.grandcentralpartnership.org
Free tours of Grand Central Terminal every Friday lunchtime at 12.30. Just show up outside Grand Central Terminal at Philip Morris at 42nd Street and Park Avenue.

THEMED WALKING TOURS

HERITAGE TRAILS
Tel 212/025-6888
Fifty landmarks on four different trails in Lower Manhattan. Free maps are available at the Federal Hall National Memorial Information Desk.

MUNICIPAL ARTS SOCIETY
Tel 212/439-1049
www.mas.org
Architectural tours of Grand Central Terminal and other sites, including Ground Zero, Madison Avenue, Rockefeller Center and Martin Luther King Boulevard in Harlem. Guides are professional architects, historians, educators and writers.

NEW YORK GALLERY TOURS
Tel 212/946-1548
Adult $15
www.nygallerytours.com
Ten modern art galleries in two hours in Chelsea, SoHo and other locations.

Eating

East 95th Street
East 95th Street
East 94th Street
East 94th Street
East 93rd Street
Jewish Museum
Sarabeth's
East 92nd Street
East 92nd Street
East 91st Street
Cooper-Hewitt National Design Museum
East 91st Street
East 91st Street
National Academy of Design
East 90th Street
Pio Pio
5th Avenue
Guggenheim Museum
East 89th Street
Gracie Mansion
East 88th Street
East 88th Street
East 87th Street
Neue Galerie
East 86th Street
86th Street
East 86th Street
Carl Schurz Park
East 85th Street
Lexington Avenue
East 84th Street
The Metropolitan Museum of Art
East 83rd Street
East 82nd Street
East 82nd Street
East 81st Street
Etats-Unis
East 80th Street
East 80th Street
East 79th Street
5th Avenue
PARK AVENUE
Lexington Avenue
3rd Avenue
2nd Avenue
1st Avenue
York Avenue
East 78th Street
East 77th Street
77th Street
John Jay Park
Café Boulud
East 76th Street
Whitney Museum of American Art
East 75th Street
Conservatory Water
East 74th Street
East 73rd Street
East 72nd Street
East 71st Street
East 71st Street
Frick Collection
East 70th Street
Asia Society and Museum
East 70th Street
East 69th Street
68th Street Hunter College
East 68th Street
Madison Avenue
East 67th Street
East 66th Street
East 65th Street
Daniel
JoJo
Maya
East 64th Street
FIFTH AVENUE
Lexington Avenue
East 63rd Street
East 62nd Street
Park Drive
The Pond
Aureole
rm
East 61st St
East 61st Street
Mount Vernon Hotel Museum and Garden
East 60th Street
5th Avenue
East 59th Street
59th Street
Felidia
HIGHWAY 25
QUEENSBORO BRIDGE
West 58th Street
East 58th Street
Main Street
Le Colonial
Dawat
WEST 57TH STREET
EAST 57TH STREET
EAST 57TH
Jimmy's Downtown
Trump Tower
Town (bers Hotel)
Dahesh Museum of Art
West 56th Street
West 56th Street
Shun Lee Palace
West 55th Street
East 55th Street
Aquavit
Oceana
West 54th Street
Vong
East 54th Street
West 5th Avenue
West 53rd Street
Brasserie
East 53rd Street
um of d Design
Museum of Television and Radio
Seagram Building
Four Seasons
East 52nd Street
"21" Club
West 51st Street
St. Patrick's Cathedral
Le Cirque 2000 (New York Palace Hotel)
East 51st Street
Municipal Art Society
51st Street
West 50th Street
G E Building
Mama Mexico
East 49th Street
Mitchell Pl
West 49th Street
Rockefeller Center
West 48th Street
East 48th Street
DIAMOND DISTRICT
West 47th Street
MIDTOWN MANHATTAN
Diwan
East 47th Street
East 47th Street
West 46th Street
East 46th Street
East 46th Street
West 45th Street
East 45th Street
East 45th Street

ROOSEVELT ISLAND
Roosevelt Island
Main Street
West Ma
FRANKLIN DELANO ROOSEVELT DRIVE
River

West 53rd Street
West 52nd Street
Museum of Arts and Design
Museum of Television and Radio
Seagram Building
Brasserie
West 51st Street
"21" Club
Le Cirque 2000 (New York Palace Hotel)
Four Seasons
Le Bernadin
Radio City Music Hall
St Patrick's Cathedral
Municipal Art Society
West 50th Street
GE Building
West 49th Street
Pam Real Thai
Noche
Rockefeller Center
MIDTOWN MANHATTAN
Blue Fin (W Times Square Hotel)
DIAMOND DISTRICT
Diwan
West 47th Street
Hell's Kitchen
BROADWAY
West 45th Street
DB Bistro Moderne
Int'l Center of Photography
Sushi Ya
Esca
Holy Cross Church
Reuters Building
Virgil's Real Barbecue
Grand Central Terminal
Chrysler Building
New Amsterdam Theater
Bryant Park
New York Public Library
Grand Central Oyster Bar
Chanin Building
L'Im
Morgan Library
Macy's
Empire State Building
34th Street Penn Station
34th Street Herald Square
Madison Square Garden
Pennsylvania Station
Artisanal
Little Church Around the Corner
Dos Caminos
Blue Smoke
Chelsea Park
Madison Square Park
Eleven Madison Park
Tabla
Red Cat
Metropolitan Life Insurance Tower
Tamarind
Union Pacific
CHELSEA
Flatiron Building
Veritas
Theodore Roosevelt Birthplace
Gramercy Tavern
Patria
GRAMERCY HISTORIC DIS
Pipa
Craft and Craftbar
Chicama
Union Square Café
Mesa Grill
UNION SQUARE
Forbes Magazine Galleries
Strip House
Pastis
Gonzo
Grace Church
Corner Bistro
Gotham Bar & Grill
Mi Cocina
Jefferson Market Library
Washington Park
Otto Enoteca Pizzeria
Babbo
GREENWICH VILLAGE
Taka
Blue Hill
Washington Square Park
NOHO
Tangerine
Annisa
McNulty's Rare Teas and Choice Coffee Shop
John's Pizzeria Pizza
Il Mulino
Mirchi
Pearl Oyster Bar
Negril Village
Dok Suni
House of Oldies Rare Records
Bond Street

264

Mesa Grill

UNION SQUARE

West 15th Street   East 15th Street
West 14th Street   14th Street Loop
14th Street   Union Square   3rd Avenue   East 15th Street
6th Avenue   WEST 14TH STREET   EAST 14TH STREET   East 14th Street   East 20th Street Service Drive

Forbes Magazine Galleries   West 13th Street   East 13th Street   Avenue   Avenue
IZO   Strip House   Ukrainian Museum

West 12th Street   East 12th Street   Angelica Kitchen   Komodo

Gotham Bar & Grill   Grace Church   St Mark's-in-the-Bowery   East 11th Street   Moustache
West 11th Street

West 10th Street   East 10th Street   Second Avenue Deli   East 10th Street
Washington Park   Holy Basil   La Palapa   I Coppi   Tompkins Square Park
West 9th Street   East 9th Street   8th Street NYU   Otto Enoteca Pizzeria   Astor Place 8th Street   EAST VILLAGE   East 8th Street

Babbo   Macdougal   WASHINGTON SQ NORTH   Wanamaker Place   Saint Marks Place
Blue Hill   Place   NOHO   East 7th Street
Waverly Place   Washington Square Park   Waverly Place   Washington Place   East 6th Street
n's Pizzeria   West 4th St-Washington   WASHINGTON SQ SOUTH   East 5th Street   Jewel Bako   Banjara   East 5th Street
za   Pearl Oyster Bar   Il Mulino   Negril Village   Merchant's House Museum   East 4th Street
chi   Dok Suni   Bleecker Street   Bar Pitti   Tomoe Sushi   Prune
Blue Ribbon Bakery   NL   Lupa   Bond Street   Chez Es Saada   Tasting Room
        HOUSTON   Katz's Deli

        New Museum of Contemporary Art   Honmura An   St Patrick's Old Cathedral   EAST HOUSTON STREET   WD-50
        Woo Lae Oak   Guggenheim Museum SoHo   Hampton Chutney   Prince Street
        Little Singer Building   Balthazar
        Fiamma Osteria   SOHO   Bread   LOWER EAST SIDE
        Aquagrill   Haughwout Building   LITTLE ITALY   Lower East Side Tenement Museum
txos   Nyonya
                Good World Bar and Grill
        LOWER MANHATTAN   Big Wong   Seward Park
        Nobu   Museum of Chinese in the Americas
        Montrachet   Vietnam
e Harrison   Chanterelle   66   CHINATOWN   Dim Sum Go Go
        Pico   Odeon   TRIBECA
        Bouley   Le Zinc   Foley Sq
        Washington Market Park   Nam   Courthouse
        Chambers Street   City Hall Park   Brooklyn Bridge City Hall and Civic Center
        Woolworth Building   BROOKLYN BRIDGE   East River
        Church of St Peter   BROOKLYN BRIDGE   River Café
        St Paul's Chapel   Mark Joseph Steakhouse   Peter Luger Steakhouse
        GROUND ZERO   Fulton Street Market
        Federal Reserve Bank   South Street Seaport
        Federal Hall National Monument
        Trinity Church   WALL ST
        Museum of American Financial History
        New York City Police Museum
        Fraunces Tavern Museum
        Museum of Irish Heritage

E   F   G   265

EATING OUT IN NEW YORK

You can dine around the world in New York City and you can spend a pittance or a fortune or somewhere in between. The choice is up to you. Some New Yorkers dine out every night, others save the top-class choices for special occasions. Dining trends change from season to season. This year the "hot" new trends are barbecue, Latin/Caribbean, and upscale Asian.

RESERVATIONS, DRESS CODES AND OTHER NOTES

In general, it's wise to make a reservation for dinner, especially on weekends. Indeed, top-class restaurants require reservations and will ask you to provide a telephone number for confirmation. If you want a table at Jean-Georges, Le Bernardin, Alain Ducasse, or similar, call well in advance. Sometimes, at these "famous" restaurants, it can be tough to get through even to the reservationists. Just keep trying. If you're on your own and want to eat on the run, you may be able to eat at the bar in one of these fancy restaurants. Note that some restaurants do not take reservations for parties under six people. In Midtown, luncheon reservations are also essential.

The United States is a more casual culture than most and strict dress codes have disappeared. A few places still do require a jacket and tie at dinner so remember to ask when making a reservation. In general, casual smart is the way to go.

Smoking is not allowed in public spaces period. The majority of restaurants have full bars; some sell beer and wine only, and a few have no liquor but will allow you to bring your own. At premier restaurants, there will be a substantial corkage fee if you bring your own wine.

Vegetarians will find a welcome. Many of the top class-dining rooms offer vegetarian menus and even fast-food joints are offering more healthful options on their menus these days.

Breakfast may be served all day at coffee shops and diners. Otherwise, the normal breakfast hours are from 7 to 11am. Lunch usually runs from 11.30am to 2 or 2.30pm and dinner from 5pm to 10 or 11pm, depending on the day of the week. Most top-class restaurants close for lunch on Saturday and Sunday. Many restaurants offer brunch on Sunday or both Saturday and Sunday.

TAXES, TIPPING AND OTHER FINANCIAL CONSIDERATIONS

A sales tax of 8.65% will be added to your dining bill. Americans tip more generously than most other nationalities. The minimum (assuming good service) is 15%; many people simply double the tax for a 17.3% tip. Many restaurants offer prix fixe menus, which often provide good value. In January and late June, a special promotion offers a $20 luncheon menu at numerous restaurants; this promotion is often continued throughout the year at many restaurants so always ask about it at a restaurant.

DESSERT AND COFFEE

Greenwich Village has been famous for its coffeehouses since the the 1950s. Of the few that remain Caffe Reggio (*119 MacDougal Street, tel 212/475-9557*) is one of the best, a genuine Italian coffeehouse where you can idle away an afternoon over a few espressos. Le Gamin (*183 Ninth Avenue at 21st Street, tel 212/243-8864*) is a similar French version. Palacinka, (*28 Grand Street, tel 212/625-0362*) is a small, busy café attracting an artsy SoHo crowd for the restaurant's namesake Eastern European crepes bathed in chocolate, or fresh fruit sauces. The Paris-inspired Payard Patisserie & Bistro (*1032 Lexington Avenue, tel 212/717-5252*) displays the creations of former Restaurant Daniel pastry chef, François Payard. The pastry case displays all kinds of gems plus handmade chocolates; sorbets are also available. Crowds make their way to the tiny storefront Magnolia Café (*401 Bleecker Street, tel 212/462-2572*) to taste the cupcakes iced with thick ultrasweet buttercream. In the East Village, Veniero's (*342 East 11th Street, tel 212/674-7070*) has been making and selling delicious Italian pastries for aeons.

EATING

TRADITIONAL AMERICAN FOOD

The United States of America is a nation of immigrants. Traditional American food has evolved out of the traditions of the immigrant populations—German, Jewish, Italian, Scandinavian, Latino, Asian—plus Native American and African-American. Each group has contributed its ingredients and techniques to the current food scene. The Germans brought sauerkraut, sausages and pumpernickel; the Hungarians goulash and stuffed cabbage; the Cubans black bean soup and Cuban sand-

cuisines, most notably Southern, Cajun, Southwestern and Tex-Mex.

DRINKS

The New York bar scene is extremely varied. Bars range from cheap dives charging a few dollars for a drink, to luxury lounges charging anywhere from $10 for a cocktail. Despite the campaign against drinking and driving, most bars offer happy hours when they charge half price for drinks or offer two for the price of one.

wiches; the Irish corned beef and cabbage; the Japanese sushi and teriyaki; the Jews chopped liver, pastrami, and knishes; the Greeks kebabs; the Lebanese baba ghanoush and falafel; the Mexicans salsa, tacos and refried beans; the Moroccans couscous; the Russians blinis and caviar; the Spanish tapas, chorizo, and paella; the Swedes gravlax, the Welsh leek and potato pie. Many of these dishes (or American modifications) have become common fare on all-American menus at standard American restaurants and even at lowly diners. The United States also boasts some distinctive regional

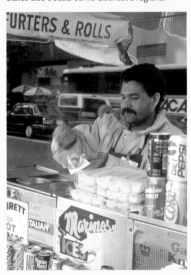

Hotdogs from a Manhattan street vendor

Note that American bartenders expect to be tipped (at least 10 percent). As far as drinks go, international beers and microbrews are readily available; cocktails are in vogue and every day brings a new concoction to light. Food is always available. It ranges from burgers and wings to more sophisticated fare. Most bars open from mid-morning to anywhere from 1am to 4am. Note that the drinking age is 21; expect to be "carded" (to show a photo ID), so carry an identification with photo. Buy wine and liquor at a liquor store; supermarkets sell beer only.

SOME NEW YORK DINING INSTITUTIONS

New York does have some unique dining institutions. The most famous is the deli. Among delis, the most traditional is the Jewish deli, which sells a variety of smoked fishes and meats, plus such items as bagels, pastrami and corned beef sandwiches, chopped liver, pickles, and knishes. The word deli is also used for small neighborhood grocery stores, often operated by Korean merchants. They sell coffee, bagels, sandwiches, salads, and other grocery items.

The coffeeshop/diner is another traditional dining haven. It will have counters and stools as well as table service. Here people secure endless cups of coffee, and breakfast, lunch, or dinner selections taken from a vast (usually laminated) menu. The city has plenty of fast-food outlets too (McDonalds, etc). Look for street vendors too. They sell everything from hot salty pretzels to soups, hot dogs, and ethnic snacks. The other dining establishment that is endemic to New York is the pizza parlor. The most visible coffee vendor is Starbucks, which seems to be on every corner, but there are plenty of independent cafés, especially in the West and East villages.

EATING

LATE NIGHT/24-HOUR

Despite New York's reputation as a 24/7 town, it's not that easy to find food in the wee hours. Among tried-and-true late-night oases, the hip but strangely unpretentious Blue Ribbon (*97 Sullivan Street, tel 212/274-0404*) draws clubbers and workers, including many chefs for sesame-glazed catfish, tofu ravioli, paella, and oysters on the half shell. It's open from 4pm to 4am daily.

The Coffee Shop (*29 Union Square West, tel 212/243-7969*), which looks like what you'd expect, is like nothing you'd find in Peoria with its Brazilian ownership and varied fare.

At Empire Diner (*210 Tenth Avenue, tel 212/243-2736*), you'll pay for the stylish chrome-and-black art deco setting as well as for the classic egg dishes, sandwiches and meat loaf. It's open around the clock.

In the Meatpacking District, Florent (*69 Gansevoort Street, tel 212/989-5779*) serves bistro-style food to night owls, clubbers, and meat-market workers—onion soup, blood sausage, steak frites, and the usual breakfast favorites. Open 24 hours.

Tip: Singles can almost always eat at the bar in Manhattan. If the place is full, or if you want to eat on the run, just ask to eat at the bar.

AMERICAN MENU READER

Bagel
An unsweetened dense egg-lessbread cooked in water and then baked. It's shaped with a hole in the middle.

Boston baked beans
Navy beans flavored with molasses and salt pork

Chicken-fried steak
Batter-dipped steak

Cobbler
Fruit pie topped with a biscuit-style crust

Chowder
Thick soup traditionally made with clams or corn

Egg Cream
A thick drink made with chocolate syrup, milk and seltzer

Eggplant
Aubergine

Eggs Over Easy
Fried eggs which have been turned over so they are cooked through

Eggs sunnyside up
Fried eggs that have not been turned over

French Toast
Bread coated with beaten eggs and sauteed. Served with maple syrup.

Grits
Corn kernels with the bran and germ removed

The famous Oyster Bar in Grand Central Terminal

Hero
An extra-large long roll

Key lime pie
Made with special lime variety from Florida

London broil
A particular cut of flank steak

Lox
cured salmon

Meatloaf
Ground beef, turkey and pork

combined with bread crumbs and egg and baked

New York Cheesecake
Jewish-style dense and creamy cake which may be plain or topped with fruit

On the Rocks
With ice

Pot roast
Braised beef

Pretzel
An elongated biscuit, which is shaped and twisted into a knot. It's sprinkled with coarse salt and sold warm from carts on the street.

Salisbury steak
A beef patty

Scotch
Scottish whiskey

Stack of pancakes
Three or four thick batter cakes served with maple syrup

Sub
Short for submarine; another name for an extra-large long roll

Straight up
No ice

Waldorf Salad
Apples, celery, and walnuts in mayonnaise; first created at the Waldorf Astoria

Whiskey
American rye

EATING

American contemporary
Annisa
Aureole
Blue Hill
Blue Ribbon Bakery
Craft and Craftbar
Eleven Madison Park
Etats-Unis
Gotham Bar & Grill
Grramercy Tavern
The Harrison
Ouest
Prune
Red Cat
River Café
Sarabeth's
Tasting Room
Tavern on the Green
Town
Union Pacific
Union Square Café
Veritas
Washington Park
WD-50

American regional
Mesa Grill

American traditional
"21" Club

Asian
Komodo
Ruby Foo's

Barbecue
Blue Smoke
Virgil's Real Barbecue

Burgers
Corner Bistro

Caribbean
Negril Village

Chinese
Dim Sum Go Go
Shun Lee Palace
66

Continental
Four Seasons

Deli
Barney Greengrass
Katz's Deli
Second Avenue Deli

French
Aix
Alain Ducasse
Artisanal
Balthazar
Bouley
Brasserie
Café Boulud
Chanterelle
Daniel
DB Bistro Moderne
Jean-Georges
JoJo
Le Cirque 2000
Le Zinc
Montrachet
Odeon
Pastis

Greek
Estiatorio Milos
Molyvos

Indian
Banjara
Dawat
Diwan
Hampton Chutney
Mirchi
Tabla
Tamarind

Italian
Babbo
Bar Pitti
Bread
Felidia
Fiamma Osteria
Gonzo
I Coppi
Il Mulino
L'Impero
Lupa

Japanese
Bond Street
Jewel Bako
Nobu
Sugiyama
Sushi Yasuda
Taka
Tomoe Sushi

Korean
Dok Suni
Woo Lae Oak

Latin American
Calle Ocho
Chicama
Jimmy's Downtown
Noche
Patria
Pio Pio

Malaysian
Nyonga

Mediterranean
Picholine

Mexican
Dos Caminos
Hell's Kitchen
La Palapa
Mama Mexico
Maya
Mi Cocina
Rosa Mexicano

Moroccan/Middle Eastern
Chez Es Saada
Moustache

Noodle shops
Big Wong
Honmura An

Pizza
John's Pizzeria Pizza
Otto Enoteca Pizzeria

Portuguese
Pico

Russian
Uncle Vanya Café

Seafood
Aquagrill
Blue Fin
Esca
Grand Central Oyster Bar
Le Bernardin
Oceana
Pearl Oyster Bar
rm

Scandinavian
Aquavit
Good World Bar and Grill

Soul
Amy Ruth's
Londel's
Sugar Hill Bistro

Spanish
Pintxos
Pipa

Steak
Mark Joseph Steakhouse
Peter Luger Steakhouse
Strip House

Thai
Holy Basil
Pam Real Thai
Tangerine
Vong

Vegetarian
Angelica Kitchen

Vietnamese
Le Colonial
Nam
Vietnam

HOTELS WITH EXCEPTIONAL DINING ROOMS

The Four Seasons

Hotel Wales

Le Parker Meridien

The Mark

The New York Palace

Sherry Netherland

Trump International Hotel

The Mercer Hotel

Ritz-Carlton (Central Park South)

The Royalton

Surrey

W-NY

EATING

The prices given are for a two-course set lunch (L) for two people and a three-course à la carte dinner (D) for two people. The wine price is for a bottle of house wine.

AIX

Map 262 C13
2398 Broadway at 88th Street
Tel 212/874-7400
www.aixnyc.com
Didier Virot has brought robust Provençal cuisine to the Upper West Side at this tri-level restaurant. He adds his twists to such dishes as pistou, with a cake of sardine tartare at the center, or foie gras rolled in pistachios on potato-quince crumble and peach coulis. Desserts are different (apple-rosemary brioche with honey Calvados sauce, anyone?).
🕐 Sun–Thu 5.30–10.30, Fri–Sat 5.30–11
🍴 D $100, wine $30
🚇 86th Street (1, 9)
🚌 M104

ALAIN DUCASSE

Map 262 D16
Essex House
155 West 58th Street between Sixth and Seventh avenues
Tel 212/265-7300
www.alain-ducasse.com

When three-Michelin-star chef Alain Ducasse opened this opulent restaurant, he was criticized for affectation, but now he draws acclaim from even the toughest critics. The crimson salon is luxe, and so is the service. Start with champagne and finish with the candy cart (caramels, nougat, macaroons). The dishes that will appear in between are sublime: scallops and caviar in watercress vichyssoise, fresh crab seasoned with citrus fruit and black pepper with a delicate velouté of sweet corn.

The 1,400 international wine selections tilt toward France.
🕐 Mon–Sat 6.30–9, closed Sun
🍴 D 3- and 4-course prix fixes $150–165, wine $56
🚇 57th Street (F, N, Q, R, W)
🚌 M6, M7

AMY RUTH'S

Off map 262 D12
113 West 116th Street between Malcolm X Boulevard and Adam Clayton Powell Jr. Blvd
Tel 212/280-8779
It's named after the owner's grandmother, who taught her Southern-style cooking. Most items on the menu are named after someone, such as the Reverend Al Sharpton (chicken and waffles). At dinner, look for lusty Southern fried chicken, oxtail stew and fried or baked catfish. No alcohol.
🕐 Daily 7.30am–11pm
🍴 $40
🚇 116th Street (2, 3, B, C)
🚌 M7, M3, M116

ANGELICA KITCHEN

Map 265 F21
300 East 12th Street between First and Second avenues
Tel 212/228-2909

This plain, 60s-like spot proves that vegetarian cuisine does not have to be bland. Go for the hearty soups, excellent chili, or tasty noodle dishes and sandwiches. No alcohol. No credit cards.
🕐 Daily 11.30–10.30
🍴 $40
🚇 14th Street/Union Square (L, N, Q, R, W, 4, 5, 6)
🚌 M15, M14

ANNISA

Map 264 D22
13 Barrow Street between Bleecker and West 4th streets
Tel 212/741-6699
www.annisarestaurant.com
At this minimalist restaurant Chef Anita Lo cooks coherent fusion cuisine. For appetizers, a

tilefish ceviche might incorporate fig, anchovy and pistachio, while roasted kabocha squash and maiiake mushrooms could be combined with bitter chocolate. Lamb tenderloin is enriched with curried golden raisins and an onion pancake. No credit cards.
🕐 Mon–Sat 5.30–10, Sun 5.30–9.30
🍴 D $95, wine $34
🚇 West 4th Street (A, C, E, F), Christopher Street/Sheridan Square (1, 9)
🚌 M20, M21

AQUAGRILL

Map 265 E23
210 Spring Street at Sixth Avenue
Tel 212/274-0505

Every day brings a fresh selection of seafood—cod, halibut, grouper, monkfish, tuna—which can be prepared to your specifications, roasted, poached or grilled, or served in such dishes as sea bass with smoked pepper and crispy bacon in thyme vinaigrette. Star of the show is the oyster bar, which offers about 24 varieties. Prices are fair.
🕐 Tue–Fri 12–3, Sat–Sun 12–3.30, Tue–Thu 6–10.45, Fri–Sat 6–11.45, Sun 6–10.30, closed Mon
🍴 L $55, D $70, wine $22
🚇 Spring Street (C, E)
🚌 M6

AQUAVIT

Map 263 E17
13 West 54th Street between Fifth and Sixth avenues
Tel 212/307-7311
www.aquavit.org
From an historic townhouse, Chef Marcus Samuelsson creates contemporary interpretations of Swedish–Scandinavian cuisine: Oysters come with a mango-curry sorbet; mushroom broth is poured over delicately smoked arctic char. There's a wide selection of aquavits, plus 250 wines (15 by the glass).

EATING

ackets are required in the dining room, but the upstairs café
is more casual and offers more
traditional Scandinavian fare.

🕐 Daily 12–2.30, 5.30–10.30
🍽 D $90, 3-course prix fixe $69,
wine $40
🚇 Fifth Avenue (E, V),
🚌 M1, M2, M3, M4, M5, M6, M7

ARTISANAL
Map 264 E19
2 Park Avenue at 32nd Street
Tel 212/725-8585

This gem is all about cheese,
and the quality of the 250
varieties in the walk-in cheese
vault is astonishing, ranging
from cabecou de Rocamadour
to callu de cabreddu. Savor
them straight or in a fondue.
Not to worry if you don't eat
cheese: Escargots, moules, and
main dishes such as crisp skate
wing with blood orange
Grenobloise, and rabbit au
Riesling complete the menu.
Some 170 wines are available
by the glass.

🕐 Mon–Thu 12–11, Fri–Sat 12–12,
Sun 12–10
🍽 L $60, D $85, wine $24
🚇 33rd Street (6)
🚌 M1

AUREOLE
Map 263 E16
34 East 61st Street between Madison
and Park avenues
Tel 212/319-1660
www.aureolerestaurant.com

Aureole's chef/owner Charlie
Palmer is one of the most
highly regarded talents on the
American culinary scene. This
elegant Upper East Side townhouse with a grand staircase
and towers of wine, liquor, and
flowers, is made for special
occasions. Palmer uses ultra-
fresh ingredients in such
signature dishes as slow-
poached Maine lobster with
heirloom tomatoes, which is
served with lemon-verbena-
infused consommé, and

BABBO
Map 264 E22
110 Waverly Place between
MacDougal Street and Sixth Avenue
Tel 212/777-0303
www.babbonyc.com

With his pony-tail and orange
clogs, Mario Batali has a lust
for life that's infectious and
an originality that is breathtaking. At Babbo, his flagship
restaurant, the welcome is
warm and the food some of
the freshest and lustiest anywhere. Try the handmade
beef cheek ravioli or the
prosciutto with spicy fig jam.
The deep all-Italian wine list
is a revelation.

🕐 Mon–Sat 5.30–11, Sun 5–11
🍽 D $100, wine $25
🚇 West 4th Street (A, C, E, F, V, S)
🚌 M5, M6

seared Hudson Valley foie gras.
The wine list features 600
selections, 25 by the glass. In
summer, sit in the courtyard.

🕐 Mon–Fri 12–2.30, Mon–Thu
5.30–11, Fri–Sat 5–11, closed Sun
🍽 L $90, prix fixe: $35 4-course, D prix
fixe $69 3-course, $85 6-course, wine
$40
🚇 59th Street (4, 5, 6), 59th
Street/Fifth Avenue (N, R, W)
🚌 M1, M2, M3, M4

BALTHAZAR
Map 265 F23
80 Spring Street between Broadway
and Lafayette Street
Tel 212/965-1414
www.balthazarny.com

Keith McNally has cloned a
classic Paris brasserie with
smoky gilded mirrors, tile floor,
red-leather banquettes and a
vast 27-foot (8m) bar. Bistro
fare includes the seafood
platter piled high with oysters,
clams, shrimp and scallops,
chicken Riesling, and roasted
bacon-wrapped monkfish. The
place is crowded and vibrant
and loaded with celebrity
cachet. Bread and pastries
come from the adjacent
bakery. The 300-selection
wine list is totally French.

🕐 Mon–Fri 7.30–11.30, 12–5, Mon–Thu
5.45–1.30, Fri 5.45–2.30, Sat 7.30–3.30,
5.45–2.30, Sun 7.30–3.30, 5.30–12.30
🍽 L $70, D $85, wine $30
🚇 Prince Street (N, R), Spring
Street (6)
🚌 M1, M5

BANJARA
Map 265 F22
97 First Avenue at 6th Street
Tel 212/477-5956

Sixth Street is lined with Indian
restaurants, but Banjara is the
best of the lot. Northern
Indian cuisine is the specialty.
The tandoori dishes are
particularly good with their
fine smoky flavor. Also
appealing are the pasanda
lamb, cooked in a yogurt-
based curry sauce and the
palak ghost—lamb cooked in a
purée of spinach, tomatoes,
ginger and cumin seeds.

🕐 Mon–Thu 3–11, Fri–Sun 12–11
🍽 $45, wine $19
🚇 Astor Place (6)
🚌 M15, M8

BAR PITTI
Map 265 E22
268 Sixth Avenue between Bleecker and
Houston streets.
Tel 212/982-3300

Actors, writers, fashion designers and Village residents gather
at this European-style boîte. In
summer, the sidewalk dining
affords great people-watching
and the chance to observe
comings and goings next door
at celebrity hot spot Da
Silvano. Your best bet is to
select one of the reliable meat,
fish, or pasta chalkboard specials. Otherwise, choose one of
the typical pastas, perhaps
spaghetti with clam sauce.
No credit cards.

🕐 Daily 12–12
🍽 $60, wine $29
🚇 West 4th (A, C, F, V, S), Houston
Street (1, 9)
🚌 M5, M6

BARNEY GREENGRASS
Map 262 C13
541 Amsterdam Avenue between West
86th and 87th streets
Tel 212/724-4707
www.barneygreengrass.com

An Upper West Side tradition
since 1929, Barney Greengrass

is frantic on weekends, when locals come to feast on huge platters of smoked fish—whitefish, sable, sturgeon and lox—or sandwiches made with similar contents, plus fresh caviar, chopped herring salad, cheese blintzes, borscht and other such specialties. During the week, it's less frenzied. Credit cards taken on bills of $25 or more only.

🕐 Tue–Fri 8.30–4, Sat–Sun 8.30–5, closed Mon
🍴 $30
🚇 86th Street (1, 9)
🚌 M7, M104, M86

BIG WONG
Map 265 F24
67 Mott Street between Bayard and Canal streets
Tel 212/964-0540
At this Manhattan restaurant you're guaranteed a cheap, tasty meal. Don't expect any decor, tablecloth or efficient service. You're here for noodles (with duck, chicken, shrimp), congee and other standard Cantonese dishes. No credit cards.

🕐 Daily 9–8.30
🍴 $30
🚇 Canal Street (J, M, N, Q, R, W, Z, 6)
🚌 M1

BLUE FIN
Map 264 D18
W Times Square Hotel
1567 Broadway at 47th Street
Tel 212/918-1400
www.Brguestrestaurants.com
The vast, theatrical Blue Fin made a culinary and design splash when it opened in 2002. Chef Paul Sale has the benefit of the freshest fish, which he prepares simply in such dishes as sautéed black bass in chive nage, or poached halibut in ancho-chili-and-vegetable broth. Sushi is available on the first floor of the two-story space, which has a dramatic floating staircase that looks out over a school of black fish suspended from the ceiling against an undulating ocean-like white wall. There are 600 wines on the list, 30 by the glass.

🕐 Daily 7–11, 11.30–4, Sun–Mon 5–12, Tue–Thu 5–12.30, Fri–Sat 5–1
🍴 L $70, D $100, wine $24
🚇 49th Street (N, R, W), 50th Street (1, 9)
🚌 M10, M20, M27, M104

BLUE HILL
Map 264 E22
75 Washington Place, between MacDougal and Sixth Avenue
Tel 212/539-1776
www.bluehillnyc.com
Candlelight and extravagant bouquets set the inviting tone of this below-ground dining room. It's named after a farm in Massachusetts where the chef finds his seasonal, locally grown ingredients. Expect corn shoots in June, squash and apples in fall. The menu offers six appetizers and seven entrées—say, fall mushrooms braised and steamed with fingerling potato tart, followed by roasted trout with a pistou of vegetables with puréed basil, or poached duck with a stew of organic carrots with toasted spices. Desserts are enticing.

🕐 Mon–Sat 5.30–11, Sun 5.30–10
🍴 D $95, wine $28
🚇 W 4th Street (A, C, E, F, V, S)
🚌 M5, M6

BLUE RIBBON BAKERY
Map 265 D22
33 Downing Street at Bedford Street
Tel 212/337-0404

Refreshing sandwiches made with house-baked breads and tasty small plates draw crowds at lunch, while such dinner entrées as New Orleans barbecue shrimp and filet mignon with tomato, onion and watercress salad and potato cake draw nighttime customers. There are so many small plates—mushroom ravioli, sweet sopressata, smoked red trout—you could eat for two months without repetition. Cheese lovers appreciate the choice of goat, cow and sheep cheeses. Extensive wine list.

🕐 Tue–Thu 12–12, Fri noon–2am, Sat 11.30am–2am, Sun 11.30am–midnight, closed Mon
🍴 L $55, D $85, wine $24
🚇 Houston Street (1, 9)
🚌 M20

BLUE SMOKE
Map 264 E20
116 East 27th Street between Park Avenue South and Lexington Avenue
Tel 212/447-7733
www.bluesmoke.com
The secret of barbecue is slow cooking and well-blended spices. Danny Meyer studied it for three years and traveled 62,000 miles before opening this rustic red-hot restaurant. Barbecue addicts drool over the rib sampler. Eight beers are on tap, while the 50-selection wine list pairs well with the food. A good jazz room downstairs shares the interesting upstairs menu.

🕐 Mon–Tue 11.30–11, Wed–Fri 11am–1am, Sat noon–1am, Sun 12–11
🍴 L $60, D $80, wine $19
🚇 23rd Street (6)
🚌 M1, M101, M102, M103

BOND STREET
Map 265 F22
6 Bond Street between Broadway and Lafayette Street
Tel 212/777-2500
The buzz has lessened at this sleek Japanese spot in a SoHo brownstone, but the glistening sushi and sashimi are as beautiful as ever. Among the appetizers, expect seared duck with shitake and truffle glaze, or monkfish filet with spicy-and-sour salsa. Desserts are innovative Japanese. Traditional tatami rooms are upstairs; downstairs there's a fashionable lounge serving exotic saketinis.

🕐 Mon–Sat 6pm–midnight, Sun 6–11; lounge Mon–Sat 5pm–2am, Sun 6pm–1am
🍴 D $60, omakase $80–100, wine $26
🚇 Broadway/Lafayette (F, V, S)
🚌 M1, M5, M6

BOULEY
Map 265 E24
120 West Broadway at Duane Street
Tel 212/964-2525
www.bouley.net

David Bouley made his name in 1987 when he opened the original Bouley. This gem is his encore. The dining rooms are gorgeous: One is in Venetian stucco with a fireplace; the other has crimson vaulted ceilings and glazed walls hung with Impressionist paintings. The exquisitely prepared cuisine makes occasional Asian references, as in the chilled lobster with Serrano ham, mango and artichoke, in a Thai curry dressing. Don't miss the Valrhona chocolate soufflé.

🕐 Daily 11.30–3, 5.30–11.30
🍴 L $120, D $130, wine $35
🚇 Chambers Street (A, C, E, 1, 2, 3, 9)
🚌 M6, M20

BRASSERIE
Map 263 F17
100 East 53rd Street between Park and Lexington avenues
Tel 212/751-4840
www.restaurantassociates.com
From its theatrical entrance ramp to its buzzing bar, Brasserie is one very cool room and so very New York. The French-Mediterranean menu is satisfying, ranging as it does from salad Niçoise and burgers (with oyster mushrooms, bacon and roasted onions) to duck cassoulet and rice-crusted black sea bass in lemongrass and lime broth. Great sushi and a raw bar, too.

🕐 Mon–Fri 7am–1am, Sat 11am–1am, Sun 11–10
🍴 $90, wine $26
🚇 53rd Street/Lexington Avenue (E, V), 51st Street (6)
🚌 M1, M2, M3, M4, M98, M101, M102, M103

BREAD
Map 265 F23
20 Spring Street between Elizabeth and Mott streets
Tel 212/334-1015
This small casual café makes delicious panini, soups, salads and daily plates. Try the gazpacho in summer and the prosciutto di Parma with truffle oil, bruschetta, spicy shrimp salad, and delicious bread and tomato soup in winter. There is a choice of wines with 12 wines sold by the glass.

🕐 Daily 11–11
🍴 $35
🚇 Spring Street (6), Bowery (J, M, Z), Grand Street (S)
🚌 M1

CAFÉ BOULUD
Map 263 E15
20 East 76th Street between Fifth and Madison avenues
Tel 212/772-2600
www.danielnyc.com
Many diners consider this casually smart 1930s-style Parisian neighborhood restaurant their favorite Daniel Boulud restaurant. Three Daniel muses inspire the menu—classics, seasons and ethnic cuisines. You will find a pot au feu and a good bouillabaisse; and entrées inspired by Tuscany, Morocco, Vietnam, Spain and the Caribbean. The 450 wine selections are categorized by varietal.

🕐 Tue–Sat 12–2.30, 5.45–11, Sun–Mon 5.45–11, closed major holidays
🍴 L $110, 2-and 3-course prix fixes $29–36, D $120, wine $20
🚇 77th Street (6)
🚌 M1, M2, M3, M4, M79

CALLE OCHO
Map 262 D14
446 Columbus Avenue between West 81st and 82nd streets
Tel 212/873-5025

Calle Ocho has brought a limited menu of very good Latin cuisine to the Upper West Side. Start with one of the refreshing ceviches (say, lobster with mango grapefruit mojo) or appetizers like arepa with spicy braised short ribs. Fish and meat dishes are tasty, both the coffee-glazed tuna or the basil chimichurri chicken with roasted almond sauce.

🕐 Sun 11.30–3, 5–10, Mon–Thu 6–11, Fri 6–12, Sat 5–12
🍴 D $90, wine $22
🚇 81st Street (B, C)
🚌 M7, M11, M79

CHANTERELLE
Map 265 E24
2 Harrison Street at Hudson Street
Tel 212/966-6960
www.chanterllenyc.com
The presentation of the superb food is simply exquisite at this ultra-spacious classic. The menu changes monthly, but the cuisine is always full-flavored. Conclude with one of the luscious desserts—molten vanilla cake with spring strawberries, for example.

🕐 Tue–Sat 12–2.30, 5.30–11 Mon 5.30–11, closed Sun
🍴 L $84, 3 course prix fixe $38, D 3 course prix fixe $84, tasting $95, wine $28
🚇 Franklin Street (1, 9)
🚌 M20

CHEZ ES SAADA
Map 265 F22
42 East 1st Street between First and Second avenues
Tel 212/777-5617
The exotic neo-Moroccan experience that begins at an unmarked door leading into a casbah-style bar continues at the rose-petal-strewn stairway leading down to a grotto-like dining room. The tagines and couscous are completely au courant, as are such house specialties as herb-crusted salmon in pomegranate sauce. The traditional mezze—katafi-wrapped prawns with harissa yogurt—make a wonderful meal in themselves.

🕐 Mon–Thu 6–midnight, Fri–Sat 6pm–1am
🍴 D $80, wine $30
🚇 Lower East Side/Second Avenue (F, V)
🚌 M15, M21

CHICAMA
Map 265 E21
35 East 18th Street in ABC Carpet and Home
Tel 212/505-2233
Chicama may be in a store, but it's still a culinary destination, thanks to the fiery cuisine and colorful Peruvian setting. For appetizers there are seven ceviches and several empanadas, plus crispy shrimp and scallops in chipotle glaze with endive, cilantro and pickled jalapeños. Among main courses, the churrasco of beef tenderloin sizzles in the chili chimichurri, and the crispy whole fish of the day can be spiced by the salsa verde on the side. Quiet it's not.

🕐 Mon–Fri 12–3, 6–11 (Fri until 12), Sat 6–12, Sun 5.30–10
🍴 L $60, D $88, wine $30
🚇 14th Street/Union Square (L, N, Q, R, W, 4, 5, 6)

CORNER BISTRO

Map 264 D21
331 West 4th Street between Jane Street
and Eighth Avenue
Tel 212/242-9502

The distressed graffiti-covered
tables and booths at this plain
West Village bar remain the
best place in town to grab
burgers. Made with 8oz (225g)
hunks of ground chuck, they
come plain or topped with
bacon or blue cheese. Other
sandwiches and decent chili
are also available. Good jukebox and beer. No credit cards.
◎ Mon–Sat 11.30am–4am, Sun
noon–4am
🍴 $15
🚇 14th Street (A, C, E)
🚌 M14, M20

CRAFT AND CRAFTBAR

Map 264 E20
43 East 19th Street between Broadway
and Park Avenue South
Tel 212/780-0880
When Tom Colicchio conceived
Craft he wanted diners to
create their own dishes from a
menu that was essentially not
any more than a list of ingredients. This is still the focus, but
the chef now supplies more
direction with superb results.
Most dishes are roasted
(striped bass, quail) or braised
(monkfish, lamb shank).
Desserts can be perfect fresh
fruits, intense sorbets, or deca-
dent confections like the toffee
steamed pudding. The cheeses
are stunning. The leather, cop-
per and steel, and plain wood
furnishings and fittings recall
the Arts & Crafts movement.
Casual Craftbar takes a similar
focus-on-the-ingredients
approach to sandwiches, fried
oysters and braised dishes.
◎ Mon–Fri 12–2, Sun–Thu 5.30–10,
Fri–Sat 5.30–11
🍴 L $90, D $105, wine $24
🚇 23rd Street (N, R, W), 23rd
Street (6)
🚌 M1, M2, M3, M6, M7

DANIEL

Map 263 E16
60 East 65th Street at Park Avenue
Tel 212/288-0033
www.danielnyc.com

Lyons-born chef Daniel Boulud
opened this restaurant in
1993. It has all the romance of
an Italian Renaissance palazzo,
and dining here is a joyous
experience. Signature dishes
include the creamy oyster
velouté with lemongrass and
caviar, roast squab stuffed with
foie gras and morels, and
chocolate bombe with
passion-fruit crème brûlée.
Warm madeleines, homemade
chocolates and petits fours
conclude the meal. The
predominantly French wine list
offers more than 900 selections. Jacket and tie required.
◎ Mon–Thu 5.45–11, Fri–Sat 5.30–11,
closed Sun
🍴 prix fixe L $85 and D $120, wine $30
🚇 63rd Street/Lexington (F),
68th Street (6)
🚌 M1, M2, M3, M4, M66

DAWAT

Map 263 F16
210 East 58th Street between Second
and Third avenues
Tel 212/355-7555
www.restaurant.com/dawat

Cookbook author Madhur
Jaffrey consults on the menu at
this comfortable Indian, aptly
named "invitation to feast." The
spices are skillfully blended to
subtle effect in such dishes as
shrimp in coconut sauce
flavored with curry leaves and
smoked tamarind; chicken
tikka; and baby goat in car-
damom sauce. Appealing rice
and vegetarian specialties.
◎ Mon–Sat 12–3, 5–11, Sun 5–11
🍴 L $60, D $65, wine $23
🚇 59th Street/Lexington Avenue (6)
🚌 M98, 1010, M102, M103, M15, M57

DIM SUM GO GO

Map 265 F24
5 East Broadway between Catherine
and Oliver streets
Tel 212/732-0797
At this small, modernist restaurant you can find the latest in
Chinese cuisine: updated dim
sum, presented in bamboo
steamers or on pupu platters.
Expect jicama and lotus root
dumplings, crabmeat stuffed in
green spinach dough, wood
mushrooms and carrot
dumplings. Pork buns and
shrimp dumplings are the
kitchen's nod to tradition.
◎ Daily 10am–10.30pm
🍴 $30
🚇 East Broadway (F), Canal Street (J,
M, Z, N, R, Q, W, 6)
🚌 M9, M15, M22

DB BISTRO MODERNE

Map 264 E18
55 West 44th Street between Fifth and
Sixth avenues
Tel 212/391-2400
www.danielnyc.com
This most casual and
contemporary of Boulud's
restaurants with its carved
wood furniture, beaded
curtains and fabric-wrapped
ceiling panels is a great
Theater District choice. It's
famous for its $27 sirloin
burger—a fistful of ground
sirloin wrapped around red
wine-braised short ribs with
truffle and foie gras, served
with tomato confit and fresh
horseradish. Other delights
include: roast salmon with
honeyed eggplant and stuffed
zucchini flowers; Muscovy
duck breast with chanterelles;
and black Mission fig
compote. Extensive wine list.
◎ Mon–Sat 12–2.30, 5.45–11,
Sun 5.45–11
🍴 L $100, D $120, wine $25
🚇 42nd Street/Grand Central (S, 4, 5,
6, 7), 42nd Street (B, D, F, V)
🚌 M1, M2, M3, M4, M42

EATING

DIWAN

Map 263 F17

148 East 48th Street between Lexington and Third avenues

Tel 212/593-5425

This uptown Indian trendsetter serves more than traditional dishes like vindaloos, chicken murgh and tandoori. You can also expect butter chicken, apricot Cornish hens, lamb in almond sauce, and sea bass with fenugreek sauce.

🕐 Daily 11.30–2.30 (Sat–Sun until 3), 5–10.30

🍴 L $60, D $80, wine $20

🚇 51st Street (6)

🚌 M98, M101, M102, M103, M50

DOK SUNI

Map 265 D22

55 Carmine Street between Bedford Street and Seventh Avenue South

Tel 212/414-1224

Here you'll experience a Korean barbecue and learn how to roll ingredients into a lettuce leaf. Start with a traditional soup—sea kelp with beef, for example. Follow with pork ribs in spicy chili pepper, garlic and ginger sauce, or with bulgogi, thin grilled slices of rib eye marinated in soy and garlic and rolled in lettuce with rice and miso. Also at 119 First Avenue *(tel 212/477-9506)*. No credit cards.

🕐 Sun–Mon 5–11, Tue–Sat 5–12

🍴 D $64, wine $25

🚇 West 4th Street (A, C, E, F, V, S)

🚌 M5, M6, M20, M21

DOS CAMINOS

Map 264 E20

373 Park Avenue South between 26th and 27th streets

Tel 212/294-1000

www.brguestrestaurants.com

This is as far from an enchilada hut as you can get. The space is celebratory, the bar stocks 150 tequilas, and the fare covers all the bases—guacamole made tableside; shrimp, scallop and tuna ceviche; chicken mole; and pan-roasted snapper with pineapple-passion fruit sauce. Desserts run to ice creams and sorbets such as tamarind chipotle or guava-mango sorbet.

🕐 Sun–Mon 11.30–11, Tue–Thu 11.30am–midnight, Fri–Sat 11.30am–1am

🍴 L $60, D $82, wine $29

🚇 28th Street (6)

🚌 M1

ELEVEN MADISON PARK

Map 264 E20

11 Madison Avenue at 24th Street

Tel 212/889-0905

This dramatic dining space, once the brokers' hall of the Metropolitan Life insurance company, is worthy of the cuisine created by Kerry Heffernan. The fish dishes are fragrant and moist (seared Arctic char in black truffle vinaigrette), and meat dishes robust (grilled hanger steak in shallot sauce). Appetizers include almond-crusted calf's brain in Calvados reduction is as much of a delicacy. The international wine list leans to the French, and there are 36 options by the glass.

🕐 Mon–Fri 11.30–2, Sat 12–2, Mon–Thu 5.30–10.30, Fri–Sat 5.30–11, Sun 5.30–10

🍴 L $70, D $105, wine $29

🚇 23rd Street (6)

🚌 M1, M2, M3

ESCA

Map 264 D18

402 West 43rd Street at Ninth Avenue

Tel 212/564-7272

Esca, another star in Mario Batali's firmament, prepares fish Southern Italian style. The menu changes daily, but you might find Mediterranean sea bass in sea salt or Amalfi-style fritto misto, with crispy scrod, skate, calamari, steamers, oysters and shrimp. Appetizers run to crispy Neapolitan-style eel and juicy morsels from a serious raw bar.

🕐 Mon–Sat 12–2.30, Mon 5–10.30, Tue–Sat 5–11.30, Sun 4.30–10.30

🍴 L $95, D $105, wine $28

🚇 42nd Street (A, C, E)

🚌 M11

ESTIATORIO MILOS

Map 262 D17

125 West 55th Street between Sixth and Seventh avenues

Tel 212/245-7400

www.milos.ca

Some 19 selections of fish are priced by the pound and range from pompano and monkfish to tuna and swordfish. Your choice will be filleted at the table. Appetizers lean to the briny, like calamari stuffed with three types of cheese and fresh mint. Honey, nuts and yogurt come to the fore in the traditional sweets.

🕐 Mon–Sat 12–3, 5.30–11, Sun 5–11

🍴 L 3-course prix fixe $35, D $110, wine $30

🚇 57th Street (F), 57th Street (N, R, Q, W)

🚌 M10, M20

ETATS-UNIS

Map 263 F14

242 East 81st Street between Second and Third avenues

Tel 212/517-8826

French though the motif maybe, this is still an American neighborhood restaurant. The bistro-style menu changes daily. Look for crispy confit of duck leg with German potato salad and mustard, a charcoal-grilled black sea bass with chive vinaigrette. Desserts are delicious and there is a good selection of cheeses.

🕐 Daily 6pm–11pm

🍴 D $105, wine $28

🚇 77th Street (6)

🚌 M98, M101, M102, M103, M15, M79

FELIDIA

Map 263 F16

243 East 58th Street between Second and Third avenues

Tel 212/758-1479

www.lidiasitaly.com

FOUR SEASONS
Map 263 F17
99 East 52nd Street between Park and Lexington avenues
Tel 212/754-9494
www.fourseasonsrestaurant.com
Titans and moguls have regular tables at this modernist power restaurant designed by Philip Johnson and Mies van der Rohe. When it opened in 1959, it helped launch the city's food revolution. The bar at the center of the rosewood paneled Grill Room is a great cocktail spot. The pièce de résistance is the Pool Room, with a large fountain as centerpiece. Chef Christian Albin's signature dish is roast duck, which is carved tableside. The soufflés are justly famous. First-rate wine list.
🕐 Mon–Fri 12–2, 5–9.30, Sat 5–11, closed Sun
🍽 L £130, D $150, wine $36
🚇 51st Street (6), Fifth Avenue/53rd Street (E, V)
🚌 M98, M01, M102, M103, M50

Owner Lidia Bastianich is a tireless promoter of Italian cuisine. Felidia is one of the city's top Italian restaurants—expensive but worth it. The Istrian wedding pillows, stuffed with rum, raisins and three cheeses, are a signature dish, but chef Fortunato Nicotra has added many regional dishes, such as pear and pecorino-filled ravioli. The wine list concentrates on great Italian selections.
🕐 Mon–Thu 12–2.30, 5–11, Fri 12–2, 5–11.30, Sat 5–11.30, closed Sun
🍽 L $110, 3-course prix fixe $28.50, D $120, wine $45
🚇 59th Street (4, 5, 6)
🚌 M15, M98, M101, M102, M103 M57

FIAMMA OSTERIA
Map 265 E23
206 Spring Street between Sixth Avenue and Sullivan Street
Tel 212/653-0100
An Italian bistro with attitude, this bi-level restaurant is as much about Hollywood styling as it is about food. Grilled octopus and cecci beans with pepper and mint, stracci with rabbit Bolognese and other exceptional pastas, plus veal chops perfumed with sage and served with caramelized sweet

and sour cipollini onions are some of the beguiling dishes.
🕐 Mon–Fri 12–2.30, Sun–Thu 5.30–11, Fri–Sat 5.30–12
🍽 L $80, D $115, wine $28
🚇 Spring Street (C, E)
🚌 M6

GONZO
Map 264 D21
140 West 13th Street between Sixth and Seventh avenues
Tel 212/645-4606
Gonzo may be moderately priced, but the rustic food is very good, made with ultra-fresh ingredients and served to a hip lively crowd in a comfortable setting. Start your meal with a plate of sliced meats and cheeses or cicchetti, such as beet and Gorgonzola salad, or chickpea and sun-dried tomato spread. The pastas and pizzas are inventive. Among entrées, the Venetian calf's liver is superb.
🕐 Daily 5.30–12
🍽 D $60, wine $22
🚇 14th Street
🚌 M5, M6, M20

GOOD WORLD BAR AND GRILL
Map 265 G24
3 Orchard Street between Canal and Division streets
Tel 212/925-9975
Distinctive Swedish cuisine is served in this lively, refreshing dining room. Here, several kinds of herring are offered, along with gravlax, Swedish meatballs and game in season. A Swedish-interpreted burger comes with capers and beets.
🕐 Daily noon–4am
🍽 L $40, D $70, wine $19
🚇 East Broadway (F), Grand Street (S)
🚌 M15

GOTHAM BAR & GRILL
Map 264 E21
12 East 12th Street between Fifth Avenue and University Place
Tel 212/620-4020
www.gothambarandgrill.com
Unique among Manhattan celebrity chefs, Alfred Portale has not yet created his own mini-chain. Which may be why his fresh-tasting dramatically presented contemporary cuisine continues to excite even after more than 20 years. Rack of lamb is Portale's signature dish, but you can't go wrong with the wild striped bass and red wine sauce or the Niman

Ranch pork with caramelized cipollini onions. The warm apple and mango tartes tatin and the warm Gotham chocolate cake are sublime. Extra-special tea selections.
🕐 Mon–Fri 12–2.15, Sun–Thu 5.30–10.15, Fri–Sat 5.30–11.15
🍽 L $80, D $120, wine $29
🚇 14th Street/Union Square (L, N, Q, R, W, 4, 5, 6)
🚌 M2, M3, M5

GRAMERCY TAVERN
Map 264 E20
42 East 20th Street between Broadway and Park Avenue South
Tel 212/477-0777
www.gramercytavern.com

Danny Meyer's stellar restaurant, under chef Tom Colicchio, still shines. Both the main dining room (a warren of several cozy rooms) and the more casual tavern in the front are striking and comfortable. The truly warm hospitality and the seamless service make this one of the city's top tables. You can't go wrong on this menu, which offers a seared foie gras paired with a rhubarb tart, arugula and sherry vinegar, and a roasted monkfish wrapped with pancetta. Twenty-five wines from the superb list are available by the glass. Desserts are equally as delightful as the main dishes.
🕐 Dining room: Mon–Fri 12–2, Sun–Thu 5.30–10, Fri–Sat 5.30–11; Tavern: Sun–Thu 12–11, Fri–Sat 12–12
🍽 D $90, 3-course prix fixe L $36, D $140; Tavern 3-course prix fixe $68, wine $19
🚇 23rd Street (N, R, W)
🚌 M1, M2, M3, M6, M7

GRAND CENTRAL OYSTER BAR
Map 264 E18
Grand Central Terminal, 42nd Street and Park Avenue
Tel 212/490-6650
www.oysterbarny.com

EATING

You don't have to love oysters to love this legendary room in the lower level of Grand Central. Since it opened in 1913 the Guastavino-tiled space has starred in many a movie. Today, it's jammed at lunch and busy in the early evening with people sampling the 20–30 fresh fish choices, or slurping down oysters in a dozen varieties, all flown in daily. The chowders and chowderlike panroasts are famous.
🕐 Mon–Fri 11.30–9.30, Sat 12–9.30, closed Sun
🍽 L $80, D $100, wine $25
Ⓜ 42nd Street/Grand Central (4, 5, 6)
🚌 M1, M2, M3

HAMPTON CHUTNEY
Map 265 F23
68 Prince Street between Crosby and Lafayette streets
Tel 212/226-9996
South Indian dosas and uttapas are the specialties of this counter-style eatery. The classic dosa is filled with spiced potato here, but many Western-inspired variations are offered, from avocado, tomato, arugula and jack cheese, to tuna with cilantro-chutney dressing. Good sandwiches on black, sourdough and other breads, too. Chai and lassi are the choice drinks.
🕐 Daily 11–8
🍽 $20
Ⓜ Prince Street (N, R), Broadway/Lafayette (F, V, S), Spring Street (6)
🚌 M1, M6

THE HARRISON
Map 265 E24
355 Greenwich Street at Harrison Street
Tel 212/274-9310
www.theharrison.com
With its tufted leather banquettes and weathered wood paneling, this friendly, inviting restaurant is the kind of neighborhood spot where people drop in regularly. The food is brimming with flavor; the skillet calf's liver comes with bacon, onion and potato strudel in a rich sherry sauce, while sautéed skate is redolent of grapefruit, red onion and green olives. The spicy French fries are superb.
🕐 Mon–Thu 5.30–11, Fri–Sat 5.30–11.30, Sun 5–10
🍽 D $95, wine $22
Ⓜ Franklin Street (1, 9)
🚌 M20

HELL'S KITCHEN
Map 264 D18
679 Ninth Avenue between West 46th and 47th streets
Tel 212/977-1588
Here, a contemporary interpretation of Mexican cuisine uses prime American ingredients. Start with mescal-cured salmon carpaccio with avocado grapefruit salad, or chayote and portobello mushroom roll with chipotle pepper sauce. The strong exotic drinks from the bar match the interesting and robust flavors.
🕐 Tue–Fri 11.30–3.30, Sun–Mon 5–11, Tue–Sat 5–12
🍽 L $50, D $70, wine $20
Ⓜ 42nd Street (A, C, E)
🚌 M11

HOLY BASIL
Map 265 F22
149 Second Avenue between East 9th and 10th streets
Tel 212/460-5557 or 645-8965

This is one of the city's best Thai restaurants. Here, the kitchen balances the flavors of sweet and salt associated with the cuisine. The stars are the fish dishes, such as the whole crisp fish, which you can order in red chili sauce or a delicious tamarind sauce. Wine selections pair well with the food.
🕐 Mon–Thu 5–11.30, Fri–Sat 5–12, Sun 5.30–11.30
🍽 D $65, wine $18
Ⓜ Astor Place (6)
🚌 M15

HONMURA AN
Map 265 E23
170 Mercer Street between Houston and Prince streets
Tel 212/334-5253
When restaurant critic Ruth Reichl chose this as one of the first restaurants she would review after arriving at the *New York Times*, she shocked the city's culinary establishment. This noodle house continues to ladle out the food she praised—hot and cold udon and soba with toppings and dipping sauces (nori, mushrooms, salmon caviar and wild greens). The tasting plates are superb (slices of duck marinated in red wine and sweet soba or blanched asparagus with sesame seed dressing).
🕐 Wed–Sat 12–2.30, Tue–Thu 6–10, Fri–Sat 6–10.30, Sun 6–9.30, closed Mon
🍽 L $45, D $60, wine $36
Ⓜ Broadway/Lafayette (F, V, S), Prince Street (N, R), Bleecker Street (6)
🚌 M1, M6

I COPPI
Map 265 G22
432 East 9th Street between First Avenue and Avenue A
Tel 212/254-2263
This restaurant is like a piece of Tuscany in Manhattan. Wood tables and rush-seated chairs create a rustic charm accompanied by music from the opera and floral bouquets. Tuna carpaccio is paper-thin and spiked with green peppercorn sauce; sliced pears with Gorgonzola and stracchino cheese make for a perfect salad. Among the secondi, there might be grilled wild boar, or wild striped bass with caper and black olives. The wine list leans to Italy.
🕐 Sat 11.30–3, 5–10, Sun 11.30–4, 5–10.30, Mon–Thu 5–11, Fri 5–11.30
🍽 D $80, wine $25
Ⓜ Astor Place (6)
🚌 M8, M14, M15

IL MULINO
Map 264 E22
86 West 3rd Street between Sullivan and Thompson streets
Tel 212/673-3783
This intimate Village Italian operated by two brothers has been a favorite for more than 20 years. It owes its success to word-of-mouth. The draw is the large portions of classic Italian dishes—fettuccine

EATING

Alfredo, spaghetti carbonara, osso buco—and the selection of tempting antipasti. Great Italian wine list.

🕐 Mon–Fri 12–2.30, 5–11, Sat 5–11
🍴 L $100, D $120, wine $30
🚇 West 4th Street (A, C, E, F, V, S)
🚌 M5, M6

L'IMPERO

Off map 264 F18
45 Tudor City Place (access from East 41st Street)
Tel 212/599-5045

Tucked away in Tudor City, L'Impero is a lovely hideaway. The dining rooms are comfortable and seductively lit, the service gracious, and the food extremely good and even affordable. Taste the roasted lobster with chickpeas, the extraordinary pastas (farfalle with sweetbreads, bitter greens, chanterelles and shallots or the duck and foie gras agnolotti), and delicious secondi like the roast cod infused with pancetta. The wine list is excellent and fairly priced.

🕐 Mon–Thu 12–2.30, 5.30–10.30, Fri 12–2.30, 5–11.30, Sat 5–11.30, closed Sun
🍴 L $90, D $100, tasting menu $48, wine $29
🚇 42nd Street/Grand Central (4, 5, 6)
🚌 M15, M27, M50, M42

JEWEL BAKO

Map 265 F22
239 East 5th Street between Second and Third avenues
Tel 212/979-1012

This tiny restaurant is the domain of sushi artist Kazuo Yoshida. Sushi cognoscenti either experience nirvana or complain because they want it done their way. Tables and golden bamboo chairs are set under a bamboo-lined barrel-vaulted ceiling. Diners are presented with slices of sea bass, pike, eel, mackerel and octopus, sprinkled variously with sea salt, yuzu pepper, sesame, or grated daikon, or smeared with wasabi paste.

🕐 Tue–Sun 6.30–10.30
🍴 D $100, wine $42
🚇 Astor Place (6)
🚌 M8, M15, M103

JIMMY'S DOWNTOWN

Map 263 G17
400 East 57th Street between First Avenue and Sutton Place
Tel 212/486-6400

Swathed in suede and red, this lavish club-like spot is way downtown from Harlem and the Bronx, home of the city's other Jimmy's. The personality of owner Jimmy Rodriguez sets the scene, along with the exotic cocktails and the robust cuisine—chimichurri sauce on the adobo-roasted chicken, papaya lemon relish on the charred garlic shrimp, and coconut in the lobster soup.

🕐 Daily 5.30–12, also Sun 11–3
🍴 D $89, wine $30
🚇 59th Street (4, 5, 6), Lexington Avenue/59th Street (N, R, W)
🚌 M31, M57, M15

JEAN-GEORGES

Map 262 D16
Trump International Hotel Tower
1 Central Park West between 60th and 61st streets
Tel 212/299-3900
www.jean-georges.com

Jean-Georges Vongerichten is the toast of the town. Thoroughly French, he has developed a signature cuisine that is intensely flavored and highly textured, based on vegetable and fruit essences, oils, vinaigrettes and broths. Stellar examples are the peekytoe crab and English pea fondue with rhubarb gelée and shiso purée, and the veal tenderloin with fricasee of mushrooms, fava beans, and Meyer lemon with liquid Parmesan. It's hard to snag a table here. There's a 300-plus-strong wine list. Terrace dining in summer.

🕐 Mon–Fri 12–2.30, 5.30–11, Sat 5.30–11, closed Sun
🍴 L $65, D 3-course prix fixe $87, tasting $118, wine $43
🚇 59th Street/Columbus Circle (A, C, B, D, 1, 9)
🚌 M7, M10, M20

JOHN'S PIZZERIA PIZZA

Map 264 D22
278 Bleecker Street between Sixth and Seventh avenues
Tel 212/243-1680

The pizza served at this John's Pizzeria is frequently touted as the best in the city, and it is extraordinarily good indeed. Note that this is not a pizza parlor; slices are not available. Instead, take a booth and order a whole pie loaded with toppings—more than 50 are available. No credit cards.

🕐 Mon–Sat 11.30–11.30, Sun 12–11.30
🍴 $30, wine $18
🚇 West 4th Street (A, C, E, F, V, S), Christopher Street/Sheridan Square (1, 9)
🚌 M5, M20

JOJO

Map 263 F16
160 East 64th Street between Lexington and Third avenues
Tel 212/223-5656
www.jean-georges.com

Jean-Georges was 29 in 1986, when he opened the bistro that made him a name in New York. The townhouse dining rooms remain sumptuous and glowing, with their plum banquettes, sconces and flattering illumination. The signature appetizer is still shrimp dusted in orange powder. Desserts are also exceptional.

🕐 Daily 12–2.30, 5.30–10
🍴 L $90, D $120, wine $25
🚇 63rd Street/Lexington (F)
🚌 M 98, M1010, M102, M103, M66

KATZ'S DELI

Map 265 G22
205 East Houston Street between Ludlow and Orchard streets
Tel 212/254-2246
www.homedelivery.com

The site of the hilarious climactic scene in *When Harry Met Sally* is the last remaining deli in what was once a thriving Jewish neighborhood. Opened in 1888, it upholds deli

EATING

traditions: nondescript surroundings and immense knishes and pastrami sandwiches. Credit cards accepted on bills of $20 and more only.

🕐 Sun–Tue 8am–10pm, Wed–Thu 8am–11pm, Fri–Sat 8am–3am
💷 $30
🚇 Lower East Side/Second Avenue (F, V)
🚌 M21, M14, M15

KOMODO
Map 265 G21
186 Avenue A between East 11th and 12th streets
Tel 212/529-2658
Chef Maggie Moore turns out Asian-Mexican dishes for a hipster crowd at this storefront. The tempura oysters with red bean-ancho sauce and the rice balls stuffed with shrimp flavored with chili, mint, coconut and cilantro are both perfection; entrées like the pork chop in miso cider glaze are exciting as well.
🕐 Mon–Sat 6–11.30, Sun 5.30–10.30
💷 D $65, wine $22
🚇 Union Square/14th Street (N, Q, R, W, 4, 5, 6), First Avenue (L)
🚌 M14

LA PALAPA
Map 265 F22
77 St. Mark's Place between First and Second avenues
Tel 212/777-2537
www.lapalapa.com

At this dark and sultry Mexican, cookbook author Diana Kennedy is the inspiration for

LE BERNARDIN
Map 262 D17
155 West 51st Street between Sixth and Seventh avenues
Tel 212/489-1515
www.le-bernardin.com
Le Bernardin, the best seafood restaurant in the city, may also be the best restaurant in the city. The teak-paneled room is spacious and comfortable, the service discreet and precise, and the food exquisite. Chef Eric Ripert's dishes are designed to show off the flavor and texture of the specific type of fish. Cod is served in a robust vinaigrette, halibut poached in saffron broth, and monkfish dropped into a reduction of beef. Signature appetizers—tuna carpaccio; a scallop wrapped in a cabbage leaf with foie gras and truffles and steamed; and black bass ceviche topped with coriander, mint, jalapenos and tomatoes—are all gems. Desserts are equally inspirational.
🕐 Mon–Fri 12–2.30, Mon–Thu 5.30–10.30, Fri–Sat 5.30–11, closed Mon
💷 L prix fixe $47, D 3-course prix fixe $84, wine $26
🚇 47th–50th streets/Rockefeller Center (B, D, F, V), 49th Street (N, R, W)
🚌 M5, M6, M7

much of the cooking, which reveals the complex flavors of epazote, cactus pads, avocado leaves and numerous chilies. The balance is always right, whether in the shrimp with red mole sauce, or the baked cod with guajillo, garlic and achiote barbecue sauce. Meat dishes are also well spiced. Then there are the extras—pinto beans with smoked bacon and chayotes in spicy cream.
🕐 Mon–Fri 12–12, Sat–Sun 11am–midnight
💷 L $35, D $50, wine $22
🚇 Astor Place (6)
🚌 M8, M15

LE CIRQUE 2000
Map 263 E17
New York Palace Hotel
455 Madison Ave between 50th and 51st streets
Tel 212/303-7788
www.lecirque.com

Sirio Maccioni and his sons rule over this legendary dining room in the extravagant Villard Houses, a magnet for celebrities and socialites. Architect Adam Tihany created the contemporary dining rooms right down to the single-armed violet and crimson chairs. Chef Pierre Schaedelin produces beautiful dishes —old standbys such as Dover sole alongside filet of rouget with shallot and black pepper marmalade in red wine and basil jus. Desserts are just as elaborate The 710 selections on the wine list are mostly French.
🕐 Mon–Sat 11.45–2.30, 5.30–11, Sun 5.30–10
💷 L $150, D $175, wine $37
🚇 Lexington Avenue/53rd Street (E,V), 51st Street (6)
🚌 M98, M101, M102, M103, M50

LE COLONIAL
Map 263 F16
149 East 57th Street between Lexington and Third avenues
Tel 212/752-0808
www.lecolonialnyc.com
The bamboo-and-fans French colonial ambience is a perfect backdrop for the southeast Asian cuisine at this striking spot. Start with chao tom (grilled shrimp wrapped around sugarcane with angel-hair noodles, lettuce, mint and peanut dipping sauce) or the delicious steamed ravioli with chicken and mushrooms. The steamed sea bass dishes are outstanding.
🕐 Mon–Fri 12–2, Sun–Mon 5.30–10.30, Tue–Thu 5.30–11, Fri–Sat 5.30–11.30
💷 $62, wine $33
🚇 59th Street (4, 5, 6), 59th Street/Lexington Avenue(N, R, W)
🚌 M57, M98, M101, M102, M103

LE ZINC
Map 265 E24
139 Duane Street
Tel 212/513-0001
www.lezincnyc.com

EATING

Lace curtains, a zinc counter and French posters may make this bistro look French, but the cuisine is international. The Waltucks, who own this place as well as Chanterelle, keep everything top quality but still affordable. Besides bistro dishes like steak frites, terrines, charcuterie and skate with black butter, you might find onion fritters with tamarind sauce, or Chinese spiced duck wings in black bean and chili sauce. Desserts are courtesy of Chanterelle's excellent pastry chef. Good wine list.

🕐 Daily 8am–midnight
🍽 L $50, D $65, wine $21
🚇 Chambers Street (A, C), Chambers Street (1, 2, 3, 9)
🚌 M1, M6

LONDEL'S

Off map 262 D12
2620 Frederick Douglass Boulevard between 139th and 140th streets
Tel 212/234-6114

The South has given the United States its most distinctive cuisine, and this restaurant serves some of the best, from the Southern fried chicken and barbecue back ribs to the blackened catfish. Order collard greens or candied yams on the side, and bread pudding with rum sauce. You'll have had a feast. Live music on Friday and Saturday.

🕐 Tue–Sat 11.30–4, 5–11, Sun 12–5, closed Mon
🍽 L $35, D $50, wine $25
🚇 145th Street (A, C, B, D)
🚌 M10

LUPA

Map 265 E22
170 Thompson Street between Bleecker and Houston streets
Tel 212/982-5089
www.luparestaurant.com

Lupa, beloved Food Channel host Mario Batali's moderately priced restaurant, has the feel of a casual Roman trattoria.

The cuisine starts with ultra-fresh staples, many of which are made on the premises, notably the pasta, sausages and cheeses featured as appetizers. The simple, intense main dishes range from a classic saltimbocca to bucatini all' amatriciana, made with bacon, onions and cilantro. Side dishes such as the braised escarole and the cauliflower with capers are worthy, too.

🕐 Mon–Fri 12–2.30, 5–11.30, Sat–Sun 12–2.30, 4.45–11.30
🍽 L $50, D $70, wine $20
🚇 West 4th Street (A, C, E, F, V, S)
🚌 M5, M6, M21

MAMA MEXICO

Map 263 F17
214 East 49th Street between Second and Third avenues
Tel 212/935-1316
www.mamamexico.com

Crowds party at this festive Mexican, which blazes with color and throbs with mariachi music. The regional Mexican cuisine is packed with flavor. There are always several robust soups, plus 20 appetizers, including ceviche and quesadillas filled with chicken and mole sauce. Among main courses, the grilled rack of lamb with chile huajillo-pineapple sauce is outstanding, and the dozen fish dishes are excellent, too. The flavored margaritas or 46 tequilas will keep you in a partying mood. No credit cards.

🕐 Sun–Wed 12–12, Thu–Sat noon–2am
🍽 L $50, D $65, wine $20
🚇 51st Street (6)
🚌 M101, M102, M103, M98, M15

MARK JOSEPH STEAKHOUSE

Map 265 F25
261 Water Street at Peck Slip
Tel 212/277-0020
www.markjosephsteakhouse.com

Those who have had enough of Peter Luger's sawdust-on-the-floor style claim that this sleek and more modern meat specialist is the city's best steakhouse. The porterhouse is the choice cut. Add a salad and an order of the addictive hash-brown potatoes, finish with the apple galette or a slice of pecan pie.

🕐 Mon–Fri 11.30–10, Fri 11.30–11, Sat 5–11
🍽 L $65, D $115, wine $25
🚇 Broadway-Nassau (A, C), Fulton Street (J, M, Z, 2, 3, 4, 5)
🚌 M9, M15

MAYA

Map 263 F16
1191 First Avenue between East 64th and 65th streets
Tel 212/585-1818
www.maya.citysearch.com

Sophisticated Mexican cuisine is the draw here. The chile relleno stuffed with seafood and sharp manchego cheese is a palate-pleasing combination and the guacamole, served in the stone pestle in which it's made, is among the best in the city. The mole that accompanies the grilled chicken is as authentic as you could find, while the pork tenderloin marinated in tamarind vinaigrette is ultra tender and richly flavored. A winner. No credit cards.

🕐 Sun–Mon 5–10, Tue–Thu 5–11, Fri–Sat 5–11.30
🍽 D $70, wine $30
🚇 Lexington Avenue/63rd Street (F) 68th Street (6)
🚌 M15

MESA GRILL

Map 264 E21
102 Fifth Avenue between 15th and 16th streets
Tel 212/807-7400
www.mesagrill.com

When Bobby Flay opened this restaurant in 1991, he introduced New Yorkers to the spices of the Southwest, and the place continues to excite. The red walls recall Sedona

EATING

rock, the shrimp and roasted garlic with corn tamale is hot off the grill, and the cactus pear margaritas cool the heat. Follow the cornmeal-crusted oysters and mango habanero sauce with sixteen-spice chicken in tangerine Mexican oregano sauce. Brunches are distinctive as well—it's not everywhere you'll find tequila-smoked-salmon quesadilla.

Mon–Fri 12–2.30, Sat 11.30–2.30, Sun 11.30–3; Sun–Fri 5.30–10.30, Sat 5–11

L $65, D $90, wine $24

14th Street/Union Square (L, N, Q, R, W, 4, 5, 6)

M2, M3, M5, M14

MI COCINA
Map 264 D21
57 Jane Street at Hudson Street
Tel 212/627-8273

Mi Cocina was one of the city's first restaurants to offer authentic regional Mexican cuisine. Start with the shrimp in spicy chile adobo or the corn tamale filled with guajillo chile sauce and Mexican white cheese. To follow, there are rich mole-coated chicken enchiladas or lighter dishes like the chicken marinated with lime, oregano and blue agave tequila. The brightly painted rooms decked with folk art strike just the right note, and the small garden courtyard is romantic on a summer evening.

Thu–Sun 11.30–2.30, Sun–Thu 4.30–10.45, Fri–Sat 4.30–11.45

L $45, D $65, wine $25

14th Street (A, C, E)

M20

MIRCHI
Map 264 D22
29 Seventh Avenue South between Bedford and Morton streets
Tel 212/414-0931
www.mirchiny.com

This sleek neo-Indian offers fiery street food and regional dishes and a list of wines that pair well with it all. Among the *chats* (snacks), try the bhel poori, made with puffed rice, onion and tomato and served with tamarind and cilantro chutneys. Peppery Chettinad chicken comes from South India; Gujarat contributes chickpea cakes with chilies and cilantro; the herb-swathed fish is a Sind specialty. The tandoor turns out succulent meats and fish spiced variously with chili, coriander, ginger and garlic.

Mon–Fri 12–3, 5.30–12, Sat noon–1am, Sun 12–11

$60, wine $22

Houston Street (1,9)

M20, M21

MOLYVOS
Map 262 D17
871 Seventh Avenue between West 55th and 56th treets
Tel 212/582-7500
www.molyvos.com

This large space with a café, a bar and two dining rooms, brings Greece to Manhattan. The Greek dips and spreads are irresistible, including the garlicky roasted eggplant purée and the tzatziki, a blend of yogurt, cucumber, garlic, mint, dill, and lemon. Also outstanding are the cold meze such as grilled baby octopus with olives, fennel, lemon and oregano, and fava beans mashed with olive oil. Marinated lamb shanks, whole grilled fish and rabbit stew are traditional main courses. The 165-bottle wine list includes more than 50 Greek wines; 10 are available by the glass.

Mon–Sat 12–3, 5.30–11.30 (Sat until 12), Sun 12–11

L $60, D $80, wine $24

Seventh Avenue (B, D, E), 57th Street (N, R, Q, W)

M10, M20

MONTRACHET
Map 265 E24
239 West Broadway between Walker and White streets
Tel 212/219-2777
www.myriadrestaurantgroup.com

The focus is on the plate in this spare, minimal classic. Chef Chris Gesualdi expresses his distinctive style in such dishes as truffle-crusted salmon with fennel, oyster mushrooms, artichokes and red wine fumet, and pan-seared duck with ramps, white asparagus, endive and port-orange sauce. Appetizers range from lobster and corn soup to foie gras with plum purée and ginger sauce. Chocolate and fruit are the core dessert ingredients.

Fri 12–2, 5.30–10.45 Mon–Thu 5.30–9.45, Sat 5.30–10.45, closed Sun

L 3-course prix fixe $20 and $28, D $105, wine $22

Canal Street (A, C, E), Franklin Street(1, 9)

M6, M20

MOUSTACHE
Map 265 G21
265 East 10th Street between First Avenue and Avenue A
Tel 212/228-2022

This unadorned restaurant serves great, inexpensive Middle Eastern cuisine. A favorite specialty is the ouzi—filo dough wrapped around fragrantly spiced basmati rice, chicken, carrots, sweet peas, onions, raisins and almonds. Pizzas come with eight different toppings. No credit cards.

Daily 12–12

$35, wine $28

First Avenue (L), Astor Place (6)

M8, M14, M15

NAM
Map 265 E24
110 Reade Street at West Broadway
Tel. 212 267 1777

Nam stands out for its style and for its authentic and often unique dishes. Particularly alluring are the appetizers. Banh xeo, for example, is a crepe filled with mushrooms, bean sprouts, coconut-flavored rice, shrimp and chicken; ca tim nuong—simple but addictive—consists of grilled Asian eggplant with ginger, lime, garlic and a little chili. Among the many main dishes, the crisp red snapper and the chicken baked with ginger are excellent dinner choices.

NOBU

Map 265 E24

105 Hudson Street between Franklin and North Moore streets

Tel 212/219-0500

www.myriadrestaurantgroup.com

Celebrities flock to Drew Nieporent's TriBeCa hotspot for the artistic sushi and sashimi fashioned by chef Nobu Matsuhisa. If you can afford it, choose the omakase menu, which will deliver the chef's inspirations for the day. Or choose from baby abalone, live scallop or sashimi drizzled with garlic and ginger-flavored olive oil. Masu sake is served in small cedar cups with salted rims; finish with green tea crème caramel. Reservations are hard to come by; the next best thing is to drop in to Next Door Nobu.

🕒 Mon–Thu 5.45pm–midnight, Fri–Sat 5.45pm–1am, Sun 5.45–11

🍴 D $90, omakase $80–120, wine $40

🚇 Franklin Street (1, 9)

🚌 M20

🕒 Mon–Fri 12–2, Sun–Thu 5.30–10, Fri–Sat 5.30–11

🍴 L $50, D $55, wine $26

🚇 Chambers Street (1, 9)

🚌 M20

NEGRIL VILLAGE

Map 265 E22

70 West 3rd Street between La Guardia Place and Thompson Street

Tel 212/477-2804

The neo-Caribbean dishes sit wonderfully on the tongue at this sultry restaurant. It's hard to choose between the succulent curried goat, and such specialties as the ackee and the saltfish. Tropical desserts incluide key lime cheesecake with mango coulis. The downstairs rum lounge pours 50 different rums.

🕒 Mon–Fri 12–12, Sat–Sun noon–2am

🍴 L $40, D $70, wine $18

🚇 West 4th Street (A, C, E, V, F, S)

🚌 M5, M21

NOCHE

Map 262 D17

1604 Broadway between 48th and 49th streets

Tel 212/541-7070

This dramatic tri-level pan-Latin restaurant is really hot.

Pass the ground-floor mojito bar and climb the circular stair or take the elevator to the sleek dining rooms. The cuisine ranges from Puerto Rican *pasteles* to Ecuadorean shrimp with spicy plantain-peanut sauce, and the rotisserie duck with mofongo and chili glaze is wonderful. Saturdays from 10pm, there are live Latino bands with dancing.

🕒 Mon–Fri 12–2.30, Mon–Wed 5–10, Thu–Sat 5–11; Lounge Mon–Wed 12–12, Thu–Fri noon–1am, Sat 5pm–3am

🍴 L $60, D $80, wine $22

🚇 50th Street (1, 9), 49th Street (N, R, W)

🚌 M6, M7, M27, M104

NYONYA

Map 265 F23

194 Grand Street between Mott and Mulberry streets

Tel 212/334-3669

Malaysian cuisine draws on many different Asian cooking traditions—Chinese, Indian, Thai and Malay. You can sample some of the country's appealing, sometimes spicy dishes at this plain favorite. You have a wide choice of rice, noodle, casserole and other dishes; start with a roti (Indian pancake) or the satays, and follow with a fiery sambal or a curry made with lemongrass, chili and coconut milk. No credit cards.

🕒 Daily 11am–11.30pm

🍴 $40

🚇 Grand Street (S)

🚌 M1

OCEANA

Map 263 E17

55 East 54th Street between Madison and Park avenues

Tel 212/759-5941

www.oceanarestaurant.com

With its nautical interior, Oceana is something like a streamlined yacht, even though it's in a handsome

townhouse. The French-Asian cuisine produced by chef Cornelius Gallagher is bold and often surprising, as exemplified by, for example, the loup de mer accompanied by a tamarind and wasabi sauce, and the salmon roulade, which is stoked up with smoked bacon and peppered green apple and served in a red wine and olive sauce. The international wine list offers 1,000 selections, 20 by the glass.

🕒 Mon–Fri 12–2.30, Mon–Fri 5.30–10.30, Sat 5–10.30

🍴 L 3-course prix fixe $45, D 3-course prix fixe $68, wine $24

🚇 53rd Street/Fifth Avenue (E, V)

🚌 M1, M2, M3, M4

ODEON

Map 265 E24

145 West Broadway between Thomas and Duane streets

Tel 212/233-0507

In the early 1980s this cafeteria-turned-hip-bistro was the incubator of the downtown scene. Odeon still has Venetian blinds on the windows and chrome stools at the bar, but nowadays it caters to neighborhood residents as well as downtown celebrities with a typical bistro menu of onion soup gratinée, moules and steak frites. This is a great late-night stop.

🕒 Mon–Fri 11.45am–2am, Sat–Sun 11am–2am

🍴 L $35, D $70, wine $21

🚇 Chambers Street (A, C, E) Chambers Street (1, 2, 3, 9)

🚌 M6, M20

OTTO ENOTECA PIZZERIA

Map 265 E22

1 Fifth Avenue at 8th Street

Tel 212/995-9559

Mario Batali continues to apply his genius to educating the average American palate to real Italian cuisine and wine. Here, the arena is pizza, which you can have with marinara, or—a better idea—in one of the combinations dreamed up by Mario, such as topped with porcini and taleggio or with tomato, fennel, bottarga (silver mullet roe), pecorino and mozzarella. The wine card is extraordinary, and the gelati are the best in the city, period.

⊙ Daily 9am–11.30pm
🍽 $55, wine $18
Ⓜ West 4th Street (A, C, E, F, V, S)
🚌 M2, M3, M5

OUEST

Map 262 C14
2315 Broadway between West 83rd and 84th streets
Tel 212/580-8700
www.ouestny.com

This lively, entertaining restaurant helped raise the Upper West Side's culinary reputation with Tom Valenti's fresh seasonal menu. Settle into one of the cherry-red booths and order the luscious short ribs, one of the braised or roasted meats such as the roast free-range chicken with garlic jus, or a fish dish such as seared tuna with white bean purée, black olive-lemon compote and red pepper coulis. The nightly specials attract crowds, especially on Monday, when the kitchen turns out the chef's signature braised lamb shanks; Friday it's Maine lobster. Desserts are Italian-inspired.

⊙ Tue–Thu 5–10.30, Fri–Sat 5–11.30, Sun 10–2, 5–10.30, closed Mon
🍽 D $80, wine $24
Ⓜ 86th Street (1, 9)
🚌 M 104

PAM REAL THAI

Map 262 C17
404 West 49th Street between Ninth and Tenth avenues
Tel 212/333-7500

At this authentic Thai, none of the of sweet, sour and salt dishes have been compromised to suit a more timid palate. The traditional favorites are all available: superb hot and milder curries, fiery salads made with green papaya, ground pork with lime dressing, noodle dishes, and, best of all, duck with chili sauce and lime leaves. BYOB. No credit cards.

⊙ Daily 11.30–11
🍽 $40
Ⓜ 50th Street (C, E, 1, 9)
🚌 M11, M50

PASTIS

Map 264 D21
9 Ninth Avenue at Little 12th Street
Tel 212/929-4844
www.balthazarny.com

At Pastis, you could just as easily be on the rue St Denis around the corner from Les Halles. Every detail rings true: the zinc bar, the smoky mirrors, the tiles and the French ads. Then there are the *plats* (dishes)—onion soup gratinée, croque monsieur, skate *au beurre noir*, steak and moules frites, and, at breakfast, wonderful brioche and egg dishes. Owner Keith McNally's heritage shows through in the fish and chips and the beans on toast. Wine is served in tumblers. Expect lines, and look out for celebrities in summer.

⊙ Mon–Fri 9–11.30, Sat–Sun 9–10 (continental breakfast), Mon–Fri 12–5, Sat–Sun 10–5 (brunch), daily 6–12 (supper Sun–Wed until 1am, Thu until 2am and Fri–Sat until 3am).
🍽 L $60, D $70, wine $21
Ⓜ 14th Street (A, C, E)
🚌 M11, M14

PEARL OYSTER BAR

Map 264 E22
18 Cornelia Street
Tel 212/691-8211

The fiercely loyal patrons of this tiny spot with a marble bar don't mind lining up for New England favorites such as oysters, creamy chowder and the fried oyster sandwiches doused in rémoulade sauce. The pièce de résistance is the delicious lobster roll encased in a toasted bun.

⊙ Mon–Fri 12–2.30, Mon–Sat 6–11
🍽 L $50, D $60, wine $27
Ⓜ West 4th Street (A, C, E, F, V, S)
🚌 M5, M6, M20

PETER LUGER STEAKHOUSE

Off map 265 E25
178 Broadway between Bedford and Briggs streets, Williamsburg, Brooklyn
Tel 718-387-7400

PATRIA

Map 264 E20
250 Park Avenue South at 20th Street
Tel 212/777-6211

Patria, the first nuevo Latin American restaurant on the scene, continues to draw crowds. The bold and spicy cuisine is inspired by the fare of Mexico, Chile, Colombia and Argentina. Traditional appetizers include a black lobster empanada served with a yellow chili aji and a shrimp ceviche made with orange, carrot, fennel, lime and habanero and served in a large martini glass. Suckling pig is also on the menu, and there are some good Chilean and Argentinian wines on the 650-bottle list. The quietest tables are on the ground floor below the bar.

⊙ Mon–Fri 12–3.30, Mon–Thu 6–11, Fri–Sat 5.30–12, Sun 5.30–10.30
🍽 L $75, D $100, wine $28
Ⓜ 23rd Street (6)
🚌 M1, M2, M3

Many people will tell you that this old-fashioned beer hall-style restaurant with its crotchety waiters serves the city's best steak, if not the nation's. The meat itself is carefully selected, aged on the premises and cooked to perfection. All the traditional cuts are available, but the most fun is the porterhouse, which is sliced tableside. Whatever you do, don't miss the creamed spinach and mashed potatoes. No credit cards.

⊙ Sun–Thu 11.45–10, Fri–Sat 11.45–11
🍽 $115, wine $25
Ⓜ Marcy Ave (J, M, Z)

PICHOLINE

Map 262 D16
35 West 64th Street between Central Park West and Broadway

EATING

Tel 212/724-8585

The Mediterranean cuisine at Picholine is superb—despite its proximity to the Lincoln Center. Among the entrées the licorice-lacquered squab is exquisite, perfectly complemented by foie gras, glazed turnips and spiced rhubarb marmalade. The wild mushroom and duck risotto is a perennial favorite. And such classics as cassoulet, bouillabaisse and a marvelously rich braised lamb shank are available daily. It's easy to fill up with such delicious entrées and the main courses on offer—but be sure to save room for one more course. Until chef-owner Terrance Brennan opened Artisanal, Picholine also had the city's most fabulous cheese tray.

🕐 Sat 11.45–2, Tue–Wed 5.15–11, Thu–Sat 5.15–11.45, Sun 5–9, closed Mon

🍴 L $60, D $112, wine $31

🚇 66th Street (1, 9)

🚌 M10, M20

PICO

Map 265 E24
349 Greenwich Street between Harrison and Jay streets
Tel 212/343-0700

Seafood and suckling pig are the stars at this plush updated Portuguese restaurant furnished with sober antique armoires and gold-tasseled chairs. The semicircular high-back booths are perfect for private dining. John Villa uses traditional Portuguese ingredients—salt cod, sardines, chorizo, pork and potatoes—but lightens and flavors them, often with spices from Goa, Angola and Macao. Black cod is flavored with a ginger and white port reduction, while salmon is swathed in a sweet and spicy curry. The roast suckling pig with wildflower honey, which turns on the spit for four hours, is extraordinary. Although Portuguese wines dominate the wine list, there is also a choice of international wines to choose from.

🕐 Mon–Fri 12–2.30, Sat–Sun 11.30–3, Mon–Thu 6–10.30, Fri –Sat 6–11.30, Sun 5–10

🍴 L $52, D $90, wine $18

🚇 Franklin Street (1, 9)

🚌 M20

PINTXOS

Off map 265 D23
510 Greenwich Street between Canal and Spring streets
Tel 212/343-9923

Pintxos are Basque tapas, and this unassuming restaurant offers 18 of them—and they are your best bet here, even though the menu also offers eight or so meat and fish entrées. Look for spicy chorizo, Basque anchovies, stuffed mussels and white asparagus, which all go wonderfully well with the available wines.

🕐 Mon–Sat 11.30–4, closed Sun

🍴 L $40, D $55, wine $22

🚇 Spring Street (C, E), Houston Street (1, 9)

🚌 M20

PIO PIO

Map 263 F13
1746 First Avenue between East 90th and 91st streets
Tel 212/426-5800

This is the Peruvian version of the Boston Chicken chain. Order a quarter, half, or whole chicken, marinated in secret spices. Then add some tostones, red beans, or yuca frita and a beer, and you've got yourself a tasty meal. Amex credit cards only.

🕐 Daily 11–11

🍴 $25

🚇 86th Street (4, 5, 6)

🚌 M15

PIPA

Map 264 E21
ABC Carpet and Home
38 East 19th Street between Broadway and Park Avenue South
Tel 212/677-2233

Nuevo Latin king Douglas Rodriguez does Spanish at this lively restaurant, whose name means "great time." You can make a meal of the wonderful tapas—succulent fried oysters with banana-and-lentil salad, horseradish aioli and crispy bacon; shrimp with garlic oil and chilies; or sautéed chorizo. Or you can follow up with a rice, meat or fish dish, or perhaps a gorgeous paella. The white or red sangria are perfect accompaniments, or go for one of the rum drinks.

🕐 Mon–Thu 12–11, Fri 12–12, Sat 11am–midnight, Sun 11–10

🍴 L $48, D $65, wine $27

🚇 4th Street/Union Square (L, N, Q, R, W, 4, 5, 6)

🚌 M1, M2, M3, M6, M7

PRUNE

Map 265 F22
54 East 1st Street between First and Second avenues
Tel 212/677-6221

Everything is meticulously prepared at this small, idiosyncratic restaurant. Dinner entrées might include roast suckling pig with pickled tomatoes, black-eyed peas and aioli, or whole grilled fish with fennel oil and salt. Order one of the carefully prepared vegetable accompaniments. Choose, perhaps, between the roast beets or the bitter greens salad with oil and lemon juice to compliment the beautifully presented dishes.

🕐 Sat–Sun 10–3.30, Mon–Thu 6–11, Fri–Sat 6–12, Sun 5–10

🍴 D $105, wine $20

🚇 Lower East Side/Second Avenue (F, V)

🚌 M15, M21

RED CAT

Map 264 C20
227 Tenth Avenue between West 23rd and 24th Streets
Tel 212/242-1122

A downtown art crowd packs this vivacious, inviting bistro, a narrow crimson room illuminated by large Moroccan lanterns. The contemporary kitchen puts plenty of flavor into its creations—take, for example, the crisp skate wing in caper brown butter, or the grilled pork chop on black-olive purée. Tasty Parmesan fries spiked with mustard aioli are one of the most popular side orders. Desserts are eclectic but equally delicious. The wine list is carefully chosen, and 17 selections are available by the glass.

🕐 Mon–Thu 5.30–11, Fri–Sat 5.30–12, Sun 5–10

🍴 D $75, wine $22

🚇 23rd Street (C, E)

🚌 M11, M23

EATING

RIVER CAFÉ

Map 265 G25
1 Water Street at Old Fulton Street, Brooklyn
Tel 718-522-5200
www.rivercafe.com

Opened in 1977, this old-timer tucked on a barge under the Brooklyn Bridge, is still one of the city's most romantic restaurants, with magical views of the river and Downtown Manhattan skyline. A dynasty of great American chefs from Larry Forgione to the current Brad Steelman have made the kitchen famous. Nowadays you might start with the tuna tartare with Asian pear splashed with coriander, sesame and chili, then go on to the roast lamb loin with mint and mustard glaze or the sautéed black sea bass with turmeric coconut sauce. The chocolate Brooklyn Bridge remains a signature dessert. 500-bottle wine list.

🕐 Mon–Thu 12–3, 5.30–10, Fri–Sat 12–3, 5.30–11, Sun 11.30–3, 5.30–10
🍴 D $95, prix fixe $70, wine $32
🚇 High Street (A, C), York Street (F)

RM

Map 263 E16
33 East 60th Street between Park and Madison avenues
Tel 212/319-3800

Rick Moonen made his name at Oceana, which this restaurant recalls with its sleek mahogany and polished surfaces. Moonen is famous for pairing pan-roasted scallops and braised oxtails, and for successfully combining multiple flavors. The halibut poached in olive oil and dropped into fennel purée textured with toasted bread-crumbs is wonderful. Truffle sauce and pickled chanterelles, might perk up the walleye, and littleneck clam vinaigrette spikes the sea bass. The pastry chef also likes to challenge the palate by pairing desserts with a cheese.

🕐 Mon–Fri 12–2, Mon–Sat 5.30–10, closed Sun
🍴 L $85, D 3-course prix fixe $58, 6-course prix fixe $100, wine $30
🚇 59th Street (4, 5, 6)
🚌 M1, M2, M3, M4

ROSA MEXICANO

Map 262 D16
61 Columbus Avenue at West 62nd Street NE corner

Tel 212/977-7700
www.rosamexicano.com

A waterfall studded with sculptures of Acapulco-style divers, among other decorative notes, sets a flashy scene at this authentic Mexican. The guacamole, which is made at the table, is fragrant with cilantro and oregano, and the menu offers unusual regional dishes such salmon al guajillo, beef short ribs marinated in lime and beer and *budin Azteca*, a flavorsome tortilla pie.

🕐 Mon–Sat 12–3, Sun 11.30–3, Sun–Mon 5–11, Tue–Fri 5–12
🍴 L $60, D $75, wine $22
🚇 59th Street/Columbus Circle (A,B,C,D,1,9)
🚌 M11, M5, M7, M104

RUBY FOO'S

Map 262 C14
2182 Broadway at 77th Street
Tel 212/724-6700
www.brguestrestaurants.com

This, the original Ruby Foo's, made a big splash when it opened in 1996 on the Upper West Side with its dramatic staircase and red lacquer walls. The pan-Asian cuisine was the other big draw then and now, ranging from dim sum and sushi to hot-and-sour shrimp with water chestnuts and coconut sticky rice, and seven-flavored beef with ginger mashed potatoes and chile-lime salsa. Have fun.

🕐 Mon 11.30–11.30, Tue–Sat 11.30am–12.30pm, Sun 11.30–4.30, 5–11.30
🍴 L $45, D $60, wine $23
🚇 79th Street (1,9)
🚌 M104

SARABETH'S

Map 263 E13
1295 Madison Avenue between East 92nd and 93rd streets
Tel 212/410-7335

Sarabeth's is the domain of Sarabeth Levine, who is most famous for her luscious baking

and breakfasts, but that does not mean that she can't turn out equally wonderful lunch and dinner fare. Try her short ribs in zinfandel or her hazel-nut-crusted sea bass, and you'll be a fan. At breakfast, don't miss the cinnamon French toast or the pumpkin waffles—and plan on a light lunch afterwards.

🕐 Daily 8am–10.30pm (breakfast until 3.30)
🍴 L $50, D $75, wine $27
🚇 96th Street (6)
🚌 M1, M2, M3, M4

SECOND AVENUE DELI

Map 265 F21
156 Second Avenue between East 9th and 10th streets
Tel 212/677-0606
www.2ndavedeli.com

The names on the sidewalk outside this deli recall the days when the neighborhood was the Yiddish Theater District. The interior is comfortable, the service swift and good-natured. Favorite dishes: chopped liver, chicken soup, hefty sandwiches filled with pastrami, corned beef and tongue and, as entrées, the goulash and boiled beef.

🕐 Sun–Thu 7am–midnight, Fri–Sat 7am–3am
🍴 L $40, D $70
🚇 Astor Place (6), Third Avenue (L)
🚌 M15, M8

SHUN LEE PALACE

Map 263 F17
155 East 55th Street between Lexington and Third avenues
Tel 212/371-8844

It's still the best Chinese restaurant in the city, even though it's been around since 1972. It may be expensive, but the dining rooms are comfort-able and elegant and the Shanghai, Szechuan and Cantonese cuisine is beautifully presented. Besides such traditional dishes as crispy sea bass Hunan style and lobster in black bean sauce, you will find such extraordinary specialties as prawns on banana leaves with curry sauce and red cooked short ribs Hang Chow style. There's a branch near Lincoln Center at 43 West 65th Street between Central Park West and Columbus Avenue (*tel 212/595-8895*)—a good bet for a leisurely meal or a pre-concert snack.

🕐 Mon–Sat 12–11.30, Sun 12–10.30
🍴 L $90, 3-course prix fixe $20, D $100, wine $35
Ⓜ Lexington Avenue/53rd Street (E, V), 51st Street (6)
🚌 M98, M1010, M102, M103, M57

66

Map 265 E24
241 Church Street between Leonard and Worth streets
Tel 212/925-0202
This is not just another Chinese restaurant; it's Jean-Georges Vongerichten's elegant and energized interpretation of Chinese cuisine. Architect Richard Meier's design pairs frosted glass and steel mesh with Eames chairs and Saarinen tables. The chefs are definitely Chinese, deftly turning out jewel after jewel, the likes of which you won't find in Chinatown—crab with lotus-seed crust, squab spiked with orange rind and crystallized ginger. Other Chinese favorites get a new twist.

🕐 Daily 12–3, Mon–Thu 6–12, Fri–Sat 6pm–1am, Sun 5.30–10.30
🍴 L $60, D $100, wine $26
Ⓜ Franklin Street(1,9)
🚌 M6

STRIP HOUSE

Map 265 E21
13 East 12th Street between Fifth Avenue and University Place
Tel 212-328-0000
www.theglaziergroup.com

Recalling a 19th-century bordello with its tufted leather

banquettes and swathe of velvet, this place serves up juicy succulent beef, notably the New York strip. Other cuts are available along with a couple of fish dishes, wild striped bass with artichokes, pancetta and basil sauce, for example.

🕐 Mon–Thu 5–11, Fri–Sat 5–11.30, Sun 5–10
🍴 D $120, wine $25
Ⓜ 14th Street/Union Square (L, N, Q, R, W, 4, 5, 6)
🚌 M2, M3, M5

SUGAR HILL BISTRO

Off map 262 C12
458 West 145th Street between Amsterdam and Convent avenues
Tel 212/491-5505
www.sugarhillbistro.com
This joyous spot in a handsome townhouse celebrates the culture of Harlem and recalls the 1920s, when the city's fun lovers came uptown to dine well and listen to jazz. The updated Southern/tropical menu, served in the lavish parlor floor of the house, features such dishes as blackened catfish with champagne shallot sauce, saffron lobster pot pie, and delicious pecan-crusted rack of lamb with rosemary demiglace. Weekends, two brunches take over (R & B on Saturday, gospel on Sunday), with a spread of about a dozen items for $22. There's live jazz Thursday to Saturday in the lounge, on the first floor.

🕐 Sat–Sun 11–4, Mon–Sat 5–11.30, Sun 5–10
🍴 D $90, wine $22
Ⓜ 145th Street (A, C, B, 1, 9)
🚌 M18, M100, M101

SUGIYAMA

Map 264 D17
251 West 55th Street between Broadway and Eighth Avenue
Tel 212/956-0670
Here, the seasons inform chef Nao Sugiyama's Kaiseki cuisine. You have a choice of four menus: 8-course, 10-course, 12-course and pre-theater. Each includes an appetizer, sashimi, soup, a sizzling dish on hot stone and dessert. The selection of sake by the glass and by the bottle is extensive.

🕐 Tue–Sat 5.30–11.45, closed Sun–Mon
🍴 D $60 8-course, $80 10-course, $100 12-course, $45 pre-theater
Ⓜ 59th Street/Columbus Circle (A, C, B, D, 1, 9)

SUSHI YASUDA

Off map 264 F18
204 East 43rd Street between Second and Third avenues
Tel 212/972-1001
www.sushiyasuda.com

Considered by many people to be the ultimate sushi restaurant in the city. Here owner Naomichi Yasuda displays his artistry, selecting the best fish, evaluating its texture, masterfully cutting it to release the best flavor, and cooking and seasoning the rice to perfection. Then he crafts a meal for the individuals who sit down at his sushi bar, according to their tastes and experience, and to the size of their mouths. It's custom-made perfection, but naturally it comes at a high price. For a delightful meal request one of his eight tuna specialties or one of the eel pieces for which he is renowned.

🕐 Mon–Fri 12–2.15, 6–10.15, Sat 6–10.15, closed Sun
🍴 L $140, D $140, wine $18 (sake)
Ⓜ 42nd Street/Grand Central (S, 4, 5, 6, 7)

TAKA

Map 264 D22
61 Grove Street between Bleecker and Seventh Avenue South
Tel 212/242-3699

Takako Yoneyama is a female sushi master, rare in a culture that has denied women such a role because their body temperature is one degree higher

EATING

TABLA

Map 264 E20
11 Madison Avenue at 25th Street
Tel 212/889-0667

Danny Meyer's Tabla delivers a superb dining experience with its plush décor, gracious service and fragrant cuisine. In the sensual coral and jade jewel box of a room upstairs, the menu offers Bombay native Floyd Cardoz's dishes, which use the spices of South India—tamarind, kokum, clove, cinnamon and black pepper. Goan-spiced crab cake, rice-flaked black bass, and duck samosa, set off by shaved fennel, almonds and dried fruit chutney are just a few favorites. The sorbets are packed with flavor. The wine selections pair beautifully with the food (16 by the glass). On the ground floor, the informal and very affordable Bread Bar serves a selection of tandoori dishes and small plates of superb Indian breads.

🕐 Mon–Fri 12–2.30, Mon–Thu 5.30–10.30, Fri–Sun 5.30–11
🍽 L $80, D $150, 3-course prix fixe $54, wine $21
🚇 23rd Street (N, R, W), 23rd Street (6)
🚌 M2, M3

than a man's. At this atypical restaurant with western-style paintings and bentwood chairs, she wields her knives creatively and delivers a bento box containing sushi, sashimi, shumai and other small dishes that's a real bargain.

🕐 Tue–Sun 5–11, closed Mon
🍽 D $55
🚇 Christopher Street/Sheridan Square (1, 9)
🚌 M20

TAMARIND

Map 264 E20
41-43 East 22nd Street between Broadway and Park Avenue South
Tel 212/674-7400
www.tamarinde22.com

Tamarind breaks all of the Indian clichés. The dining room is sleek, modern and comfortable, the cuisine fresh and the wine list expansive. The flavor of the restaurant's namesake fruit infuses many

of the wonderful dishes, such as the shrimp cooked in coconut sauce flavored with curry leaves and smoked tamarind, but there are other flavors as well—the she-crab soup with sweet spices, ginger and saffron is another winner. The lamb vindaloo is authentically spiced, as are many of the vegetarian dishes. Some are refreshingly new—*bhindi do piazza*, which is okra flavored with brown onions and dried mango, for example. Even the desserts shine.

🕐 Daily 11.30–3, 5.30–11.30
🍽 L $55, D $70, wine $30
🚇 23rd Street (N, R), 23rd Street (6)
🚌 M1, M2, M3, M6, M7

TANGERINE

Map 264 D22
228 West 10th Street between Bleecker and Hudson streets
Tel 212 463-8585
www.tangerinebarandrestaurant.com

The lighting at this sleek dining room is worthy of the stage. And so too is the beautifully presented food. The limited menu makes for some carefully crafted dishes. Curries (yellow, green and masaman) are well spiced and the salads wonderfully piquant, whether mango, papaya or beef. The specialties, though, are the combination plates—towers of tasting delights made with meat, seafood or vegetables.

🕐 Daily 5.30pm–midnight
🍽 D $55, wine $32
🚇 Christopher Street/Sheridan Square (1, 9)
🚌 M20

TASTING ROOM

Map 265 F22
72 East 1st Street between First and Second avenues
Tel 212/358-7831

This small restaurant offers just a dozen jewel-like tasting dishes. Based on seasonal vegetables, fish, and meat,

they range from asparagus terrine with crayfish jus, radishes and bacon vinaigrette, to Rhode Island oysters with vanilla oil, tapioca and sherry vinaigrette. Every dish has a surprise element, like the candied fennel that comes with the brown butter-lemon tart. The 300 American wines, 10 by the glass, include some hard-to-find selections.

🕐 Tue–Sat 5.30–11.30, closed Sun–Mon
🍽 D $75, wine $19
🚇 Lower East Side/Second Avenue (F, V)
🚌 M15

TAVERN ON THE GREEN

Map 262 D16
Central Park West at 67th Street
Tel 212/873-3200
www.tavernonthegreen.com

Visitors are drawn to this bauble of a restaurant at the edge of Central Park, shaded by stately trees outlined after dark by thousands of twinkling fairy lights. The view from the Crystal Room and the summer dining terrace creates a certain magical, festive look. Against all odds, the Tavern delivers a memorable dining experience—despite its stature as a prime visitor destination, despite its size, and despite the breadth of its menu, which ranges from prime rib with Yorkshire pudding to sautéed rainbow trout in brown butter sauce. The wine list boasts 1,000 selections, a 1975 Chateau Petrus among them. From May to mid-October you can dance under the stars in the garden areas from 9pm.

🕐 Mon–Fri 11.30–3.30, Sat–Sun 10–3.30, Sun–Thu 5–10.30, Fri–Sat 5–11.30
🍽 L $100, prix fixe $25, D $115, prix fixe $45, pre-theater $35, wine $29
🚇 66th Street (1, 9)
🚌 M10

EATING

TOMOE SUSHI
Map 265 E22
172 Thompson Street between Bleecker and Houston streets
Tel 212/777-9346
Around the corner from New York University, this plain sushi parlor does a brisk trade among students and other sushi aficionados, drawn by its reasonable prices. About 30 different sushi choices and 30 varieties of maki rolls are available, along with traditional hot dishes and noodles.
🔵 Mon 5–11, Wed–Sat 1–3, 5–11, closed Tue and Sun
🍴 L $40, D $60
🚇 West 4th Street (A, C, E, F, V, S)
🚌 M5, M6, M21

TOWN
Map 262 E17
Chambers Hotel
15 West 56th Street between Fifth and Sixth avenues
Tel 212/582-4445
www.townnyc.com
Strands of crystal beads suspended in the two-story loft space in this stylish subterranean dining room swathed in suede and blond wood sparkle magically. Chef Geoffrey Zakarian's fusion cuisine sparkles, too. Start with the fragrant octopus fricassee in lemongrass broth, or the lobster bisque, zapped with ginger, coconut and wood sorrel. Zakarian poaches or roasts his fish to retain moisture, wrapping cod in pancetta and drizzled with porcini curry foam, for instance; the venison is simply slow-roasted to exquisite tenderness. Desserts are showstoppers.
🔵 Daily 7am–10.30am, Mon–Fri 12–2, Mon–Thu 5.30–10.30, Fri–Sat 5.30–11, Sun 11–2, 5.30–9
🍴 D $90, 3-course prix fixe $68, wine $30
🚇 53rd Street/Fifth Avenue (E, V)
🚌 M1, M2, M3, M4, M57

'21' CLUB
Map 262 E17
21 West 52nd Street between Fifth and Sixth avenues
Tel 212/582-7200
www.21club.com
The hamburger makes headlines for its price ($27 and climbing), but this storied locale is about so much more than the sandwich. Two college students opened it as a speakeasy in Greenwich Village in 1920; it was frequented by Humphrey Bogart, F. Scott Fitzgerald and Joe Di Maggio after relocating to this townhouse in 1929. Old-fashioned and masculine, it purveys fist-sized medallions of beef flambéed with cognac and Dijon, chicken hash and Dover sole, along with newer, lighter dishes like black sea bass in champagne sauce. The daily special ice creams, gussied up or plain, are the choice desserts, and the wine cellar is renowned. Jacket and tie required.
🔵 Mon–Fri 12–2.30, Mon–Sat 5.30–9, closed Sun
🍴 L $160, D $180, wine $45
🚇 47th–50th streets (B, D, F, V)
🚌 M1, M2, M3, M4, M5, M6, M7

UNCLE VANYA CAFE
Map 262 D17
315 West 54th Street between Eighth and Ninth avenues
Tel 212/262-0542
Russian home cooking starts at this plain storefront restaurant: hearty borscht, beef dumplings with sour cream, stuffed cabbage rolls and beef Stroganoff with kasha. It's all good and filling and costs very little. Try one of the Georgian wines, if you dare.
🔵 Mon–Sat 12–11, Sun 2–10
🍴 $40, wine $25
🚇 50th Street (C, E)
🚌 M10, M11, M20

UNION PACIFIC
Map 264 F20
111 East 22nd Street between Park Avenue South and Lexington Avenue
Tel 212/995-8500
www.unionpacificrestaurant.com
Celebrity Chef Rocco DiSpirito's dazzling French-Asian cuisine suits the dining room, with its Asian-inspired bridge of life and falling water. Foie gras comes with garlands of green papaya with tamarind sauce, while uni, tomato water and mustard oil enliven the Taylor Bay scallops. Seafood dishes stand out—tuna with yuzu juice and fresh wasabi, or black cod with saffron sauce, for example. Wines are categorized by varietal.
🔵 Mon–Fri 12–2, 5.30–10, Sat 5.15–10.30, closed Sun
🍴 L $90, D prix fixe: $68, wine $38
🚇 23rd Street (6)
🚌 M1, M2, M3

UNION SQUARE CAFÉ
Map 264 E21
21 East 16th Street between Fifth Avenue and Union Square West
Tel 212/243-4020

Union Square Café remains a darling of the downtown publishing industry because it delivers on every aspect of the dining experience from the comfortable but not-too-fussy setting to the warm but thoroughly professional service. Michael Romano's bold Tuscan cuisine is thoughtfully imaginative and always flavorful. The meats and fishes are grilled to perfection and enhanced with just the right combination of ingredients. Try the pan-roasted black sea bass with chick peas, roasted peppers, toasted almonds and cumin, or the organic chicken with buttermilk-sage potatoes and sautéed Savoy cabbage. The signature warm banana tart with honey-vanilla ice cream and macadamia brittle is perfect. The 200-plus wine list is organized by varietal.
🔵 Mon–Sat 12–2.30, Mon–Thu 6–10.30, Fri–Sat 6–11.30, Sun 5.30–10
🍴 L $70, D $90, wine $20
🚇 14th Street/Union Square (L, N, Q, R, W, 4, 5, 6)
🚌 M2, M3, M5, M7

VERITAS
Map 264 E20
43 East 20th Street between Broadway and Park Avenue South
Tel 212/353-3700
With 2,700 selections Veritas has the most comprehensive wine list in the city; in fact, the list itself sells for $70. And the kitchen offers some gutsy cuisine to go with the wines. Expect pepper-crusted venison with Armagnac or juniper, or braised short ribs in Barolo reduction. Even a dish like black bass brings a surprise—here it arrives in lemon truffle vinaigrette and foie gras butter.

EATING

Hot chocolate and doughnuts is the signature dessert.

🕐 Mon–Sat 5.30–10, Sun 5–9.30
🍽 D 3-course prix fixe $68, wine $14
🚇 23rd Street (N, R), 23rd Street (6)
🚌 M1, M2, M3, M6, M7

VIETNAM
Map 265 F24
11 Doyers Street between Bowery and Pell Street
Tel 212/693-0725

Tasty and authentic Vietnamese fare is the draw at this plain subterranean dining room. On the vast menu, the satay is good, and so are the spicy black bean dishes. Other hits include shrimp paste on sugar cane with thin rice noodle, and the papaya salad made with shrimp, grilled beef or pork. No credit cards.

🕐 Sun–Thu 11–9.30, Fri–Sat 11–10.30
🍽 L $20, D $24
🚇 Canal Street (J, M, Z, N, Q, R, W, 6)
🚌 M103

VIRGIL'S REAL BARBECUE
Map 264 D18
152 West 44th Street between Sixth Avenue and Broadway
Tel 212/921-9494
www.virgilsbbq.com

The aroma of hickory wood smoke alone is enough to draw you into this vast barbecue emporium. Here, the huge platters of Memphis-style barbecue or fried chicken arrive with grits or mashed potatoes and biscuits and gravy. Po'boys, also known as hero sandwiches, round out the southern-style menu.

🕐 Tue–Sat 11.30am–midnight, Mon 11.30–11, Sun 11.30–10
🍽 L $50, D $65, wine $24
🚇 42nd Street/Times Square (N, Q, R, S, W, 1, 2, 3, 7, 9), 42nd Street (B, D, F, V)
🚌 M5, M6, M7

VONG
Map 263 F17
200 East 54th Street at Third Avenue

Tel 212/486-9592

When Jean-Georges launched his French-Asian cuisine, it was revolutionary. Today, it's just plain beautiful, and the explosive flavors still dance on the tongue. Vongerichten worked in Thailand, Hong Kong and Singapore in the 1980s, and the flavors of lemongrass, cilantro, ginger and coconut milk changed his life.

🕐 Mon–Fri 12–2.30, 6–11, Sat 5.30–11.30, Sun 5.30–10
🍽 L$85, 3-course prix fixe $20, D tasting menu $68, 3-course pre-theater $38, wine $38
🚇 53rd Street/Lexington Avenue (F, V), 51st Street (6)
🚌 M98, M101, M102, M103

WASHINGTON PARK
Map 265 E22
24 Fifth Avenue at 9th Street
Tel 212/529-4400
www.washingtonparknyc.com

Jonathan Waxman, who apprenticed at Berkeley's Chez Panisse, brought California cuisine to New York in the 1980s, and then disappeared. Now he's back at this elegantly casual Village bistro a few blocks north of Washington Square Park. Chiogga and golden yellow beets and asparagus are dressed in tangy, blood orange vinaigrette; the mushroom dishes are always extraordinary. Pork tenderloin brined in salt, maple sugar, juniper berries, peppercorns, bay leaves and coriander, and sake-marinated sable with tangerine butter are among the accomplished entrées. Finish with brioche pudding with lemon curd and blueberries. The international wine list offers 1,000 selections. The prix fixe luncheon is a phenomenal value.

🕐 Mon–Fri 12–2.30, Mon–Sat 5.30–11, Sun 5–10
🍽 L $80, prix fixe $20, D $105, wine $12

🚇 West 4th Street (A, C, E, F, V)
🚌 M2, M3, M5, M8

WD-50
Map 265 G23
50 Clinton Street between Stanton and Rivington streets (east side of the street)
Tel 212/477-2900

Wylie Dufresne made the Lower East Side a dining destination when he cooked at 71 Clinton Street. Now he has his own place, a sleek postmodern dining room where he mixes exciting but harmonious flavor combinations—oysters with Granny Smith apple and pistachios, monkfish with black trumpet mushrooms and snow peas in bonito broth with mint oil. Desserts are also creative.

🕐 Mon–Sat 6–11, closed Sun
🍽 D $100, wine $30
🚇 Delancey (F), Essex (J, M, Z)
🚌 M9, M21

WOO LAE OAK
Map 265 E23
148 Mercer Street between Houston and Prince streets
Tel 212/925-8200
www.woolaeoaksoho.com

Here, you'll find a stylized American version of Korean cuisine. Start with the hot Dungeness crab wrapped in spinach crèpes, or tuna tartare served over Korean pear. Among the selections for the on-the-table barbecue there are 17 meats, fishes and vegetables, including ostrich, squid and tripe. Among other dishes, short ribs are swathed in sweet soy sauce, and then there are soups, casseroles and rice dishes. Don't forget the kimchi—the pickle dishes that are a perennial presence on the Korean table.

🕐 Sun–Thu 12–11, Fri–Sat 12–11.30
🍽 $66, prix fixe $15 and $20, wine $30
🚇 Broadway/Lafayette (F, V, S), Prince Street (N, R), Bleecker Street (6)
🚌 M1, M5

EATING

MAJOR RESTAURANT CHAINS

New York is a good place for eclectic and unusual eating, but there are also plenty of tried and tested chains, where you know exactly what you're getting and how much you'll have to pay.

	Price range ($–$$$)	Alcohol	Child Menu	Takeaway	Phone Number	Website
RESTAURANTS						
Baluchi's	$$	Yes	No	Yes	212/594-5533	www.baluchis.com
Burritoville	$	No	Yes	Yes	212/563-9010	Www.burritoville.com
California Pizza Kitchen	$$	Yes	Yes	Yes	310/342-5000	www.californiapizzakitchen.com
Lemongrass Grill	$$	Yes	No	Yes	718/399-7100	www.lemongrassgrill.com
Patsy's Pizzeria	$$	Yes	No	Yes	212/688-5916	www.patsyspizzeria.com
Pizzeria Uno	$$	Yes	Yes	Yes	617/323-9200	www.pizzeriauno.com
TGI Friday's	$$	Yes	Yes	Yes	972/450-5400	www.Fridays.com
Pizza Hut	$	some	Yes	Yes	972/338-7700	www.pizzahut.com
Two Boots Pizzeria	$	No	Yes	Yes	212/777-2668	www.twoboots.com
Xando Cosi	$	Yes	Yes	Yes	212/653-1600	www.xandocosi.com
Zen Palate	$$	No	No	Yes	212/614-9345	Www.zenpalate.com

	Price range ($–$$$)	Alcohol	Child Menu	Takeaway	Phone Number	Website
SANDWICHES AND FAST FOOD						
Au Bon Pain	$	No		Yes	617/423-2100	www.aubonpain.com
Burger King	$	No	Yes	Yes	305/378-3000	www.burgerking.com
Cosí Sandwich Bar	$	Yes		Yes	212/653-1600	www.getcosi.com
Kentucky Fried Chicken	$	No	Yes	Yes	800/225-5532	www.kfc.com
Le Pain Quotidien	$	No	No	Yes	212/625-9009	www.painquotidien.com
Little Pie Company	$	No		Yes	212/414-2324	www.littlepiecompany.com
McDonald's	$	No	Yes	Yes	800/244-6227	www.mcdonalds.com
Pret à Manger	$	No	No	Yes	646/728-0750	www.pretamanger.com
Subway	$	No	Yes	Yes	203/877-4281	www.subway.com
Wendy's	$	No	Yes	Yes	614/764-3100	www.wendys.com

	Price range ($–$$$)	Alcohol	Child Menu	Takeaway	Phone Number	Website
COFFEE SHOPS						
Dean and DeLuca	$	No	No	Yes	877/826-9246	www.deananddeluca.com
Krispy Kreme Donuts	$	No	No	Yes	800/457-4779	www.krispykreme.com
Starbucks	$	No	No	Yes	800/782-7282	www.starbucks.com

TASTING & STAYING

Staying

Hostelling International

Newton

West 95th Street

UPPER WEST
SIDE

West 94th Street

West 93rd Street

West 92nd Street

West 91st Street

West 90th Street

West 89th Street

West 88th Street

West 87th Street

West 86th Street

86th
Street

86th
Street

West 85th Street

West 84th Street

West 83rd Street

West 82nd Street

81st Street
Museum
of Nat Hist

Excelsior

West 81st Street

West 80th Street

Lucerne

American Museum
of Natural History

West 79th Street

79th
Street

West 78th Street

On the
Avenue

West 77th Street

New-York
Historical
Society

West 76th Street

Milburn

West 75th Street

San Remo
Apartments

Beacon

West 74th Street

Ansonia
Building

West 73rd Street

The Dakota

West 72nd Street

72nd
Street

72nd
Street

West 71st Street

West 70th Street

West 69th Street

West
69th
Street

West
68th
Street

West 68th Street

West 67th Street

66th Street
Lincoln Center

Juilliard School

West 66th Street

West 65th Street

Tavern on
the Green

West 64th Street

Lincoln
Center

Empire

West Side YMCA

West 63rd Street

West 63rd Street

West 62nd Street

American
Bible Society

Mayflower Hotel
on the Park

West 61st Street

West 61st Street

Trump International
Hotel & Tower

West 60th Street

59th Street
Columbus
Circle

West 59th Street

COLUMBUS
CIRCLE

West 59th
street

West 58th Street

West 57th Street

Hudson

Westpark

57th
Street

WEST 57TH STREET

West 56th Street

Moderne

Wellington

West 55th Street

West 54th Street

7th
Avenue

West 53rd Street

De Witt
Clinton Park

West 52nd Street

West 51st Street

West 50th Street

50th
Street

50th
Street

49th
Street

West 49th Street

West 48th Street

Belvedere

West 47th Street

Edison

BROADWAY

Paramount

West 46th Street

Broadway
Inn

West 45th Street

Intrepid Sea-
Air Space Museum

West 46th
Street

Hudson River

Riverside Park

Riverside Drive

Highway 9A

West End Avenue

BROADWAY

Amsterdam Avenue

Columbus Avenue

Central Park West

Central Park

Strawberry
Fields

The
Lake

CE
P

79th street

65th

Freedom
Place

Riverside
Boulevard

West 64th Street

West End Avenue

Amsterdam Avenue

Columbus Avenue

Central Park West

Central
Park

12th Av

11th Avenue

10th AVENUE

9th AVENUE

8th
Avenue

7th
Avenue

BROADWAY

12TH
AVENUE

B   C   D

STAYING IN NEW YORK

There are plenty of hotel rooms in New York City, but it is hard to find a comfortable room under $150. If money is no object, then reserve a room at the Carlyle or the Four Seasons.

For less expensive options, check out the inexpensive chains—Red Roof, Super 8, and others. The city also has some bed-and-breakfasts, which charge less than the average hotel and provide good-value extras. Hostels are the least expensive lodging options.

It used to be that all the best hotels were in Midtown but that has changed dramatically. Now, there are first-class luxury hotels downtown in SoHo, Greenwich Village and the Financial District. Still, there are more bargains away from Midtown. New York City hotels range in size from vast 2,000-room monstrosities to smaller establishments with 250 rooms or less. If you stay at a large convention hotel, expect to find crowded lobbies, more lines, and slower service. Most hotels have similar amenities. The average hotel room comes with air-conditioning, private bathroom, cable TV, telephone, coffeemaker, hairdryer, iron and ironing board. The level of luxury and the quality and range of the service are the real distinctions between hotels. Top-class hotel rooms boast luxe fabrics and linens (Frette, Pratesi), high-tech electronics and telephony, and high staff-to-guest ratios, which guarantees prompt courteous service. Space is at a premium in Manhattan, so expect rooms to be on the small side. Double-glazed windows, which are usually standard, help reduce noise. Most hotels have complimentary coffee/tea service and newspapers either in the lobby or delivered to the room.

Today there is no such thing as a standard rack rate. Prices fluctuate with customer demand. To get the best rate on a hotel room, always call the hotel directly and ask for the best available rate and what special discounts are available. Alternatively, go online to such discount services as hotel.com, quickbook.com or hoteldiscounts.com to secure the best rates. Winter (Jan–Feb) is the least expensive season. Parking charges of $30 and up will add substantially to any bill. Note, too, that 13.625% will be added to your bill, plus $2 occupancy tax on a standard room and $4 on a one-bedroom suite.

PRICES

Prices are for a double room for one night, including breakfast and sales tax. All the hotels listed accept credit cards unless otherwise stated.

ABINGDON GUEST HOUSE
Map 294 D21
13 Eighth Avenue at West 12th Street, 10014
Tel 212/243-5384
www.abingdonguesthouse.com
Located in two historic three-story red-brick town-houses above a coffee shop in Greenwich Village, the guest house is unmarked. The nine rooms are individually decorated and well furnished with antiques. Amenities include private bath (with hairdryer), cable TV and telephone. The patio garden is a bonus.
🅑 $147–232
🅘 9
🅜 14th Street (A, C, E), Christopher Street/Sheridan Square (1, 9)
🚌 M20, M14

ALGONQUIN
Map 294 E18
59 West 44th Street between Fifth and Sixth avenues, 10036
Tel 212/840-6800
www.algonquinhotel.com
It's famous for being the place where in the 1920s Robert Benchley, Dorothy Parker, and the rest of the *Vanity Fair/New Yorker* crowd gathered regularly for lunch at the Round Table. The rooms are moderate in size and furnished with reproductions of American antiques. The wood-paneled Oak Room is the city's best cabaret, and there's a fitness center.
🅑 $199–259, suite from $299
🅘 150 rooms, 24 suites
🅜 42nd Street (B, D, F, V)
🚌 M5, M7, M42

AMERICANA INN
Map 294 E18
69 West 38th Street between Fifth and Sixth avenues, 10018
Tel 212/840-6700
www.newyorkhotel.com
Rooms here are bright, modern and comfortable, if plainly decorated. They are equipped with cable TV and telephone. All rooms share a bath, and each floor has a kitchenette.
🅑 $85
🅘 51
🅜 42nd Street (B, D, F, V)
🚌 M5, M6, M7

AVALON
Map 294 E19
16 East 32nd Street at Madison Avenue, 10016
Tel 212/299-7000
www.theavalonny.com

This small hotel is near the Empire State Building and has traditionally furnished rooms. Executive suites have fax, Bose radio and cordless phone. Complimentary breakfast and afternoon tea are set out in the mahogany-paneled library off the lobby. The Avalon Bar and Grill serves contemporary American cuisine. Guests have access to a gym nearby.

STAYING

$179–249, suite from $229, including breakfast
🛏 20 rooms, 80 suites
Ⓜ 33rd Street (6)
🚌 M1, M2, M3, M4, M34

BEACON
Map 292 C15
2130 Broadway between 74th and 75th streets, 10023
Tel 212/787-1100
www.beaconhotel.com

Less than 10 blocks from Lincoln Center and close to Central Park, this 25-story hotel offers good value. Guests can save money using the kitchenette with stove, microwave and refrigerator. Amenities include TV, telephone and hairdryer. 24-hour restaurant and fitness center.
$195–235, suite from $275
🛏 120 rooms, 110 suites
Ⓜ 72nd Street (1, 2, 3, 9)
🚌 M7, M11, M104

BEEKMAN TOWER
Map 293 F17
3 Mitchell Place (East 49th Street and First Avenue), 10017
Tel 212/355-7300
www.mesuite.com
This all-suite hotel, in a 1928 art-deco building near the UN, has accommodations that include bedroom, sitting room and fully equipped kitchen. The deluxe suites have such extras as VCRs and two-line phones. The bar/ restaurant on the top floor is one of the most romantic aeries in the city. Fitness center on-premises.

$380–440, 2-bedroom suite $700
🛏 174 suites
Ⓜ 51st Street (6)
🚌 M15

BELVEDERE
Map 292 D17
319 West 48th Street between Eighth and Ninth avenues, 10036
Tel 212/245-7000
www.newyorkhotel.com
The most expensive hotel in the Empire Hotel group, the Belvedere has handsome sizable rooms with kitchenettes fitted with microwave, refrigerator and coffeemaker. Executive rooms are also available. On premises, the Churrascaria Plataforma is a Brazilian steakhouse.
$160–420
🛏 400 rooms and suites
Ⓜ 50th Street (C, E)
🚌 M11, M20, M50

BENJAMIN
Map 293 F17
125 East 50th Street at Lexington Avenue, 10022
Tel 212/320-8002
www.thebenjamin.com
Conveniently situated in Midtown, this Manhattan Suites hotel offers good-looking rooms and excellent facilities in a handsome 1927 building. The rooms are furnished with mahogany pieces. Guests can select from a ten type pillow menu. The Woodstock spa and fitness studio is a bonus. Seafood restaurant and chop house.

$389–420
🛏 209
Ⓜ 51st Street (6)
🚌 M98, M101, M102, M103, M50

BIG APPLE HOSTEL
Map 294 D18
119 West 45th Street between Sixth and Seventh avenues, 10036
Tel 212/302-2603
www.bigapplehostel.com
You can't beat the location of

CARLYLE
Map 293 E14
35 East 76th Street between Madison and Park avenues, 10021
Tel 212/744-1600
www.rosewoodhotels.com

This is a striking art-deco building. The rooms boast large bathrooms and every conceivable amenity. The public areas are classics, particularly Bemelman's Bar with its charming murals and the Café where Bobby Short plays. Facilities include fitness center and pool.
$525–850, suite from $950
🛏 124 rooms, 56 suites
Ⓜ 77th Street (4,5)
🚌 M1, M2, M3, M4

this hostel. It's large and busy. Accommodations are in single-sex or coed dorms with 4 beds per room, or in private rooms with shared bath. Amenities are good and furnishings are modern. International visitors meet one another in the common room and kitchen, or on the back deck with grill.
Dorm $35–45, private room $85–116
🛏 116 beds
Ⓜ 42nd Street (B, D, F, V)
🚌 M6, M7

BROADWAY INN
Map 294 D18
264 West 46th Street between Broadway and Eighth Avenue, 10036
Tel 212/997-9200
www.broadwayinn.com
In the Theater District, this cozy small hotel could be found in London, or any other European city. The second-floor lobby welcomes guests to a comfortable hearth and book-lined aerie. The rooms vary in size, but it's one of the few places in town where a solo traveler

STAYING

can rent a single room—and save money doing so. They are basically decorated and have such amenities as cable TV, telephone and hairdryer. Suites have extras such as a refrigerator and microwave. Quietest rooms are in the back. No elevator. Restaurant on premises.

💵 $159, suite from $250, including breakfast
🛏 31 rooms, 10 suites
🚇 42nd Street (A, C, E), 42nd Street/Times Square (N, Q, R, S, W, 1, 2, 3, 7, 9)
🚌 M6, M7, M20, M27, M104

CASABLANCA
Map 294 D18
147 West 43rd Street between Sixth and Seventh avenues, 10036
Tel 212/869-1212
www.casablancahotel.com
Close to the Theater District, the boutique-style Casablanca is small and personal and offers stylish, modern, well-equipped rooms. The public areas have a Moroccan feel with tiles and rattan chairs.

💵 $275–325, suite from $395, including breakfast and evening wine and cheese (weekdays only)
🛏 40 rooms, 8 suites
🚇 42nd Street/Times Square (N, Q, R, S, W, 1, 2, 3, 7, 9), 42nd Street (B, D, F, V)
🚌 M6, M7, M10, M20

CHELSEA
Map 294 D20
222 West 23rd Street between Seventh and Eighth avenues, 10011
Tel 212/243-3700
www.chelseahotel.com

Many artists and bohemians have stayed or lived here since it opened in 1884, including Mark Twain and Dylan Thomas. The most lurid recorded event here was the killing of Nancy by Sid Vicious supposedly in room 100. The rooms vary in size and décor. Serena's, the bar opened by Serena Bass, attracts a Brit-pack crowd.

💵 $200–325, suite from $330
🛏 375 rooms (250 permanent residents)
🚇 23rd Street (C, E), 23rd Street (1, 9)
🚌 M20, M23

CHELSEA CENTER HOSTEL
Map 294 D19
313 West 29th Street between Eighth and Ninth avenues, 10031
Tel 212/643-0214
www.chelseacenterhostel.com
What makes the difference at this small friendly hostel is that it's owner operated. It has a good location and some extra special facilities including a small garden. There's also a kitchen and common rooms. Rooms are dormitory style.

💵 $35
🛏 20 beds
🚇 34th Street (A, C, E)
🚌 M11, M20

CHELSEA INTERNATIONAL HOSTEL
Map 294 D20
251 West 20th Street between Seventh and Eighth avenues, 10011
Tel 212/647-0010
www.chelseahostel.com
This large hostel has single-sex dormitory-style accommodations and some private rooms.

💵 Dorm $30, private rooms $65
🛏 350 beds
🚇 18th Street (1, 9)
🚌 M20

CHELSEA LODGE
Map 294 D20
318 West 20th Street between Eighth and Ninth avenues, 10001
Tel 212/243-4499
www.chelsealodge.com
In very fashionable Chelsea, this small hotel occupies a handsome red-brick townhouse, which has been lovingly restored by the owners. The rooms are decorated in plain American country style with patterned wallpaper and eclectic furnishings. Most have hardwood floors and small TVs, plus sink and shower. Toilet is down the hall.

💵 $110
🛏 22
🚇 23rd Street (C, E)
🚌 M11, M20

CHELSEA SAVOY
Map 294 D20
204 West 23rd Street at Seventh Avenue (southwest corner) 10011
Tel 212/929-9353
www.chelseasavoynyc.com
This modern hotel offers good, if unexciting, value. The motel-style furnished rooms (floral bedspreads, etc.), feature such extras as small refrigerators, hairdryers and phones with data ports.

💵 $99–185, including breakfast
🛏 90
🚇 23rd Street
🚌 M20

COSMOPOLITAN HOTEL–TRIBECA
Map 295 E24
95 West Broadway at Chambers Street, 10007
Tel 212/566-1900
www.cosmohotel.com

This hotel has a great downtown location and good-looking rooms. They're all furnished with industrial-style carpeting and Scandinavian-style pieces, but they have private bath, TV and telephone.

💵 $119–129
🛏 105
🚇 Chambers Street (1, 2, 3, 9), Chambers Street (A, C)
🚌 M20

EDISON
Map 294 D18
228 West 47th Street between
Broadway and Eighth Avenue, 10036
Tel 212/840-5000.
www.edisonhotelnyc.com
Theater patrons appreciate this
art-deco 1931 hotel in the
center of the Theater District.
The entrance lobby is somewhat bland but functional. The
rooms are moderately priced
and have cable TV and telephone. Restaurant and bar too.
🅗 $155–190, suite from $250
ℹ 1,000 rooms, 30 suites
🅢 50th Street (C, E), 50th Street (1, 9)
🚌 M6, M7, M20, M27, M104

ELYSEE
Map 293 E17
60 East 54th Street, 10022
Tel 212/753-1066
www.elyseehotel.com

This little gem of a hotel, built
in 1926, has comfortable
rooms decorated with fine
French antique reproductions
and luxurious fabrics.
Bathrooms are marble and
brass. The Monkey Bar, named
for its murals, was once home
to such regulars as Tallulah
Bankhead. Guests have use of
a nearby sports club.
🅗 $350–395, suite from $400, including Continental breakfast and wine and
cheese (weekday evenings)
ℹ 85 rooms, 14 suites
🅢 53rd Street/Fifth Avenue (E, V), 51st
Street (6)

EMPIRE
Map 292 D16
44 West 63rd Street between Broadway
and Amsterdam Avenue,
10023
Tel 212/265-7400
www.empirehotel.com
Right across the street from
the Lincoln Center, the
Empire's rooms are well
equipped with dual-line
phones, CD players and VCRs.
Guests may use the nearby
New York Sports Club. The

West 63rd Street Steakhouse
serves breakfast and lunch.
🅗 $119–239, suite from $209
ℹ 381 rooms and suites
🅢 66th Street (1, 9)
🚌 M5, M7, M11, M104

EXCELSIOR
Map 292 D14
45 West 81st Street between Columbus
Avenue and Central Park West, 10024
Tel 212/362-9200
One of the few hotels on the
Upper West Side, near the
Natural History Museum, the
Excelsior offers spotless
modern rooms equipped with
cable TV, dual-line phone with
data port, and such niceties as
bathrobes. Small, decently
equipped exercise room.
🅗 $199–339, suite from $269
ℹ 116 rooms, 80 suites
🅢 81st Street (B, C)
🚌 M7, M11, M10, M79

SPECIAL
FOUR SEASONS
Map 293 E16
57 East 57th Street between Madison
and Park avenues, 10022
Tel 212/758-5700
www.fourseasons.com

The service at this hotel is
legendary; staff are trained to
cater to a guest's every whim.
I. M. Pei designed the 53-
story building, which opened
in 1993. The rooms, averag-
ing 600-square feet (55sq.
meters) are the largest in the
city and include a dressing
area. The suites have walk-in
closets and balconies with
grand city views. The large
fitness center contains a full
spa, and the restaurant and
bar are both top-of-the-line.
🅗 $530–895, suite from $1075
ℹ 305 rooms, 63 suites
🅢 59th Street (4, 5, 6)
🚌 M1, M2, M3, M4

FRANKLIN
Map 293 F13
164 East 87th Street between Lexington
and Third avenues, 10128
Tel 212/369-1000
www.franklinhotel.com
Well located for the Museum
Mile on the Upper East Side,
this small boutique hotel is
stylish and reasonably
priced. Standard equipment
includes VCRs.
🅗 $159–249, including breakfast
ℹ 48
🅢 86th Street (4, 5, 6)
🚌 M98, M101, M102, M103, M86

GERSHWIN
Map 294 E20
7 East 27th Street between Fifth and
Madison avenues, 10016
Tel 212/545-8000
www.gershwinhotel.com
The Gershwin attracts young
budget travelers, who stay in
plain doubles or dormitory-
style rooms with ten beds.
Rooms have cable TV and
phone. Every night live bands
play in the rough-and-ready
Red Room bar.
🅗 $109–229, suite from $269, dorm
for two $53, women only dorm $43,
coed dorm $33
ℹ 130 rooms, 6 suites
🅢 28th Street (N, R, W)
🚌 M2, M3

GIRAFFE
Map 294 F20
365 Park Avenue South between 26th
and 27th streets, 10016
Tel 212/685-7700
www.hotelgiraffe.com

A small boutique hotel in the
Flatiron neighborhood evokes
the 1920s and 1930s. Each
floor has only seven rooms,
decorated in glamorous colors
and materials. Many have
balconies. On-premises
restaurant, plus access to a
nearby health club.
🅗 $285–350, suite from $450, including breakfast and wine and cheese
(weekday evenings)

ⓘ 52 rooms, 21 suites
Ⓜ 23rd Street (6)
🚌 M1

GORHAM
Map 292 D17
136 West 55th Street between Sixth and
Seventh avenues, 10019
Tel 212/245-1800
www.gorhamhotel.com

Chandeliers hang in the lobby,
and the rooms are traditionally
decorated with dark cabinetry
and equipped with kitchenette
(microwave, refrigerator, coffeemaker), two-line telephone,
modular jack, cable TV, fax and
VCR. The marble bathrooms
have hair dryers and bathrobes
(whirlpool tubs in suites). Bar
and fitness center on premises.
💰 £235–460, suite from $275
ⓘ 71 rooms, 44 suites
Ⓜ 57th Street (N, R, Q, W), 57th
Street (F)
🚌 M5, M6, M7, M57

GRACIE INN
Map 293 G14
502 East 81st Street between York and
East End avenues, 10028
Tel 212/628-1700
www.thegracieinn.com
Slightly off the beaten track,
near the Mayor's mansion, this
inn attracts long-term guests to
12 apartments in a five-story
building. Each has a kitchenette, plus TV and phone
with data port. The penthouses
have waterbeds, whirlpool
tubs and sundecks. Breakfast
delivered to the room is a welcome indulgence.
💰 $139–179 studio, 1-bedroom suite
from $189
ⓘ 12 rooms, 2 suites
Ⓜ 77th St (6)
🚌 M15, M31, M79

GRAND UNION
Map 294 E19
34 East 32nd Street between Madison
and Park avenues, 10016
Tel 212/683-5890
This old-fashioned hotel in the

trend-setting Flatiron neighborhood has clean basic rooms
that are equipped with small
refrigerators and phones with
data ports. Coffee shop.

💰 $109–160
ⓘ 95
Ⓜ 33rd Street (6)
🚌 M1, M2, M3, M34

HABITAT
Map 293 F17
130 East 57th Street at Lexington, 10022
Tel 212/753-8841
www.habitatny.com
Little wonder that budget travelers love this place. It has a
great location, and the contemporary rooms are clean,
comfortable and attractively
decorated. Some have shared
bath. All have cable TV and
telephone with data port.
💰 Shared bath $95–135, private bath
$135–195, suite from $250, including
breakfast
ⓘ 250 rooms, 50 suites
Ⓜ 59th Street (4, 5, 6)
🚌 M98, M101, M102, M103, M59

HOSTELLING INTERNATIONAL
Off map 292 C12
891 Amsterdam Avenue at 104th Street
Tel 212/932-2300
www.hinnewyork.org/home
This large facility on the Upper
West Side, a dozen blocks
south of Columbia University,
has dormitory-style accommodations with 4 to 12 beds.
Extra conveniences include
laundry, kitchen, and store plus
lounge, game room and café.
💰 Members $32–38, non-members
$36–42, private room $135
ⓘ 624 beds and 3 private rooms
Ⓜ 103 Street (1, 9)
🚌 M7, M11

HUDSON
Map 292 D16
356 West 58th Street between Eighth
and Ninth avenues, 10019
Tel 212/554-6000
www.hudsonhotel.com
The Hudson is Ian Schrager's

and Philippe Starck's latest
"hotel as on-going party".
Guests arrive in the ivy-draped
lobby via escalators encased in
a chartreuse-green tube. Starck
trademarks include oversized
chairs and other objects like
the 500-gallon watering can in
the garden courtyard. The
rooms are small and furnished
with minimalist stainless steel
pieces, plus the latest technical
amenities. The Library lounge
has plenty of leather, a hearth
and a dramatically lit antique
billiard table. A long gilded
table serves as a bar in the
lounge, which converts into a
dance club at night.
💰 $175–325, suite from $345
ⓘ 1000 rooms, 11 suites
Ⓜ 59th Street/Columbus Circle (A, B,
C, D, 1, 9)
🚌 M1, M20, M57

INN AT IRVING PLACE
Map 294 F21
56 Irving Place between East 17th and
18th Streets, 10003
Tel 212/533-4600
www.innatlrving.com.
These two 1834 town-houses
have plenty of ersatz atmosphere. Rooms have fireplaces
and four-poster beds dressed
with Frette linens, plus antique
reproductions. Amenities
include two-line telephones
with data port, VCRs, and CD
players. Guests sit on tufted
chairs around the fireplaces in
Lady Mendl's at afternoon tea.
Martini lounge, plus a café and
two restaurants.
💰 $295–435, suite from $500, including breakfast
ⓘ 5 rooms, 6 junior suites
Ⓜ 14th Street/Union Square (L, N, Q,
R, W, 4, 5, 6)
🚌 M1, M2, M3, M14

INN ON 23RD STREET
Map 294 D20
131 West 23rd Street between Sixth and
Seventh avenues, 10011
Tel 212/463-0330
www.www.bbonline.com/newyork
If you prefer a bed-and-break-
fast, then this inn located in a
19th-century townhouse (with
an elevator!) has much to
offer. The Fisherman family has
furnished it with family heirlooms and eclectic pieces. The
rooms have such modern
amenities as dual-line phone
(local calls are free).
Bathrooms are small. Guest
amenities include an inviting

second-floor library and an honor bar with liquor, wine and beer, plus a microwave.

🏨 $189–269, suite from $329, including breakfast
🛏 11
🚇 23rd Street (F, V), 23rd Street (1, 9)
🚌 M5, M6, M7, M20, M23

IROQUOIS

Map 294 E18
49 West 44th Street between Fifth and Sixth avenues, 10036
Tel 212/840-3080
www.iroquoisnyc.com

Fifty years ago this was James Dean's residence. When the 1923 building was renovated in 1998, the marble and stucco architectural details were retained. The rooms are equipped with 25-inch TV, dual phone with data port, VCR and CD player. Marble bathrooms have Frette robes and Molton Brown toiletries. There is 24-hour coffee and cappuccino in the tiny library-lounge, and a restaurant and fitness center.

🏨 $365–465, suite from $600
🛏 114 rooms, 9 suites
🚇 42nd Street/Grand Central (4, 5, 6), 42nd Street (B, D, F, V)
🚌 M1, M2, M3, M4, M42

KIMBERLY

Map 293 F17
145 East 50th Street between Third and Lexington avenues, 10022
Tel 212/755-0400
www.kimberlyhotel.com

This small personal hotel in Midtown has a European

flavor. Originally built in 1985 as an apartment house, it has large rooms with fully equipped kitchens. Some rooms have balconies; they all have three dual-line phones and fax/printer. Restaurant, bar and supper club round out the amenities. Guests have membership at the New York Health and Racquet Clubs.

🏨 $259–369, suite from $329
🛏 26 rooms, 158 suites
🚇 51st Street (6)
🚌 M98, M101, M102, M103, M50

LARCHMONT

Map 295 E21
27 West 11th Street between Fifth and Sixth avenues, 10011
Tel 212/989-9333
www.larchmontHotel.com

This is a great buy on an extra-quiet side street in Greenwich Village. It has plenty of character and appeals to European travelers who don't mind shared baths (bathrobe and slippers provided). The rooms are attractively decorated, ultra clean and well equipped with air conditioning, cable TV and telephone.

🏨 $100–125 including breakfast
🛏 58
🚇 14th Street (F, V), Sixth Avenue (L)
🚌 M2, M3, M5, M6

LE MARQUIS

Map 294 E19
12 East 31st Street between Fifth and Madison avenues, 10016
Tel 212/889-6363
www.lemarquisny.com

This 14-floor boutique hotel in the Murray Hill neighborhood occupies a 1903 Beaux-Arts building, which has been carefully renovated and decorated in retro style. Rooms are small but chic with CD and DVD. The library room has a desktop PC and 40-inch flat screen TV, and the 12:31 bar attracts a hip after-work crowd. There is a fitness room with sauna.

LE PARKER MERIDIEN

Map 292 D17
118 West 57th Street between Sixth and Seventh avenues, 10019
Tel 212/245-5000
www.parkermeridien.com

The rooms in this French hotel are furnished with sleek modernist pieces and contain the latest amenities—32-inch TV, ergonomic chairs, fax, DVD, CD player and free high-speed Internet access. Hip bistro-style Seppi's serves Mediterranean fare, while Norma's luxury all-day breakfast is famous. Jack's Lounge produces exotic cocktails. There is an excellent 42nd-floor fitness center with a rooftop jogging track.

🏨 $255–495, suite from $560
🛏 600 rooms, 100 suites
🚇 57th Street (N, R, Q, W)
🚌 M6, M7, M57

🏨 $229–329, suite from $495
🛏 120 rooms, 8 suites
🚇 33rd Street (6)
🚌 M2, M3, M5

LOWELL

Map 293 E16
28 East 63rd Street between Madison and Park avenues, 10021
Tel 212/838-1400
www.lhw.com

This little-known hotel, located in an elegant 1920s town-

STAYING

LIBRARY
Map 294 E18
299 Madison Avenue at 41st Street, 10017
Tel 212/983-4500
www.libraryhotel.com
It's not just the design concept that book lovers appreciate at this boutique property, it's also the service. Each floor of the hotel is dedicated to a subject category from the Dewey Decimal system and each room has a collection of art and books related to a sub-category. The décor is modern and minimalist. Amenities include multi-line phones with high-speed Internet access. Refreshments are served in the second-floor book-lined Reading Room. There's also an Italian restaurant and complimentary passes to a nearby fitness center.

🍽 $225–325, suite from $325, including breakfast
🛏 52 rooms, 8 suites
🚇 Grand Central/42nd Street (S, 4, 5, 6, 7)
🚌 M1, M2, M3, M4, M42

STAYING

house, draws a regular clientele. The rooms are furnished with antiques and the suites are spectacular, with fireplaces and large garden terraces. There's 24-hour room service and concierge, and also a restaurant and fitness center.
🍽 $550–600, suite from $800
🛏 23 rooms, 47 suites
🚇 59th Street (4, 5)
🚌 M1, M2, M3, M4

LUCERNE
Map 292 C14
201 West 79th Street between Broadway and Amsterdam Avenue, 10024
Tel 212/875-1000
www.newyorkhotel.com

This hotel, in a 1903 landmark building, is a bargain. Rooms are spacious enough for queen or king beds, and have marble bathrooms. The suites have sitting areas as well as kitchenette with refrigerator and microwave. Facilities include a decent fitness center.
🍽 $150–300, suite from $220, including breakfast
🛏 190 rooms, 60 suites
🚇 79th Street (1, 9)
🚌 M7, M11, M79

LYDEN GARDENS
Map 293 F16
215 East 64th Street, between Second and Third avenues, 10021
Tel 212/320-3022
www.mesuite.com
The suites at this well-located hotel have fully equipped kitchens, grocery shopping service and guest laundry. There's also a fitness center.
🍽 £380–420
🛏 131
🚇 68th Street (6)
🚌 M15, M101, M103, M98, M72

MANSFIELD
Map 294 E18
12 West 44th Street between Fifth and Sixth avenues, 10036
Tel 212/944-6050
www.mansfieldhotel.com
Occupying a 1904 Beaux-Arts building with many original features, the hotel is convenient for the theater and midtown shopping. The elegantly furnished rooms have sleigh beds with steel mesh headboards, metal and fabric armoires, plus CD players and VCRs. Nearby health club.
🍽 $159–279, suite from $300, including breakfast
🛏 100 rooms, 24 suites
🚇 42nd Street (B, D ,F, V)
🚌 M1, M2, M3, M4, M5, M42

MARK
Map 293 E14
25 East 77th Street between Fifth and Madison avenues, 10021
Tel 212/744-4300
www.mandarinoriental.com
In the center of the fashionable Upper East Side, the Mark is the city's first boutique hotel. Small and elegant, it has a neoclassic Italian style. Piranesi prints accent the marble lobby. Rooms incorporate dressing areas, and bathrooms have large soaking tubs, heated towel racks and Molton Brown

MARCEL
Map 294 F20
201 East 24th Street between Second and Third avenues, 10011
Tel 212/696-3800
www.nychotels.com
The rooms at this hotel are serene and minimal. Sheathed in blond wood and furnished in taupe, they have such modern clever design accents as high hats over the beds. They also have exceptional amenities for the price: dual-line phones with data ports and CD players, for instance. Spread is a trendy retro restaurant and there's also a subterranean lounge.
🍽 $135–187
🛏 100
🚇 23rd Street (6)
🚌 M15, M101, M102, M103, M23

toiletries. Fax and VCR are standard. Facilities include a well-equipped fitness center.

🍽 £565–725, suite from $750
🛏 116 rooms, 60 suites
🚇 77th Street (6)
🚌 M1, M2, M3, M4, M79

MAYFLOWER HOTEL ON THE PARK
Map 292 D16
15 Central Park West at 61st Street, 10023
Tel 212/265-0060
www.mayflowerhotel.com
The Mayflower is excellent value, conveniently located for Lincoln Center and midtown. Because this hotel was built before World War II, it has extra-large rooms with high ceilings, some of which also have separate pantries with sink and refrigerator. Front rooms overlook Central Park. Furnishings are old-fashioned and somewhat worn, but the rooms have all the expected

amenities including VCRs. Restaurant/bar and fitness center, too.

💵 $245–260, suite from $340
🛏 365 rooms, 177 suites
Ⓜ 59th Street/Columbus Circle (A, B, C, D, 1, 9)
🚌 M10

MERCER

Map 295 E23
147 Mercer Street between Prince and Spring streets, 10012
Tel 212/966-6060
www.mercerhotel.com
The Hollywood crowd loves this East Coast version of Andre Balaz's Château Marmont. The SoHo location is ultra-hip, but the place is discreet, comfortable and tranquil. The loft-style rooms are spacious and minimalist. Christian Liaigre used neutral colors, glass, fabrics like linen, and rich woods from Africa. Extras include a mini-bar stocked by Dean and DeLuca and three telephones including a portable. If that's not enough, then the Mercer Kitchen under star chef Jean Georges Vongerichten is the clincher. Access to a nearby fitness center is provided.

💵 $425–650, suite from $1100
🛏 68 rooms, 8 suites
Ⓜ Prince St (N, R, W)
🚌 M1, M6

MILBURN

Map 292 C15
242 West 76th Street between Broadway and West End Avenue, 10023
Tel 212/362-1006
www.milburnhotel.com
An old-fashioned hotel in an historic building on the residential Upper West Side, the Milburn offers good value. The lobby decorated with stucco, tapestries and Oriental rugs sets the tone. The traditionally decorated rooms are well equipped with kitchenettes (refrigerator, microwave, coffeemaker), dual-line phones with data ports, and VCRs; tiled bathrooms have hairdryers. One-bedroom suites have CD players. There's an exercise room, plus access to a nearby swimming pool and health club.

💵 $139–189, studios $159–195, junior suites $179–239
Ⓜ 79th Street (1, 9)
🚌 M5, M104

METRO

Map 294 E19
45 West 35th Street between Fifth and Sixth avenues, 10001
Tel 212/947-2500
www.hotelmetronyc.com
This has to be one of the best hotel values in the city. It has a good Midtown location and plenty of art-deco style. The rooms are nicely decorated with good-looking beds, nightstands and chairs and equipped with cable TV, and phone with data port. The marble bathrooms have hairdryers. Guests can relax in the library, which actually has books, or on the rooftop garden terrace. The sleek Metro Grill provides room service.

💵 $155–260, suite from $220, including breakfast
🛏 179 rooms and suites
Ⓜ 34th Street (B, D, F, N, Q, R, V,W)
🚌 M2, M3, M5, M6, M7

MILLENNIUM UN PLAZA

Off map 293 G18
1 UN Plaza at 44th Street and First Avenue, 10017
Tel 212/758-1234
www.millenniumhotels.com
Across the street from the UN, this flashy hotel attracts international diplomats and other wealthy visitors. Many of the rooms, which are located from the 28th floor and up, have splendid views of the skyline and the East River. They are well equipped with two-line phones with data port and printer/fax/copier. Traditional rooms feature mahogany and cherry furnishings, while more classicly furnished rooms with their blond woods look more contemporary. The fitness center has indoor pool and tennis court. The Ambassador Grill and lounge serves contemporary American cuisine.

💵 $229–429, add $100 for suite
🛏 382 rooms, 45 suites
Ⓜ 42nd Street/Grand Central (S, 4, 5, 6, 7)
🚌 M15, M27, M50

MODERNE

Map 292 D17
243 West 55th Street between Broadway and Eighth Avenue, 10019
Tel 212/397-6767
www.nychotels.com

This small retro-style hotel in a fine location near Carnegie Hall is reliable. The rooms are sleekly decorated (padded high back bed, built-in nightstands, op art), and equipped with the latest gadgetry—VCR, CD player, and telephone with data port—plus hairdryer and an extra phone in the bathroom.

💵 $125–195, suite from $245
🛏 29 rooms, 5 suites
Ⓜ Seventh Avenue (B, D, E), 59th Street/Columbus Circle (A, B, C, D, 1, 9)
🚌 M10, M20, M104

MORGANS

Map 294 E19
237 Madison Avenue between East 37th and 38th streets, 10016
Tel 212/686-0300
www.ianschragerhotels.com

In 1984 Ian Schrager opened this hotel, his first in New York City. It's discreet (no name-plate visible) and more sedate than most. Minimalist furnishings decorate the rooms, which are ultra-comfortable with their club chairs, ottomans and window seats, and good looking, too, with suede headboards and bird's-eye maple cabinets. Bathrooms have whirlpool tubs and stainless-steel fixtures, granite floors and eye-catching black and white tile. The rooms also have the latest amenities. Morgans cellar bar and the restaurant Asia de Cuba attract a fashion-conscious crowd. Residents have complimentary access to a nearby fitness club.

💵 $325–400, suite from $389
🛏 113 rooms, 28 suites
Ⓜ 33rd Street (6), 42nd Street/Grand Central (S, 4, 5, 6, 7)
🚌 M1, M2, M3, M4, M42, M34

NEW YORK PALACE

Map 293 E17
455 Madison Avenue between 50th and 51st streets, 10022

STAYING

Tel 212/888-7000
www.newyorkpalace.com
Six landmark brownstones designed by McKim, Mead and White make up the core of this luxury hotel. Owner Sultan of Brunei has spent lavishly on the décor of the public areas and the guest rooms. Several gorgeous Louis Comfort Tiffany windows and alabaster sculptures by Saint-Gaudens grace the interiors. The accommodations are located in a 55-story tower. Business travelers appreciate the executive amenities: fax, three phones and spacious desk. The restaurant, Le Cirque 2000, is the darling of many celebrities. Istana offers an olive bar (30-plus), numerous sherries, and tapas at afternoon tea. Fitness center available.

🛏 $580–625, suite from $1000
🛎 821 rooms, 75 suites
Ⓜ 51st Street (6)
🚌 M1, M2, M3, M4, M50

NEWTON
Map 292 C13
2528 Broadway between 94th and 95th streets, 10025
Tel 212/678-6500
www.newyorkhotel.com
This reliable hotel caters to the workers in the entertainment industry who appreciate the value of the rooms here. They are equipped with cable TV and phone and prettily decorated in an old-fashioned way.

🛏 $95–170
🛎 98 rooms, 12 suites
Ⓜ 96th Street (1, 2, 3, 9)
🚌 M104

OFF-SOHO SUITES
Map 295 F23
11 Rivington Street between Chrystie and Bowery streets, 10002
Tel 212/979-9815
www.offsoho.com

It's pushing the envelope when the location is described as SoHo. It is, in fact, on the

Lower East Side, the last of Manhattan's gentrified neighborhoods. Savvy travelers will appreciate the low prices of these suites, which have bedroom living/dining area. Ideal for two couples traveling together, as each suite shares a kitchen and bath. They are well equipped with cable TV, telephone, modular jack, VCR and minibar. Fitness center available.

🛏 $89–99, quads $159–189
🛎 36 suites
Ⓜ Bowery (J, M, Z)
🚌 M103

ON THE AVENUE
Map 292 C14
222 West 77th Street between Broadway and Amsterdam, 10024
Tel 212/362-1100
www.ontheave-ny.com
A few blocks from the Natural History Museum, this small hotel built in 1922 is part of the Citylife Hotel Group, which has rescued and refurbished several historic buildings in Manhattan. The rooms, furnished in sleek modern style (duvets on beds, retro chairs), feature vibrant paintings by Alfonso Muñoz. Amenities include two phones. The three floors of penthouse suites have fine views.

🛏 $139–235, suite from $285
🛎 251 rooms, 9 suites
Ⓜ 79th Street (1, 9)
🚌 M104, M79

PARAMOUNT
Map 294 D18
235 West 46th Street between Broadway and Eighth Avenue, 10036
Tel 212/764-5500
www.ianschragerhotels.com
If you want to stay in a hip Schrager-Starck hotel, but don't want to overpay, then try this Theater District choice. The rooms are small and the furnishings seem too large for them, but they are equipped with the latest technology. Enlarged Vermeer reproductions loom from the headboards. Stainless-steel sinks and similar Starck elements set the tone in the bathrooms. The Mezzanine restaurant affords views of the action in the lobby. Whiskey Bar is a sultry hideaway; there's also a comfortable Library Bar on the mezzanine. 24-hour fitness center.

🛏 $200–395, suite from $400
🛎 593 rooms, 12 suites
Ⓜ 50th Street (1, 9), 50th Street (C, E)
🚌 M10, M20, M27, M104

PENINSULA
Map 293 E17
700 Fifth Avenue at 55th Street, 10019
Tel 212/956-2888
www.peninsula.com

This small hotel in a beautiful 23-story 1902 Beaux-Arts building, has a premier location, luxurious interiors and superb service. The rooms contain the latest amenities: fax, hands-free telephone, TV in the bathroom, dual-line phone with data port, and bedside electronic control of all the electrical systems. The furnishings are luxurious and made even more so by the mood lighting. The Pen-Top Bar & Terrace is ideal for summer-time trysts and Fives is an inviting bar/restaurant overlooking Fifth Avenue. Large outstanding fitness center, too, with an indoor pool, sundeck and spa.

🛏 $600–750, suite from $825
🛎 184 rooms, 55 suites
Ⓜ 59 Street/Fifth Avenue (E,V)
🚌 M1, M2, M3, M4, M57

PICKWICK ARMS
Map 293 F17
230 East 51st Street, between Second and Third avenues, 10022
Tel 212/355-0300
www.pickwickarms.com
One of the most reliable

budget hotels in Manhattan, the Pickwick Arms attracts many international tour groups to its central and safe location. Single women in particular appreciate the last. The rooms are plain and comfortable with cable TV and telephone as standard amenities. Some single rooms have shared or corridor bath. It has a restaurant, wine bar and a rooftop terrace.

🛁 Shared bath $79–109, double $139–160
🛏 350
🚇 51st Street (6)
🚌 M15, M98, M101, M102, M103, M50

PIERRE
Map 293 E16
2 East 61st Street at Fifth Avenue, 10021
Tel 212/940-8101
www.fourseasons.com

Overlooking Central Park, this 41-story hotel, built in 1930, is the quintessence of luxury, service and refinement. Named after the son of Jacques Pierre, owner of the Hotel Anglais in Monte Carlo, it is currently under Four Seasons management and offers the same premier service. Both the rooms and the public areas are traditionally decorated with antiques. Trompe-l'oeil work decorates the Rotunda, where breakfast, afternoon tea, and cocktails are served, and the marble, etched glass, silk and satin of the Café Pierre are extravagant. Even the fitness center is elegant.

🛁 $525–975, suite from $750
🛏 150 rooms, 52 suites
🚇 59th Street/Fifth Avenue (N, R, W)
🚌 M1, M2, M3, M4

PIONEER OF SOHOTEL
Map 295 F23
341 Broome Street at Bowery
Tel 212/226-1482
www.pioneerhotel.com
The Bowery was once a fashionable area and the Pioneer

Hotel, which was built in 1822, was a favorite gathering place. Today, spruced up, it offers really inexpensive rooms. It's still in a seedy neighborhood, and the rooms still have old-fashioned decor and sinks and showers only. Still they're clean and you can't beat the price.

🛁 With sink $70, with private facilities $85–105
🛏 130
🚇 Bowery (J, M, Z)
🚌 M103

PLAZA
Map 293 E16
768 Fifth Avenue at Central Park South, 10019
Tel 212/759-3000
www.fairmont.com

This is the one hotel that out-of-towners invariably know, thanks to the role it played in author Kay Thompson's Eloise books and to its many appearances in such films as *Arthur* and *Home Alone 2*. The opulent 1907 Belle Epoque building has a superb location overlooking Central Park. It's large, and rooms do vary in size. Some lack views, but they all have high ceilings, crystal chandeliers, ornamental moldings and, sometimes, marble fireplaces. The public areas are New York gems. The Palm Court is famous for afternoon tea and brunch, while the Oak Bar is notable for its murals. The fitness center has a spa.

🛁 $369–849, suite from $869
🛏 738 rooms, 67 suites
🚇 59th Street/Fifth Avenue (N, R, W)
🚌 M1, M2, M3, M4

REGENT WALL STREET
Map 295 F26
55 Wall Street at William Street, 10005
Tel 212/845-8600
www.regenthotels.com
For moguls with business downtown, this hotel is the best choice. It occupies a magnificent 1842 Greek Revival

RITZ CARLTON
Map 293 E16
50 Central Park South, 10019
Tel 212/308-9100
www.ritzcarlton.com
On the corner of Sixth Avenue and Central Park, this sparkling 33-story hotel has magnificent views. The lobby sets an opulent tone with its limestone walls, inlaid onyx floor and Samuel Halpert paintings. The rooms are luxuriously decorated in soft shades with brocade drapes and other plush fabrics. Room amenities include flat-screen TVs, DVDs and multi-line cordless phones. Park-view rooms have telescopes for bird-watching. Bathrooms have deep tubs with neck pillows, Frederic Fekkai toiletries, and Frette candles. Pratesi linens and Bang and Olufsen stereo grace the suites. The Ritz Carlton is famous for its exceptional service, which here even extends to complimentary Burberry trench coats. The modern Restaurant Atelier under the direction of Alsatian Gabriel Kreuther is generating culinary excitement. Legendary bartender Norman Bukofzer, who reigned for 30 years at the old Ritz Carlton, now presides over the Star Lounge. The full service La Prairie spa is the first to open in the US. Fitness center too. Note that Ritz Carlton also has another hotel overlooking the Statue of Liberty at Battery Park *(tel 212/344-0800)*.

🛁 $675–1,100, suite from $1,495
🛏 237 rooms, 40 suites
🚇 59th Street/Fifth Avenue (N, R, W), 57th Street (F)
🚌 M5, M6, M7

STAYING

McKim, Mead & White building across from the Stock Exchange. The rooms are arranged around the dome of the old National City Bank below. Inner rooms overlooking a landscaped roof garden are the quietest. The spacious rooms (minimum 525 sq. ft./48sq. meters) are modern and well decorated. The large bathrooms contain two vanities, plus double tub and separate shower. Amenities include DVD, fax/copier and cordless phone. The restaurant, 55 Wall, has become a destination dining room. There's also a lounge and an outdoor terrace. The large fitness center/spa is busy, too.

🛏 $525–625, suite from $650
🛌 97 rooms, 47 suites
🚇 Wall Street (2, 3)
🚌 M1, M6, M9, M15

ROGER SMITH
Map 293 F18
501 Lexington Avenue at 47th Street, 10017
Tel 212/755-1400
www.rogersmith.com
This centrally located hotel is one of Manhattan's few remaining whimsical/personal hotels. Owner James Knowles is a sculptor and has decorated the hotel with paintings and sculpture. The spacious rooms are furnished in Colonial style with Windsor and wing chairs, chintz and antique reproductions. Some even have four-posters. They are equipped with small refrigerators, coffeemakers and such rare amenities as books. There's also a video lending library. Lily's is the quirky bar/restaurant decorated with murals and sculpture and host to unique events (Iberian festivals, flamenco, Avignon Film Festival). Access to a nearby health club.

🛏 $275–300, suite from $325, including breakfast
🛌 102 rooms, 28 suites
🚇 51st Street (6)
🚌 M98, M101, M102, M103

ROGER WILLIAMS
Map 294 E19
131 Madison Ave at 31st Street, 10016
Tel 212/448-7000
www.rogerwilliamshotel.com
In 1997 Unique Hotels Group renovated this fine old hotel (1928). They transformed the lobby, lining it with limestone and coating the fluted columns with zinc. In the good-sized rooms they installed sleek contemporary maple furnishings, shoji window screens, and such amenities as VCRs, CD players, 27-inch TVs, and three phones. Bathrooms have hairdryers, Frette robes and Aveda toiletries. Cappuccino and espresso are available 24 hours. There's also a fitness studio.

🛏 $159–339, suite from $279
🛌 183 rooms, 2 suites
🚇 33rd Street (6)
🚌 M1, M2, M3

ROYALTON
Map 294 E18
44 West 44th Street between Fifth and Sixth avenues, 10036
Tel 212/869-4400
www.ianschragerhotels.com

The first hotel conceived by Ian Schrager, the late Steve Rubell and Philippe Starck became an instant sensation and a Mecca for the city's movers and shakers. Some even dubbed the lobby-restaurant 44 the Condé Nast cafeteria. The rooms are sleekly decorated in contemporary minimalist style using trendy materials like slate, steel and glass. Bathrooms have oval tubs, and rooms come equipped with VCRs, fax and cassette players as standard. The Round Bar is a pleasant place for a drink. The fitness center is open 24 hours.

🛏 $325–550, suite from $550
🛌 161 rooms, 8 suites
🚇 42nd Street (B, D, F, V)
🚌 M1, M2, M3, M4

SHERRY-NETHERLAND
Map 293 E16
781 Fifth Avenue between 59th and 60th streets, 10022
Tel 212/355-2800
www.sherrynetherland.com
The Sherry-Netherland is

ST. REGIS
Map 293 E17
2 East 55th Street at Fifth Avenue, 10022
Tel 212/753-4500
www.stregis.com

Colonel John Jacob Astor IV conceived this beautiful 1904 Beaux-Arts style hotel. The hallmarks of luxury, marble, gold leaf, tapestries, Louis XVI furniture, are joined by the latest in technical wizardry. The service—each floor has 24-hour butler service—is also extraordinary. Suites have such extras as CD player/stereo, VCR, fax and a daily delivery of roses. The King Cole Bar is famous for the 1932 murals painted by Maxfield Parrish and for the creation of the first Bloody Mary in 1934 (originally called the "Red Snapper"). Tea in the Astor Court is one of the city's best. Carita of Paris spa and a fitness center.

🛏 $630–750, suite from $1,200
🛌 222 rooms, 93 suites
🚇 Fifth Avenue/53rd Street (E, V)
🚌 M1, M2, M3, M4

unique because it's a building cooperative, which means that the owners individually decorate their units, and that the number of guest rooms available fluctuates between 100 and 150. It's also one of the best situated and most opulent cooperatives. The building dates from 1927 and much of its luxury detailing was taken from a nearby Vanderbilt mansion that was being torn down. It has plenty of genuine European style—there are even elevator operators—so it's not surprising that Harry Cipriani chose to open a restaurant here. There is a bar and fitness center for guests, too.

$400–575, suite from $650
150 rooms and suites
59th Street/Fifth Avenue (N, R, W)
M1, M2, M3, M4

SHOREHAM
Map 293 E17
33 West 55th Street between Fifth and
Sixth avenues, 10019
Tel 212/247-6700
www.shorehamhotel.com
This mid-size Midtown hotel,
right behind the Museum of
Modern Art, has been imagina-
tively updated and now boasts
the latest looks and the most
up-to-date technology and
amenities in the rooms. Mesh
headboards shimmer above
the beds. The decor includes
plenty of aluminum, plus
entertainment musts such as
VCRs and CD players. Choice
rooms are in the back. The
three-star La Caravelle
Restaurant is in the hotel and
there is also a comfortable bar.
$159–300, suite from $259, including Continental breakfast
143 rooms, 31 suites
53rd Street/Fifth Avenue (E, V),
M1, M2, M3, M4, M5, M6, M7

STANFORD
Map 294 E19
43 West 32nd Street between Fifth
Avenue and Broadway, 10001
Tel 212/563-1500
www.hotelstanford.com
This Garment District economy
hotel is a reliable standby.
The small rooms are excellent
for the price. Amenities include
TV/VCR, phone and small
refrigerator. There's a
second-floor café-bakery.
$99–159, suite from $199
85 rooms, 36 suites
28th Street (N, R, W)
M2, M3, M5, M6, M7

STANHOPE PARK HYATT
Map 293 E14
995 Fifth Avenue at 81st Street, 10028
Tel 212/774-1234
www.stanhopepark.hyatt.com

SOHO GRAND
Map 295 E23
310 West Broadway between Canal
and Grand streets, 10013
Tel 212/965-3000
www.sohogrand.com
**Since the CEO of Hartz pet
food owns this stylish
downtown hotel it puts out a
welcome mat for animals. It
was a pioneer, too, when it
opened in art-oriented SoHo.
A cast-iron staircase studded
with coke-bottle glass leads
up to the vibrant lobby. Cool
tones create the ambience
in the rooms, but there are
plenty of guest comforts—
bathrobes, Frette linens and
velvet drapes, plus VCR and
CD player. Restaurant, bar,
and fitness center.**
$299–529, suite $1799
358 rooms, 2 suites
Canal Street (A, C, E)
M5

The dining terrace looking
across Fifth Avenue to the
Metropolitan Museum and
Central Park gives this elegant
hotel a Parisian air. Opened in
1926, the Beaux-Arts building's
public areas are lavishly
decorated in Empire style.
The rooms are furnished with
antique reproductions and a
hint of the Orient. They are, of
course, well equipped with CD
players, VCRs, fax and two-line
phones. There are two bars
(one paneled and book-lined),
plus a fine restaurant serving
Mediterranean cuisine.
$350–575, suite from $475
142 rooms, 43 suites
77th Street (6)
M1, M2, M3, M4

SURREY
Map 293 E15
20 East 76th Street at Madison Avenue,
10021
Tel 212/288-3700
www.mesuite.com
The Surrey's large suites with
kitchenettes and dining area
are attractively decorated and
well equipped, with two-line
phones, VCRs, irons and ironing boards and bathrobes.
Another reason to stay here?
Eminent chef Daniel Boulud's
Café Boulud is on the
premises. Facilities include
fitness center.

$420–530
131 suites
77th St(6)
M1, M2, M3, M4, M79

THIRTY THIRTY
Map 294 E13
30 East 30th Street between Madison
and Park avenues, 10016
Tel 212/689-1900
www.thirtythirty-nyc.com
On the edge of the burgeoning
Flatiron District in a refurbished 1902 building, this
hotel is decent value. The
rooms sport the latest minimal
look, but they are small and
exhibit some European-style
solutions—TVs suspended on
the walls and very limited
furnishings. Still, they do
have such conveniences as
telephone with data port and
hairdryer. Superior rooms
have 27-inch TVs. Bathrooms
are tiled and have glass
shower doors.
$125–195
235 rooms, 15 suites
33rd Street (6)
M1, M101, M103, M103

TRAVEL INN
Map 294 C18
515 West 42nd Street between Tenth
and Eleventh avenues, 10036
Tel 212/695-7171
www.newyorkhotel.com
The great benefits of this
Manhattan hotel are the outdoor pool and the free parking.
The rooms are decorated in
typical motel style. Coffeeshop
and fitness center.
$135–210
160
42nd Street (A, C, E)
M42, M11

TRIBECA GRAND
Map 295 E24
2 Avenue of the Americas at White
Street, 10013
Tel 212/519-6600
www.tribecagrand.com
With its luxurious 98-seat private screening room, this
hotel, close to SoHo and the
Village, caters to the independent film crowd. The lobby
opens to a dramatic atrium
lounge/restaurant. The rooms
are modern and come with
such gadgets as wireless key-
boards, a bathroom TV with
waterproof remote, Bose radio
and fax/printer. Bliss and Kiehl
products in the bathroom and
the Dean and DeLuca snacks

STAYING

are alluring extras. The business center is exceptionally well equipped, and the workstations have flat-panel screens. Hartz owns the place, so pets are welcome. Fitness center.

🖐 $299–469, suite from $1299
ⓘ 365 rooms, 4 suites
Ⓢ Franklin Street (1, 9)
🚌 M6

TRUMP INTERNATIONAL HOTEL AND TOWER

Map 292 D16
1 Central Park West at Columbus Circle, 10023
Tel 212/299-1000
www.trumpintl.com

You have to admire Donald Trump for taking one of the worst buildings in the country, recognizing its strengths, and transforming it into such a stylish hotel. The location is superb, with breathtaking views of Central Park and easy access to Lincoln Center and midtown. The rooms, located between the third and 17th floors, are stylish, and each has fax, CD player and VCR; suites have whirlpool tubs and even telescopes. The restaurant Jean-Georges is another draw. Excellent fitness center with lap pool and spa.

🖐 $550–600, suite from $825
ⓘ 38 rooms, 129 suites
Ⓢ 59th Street/Columbus Circle (A, B, C, D, 1, 9)
🚌 M10, M20

UNION SQUARE INN

Map 295 F21
209 East 14th Street between Second and Third avenues
Tel 212/614-0500
www.unionsquareinn.com

Even though most rooms are small with wall pegs for closets and only showers in the tiled bathrooms, this place is attractive and modern and offers decent value. No elevator. Coffeeshop.

🖐 $139–159, including breakfast
ⓘ 43
Ⓢ 14th Street/Union Square (L, N, Q, R, W, 4, 5, 6)
🚌 M14, M101, M102, M103, M15

W-NEW YORK

Map 293 F17
541 Lexington Avenue between East 49th and 50th streets, 10022
Tel 212/755-1200
www.whotels.com

W is the hip Starwood Hotels chain. Here, as elsewhere in the group, the lobby is a living room space, where you can relax on ottomans or play board games. Natural elements are always evident, too: pots of grass, waterfalls, polished chunks of tree trunk as coffee tables and bouquets of grasses and seedpods, for example. Rooms are modern and equipped with Web TV, two-line phones, VCRs, and CD players. Good food and beverage outlets polish the image—Rande Gerber's Whiskey Blue and Drew Nieporent's Heartbeat Restaurant. The spa and fitness center is a standout.

🖐 $259–500, suite from $499
ⓘ 647 rooms, 67 suites
Ⓢ 51st Street (6)
🚌 M101, M102, M103, M50

WALDORF-ASTORIA HOTEL AND TOWERS

Map 293 F17
301 Park Avenue between 49th and 50th streets, 10022
Tel 212/355-3000
www.waldorfastoria.com or www.waldorf-towers.com

The Waldorf opened in 1931 to rave reviews. The largest hotel in the world at the time, it remains monumental—some would say overwhelming. The Towers, which occupies the 28th to 42nd floors, have a separate entrance and the most luxurious rooms; this is where residents and heads of state stay when they come to town. The clubby Bull and Bear is popular for steaks, while Peacock Alley is famous for its Sunday brunch, and Oscar's is a very chic coffeeshop, and Inagiku is authentically Japanese. Large fitness center, excellent business center.

🖐 Waldorf $225-525, suite from $275; Waldorf Towers $349-779, suite from $500

ⓘ 1,049 rooms, 197 suites (Waldorf), 79 rooms, 101 suites (Towers)
Ⓢ 51st Street (6)
🚌 M1, M2, M3, M4, M50

WALES

Map 293 E13
1295 Madison Avenue between 92nd and 93rd streets, 10128
Tel 212/876-6000
www.waleshotel.com

The Hotel Wales is a study in old-fashioned luxury in a nine-story building on the quiet Upper East Side near Museum Mile and Central Park. The rooms are traditional with plush chairs and half-poster beds, with VCRs and CD players; some have views of Central Park, just two blocks away. Sarabeth's Kitchen, with yummy breakfast pastries and teas, and the charming rooftop terrace are bonuses. Small fitness studio.

🖐 $175–349, suite from $300
ⓘ 46 rooms, 41 suites
Ⓢ 96th Street (6)
🚌 M1, M2, M3, M4, M96

WARWICK

Map 293 E17
65 West 54th Street at Sixth Avenue, 10019
Tel 212/247-2700
www.warwickhotels.com

William Randolph Hearst built this impressive hotel in 1927 as his East Coast hideaway and guest facility. Many a Hollywood celebrity settled into residence here, including Cary Grant. The rooms are large with such old-fashioned and rare amenities as walk-in closets and extra-large marble bathrooms, plus modern ones such as fax machines and two dual-line phones. They are furnished in English style with Asian accents. Facilities include restaurant, bar and well-equipped fitness center.

🖐 $300–350, suite from $325
ⓘ 359 rooms, 67 suites

STAYING

📷 57th Street (F)
🚌 M5, M6, M7, M57

WASHINGTON SQUARE
Map 295 E22
103 Waverly Place between Fifth and
Sixth avenues, 10011
Tel 212/777-9515
www.wshotel.com

On the northwest corner of
Washington Square Park, this
small hotel has a casual
bohemian air (in the 60s Joan
Baez and Bob Dylan were frequent visitors). The rooms are
small, basic and unimagina-
tive, but the price is right. They
do have cable TV and telephone with data port. Facilities
include an attractive restau-
rant-lounge (with occasional
jazz) and exercise room.
💲 $170–190, including breakfast
🛏 175
📷 West 4th Street (A, C, E, F, V, S)
🚌 M5, M6, M8

WELLINGTON
Map 292 D17
871 Seventh Avenue at West 55th
Street, 10019
Tel 212/247-3900
www.wellingtonhotel.com
The Wellington has a great
location two blocks south of
Carnegie Hall and is a popular
budget choice for business
travelers and tour groups. The
hotel is uninspiring, but the
rooms are clean. Tower rooms
are more expensive.
💲 $125–220, suite from $200
🛏 617 rooms, 83 suites

📷 57th Street (N, R, Q, W)
🚌 M6, M7

WEST SIDE YMCA
Map 292 D16
5 West 63rd Street between Central
Park West and Broadway, 10023
Tel 212/875-4100
www.ymcanyc.org
Local residents pay plenty to
live in this neighborhood by
Lincoln Center and Central
Park, but visitors can stay here
for very little. The biggest "Y" in
New York City, located in a
Spanish Revival style building,
it has rooms that share a bath
down the hall. The rooms have
plain furnishings and TV. There
are also a few rooms with private bath. Guests have use of
the extensive, if somewhat
scruffy, sports facilities, which
include two pools, racquetball
and squash courts, and a short
indoor running track.
💲 $72–89, with private bath $109–120
🛏 365 and 30 with private bath
📷 66th Street (1, 9)
🚌 M5, M7, M10, M20, M104

WESTPARK
Map 292 D16
6 Columbus Circle (between Eighth and
Ninth avenues) 10019
Tel 212/246-6440
www.westparkhotel.com
Conveniently situated near
Carnegie Hall in an attractive
historic building, this hotel's
rooms are quite plain, but are
equipped with all the necessary amenities: air
conditioning, cable TV, dual-
line telephone with data port,
hairdryer. Some of the rooms
have views of Central Park.
💲 $100–150, suite from $220
🛏 87 rooms, 3 suites
📷 59th Street/Columbus Circle (A, B,
C, D, 1, 9)
🚌 M10, M11, M20, M57

WHITEHOUSE
Map 295 F22
340 Bowery between 2nd and Great
Jones streets, 10012
Tel 212/477-5623
www.whitehousehotelofny.com
This NoHo hostel is in an
excellent position right in the
center of the downtown
action. It offers air-conditioned
rooms with hallway bath-
rooms. There's a lounge
equipped with a microwave
and a refrigerator as well as a
laundry room for guest use.
💲 $53–59

🛏 200
📷 Bleecker St (6)
🚌 M103

WOLCOTT
Map 294 E19
4 West 31st Street between Fifth Avenue
and Broadway, 10001
Tel 212/268-2900
www.wolcott.com.
Close to the Empire State
Building, this hotel has comfortable rooms decorated in a
quaint, old-fashioned style
(candy-stripe wallpaper, patterned bed cover, wing chair,
swing arm lamps). The standard amenities you can expect
in the rooms include cable TV,
telephone with data port,
hairdryer and air conditioning.
There is a fitness room for
guests use.
💲 $99–150, suite from $150
🛏 144 rooms, 23 suites
📷 28th Street (N, R, W), 34th
Street/Herald Square (B, D, F, N, Q, R,
V, W)
🚌 M2, M3, M5, M6, M7

SPECIAL

WYNDHAM
Map 293 E16
42 West 58th Street between Fifth and
Sixth avenues, 10019
Tel 212/753-3500
Given its location and
attributes, this place is a
great value. After all, you're
staying across from the Plaza
for half the price. Although it
has the name Wyndham, it is
not part of that chain. It's a
quirky place relying on its
good word-of-mouth and
a great midtown location, just
a block from Central Park
and a short walk from both
Lincoln Center and the
Theater District. The decor
is old-fashioned, as is the
service and the attitude,
which is a pleasant bonus.
Suites come with pantries,
refrigerators and walk-in
closets. All rooms have cable
TV and telephone.
💲 $155–200, suite from $210
🛏 100 rooms, 100 suites
📷 57th Street (F), 59th Street/Fifth
Avenue (N, R, W)
🚌 M1, M2, M3, M4, M5, M6, M7

STAYING

MAJOR HOTEL CHAINS

Company	Company Statement and Regional Coverage	Number of Hotels	Contact Number and Website
Best Western	Decent quality, budget accommodation	5	602-957-4200; www.bestwestern.com
Clarion Hotels	A Choice Hotels International brand. It's moderately priced and offers full amenities.	3	301-592-5000; www.clarionhotel.com
Comfort Inn	Strictly budget. Rooms-only; no extras (restaurants, for example). Owned by Choice Hotels International	8 (4)	301-592-5000; 800-228-5150; www.comfortinn.com
Courtyard Marriott	A moderately priced Marriott brand that appeals to business travelers.	4	301-380-3000; www.courtyard.com
Crowne Plaza	The second tier full service brand of Intercontinental	4 (2)	770-604-2000; 800-227-6963 www.crowneplaza.com
Days Inns/Hotels	Decent quality budget accommodations.	1	973-428-9700 800-329-7466; www.daysinn.com
Doubletree Suites	Hilton's all-suite hotel	2 (1)	310-278-4321; www.doubletree.com
Embassy Suites	Another Hilton all suite hotel; trademark is complimentary breakfast and evening hors d'oeuvres	1	800-362-2779; www.embassysuites.com
Hampton Inn	Hilton's moderately priced brand	3	800-426-7866 www.hamptoninn.com
Hilton	International full-service hotel chain	4	800-445-8667; www.hilton.com
Four Points	Starwood's budget brand	1	914-540 or 640-8100 www.fourpoints.com
Holiday Inn/ Holiday Inn Express	Consistent good-value accommodations. Express is the budget line. Owned by Intercontinental	5	770-604-2000; www.holiday-inn.com
Howard Johnson	Moderately priced accommodations	6 (3)	800-446-4656; www.hojo.com
Hyatt	International full-service hotel chain.	2	312-750-1234; 800-233-1234 www.hyatt.com
La Quinta	Budget chain	1	866-725-1661 or 800-642-4241 www.lq.com
Marriott Hotels	The premier brand of this international chain	4	301-380-3000; www.marriott.com 800-228-9290
Quality Inns	Decent quality hotels for business and leisure travelers. Owned by Choice Hotels	2	301-592-5000 800-4choice; www.qualityinn.com
Radisson	Full-service international chain	2 (1)	800-333-3333 www.radisson.com
Ramada Inns	Full-service moderately priced hotel chain. Ramada Limited brand lacks in-house dining.	4 (2)	973-428-9700; www.ramada.com; 800-272-6232
Red Roof Inns	Modern, high-quality budget accommodations.	1	972-360-900 or 800-567-7720 or 800-843-9999; www.redroof.com
Renaissance	Marriott's moderately priced full service brand	1	301-380-3000; www.renaissancehotels.com
Sheraton	Owned by Starwood, Sheraton offers good-quality modern full-amenity hotels	4	914-540 8100 or 640-8100; www.sheraton.com
W Hotels	The hip brand owned by Starwood Hotels	5	914-540 8100: www.whotels.com
Westin	This Starwoods brand appeals to business travelers	2	914-540-8100 or 640-8100; www.starwood.com

Planning

BEFORE YOU GO

GEOGRAPHY

New York City is in the northeast United States. Four of the five boroughs that comprise New York City are islands. Manhattan, the most populous, is bordered on the east by the East River and on the west by the Hudson River. The narrow Harlem River separates it from the Bronx to the north, and Long Island Sound separates it from Long Island to the south. The city has a waterfront of 578 miles (930km). The Bronx is the only borough on the mainland and it is bounded by water to the south, east and west. The surrounding landscape is flat, although the highest point, at Todt Hill on Staten Island, is the highest point on the Atlantic coast south of Maine at 409ft (124m) .

During the Ice Age, most of New York State was covered by glaciers, with southern Long Island and Staten Island being the exceptions. The movement of the glaciers produced nine distinct physiographic regions.

The four seasons are very distinct in this region, and New Yorkers endure, without too many complaints, the cold, damp winters and hot, humid summers.

DAYLIGHT HOURS

Be aware of the number of daylight hours you have when planning your days out in and around the city. There are some areas, away from central tourist areas, that are best avoided after dark (see page 319).

TEMPERATURE

Right are the average daily maximum and minimum

Carl Schurz Park (above); cooling off at a fire hydrant (left)

temperatures for New York City. Precipitation in December, January, February and March can fall in the form of snow.

WINTER

In 2003, a total of 29 inches (0.73m) of snow fell, most of it in January and February. However, even after heavy snowfall, plows quickly remove it and disruptions are minimal. The strong winds, more pronounced as you approach the East River or the Hudson, makes it feel colder than it really is.

SUMMER

In July and August, the hottest months, humidity can be as high as 90 percent, the sun can be fierce, and everyone feels lethargic and sticky. Avoid these months if you suffer from the heat. If you do decide to visit then, make sure to wear sunscreen during the day both in the city and at the beaches.

THE BEST TIME TO VISIT

The most pleasant time to visit, and therefore the most expensive, as it is peak season, is May to early June and September to mid-November.

From May to early June, the days are delightfully comfortable and the evenings cool; showers are always a possibility. From September to late October, days are still warm but evenings start getting cooler. The leaves change to gold and red in mid- to late October, which is very pretty but not as spectacular as in New England, farther north. By November, days are much cooler and there is more rain and wind.

AVERAGE SUNRISE/SUNSET TIMES

	Sunrise	Sunset
Jan	7.15	4.45
Feb	6.50	5.30
Mar	6.10	6.00
Apr	5.15	6.30
May	4.30	7.00
June	4.30	7.30
July	4.35	7.30
Aug	5.00	7.00
Sep	5.30	6.00
Oct	5.30	5.20
Nov	6.35	4.45
Dec	7.15	4.30

PLANNING

WEATHER REPORTS

- Radio and television news end with a weather report and a short-range forecast (see page 321).
- Visit www.weather.com, the Weather Channel's 10-day forecast.
- Visit www.cnn.com/weather for CNN's five-day forecast and satellite pictures.
- In New York, you can get up-to-minute reports from 212/976-1212.

TIME ZONES

New York is on Eastern Standard Time, five hours behind GMT. Daylight Saving time, four hours behind GMT, is from early April to late October. An easy way to remember this is: In April, the clocks "spring" ahead one hour, and in October they "fall" behind one hour. Phone 212/976-1616 to get the correct time.

TIME ZONES		
City	Time difference	Time at 12 noon
Amsterdam	+4	4pm
Berlin	+4	4pm
Brussels	+4	4pm
Chicago	-1	11am
Dublin	+5	5pm
Johannesburg	+7	7pm
London	+5	5pm
Madrid	+4	4pm
Montreal	0	12 noon
Paris	+4	4pm
Perth, Australia	+13	1am
Rome	+4	4pm
San Francisco	-3	9am
Sydney, Australia	+15	3am
Tokyo	+14	2am

DOCUMENTATION FOR NON-U.S. VISITORS

SECURITY
Since 9/11, security in the U.S. has been stepped up. Restrictions are tight on what baggage you can check in and what you can carry on board, both for domestic and international flights (see www.tsa. gov for the latest information). Expect your belongings to be searched at airports, at museums and at the entryways of many office buildings. Prohibited items may be confiscated. If you are carrying bottled water, you may be asked to take a sip of it, as proof that it is not chemically suspicious. Co-operation will facilitate easy access. For the most up-to-date information on security in and around the city visit the city's official tourism office at www.nycvisit.com.

VISA AND PASSPORT REQUIREMENTS
Canadian citizens do not require a passport, but all other nationalities must have a passport to enter the United States. Canadians may be asked for identification and proof of citizenship before entering the country, such as a birth certificate or photo ID. From October 26, 2004, visitors to the U.S. may need a visa, even if you did not need one before. For up to date information on visa requirements and how to obtain one, contact the American embassy in your home country or check www.usembassy.org.uk. Non-resident foreign visitors must show their passport, their visa if required, and their round-trip ticket when entering the United States.

CUSTOMS ALLOWANCES
Visitors arriving in New York from outside the country are required to fill in a Customs Declaration before landing in the United States, and they must declare everything except personal effects, which include either 200 cigarettes or 50 cigars or 2.2lbs (1kg) of smoking tobacco, providing you are 21 or older. You may also bring in 1 liter (33.8fl oz) of alcohol.

Visitors are not allowed to bring in any fruits, vegetables, plants, meat or meat products, firearms or ammunition to the United States, except for sporting purposes.

If you have any questions, telephone the Customs Information Line on 202/354-1000 or contact your nearest United

CUSTOMS WEBSITES

Australia
1-300-363-263 or 61-2-6275-6666
www.customs.gov.au

Canada
800/461-9999 or 204/983-3500
or 506/636-5064
www.ccraadrc.gc.ca

New Zealand
(0800) 428-786 or 64-(09) 300-5399
www.customs.govt.nz

United Kingdom
0845 010 9000 or 44 208 929 0152
www.hmce.gov.uk

States consulate or embassy before departing, or visit www. customs.ustreas.gov and click on "Traveler Information." If you are bringing more than $10,000 into the country, there are no restrictions on the amount, but you must declare it on the Customs form given to passengers during your inbound flight. You may bring in only $100 worth of gifts duty-free, however.

WHAT YOU CAN TAKE HOME
If you buy expensive items, you can often avoid paying New York City's 8.25% sales tax by having the items shipped back to your home. Ask when making the purchase, but before paying. Because rules vary for each country, contact the customs service in your country by telephone or check its website.

PLANNING

DOCUMENTATION FOR NON-U.S. VISITORS 313

Country	Address	Website
Australia	31 Market Street, St. Martin Tower, Level 26, Sydney, NSW 2000, tel 02 92 61 57 79	www.consulfrance-sydney.org
Canada	1 place Ville Marie, Bureau 2601, Montréal, Québec, H3B 4S3, tel 514 878-4385	www.consulfrance-montreal.org
France	2 avenue Gabriel, Paris 75008, tel 1 43 12 22 22	www.amb-usa.fr
Germany	Pariser Platz 5, 10117 Berlin, tel 590 03 90 00	www.botschaft-frankreich.de
Ireland	36 Ailesbury Road, Ballsbridge, Dublin 4, tel 01 260 1666	www.ambafrance.ie
Italy	Via Giulia 251, 00 186 Rome, tel 06 68 60 11	www.france-italia.it/consulat/rome
New Zealand	34–42 Manners Street, 12th floor, Wellington, P.O. Box 11-343, tel 64 4 384 25 55	www.ambafrance-nz.org
Spain	Calle Marqués de la Ensenada 10, 28004 Madrid, tel: 91 700 78 00	www.consulfrance-madrid.org
South Africa	3rd floor, Standard Bank Building, 191 Jan Smuts Avenue, Rosebank, tel 011 778 56 00	www.consulfrance-jhb.org
U.K.	21 Cromwell Road, London, SW7 2EN, tel 020 7073 1200	www.frenchembassy.org.uk

TRAVEL INSURANCE

The United States does not have reciprocal healthcare arrangements with other countries. Ensure you purchase travel insurance in your country before departing. Check that it covers cancellations, lost luggage and medical expenses up to $1 million, including dental care. Medical costs in the U.S. are high, so make sure you have good medical coverage. The cost of insurance depends on your age, health, type and length of your trip. One-year coverage is very economical if you are planning more than one trip per year. Family coverage is also good value if you are traveling with a spouse and children.

PRACTICALITIES

CLOTHING

Casual clothing is acceptable in restaurants, museums and attractions throughout New York City. In summer, men must wear a shirt to enter most restaurants, although only a handful of the city's restaurants require men to wear a jacket and tie. Of course, there is no shortage of stores where you can buy any clothing that you may have forgotten to bring with you. In public places, you will be expected to wear shoes (no bare feet), and men are expected to remove their hats in churches.

Comfortable walking shoes are a must. In winter, you will need a hat or earmuffs, scarf, gloves or mittens, boots, a sweater and a warm coat or jacket. If you want to go ice-skating or sledding in Central Park, you can either bring your own gear or rent skates on site.

In spring, bring a sweater and a spring coat or jacket. In summer, prepare for hot, humid weather, and be sure to bring a sun hat or cap and sunglasses. In fall, pack a sweater and a light jacket or coat as well as lighter clothes in the event of warm weather. Rainwear and an umbrella, however, are a must all year round.

SHOPPING

Don't overpack—shopping in New York is fun, and you can readily find anything you may need—umbrella vendors seem to materialize on almost every significant street corner when it rains (you can pick an umbrella up for just $5), and you can readily acquire sunglasses on the street on fine days.

Clothes, accessories, electronic equipment and many other items come in wider selections than in most of the rest of the United States and are cheaper than in many European countries.

For every shopper, bargain-hunting can be rewarding. Be aware, however, that the "Going out of business" sales advertised on posters at electronic equipment stores in the Theater District are bogus—these "sales" are a come-on to attract naïve customers. Before buying, get the model number of the product you want and check other retailers' prices online or you will almost certainly pay too much; if you're spending a significant sum of money, it's better to patronize a reputable specialist retailer. In vintage and second-hand shops it is always worthwhile to ask for a better price—sometimes you will get it.

Keep in mind that many stores close on public holidays; SoHo is fairly closed on Mondays; and the Lower East Side is shuttered on Saturdays—and is very slow on Friday afternoons.

MEASUREMENTS

If you are more used to metric measurements than imperial, the conversion table below will be very useful.

CONVERSION CHART		
From	To	Multiply by
Inches	Centimeters	2.54
Centimeters	Inches	0.3937
Feet	Meters	0.3048
Meters	Feet	3.2810
Yards	Meters	0.9144
Meters	Yards	1.0940
Miles	Kilometers	1.6090
Kilometers	Miles	0.6214
Acres	Hectares	0.4047
Hectares	Acres	2.4710
Gallons	Liters	4.5460
Liters	Gallons	0.2200
Ounces	Grams	28.35
Grams	Ounces	0.0353
Pounds	Grams	453.6
Grams	Pounds	0.0022
Pounds	Kilograms	0.4536
Kilograms	Pounds	2.205
Tons	Tonnes	1.0160
Tonnes	Tons	0.9842

PLANNING

CLOTHING SIZES
The chart below indicates how U.K. and
Australian clothing and shoe sizes
compare with those in the U.S.

Australia	U.K.	U.S.	
90	36	36	SUITS
96	38	38	
102	40	40	
108	42	42	
114	44	44	
120	46	46	
7	6	8	SHOES
8	7	8.5	
9	8	9.5	
10	9	10.5	
11	10	11.5	
12	11	12	
37	14.5	14.5	SHIRTS
38	15	15	
39/40	15.5	15.5	
41	16	16	
42	16.5	16.5	
43	17	17	
8	8	6	DRESSES
10	10	8	
12	12	10	
14	14	12	
16	16	14	
18	18	16	
20	20	18	
6	4.5	6	SHOES
6.5	5	6.5	
7	5.5	7	
7.5	6	7.5	
8	6.5	8	
8.5	7	8.5	
9	7.5	9	

VOLTAGE AND ADAPTERS
The power supply in the U.S. is
110/120 volts AC (60 cycles).
American plugs have two-prong
flat pins, so you will need an
adapter if you have plugs with
two round pins, or three pins.

It is best to buy an adapter
before departing or in the airport
shop as they can be difficult to
find in the U.S., although some
department stores and pharmacies stock them. You will also
need a voltage transformer for
European appliances.

COMFORT AND ETIQUETTE

Public restrooms
Restrooms are normally labeled
"Women" and "Men" or use a
male/female symbol. You may
notice that they are labeled in
Spanish as well as English in
airports, some restaurants and
clubs. Public restrooms are found
in visitor centers (see page 324)
and in Grand Central Terminal
(see pages 102–104), but New
Yorkers stop in hotels, large
bookstores, department stores,
or cafés—theoretically restrooms
in eating places are for patrons
only, but in some restaurants it's
an option. Restrooms in public
buildings are wheelchair accessible and may offer facilities for
baby-changing. Restrooms in
most parts of the city are clean
and well supplied with soap,
hand-dryers and paper. A few in
Chinatown are substandard.

Traveling with children
New York is family-friendly for the
most part, with special discounts
for children, special prices for
meals and plenty of attractions to
keep them happy. Many hotels
let kids stay for free and most
museums do not charge for
young children. Look for special
things to do in the "Weekend"
section of the Friday *New York
Times*, *New York* magazine's
"Cue" section, and in *Time Out
New York*. Special performances
can sell out or fill up early, so
expect to plan ahead. For baby-
sitting services there's the Baby
Sitters' Guild (tel 212/682-0227
or www.babysittersguild.com).

Laundry services
Most hotels either offer laundry
services or will recommend one.
Before you make your reservation,
check what the hotel offers.

Smoking
Smoking has been more controversial than ever in New York
since Mayor Michael Bloomberg's
April 2003 law banning smoking
in all public places, including
restaurants, clubs, bars and
anywhere an employee may be
exposed to a patron's smoke.
People who want to smoke must
go outside. There is no smoking
on buses, subways or trains, but
you may smoke in the privacy of
your hotel room—providing it is a
designated smoking room.

Dealing with beggars
It is your choice whether to give
money to beggars. If you would
prefer not to, simply keep on
moving if a beggar approaches
you on the street and asks for
money. Don't make eye contact
and don't engage in conversation.
On the subway, you may come
across beggars who deliver a
monologue about their hard
times and about how your
donation will help their family.
Again, if you prefer not to give,
don't make eye contact, and
shake your head "no" if you are
approached personally.

On subways
If all seats are taken, move to the
center of the subway car so you
don't block the doors. If a senior
citizen, an adult with a young
child, a pregnant woman or
person with a disability gets on
and there are no available seats,
offer yours. It's the civilized thing
to do, and your fellow passengers
—at least the civilized ones—will
admire you for it.

GAY AND LESBIAN NEW YORK
The Stonewall Riot on Christopher
Street in Greenwich Village is
credited with starting the gay
liberation movement in New York
City in 1969. Today, gay and
lesbian visitors will find New York
an easy place to visit. The West
Village, especially Christopher
Street, is full of shops, restaurants
and services with a gay orientation, as is Chelsea, on Eighth
Avenue from 16th to 23rd streets.

Finding help
● The International Gay &
Lesbian Travel Association
(Tel 800/448-8550 or 954/776-
2626, www.iglta.org) is a
specialist travel agency.
● Lesbian, Gay, Bisexual &
Transgender Community
Center (208 West 13th Street,
between Seventh and Eighth
avenues, tel 212/620-7310,
www.gaycenter.org) is an
excellent source of information
on what's happening in the city
and where to stay.
● Gay and Lesbian Switch-
board of N. Y. Project (Tel
212/989-0999, www.glnht.org)
offers peer counseling and
information on events.

What's happening
For current gay and lesbian
nightlife, pick up a copy of *HX,
New York Blade, Next, Village
Voice* and *Gay City News*, all of
them free publications. *Time Out
New York*, available at all street
news-stands and many other
retail outlets, has an excellent
section on what's on for gay and
lesbian visitors.

PLACES OF WORSHIP

With its rich cultural mix, this city of immigrants offers a place to worship for every kind of belief. Listings in newspapers note the topic of the current week's theme. For the most extensive list of churches, temples, synagogues and mosques, look in the *Yellow Pages*.

PLACES OF WORSHIP	
Baptist	Abyssinian Baptist Church (132 Odell Clark Place at West 138th Street between Adam Clayton Powell Boulevard and Lenox Avenue, tel: 212/862-7474).
Buddhist	New York Buddhist Church (Riverside Drive between 105th and 106th streets, tel: 212/678-0305).
Greek Orthodox	St. Nicholas Greek Orthodox Church (155 Cedar Street, tel: 212/227-0773).
Interfaith	Cathedral of St. John the Divine (1047 Amsterdam Avenue at 112th Street, tel: 212/316-7540)
Jewish	Temple Emanu-El (1 East 65th Street at Fifth Avenue tel: 212/744-1400) is reform.
Muslim	Mosque of the Islamic Culture Center (Third Avenue at 96th Street, tel: 212/722-5234).
Roman Catholic	St. Patrick's Cathedral (Fifth Avenue between 50th and 51st streets, tel; 212/753-2261).

St. Patrick's Cathedral, with its two spires, is dwarfed by Midtown skyscrapers

MONEY

TAXES

In New York City an 8.25% sales tax is added at the cash register. You will pay this on most purchases, except on clothing under $110. The hotel tax is 13.25%, plus $2 per room per night. The parking garage tax is 18.25%.

TIPPING

You must tip people in the service sector because their livelihood depends on tips. Employers pay them a minimum wage, in most cases, and expect tips to make up the rest of their income. If you tip less than expected, you are sending a message that the service was less than satisfactory.

● **In restaurants**, tip waiters, waitresses and bartenders at least 15% of the bill—to figure it out quickly just double the 8.25% sales tax listed on the bill. Tip 20% in expensive restaurants, and always round up for good service. The head waiter in upscale restaurants expects 5% and the cloakroom attendant expects $1 when they give you back your coat.

● **In taxis**, tip the driver 15%, more if the journey is short.

● **In hotels**, tip the bellboy $1 or $2 for each suitcase he carries up to your room or down to the lobby. The chambermaid expects $2 for a few nights' stay. The hall porter expects $1 or $2 for getting you a taxi.

● **At the airport or train station,** tip the porter who transports your luggage $1 or $2 per bag.

FOR NON-U.S. VISITORS

Changing money

If you are coming from outside the United States, change money before you leave home so that you can pay taxis, trains or buses on arrival. The commissions at airport bureaux de change is higher than in most banks. Dollar bills of a higher denomination than $20 may not be accepted by taxi drivers, so it is best to always have small bills available. There are bureaux de change throughout Manhattan, but you get better service in banks and at the visitor center in Times Square (see page 324). There are ATMs all over the city. Expect to pay up to $3 per transaction if you are using a bank other than your own.

● **American Express Travel Services** has many offices in the city, including one on the mezzanine level at Macy's in Herald Square (tel 212/695-8075).

● **Thomas Cook Foreign Exchange** has a number of offices (tel 212/265-6063 or www.us.thomascook.com).

● **Chase Manhattan Bank** (tel 212/935-9935 or www.chase.com) has more than 400 branches with bureaux de change.

How to get money

Most people use credit cards to pay for hotels, restaurant meals and shopping. However, some restaurants and other establishments accept only cash. If you rent a car, a credit card will be essential. MasterCard, Visa and American Express are the cards most often accepted (but Amex occasionally is not accepted). Diner's Club and Carte Blanche are accepted by most restaurants and many hotels, but not all. Discover, enRoute, Eurocard and JCB are also often accepted, but not always.

Traveler's checks in U.S. dollars, although less common than in the past, remain a safe way to

MONEY VOCABULARY	
$	dollar
¢	cent
a penny	1 cent
a nickel	5 cents
a dime	10 cents
a quarter	25 cents
a half dollar	50 cents
5 bucks	5 dollars

PLANNING

carry money. Keep a copy of the serial numbers separate from the checks and record the ones you cash, so that any lost or stolen checks can be replaced quickly. Checks from American Express (tel 800/221-7282 or www.americanexpress. com) are the most widely accepted. Most restaurants and large stores will accept traveler's checks as payment but will ask to you to produce your passport. Most banks will cash them, but charge between 1% and 4% on the value for doing so. American Automobile Association members can avoid fees by purchasing checks from a AAA office.

Stolen credit cards or traveler's checks

If your credit card is stolen, report the theft to the bank so that charges can be blocked. Also notify the police. The bank's toll-free number is usually on the back of the credit card. It's a good idea to photocopy the front and back sides of everything in your wallet, or at least write down

LOST/STOLEN CREDIT CARDS

American Express
800/221-7282
www.americanexpress.com

Diners Club
1800 360 060
www.dinersclub.com

MasterCard
800/307-7309
www.mastercard.com

Visa
800/336-8472
www.visa.com

the numbers you need to report the card lost, and carry this information separately.

Exchange rates
For the latest market conversion rates, visit www.oanda.com or www.x-rates.com.

MONEY-SAVING TIPS
● CityPass (Tel 707/256-0490, www.citypass.com), is a book of tickets to seven attractions and will save you hours of waiting in line at attractions, as well as 50%

10 EVERYDAY ITEMS AND HOW MUCH THEY COST

Takeaway sandwich	$6
Bottle of water	$2
Cup of tea or coffee	$1
Pint of beer	$6
Glass of wine	$10
Daily newspaper	25c–$1.25
Roll of camera film	$8
20 cigarettes	$7.75
An ice-cream	$2.50
A gallon of fuel (petrol)	$2

on admission to the American Museum of Natural History (see pages 68–72), Empire State Building Observatory (see pages 94–96), Guggenheim Museum (see pages 110–111), *Intrepid* Sea-Air-Space Museum (see page 109), MoMA QNS (see page 125) and the Whitney Museum of American Art (see pages 148–151), as well as on two-hour Circle Line harbor cruises (see page 000). The CityPass costs $38 ($31 for ages 12–17) and can be purchased at any attraction. It is good for nine days once you begin using it.

BANKNOTES AND COINS

Local currency One U.S. dollar is worth 100 cents. Paper bills come in denominations of $1, $5, $10, $20, $50 and $100. Bills are all the same size and color, so look carefully at the numbers on them before handing them over. Each type of coin is a different size, so they are easier to differentiate (coins and bills are not shown actual size).

1 cent
penny

5 cents
nickel

10 cents
dime

25 cents
quarter

50 cents

Dollar

Coin images courtesy United States Mint.

- **New York Pass** *(250 West 49th Street, New York 10019, tel 877/714-1999, www. newyorkpass.com)* an all-inclusive passport to New York City that gets you admission to and discounts at 65 attractions, as well as a MetroCard (see page 43) for unlimited bus and subway travel. The New York Pass can be purchased at Madame Tussaud's *(234 West 42nd Street)*, the Empire State Building's Skyride *(350 Fifth Avenue)* or online. Passes cost $39 ($25 for children) and are good for 1, 2, 3 or 7 days.
- **"Pay-what-you-wish"** is the admission scheme adopted by some attractions; a suggested admission is posted, but you decide how much you actually pay. Some museums are free one day a week or for a couple of evening hours. To save on museum admission prices, visit during the hours given in the table above.
- **The Official NYC Guide** *(810 Seventh Avenue, New York 10019, tel 800/NYC-VISIT or*

MUSEUM ADMISSION		
Attraction	**Pay-what-you-wish**	**Free**
American Folk Art Museum		Fri 6–8pm
Bronx Zoo	All day Wed	
Brooklyn Botanic Garden		Sat 10–noon, All day Tue
Brooklyn Museum of Art	1st Sat each month	After 5pm
Guggenheim Museum	Fri 6–8pm	
Jewish Museum	Thu 5–8pm	
MoMA QNS	Fri 4–7.45pm	
Museum of Arts and Design	Thu 6–8pm	
New York Botanical Garden	All day Wed	Sat 10–noon
Whitney Museum of American Art	Fri 6–9pm	

212/397-8222, www.nycvisit. com) is published by NYC & Company, the city's official tourism marketing organization, and contains discount vouchers for hotels, stores, restaurants, cruises and museums. Buy the book online, or pick up a copy from one of the visitor centers.
- **New York forLess™** *(tel 888/463-6753 or 937/846-1411, www.for-less.com)* includes discount vouchers and a discount card for participating attractions, tours and cruises,

hotels, restaurants, stores and nightspots, and buys you $8-worth of free international telephone calls.

The card is good for up to four people for eight consecutive days. If three or four of you are using the card, you can recoup the $19.95 cost on your first meal, and the more places you visit, the more you save.

HEALTH

New York City has some of the best hospitals and doctors in the country, so if you should be in need of care, you have come to the right place.

INOCULATIONS
If you are arriving in the United States from Canada or from a European Union member country, you will probably not need inoculations. However, check with your travel agent or with a U.S. consulate or embassy (see page 314). All visitors to the United States are advised to be fully immunized against tetanus and diptheria.

WHAT TO TAKE
If you will be in New York during the summer, make sure to have sunscreen, which you can easily purchase from any pharmacy upon arrival. Any medication that you require, you should bring with you and if it is prescription medicine, pack it in your in-flight baggage. Take copies of your prescription to be on the safe side. If the bag in which you are carrying medication gets lost or

A New York pharmacy

stolen, the copy of the prescription will make it easier to get a replacement.

If you require medication containing habit-forming drugs or narcotics, such as some cough medicines, diuretics, heart drugs, tranquilizers, sleeping pills, anti-depressants, stimulants, etc., make sure they are properly labeled and that you have a prescription or written statement from your doctor confirming that you are taking these under a doctor's direction and that you require them while traveling.

If you suffer from heart problems, epilepsy or diabetes, it is a good idea to wear a Medic Alert Identification Tag so that the doctor can easily get access to your medical records through the 24-hour hotline in case of an emergency. You can get this tag by phoning 800/825-3785 or visit www.medicalert.org.

DRINKING WATER
The tap water in New York is safe to drink, as is water from public water fountains. However, bottled water is sold throughout the city in stores, restaurants and vending machines.

BUYING MEDICATIONS
The 24-hour pharmacies listed opposite are all located in convenient places.

Travelers from abroad may require a prescription in the United States to purchase certain medications, such as birth control pills, inhalers and codeine, that they can buy over the counter in their own country. Pharmacies are generally open from 9am to 5pm and can be

PLANNING

Dial 911
for fire, police and
ambulance

Poison Control
800/222-1222

**Rape and Sexual Abuse
Hotline**
212/267-7273 (24-hour)

Crime Victims' Hotline
212/577-7777

Dentists
800/336-8478 or
800/400-1800

**N.Y. Hotel Urgent Medical
Center**
212/737-1212
(medical/dental 24-hour)

recognized by signs in the window, either a mortar and pestle or a caduceus (a staff with two entwined snakes and two wings at the top, which symbolize a physician).

FINDING A DOCTOR

If you need to find a doctor in New York, contact any one of the health services listed below. They are reputable providers accustomed to treating visitors.

DOCS at New York Healthcare *(55 East 34th Street, between Park and Madison avenues, tel 212/252-6001)* is a walk-in medical center for non-emergency cases. New York University Downtown Hospital *(tel 212/698-3362)* offers referrals. N.Y. Hotel Urgent Medical Services *(952 Fifth Avenue between 76th and 77th streets, tel 212/737-1212, www.travelmd.com)* was set up by a New York City doctor to treat visitors. Whether you need a prescription, a medical examination or a dentist, a specialist will come to your hotel room. He or she will produce appropriate identification. The hotel visit fee is $200 to $300, with higher rates at night and on

weekends. You can also go to the office for a fee of between $55 and $155, depending on treatment—either drop in or phone for an appointment. Emergency rooms (ER rooms) in some hospitals have walk-in

clinics where you can go for non-emergencies (and pay a slightly lower rate than in the emergency area), but you will probably have to wait for a long time. Or you can always ask the hotel staff to suggest a doctor.

- Visitors from Europe, Australia or New Zealand may be concerned about the effect of a long-haul flight on their health. The most widely publicized concern is Deep Vein Thrombosis (DVT). Misleadingly labeled "economy class syndrome," DVT is when a blood clot forms in the body's deep veins, particularly in the legs. The clot can move around the bloodstream and can be fatal.
- You are most at risk if you are elderly, pregnant, using the contraceptive pill, smoke or are overweight. If you think you are at increased risk of DVT, see your doctor before departing. Flying increases the likelihood of DVT because passengers are often seated in a cramped position for long periods of time and may become dehydrated.
- Other health hazards for flyers are airborne diseases and bugs spread by the air-conditioning system on board. These hazards are largely unavoidable but if you have a serious medical condition, seek advice from a doctor before flying.

To minimize risk:
- drink water (not alcohol)
- don't stay immobile for hours at a time
- stretch and exercise your legs periodically
- wear elastic flight socks, which support veins and reduce the chances of a clot forming
- a small dose of aspirin, which thins the blood, may be recommended.

EXERCISES

1 ANKLE ROTATIONS **2 CALF STRETCHES** **3 KNEE LIFTS**

Lift feet off the floor. Draw a circle with the toes, moving one foot clockwise and the other counter-clockwise.

With heel on the floor, point foot upward as high as you can. Then lift heel, keeping ball of foot on the floor.

Lift leg with knee bent while contracting your thigh muscle. Straighten leg, pressing foot flat to the floor.

IF YOU HAVE TO GO TO THE HOSPITAL

Before you go, phone your travel insurance company's emergency number to find out which hospitals accept your insurance. You will need to show your insurance card at the hospital

PHARMACIES OPEN 24 HOURS		
Name	**Address**	**Telephone**
Duane Reade	224 West 57th Street/Broadway	212/541-9708
Duane Reade	485 Lexington Avenue/47th Street	212/682-5338
Duane Reade	2025 Broadway/70th Street	212/579-9955
Rite Aid	146 East 86th Street/Lexington Avenue	212/876-0600

PLANNING

before any treatment will be given.

INSURANCE FOR NON-U.S. VISITORS

Although you are not required to have health insurance in order to visit the United States, it would be extremely unwise not to. The U.S. does not have reciprocal health agreements with other countries and the cost of healthcare is very high, whether you need a doctor's visit or dental care or have a medical emergency. An emergency room visit usually carries a minimum charge of $300, and that's before you begin receiving treatment. Make sure that you have a good insurance policy that covers all healthcare, including dental care (see page 313).

New York Opticians
American Vision Center, 2301 Broadway, tel: 212/580-1600

Morgenthal Frederics Opticians
699 Madison Avenue, tel: 212/838-3090
399 West Broadway, tel: 212/966-0099

ALTERNATIVE MEDICINE

Alternative medical treatments are widely available in New York City.

American Academy of Medical Acupuncture
www.medicalacupuncture.org

North American Society of Homeopaths
www.homeopathy.org

Chiropractic Federation of New York
64 East 34th Street
tel 212/532-0185

Chinatown offers a wide selection of herbal and alternative treatments, including acupuncture. In Chinatown you will find, among others:

Zon Foo Acupuncture and Medical
36 East Broadway, 2nd Floor, New York 10002, tel 212/925-2501

Kamwo Herbs
211 Grand Street, New York 10013, tel 212/966-6370

Grand Meridian Herbs, Acupuncture and Massage
209–211 Grand Street, New York 10013, tel 212/965-1503

COMMUNICATIONS

TELEPHONE CHARGES

Public pay phones

Local calls cost 25 cents for the first three minutes. Even if you are making a local call, one that has the 212 or 646 area code, you must still dial 1, then the area code, before the seven-digit number. From Manhattan, calls to other boroughs, though these are charged as local calls, also require you to dial 1 followed by the area code 718 or 347.

All calls that are not local are so-called long-distance calls, which cost more; for these, dial 1 followed by the area code and seven-digit number.

Paying by card

Prepaid calling cards, sold at many convenience stores and news-stands in denominations up to $50, are the easiest and

probably the cheapest way to phone home.

Public pay phones throughout New York City take phonecards. Airport public telephones all accept MasterCard, Visa and American Express.

TELEPHONES AND NON-U.S. VISITORS

Telephone numbers

Local and long distance calls: dial 1 + area code + 7-digit number

Word telephone numbers: Some numbers are made easy to remember by using the letters on the dial rather than the numbers, for example, 1-800/ WHITNEY. Find the letters on the dial to call these numbers.

Toll-free numbers

There is no charge for telephone numbers with area codes 800,

COUNTRY CODES FROM THE UNITED STATES

Dial 011 followed by the country code, the city code, then the telephone number

Australia	(011) 61
Belgium	(011) 32
France	(011) 33
Germany	(011) 49
Greece	(011) 30
Ireland	(011) 353
Italy	(011) 39
Netherlands	(011) 31
New Zealand	(011) 64
Spain	(011) 34
Sweden	(011) 46
United Kingdom	(011) 44

888 and 877. The 911 emergency number is also free.

High-toll numbers

Telephone numbers with area codes 700 and 900 are chat lines, dating services or other specialized services that can charge anywhere between 95¢ to $15 per minute.

Cell phones and laptops

If your cell phone is not equipped to make calls from the U.S., you may as well leave it at home. If you plan to use a laptop while traveling, make sure that the battery is fully charged before you leave home. At airport

PLANNING

TIP

Hotel-room phones may be convenient but they are costly, because most hotels impose a high surcharge on calls dialed from rooms. To avoid these surcharges, use a public pay phone. Many hotels have Internet access in the lobby, so you can email, as long as you have a credit card.

TIP

The New York for Less guidebook not only saves you money on hotels, restaurants, and attractions but also includes a phonecard with $8-worth of free international phone calls. To order, call 888/463-6753 or 937/846-1411 or visit www.for-less.com.

USEFUL TELEPHONE NUMBERS AND WEBSITES

Emergency
(Police, Fire, Ambulance)
911

Traveler's Aid
718/656-4870 or
973/623-5052

U.S. Postal Information
800/275-8777 or
www.usps.com

Directory Assistance
212/555-1212

Mail boxes are blue

Alternatively, use the free terminals at the Times Square Visitor Center at 1560 Broadway (see page 324).

CYBER-CAFÉS
There are more and more of these around town (see below for two well-known cafés).

POST OFFICES
The main post office is on Eighth Avenue between 31st and 33rd streets (tel 212/967-8585). Throughout the city there are numerous branches, which are listed in the *Yellow Pages*. Most branches are open Monday to Friday 8am to 6pm and Saturday 8am to 1pm.

security, you may be asked to take the laptop out of the case. Security officers may ask you if it is yours, if it is new and if anyone else has been using it. Make sure that you have an adapter for your laptop, and a converter for voltage if necessary, if it does not have a U.S. two-prong, flat-pin plug and does not work on 110/120 volts. If you plan to use it a lot, bring an extra battery.

EMAIL
Go to www.mail2web.com and type in your email address and password to retrieve your email from any Web browser. You can also open a free email account

via www.hotmail.com or www.mail.yahoo.com.
   You can check your email from most hotel lobbies, at Internet cafés or Kinko's copy shops (www.kinkos. com), which are found throughout the city.

POSTAGE RATES

As of June 2003, a regular letter costs:
Within the U.S., minimum of 37 cents
Across the border to Canada, minimum of 60 cents
Overseas, minimum of 80 cents

CYBER CAFES

Cyber Café
Times Square, 250 West 49th Street
tel 212/333-4109
www.cyber-café.com
Mon–Fri 11am–10pm
Sat–Sun 11am–1am

N.Y. Computer Café
247 East 57th Street
tel 212/872-1704
www.nycomputercafe.com
Mon–Fri 8am–11pm
Sat 10am–11pm
Sun 11–11

FINDING HELP

The crime rate in New York has plummeted over the past ten years and it is now one of the safest large cities in the United States. However, it is big and crowded, and crimes do occur, so always be aware of your surroundings. If someone does try to steal your property, let them take it, then report the crime to the police.

PERSONAL SECURITY
● Do not keep all your money, credit cards and traveler's checks in the same place. Wear a money belt.
● Do not carry large sums of money with you. Use the

New York City policeman

hotel safe if you have brought valuables or have large amounts of cash.
   ● Do not walk alone at night in deserted areas, and do not go into parks after dark unless there is a concert and a large crowd is already there.
● If someone "falls" in front of you, be aware that this may be a ploy to distract you while an accomplice picks your pocket. Stop to help, but be aware of your surroundings.
● Wear shoulder bags and cameras over one shoulder and across your front—in bandolier style. Do not let your handbag dangle from the back of your chair in restaurants; put it on your lap rather than risk making it an easy target.

OBEY THE LAWS
● Drinking laws are strictly enforced in New York. It is against the law to drive with an open container of alcohol in the

LEGAL AGE	
To purchase tobacco	18 years
To purchase pornography	18 years
To gamble or play the lottery	18 years
To purchase/consume alcohol	21 years
To rent a car	25 years

car and also, of course, to drive while intoxicated.

● Smoking in all public places, such as restaurants, museums, on public transportation or in public offices, is now illegal in New York (since new laws were passed in April 2003). You must smoke outside—as you will see many New Yorkers doing.

IF YOU ARE ARRESTED

● Remember that New York has been on high alert at different times since 9/11 and that even when these alerts are not in effect, there is a high police presence in the streets, at public places, in airports and at other metropolitan locations. Never joke about matters of security—it's a crime.

● Visitors from abroad need to be aware that the police can arrest you if you break the law, if they have a strong suspicion that you have been involved in a

crime, or if your behavior or activities make them suspect that you are involved in criminal activities.

If you are arrested, you have the right to remain silent, to make a telephone call, and you have the right to contact a lawyer. Anything you say can be used as evidence against you. Your best option is to contact your embassy or consulate (see below) and ask for their assistance.

CONSULATES FOR VISITORS FROM OVERSEAS	
Australia	212/351-6500
Canada	212/596-1700
Ireland	212/319-2555
New Zealand	212/832-4038
United Kingdom	212/745-0200

EMBASSIES FOR VISITORS FROM OVERSEAS			
Country	**Address**	**Telephone**	**Website**
Australia	1601 Massachusetts Avenue, NW, Washington, D.C. 20036	202/797-3000	www.austemb.org
Canada	501 Pennsylvania Avenue, NW, Washington, D.C. 20001	202/682-1740	www.canadianembassy.org
Ireland	2234 Massachusetts Avenue, NW, Washington, D.C. 20008	202/462-3939	www.irelandemb.org
New Zealand	37 Observatory Circle, Washington, D.C. 20008	202/328-4800	www.nzemb.org
United Kingdom	3100 Massachusetts Avenue, NW, Washington, D.C. 20008	202/588-6500	www.britainusa.com

MEDIA

At the newspaper stands on many streets citywide, you can buy newspapers in English, Spanish and, at some, a few other languages, as well as a wide variety of magazines.

NEWSPAPERS

● *The New York Times* is the city's most widely read daily (www.nytimes.com), published seven days a week. The Sunday Edition includes a magazine and special sections for sports, travel, real estate, etc.

● The *Daily News* is a tabloid published seven days a week and offers a large quantity of Sunday supplements.

● The *New York Post* is another tabloid published Monday to Saturday.

● The *Wall Street Journal* is the much-respected New York-based national financial newspaper.

● The *New York Observer* is the pink-hued weekly full of media and political gossip.

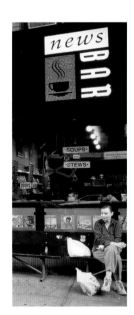

Taking the time out to sit and watch the world go by—and possibly to log on to the Internet

MAGAZINES

● *The New Yorker* (www.new yorker.com) is a national literary and news magazine with New York listings and reviews; published every Monday.

● *New York Magazine* (www.newyorkmetro.com), published every Monday, is a good source of information on restaurants, theaters, movies, books, art, television and bargains around town.

● *The Village Voice* (www. villagevoice.com) is published weekly every Tuesday, with extensive listings of music, clubs, arts and entertainment.

● *Time Out* (www.timeoutny. com) is a very good comprehensive weekly magazine with plenty of listings on just about everything going on around town.

To buy newspapers from other countries, go to **Universal News & Magazines** (*234 West 42nd Street between Seventh and*

MAJOR RADIO STATIONS	
www.nyradioguide.com	
AM:	
Sports	620 (WSNR)
News and Talk	820 (WNYC feeds from NP Rand; the BBC World Service)
Multi-ethnic	930 (WPAT)
News	1130 (WBBR)
News around the clock	880 and 1010 (WINS)
FM:	
Classic and talk	93.9 (WYNC-FM)
Classical	WQXR, the radio station of the New York Times
Top 40	108.3 (also known as Z-100).

NATIONAL TV STATIONS
2 (CBS)
4 (NBC)
5 (Fox)
7 (ABC)
9 & 11 (independent)
13 (PBS)

Eighth avenues, tel 212/221-1809) or **Hotaling News Agency** *(624 West 52nd Street between Eleventh and Twelfth avenues, tel 212/974-9419).*

MAJOR TV STATIONS
On cable, NY1 is all about New York, and more than 50 stations on cable, available in most hotels, supply movies, weather updates and home shopping. If you're traveling with kids, ask when Disney Channel is available.

Number 9 West 57th Street (right); billboard for one of New York's radio stations (below)

OPENING TIMES AND PUBLIC HOLIDAYS

New York never sleeps. The working week is Monday through Friday, 9am to 5pm, but some banks are open on Saturday mornings and many stores are open longer hours; most stores are open all weekend. Some pharmacies are open 24/7, as are some coffee shops and bureaux de change.

Always phone in advance if timing is critical or if you're making a detour to visit a particular place.

PUBLIC HOLIDAYS
On public holidays many museums, some restaurants, and all public office buildings close. New Year's Day, Christmas and Thanksgiving are the biggest, most widely celebrated holidays, when most New York businesses grind to a halt. Airports and train stations are particularly busy in the period leading up to these holidays, when many New Yorkers travel out of town to be with family or friends. However,

it is also a time when the city is festive and celebrations are enjoyed by visitors as well as New Yorkers (for a list of parades see page 324). Much of the city closes down or slows during the Jewish High Holidays—Rosh Hashanah and Yom Kippur—in September and early October.

PUBLIC HOLIDAYS
January 1
New Year's Day
3rd Monday in January
Martin Luther King Day
3rd Monday in February
Presidents' Day
March/April
Easter (half day Good Friday)
Last Monday in May
Memorial Day
July 4
Independence Day
1st Monday in September
Labor Day
2nd Monday in October
Columbus Day
November 11
Veterans' Day
4th Thursday in November
Thanksgiving Day
December 25
Christmas Day

OPENING HOURS			
	Open	**Closed**	**Comments**
Stores	Mon–Sat, 10–7		Many closed Sun Upper East
	Sun noon–6		Side, Sat on Lower East Side
Banks	Mon–Fri 9.30–3.30	Sat–Sun	Some close at 3, some open
			Sat morning
Offices	Mon–Fri 9–5	Sat–Sun	
Museums	Tue–Sun		Some open Mon or close
			another day
Galleries	Tue–Sat 10–6	Mon	
Doctors	Mon–Fri 9–5	Sat–Sun	See page 000
Pharmacies	Daily 9–7 or 9–9		Shorter hours and Sunday
			closing in commercial
			neighborhoods, some 24hrs
Grocery stores	Daily 7am–9pm		As above
Restaurants	Daily (see listings)	Some close one	Many serve until 11pm or
		day a week	midnight, a few between 4pm
			and 5.30

TOURIST INFORMATION

EVENTS AND PARADES

Lively events worth planning a trip around take place throughout the year. If you are in New York during a parade, don't miss it. The two biggest are the St. Patrick's Day Parade and the Macy's Thanksgiving Day Parade, which is televised nationwide. The crowd scene is almost as entertaining as the parade. Check local listings for dates, times and parade routes, and plan to show up early for either of them to get a choice viewing spot.

TOURIST OFFICES

Major visitor centers, listed below, are well worth visiting on your first or second day. Many brochures offer discount vouchers, which will save you a few dollars at attractions or restaurants. In addition, most hotels offer a good selection of maps and free brochures.

Times Square Visitors Center

(1560 Broadway, between 46th and 47th streets, tel 212/768-1560, www.timessquarebid.org, daily 8am to 8pm)
This is New York's central tourist office and has free brochures, maps, helpful staff, a Broadway Ticket Center and a Metropolitan Transportation Authority that sells MetroCards (see page 000), as well as providing ATMs, currency-exchange machines and free Internet. It's worth visiting even if

New York's marathon goes from Staten Island to Central Park

EVENTS
January or early February
Chinese New Year in Chinatown
April–October
Baseball Season
May
Ninth Avenue International Food Festival
June
Metropolitan Opera park concerts, Museum Mile Celebration
July
Independence Day Fireworks over the East River
July–August
Shakespeare in the Park
August–September
Lincoln Center Out-of-Doors Festival; Harlem Week
September
Feast of San Gennaro, in Little Italy
September–October
New York Film Festival
Early November
New York Marathon
December
Tree lighting at Rockefeller Center, New Year's Eve celebrations

PARADES
January
Three Kings' Day, tel 212/831-7272
March
St. Patrick's Day
Greek Independence Day Parade (parade of circus animals to Madison Square Garden)
March or April
Easter Parade, Fifth Avenue between 44th and 59th streets
May
Martin Luther King Day Parade
June
Puerto Rican Day Parade
Lesbian and Gay Pride
October
Columbus Day Parade
Halloween Parade in Greenwich Village
November
Macy's Thanksgiving Day

you think you don't need to. Some of the free walking tours start from here.

NYCVB Visitor Information Center

(810 Seventh Avenue between 52nd and 53rd streets, tel 212/484-1222, Monday to Friday 8.30am to 6pm)
Smaller than the Times Square complex, this information center has free brochures and leaflets. The interactive terminal with touch-screen access to visitor

information is extremely useful. Buy advance tickets to major attractions here, your CityPass (see page 317), and pick up an *Official New York City Guide*.

The center provides an ATM (cashpoint), plus telephones that are directly connected to American Express offices.

Lower East Side Visitors Center

(261 Broome Street, between Orchard and Allen streets, tel 888/825-8374 or 212/226-9010, www.lowereastsideny.com, daily 10am to 4pm)
Provides pamphlets covering local shopping, dining and nightlife entertainment.

PLANNING

BOOKS, MAPS, MOVIES AND TELEVISION

BOOKS

Non-fiction

The Historical Atlas of New York City: Eric Homberger, Henry Holt and Company, New York, 1998
A fascinating book on the history of New York, always a pleasure to read. Excellent graphics, maps and photographs.

New York City (A Short History): George J. Lankevich, New York University Press, New York, 2002
A fascinating look at New York political and social history from the first settlers to the election of Mayor Michael Bloomberg.

New York: Songs of the City: Nancy Groce, Watson-Guptill Publications, New York, 1999
A delightful musical journey through New York's five boroughs, with anecdotes and facts about people in the music industry, lyrics of old tunes about New York, and beautifully reproduced music sheet covers and posters.

Fiction

Novelists and short-story writers have always been attracted to New York, and many American classics have been set here. For short stories pick up O. Henry's *The Voice of the City* (1908) or Damon Runyon's *Guys and Dolls*. Novels such as F. Scott Fitzgerald's *The Beautiful and the Damned* (1922), John Dos Passos's *Manhattan Transfer* (1925), J. D. Salinger's *The Catcher in the Rye* (1951) and Truman Capote's *Breakfast at Tiffany's* (1958) are all popular reads. More recent novels include Tom Wolfe's *Bonfire of the Vanities* and The *New York Trilogy* by Paul Auster.

MAPS AND OTHER PUBLICATIONS

Fodor's *New York City 2004*
Fodor's shows you the way on and off the beaten path, with detailed reviews and expert inside track knowledge.

Fodor's *Gold Guide to New York City* has information on where to go, what to see and how to get there, written by New

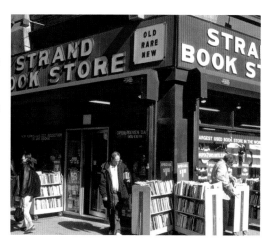

York City-based shopping experts, restaurant critics and other specialists. It includes detailed descriptions of hundreds of restaurant and hotel choices, information on sights, and listings of stores and sports opportunities. Useful web links and Smart Travel Tips help in planning.

AIA *Guide to New York City*: Norval White & Elliot Willensky, Three Rivers Press, New York, 2000
The American Institute of Architects' guide to parks and buildings in all five boroughs is a treasure of architectural knowledge and opinion. With structures arranged in geographical order, it's fun to have as you amble around town, but it's hefty.

Guide to New York City Landmarks: John Wiley & Sons, Inc. 1998
This guide to the city's landmarks and historic districts is ideal for walking tours.

MOVIES
New York has been the setting of great movies by some great directors. Why not watch a few of them before you visit.

42nd Street (1933), Hal Wallis
King Kong (1933), Merian C. Cooper
Guys and Dolls (1955), Samuel Goldwyn
Breakfast at Tiffany's (1961), M. Jurrow, R. Shepherd
West Side Story (1961), Robert Wise

The place for literary bargains

Mean Streets (1973), Martin Scorsese
Taxi Driver (1976), Martin Scorsese
New York, New York (1977), Martin Scorsese
Saturday Night Fever (1977), John Badham
Manhattan (1979), Woody Allen
Broadway Danny Rose (1984), Woody Allen
The Cotton Club (1984), Francis Ford Coppola
Desperately Seeking Susan (1985), Susan Seidelman
Radio Days (1987), Woody Allen
When Harry Met Sally (1989), Rob Reiner
A Bronx Tale (1993), Robert De Niro
Pollock (2000), Ed Harris
Gangs of New York (2002), Martin Scorsese
The Hours (2002), Stephen Daldry

TELEVISION
High drama, farce and comedy are played out on the streets of New York daily, and on the screens in people's homes throughout the world when they tune into the following popular TV shows set in or about New York City. Many of them can also be seen on video or DVD.

"Friends"
"Law & Order"
"NYPD Blue"
"Seinfeld"
"Sex and the City"
"Will & Grace"

PLANNING

USEFUL WEBSITES

ACCOMMODATIONS
● All New York Hotels
www.allnewyorkhotels.net
Search for a hotel (including
discount hotels) by name or
criteria
● Hotel Conxions
www.hotelconxions.com
Finds great deals on city hotels
● New York hotels
www.new-york.hotels-nb.com
Assists with reservations at any of
the hotels they list
● Room Connection
www.RoomConnection.com
A central reservation service for
hotels in New York City
● YMCA Guest Rooms
www.ymcanyc.org
The main site for YMCA, with
links to YMCAs around Greater
New York

BROADWAY AND OFF-BROADWAY TICKETS
● Playbill's Online Theater
Club www.playbillclub.com
A membership club that gives
discounts to top shows
● TeleCharge
www.telecharge.com
● Theater Direct International
www.broadway.com
● TheaterMania
www.theatermania.com
● Ticketmaster
www.ticketmaster.com

MONEY
● Comprehensive Guide to
ATMs, banks, currency
exchanges
www.money-map.com
● Thomas Cook Foreign
Exchange
www.us.thomascook.com

NEW YORK CITY INFORMATION
● Alliance for Downtown New
York www.downtownny.com
Everything you need to know
about Downtown, including links
to a free bus service and an
interactive map
● The Bronx Tourism Council
www.ilovethebronx.com
● Brooklyn Tourism Council
www.brooklynX.org
● Citysearch
www.newyork.citysearch.com
Attractions, events, hotels, real
estate, restaurants and shopping
● Customs information for
entering New York City
www.customs.ustreas.gov

● New York Convention &
Visitors Bureau
www.nycvisit.com
● New York Metro
www.nymetro.com
New York magazine and Metro
TV website
● New York Today
www.nytoday.com
The *New York Times* site, a guide
for New Yorkers and visitors to
what's on and what to do
● Times Square Business
Improvement District
www.timessquarebid.org
The official site for Times Square
and what's going on there

NEWS, REVIEWS AND WHAT'S ON
● *New York* magazine
www.newyorkmag.com
● The *New York Times*
www.nytimes.com
● *The New Yorker*
www.newyorker.com
● *New York Press*
www.nypress.com
A free weekly newspaper
● *New York Today*
www.nytoday.com
● *Time Out New York*
www.timeoutny.com
● *Village Voice*
www.villagevoice.com
A major gay publication

RADIO
New York City is the United
States's top radio outlet. The
radio dial is literally cacophonous,
and if you live in an area without
a similar level or choice, just
turning on the radio and flipping
the dial is an experience. A few
top stations are:

Keeping in touch is easy

● WYNC-FM 93.9 (820-AM)
www.wnyc.org
● 1010 WINS-AM Radio
www.1010wins.com
● WBGO-FM 88.3 Radio
www.wbgo.org
● WQXR-FM 96.3
www.wqrx.com
New York Times radio station,
with classical music
● WFAN-AM 660
www.wfan.com
Sports and news talk
● WOR-AM 710
www.wor710.com
Venerable NYC talk radio

TRANSPORTATION
● Airports
www.panynj.gov/airports
● Trains www.amtrak.com
● Airtrain Newark
www.airtrainnewark.com
An on-airport service and shuttle
from Newark Liberty International
Airport Train Station to Newark
Liberty Airport
● American Automobile
Association
www.aaa.com
● Subways and buses
www.mta.info

GENERAL
● The Baby Sitters' Guild
www.babysittersguild.com
To get child care at any time
● Smart Pages
www.smartpages.com
Telephone numbers in the U.S.
● www.weather.com or
www.cnn.com/weather
A comprehensive weather
service

GLOSSARY FOR NON-U.S. VISITORS

You will see signs in Spanish throughout the city, especially in subways, and hear a wide variety of languages in various neighborhoods. But the New York vocabulary also has its idiosyncrasies, as you will see below.

arugula	rocket
automated teller machine (ATM)	cashpoint
Band-Aid/bandage	plaster
car (on a train)	carriage
cart	trolley
check (restaurant)	bill
cilantro	coriander
cookie	biscuit
cot	camp bed
counterclockwise	anticlockwise
crib	cot
crosswalk	zebra-crossing
day care	crèche
desk clerk	receptionist
dessert	pudding
diaper	nappy
directory assistance	directory enquiries
eggplant	aubergine
elevator	lift
emergency room (hospital)	casualty
faucet	tap
flashlight	torch
french fries	chips
gas	petrol
gas station	garage
hood (car)	bonnet
house trailer/RV	caravan
Jello™	jelly
jelly	jam
license plate	number plate
liquor store	off-licence
long-distance bus	coach
mail	post
main street	high street
one-way ticket	single ticket
pants	trousers
panty-hose	tights
parking lot	car park
pavement	road surface, usually referring to the street
pharmacy	chemist
phone booth	phone box
potato chips	crisps
private school	public school
public holiday	bank holiday
pull-off	layby
rent	hire
restrooms	toilets
roundtrip ticket	return ticket
row houses	terrace
sidewalk	pavement
soccer	football
soda	fizzy soft drink
street musician	busker
stroller	pushchair/buggy
sweater	jumper, jersey
takeout	takeaway
taxi stand	taxi rank
two-lane highway	dual carriageway
traffic circle	roundabout
truck	lorry
trunk (car)	boot
underpass	subway
underpants (men's)	pants
undershirt	vest
vest	waistcoat
washcloth	face flannel
wharf/pier	quay
yard (residential)	garden
zucchini	courgette

NEW YORK GLOSSARY

first balcony	dress circle
balcony	gallery
orchestra seats	stalls
checkroom	cloakroom
brownstones	four- and five-story 19th-century row houses originally faced with cheap brown sandstone
crosstown	an east–west direction across the city
downtown	a direction south of any point
uptown	a direction north of any point
upstate	the state of New York north of New York City
jaywalking	crossing the street illegally, or not at the crosswalk

BUILDING FLOOR NUMBERING

The first floor in America is the ground floor to British visitors, the second floor is the first floor and so on. This is worth watching out for when visiting museums, galleries and other public buildings.

NEW YORK NEIGHBORHOODS

New York is divided into the five boroughs of Manhattan, Brooklyn, the Bronx, Queens and Staten Island, each with their own distinct character.

MANHATTAN

Attractions, many of them world famous, line the streets of Manhattan, the area stretching from Battery Park at its tip to Harlem in the north, beyond Central Park.

Financial District

The oldest part of the city and the nexus of the securities industry anchored by the New York Stock Exchange and Wall Street. It's still primarily a business district, although residents have moved in over the last decade.

Battery Park City

A 92-acre (35ha) complex, built on landfill from the creation of the World Trade Center in 1974. It includes housing, commercial and retail space, plus a marina and the Museum of Jewish Heritage.

TriBeCa

It means *Tri*angle *Be*low *Ca*nal and is defined by Canal and Barclay streets and Broadway and the Hudson River. In 1980, the Odeon restaurant opened and pioneer residents followed, settling into the warehouses and manufacturing buildings. It now has the highest real-estate values in the city and plenty of celebrity cachet. Home to TriBeCa Film Studios, it's still a mixed-use neighborhood of gritty ware-house lofts, loft-style restaurants and low-end retail.

Civic Center

The focal point of City govern-ment, incorporating the courts, police and immigration. City Hall is at the center of the area. It's dwarfed by the nearby Municipal Building, designed by McKim, Mead and White.

Chinatown

In the 1840s Chinatown was just eight blocks. Today it includes about 30 blocks, from Kenmare and Delancey streets to East Broadway and Worth Street, and from Broadway to Allen Street.

Shop for fish, meat, vegetables and herbal remedies or dine in the many affordable restaurants.

Little Italy

Very little of this once vibrant community survives. Most of the Italians have moved to the suburbs and Chinese residents have replaced them. It consists largely of Mulberry Street, which is lined with tourist-oriented restaurants, plus one or two genuine delis.

Nolita

It stands for North of Little Italy. The narrow streets around St. Patrick's Cathedral, once the heart of the Italian community, are now lined with hip designer boutiques.

SoHo

In 1973 the 20 blocks between Houston, Canal, West Broadway and Broadway were designated a Historic District, protecting the best stock of cast-iron buildings in the city. Artists had already begun reclaiming the manufact-uring and warehouse spaces and pioneering a loft lifestyle. Today the artists and most of the art galleries have moved on; the area is now an ultra-expensive, chic shopping mall crowded with non-residents on weekends.

Bowery

A long street connecting Chinatown to the East Village, it was once the city's Skid Row, lined with flophouses and numerous stores selling kitchen supplies and lighting fixtures. Today it is being gentrified.

Lower East Side

The traditional gateway for every wave of immigrants, from the Jewish and the Italians to the Puerto Ricans, this was the last Manhattan neighborhood to be updated. Today, young profes-sionals and artists occupy the tenements and congregate at the clubs and bars along Orchard, Clinton and other streets. Remnants of the Puerto Rican community survive, and so does the bargain bazaar on Sunday along Orchard Street. The boundaries stretch from 14th Street to Fulton and Franklin and from the East River to Broadway,

incorporating Chinatown, Little Italy and the East Village neighborhoods.

Greenwich Village/ West Village

This area stretches from 14th to Houston streets and from the Hudson River to Bowery and Fourth Avenue. Originally a poor neighborhood housing the workers and stevedores who worked the waterfront, it became a bohemia around 1900, attracting a mixture of artists, writers and anarchists. Today, it's a mixed neighborhood. The gay population has mostly moved to Chelsea, and now "successful" singles and families occupy the townhouses and apartments. Small boutiques line the west end of Bleecker Street. The southern section around Bleecker Street and Sixth Avenue still has an Italian flavor.

Meatpacking District

Sandwiched between the West Village and Chelsea around 14th Street, this gritty neighborhood is being redeveloped. Restaurants, bars, clubs and stores are opening and a new hotel is being constructed.

NoHo

Between SoHo and Greenwich Village (from Houston to Eighth Streets and Mercer to Bowery/ Third Avenue), this youth-oriented neighborhood has plenty of fashionable shopping, bars and restaurants. The acronym stands for *No*rth of *Ho*uston.

East Village

This was originally an extension of the Lower East Side, settled by Jewishs and Ukrainian/Polish communities. In the 1960s and 70s it became the center of the counter culture. It has rapidly redeveloped and is now filled with restaurants, bars and a young street scene.

Alphabet City

It refers to avenues A, B, C and D between Houston and 14th streets. In the 1970s, First Avenue marked the DMZ and the streets east of First were considered dangerous drug supermarkets. Gentrification began in 1983 when Operation Pressure Point started cleaning up the drug trade and buildings on Tompkins Square became co-ops. Today young professionals occupy the tenement apartments; there's a thriving dining and bar scene, including a substantial number of gay bars and clubs. The original Hispanic population has been dispersed.

Gramercy Park
This genteel and dignified neighborhood radiating from the eponymous gated garden square remains primarily residential. It stretches from 18th to 23rd streets and from Park Avenue South to Third Avenue.

Union Square/Flatiron District
This hot new neighborhood leading south from the Flatiron Building on 22nd Street and around Madison Square has plenty of bars, restaurants and clubs. The Green Market at Union Square is a must on Saturday. The former Ladies' Mile along Sixth Avenue between 15th and 24th streets is now occupied by large national chain stores. The boundaries go from 14th to 23rd streets and from Park Avenue to Sixth Avenue.

Chelsea
Today Chelsea is the center of the gay community and the new focus for contemporary art anchored by DIA on 22nd Street and numerous warehouse/garage galleries along 24th Street. It has a lively club and restaurant scene. The boundaries stretch from 14th to 30th streets and from Sixth Avenue to the Hudson River.

Murray Hill
A quiet residential neighborhood between 34th and 40th streets between Madison and Third avenues. It is becoming increasingly commercial on the fringes. The Morgan Library and the Episcopalian church, where the Roosevelts worshiped, set the tone.

Midtown
The commercial heart of the city between 34th and 59th streets on the West Side and from 40th to 59th streets on the East Side. It includes major attractions, shops, restaurants, theaters, TV studios, Nasdaq and corporate offices.

Times Square/Theater District
The old peep shows, hookers and junkies have been displaced, and the area around 42nd Street and Broadway is now occupied by an array of major corporations and national chain stores—Condé Nast, Reuters, ESPN Zone, Toys R-Us and many others, who share the area with new hotels, clubs and theaters.

Clinton
Real-estate developers have rediscovered this neighborhood from 42nd to 59th streets between Eighth Avenue and the Hudson River. It was formerly known as Hell's Kitchen and was the site of slaughterhouses, freight yards and factories.

Upper East Side
It stretches from 59th to 96th streets from Fifth Avenue to the East River. The section from 59th to 78th streets between Fifth and Park avenues is often referred to as the Gold Coast, where those who can afford it live. Farther east it was not always elegant, but it became more so in 1956 when the Third Avenue El was demolished and Madison Avenue became an ultra-chic shopping street. Today it is filled with private clubs, consulates, art galleries, restaurants and fine residences. Museum Mile extends along Fifth Avenue from 81st Street north past the Metropolitan Museum of Art.

Yorkville
High-rise apartments line the streets of what was formerly the German section between Lexington and Third avenues on 86th Street.

Carnegie Hill
Between 86th and 96th streets between Fifth and Third avenues, this is primarily a low-key wealthy residential district, anchored by the Carnegie mansion (now the Cooper-Hewitt National Design Museum). The area is home to such prestigious private schools as Dalton, Spence and Horace Mann, plus the Guggenheim and the Jewish Museum.

East Harlem/Spanish Harlem
From 96th to 142nd streets, between Park Avenue and the East River, this area is still home to El Barrio, the community

established by the Puerto Ricans, who first arrived at the end of World War I and increased in numbers after World War II. Today it's a mixed neighborhood of Italians, African-Americans and Hispanics.

Lincoln Square
The square is the area around Lincoln Center. Wealthy individuals, many of them successful performers, occupy the towers, and the area buzzes with bars, restaurants and stores. The ABC and CNN studios are a major presence.

Upper West Side
Broadway cuts right through this section that extends from 59th to 125th streets between the Hudson River and Central Park West. The blocks around 72nd Street were the center of an old German/East-European, primarily Jewish, liberal intellectual community. In the 1970s and 80s Columbus and Amsterdam avenues were gentrified and the old single-room occupancy hotels returned to handsome residences. Today, it's often referred to as a Manhattan suburb, because of its family orientation, although it has become more fashionable recently, as new chic restaurants have opened. Central Park West is lined with expensive cooperatives overlooking Central Park. Notable attractions include the American Museum of Natural History .

Morningside Heights
Columbia University dominates this neighborhood, along with Barnard, Teachers College, the Cathedral of St. John the Divine and the Union Theological and Jewish Theological seminaries.

Harlem
Stretching from 110th Street to the Harlem River and from Fifth to St. Nicholas avenues, Harlem is the city's most famous black community. Originally a suburb for the wealthy, it was settled in the late 19th century by Jewish immigrants from Germany. When the subway arrived in the early 20th century, most of the black community moved in from midtown Manhattan and also from the southern states, and it became a mecca for black artists, writers and musicians. In the 1920s the Harlem Renaissance

brought whites and blacks together to the clubs, theaters and jazz joints. Later it became a blighted community, destroyed by the riots of the 1960s. Today it has been rediscovered by the middle classes and increasingly by whites in search of reasonably priced houses. The restaurants and churches attract visitors.

Washington Heights/Inwood
The last stop in Manhattan. It has been home to many different immigrant groups. Today, it's largely a Dominican Republic community, although young professionals are moving in. It's also home to the Cloisters.

BROOKLYN
With the highest population of the five boroughs (2.5 million), Brooklyn is a healthy rival to Manhattan. It's full of world-class museums, spacious parks, landmark buildings and lively neighborhoods.

Greenpoint
An old Polish neighborhood where young professionals are moving in because of its proximity to Manhattan.

Williamsburg
Primarily a Jewish and African-American neighborhood, recently it has been discovered by the young and hip. It's now reminiscent of 1950s Greenwich Village.

DUMBO
One developer alone has created this neighborhood (Down Under the Manhattan Bridge Overpass) by renting to artists and musicians. It's likely to become the next "hot" neighborhood à la SoHo.

Brooklyn Heights
A former premier residential neighborhood. The Promenade has magnificent views of the Manhattan skyline.

Cobble Hill
This is another affluent residential neighborhood where the streets are lined with elegant brownstones. Atlantic Avenue supports a major Middle Eastern community.

Prospect Park
The Brooklyn Botanic Gardens are in Prospect Park and the Brooklyn Museum of Art is adjacent to the gardens.

Carroll Gardens
Fine brownstones made this primarily Italian neighborhood an attractive residential area for those who could not afford to buy in Manhattan.

Fort Greene
After it was designated a historic district in 1978, professionals started buying the handsome brownstones. It's home to the Brooklyn Academy of Music.

Park Slope
Brooklyn's "alternative" village on the western edge of Prospect Park. The main commercial streets are 7th and 5th avenues.

Crown Heights
The city's largest West Indian community, plus a thriving Hasidic Jewish community.

Brighton Beach/Coney Island
Often called Little Odessa due to its Russian Jewish community, Brighton Beach has a boardwalk, clubs, restaurants and stores servicing the Russian community.

Next door, Coney Island was the city's great blue-collar playground from the late 1890s to the early 1930s. In the 1960s it became drug infested and dangerous. Today it is being revived. It's home to the New York Aquarium.

QUEENS
An international melting-pot, Queens has the most diverse population of the five boroughs, and is also the largest. Named after Queen Catherine of Braganza, Charles II's wife, it is a good place to go to sample ethnic life and cuisine.

Astoria
The old Greek neighborhood has survived. Astoria was also a film-making area and some of the studios have been revived, including one that houses the Museum of the Moving Image.

Long Island City
Queens' most industrialized area. Art has come to this gritty waterfront area with the arrival of MoMA QNS up to 2005.

Forest Hills
This wealthy, largely Jewish enclave, only a short commute from Manhattan, has handsome apartment houses, and good restaurants and social services.

Jackson Heights
A major South American and Indian enclave on 82nd Street..

Corona, Shea Stadium and Flushing Meadow Park
The stadium is the home of the Mets. The park has the National Tennis Center, the New York Hall of Science and the Queens Museum of Art. Corona is mainly a Dominican Republic, Colombian and Mexican community.

Flushing Meadows
An area populated by Chinese, Koreans, Vietnamese, Malaysians and Japanese.

THE BRONX
The Bronx was once an expensive retreat for the wealthy. Development in the 1920s brought more well-heeled residents, then it got a reputation as a crime-laden area, and now has been turned into a much more tourist-friendly borough, with plenty of attractions and beautiful parks.

Fordham
The Bronx Zoo and the New York Botanical Gardens are in this neighborhood. Arthur Avenue is a colorful Italian area.

Riverdale
The most desirable residential neighborhood in the borough and the location of Wave Hill home, an 1843 estate once home to Mark Twain and Teddy Roosevelt and now a public garden and cultural center.

Van Cortlandt Park and Woodlawn Cemetery
IMany famous people are buried at Woodlawn, including F. W. Woolworth, Irving Berlin and Duke Ellington. Van Cortlandt Park is a delightful space with forests and hills to explore.

City Island
New Yorkers come to this historic fishing community for fresh fish.

STATEN ISLAND
Staten Island is more than twice the size of Manhattan. It's residents are largely blue collar, still living a fairly autonomous, rural life away from busy Manhattan. Attractions include Alice Austen House, Snug Harbor Cultural Center and Historic Richmond Town.

PLANNING

	Main road
	Other road
	Minor road/path
	Railway
	Park
	Important building
	Featured place of interest
	Subway station:
	1, 2, 3, 9
	4, 5, 6
	7
	A, C, E
	B, D, F
	L
	M, J, Z
	N, R, Q, W
	S (42 St Shuttle)
	S (Grand St Shuttle)
	S (Franklin Av Shuttle)
	V (0530-2300 Mon-Fri)
	Railway station
P	Parking

	0	300 m
332-345		
	0	250 yds

	0	8 km
346-347		
	0	5 m

Maps

West 92nd Str

UPPER WE

West 91st Stre

SIDE

West 90th Str

West 89th Stre

West 88th Str

West 87th Stre

West 86th Str

West 85th Stre

West 84th Str

West 83rd Str

West 82nd Stre

West 81st Str

West 80th Str

West 79th Stre

West 78th Stre

West 77th Stre

West 76th Str

West 75th Stre

West 74th Stre

West 73rd Str

West 72nd Stre

West 71st Str

West 70th Str

West 69th Str

West 68th Str

West 67th Str

66th Street Lincoln Center

West 66th Stre

West 65th Str

West 64th Street

West 63rd Street

West 62nd Street

Lincoln Center

West 62nd Str

West 61st Street

West 60th Str

West 59th Street

HIGHWAY 9A

Riverside Drive

West End Avenue

BROADWAY

Amsterdam Avenue

Riverside Park

Hudson River

79th Street

86th Street

72nd Street

Ansonia Building

BROADWAY

Riverside Drive

Freedom Place

West 69th Street

West 68th Street

Riverside Blvd

West 61st Drive

West End Avenue

Amsterdam Avenue

Juilliard School

13

14

15

16

D

Central
Park
Reservoir

E

Jewish
Museum

East 92nd Street

East 91st Street

Cooper-Hewitt
National Design Museum

East 90th Street

National
Academy
of Design

13

Guggenheim
Museum

East 88th Street

East 87th Street

86th
Street

86th Street Transverse Road

West

Drive

86th
Street

CENTRAL PARK

East 86th Street

Neue
Galerie

East 85th Street

East 84th Street

81st Street
Museum of
Nat Hist

East 83rd Street

The Metropolitan
Museum of Art

East 82nd Street

Central Park

East 81st Street

14

East 80th Street

*Belvedere
Lake*

79th Street Transverse Road

East 79th Street

can Museum
ural History

Central Park West

East 78th Street

5th Avenue

PARK AVENUE

New-York
cal Society

East 77th Street

77th
Street

*The
Lake*

East 76th eet

334

an Remo
artments

East 75th Street

Whitney Museum
of American Art

*Conservatory
Water*

East 74th
Street

he Dakota
Building

East 73rd Street

72nd
Street

East 72nd Street

*Strawberry
Fields*

East 71st Street

15

Olmsted Drive

Frick
Collection

Asia Society
and Museum

East 70th Street

West

Drive

East 69th Street

Madison Avenue

68th Street
Hunter College

East 68th Street

East Drive

East 67th Street

*The
Sheep
Meadow*

East 66th Street

Tavern on
the Green

East 65th Street

65th Street Transverse Road

Park Drive

East 64th Street

t 64th Street

West
63rd Street

Center Drive

FIFTH

East 63rd Street

16

ton
nue

erican
Society

*Central
Park*

East 62nd Street

PARK AVENUE

AVENUE

61st Street

East 61st Street

Park Drive North

*The
Pond*

East 60th Street

D

Central Park South

337

E

5th
avenue

East 59th Street

333

59th Street
Columbus
Circle

COLUMBUS
CIRCLE

Jewish
Museum

East 92nd Street

East 91st Street

**Cooper-Hewitt
National Design Museum**

East 91st Street

East 90th Street

**National
Academy
of Design**

East 90th Street

PARK AVENUE

Lexington Avenue

3rd Avenue

2nd Avenue

1st Avenue

York Avenue

5th Avenue

East 89th Street

13

**Guggenheim
Museum**

East 88th Street

East 88th Street

East 87th Street

East 87th Street

86th
Street

East 86th Street

East 86th Street

**Neue
Galerie**

East 85th Street

East 85th Street

East 84th Street

East 84th Street

East 83rd Street

East 83rd Street

**The Metropolitan
Museum of Art**

East 82nd Street

East 82nd Street

East 81st Street

East 81st Street

14

East 80th Street

East 80th Street

East 79th Street

East 79th Street

PARK AVENUE

Lexington Avenue

3rd Avenue

2nd Avenue

1st Avenue

York Avenue

5th Avenue

East 78th Street

East 78th Street

East 77th Street

East 77th Street

77th
Street

East 76th Street

East 76th Street

333

East 75th Street

East 75th Street

*Conservatory
Water*

**Whitney Museum
of American Art**

East 74th Street

East 74th Street

East 73rd Street

East 73rd Street

East 72nd Street

East 72nd Street

15

East 71st Street

East 71st Street

**Frick
Collection**

Madison Avenue

**Asia Society
and Museum**

East 70th Street

East 70th Street

East 69th Street

68th Street
Hunter College

East 69th Street

East 68th Street

East 68th Street

East 67th Street

East 67th Street

FIFTH

East 66th Street

East 66th Street

AVENUE

East 65th Street

East 65th Street

East 64th Street

East 64th Street

16

East 63rd Street

Lexington
Avenue

East 63rd Street

PARK AVENUE

Lexington Avenue

3rd Avenue

2nd Avenue

1st Avenue

York Avenue

East 62nd Street

East 62nd Street

**Mount Vernon Hotel
Museum and Garden**

East 61st Street

East 61st St

North

East 60th Street

**Lexington
Avenue**

East 60th Street

HIGH

334 5th
Avenue

E

59th
Street

338

F

East 59th Street

East 59th Street

Gracie
Mansion

Carl
Schurz
Park

H

1st
Street

27th
Avenue

8th
Street

12th
Street

Astoria Boulevard

J

29th
Avenue

I3

30th
Astoria
Boulevard

Welling
Court

30th
Avenue

Hallets
Cove Playground

Vernon

30th
Road

East River

30th
Drive

31st
Avenue

31st Road

Boulevard

31st
Drive

31st Road

Socrates
Sculpture
Park

Broadway

33rd Avenue

33rd
Avenue

I4

33rd
Road

13th
Street

33rd Road

Main
Street

Rainey
Park

Vernon
Boulevard

9th
Street

10th
Street

11th
Street

12th
Street

14th
Street

Ravenswood
Playground

34th
Avenue

FRANKLIN DELANO ROOSEVELT DRIVE

35th
Avenue

QUEENS

River
Road

21st
Street

P

Roosevelt Island
Bridge

36th
Avenue

14th
Street

I5

Main
Street

37th
Avenue

**Roosevelt
Island**

38th
Avenue

9th
Street

10th
Street

11th
Street

12th
Street

13th
Street

Roosevelt
Island
Main
Street

East
Road

40th
Avenue

I6

West
Road

Vernon
Boulevard

41st
Avenue

Queensbridge
Park

21ST STREET

21st Street
Queensbridge

J

Main   Street

QUEENSBORO BRIDGE

339

H

HIGHWAY 25
Queens Plaza South

**Museum of
Modern Art,
Queens**

J

41st   Road

Main   Street

West 59th Street

12th Av

West 59th Str

West 58th Stre

West 57TH STRE

12th
Avenue

12th Av

12TH AVENUE

11th Avenue

10TH AVENUE

West 56th Str

West 55th Str

West 54th Str

*De Witt
Clinton Park*

17

Avenue

West 53rd Stre

West 52nd St

West 51st Str

12th

West 50th Str

West 49th Str

West 48th St

West 47th Str

*Intrepid Sea-Air-
Space Museum*

West 46th
Street

West 46th Str

West 45th Str

Hudson River

9A

11th Avenue

10TH AVENUE

West 44th St

West 43rd St

18

WEST 42ND ST

West 41st Str

West 40th Str

West 39th Str

HIGHWAY 495

DYER AVENUE

West 38th Str

**Jacob K
Javits
Convention
Center**

West 37th Str

West 36th St

West 35th Str

West 34th St

19

West 33rd Str

12TH AVENUE

11th Avenue

10TH AVENUE

West 31st Stre

West 30th St

West 29th Str

West 28th Str

Chelsea Par

West 27th Street

20

West 26th St

West 25th St

CIRCLE
59th Street
Columbus
Circle

D Central Park South E Avenue East 59th Street 16
333
West 58th Street East 58th Street

57th
Street
57th
Street
WEST 57TH STREET EAST 57TH STREET

Carnegie
Hall
Trump
Tower
Dahesh Museum of Art

West 56th Street East 56th Street

8TH AVENUE
BROADWAY
7TH AVENUE
West 55th Street East 55th Street

Madison Avenue
5TH AVENUE
PARK AVENUE
PARK AVENUE

West 54th Street East 54th Street

7th
Avenue
5th
Avenue
Seagram
Building

West 53rd Street East 53rd Street

Museum of
Arts and Design
Museum of
Television and Radio
17

West 52nd Street East 52nd Street

Radio City
Music Hall
St Patrick's
Cathedral
Municipal
Art Society
51st
Street

West 51st Street East 51st Street

West 50th Street East 50th Street MIDTOWN

50th
Street
50th
Street
49th
Street
47th - 50th Streets
Rockefeller Center
GE
Building
West 49th Street East 49th Street MANHATTAN

Rockefeller
Center
Rockefeller Plaza
West 48th Street East 48th Street

DIAMOND
DISTRICT
West 47th Street East 47th Street

BROADWAY
West 46th Street East 46th Street

West 45th Street East 45th Street

West 44th Street East 44th Street

Vanderbilt Avenue
PARK AVENUE
Grand
Central
Terminal

Times
Square
Int'l Center of
Photography
West 43rd Street East 43rd Street 18

42nd
Street
5th
Avenue
Grand
Central
42nd St

Holy Cross
Church
Reuters
Building
WEST 42ND STREET EAST 42ND STREET 338

42nd Street
Port Authority
Bus Terminal
Candler
Building
New
Amsterdam
Theater
Bryant
Park
New York
Public
Library
East 41st Street Chanin
Building

FASHION AVENUE
BROADWAY
West 40th Street East 40th Street

Times Square
42nd Street
West 39th Street East 39th Street

West 38th Street East 38th Street

West 37th Street East 37th Street

Morgan Library

West 36th Street East 36th Street

West 35th Street East 35th Street

Macy's
WEST 34TH STREET EAST 34TH STREET

34th Street
Penn Station
34th Street
Penn Station
34th Street
Herald Square
Empire State
Building
19

West 33rd Street East 33rd Street 33rd
Street

Madison
Square
Garden
Pennsylvania
Station
West 32nd Street East 32nd Street

5TH AVENUE
Madison Avenue
PARK AVENUE

West 31st Street East 31st Street

West 30th Street East 30th Street

Little Church
Around the Corner
West 29th Street East 29th Street

8TH AVENUE
7TH AVENUE
28th
Street
28th
Street
West 28th Street East 28th Street 28th
Street

28th
Street
West 27th Street East 27th Street 20

D West 26th Street East 26th Street 337
341 E

West 25th Street East 25th St
Madison

5th
Avenue

East   E   Street   59th   334   F   East   59th   Street

16

Street   East   58th   Street   East   58th   Street

STREET   EAST   57TH   STREET   EAST   57TH   STREET

Trump   Dahesh Museum of Art   West   56th   Street
Tower

Street   East   56th   Street   West   56th   Street

Street   East   55th   Street   PARK   Lexington Avenue   3rd   P   East   55th   1st   Street   Sutton Place
5th   AVENUE   Avenue   Avenue   2nd
Avenue   PARK AVENUE   Avenue

Street   East   54th   Street   East   54th   Street

5th
Avenue

Street   East   53rd   Street   Lexington   East   53rd   Street
Avenue

Seagram
Building

17   Street   East   52nd   Street   East   52nd   Street

Museum of Television   St Patrick's   East   51st   Street
and Radio   Cathedral   Municipal   5 1st
Art Society   Street

Street   East   50th   Street   East   50th   Street   Mitchell Pl

MIDTOWN   East   49th Street
Rockefeller
Plaza   Street   East   49th   Street

MANHATTAN   East   48th Street
Street   East   48th   Street

P   Street   East   47th   Street   East   47th   Street

Street   East   46th   Street   East   46th   Street   United Nations Plaza   United Natio
Headquarte

Street   East   45th   Street   East   45th Street

5th   East 44th   Madison Avenue   Vanderbilt Avenue   PARK AVENUE   Lexington Avenue   3rd Avenue   2nd Avenue   East   44th Street
Avenue   Street   Grand
Street   East   43rd   P   Central   Chrysler   P   P   East 43rd Street   Tudor
18   Street   Terminal   Building   City
5th   East   Grand   STREET   Central   EAST   42ND   STREET   Place
Avenue   337   42nd St
STREET   EAS   Chanin   Daily News   EAST   42ND   STREET   4

New York   Building   Building   East 41st
Public   Street
Library   East   41st   Street

Street   East   40th   Street   TUNNEL   East   40th   Street

Street   East   39th   Street   TUNNEL   East   39th Street

Street   East   38th   Street   EXIT   ENTRANCE   East   38th Street

Street   East   37th   Street   East   36th   Street
Morgan Library

Street   East   36th   Street   PARK   STREET   STREET   East   35th   Street
AVENUE

P   Street   East   35th   Street   East 35th   Street

STREET   EAST   34TH   STREET   EAST   34TH   STREET

19   Empire State
Building   East   33rd   Street   33rd   East   33rd   Street   FDR DRIVE SERVICE ROAD
Street   Street

Street   East   32nd   Street   P

Street   East   31st   Street

5th   East   30th   Street   Lexington Avenue   3rd Avenue   2nd Avenue   1st Avenue   East   30th   Street
Little Church   Avenue
Around the Corner
Street   East   29th   Street   East   29th   Street

Street   East   28th   Street   East   28th   Street   Mt. Carmel   Street.

20   Street   East   27th   Street   28th   East   27th
Street   Street

338   East   E   Street   342   F   East   26th   Street

Street   East   25th St   East   25th   Street

Main Street

Museum of
Modern Art,
Queens

22n

West Road

East Road

Vernon Boulevard

43rd

43rd Street

9th Street

10th Street

11th Street

12th Street

13th Street

21ST STREET

22nd St

Avenue

Road

44th Avenue

44th Road

45th Road
Court House Square

17

44th Drive

45th Avenue

45th Avenue

45th Road

46th Avenue

46th Road

21st Street
(Van Alst)

QUEENS

47th Avenue

47th Road

JACKSON AVENUE

21ST STREET

5th Street

Vernon Boulevard

49th Ave

50th Av

Gantry
Plaza
State Park

8th Avenue

18 **495**

49th Avenue

Center Blvd

Vernon Blvd
Jackson Av

50th Avenue

11th STREET

Avenue

51st Avenue

Borden Avenue

2nd Street

53rd Avenue

QUEENS MIDTOWN TUNNEL

54th Avenue

2nd Street

Ash Street

Box Street

Commercial Street

Manhattan Street

Clay Street

Dupont Street

19

Ave

Eagle Street

Freeman Street

Green Street

Franklin Street

East River

West Street

Huron

Ind

20

336

West 25th Stre

West 24th Stre

10TH AVENUE

West 23rd Stre

West 22nd Str

West 21st Stre

West 20th Stre

West 19th Str

West 18th Str

West 17th Str

West 16th Str

West 15th Stre

WEST 14TH STR

West

Washington

Little West 12th S

Street Gans

Bloomfield
Street

10TH AVENUE

Horatio

Gansevoort
Street

WEST STREET

Jane

Wes

Be

*Chelsea
Waterside Park*

20

P

11TH AVENUE

9A

21

Hudson River

22

23

West 26th Street East 26th Street

D **337** **E** West 25th Street East 25th St

Madison Square Park

Metropolitan Life Insurance Tower

East 24th St East

West 24th Street

23rd Street 23rd Street East 23rd Street **20**

West 23rd Street East 23rd Street

23rd Street Flatiron Building

West 22nd Street East 22nd Street

CHELSEA

West 21st Street East 21st Street Grame

West 20th Street East 20th Street Grame

Theodore Roosevelt Birthplace

West 19th Street East 19th Street

18th Street

West 18th Street East 18th Street

West 17th Street East 17th Street

Union Square Park

West 16th Street East 16th St

West 15th Street East 15th Street

14th Street 8th Street 14th Street 14th Street **UNION SQUARE** 14th Street Union Square **21**

WEST 14TH STREET EAST 14TH STREET

6th Avenue

West 13th Street East 13th Street

Forbes Magazine Galleries

West 12th Street East 12th Street

Grace Church

West 11th Street East 11th Street

Jefferson Market Library

West 10th Street East 10th Street

West 9th Street East 9th **342**

8th Street NYU

West 8th Street East 8th Street

Macdougal Aly Washington Mews

Waverly Place

Christopher Street - Sheridan Square Christopher Park

GREENWICH VILLAGE

Washington

Place

WASHINGTON SQ NORTH

Washington Square Park

Waverly Place

Washington Place **22**

West 4th St Washington Square

WASHINGTON SQ SOUTH West 4th Street

McNulty's Rare Teas and Choice Coffee Shop

Church of St Luke-in-the-Fields

West 3rd Street

Minetta Lane

Bleecker Street Gre

Bor

House of Oldies Rare Records

Jon Al

J J Walker Park

WEST HOUSTON STREET

Broadway Lafayette Street

9A

New Museum of Contemporary Art

Guggenheim Museum SoHo

Prince Street

Little Singer Building

Houston Street

Spring Street

Prince Street

23

New York City Fire Department Museum

SOHO

Haughwout Building

Broome Street

Tony Shafrazi Gallery

341

AND TUNNEL **D** CANAL ST Canal Street Canal Street **344** Grand **E** Canal Street

20

East River

21

FRANKLIN DELANO ROOSEVELT DRIVE

Avenue C Loop

esant
val

Avenue

East 16th
Street

East 15th Street

ce Drive

EAST 14TH STREET

Avenue

East 13th Street

Avenue

Avenue D

East 12th Street

Szold Place

East 11th Street

East 10th Street

East 9th Street

East 8th Street

East 7th Street

East 6th Street

East 5th Street

East 5th Walk

22

East 4th Street

East 4th Walk

East

Avenue

Avenue D

East 3rd Street

East 3rd
Street

Louis Street

River

FRANKLIN DELANO ROOSEVELT DRIVE

Manglin Street

Park

Avenue B

Avenue C

EAST HOUSTON STREET

Attorney
Avenue

Hamilton
Fish Park

Columbia

Baruch
Place

Franklin D Roosevelt Drive

Stanton Street

Clinton Street

Attorney

Ridge Street

Pitt Street

Baruch Drive

Rivington Street

street

WILLIAMSBURG BRIDGE APPROACH

P

Franklin D Roosevelt Drive

23

**LOWER
EAST SIDE**

Broome

Ridge Street

Pitt Street

Willett Street

Broome Street

Columbia Street

Lewis Street

Suffolk Street

Grand Street

Montgomery Street

Henry Street

Madison Street

Jackson Street

Henry Street

ard
k

Broadway

Corlears
Hook
Park

Corlears
Hook
Park

24

Seward
Park

East
Broadway

Hester

Canal

Street

Street

Street

Street

Street

Jefferson St

East
Broadway

Broadway

Clinton

Madison

Monroe
Street

Couvenneur
Street

Water

Street

Street

Division
Street

Rutgers

Street

Pike
Street

Monroe St

Street

Falcon
Drive

Rutgers
Slip

Rutgers
Street

Cherry

Rutgers
Park

South

Division

East

Broadway

Henry

Street

Catherine

Street

Monroe

Cherry

Street

Street

Market
Slip

Catherine
Slip

Water

Catherine
Slip

FRANKLIN DELANO ROOSEVELT DRIVE

MANHATTAN BRIDGE

Oliver
Street

James
Street

Madison

Street

Street

Street

East River

BROOKLYN BRIDGE

Finest

Front

Street

SOUTH STREET

SOUTH STREET

Slip

**Fulton Street
Market**

South Street Seaport

New Dock
Street

Empire-
Fulton Ferry
State Park

Water

Front
Street

York

Plymouth
Street

Main Street

Washington St

Adams
Street

York
Street

25

Pearl

John
Street

Plymouth

Water

St

Street

CADMAN

Cadman Plaza East

278

Doughty Street

Vine
Street

Hicks

Middagh

Street

High Street
Brooklyn Bridge

Cadman
Plaza
Park

FURMAN ST

Willow

**Plymouth Church
of the Pilgrims**

Columbia

Orange

Street

BROOKLYN

PLAZA

WEST

Pineapple

Street

HEIGHTS

Street

Clark

Clark
Street

Monroe

26

Clinton Street

Heights

Street

College
Place

Place

Love Lane

Street

Pierrepont

Cathedral of
Our Lady of
Lebanon

Street

Montague

Street

Remsen

Grace
Court

Hunts Lane

BROOKLYN-QUEENS EXPRESSWAY

Grace

Court

Grace
Court
Aly

**Grace
Church**

Street

Garden Place

Joralemon

Joralemon
Street

Willow Place

Columbia Pl

State

Columbia Place

Place

27

ATLANTIC AVENUE

84th Street, West 332 C14
85th Street, East 334 F14
85th Street, West 332 C14
86th Street Transverse Road
  333 D13
86th Street, East 334 F13
86th Street, West 332 C13
87th Street, East 334 F13
87th Street, West 332 C13
88th Street, East 334 F13
88th Street, West 332 C13
89th Street, East 334 F13
89th Street, West 332 C13
90th Street, East 334 F13
90th Street, West 332 C13
91st Street, East 334 F13
91st Street, West 332 C13
92nd Street, East 334 F13
92nd Street, West 332 C13
93rd Street, East 334 F13
93rd Street, West 332 C13

A

Adams Street 345 H25
Admiral George Dewey
  Promenade 344 E27
Albany Street 344 E26
Allen Street 342 G23
Amsterdam Avenue 332 C14
Anew Street 338 G20
Ann Street 344 E25
Ash Street 339 J19
Asser Levy Place 342 G20
Astor Place 342 F22
Astoria Boulevard 335 H13
Atlantic Avenue 345 H27
Attorney Avenue 343 G22
Attorney Street 343 G23
Avenue A 342 G21
Avenue B 343 G21
Avenue C 343 G21
Avenue C Loop 343 G21
Avenue D 343 H21
Avenue of the Americas 337 E18
Avenue of the Finest 345 F25

B

Bank Street 341 D22
Barclay Street 344 D25
Barrow Street 341 D22
Baruch Drive 343 H22
Baruch Place 343 H22
Battery Place 344 E26
Baxter Street 344 F24
Bayard Street 344 F24
Beach Street 344 E24
Beaver Street 344 E26
Beekman Street 344 F25
Bethune Street 340 C22
Bleecker Street 341 D22
Bloomfield Street 340 C21
Bond Street 342 F22

Borden Avenue 339 J18
Bowery 342 F23
Box Street 339 J19
Broad Street 344 E26
Broadway 337 D18
Broadway, Queens 335 J14
Brooklyn Battery Tunnel 344 F27
Brooklyn Bridge 345 G25
Broome Street 341 E23

C

Cadman Plaza East 345 H26
Cadman Plaza West 345 H26
Canal Street 344 F24
Cardinal Hayes Place 344 F24
Carmine Street 342 D22
Catherine Slip 345 F25
Catherine Street 345 F24
Cedar Street 344 E25
Center Boulevard 339 H18
Center Drive 333 D16
Central Park South 337 D16
Central Park West 333 D14
Centre Market Place 342 F23
Centre Street 344 F24
Chambers Street 344 E24
Charles Lane 341 D22
Charles Street 341 D22
Charlton Street 341 D23
Cherry Street 345 G24
Christopher Street 341 D22
Chrystie Street 342 F23
Church Street 344 E24
Clark Street 345 H26
Clarkson Street 342 D23
Clay Street 339 J19
Cliff Street 344 F25
Clinton Street 343 G23
Clinton Street, Brooklyn 345 H26
College Place 345 H26
Columbia Heights 345 G26
Columbia Place 345 H27
Columbia Street 343 G22
Columbus Avenue 332 D15
Commerce Street 341 D22
Commercial Street 339 J19
Cooper Square 342 F22
Cornelia Street 341 E22
Cortlandt Street 344 E25
Crosby Street 342 F23

D

Delancey Street 342 F23
Desbrosses Street 344 D24
Dey Street 344 E25
Division Street 345 F24
Dominick Street 341 E23
Doughty Street 345 G25
Dover Street 344 F25
Downing Street 341 D23
Duane Street 344 E24
Dupont Street 339 J19

Dutch Street 344 F25
Dyer Avenue 336 C19

E

Eagle Street 339 J19
East 20th Street Service Drive
  342 G20
East Broadway 344 F24
East Drive 333 E15
East Houston Street 343 G22
East Road 339 G17
Eldridge Street 342 F23
Elizabeth Street 345 F24
Ericsson Place 344 E24
Essex Street 342 G23
Exchange Alley 344 E26
Exchange Place 344 E26
Falcon Drive 345 G24
Fashion Avenue 337 D19

F

FDR Drive Service Road 338 G19
Fletcher Street 344 F25
Foley Square 344 F24
Forsyth Street 342 F23
Franklin Delano Roosevelt Drive
  338 G17
Franklin Place 344 E24
Franklin Street 344 E24
Franklin Street, Queens 339 J19
Freedom Place 332 B15
Freeman Street 339 J19
Front Street 344 F26
Front Street, Brooklyn 345 H25
Fulton Street 344 E25
Furman Street 345 G26

G

Gansevoort Street 340 C21
Garden Place 345 H27
Gay Street 341 E22
Gold Street 344 F25
Gouverneur Lane 344 F26
Gouverneur Street 345 H24
Grace Court 345 H27
Grace Court Alley 345 H27
Gramercy Park North 342 F20
Gramercy Park South 342 F20
Grand Street 342 F23
Great Jones Street 342 F22
Green Street 339 J19
Greene Street 342 E22
Greenwich Avenue 341 D21
Greenwich Street 341 D23

H

Hanover Street 344 F26
Harrison Street 344 E24
Henry Street 345 F24
Hester Street 344 F24
Hicks Street 345 H26
Highway 25 334 G16

Highway 9A 332 B14
Hogan Place 344 F24
Holland Tunnel 341 D23
Horatio Street 340 C21
Howard Street 344 F24
Hubert Street 344 D24
Hudson Street 341 D22
Hunts Lane 345 H26
Huron Street 339 J20

I

India Street 339 J20
Irving Place 342 F21

J

Jackson Avenue 339 J18
Jackson Street 343 H23
James Street 345 F24
Jane Street 340 C22
Java Street 339 J20
Jay Street 344 E24
Jefferson Street 345 G24
John Street 344 F25
John Street, Brooklyn 345 H25
Jones Alley 342 F22
Jones Street 341 D22
Joralemon Street 345 G27

K

Kenmare Street 342 F23
King Street 341 D23

L

La Guardia Place 341 E22
Lafayette Street 342 F22
Laight Street 344 D24
Leonard Street 344 E24
Leroy Street 341 D23
Lewis Street 343 H23
Lexington Avenue 338 F18
Liberty Street 344 E25
Lispenard Street 344 E24
Little West 12th Street 340 C21
Little West Street 344 E26
Louis Street 343 H22
Love Lane 345 H26
Ludlow Street 342 G23

M

Macdougal Alley 341 E22
Macdougal Street 341 E22
Madison Avenue 337 E18
Madison Street 345 F24
Maiden Lane 344 E25
Main Street 335 G16
Main Street, Brooklyn 345 H25
Mangin Street 343 H22
Manhattan Avenue 339 J19
Manhattan Bridge 345 G24
Market Slip 345 G24
Market Street 345 G24
Matterhorn Drive 344 E26

The following indexes list hotels, restaurants and cafés, stores, theaters and music and dance venues.

ACKNOWLEDGMENTS

Abbreviations for the credits are as follows:
AA = AA World Travel Library, t (top), b (bottom), c (center), l (left), r (right)

UNDERSTANDING NEW YORK

5 AA/C Sawyer; 8tl AA/C Sawyer; 8tr AA/S McBride; 8ctr AA/C Sawyer; 8cbr AA/R Elliott; 8br AA/P Kenward; 9tl Jean-Georges; 9cl Photodisc; 9bl AA/D Corrance; 9cr AA/T Souter; 9b AA/C Sawyer; 10tl AA/C Sawyer; 10cl AA/C Sawyer; 10bl AA/P Kenward; 10tr AA/D Corrance; 10cr AA/C Sawyer; 10br AA/C Sawyer.

LIVING NEW YORK

11 AA/P Kenward; 12/3bg AA/C Sawyer; 12tl AA/C Sawyer; 12/3t AA/C Sawyer; 12c AA/R Elliott; 12cr AA/C Sawyer; 12cl AA/P Kenward; 12bl AA/C Sawyer; 13tr AA/R Elliott; 13cl AA/C Sawyer; 13c AA/R Elliott; 13cr AA/R Elliott; 13br AA/C Sawyer; 14/5bg AA/C Sawyer; 14tl AA/S McBride; 14tc AA/C Sawyer; 14tr AA/S McBride; 14c AA/R Elliott; 14cl AA/C Sawyer; 14bl AA/C Sawyer; 14/5c AA/S McBride; 15tl AA/C Sawyer; 15cl AA/C Sawyer; 15tr AA/R Elliott; 15cr AA/C Sawyer; 16/7bg AA/C Sawyer; 16tl AA/D Corrance; 16tr AA/S McBride; 16c AA/E Rooney; 16cr AA/C Sawyer; 16br AA/D Corrance; 16/7c AA/C Sawyer; 17tl AA/C Sawyer; 17tr AA/C Sawyer; 17cl AA/C Sawyer; 17c AA/C Sawyer; 17cr AA/R Elliott; 18/9bg AA/C Sawyer; 18tl AA/C Sawyer; 18tc AA/C Sawyer; 18tr AA/C Sawyer; 18cl AA/D Corrance; 18cr AA/S McBride; 18cbl AA/R Elliott; 18bl AA/C Sawyer; 19tl AA/P Kenward; 19tr AA/C Sawyer; 19cl AA/C Sawyer; 19cr AA/C Getty Images; 20/1bg AA/C Sawyer; 20tl AA/C Sawyer; 20tr AA/C Sawyer; 20cl AA/C Sawyer; 20cr AA/D Corrance; 20cr AA/C Sawyer; 20bc AA/C Sawyer; 21tl The Kobal Collection; 21tc AA/C Sawyer; 21c AA/R Elliott; 21r AA/P Kenward; 22/3bg AA/C Sawyer; 22tl AA/C Sawyer; 24tr AA; 22cl Nova Development Corp; 22cr Getty Images; 22b AA/D Corrance; 22/3t Nova Development Corp; 23cl Getty Images; 23tc AA/C Sawyer; 23tr AA/C Sawyer; 23c Nova Development Corp; 24bg AA/C Sawyer; 24l Getty Images; 24tc Federal Reserve Board, Washington, D.C; 24tr AA/C Sawyer; 24cr AA/C Sawyer.

THE STORY OF NEW YORK

25 Illustrated London News; 26/7bg AA; 26cl Mary Evans Picture Library; 26cr Corbis; 26bl Corbis; 26/7b AA; 26/7c Mary Evans Picture Library; 27l Mary Evans Picture Library; 27c AA; 27br Mary Evans Picture Library; 28/9bg AA; 28cl Mary Evans Picture Library; 28cr Mary Evans Picture Library; 28bl AA/R Elliott; 28/9 Representation of the Terrible Fire of New York in 1776 (engraving) by French School th(18th century), Museum of the City of New York, USA/Bridgeman Art Library; 29cl AA; 29c Mary Evans Picture Library; 29bl AA; 29br Mary Evans Picture Library; 30/1bg New York Looking South from Union Square, pub. By John Bachman, 1849 (litho) by C Bachman (19th century), Museum of the City of New York, USA/Bridgeman Art Library; 30cl View of the Ruins after the Great Fire in New York, Dec. 16th & 17th 1835, engraved by W I Bennett, pub, by L P Glover, by Bernardo Belottto Canaletto (1720-80), Museo di Goethe, Rome, Italy/Bridgeman Art Library; 30c Hulton Archives/Getty Images; 30cr Mary Evans Picture Library; 30/1 New York Looking South from Union Square, pub. by John Bachman, 1849 (Litho) by C Bachman (19th century), Museum of the City of New York, USA/Bridgeman Art Library; 31cl Hulton Archives/Getty Images; 31c Hulton Archives/Getty Images; 31bl AA/C Sawyer; 31br Hulton Archives/Getty Images; 32/3bg AA; 32c Illustrated London News; 32cr Mary Evans Picture Library; 32bl AA; 33cl Illustrated London News; 33c AA; 33bl Hulton Archives/Getty Images; 33br AA/R Elliott; 34/5bg AA/C Sawyer; 34cl AA/C Sawyer; 34cr AA/C Sawyer; 34bl Hulton Archives/Getty Images; 34br Mary Evans Picture Library; 34/5 AA/C Sawyer; 34cl Mary Evans Picture Library; 35c Hulton Archives/Getty Images; 35bc AA/R Elliott; 35br AA/C Sawyer; 36/7bg AA/R Elliott; 36cl AA/P Kenward; 36cr Corbis; 36bl AA/R Elliott; 36/7 AA/R Elliott; 37cl Corbis; 37c Hulton Archives/Getty Images; 37cr Hulton Archives/Getty Images; 3br AA/C Sawyer; 38bg AA/C Sawyer; 38c Getty Images; 38cr AA/S McBride; 38bl AA/C Sawyer; 38br AA/C Sawyer.

ON THE MOVE

39 AA/C Sawyer; 40/1 Digital Vision; 42t Digital Vision; 42b NY Airport Service; 43t AA/S L Day; 43b AA/C Sawyer; 44/5 AA/S L Day; 44 AA/C Sawyer; 46/7 AA/S L Day; 46 AA/C Sawyer; 47c AA/R Elliott; 47b AA/S McBride; 48/9 AA/C Sawyer; 48tr AA/C Sawyer; 48br AA/C Sawyer; 49tl AA/C Sawyer; 50 AA/C Sawyer; 51t AA/D Corrance; 51cr AA/D Corrance; 51br AA/C Sawyer; 52/3 Digital Vision; 52 AA/E Rooney; 53t AA/C Sawyer; 53b AA/C Sawyer; 54/5 AA/C Sawyer; 54cr AA/C Sawyer; 54b AA/C Sawyer; 55 Printed by Permission Greyhound Lines, Inc; 56t AA/C Sawyer; 56c AA/N Sumner.

THE SIGHTS

57 AA/C Sawyer; 62L AA/R Elliott; 62r AA/C Sawyer; 63l AA/D Corrance; 63r AA/R Elliott; 64l AA/E Davies; 64r AA/C Sawyer; 65l AA/C Sawyer; 65r AA/D Corrance; 66l AA/C Sawyer; 66r AA/C Sawyer; 67tl American Bible Society; 67tr American Numistic Society; 67bl Asia Society & Museum/Frank Oudeman; 68 AA/C Sawyer; 69t American Museum of Natural History; 69cr AA/C Sawyer; 69c American Museum of Natural History; 69r D Finnin/American Museum of Natural History; 69b American Museum of Natural History; 70t AA/R Elliott; 70cl American Museum of Natural History; 70c American Museum of Natural History; 70cr American Museum of Natural History; 70bl American Museum of Natural History; 72 D Finnin/American Museum of Natural History; 73t AA/C Sawyer; 73cr AA/C Sawyer; 73br AA/C Sawyer; 74t AA/C Sawyer; 74cl AA/C Sawyer; 74cr AA/C Sawyer; 75 AA/D Corrance; 76t Don Perdue; 76cl Don Perdue; 77tl AA/C Sawyer; 77tc AA/C Sawyer; 77tr AA/C Sawyer; 78t AA/E Rooney; 78cl AA/C Sawyer; 78c AA/C Sawyer; 78cr AA/C Sawyer; 79t AA/S McBride; 79br AA/S McBride; 80tl AA/S McBride; 80tr AA/S McBride; 80c AA/S McBride; 80cr AA/S McBride; 82 AA/D Corrance; 83l AA/S McBride; 83c AA/C Sawyer; 83r AA/C Sawyer; 84t AA/C Sawyer; 84l AA/S McBride; 85t AA/C Sawyer; 85cr AA/C Sawyer; 85br AA/S McBride; 86t AA; 86l AA/C Sawyer; 87tl Dahesh Museum of Art; 87tc AA/C Sawyer; 87tr AA/D Corrance; 88t AA/C Sawyer; 88cl AA/C Sawyer; 88c AA/S McBride; 88cr AA/C Sawyer; 88bl AA/S McBride; 89 AA/C Sawyer; 90 AA/C Sawyer; 91 Corbis; 92t By courtesy of the Ellis Island Immigration Museum; 92cl By courtesy of the Ellis Island Immigration Museum; 92c Corbis; 92cr AA/R Elliott; 92bl AA/S McBride; 94 AA/C Sawyer; 95 AA/C Sawyer; 95cl AA/C Sawyer; 95cr AA/S McBride; 96 AA/C Sawyer; 97t AA/P Kenward; 97r Federal Hall; 98t AA/C Sawyer; 98cl AA/C Sawyer; 99tl AA/C Sawyer; 99tc AA/C Sawyer; 99tr AA/C Sawyer; 100t Frick Collection; 100cl Frick Collection; 101tl AA/C Sawyer; 101tc AA/C Sawyer; 101tr AA/C Sawyer; 102 AA/S McBride; 103t AA/S McBride; 103cl AA/S McBride; 103c AA/S McBride; 103cr AA/S McBride; 104tl AA/S McBride; 104tr AA/S McBride; 105t AA/S McBride; 105cl AA/C Sawyer; 105c AA/S McBride; 105cr AA/C Sawyer; 106 AA/S McBride; 107cl AA/C Sawyer; 107c AA/P Kenward; 107cr AA/S McBride; 107b AA/C Sawyer; 108t AA/C Sawyer; 108cl AA/C Sawyer; 109tl AA/R Elliott; 109tc Jewish Museum; 109tr AA/C Sawyer; 110t AA/C Sawyer; 110cl AA/S McBride; 110c Flask, Glass and Fruit, 1877 by Paul Cezanne (1839-1906) Solomon R Guggenheim Museum, New York, USA/Bridgeman Art Library; 110cr AA/C Sawyer; 111t Robert Harding Picture Library; 111br Jeanne Hebuterne in a Yellow Jumper, 1918-19 (oil on canvas) by Amedeo Modigliani (1884-1920), Solomon R Guggenheim Museum, New York, USA/Bridgeman Art Library; 112t AA/P Kenward; 112cl AA/C Sawyer; 112c Lincoln Center/Steve J Sherman; 112cr AA/E Rooney; 113 AA/P Kenward; 114t AA/C Sawyer; 114cl AA/C Sawyer; 114c Lady at the Tea Table, 1885 (oil on canvas) by Mary Stevenson Cassatt (1844-1926), Metropolitan Museum of Art, New York, USA/Bridgeman Art Library; 114cr AA/R Elliott; 115 AA/R Elliott; 116 AA/D Corrance; 118 Corbis; 119t AA/D Corrance; 119cl AA; 119c The Dance Lesson, c 1879 (pastel) by Edgar Degas (1834-1917) Metropolitan Museum of Art, New

York, USA/Bridgeman Art Library; 119cr AA/C Sawyer; 120tl Lower East Side Tenement Museum; 120tc AA/R Elliott; 120tr Mount Vernon Hotel Museum; 121t AA/R Elliott; 121cr AA/C Sawyer; 122t © Photo SCALA, Florence,The Pierpont Morgan Library, 2001; 122cl AA/C Sawyer; 123tl Museum of the Chinese in Americas; 123tr Museum of Arts and Design; 124tl AA/R Elliott; 124tc Maika, Neue Galerie, © Christian Schad Stiftung Aschaffenburg/VG Bild-Kunst, Bonn and DACS, London 2004; 124tr AA/R Elliott; 125t © Photo SCALA, Florence, Museum of Modern Art, 2003; 125cr MOMA/Jack Pottle/Esto; 126tl Courtesy of the NY City Police Museum; 126tc New York Historical Society; 126tr AA/C Sawyer; 127t AA/R Elliott; 127cr AA/E Rooney; 128t AA/S McBride; 128cl AA/S McBride; 128c AA/S McBride; 128cr AA/C Sawyer; 129 AA/C Sawyer; 130tl AA/C Sawyer; 130cl AA/C Sawyer; 130r AA/C Sawyer; 130bl AA/S McBride; 131tl AA/C Sawyer; 131tc AA/P Kenward; 131tr AA/S McBride; 132t AA/S McBride; 132cl S McBride; 132c AA/C Sawyer; 132cr AA/C Sawyer; 132bl AA/C Sawyer; 133 AA/C Sawyer; 134t AA/C Sawyer; 134cl AA/S McBride; 134cr AA/C Sawyer; 134bl South Street Seaport; 135t AA/C Sawyer; 135b AA/C Sawyer; 136t AA/E Rooney; 136cl AA/C Sawyer; 136c AA/E Rooney; 136cr AA/P Kenward; 136bl AA/R Elliott; 137 AA/C Sawyer; 138 AA/C Sawyer; 139 AA/C Sawyer; 140tl AA/C Sawyer; 140cl AA/C Sawyer; 141tl AA/C Sawyer; 141tc AA/C Sawyer; 141tr AA/C Sawyer; 142t AA/C Sawyer; 142cl AA/P Kenward; 142c AA/C Sawyer; 142cr AA/C Sawyer; 143 AA/P Kenward; 144tl AA/C Sawyer; 144tc AA/C Sawyer; 144tr AA/C Sawyer; 145t AA; 145r AA/C Sawyer; 146 AA/C Sawyer; 147t AA/C Sawyer; 147cl AA/C Sawyer; 147c AA/C Sawyer; 147cr AA/C Sawyer; 148/9 AA/R Elliott, ©ADAGP, Paris and DACS, London 2004; 148c Whitney Museum of American Art View 2/Jeff Goldberg, Esto; 148bl AA/R Elliott; 150cl AA/P Kenward; 150cr Whitney Museum of American Art View 1/Jeff Goldberg, Esto; 150b Corbis; 151 Railroad Crossing, 1922-23 by Edward Hopper (1882-1967) Whitney Museum of American Art, New York, USA/Bridgeman Art Library; 152tl AA/R Elliott; 152tr AA/C Sawyer; 152b Brooklyn Historical Society; 153t The Peaceable Kingdom, c 1840-45) by Edward Hicks (1780-1849), Brooklyn Museum of Art, New York, USA/Bridgeman Art Library; 153cr AA/C Sawyer; 154tl AA/R Elliott; 154tc AA/C Sawyer; 154tr AA/C Sawyer; 154bl NY Transit Museum; 155tll NY Hall of Science; 155tc AA/C Sawyer; 155tr Waterfront Museum/Frank Zimmerman; 155c AA/R Elliott; 156tl Garibaldi Meucci Museum; 156tc AA/C Sawyer; 156tr AA/C Sawyer; 156bl Historic Richmond Town; 157t AA/R Elliott; 157cr Bronx Zoo; 158t Getty Images; 157l Photodisc.

WHAT TO DO

159 Photodisc; 164t AA/M Jourdan; 164cl Screaming Mimi's; 164c AA/C Sawyer; 165/5c AA/C Sawyer; 165cl AA/C Sawyer; 165cr AA/C Sawyer; 166cl AA/S McBride; 166cr AA/S McBride; 166b Me & Ro; 167cl AA/C Sawyer; 167c Jimmy Choo; 167cr AA/C Sawyer;168 AA/C Sawyer; 169 AA/M Jourdan; 170t AA/M Jourdan; 170c Jazz Record Store; 170b Footlight Records; 171t AA/M Jourdan; 171ct AA/C Sawyer; 171cl AA/P Kenward; AA/C Sawyer; 172t AA/M Jourdan; 173t AA/M Jourdan; 173tl AA/C Sawyer; 173cr AA/C Sawyer; 173bl AA/C Sawyer; 174t AA/M Jourdan; 174tl AA/S McBride; 174tc AA/C Sawyer; 174c AA/C Sawyer; 174cr AA/S McBride; 175t AA/M Jourdan; 175tl AA/C Sawyer; 175bl AA/C Sawyer; 175br Kirna Zabete; 176t AA/M Jourdan; 177t AA/M Jourdan; 177c Screaming Mimi's; 177cr AA/C Sawyer; 177bl Mark Bulkin; 178t AA/M Jourdan; 178ct Eye Candy; 178cr Jimmy Choo; 179t AA/M Jourdan; 179b Me & Ro; 180t AA/M Jourdan; 180tl AA/C Sawyer; 181t AA/M Jourdan; 181tc AA/C Sawyer; 181cl Broadway Panhandler; 181cr AA/C Sawyer; 181b AA/C Sawyer; 182t AA/M Jourdan; 183t AA/M Joudan; 184t AA/M Jourdan; 184tc AA/C Sawyer; 184bc AA/C Sawyer; 185t Digital Vision; 185cl Digital Vision; 185c Digital Vision; 190t AA/C Sawyer; 190tc AA/S Collier; 190cl AA/R Elliott; 190tr AA/S Collier; 191t AA/C Sawyer; 191ct AA/S Collier; 191cb Jonathan B Ragle; 192/3t Digital Vision; 192cl AA/C Sawyer; 192bc AA/C Sawyer; 193b John Bigelow Taylor; 194/5t Digital Vision; 194c AA/P Kenward; 196/7t Brand X Pics; 196tc

Chicago City Limits; 196cr Gotham Comedy Club; 197tr Michael Moran; 197cl AA; 198/9t Digital Vision; 198tl Digital Vision; 198c AA/C Coe; 199tl © Bob Colton/Black Star; 199tc Digital Vision; 200tl Cornelia Street Café; 200/1t Digital Vision; 200cl AA/C Sawyer; 202bl AA/C Sawyer; 200br AA/P Kenward; 200cr Iridium Jazz Club; 202/3t Digital Vision; 202cl AA/C Sawyer; 203tl AA/C Sawyer; 204t Digital Vision; 204tl Luna Lounge; 204bc Sob's; 205t AA/C Sawyer; 206/7t AA/C Sawyer; 206c AA/C Sawyer; 207cl AA/C Sawyer; 207cb AA/C Sawyer; 207ct AA/C Sawyer; 208/9t AA/C Sawyer; 207cr AA/C Sawyer; 208c AA/C Sawyer; 209cl Bowerie Lane; 209bl Bengt Wanselius; 210/1t AA/C Sawyer; 210c AA/P Kenward; 210l Rendering by Sean Daly/Windtunnel Visualization; Architect: Michael Kurtz Architect PC; 210ct Public Theater; 210cr Carol Rosegg; 212/3t AA/T Souter; 212c Brand X Pics; 212b Brand X Pics; 213c Bubble Lounge; 214/5t AA/T Souter; 214c Happy Ending; 216/7t AA/T Souter; 217bc AA/R Elliott; 217t AA/P Kenward; 217cl AA/C Sawyer; 218/9t Pianos; 218c Pianos; 219tc Nell's Inc; 219cr Supper Club; 219b Pianos; 220t Pianos; 220tl Photodisc; 220b Larry Bullock; 221t Photodisc; 222/3t Photodisc; 224/5t Photodisc; 224tl AA/C Sawyer; 224tc Bowlmor Lanes; 225c AA/P Kenward; 226/7t Photodisc; 226cl Asphalt Green; 226cr New York Health and Racquet Club; 228r (La Prairie); 227b (Clay); 228t Photodisc; 227cr (Greenhouse Spa); 228ct (Oasis Day Spa); 229t AA/R Elliott; 229b New Victory Theater; 230/1t AA/R Elliott; 230c Children's Museum of Manhatten; 231cl Steve Williams © 2003; 231cr AA/D Corrance; 232tl (Liberty Helicopters); 232t AA/R Elliott; 232c AA/C Sawyer; 233t AA/S L Day; 233c AA/P Kenward; 234t AA/S L Day; 234cl AA/C Sawyer; 234cr AA/C Sawyer.

OUT AND ABOUT

235 AA/P Kenward; 237tl AA/C Sawyer; 237tc AA/C Sawyer; 237tr AA/C Sawyer; 237cr AA/C Sawyer; 238 AA/N Lancaster; 239t AA/C Sawyer; 239ct AA/R Elliott; 239cb AA/N Lancaster; 239b AA/N Lancaster; 241tl AA/N Lancaster; 241tr AA/C Sawyer; 241cr AA/C Sawyer; 241bl AA/N Lancaster; 242 AA/C Sawyer; 243tl AA/C Sawyer; 243tr AA/C Sawyer; 243bc AA/C Sawyer; 243br AA/C Sawyer; 244 AA/C Sawyer; 245tl AA/C Sawyer; 245tr AA/C Sawyer; 245cr AA/C Sawyer; 245br AA/E Rooney; 246 AA/R Elliott; 247tr AA/C Sawyer; 247ctr AA/C Sawyer; 247cbr AA/C Sawyer; 247br AA/C Sawyer; 248 AA/C Sawyer; 249tr AA/C Sawyer; 249c AA/S McBride; 249cr AA/C Sawyer; 249b AA/C Sawyer; 251tl AA/C Sawyer; 251tr AA/C Sawyer; 251b AA/C Sawyer; 252/3 AA/N Lancaster; 253tr AA/P Kenward; 253ctr AA/C Sawyer; 253cb AA/N Lancaster; 253b AA/N Lancaster; 254 AA/N Lancaster; 255tl AA/N Lancaster; 255tr AA/N Lancaster; 255c AA/C Sawyer; 255b AA/N Lancaster; 256 AA/R Elliott; 257t AA/R Elliott; 257c AA/R Elliott; 257b AA/R Elliott; 258c AA/R Elliott; 258/9 AA/R Elliott; 259t AA/R Elliott; 259c AA/R Elliott; 260l AA/C Sawyer; 260c AA/C Sawyer; 260r AA/C Sawyer.

EATING AND STAYING

261 AA/C Sawyer; 266l AA/C Sawyer; 266cl AA/P Kenward; 266cr AA/C Sawyer; 266r AA/P Kenward; 267l AA/C Sawyer; 267c AA/C Sawyer; 267r AA/R Elliott; 267bl AA/R Elliott; 268l AA/C Sawyer; 268c AA/C Sawyer; 268r AA/D Corrance; 268cb AA/S McBride; 270c AA/S Collier; 270r S Collier; 271r AA/S McBride; 272c AA/S Collier; 275bc AA/S Collier; 275r AA/S Collier; 277l AA/S McBride; 277c AA/S Collier; 278r AA/S McBride; 279tl AA/S McBride; 280br AA/S Collier; 280bl AA/S Collier; 280c AA/S Collier; 281br AA/S Collier; 281bl AA/S Collier; 283tc AA/S Collier; 283bc AA/S Collier; 286bl AA/S Collier; 286tr AA/S Collier; 286br AA/S Collier; 287tc AA/S Collier; 288br AA/S McBride; 288 AA/S Collier; 289cl AA/S Collier; 289c AA/S Collier; 290t AA/S McBride; 290c AA/S McBride; 290b AA/N Lancaster; 291 AA/C Sawyer; 305c AA/C Sawyer.

PLANNING

311 AA/C Sawyer; 312t AA/C Sawyer; 312c AA/E Rooney; 316 AA/C Sawyer; 318 AA/C Sawyer; 321t AA/C Sawyer; 321b AA/C Sawyer; 322 AA/S Collier; 323tr AA/P Kenward; 323cr AA/R Elliott; 324 AA/E Rooney; 325 AA/R Elliott; 326 AA/S Collier.

Project editor
Betty Sheldrick

Interior design
David Austin, Glyn Barlow, Alan Gooch, Kate Harling, Bob Johnson,
Nick Otway, Carole Philp, Keith Russell

Additional design
Jo Tapper, Nautilus Design

Picture research
Carol Walker

Cover design
Tigist Getachew

Internal repro work
Susan Crowhurst, Ian Little, Michael Moody

Production
Lyn Kirby, Caroline Nyman

Mapping
Maps produced by the Cartography Department of AA Publishing

Main contributors
Coleen Degnan-Veness, Marilyn Wood

Copy editors
Sheila Hawkins, Sarah Hudson, Jo Perry

ISBN 1-4000-1387-9

Colour separation by Keenes
Printed and bound by Leo, China

Special Sales: Fodor's Travel Publications are available at special discounts for bulk purchases for
sales promotions or premiums. Special editions, including personalized covers, excerpts of existing
guides, and corporate imprints, can be created in large quantities for special needs. For more
information, contact your local bookseller or write to Special Marketing, Fodor's Travel Publications,
1745 Broadway, New York, NY 10019. Inquiries from Canada should be directed to your local
Canadian bookseller or sent to Random House of Canada, Ltd., Marketing Department,
2775 Matheson Blvd. East, Mississauga, Ontario L4W 4P7.

A01516
Mapping in this title produced from New York data © Tele Atlas N. V. 2003
Relief map images supplied by Mountain High Maps ® Copyright © 1993 Digital Wisdom, Inc
Weather chart statistics supplied by Weatherbase © Copyright 2003 Canty and Associates, LLC

Important Note: Time inevitably brings changes, so always confirm prices, travel facts, and
other perishable information when it matters. Although Fodor's cannot accept responsibility
for errors, you can use this guide in the confidence that we have taken every care to ensure its
accuracy.

Fodor's Key to the Guides

AMERICA'S **GUIDEBOOK LEADER** PUBLISHES GUIDES FOR **EVERY KIND OF TRAVELER**. CHECK OUT OUR MANY SERIES AND FIND YOUR **PERFECT MATCH**.

FODOR'S GOLD GUIDES
America's favorite travel-guide series offers the most detailed insider reviews of hotels, restaurants, and attractions in all price ranges, plus great background information, smart tips, and useful maps.

COMPASS AMERICAN GUIDES
Stunning guides from top local writers and photographers, with gorgeous photos, literary excerpts, and colorful anecdotes. A must-have for culture mavens, history buffs, and new residents.

FODOR'S CITYPACKS
Concise city coverage in a guide plus a foldout map. The right choice for urban travelers who want everything under one cover.

FODOR'S WHERE TO WEEKEND
A fresh take on weekending, this series identifies the best places to escape outside the city and details loads of rejuvenating activities as well as cool places to stay, great restaurants, and practical information.

FODOR'S AROUND THE CITY WITH KIDS
Up to 68 great ideas for family days, recommended by resident parents. Perfect for exploring in your own backyard or on the road.

FODOR'S TRAVEL HISTORIC AMERICA
For travelers who want to experience history firsthand, this series gives in-depth coverage of historic sights, plus nearby restaurants and hotels. Themes include the Thirteen Colonies, the Old West, and the Lewis and Clark Trail.

FODOR'S FLASHMAPS
Every resident's map guide, with 60 easy-to-follow maps of public transit, parks, museums, zip codes, and more.

FODOR'S LANGUAGES FOR TRAVELERS
Practice the local language before you hit the road. Available in phrase books, cassette sets, and CD sets.

THE COLLECTED TRAVELER
These collections of the best published essays and articles on various European destinations will give you a feel for the culture, cuisine, and way of life.

FODOR'S HOW TO GUIDES
Get tips from the pros on planning the perfect trip. Learn how to pack, fly hassle-free, plan a honeymoon or cruise, stay healthy on the road, and travel with your baby.

KAREN BROWN'S GUIDES
Engaging guides—many with easy-to-follow inn-to-inn itineraries—to the most charming inns and B&Bs in the U.S.A. and Europe.

BAEDEKER'S GUIDES
Comprehensive guides, trusted since 1829, packed with A–Z reviews and star ratings.

OTHER GREAT TITLES FROM FODOR'S
Baseball Vacations, The Complete Guide to the National Parks, Family Vacations, Golf Digest's Places to Play, Great American Drives of the East, Great American Drives of the West, Great American Vacations, Healthy Escapes, National Parks of the West, Skiing USA.

At bookstores everywhere.   www.fodors.com/books

Dear Traveler

From buying a plane ticket to booking a room and seeing the sights, a trip goes much more smoothly when you have a good travel guide. Dozens of writers, editors, designers, and cartographers have worked hard to make the book you hold in your hands a good one. Was it everything you expected? Were our descriptions accurate? Were our recommendations on target? And did you find our tips and practical advice helpful? Your ideas and experiences matter to us. If we have missed or misstated something, we'd love to hear about it. Fill out our survey at www.fodors.com/books/feedback/, or e-mail us at seeit@fodors.com. Or you can snail mail to the See It Editor at Fodor's, 1745 Broadway, New York, New York 10019. We'll look forward to hearing from you.

Karen Cure
Editorial Director